THE MANAGEMENT OF SPORT

Its Foundation and Application

THE MANAGEMENT OF SPORT

Its Foundation and Application

Fourth Edition

Bonnie L. Parkhouse, Ph.D.

Temple University

EDITOR

With the Endorsement of
The National Association for Sport and Physical Education (NASPE)
an association of the American Alliance for Health,
Physical Education, Recreation and Dance (AAHPERD)

National
Association
for Sport &
Physical Education

Boston   Burr Ridge, IL   Dubuque, IA   Madison, WI   New York   San Francisco   St. Louis
Bangkok   Bogotá   Caracas   Kuala Lumpur   Lisbon   London   Madrid   Mexico City
Milan   Montreal   New Delhi   Santiago   Seoul   Singapore   Sydney   Taipei   Toronto

Higher Education

THE MANAGEMENT OF SPORT: ITS FOUNDATION AND APPLICATION

Published by McGraw-Hill, a business unit of The McGraw-Hill Companies, Inc., 1221 Avenue of the Americas, New York, NY, 10020. Copyright © 2005, 2001, 1996, 1991, by The McGraw-Hill Companies, Inc. All rights reserved. No part of this publication may be reproduced or distributed in any form or by any means, or stored in a database or retrieval system, without the prior written consent of The McGraw-Hill Companies, Inc., including, but not limited to, in any network or other electronic storage or transmission, or broadcast for distance learning.

Some ancillaries, including electronic and print components, may not be available to customers outside the United States.

This book is printed on acid-free paper.

1 2 3 4 5 6 7 8 9 0 FGR/FGR 0 9 8 7 6 5 4

ISBN 0-07-284412-4

Vice President and Editor-in-Chief: *Emily Barrosse*
Publisher: *William Glass*
Sponsoring editor: *Nicholas Barrett*
Director of Development: *Kate Engelberg*
Developmental editor: *Lynda Huenefeld*
Senior marketing manager: *Pamela S. Cooper*
Media producer: *Lance Gerhart*
Project manager: *Jill Moline-Eccher*
Associate production supervisor: *Jason I. Huls*
Associate designer: *Srdjan Savanovic*
Media project manager: *Meghan Durko*
Manager, Photo research: *Brian Pecko*
Art editor: *Emma Ghiselli*
Art director: *Jeanne Schreiber*
Cover design: *Srdjan Savanovic*
Interior design: *Srdjan Savanovic*
Typeface: *9.5/11 Palatino*
Compositor: *Interactive Composition Corporation*
Printer: *Quebecor World Fairfield Inc.*

Library of Congress Cataloging-in-Publication Data

The management of sport : its foundation and application / Bonnie L. Parkhouse, editor.—
4th ed.
p. cm.
"With the endorsement of the National Association for Sport and Physical Education (NASPE), an association of the American Alliance for Health, Physical Education, Recreation and Dance (AAHPERD)."
Includes bibliographical references and index.
ISBN 0-07-284412-4 (alk. paper)
1. Sports administration—Study and teaching—United States. I. Parkhouse, Bonnie L. II. National Association for Sport and Physical Education.
GV713.M35 2005
796'.06'9—dc22
2004052434

www.mhhe.com

In memory of Harmon Gallant.

This fourth edition is dedicated to the memory of Harmon Gallant, J. D., who contributed the chapter on "Labor Relations in Professional Sports" to the second and third editions. He was a brilliant scholar regarding antitrust and labor law issues in professional sports. Thank you, Harmon, for gracing our lives with yours.

—Bonnie L. Parkhouse

Brief Table of Contents

Contents

ix

PART V   PROFESSIONAL
  RELATIONS

**16   Group Decision Making and Problem
   Solving,** 272

Laurence Chalip
Judith A. Switzer

**17   Human Resource Management
   in Sport,** 286

Frank Linnehan

**18   Labor Relations in Professional
   Sports,** 301

Harmon Gallant
Lloyd Zane Remick
Bernard M. Resnick

Preface

This book represents a "labor of love" for me personally. Although it is virtually impossible to exhaustively describe the body of knowledge that constitutes a profession in one volume, *The Management of Sport: Its Foundation and Application*, fourth edition, reestablishes the precedent set by the previous editions, serving as the most comprehensive and current entry in its market. This edition is tailored around the informational needs of the sport manager.

In the era of the fitness entrepreneur, sport has become even more significant (especially financially) and pervasive in our society. This multibillion-dollar industry places unique demands on its personnel and increasingly requires specialized training. Jobs in the sport industry involve myriad skills applicable to the sport setting and specific to the increasingly complex and multifaceted areas it represents. As a result, a new breed of specialists has emerged. Sport management is now recognized as a legitimate field of study in colleges and universities throughout the world. *The Management of Sport: Its Foundation and Application*, fourth edition, is the most comprehensive compilation of subject matter published to date for the sport management profession.

AUDIENCE

In increasing numbers, students with a wide variety of backgrounds are choosing a course of study in sport management. Our intention with this book is to cater to this changing and rapidly growing audience.

Also, although this book was primarily written as an introductory text for undergraduates, graduate students and instructors at other levels are encouraged to review its content for potential use as well. **Practitioners will also find it to be a valuable resource.**

FEATURES
Organization
This book uses a unique approach in addressing the substantive aspects of the profession by presenting both the theoretical foundations and subsequent application of these principles.

Content
This book is a compilation of great minds and talent from around the world. Over twenty contributors lent their expertise, providing credibility in regard to content and expanding the student's understanding of the concepts as applied worldwide. For example, there are two chapters on sport governance, which address international, scholastic, collegiate, and professional sports. These chapters show readers the importance of how sports organizations govern themselves. This topic and all of the other core topics integral to a career in sport management (e.g., finance, human resources, budgeting, diversity, and so on) are captured and bound in this book.

Current events in the field are also included, such as an updated history of employer-employee relationships within four professional team sports. It examines crisis situations, their influence on the industry, and how opposing sides worked through differences.

Pedagogy

This text uses many pedagogical features to aid students' comprehension of many diverse topics.

- Each author has indicated **key terms** with which the student will become familiar while reading the chapter. These terms are located at the beginning of each chapter, as well as in bold face type either in headings or text when they are discussed within the chapter.
- Each major section ends with a **Concept Check** that highlights the main discussion.
- A succinct, enumerated **Summary** emphasizes the key points in each chapter.
- Each chapter includes a complete list of **References.** It is recommended that students read these references carefully for supplemental information.
- **Review Questions and Issues and Case Studies** give students further insight into how to apply the theoretical principles.
- **Critical Thinking Exercises** ask readers to take what they've learned in each chapter and find the solution to a real-world problem facing sport management.
- Annotated **Web Sites** provide additional information not addressed in each chapter.
- A **Fostering Your Work Skills** section provides students with the experience of applying what they have learned.

ACKNOWLEDGMENTS

I would like to express my gratitude to all who contributed to *The Management of Sport: Its Foundation and Application,* 4th edition. Jill Moline-Eccher, project manager, and Lynda Huenefeld, developmental editor, made an invaluable contribution to this work. Their tireless effort, expertise, and professionalism are greatly appreciated. They kept all of us on schedule under very challenging circumstances.

The ultimate success of a book is contingent upon the quality of subject matter presented. Drawing on the expertise of a "Who's Who" list of contributors, this work—as forementioned—is the most comprehensive compilation of subject matter ever published for the sport management profession. Without question, the authors made a commitment to excellence and set other priorities aside to meet extremely demanding deadlines.

A special thanks goes to the reviewers, who reviewed the current edition; their feedback was tremendously helpful in focusing the revision.

Benjamin D. Goss, Clemson University
Jeffrey R. Meyer, Wayne State University
Bonnie Tiell, Tiffin University
John Wolohan, Ithaca College

Many thanks to everyone who contributed to this book. In my opinion, it's an accomplishment we can all be proud of.

Bonnie L. Parkhouse, Editor

Editor

BONNIE L. PARKHOUSE
Temple University

Bonnie L. Parkhouse, Professor, received a Ph.D. in Administration from the University of Minnesota. She is currently a member of the faculty in the School of Tourism and Hospitality Management. Previous faculty appointments include the University of Southern California and California State University, Fullerton. Twenty of her studies have been published in distinguished refereed research journals. Numerous articles she has written have appeared in trade and commercial publications, and she is the senior author of previous books and the editor of the first, second and third edition of this revision.

Dr. Parkhouse is a former member of the editorial boards for the *Journal of Sport Management* and *Quest*. She is currently a member of the review board for the *International Journal of Sport Management*. She also served as one of the original seven members of the Sport Management Program Review Council (SMPRC), which acts as an entity for the purpose of reviewing sport management programs in the United States. On invitation, she has served as a consultant in sport management curricular matters at numerous institutions in the United States, as well as in England, Australia, and the Caribbean. Dr. Parkhouse is recognized as a progenitor of sport management curricula and theory; her publications are frequently cited by other authors. She received an outstanding alumnae award from the University of Minnesota in 2002.

Contributing Authors

JOHN M. AMIS
University of Memphis

John Amis is an Associate Professor in the College of Education. He obtained a Ph.D. in sport management from the University of Alberta in 1998 and was employed by De Montfort University in England before joining The University of Memphis in 2001. Amis's research interests are centered on organizational change and the identification, utilization and management of intangible resources. In addition to two books, he has had thirty articles and book chapters published in journals such as *Academy of Management Journal, Journal of Applied Behavioral Science, European Marketing Journal, Journal of Sport Management, European Sport Management Quarterly,* and *Leisure Studies.* A paper published in *European Marketing Journal* (with Trevor Slack and Tim Berrett) received an ANBAR citation (Highest Quality Rating). He has delivered 26 papers at international conferences, several of which have been published in conference proceedings, and has been invited to provide keynote addresses in Europe and North America. Dr. Amis has conducted academic and proprietary research on and for a number of high-profile North American, European and Australian organizations, including Guinness, Next, Telstra, Sport Canada, Ski Canada, the Canadian Soccer Association, and the Memphis Grizzlies.

SCOTT BRANVOLD
Robert Morris University

Scott Branvold is currently a Professor in the Management and Marketing Department at Robert Morris University in Pittsburgh, PA, and the internship coordinator for the Sport Management Program. He has 19 years of college teaching experience in sport management programs at both the undergraduate and graduate levels at Robert Morris and the University of Oklahoma. He has taught Sport Marketing, Sport Sociology, Legal Issues in Sport, and a variety of other courses in the field of sport management. Scott has been involved in sports as an athlete, coach, facility manager, and sports information assistant. He is currently Robert Morris University's Faculty Athletics Representative. During his career he has presented papers at various conferences including the North American Society for Sport Management, American Alliance for Health, Physical Education, Recreation & Dance, and the International Sports Business Conference. He has had articles published in the *Sport Management Journal* and the *Sport Marketing Journal,* and has written a chapter on quality management in *Sport Business: Operational and Theoretical Aspects.* He has an undergraduate degree in business from the University of North Dakota, a Master's degree from Minnesota State University–Mankato, and a Doctorate from the University of Utah.

PACKIANATHAN CHELLADURAI
The Ohio State University

Professor Packianathan (Chella) Chelladurai (Ph.D., University of Waterloo) is currently

Professor of Sport Management in the School of Physical Activity and Educational Services at The Ohio State University. Earlier he was a professor at The University of Western Ontario, London, Canada. He specializes in organizational theory and organizational behaviors applied to the sporting context. He has published over 70 articles in refereed journals. He has written three textbooks and two monographs. He is on the editorial boards of the *Journal of Sport Management* and the *European Sport Management Quarterly.* He is a frequent reviewer for journals such as the *Journal of Sport and Exercise Psychology,* the *Journal of Applied Sport Psychology, Research Quarterly for Exercise and Sports,* and *Perceptual and Motor Skills.* He was honored by the North American Society for Sport Management as the first recipient of its prestigious Earle F. Zeigler award. He is a Fellow of the American Academy of Kinesiology and Physical Education. He has been invited to speak and consult on a worldwide basis, presenting keynote addresses at national and international conferences held in the Republic of South Africa, Korea, Netherlands, Japan, Hungary, France, England, Finland, Norway, Italy, Portugal, and Spain. He serves the Olympic Solidarity by presenting lectures for its MEMOS program (master's program for administrators of sport governing bodies in Europe and Asia).

ANNIE CLEMENT
Barry University

Annie Clement, author, researcher, attorney, and academic leader, is professor at Barry University. Dr. Clement is currently best known for her texts, *Law in Sport and Physical Activity, Legal Responsibility in Aquatics,* and *Teaching Physical Activity.* One additional book, 20 book chapters, 70 articles, and over 150 presentations are among her achievements. In-depth study of risk management, aquatics, intellectual property, antitrust, equal pay, and gender equity are a few of the areas in which her research and writing have been continuous. Dr. Clement holds a Bachelor's degree and a Master's degree from the University of Minnesota. Her Doctorate is from the University of Iowa and her Jurisdoctorate from Cleveland State University. She also studied at Cambridge University and the University of Oslo. Unique honors awarded to Dr. Clement are the Fellow of the American Bar Foundation (ABA), a distinction given to only one-third of one percent of the ABA membership; the Nonprofit Lawyers Award; distinguished speaker at ten different universities; President of the National Association for Sport and Physical Education (NASPE); President, Ohio Teacher Educators; The American Alliance for Health, Physical Education, Recreation, and Dance (AAHPERD) Honor Award; Aquatic Council Merit Award; and the NASPE Joy of Effort Award. She also received the Ohio AHPERD Honor Award, Tsunami Spirit Award from the Aquatic Therapy and Rehab Institute, the Susan B. Anthony Award from Ohio National Organization of Women (NOW), and Honor Award from the Council for National Cooperation in Aquatics (CNCA).

DIANNA P. GRAY
University of Northern Colorado

Dianna Gray, Professor, currently serves as the Director of the School of Sport and Exercise Science (SES) in the College of Health and Human Sciences. She joined the UNC faculty in 1995 after teaching appointments at Indiana University, Bloomington, and Kent State University, in Ohio. She has worked in education since 1973, at both the public school and university levels. Dr. Gray is a member of the Sport Administration faculty and teaches in the areas of management, sport marketing, public relations and finance. She is the founder of the UNC Sport Marketing Research Institute (SMRI), a university-based center that researches issues in the sport industry and assists sport organizations at all levels with improving the delivery of sport services. She has served in a consulting capacity for a number of sport organizations and is a Past President of the North American Society for Sport Management (NASSM). She received her Ph.D. and M.A. from The Ohio State University, and a B.S. from Madison College.

LAWRENCE (LARRY) HAM
James Madison University

Larry worked as a practitioner in Virginia Beach, Virginia, as the Parks Construction Supervisor after approximately 15 years in Civil Engineering. After working with professionals in Parks and Recreation, he decided to return to school and complete his Bachelor's degree in Leisure Studies at Central Washington University in Ellensburg, Washington. Larry then returned to Virginia to serve as Superintendent of Recreation in Staunton, Virginia, before deciding to continue his education at the graduate level. Larry completed his Master's and Doctoral education at Temple University, Philadelphia, Pennsylvania, in Sport and Recreation Administration. His dissertation on *The Use of the Enterprise Fund in Municipal and County Parks and Recreation Departments* was awarded the Best Dissertation Award in 1997 by the American Academy for Parks and Recreation Administration. Larry has expertise in and presently teaches students in Recreation Administration; Fiscal Administration of Sport, Recreation and Leisure; Legal Aspects and Risk Management of Sport and Recreation Facilities; Planning, Design and Construction of Recreation Facilities; Facility Maintenance Management and Operations; Special Events Planning and Management; Commercial Recreation, Park Planning, Design, Construction, and Maintenance; and Outdoor Recreation.

SUE INGLIS
McMaster University

Sue Inglis is an Associate Professor in the Department of Kinesiology. She earned her Ph.D. from The Ohio State University, and M.A. and B.P.E. degrees from the University of Alberta. Dr. Inglis' experience includes teaching, coaching and athletic administration, and leadership positions in the North American Society for Sport Management (NASSM), including president, member of the NASPE-NASSM Sport Management Task Force and Sport Management Program Review Council, and Strategic Planning group. Dr. Inglis' research interests and published work focuses on two areas, organizational behavior issues of board of director governance and student inquiry.

BETTE B. KEYSER
Illinois State University

Bette B. Keyser, Associate Professor Emerita, received an Ed.D. in Curriculum and Instruction from Illinois State University. As former Coordinator of Clinical Experiences in Health Education, she supervised both health education interns and student teachers. She has provided guidance to undergraduate students in portfolio development and to faculty interested in integrating student portfolios into professional preparation programs. Her publications and presentations have been in the area of student portfolios, pedagogy, in-service design, and critical thinking.

MICHAEL LEEDS
Temple University

Michael Leeds is Associate Professor of Economics in the Fox School of Business at Temple University. His areas of research include labor economics and the economics of sports. His most recent research includes work on the impact of major college football on Title IX compliance and on the economic value of naming rights purchases. Since 1994, he has served as Director of the Honors Program in the Fox School of Business.

FRANK LINNEHAN
LeBow College of Business
Drexel University

Dr. Frank Linnehan is an Associate Professor of Organizational Behavior and Human Resources in the Department of Management at Drexel University. Dr. Linnehan received his Ph.D. in Human Resources Administration from Temple University and has taught both graduate and undergraduate courses in Human Resources, Compensation, Organization Behavior, Leadership and Management. Prior to receiving his Ph.D., Dr. Linnehan worked for seventeen years in both line and Human Resource management in the financial services industry. Dr. Linnehan's research interests include Affirmative Action, Equal Employment and workforce diversity initiatives, along with school-to-work transitions for high school students. He has authored or co-authored papers that have appeared in the *Academy of Management Journal, Journal of Vocational Behavior, Group and Organization Management, Applied Psychology: An International Journal, Journal of Management Inquiry, Social Psychology of Education* and *Educational Evaluation and Policy Analysis*. He is also a member of the editorial board of the *Journal of Vocational Behavior*.

MIREIA LIZANDRA

Mireia Lizandra attended the University of Barcelona, Spain, where she received her degree in physical education as well as her J.D. In the United States, she received her Master's and Doctorate degrees in sport administration from Temple University, Philadelphia, PA. While in Philadelphia, she worked with the Philadelphia Eagles Football Club. In 1990, she began working for the United States Olympic Committee in Colorado Springs, CO, as an International Relations Coordinator. In that position, she was involved with the 1991 Pan American Games in Cuba, the 1992 Winter Olympic Games in Albertville, and the 1992 Summer Olympic Games in Barcelona. Later on, she took a position with the Atlanta Committee for the Olympic Games (ACOG) as the Director of the National Olympic Committee Relations Department. In that capacity, she orchestrated the communications between ACOG and the 197 National Olympic Committees. After the 1996 Summer Olympic Games, Mireia worked as a freelance consultant conducting and developing different national and international projects for several clients. In 1998, she took a position with The Marquee Group as Managing Director for Olympic and Pan American Projects. In 2000, she started to do consulting. She has combined her jobs with teaching at the graduate level at Georgia State University, Georgia Institute of Technology and Temple University.

JOANNE MACLEAN
Brock University

Joanne Maclean is an Associate Professor in the Department of Sport Management. She has extensive administrative and coaching experience in Canada and internationally, including fifteen years as a University Athletic Coordinator and Director, and Chef de Mission for Canada at the 2003 World University Games in South Korea. Dr. Maclean earned her Ph.D. from The Ohio State University, and M.P.E. and B.P.E. from the University of New Brunswick. She has authored two books and several articles in her specialty of human resource management, and currently holds the position of Treasurer on the Executive Committee of the North American Society for Sport Management.

CHAD D. MCEVOY
Illinois State University

Dr. McEvoy is an assistant professor in the School of Kinesiology and Recreation. He earned his Ed.D. in sport administration from the University of Northern Colorado, his M.S. in sport management from the University of Massachusetts, Amherst, and his B.S. in sport management from Iowa State University. Dr. McEvoy's professional experience includes four years of marketing and fund raising for two Division I-A intercollegiate athletics programs, as well as consulting projects for intercollegiate, professional, and Olympic sport organizations. Dr. McEvoy's primary teaching and research interests are in the areas of sport marketing and finance.

MARK E. MOORE
St. Cloud State University

Dr. Mark Moore, Assistant Professor of Health, Physical Education, Recreation and Sport Science at St. Cloud State University, received a Ph.D. in Sport Management and an MBA from the University of Pittsburgh. In addition, Dr. Moore completed postdoctoral work in sport management at Temple University. As graduate coordinator of the Sport Management Program, Dr. Moore teaches undergraduate recreation administration courses as well as graduate courses in sport management, sport finance and sport marketing. Prior to his St. Cloud State appointment, he taught at Temple University, Harcum College and Lakeland College. Dr. Moore's research interests include educational and employment diversity issues, along with marketing planning and consumer behavior aspects pertaining to sport. He has authored or co-authored manuscripts that have appeared in the *Women in Management Review, Journal of Sport Management, and Sport Marketing Quarterly*. In addition to his teaching and research, Dr. Moore has also consulted for various sport and non-sport organizations.

MARILYN MORROW
Illinois State University

Marilyn Morrow, Associate Professor and Chairperson in the Department of Health Sciences, holds a Ph.D. from Southern Illinois University at Carbondale and an M.A. and B.S. from Eastern Illinois University. Her teaching and research interests include publications and presentations in the area of professional preparation issues, including program assessment and portfolio development. She has coauthored a book designed to help students practice and build competency in a number of essential professional skills.

AARON MULROONEY
Kent State University

Aaron L. Mulrooney is currently an Associate Professor in the School of Exercise, Leisure, and Sport. He holds an M.B.A. in Finance and a J.D. from the University of Akron and currently teaches graduate courses in sport law, finance, and facility management, as well as coordinating the sport administration program at Kent. His primary publications have been in facility management and law, and he has developed presentations for various audiences at state, national, and international conferences. Along with Peter Farmer and Rob Ammon, he is currently completing a text specifically devoted to the topic of facility planning and management.

DANNY O'BRIEN
Griffith University, Australia

Danny O'Brien earned his doctorate in sport management in 2000 from DeMontfort University, Bedford, England. His thesis explored organizational change and the professionalization of English rugby union. While undertaking his doctoral studies, Danny won the 1997 North American Society for Sport Management (NASSM) Student Research Paper Competition. His other degree qualifications were earned from California State University, Long Beach; and Australian Catholic University. Currently, Danny lectures in sport event management, strategic management, and sport organization and governance in Griffith University's Department of Tourism, Leisure, Hotel and Sport Management on the Gold Coast in Queensland, Australia. He has published a number of book chapters, as well as articles in *Journal of Sport Management* and *Sport Management Review.* His research interests have focused primarily on organizational and strategic change in sport organizations. More recently, Danny's research has explored the potentials presented through strategically leveraging the nexus among sport, tourism and economic, social and community development. Now considering himself too old and beat up to play his beloved rugby, Danny's sporting passion is surfing—he is currently a committee member and secretary of his local longboard club.

BRENDA G. PITTS
Georgia State University

Dr. Brenda G. Pitts is currently Professor and Director of the Master's Degree Program in Sport Management (one of only 26 approved programs in the U.S.A.), and Director of the Sport Business Research Center at Georgia State University in Atlanta, Georgia (June, 2002– present). Previously, Dr. Pitts spent 6 years at Florida State University and 12 years at the University of Louisville. She is distinguished as the Dr. Earle F. Zeigler Scholar of 2000, received the 2004 Dr. Garth Paton Distinguished Service Award of the North American Society for Sport Management (NASSM), and was one of the first Research Fellows of NASSM in 2001. Dr. Pitts is author/coauthor of four sport marketing textbooks and numerous publications and presentations, and is published in several scholarly journals such as the *Journal of Sport Management, Sport Marketing Quarterly, Journal of Vacation Marketing, International Journal of Sports Marketing and Sponsorship,* and *the International Journal of Sport Management.* She is a consultant in sport marketing for various sport businesses. Her international stops have included Sweden, South Africa, Hong Kong, Singapore, Malaysia, Spain, France, Australia, Germany, Hungary, England, The Netherlands, Canada, Scotland, and France. Some of Dr. Pitts' service accomplishments have included: member of the committee that wrote the Sport Management Curriculum Standards (first published in 1993), served on the first Sport Management Program Review Council, Program Chair of 2 NASSM conferences, hosted the 1990 NASSM Conference in Louisville and the 2004 NASSM Conference in Atlanta, and was Council Member, President-Elect, President, and Past-President of NASSM during 1990–1995, and is currently serving a three-year appointed term as Vice President of Academic Affairs for the new Sport Marketing Association (SMA) and as Editor for an annual SMA book of papers. In addition, she was an Editorial Board Member (1991–1998) and later Co-Editor-in-Chief of The Sport Management Library (1998–2000), a project that has produced 18 textbooks in sport management since 1991.

TOM H. REGAN
University of South Carolina

Dr. Tom H. Regan is the Chairman of the Department of Sport and Entertainment Management at the University of South Carolina. Research emphasis focuses on the economic impact of sport and entertainment events on regional economies and the financing and feasibility of live entertainment events. He has completed numerous studies on professional, collegiate, and touring sports. Publications have highlighted his work on the Denver

Broncos Football Club, the University of South Carolina athletic department, NASCAR, golf in South Carolina, USTA and WTA professional tennis, and other studies involving live entertainment. He was invited to the Brookings Institute to discuss the impact of professional sport facilities on regional economies.

Dr. Regan's work experience includes working as a staff accountant for Fox & Co., CPAs and eight years as a comptroller for a fully integrated oil and gas company. He has consulted with many professional organizations concerning financing venues and determining the economic benefit of facilities, events and teams. Dr. Regan's education experience includes Bachelor's and Master's of Accounting degrees from the University of Wyoming and a Doctorate degree in Sports Administration at the University of Northern Colorado.

LLOYD ZANE REMICK

Lloyd Z. Remick, Esquire, is an attorney who concentrates his practices in the areas of entertainment, sports, hospitality and communications law. He is President of Zane Management, Inc., a Philadelphia-based sports, entertainment and communications consulting and management firm.

Mr. Remick is a nationally recognized entertainment and sports attorney and manager of athletes, recording artists, writers, producers, television, radio and entertainment personalities. He is a registered contract advisor with The National Football League Players Association and the NCAA, representing professional athletes with their careers in football, basketball, ice skating, crew, boxing and track and field. He has represented a number of award winning recording artists and producers, and for twenty years he represented and managed Grammy Award winning musician Grover Washington, Jr. A graduate of Wharton School at the University of Pennsylvania, he received his J.D. Degree from Temple University School of Law and received his Master's in Tax Law from Villanova Law School. Mr. Remick has been a guest lecturer at various organizations and universities throughout the country, lecturing on power negotiations, contracts and various law-related topics. He is an Adjunct Professor at Temple University School of Law where he teaches an entertainment and sports law course and has written several articles and a text-

book on entertainment law-related subjects. Additionally, he is adjunct professor at the Temple University School of Hospitality and Tourism.

BERNARD M. RESNICK

Bernard Resnick is a Philadelphia-based entertainment and sports attorney and manager. Before forming Bernard M. Resnick, Esq., P.C. in 1999, Mr. Resnick served as counsel to Zane Management, Inc., where he was involved in the representation of entertainers including Grover Washington, Jr., Charles Fambrough and Pieces of a Dream, as well as many NFL, NBA, and MLB players, professional boxing champions and Olympic medalists. Mr. Resnick received his J.D. from the Villanova University School of Law. He has taught university classes and he has lectured widely on entertainment and sports law at bar association-sponsored continuing legal education seminars and entertainment industry conferences such as MIDEM, Billboard Magazine/American Urban Radio Network's 2003 Hip Hop/R&B Conference and Awards, The Independent Music Conference, The Philadelphia Music Conference, Music and Entertainment Industry Educators Association, The Independent Music Conference and The Millennium Music Conference. He has also served as an "expert witness" in several lawsuits.

MATTHEW J. ROBINSON
University of Delaware

Dr. Matthew J. Robinson is Associate Professor of Sport Management and Director of the Sport Management Program at the University of Delaware. He earned his Doctorate in sport administration from Temple University in 1995. Dr. Robinson has conducted market research for professional and minor league sport franchises and leagues, NCAA Division I & III athletic departments and LPGA and PGA tour events. He has also been involved in planning marketing strategies with these organizations. Dr. Robinson was the lead author for the book *Profiles of Sport Industry Professionals: The People Who Make the Games Happen.* He has published over 15 articles on sport management and marketing topics and serves on the editorial boards of *Sport Marketing Quarterly, International Sports Journal* and *Athletic Management.* He has also made over 25 national and international presentations on topics related to the sport management field.

DAVID K. STOTLAR
University of Northern Colorado

Dr. David K. Stotlar teaches on the University of Northern Colorado faculty in the areas of sport marketing and sport law. He has had over fifty articles published in professional journals and has written several textbooks and book chapters in sport marketing, fitness risk management, and sport law. He has made numerous presentations at international and national professional conferences. On several occasions, he has served as a consultant in sport management to various sport professionals; and in the area of sport law, to attorneys and international sport managers. David was selected by the USOC as a delegate to the International Olympic Academy in Greece and the World University Games Forum in Italy. He has conducted international seminars in sport management and marketing for the Hong Kong Olympic Committee, the National Sports Council of Malaysia, Mauritius National Sports Council, the National Sports Council of Zimbabwe, the Singapore Sports Council, the Chinese Taipei University Sport Federation, the Bahrain Sport Institute, the government of Saudi Arabia, the South African National Sports Congress and the Association of Sport Sciences in South Africa. Dr. Stotlar's contribution to the profession includes an appointment as Coordinator of the Sport Management Program Review Council (NASPE/NASSM) from 1999–2001. He previously served as Chair of the Council on Facilities and Equipment of the American Alliance for Health, Physical Education, Recreation and Dance and as a Board Member and later as President of the North American Society for Sport Management. Dr. Stotlar was a member of the initial group of professionals inducted as NASSM Research Fellows. He is also a founding member of the Sport Marketing Association.

ALVY E. STYLES
Ashland University

Alvy Styles, Ph.D., is an Assistant Professor in the Sport Sciences Department at Ashland University. She earned her Ph.D. in Educational Administration and an M.A. in Physical Education–Sport and Recreation Management from Kent State University. She currently teaches graduate and undergraduate courses in recreation and sport management. Her areas of scholarly interest include risk management in sport and recreation, volunteerism, and social issues in sport.

JUDITH A. SWITZER
Bucks County Community College

Judith A. Switzer received a Ph.D. and M.A. from the Graduate School of Arts and Sciences at New York University, an M.A. in Public Speaking and Rhetoric from Temple University, and a B.A. in Theatre Arts from the Pennsylvania State University. She has taught speech and film courses at Bucks County Community College for 35 years, and formerly she taught film history at Villanova University where she pioneered their Women and Film course. Apart from publishing in scholarly film journals, she is also an independent filmmaker whose films have been shown on PBS. Recently she was nominated for the third time for Who's Who Among America's Teachers.

SUSAN E. VAIL
York University

Susan is an Associate Professor and the Coordinator of the Sport Administration Program at York University in Toronto, Ontario, Canada. She teaches Politics and Policy in the Sport Industry. Dr. Vail developed our Canadian content for this edition based on her extensive knowledge of the Canadian sport system and her experience in working with Sport Canada (federal government) and a number of National Sport Organizations such as Tennis Canada, Hockey Canada and Canada Basketball.

M. ELIZABETH VERNER
Illinois State University

Dr. M. Eliza(Beth) Verner is a Professor at Illinois State University and currently serves as the President for the Illinois Association for Health, Physical Education, Recreation and Dance, a 4,000 member state organization of the American Alliance for Health, Physical Education, Recreation and Dance. At Illinois State University Dr. Verner teaches fitness management at the undergraduate level, athletics administration at the graduate level, and coordinates the professional practice program (senior field experience) for undergraduate exercise science and athletic training students. She has authored/presented over 100 articles and presentations related to experiential learning, curriculum design, and management, and is exploring a model based on social cognitive theory to study factors which influence the preferences and contribution patterns of those who financially donate to inter-collegiate athletics. Recently she assumed project coordinator responsibilities of an Illinois group dedicated to securing state, federal and foundation funding to establish and manage a statewide health-related fitness assessment and intervention program supported by an online data management system.

PART I

Developing the Fundamentals

Discussion Topic One

"History repeats itself" is not just an adage, it's a reality! The future of sport management relies on individuals, like you, who understand its fascinating evolution. This historical process was pioneered by selfless and committed men and women who devoted their lives to the field. History is cyclical: that is, it is a series of events that reoccur.

Group Discussion Question: What sport management–related examples come to mind? What are the implications?

Discussion Topic Two

The structure of intercollegiate departments of athletics is indeed changing. Recently, Chancellor Gordon Gee of Vanderbilt University restructured the Department of Intercollegiate Athletics at his institution by merging it into another unit within the Department of Student Affairs. The Vice Chancellor of Student Affairs was given the responsibility for leading this new unit. The Director of Intercollegiate Athletics was offered reassignment as a consultant. The rationale for restructuring the department was to bring athletics back into the mainstream of university activities.

Group Discussion Question: Other universities are now interested in adopting this new structure. The president of Grand University in Cedar Rapids, Minnesota, has appointed a task force to identify diversity issues and strategies for resolving those issues. How should the task force proceed?

CHAPTER 1

History of Sport Management

Bonnie L. Parkhouse and Brenda G. Pitts

In this chapter, you will become familiar with the following terms:

Sport administration	Sport Management Program
Sport management	Review Council

Learning Goals
By the end of this chapter, students should be able to:

- Explain why sport is a dominant influence in American society. Provide examples in spectator and participant sports.
- Identify sports media businesses and industries whose sole purpose is producing, televising, broadcasting, and printing information about spectator-driven sporting events.
- Explain why sports, once unique or indigenous to certain regions, have become global. Provide examples.

SPORT MANAGEMENT DEFINED

From an *applied* perspective, sport management has existed since the time of the ancient Greeks, when combat among gladiators or animals attracted crowds of spectators. Herod, king of Judaea, was honorary president of the eleventh-century Olympics. A magnificent ceremony opened the Games, followed by athletic competition where thousands of spectators were entertained lavishly (Frank, 1984). According to Parks and Olafson (1987), given the magnitude of such events, there must have been purveyors of food and drink, promoters, purchasing agents, marketing personnel, and management directors. Sport management has emerged both as an academic discipline and a professional occupation. It is the main source of income and a full-time job for a significant number of people (Soucie and Doherty, 1996). Today, all of these individuals are known as *practitioners*; this term includes all persons employed in the applied field of sport management.

Although the terms **sport(s) management** and **sport(s) administration** are often used interchangeably, the first most accurately describes this field from a universal, or global, perspective. That is, *management* is all-encompassing and represents the myriad of sport-related areas identified by DeSensi et al. (1990), including facilities, hotels and resorts, public and private fitness and racquet clubs, merchandizing, and collegiate and professional sports. They defined sport management as "any combination of skills related to planning, organizing, directing, controlling-budgeting, leading and evaluating within the context of an organization or department whose primary product or service is related to sport" (p. 33).

Although some scholars have made the distinction that the function of administration is to set goals and policies while management executes those policies, it is an accepted practice to use these two terms synonymously. The term *management* is most commonly used in the field of sport management. For example, our professional organization is the North American Society for Sport Management (NASSM). The *Journal of Sport Management (JSM)*, which has garnered a high standard of scholarship in a relatively short time (Weese, 1995), has become a major resource for disseminating significant knowledge in sport management (Parkhouse, 1996). (See Table 1-1 for an acronym "Cheat Sheet.")

The terms *sport* and *sports* are also used interchangeably. According to Parks, Zanger, and Quarterman (1998), sports is singular in nature, whereas sport is a more all-encompassing term. The North American Society for Sport Management (NASSM) has elected to use the collective noun "sport" and encourages its use.

As previously mentioned, *sport* has several definitions (Loy, 1968; Snyder and Spreitzer, 1989; vander Zwaag, 1988). For contemporary sport management as an academic field of study, the term *sport* must now be more broadly defined. Because sport management is the academic area that encompasses the study of the sport business industry, the word *sport* must encompass all of the segments of the industry, such as sporting goods, sports tourism, and other previously mentioned areas. It is necessary to develop a more contemporary definition of sport management as it relates to the academic field. A review of the current sport management literature revealed different definitions for sport management. However, the one chosen for this textbook that we believe reflects the contemporary broad concept of the sport business industry is the following:

Sport management is the study and practice involved in relation to all people, activities, organizations, and businesses involved in producing, facilitating, promoting, or organizing any product that is sport, fitness, and recreation related; and, sport products can be goods, services, people, places, or ideas (Parks, Zanger, and Quarterman, 1998; Pitts, Fielding, and Miller, 1994; Pitts and Stotlar, 2002).

The NASPE-NASSM Joint Task Force on Sport Management Curriculum and Accreditation (2000) defined sport management as "the field of study offering the specialized training and education necessary for individuals seeking careers in any of the many segments of the industry."

CONCEPT CHECK

From an applied perspective, sport management has been in existence for centuries. Only recently, however, has sport management been acknowledged as an academic pursuit. This field shares two basic elements—sport and business administration, or management. The business component includes not only such management functions as planning, organizing, directing, and controlling, but also such areas as accounting, marketing, economics and finance, and law. From a sport management perspective, the term sport includes the spectator sport industry, which focuses on consumer entertainment, and the fitness industry, which concentrates on consumer participation in fitness-related activities. Although the terms sport management, sport administration, and athletic administration are often used interchangeably, the first most accurately describes this field from a universal, or global perspective.

THE EVOLUTION OF SPORT MANAGEMENT

Although sport management is still a relatively new concept in academe, its acceptance as a legitimate area of study that is gaining credibility is well documented in the literature (Crosset et al., 1998; Danylchuk and Boucher, 2003; Parkhouse and Ulrich, 1979; Parkhouse, 1987; Parks and Quarterman, 2003; Soucie and Doherty, 1996). Sport business is also the topic of numerous publications and media

TABLE 1-1   *Acronyms and Their Descriptions*

Acronym	Description
NASSM	North American Society for Sport Management. Started in 1985, NASSM was the first academic association for sport management in the United States. NASSM's "purpose is to promote, stimulate, and encourage study, research, scholarly writing, and professional development in the area of sport management—both theoretical and applied aspects." NASSM hosts an annual scholarly conference and publishes the *Journal of Sport Management.*
NASPE-NASSM	National Association for Sport and Physical Education. NASPE "seeks to enhance knowledge and professional practice in sport and physical activity through scientific study and dissemination of research-based and experiential knowledge to members and the public." The first sport management curriculum standards were written by a joint task force of members of NASPE and NASSM.
JSM	*Journal of Sport Management.* JSM is the official journal of NASSM. The journal publishes articles that focus on the theoretical and applied aspects of management related to sport, exercise, dance, and play.
EASM	European Association for Sport Management. Similar to NASSM, EASM is the scholarly association that serves primarily European countries. EASM hosts an annual conference and publishes a journal, the *European Sport Management Quarterly.*
ESMQ	*European Sport Management Quarterly.* The official journal of EASM.
SMAANZ	Sport Management Association of Australia and New Zealand. Similar to NASSM, SMAANZ is the scholarly association for Australia and New Zealand. SMAANZ hosts an annual conference and publishes a journal, the *Sport Management Review.*
AAHPERD	American Alliance for Health, Physical Education, Recreation and Dance. AAHPERD is the scholarly association for people in the many fields related to fitness and sports, such as physical education, recreation, sport management, and leisure studies.
SMA	Sport Marketing Association. This is the newest academic association. The SMA started November 2002 and held its inaugural conference November 2003.
SRLA	Sport and Recreation Law Association. Started in 1987, this academic association focuses on the sport law content area of sport management. SRLA hosts an annual scholarly conference and publishes the *Journal of Legal Aspects of Sport and Physical Activity.*

outlets, such as CNNSports, *USA Today,* and *Time,* and can be found in a multitude of Internet sites.

Although there has been no historical study to determine the history of sport management as a university program, Ohio University claims to have had the first in 1966. Two decades earlier, however, between 1949 and 1959, Florida Southern University offered a sport management curriculum approved by the State Department of Education of Florida. The program, titled "Baseball Business Administration," was considered to be the first and only one of its kind (Isaacs, 1964). The curriculum consisted of nine content areas, some of which were similar to those today required in the Sport

Management Curriculum Standards. Some of the courses were "Tickets and Tax Laws," "Legal Responsibility and Insurance," "Promotion and Public Relations," "Park Maintenance," and "Finances, Accounting, and Payroll Systems."

It is quite possible that the first time sport management jobs and careers were written about was in 1964 in a book titled "Careers and Opportunities in Sports" (Isaacs, 1964). Throughout the book, a variety of jobs in sport business are presented, some of which are listed in Table 1-2.

The Sports Administration Program at Ohio University was a master's offering that actually had its roots at the University of Miami in Coral Gables,

TABLE 1-2 *Sport Administration Jobs and Careers Presented in Stan Isaacs' 1964 book "Careers and Opportunities in Sports"*

sports trading cards	sports themed restaurants
sports art	sports agent
sports merchandising	sports journalism
sports reporter	sports photographer
sports TV	sports radio
sports books	sports concessions
sports promoter	sports statistics organization
sporting goods	sports lawyers
sports accountant	

Note: Refer to Chapter 20 for current career opportunities in sport management.

TABLE 1-3 *Current Sport Management Program Review Registry*

Approved programs	Institutions currently in folio review
Undergraduate 33	Undergraduate 6
Master's 26	Master's 2
Doctorate 4	Doctorate 0
Total: 63	8

Florida. James G. Mason, a physical education professor there, prepared a curriculum for a proposed program in sport management at the encouragement of Walter O'Malley, then president of the Brooklyn (soon to become Los Angeles) Dodgers. O'Malley first approached Mason in 1957 with the idea. Although it was never implemented, this curriculum became the basis of the Ohio University program (Mason et al., 1981). A few years later, Biscayne College (now St. Thomas University) and St. John's University became the first institutions granting baccalaureate degrees in sport management. The second master's program was established in 1971 at the University of Massachusetts.

In 1980, 20 colleges and universities in the United States offered graduate programs in sport management. By 1985, this number had grown to 83 programs in the United States (40 undergraduate, 32 graduate, and 11 at both levels), as identified by the National Association for Sport and Physical Education (NASPE). The May 23, 1988, issue of *Sports, Inc.* published a compendium of 109 colleges and universities with programs in sport management. Of the 109 institutions identified, 51 offered undergraduate degrees, 33 were at the master's level, and 25 sponsored both undergraduate and master's programs (Brassie, 1989). A follow-up survey of colleges and universities in the United States conducted by NASPE in 1993 identified 201 sport management programs, including six doctoral programs.

More recent surveys indicate that more than 200 programs existed at the end of the millennium in the United States. That's a growth of 5,000 percent over thirty years. According to the Sport Management Program Review Registry, 63 programs have been approved and 8 are currently in folio review. (See Table 1-3.)

Although the first sport management programs were established between the 1940s and 1970s, the significant proliferation in curricular development was not observed until the mid-1980s. As a result, by 1988 only 10 percent of the programs had been in existence for more than five years.

Unlike the United States, the number of programs in Canada has not changed significantly in the past twenty years. In 1980 Bedecki and Soucie reported that ten undergraduate, nine master's, and two doctoral programs existed there. Eight years later, Soucie (1988) reported six undergraduate, nine master's and two doctoral programs. Today, ten undergraduate, seven master's, and two doctoral programs exist. Most Canadian campuses offer a course or two in sport management.

Present programs in the United States are more applied in nature, focusing on such areas as collegiate and professional sports, facility management, and health and fitness club management, whereas those in Canada are more theoretical. That is, the focus is on such subdisciplines as historical and cultural perspectives of sport and physical activity, psychological and sociological dimensions, and physiological and biomechanical aspects.

The timeline of growth and development in the international arena in sport management academe is shorter and has been slower to develop than in North America. The international community, however, looks to developments in North America as a paradigm, especially one that forms the basis of a methodology or theory. Sport management faculty in many countries have looked to North America for models of curriculum, course content, textbooks, associations, conferences, research, journals, and curriculum standards.

As a field of study and degree program, sport management is growing internationally. In the past decade, universities and colleges in the following countries have developed degree programs in sport management: Japan, China, Greece, Italy, South Africa, France, the United Kingdom, Sweden, Spain, Korea, Taiwan, Hong Kong, Singapore, Germany, Malaysia, Ireland, Norway, Finland, India, the Netherlands, and Scotland.

Sport management academic associations are being developed around the world. Most recently came the announcement of the initiation of the Asian Association for Sport Management. Others include the European Association for Sport Management, the Sport Management Association of Australia and New Zealand, and the Korean Association for Sport Management. There are similar associations now in countries such as Taiwan, Japan, Italy, South Africa, and France.

Recently the Japanese physical education curriculum has also undergone a significant transformation. The major reason is the decreasing demand for physical education teachers and the increasing need for personnel in the commercial sport sector. Specifically, the demand in the driving range industry is unique to Japan. Unlike the United States and other European countries, Japan has had tremendous growth in this area; more than 100 million people use driving range facilities there each year. These facilities require personnel who have exceptional management skills. Management of spectator sports has also become increasingly important because this industry continues to grow rapidly not only in Japan, but worldwide as well. The curricular standards (discussed in the curriculum section) that were developed for the preparation of students for the sport management profession serve as an American model for curriculum development. As

sport management becomes more global in nature, country-specific curricula will serve the same purpose (Crosset, Bromage, & Hums, 1998).

Four professional associations in North America serve the sport management profession. The North American Society for Sport Management (NASSM), the National Association for Sport and Physical Education (NASPE), the Sport Marketing Association (SMA), and the Sport and Recreation Law Association (SRLA), have monitored the rapid growth in this profession.

In 1985 NASSM was established to promote, stimulate, and encourage study, research, scholarly writing, and professional development in sport management (Zeigler, 1987). NASSM is the successor of the Sport Management Arts and Science Society (SMARTS), which was conceived in the 1970s by faculty at the University of Massachusetts. Like the members of SMARTS, those of NASSM focus on the theory, applications, and practice of management specifically related to sport, exercise (fitness), dance, and play. In addition to an annual conference, NASSM sponsors the *Journal of Sport Management (JSM)*. *JSM* publishes refereed articles relative to the theory and applications of sport management. Published since January 1987, this journal has become the major resource for disseminating significant knowledge in the field.

The Sport Marketing Association (SMA) is the newest academic association in the United States. As has been predicted by sport management scholars, this new association is one that focuses on one content area within sport management—sport marketing. The SMA was initiated in November 2002 by sport marketing professors and scholars. In November 2003, the inaugural SMA conference convened in Gainesville, Florida.

The Sport and Recreation Law Association (SRLA; until 2003 this association's title was Society for the Study of Legal Aspects of Sport and Physical Activity) was started in 1987. SRLA focuses on one content area of sport management, the legal aspects of sport. SRLA hosts an annual scholarly conference and publishes a journal, *Journal of Legal Aspects of Sport*.

NASPE, an association of the American Alliance for Health, Physical Education, Recreation, and Dance (AAHPERD), approved a sport management task force in 1986 to meet the needs of its members who were involved in sport management curricula. The NASPE task force included five professors and four practitioners. In an attempt to avoid duplication of the services offered by NASSM, the task force identified three agenda items: (1) curricular guidelines, (2) student guidelines for selecting programs, and (3) a directory of college programs preparing professionals in sport management. The task force drafted curricular guidelines and disseminated them to those directors of sport management programs identified by NASPE for input. Suggestions were then incorporated into the final document. In the fall of 1987, the NASPE Cabinet approved this document as NASPE's official curricular guidelines and published it as *Guidelines for Programs Preparing Undergraduate and Graduate Students for Careers in Sport Management* (Brassie, 1989).

When NASPE published its 1987 guidelines for programs preparing undergraduate and graduate students for careers in sport management, NASSM was invited to endorse the guidelines. Many members of NASSM believed the NASPE guidelines were too limited, which led to a discussion of developing curricular standards endorsed jointly by NASPE and NASSM. A joint task force of five NASPE and five NASSM members was appointed by the respective associations to develop standards that could shape the preparation of prospective sport management students. The joint task force was also mandated to investigate the feasibility of accrediting sport management curricula as a means to provide an incentive for institutions to upgrade their respective programs. The members of the task force agreed that program review and approval was an approach that could help assure students and potential employers that graduates of an approved program had been prepared in content areas that would result in the development of appropriate knowledge and skills required of an effective professional. The joint task force convened in 1989 to begin identifying the essential curricular content areas, establishing standards, and developing a program approval protocol that could evaluate programs for compliance with the standards.

The curricular standards were approved by the NASSM board of directors in 1990 after discussion by the entire membership in attendance at both its 1989 and 1990 conferences. NASPE conducted presentations at its conventions in 1990 and 1991. After the presentation at the 1991 convention, a referendum card and descriptive documents were sent to the 181 institutions with sport management programs, and a vote was taken. The NASPE Cabinet, as a result of the positive vote, approved the standards in 1992.

After the adoption of the standards, the joint task force continued working on a protocol that could be used to evaluate an institution's sport management program. Both associations agreed on a protocol and decided to adopt a voluntary "program review" procedure rather than an "accreditation process" so that the evaluation would be viewed more positively and less threateningly by an institution. In May 1993, the first NASPE-NASSM Sport Management Curriculum Standards and Program Review Process was published. The **Sport Management Program Review Council** (SMPRC) was created to govern the review process, which officially began in 1994. For information about the content (curricular) standards, call 1-800-321-0789.

SPORT MANAGEMENT TODAY AND IN THE FUTURE

Sport management has grown tremendously as an academic field of study in a short period of time. The number of journals, for example, has grown in number and content just within a decade (see Table 1-4). The number of programs, students, and faculty continue to grow. Most programs today have an average

---

TABLE 1-4   *Some Sport Management and Related Journals*

Australian Leisure Management
Entertainment and Sports Law Forum
European Sport Management Quarterly
  (formerly the *European Journal of Sport Management*)
International Journal of Sport Management
International Sports Journal
Journal of Hospitality and Leisure Marketing
Journal of Legal Aspects of Sport and Physical Activity
Journal of Sports Economics
Journal of Sport Management
Journal of Sport Tourism
International Journal of Sports Marketing and Sponsorship
Marquette Sport Law Journal
Seton Hall Journal of Sport Law
Southern California Sports & Entertainment Law Journal
Sport Management Review
Sport Marketing Quarterly
The Sport Lawyer Journal
Women in Sport and Physical Activity Journal

---

of two full-time sport management faculty, while a few have five or more. As you will learn in the next section, there are primarily ten, nine, and five content areas required as a base of knowledge across the undergraduate, master's and doctoral curricula: management in sport, ethics in sport, marketing in sport, legal aspects of sport, social and behavioral dimensions in sport, and finance in sport. These areas are growing as areas of specialization as the number of faculty increases and develops specialized areas of research. Recently, Mahony and Pitts (1998) called for increased attention to developing areas of specialization in sport management. They believe and state the following:

It is critical for the future of the field that sport management researchers produce strong, theoretically grounded research that will be respected by colleagues in other fields and by the universities that employ sport management faculty. While publishing articles geared to practitioners is good for the field, a decision to focus the efforts of researchers too much on the needs of current practitioners could prevent the field's young professionals from developing a strong theoretical research agenda. This may not always affect practitioners today but will affect their efforts in the future. . . . We expect to see increased specialization in a number of sport management content areas. As programs expand, add more faculty, and broaden their course offerings, specialization is imminent. Specialization is critical for developing a unique body of knowledge . . . the more focused sport management faculty become in their research, the better their production will be as scholars. (pp. 262–63, 269–70)

Perhaps the field will grow to the extent that one day there will be colleges of sport management. Currently, there is a school of Tourism and Hospitality management in the United States with programs in sport, recreation, tourism, and hospitality management. Within a college there will be departments that focus on the different areas, such as a department of sport marketing and a department of sport finance, with large numbers of faculty who specialize in that area and students who want their sport management education focused on that area.

Today, one out of every ten people in the United States is working in the leisure industry. In addition, one-third of the nation's land is devoted to leisure, and Americans spend approximately one-third of their time and income on leisure pursuits. Tourism is the world's number one industry and one of four "markets" driving our economic future (AALR, 1994). Given these facts, it is probable that a signifi-

cant number of sport management programs will expand to include such areas as tourism, sport tourism, gaming, and hospitality.

CONCEPT CHECK

Although the number of programs in Canada has not changed much in the past fifteen years, a significant proliferation in sport management curricula has occurred since the mid-1980s in the United States. Several other countries have also begun offering academic programs in sport management.

CURRICULUM

Curriculum in sport management has changed dramatically over the past thirty-five years. Historically, sport management has had a strong physical education orientation. Required courses for the sport management student twenty years ago typically included physiology of exercise, motor learning, and measurement in physical education. Electives often included sociology or psychology of sport and perhaps a course in the history or philosophy of physical education and sport. A course in the organization and administration of physical education and sport was about the only course with a managerial focus available. Sometimes electives were available in business or journalism, and the more sophisticated programs may have created internship opportunities. Sport management was often promoted as a nonteaching option in physical education, which physical education faculty tolerated primarily to offset the declining enrollment in teaching and coaching.

Unfortunately, many schools during this early period merely repackaged an existing physical education curriculum and added some catchy course titles to create a sport management curriculum (Berg, 1989). Parkhouse (1987) reported that a significant number of sport management programs still included physical education–related coursework that is questionable in meeting the educational or job-related needs of this industry. In 1989 Berg reported that only a handful of programs were sufficiently developed in terms of faculty and curriculum to produce qualified graduates.

In 1989 NASPE and NASSM created a joint task force to further develop curricular standards for the

TABLE 1-5   *Sport Management Curriculum Standards: Undergraduate Content Areas*

Content Area 1—Sociocultural dimensions
Content Area 2—Management and leadership in sport
Content Area 3—Ethics in sport management
Content Area 4—Marketing in sport
Content Area 5—Communication in sport
Content Area 6—Budget and finance in sport
Content Area 7—Legal aspects of sport
Content Area 8—Economics in sport
Content Area 9—Governance in sport
Content Area 10—Field experience in sport management

TABLE 1-6   *Sport Management Curriculum Standards: Master's Program Content Areas*

Content Area 1—Sociocultural context of sport
Content Area 2—Management and leadership in sport
Content Area 3—Ethics in sport management
Content Area 4—Marketing in sport
Content Area 5—Public relations in sport
Content Area 6—Financial management in sport
Content Area 7—Legal aspects of sport
Content Area 8—Research in sport
Content Area 9—Field experience in sport management

TABLE 1-7   *Sport Management Curriculum Standards: Doctoral Program*

Content Area 1—Background requirements
Content Area 2—Research foundations
Content Area 3—Sport management theory in an area of specialization
Content Area 4—Advanced cognate consisting of a minimum of two courses outside the department that support the specializations cited in content area 3.
Content Area 5—Field experience

From: NASPE-NASSM (2000). *Sport Management Program Standards.*

preparation of students for the sport management profession. The approach differed from the NASPE Guidelines approved in 1987. Rather than identifying specific courses, content areas were developed that could be met in a single course or in multiple courses in the curriculum. Rather than identifying foundational and applied areas of the curriculum, each content area included a body of knowledge needed by those preparing for careers in sport management. The standards were divided into the core content required at the baccalaureate, master's, and doctoral levels.

Today, the NASPE-NASSM Sport Management Curriculum Standards outline the minimum body of knowledge that a sport management program should offer at the undergraduate, master's, and doctoral levels. The Content Areas for Curriculum are presented in Tables 1-5 to 1-7 (NASPE-NASSM, 2000).

Parkhouse and Pitts have frequently made the following statements: (1) "A field of study without curriculum standards is a field of study without credibility" (2) "Many of these programs are more on paper than in practice."

FUTURE OF SPORT MANAGEMENT AS AN ACADEMIC PROGRAM OF STUDY

The future of sport management has great potential, although major hurdles must be confronted. First, although sport management is becoming increasingly more accepted as a profession—an appropriate prerequisite for employment in the sport industry—it will become legitimate only when graduates of sport management programs are able to demonstrate that they have the knowledge necessary to be successful in the marketplace, are able to perform the functions expected of a manager, and qualify for advancement through the ranks of the organization. NASPE and NASSM are working collectively to encourage administrators of sport management programs to submit their curricula for evaluation through the program review process so that every sport management student is subjected to the rigor of those content areas that are necessary for successful management.

Second, the potential of sport management will be influenced by the quality of its faculty. The new doctoral graduates of sport management programs compose the faculty of tomorrow. Many more talented and energetic students are needed in our doctoral programs to supply these faculty with quality pedagogy and scholarship, which is imperative for the growing number of programs in this profession.

Third, sport management must continue its development as an area of scholarship. Considerable research predicated on management theories that are specific to sport need to be developed. The extent to which the latter is accomplished will largely determine whether sport management will take its place among the widely accepted professions or decline as an area with little substance.

Lastly, faculty and students in sport management and industry professionals must continue to insist on sustaining and improving sport management curriculum standards. Curriculum standards and an approval or accreditation process serve to ensure that programs are of a quality level deserving recognition and credibility, and that the knowledge and skills needed to work in the sport industry are developed in programs of study in sport management.

CONCEPT CHECK

Historically, sport management has had a strong physical education orientation. Today the focus is on foundation areas of study, with a strong emphasis on sport management courses, application areas of study that build on foundation subject matter and are specific to the sport industry, and field experiences. Given its nature, sport management is a multidisciplinary field of study. It requires the cooperation of several disciplines, especially business administration (management) and physical education (now commonly referred to as "sport studies," "exercise and sport sciences," or similar titles that more accurately describe the academic components of physical education).

SOME THOUGHTS ON THE GROWTH OF THE FIELD OF SPORT MANAGEMENT

The sport management discipline has come a long way since Earle F. Zeigler planted its first seed when he introduced, approximately forty years ago, the first major textbook on the administration of physical education and athletics. In that relatively short period of time, sport management has created a solid niche for itself. It now has a clear social identity, and it is fully integrated within the broader academic sector of sport and business sciences and physical education.

From a professional practice perspective, administrators in sport have evolved from being volunteer and part-time administrators to full-time university-trained professionals. All over the world, sport management university graduates are now at work managing the sport sector. Over the years, academic programs have mushroomed in order to meet the increasing demand for competent graduates for this new industry. Furthermore, the quality of academic programs has also increased as curriculum standards for the discipline were developed and implemented. Hence, not only is sport management now recognized as a unique professional occupation, but also practitioners with proper academic credentials have taken over this field of practice.

From a disciplinary perspective, sport management has been embraced as a distinct academic subject, and it is now accepted as a legitimate and unique field of inquiry. Such rapid progress is largely due to the emergence of continental and international organizations and societies like NASSM, EASM, and SMAANZ. These organizations, particularly through their publications and annual conferences, have considerably enhanced the credibility of the discipline. Past and present academic leaders behind these organizations deserve a lot of credit as they have contributed a lot to the construction and advancement of the field.

From a research perspective, excellent sport management journals are now published regularly by these organizations. As a consequence, the quantity of published research has clearly increased as more avenues for publication emerged, and as doctoral students joined the ranks of active sport management scholars. Still, sport management research is in its infancy, and there remains a vast research agenda. Also, in comparison with other sport science disciplines, there are still relatively few active researchers in sport management. The development of more scholars needs to be an area of focus in the new millennium. Nevertheless, it appears that the initial call by early pioneers for a more solid theoretical foundation has been heard. In less than half a century, sport management has clearly matured and become a respected discipline in the sport sciences.

Dan Soucie, Ph.D.
Nanyang Technological University
Singapore

As the numbers of sport management programs have increased, I have seen both positive and negative results. The negative is that the supply of graduates in sport management has exceeded demand. This has had a tendency to depress salaries and increase the competition for the positions that are available. However, the positive is that only the most qualified students are hired. Colleges and universities have upgraded the curricula and the experiences they provide for their students to enable their students to be competitive in the job market. As a result, sport management programs today are much stronger and the quality of graduating students is much higher.

Another positive today is that sport management degrees have much higher visibility and acceptance in the sport industry. As administrators with sport management degrees climb the career ladder, they will be in a position to hire graduates of sport management programs.

In summary, the growth of sport management as a profession is still in its infancy, but only those students who are bright and well prepared will enjoy a rewarding career. Students who are non-committed and not well prepared need not apply!

Stan Brassie, Ph.D.
Professor Emeritus
Athens, GA

When I entered the academic field of sport management in 1981, most sport management curricula were specializations within physical education programs, most faculty were physical educators, there were no sport management textbooks, and there were no scholarly associations or journals. Moreover, many sport management programs had only one or two faculty members, and most curricula still included physical education courses. It has been most gratifying for me to witness and to participate in the evolution of sport management from its humble beginnings to its current position as a respected entity in the academy. An essential feature of this evolution has been the large number of people involved in the process and their selfless commitment to the development of our field. Sport management has clearly been a team effort!

Sport management has made many advances, but there are challenges yet to be addressed. Three actions I believe would enhance the quality of sport management as an area of academic study are (a) a greater emphasis on the sport studies component of the curriculum; (b) an increase in the number of qualified faculty required to constitute a critical mass in NASPE-NASSM approved programs; and (c) the continuation of our quest to establish a unique body of knowledge.

Much of the responsibility for the future of sport management rests with the individuals who are reading this chapter. I encourage each of you to learn about the history of the field through the many publications available to you, to determine to have a positive impact on the continued development of sport management, and to dedicate your intellect and energy toward that objective. Your lives as well as sport management will be all the richer for your efforts!

Janet Parks, DA
Bowling Green State University
Bowling Green, OH

As we move into the new millennium there are over a hundred books in sport law, and courses in sport law are found in over half of the law schools in the United States and in over 80 percent of the sport management curricula. Today, most sport law authors specialize in one or more areas of law.

The American Bar Association (ABA) has an Entertainment and Sport Law Section and a Committee on Sport in the Section of Business.

As society develops an appetite for risk management, supervision, and compliance in the workplace, a need for persons knowledgeable in law is a must. When the workplace is sport with its inherent risks, the need for an expert in sport law is a must. The sport lawyer will be a multidisciplinary specialist with skills appropriate to teach, advise, and practice in both law and in sport.

Annie Clement, Ph.D., J.D.
Barry University
Miami, FL

In the second half of the twentieth century, sport management "came on like gangbusters." By that statement I am simply affirming the tremendous interest in this area of endeavor that has resulted in the establishment of several hundred professional training programs in North America alone. Yet at the moment, I am finding it necessary to analyze philosophically what I anachronistically am calling the "plight" of sport management as the profession strives to cross the so-called postmodern divide from one epoch to another.

It can be argued that indeed the world is moving into a new epoch as the proponents of postmodernism have been affirming over recent decades. An epoch approaches closure when many of the fundamental convictions of its advocates are challenged by a substantive minority of the populace. Within such a milieu there are strong indications that sport management is going to have great difficulty crossing this postmodern chasm.

Scholars argue that many in democracies, undergirded by the relative achievement of various rights being propounded (e.g., individual freedom, privacy), have come to believe that they require a supportive "liberal consensus" within their respective societies. Conversely, conservative, essentialist elements functioning in such political systems feel that the deeper foundation justifying this claim of a (required) liberal consensus has never been fully rationalized (keeping their more authoritative orientation in mind, of course).

However, postmodernists form a growing, substantive minority that supports a more humanistic, pragmatic, liberal consensus. Within such a milieu there are strong indications that present sport management is going to have difficulty crossing the postmodern divide. I say this because at present competitive sport appears to be a social institution with an implied theory that daily gives indications of not being able to live up to its assertive, yet vague proclamations.

There is a need to answer such questions as (1) where sport *has been,* (2) where it *is now,* (3) where it *is heading,* and (4) where it *should be heading.* Further questions that should be considered are (5) what competitive sport's prevailing drift is, (6) what various kinds of sport forms are available today, (7) what the advantages and disadvantages of sport involvement in life are, and (8) what sport's residual impact is.

In response to these questions, sport may be postulated as "the destroyer," "the redeemer," the institution being tempted by "technology and science," the social phenomenon where heroes and villains are created, and, finally, the institution surviving within an era characterized by a vacuum of belief. I firmly believe that the sport manager of the twenty-first century needs to understand competitive sport's dilemma fully, since he or she will be confronted inevitably by the postmodern divide.

In crossing this frontier, many troubling and difficult decisions, often ethical in nature as well, will have to be made as the sport management profession seeks to prepare prospective professionals capable of guiding sport into becoming a truly responsible social institution.

Earle F. Zeigler, Ph.D.
The University of Western Ontario
Emeritus Graduate Faculty
Oregon State University

SUMMARY

- Although sport management is relatively new to academia, its acceptance as a legitimate area of study is well documented in the literature.
- Although the terms *sport management* and *sport administration* are often used interchangeably, the first most accurately describes this field from a universal, or global perspective.
- In 1993, the NASPE-NASSM Sport Management Curriculum Standards were initially published and again in 2000 with minor changes. Sport management programs should use the standards to develop curricula.
- The North American Society for Sport Management (NASSM) and the National Association for Sport and Physical Education (NASPE) Task Force on Sport Management corroborate a rapid growth in this profession. NASSM was established to promote, stimu-

late, and encourage research, scholarly writing, and professional development in the area of sport management. The Task Force focuses on curricular needs. The *Journal of Sport Management* is the major resource for disseminating significant knowledge in this field.
- This relatively new field has great potential, but its destiny is still in question. It is imperative that those responsible for the curricular development of sport management programs at both the national and institutional levels accept this responsibility for ensuring quality professional preparation. At the institutional level, proliferation in the interest of increasing student enrollment must give way to a commitment to excellence.
- Quality control is currently a major concern of academicians and practitioners in this field. In this endeavor, an "accrediting" agency comparable to those in business administration and communications is now being operationalized in sport management.

 ## CRITICAL THINKING EXERCISE

You are a first-year college professor of sport management with a personal interest in major league baseball and other men's professional sports. You would love to focus on these for case studies and examples in class, even though you know that there is much more to the sport business industry. Should you compromise your personal interests in a couple of sports to be sure you teach your students about the true breadth and depth of the sport business industry? Why or why not? What is your responsibility to the students, to the program, and to the growth of sport management as a field of study? What material exists in the literature that will help you determine the content of your sport management curriculum, courses, and lectures?

 ## REVIEW QUESTIONS AND ISSUES

1. What is sport management? What is the sport business industry?
2. What is the purpose of accreditation? What is the difference between accreditation and

program approval? How can program approval resolve the quality control problem that currently exists in sport management programs? Why have some academicians been reluctant to support accreditation?

3. Why does the term *sport management* more accurately describe this field than *sport administration*?

4. How has the sport management curriculum changed over the past twenty-five years?

 SOLUTION TO CRITICAL THINKING EXERCISE

Help in solving this dilemma: The majority of students in sport management do not go into jobs and careers with the few large men's professional sports, such as MLB, the NBA, and the NFL. Therefore, your first consideration is the depth and breadth of the sport business industry and the enormous variety of jobs and careers into which sport management students will be going. The sport management curriculum standards will guide you in the development of content for programs and courses. The curriculum standards provide the base knowledge applicable to any sport business job or career that every sport management student should know. Current textbooks and academic journals will help in developing courses and lecture material. You will discover, however, that there is an overemphasis on men's professional sports and college athletics in many of these materials. Therefore, use a variety of materials and books from a variety of sources. For example, for every industry segment, there are trade journals and magazines to which you could subscribe that would help with disseminating information on those segments. The Sporting Goods Manufacturers Association publishes several newsletters, magazines, and reports. They also have a Website and stage annual meetings and conventions. As another source for another type of industry segment, the Snowsports Industries of America is an umbrella organization for many different sport businesses, such as equipment, marketing, financial, facilities, and clothing, relating to a variety of snow sports. The SIA also publishes several newsletters, magazines, and reports. Moreover, you could assign the students to seek information on

different industries, bring the materials to class, and use them to share with the class.

FOSTERING YOUR WORKPLACE SKILLS

1. On the Web, go to a sport management careers/jobs Website. Study the jobs listed during a two-week or one-month period of time. Develop categories for the jobs listed, such as sport marketing, athletic administration (college sports), and sports finance. Develop a matrix of the job requirements, such as education requirements, years of experience, city and state. Give a presentation of this to the class.

2. Develop your résumé and a business card based on your qualifications.

3. Schedule a meeting and interview with two local sport management professionals in different jobs and sport businesses. Interview them to learn about their backgrounds, their jobs, and their advice about working in the sport business industry.

 WEBSITES

www.nassm.com—Website of the North American Society for Sport Management

www.sportscareers.com—Website listing sport business jobs

http://www.griffith.edu.au/text/school/gbs/tlhs/smaanz/home.html—Website for the Sport Management Association of Australia and New Zealand

www.easm.org—Website of the European Association for Sport Management

www.naspe.org—Website for the National Association for Sport and Physical Education

www.sportmanagementclub.com—Website for a student Sport management club

www.sportmarketingassociation.com—Website for the Sport Marketing Association

www.womensportsjobs.com—Website for sport business jobs

www.workinsports.com—Website for sport business jobs

www.ithaca.edu/srla—Website for the Sport and Recreation Law Association

REFERENCES

American Association for Leisure and Recreation (AALR) (1994). *Guide for Department Chairs of Leisure, Parks, & Recreation Curricula.* Reston, VA.

Bedecki, T., and Soucie, D. (1980). Trends in physical education, sport, and athletic administration in Canadian universities and colleges. Paper presented at the 26th Annual

Conference of the Canadian Association for Health, Physical Education, and Recreation. St. John's, Newfoundland.

Berg, R. (1989). The quest for credibility. *Athletic Business,* 13(11), 44–48.

Brassie, S. (1989). Guidelines for programs preparing undergraduate and graduate students for careers in sport management. *Journal of Sport Management,* 3(2), 158–64.

Crosset, T. W., Bromage, S., and Hums, M. A. (1998). History of sport management. In L. P. Masteralexis, C. A. Barr, and M. A. Hums (eds.), *Principles and practice of sport management.* Gaithersburg, MD: Aspen Publishers.

Danylchuk, K., and Boucher, R. (2003). The future of sport management as an academic discipline. *International Journal of Sport Management,* 4, 281–300.

DeSensi, J., Kelley, D., Blanton, M., and Beitel, P. (1990). Sport management curricular evaluation and needs assessment: A multifaceted approach. *Journal of Sport Management,* 4(1), 31–58.

Frank, R. (1984). Olympic myths and realities. *Arete: The Journal of Sport Literature,* 1(2), 155–61.

Isaacs, S. (1964). *Careers and opportunities in sports.* New York: E. P. Dutton & Co.

Loy, J. (1968). The nature of sport: A definitional effort. *Quest,* 10, 1–15.

Mahony, D., and Pitts, B. G. (1998). Research outlets in sport marketing: The need for increased specialization. *Journal of Sport Management,* 12, 259–272.

Mason, J., Higgins, C., and Owen, J. (1981). Sport administration education 15 years later. *Athletic Purchasing and Facilities* (January), 44, 45.

Meek, A. (1997). An estimate of the size and supported economic activity of the sports industry in the United States. *Sport Marketing Quarterly,* 6(4), 15–21.

NASPE-NASSM. (2000). *NASPE-NASSM Sport Management curriculum standards and program review.* Reston, VA: AAHPERD Publications. (www.aahperd.org/naspe)

Parkhouse, B. L. (1987). Sport management curricula: Current status and design implications for future development. *Journal of Sport Management,* 1(2), 93–115.

Parkhouse, B. L., and Ulrich, D. (1979). Sport management as a potential cross-discipline: A paradigm for theoretical application. *Quest,* 31(2), 264–76.

Parkhouse, B. L. (1996). Definition, evolution, and curriculum. In B. L. Parkhouse (ed.), *The Management of Sport: Its Foundation and Application* (pp. 3–12). 2nd ed. St. Louis: Mosby.

Parks, J., and Olafson, G. (1987). Sport management and a new journal. *Journal of Sport Management,* 1(1), 1–3.

Parks, J., and Quain, R. (1986). Curriculum perspectives. *Journal of Physical Education, Recreation and Dance,* 57(4), 22–26.

Parks, J. B., and Quarterman, J. (eds.). (2003). *Contemporary Sport Management.* Champaign, IL: Human Kinetics.

Parks, J. B., Zanger, B., and Quarterman, J. (1998). *Contemporary sport management.* Champaign, IL: Human Kinetics.

Parks, J., Zanger, B., and Quarterman, J. (1998). Introduction to sport management. In J. Parks, B. Zanger and J. Quarterman (eds.), *Contemporary sport management.* Champaign, IL: Human Kinetics.

Pitts, B. G. (March 19, 2003). Personal communication.

Pitts, B. G., Fielding, L. W., and Miller, L. K. (1994). Industry segmentation theory and the sport industry: Developing a sport industry segmentation model. *Sport Marketing Quarterly,* 3(1), 15–24.

Pitts, B. G., and Stotlar, D. K. (2002). *Fundamentals of sport marketing.* Morgantown, WV: Fitness Information Technology.

Sandomir, R. (1988). The $50 billion sport industry. *Sports Inc.* (November 14).

Snyder, E., and Spreitzer, E. (1989). *Social aspects of sport.* Englewood Cliffs, NJ: Prentice Hall.

Soucie, D. (1988). Promotion of sport management programs in Canada. Paper presented to the North American Society for Sport Management. Champaign, Illinois.

Soucie, D., and Doherty, A. (1996). Past endeavors and future perspectives for sport management research. *Quest,* 48, 486–500.

Street & Smith's *SportBusiness Journal* (1999). Research Department.

vander Zwaag, H. (1988). *Policy development in sport management.* Indianapolis: Benchmark Press.s

Weese, W. J. (1995). If we are not serving practioners, then we're not serving sport management. *Journal of Sport Management,* 9, 237–43.

Zeigler, E. (1987). Sport management: Past, present, future. *Journal of Sport Management,* 1(1), 4–24.

CHAPTER 2

Research and Inquiry

Sue Inglis and Joanne Maclean

In this chapter, you will become familiar with the following terms:

Academic dishonesty	Grounded theory	Qualitative
Action research	Human ethics	Quantitative
Biography	Independent variable	Reliability
Case study	Inductive reasoning	Semiotics
Deductive reasoning	Inquiry	Survey research
Dependent variable	Organizational behavior	Theory
Descriptive research	Organizational theory	Triangulation
Ethnography	Paradigm	Validity
Experimental designs	Peer review	
Experimental research	Phenomenology	

Learning Goals
By the end of this chapter, students should be able to:

- Discuss a range of topic areas in sport management research.

- Understand validity and reliability in research.

- Explain key concepts in qualitative and quantitative research.

- Identify types of published resources and how to evaluate them.

- Discuss ethics in research and inquiry.

- Explain how to avoid plagiarism and academic dishonesty.

Managing sport is full of challenges and complexities! In this chapter we take a look at the importance research and inquiry play in advancing our understanding of the management of sport. Research and inquiry represent our curiosity about how sport is managed and how management practices can be improved by asking good questions and seeking new information that will ensure that sport is effectively managed within society.

Learning about key concepts of research and inquiry sharpens critical thinking skills and makes us better students, practitioners, and scholars of management, thus enhancing our potential to understand and anticipate organizational life, and work effectively toward desired change. There is a certain air of excitement associated with research; this chapter is written in the hope that the reader catches a bit of it!

As long as sport has existed, so has its management. The citizens of Elis, Greece, for example, managed the ancient Olympic Games (Harris, 1967; Kyle, 1987). In the nineteenth and twentieth centuries professional organizations emerged to manage amateur and professional sport (Hardy, 1986; Hardy and Berryman, 1983). The study of sport and its management, however, is a relatively new field in contemporary society and is characterized by emerging specializations and refined ways of conducting inquiry and research. The purpose of inquiry and research is to understand sport management and to allow for a meaningful contribution to the practical side or "the doing" of the management of sport.

This chapter begins with an organizational behavior and theory and work-related functions framework that is helpful in understanding relevant topics within sport management. A major portion of the chapter is concerned with knowledge development in the field of sport management. Within knowledge development, the concepts of theory and deductive and inductive reasoning are pertinent. Also introduced are the foundations of sport management, including sport and business administration and areas such as sociology and psychology from which theory can be derived. The importance of working with theory as the field of sport management develops is a theme stressed throughout the chapter.

Various types of validity and reliability are introduced as important concepts in conducting research and in evaluating published research. Next, key steps involved in the research process and qualitative and quantitative approaches to research design are outlined.

Guidelines for evaluating various types of published research are included. These should be helpful in identifying a variety of sources, including books and peer-reviewed journal articles, as well as understanding key questions to ask in assessing published work.

Individuals engaged in research have an obligation to adhere to ethical guidelines. The reader is introduced to some of the ethical areas through practical examples of communication between the researcher and respondents. Information on how to avoid plagiarism and academic dishonesty is explained.

Although the topics and concepts cannot be fully explored in one chapter, hopefully the chapter will serve as an introduction for the reader and inspire more reading and application of sound research in this field of study.

FRAMEWORK FOR SPORT MANAGEMENT

A useful way of depicting some of the topics in sport management follows the organizational behavior and organizational theory framework used in the management literature (Daft, 1995; Johns, 1992; Steers et al., 1996). Recently, scholars in sport management have published textbooks using this framework. See Slack (1997) and Chelladurai (2001) for two excellent examples. **Organizational behavior** includes areas such as individual perceptions, individual differences, learning styles, motivation, communication, leadership, decision making, conflict, and work group behavior. Organizational behavior helps us understand why people behave the way they do in their organizational lives and is thought of as taking a micro perspective, that is, a concern with individuals and groups as basic components for the analysis of work behavior. Questions such as "How do individual differences affect the way we perceive others?" "What factors are involved with motivating individuals to perform on the job?" "How do group norms affect work behavior?" "What leadership styles are most prominent in the managing of change?" and "How do conflict management strategies apply to sport management?" are the types of questions typical of the organizational behavior perspective.

Organizational theory includes the study of areas such as the design, technology, and environment of organizations. Organizational theory takes a macro perspective, with the organization as the unit of analysis. Questions and areas include "What are useful ways of describing the structures of our sport organizations?" "What effect does size have on the design and function of the organization?" "What role does a turbulent environment have on the design and operations of our work sites?" and "How do similar organizations compete for scarce resources?"

Organizational behavior and organizational theory fit under the umbrella term of organizational science. Organizational behavior and theory provide a useful way of understanding organizational life. Introductions to a number of organizational behavior and theory topics are provided in this textbook. The other range of topics actively pursued by researchers and writers of sport management include work-related functions of marketing (including advertising, sponsorship, and promotions), facility management, finance, computer application in sport environments, product development, and case law and its application to sport environments. These are just a few examples of the range of topics of interest to scholars in sport management. The inquiry and research into these topics will advance the understanding of how sport is managed and can be most effectively delivered to the benefit of the participants, spectators, and communities. How knowledge is acquired and the meaning of theory are also important to understand, and they are the focus of the next section.

CONCEPT CHECK

An organizational science framework for understanding specializations within sport management includes organizational behavior with an emphasis on the individual and group, and organizational theory with an emphasis on the organization as the unit of analysis. A number of work-related functions (e.g., marketing, legal liability, and facility management) are also important areas within sport management.

INQUIRY AND KNOWLEDGE DEVELOPMENT

Inquiry is the art and skill of arriving at new understandings about a problem, issue, or phenomenon through the process of asking good questions, identifying and evaluating good sources of information, drawing reasoned conclusions and emergent questions and communicating to others.

Developing knowledge through research and inquiry in the field of sport management involves creating theory and testing theory. In simple terms, a **theory** is an explanation of how concepts are related.

For researchers, a theory will be a series of statements that capture what is currently known about related concepts and assumptions about the concepts. Assumptions represent the ideas and views we think are true about particular issues without knowing for sure. Often, assumptions are the answers to our research questions we have before we begin the research (Hubbuch, 1996). The theory may be derived from the "field," that is, where the theory is played out in practice and may be tested and explored in various types of studies. Managers use theories, too. Although managers may not formally write down their ideas about particular concepts, their behavior at work often reflects trial-and-error attempts related to different theories they hold.

Using theories in research helps in three important ways (Hamner and Organ, 1978). First, theories provide a practical way of organizing knowledge and therefore provide a structure for understanding. Second, a good theory will summarize or capture a great deal of information in a few critical propositions. Third, theories help direct future study and practice. Good theories help to explain real behavior in real organizational settings, thus good theory development is inextricably linked to practice. Daft and Steers (1986) offer the well-known quote of Kurt Lewin, "There is nothing so practical as a good theory." This is true for sport management.

To evaluate what makes a good theory, Kaplan's (1964) framework can be used.

1. *Internal consistency.* Are the concepts and relationships between the concepts in the theory free from contradiction? Do the concepts and relationships make sense?
2. *External consistency.* Does the theory seem to make sense when viewed in relation to real life examples?
3. *Scientific parsimony.* Is the theory simple? Does the theory include only the main concepts that explain a phenomenon?
4. *Generalizability.* Does the theory apply to a variety of situations? For example, if we have a theory about why there are so few women in management positions within those organizations, does the theory hold true for other situations of few women in management?
5. *Verification.* Can we test the theory? For the theory to be useful, it would need to be tested or explored in a research setting.

When a theory satisfies these characteristics, it has greater meaning and usefulness to both researchers and managers.

The work of Thibault et al. (1993) is a good example of a research program reflecting Kaplan's framework for good theory. These authors were interested in understanding how sport organizations develop strategies to anticipate change and environmental challenges. They developed a relatively simple and meaningful theory, of value to sport managers and theorists, that explains how different nonprofit amateur sport organizations develop different strategies and plans for their organizations. Their framework (theory) incorporated the two main dimensions of program attractiveness and competitive position with a number of imperatives in both dimensions. The imperatives for program attractiveness were "fundability," size of client base, volunteer appeal, and support group appeal. For competitive positions the imperatives were equipment costs and affiliation fees. When plotted on a matrix, these two dimensions produced four strategic types called *enhancers, innovators, refiners,* and *explorers.* In a subsequent study (Thibault et al., 1994), the theory was tested on a sample of thirty-two national sport organizations. The findings supported the theory and, most importantly, provided a contingency framework for understanding how different sport organizations employ differing strategies to cope with environmental variances.

DEDUCTIVE AND INDUCTIVE REASONING

Deductive and inductive reasoning are two ways of working with theories and knowledge development. They are illustrated in Figure 2-1. **Deductive reasoning** is a process of inquiry in which one works from general principles to specific instances or observations. For example, if a study worked from the principle that involving employees in decisions concerning scheduling of work will lead to lower absenteeism, then the study would be designed or a situation found in which employees are involved in these scheduling decisions. Ways of assessing and measuring whether the reality of the employee involvement did in fact fit with the initial theory or principle would be developed. **Inductive reasoning** works the other way. Inquiry from a number of observations and situations leads to a general theory or principle. What principle is captured in the reality of the observations?

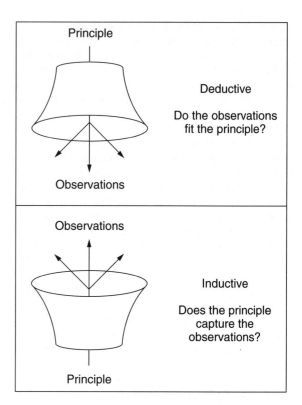

FIGURE 2-1 Deductive and inductive reasoning.

USING FOUNDATIONS AND THEORY IN SPORT MANAGEMENT

Good researchers have substantive knowledge in the area they are studying. Moving to more theoretical-based research in sport management implies that for the phenomena under study, the foundations and frameworks informing the research area will be used. Lambrecht (1991), drawing on Parkhouse's 1987 work, depicted sport management as originating from the two primary disciplines of sport studies and business administration. We can add to this depiction the parent disciplines such as anthropology, economics, sociology, political science, and psychology that inform sport studies and business administration. This is an important message within sport management. To develop substantive knowledge and theory in sport management, exposure to other areas and parent disciplines, such as labor studies and women's studies, is necessary. From new insights and knowledges, combined with working knowledge and experience in sport management, greater understanding will be possible.

CONCEPT CHECK ✓

Understanding theory is important in developing new knowledge that will be useful to the practice of sport management. Deductive and inductive reasoning represent ways we work with theory. The two major academic disciplines of sport studies and business administration inform sport management. Additional disciplines (psychology and sociology as examples) also inform the field. New interdisciplinary alliances with areas like labor studies and women's studies are encouraged.

VALIDITY AND RELIABILITY

An understanding of the concepts of validity and reliability are important in developing knowledge and theory about sport management. **Validity** addresses the question, "To what degree does this measure or capture what it is intended to measure or capture?" A number of types of validity help the researcher and reviewer of published work to determine how accurately the measure reflects reality. Researchers working in qualitative and quantitative designs approach validity from distinct perspectives (Lather, 1986). Five types of validity (there are more!) defined here help in constructing research designs that validate social knowledge and give confidence to the trustworthiness of the data.

Face validity is the most basic and answers the question, "does the indicator measure the concept?" (Neuman, 1997). This can be asked of the scientific community or the research participants. Fletcher and Bowers (1991) use face validity in advertising research to assess whether the results seem logical or predictable. In qualitative designs, member checks (Guba and Lincoln, 1981; Reason and Rowan, 1981) are used. Member checks involve the participants of the research reviewing the tentative results, with subsequent refinements made in light of these reactions.

Content validity is the extent to which the items/variables most fully represent the theoretical construct under study (Neuman, 1997). In survey research, a "panel of experts" is often used during the development of the questionnaire to ensure that the concept under study is being fully captured.

Construct validity refers to situations in which multiple indicators of a concept must be measured. It is concerned with assessing the consistency with which the different indicators operate (Neuman, 1997). Similar to content validity, experts may be used to assess the conceptual appropriateness of measures. Statistical analysis is also used.

Predictive validity suggests that results from one measure can be verified by comparing them with another (Fletcher and Bowers, 1991). For example, if an advertising campaign designed to solicit inquiries about season ticket sales does in fact generate a high number of inquiries, the advertising campaign could be considered to have high predictive validity.

Catalytic validity as described by Lather (1986) is that in which individuals who have been part of the research develop self-understanding and self-determination through the research process. This is a term specific to qualitative methodology.

Reliability addresses the question, "To what degree will the measure be consistent over time?" Reliability in research can be improved by taking care in developing questions and instructions that will be used in interviews, focus groups, surveys, or experiments. Questions need to be pretested with a small group before the actual research is conducted. Interviewers must be well trained. A common measure of estimating internal consistency reliability used in survey research is on the basis of a coefficient alpha (Mueller, 1986; Nunnally, 1970). Nunnally stresses the importance of assessing reliability and outlines various ways reliability can be assessed. Reliability coefficients of 0.70 or higher for subscale or item measures are considered satisfactory; if, however, decisions are to be made with respect to specific scores, a reliability of 0.90 is considered minimal and 0.95, desirable (Nunnally, 1978).

The analogy of a target to measures of validity and reliability from Babbie (1995, p. 128) is helpful in understanding these important concepts. In target practice the results are reliable when they consistently hit the target in the same place (e.g., on the outside ring). The problem is, the results are off the mark and therefore not valid. When the results are closer to the mark but scattered all around the center, they are considered to be valid but lacking in reliability. The ideal situation of validity and reliability is when you consistently hit on the mark!

A research study by Doherty and Carron (2003), which examined cohesion in volunteer sport executive committees, was "on the mark" in terms of its reported validity and reliability. Several instruments were adapted in order to measure cohesion, satisfaction, and other factors of cohesion for volunteers. The face and construct validity of the instruments was based on a panel of experts' feedback that assessed the clarity and conceptual relevance of the items to group cohesion in volunteer sport executive committees. Additionally, the internal consistency and item-to-total correlation estimates were substantial and added empirical support to the instrument.

QUALITATIVE AND QUANTITATIVE PARADIGMS

In their simplest form, our "ways of knowing" by inquiry through research can be thought of as qualitative and quantitative paradigms. The term **paradigm** refers to a way of conceptualizing the theoretical perspective in which we look at the world (Esterberg, 2002). Table 2-1 presents selected characteristics of qualitative and quantitative paradigms. Table 2-1 is useful in acquiring an initial understanding of some of the differences between the two perspectives. The qualitative-quantitative perspective is important for introducing readers to designs and underlying philosophies.

Qualitative

Qualitative methodologies involve the exploration of situations that are lived or observed in everyday life. Interaction with people who are closely connected to the phenomena under study provide rich insights into people's conditions, behavior, and perceptions. Qualitative data provide the basis for developing theory.

Morse (1994) describes qualitative processes as following an analytical scheme that includes *comprehending* what is being observed or talked about, *synthesizing* to make generalized statements about the individuals or things, *theorizing* by offering explanations that connect the data to real-world experiences, and *recontextualizing* by thinking about the theory in different settings.

The qualitative paradigm involves seven different traditions or strategies of research design depending on the question being investigated. These traditions of qualitative inquiry include:

- Case study
- Ethnography
- Action research
- Grounded theory
- Phenomenology
- Semiotics
- Biography

Case study identifies and examines a "case," which might include a program, organization, event, activity, or individuals. The case has clear boundaries, and multiple sources of information are examined in order to understand the peculiarity and complexity of a particular problem or unique situation in greater depth. **Ethnography** is a research technique that places researchers in the middle of whatever they are studying to examine the phenomena as perceived by the participants involved. The author tells a story from the insiders' perspective to "draw a portrait" of the roles, behaviors, norms, values, or language of a particular group of people. **Action research** involves a form of qualitative inquiry in which the researcher not only studies a set of circumstances but also tries to help make those circumstances better for the people involved. Action research facilitates positive, fundamental change. The purpose of **grounded theory** research is to generate a theory or visual model that helps to explain a question or problem in detail. **Phenomenology** involves research into understanding the meaning of a single concept or phenomenon through investigating the participants' lived experiences and attributed meanings. **Semiotics** is the general science of signs, or finding meaning for something that actually stands for something else. Semiotic research is about learning to discover and use a system of signs. Finally, **biography** is the study of an individual's experience as told to the researcher or found in documents and archival materials. Qualitative researchers must have the technical understanding to choose the tradition most suited to answering their research question.

In addition to choosing the best research tradition, the researcher must have the personal skills to conduct the work, since qualitative research often requires significant involvement of the researcher. Shank (2002) contends there are four core personal skills required of the qualitative researcher: observing, conversing, participating, and interpreting. The researcher will collect data by doing one or more of the following: observing the group under study, interviewing participants, investigating the content of documents, or acting as a subject. She then works

TABLE 2-1   *Selected Characteristics of Qualitative and Quantitative Paradigms*

Selected characteristics	Qualitative	Quantitative	
		Survey research	Experimental
Goal	Discovering the experience Developing theory	Show relationships Hypothesis testing	Hypothesis testing Prediction
Research site	Participants' locale, close to natural location as possible	Mail	Researchers' locale Laboratory or other experiment setup
Data			
Collection method	Observation, interviewing	Participant responses	Experiments using scientific method
Using	Interview guides, probes	Surveys	
From	Informants, participants	Respondents	Testing protocol
Sources	Field notes, personal documents, official documents, photographs		Subjects
Variables	Not controlled	Controlled	Controlled
Empiricism	Words as the information		Numbers as the information
Analysis	Content of the experience	Descriptive and/or predictive statistics Bounded by study	
Findings based on	Inference as results emerge from coherent whole, insight, intuition	Survey results	Direct product of observable processes
Theory	Emerges from data to support previous theory or to build new theory	Supported or not supported by data, based on probabilistic model, a prior set alpha level of significance	
Phrases and designs associated with approach	Action research, grounded theory, fieldwork, focus groups, case studies, participant observation, naturalistic	Social survey, descriptive, correlational	Experiment, positivist, statistical

Modified from Bogdan and Biklen (1992). *Qualitative research for education: An introduction to theory and methods.* Boston: Allyn and Bacon; and Morse, J. M. (ed.). (1994). *Critical issues in qualitative research methods.* Thousand Oaks, CA: Sage.

with the observations, interview scripts, or notes from participating in order to interpret or understand the findings. In addition to these activities, qualitative inquiry requires the advanced skills of conceptualizing, reasoning, analyzing, narrating, and writing. These skills help the researcher to better understand the issue and its meaning.

Case study is the dominant tradition of qualitative research used in sport management, and interviews, focus groups, and content analysis are the personal skills most often employed in our field. For example, O'Brien and Slack (2003) investigated change in the case of the professionalization of the English Rugby Union by interviewing 43 key individuals within that organizational field. Marketing research often employs focus groups in order to solicit specific feedback on products or ideas because in-depth input from potential consumers is important. Focus groups are moderated discussion groups of five to ten people (therefore considered an interview or conversation technique) brought together on the basis of some important interest or similarity (Inglis, 1992; Morgan, 1988). Content analysis involves checking written documents for the presence or absence of information relevant to the research question.

Sometimes research designs incorporate both qualitative and quantitative research designs. Using both research methods generates multiple data sources that can create better depth of understanding. The technique is called **triangulation,** and it can be extremely helpful in furthering the depth of understanding when answering research questions.

Quantitative

Research is a structured method of problem solving, and **quantitative** methodologies are systematic in that they involve specifically identified variables that are studied under conditions that are as controlled as possible. The variables under study are labeled independent or dependent. The **independent variable** is the part of the study that the researcher manipulates. The **dependent variable** is the effect or result of the manipulation of the independent variable. For example, a survey could be designed to look at the effect of ticket prices (independent variable) on fan support (dependent variable). Other characteristics of quantitative research designs involve data collection procedures, which include structured, replicable (repeatable)

methods defined in advance of the data collection, and the use of empirical methods, meaning that conclusions are made on the basis of actual data collected (Thomas and Nelson, 2001).

There are different types of quantitative research; however, descriptive methods are the most commonly used in sport management. **Descriptive research** literally describes some activity, perception, behavior, or event. Survey or questionnaire designs, along with case and correlation studies, are most common. Although used to a lesser extent in sport management, experimental research is an important quantitative methodology.

Conducting good **survey research,** like other types of research, requires knowledge of the subject matter and theoretical foundations, as well as knowledge about the design and conduct of the survey, coding of the survey, and analysis. The analysis often requires computers. The type of statistical analysis required will depend on the research question, the design, and the response format of the survey. Some research questions involve simple yet meaningful analysis, whereas others involve more complex analysis. Survey research should not be conducted unless the individuals involved have the knowledge, expertise, and time, and the research question has been carefully developed.

Experimental designs allow for the manipulation of variables under closely controlled, laboratory-like settings. In these settings, issues of causation and prediction can be addressed. Although experimental research is conducted in many management environments, sport management has not, to any great extent, utilized this research design. Hopefully this will soon change, because there are appropriate areas in which experimental research designs would make a meaningful contribution to the understanding and practice of sport management.

For example, consider a closely controlled laboratory setting in which sport managers are engaged with consumers in simulated decision-making activities involving event ticket pricing, augmented product pricing, and consumer behavior. Similarly, consider the use of a computer program and conditions in which individuals (subjects) are involved in decisions about strategies, expenditures, or organizational crises. These testing conditions would allow the researcher to replicate an organization's environment while controlling for time and access to information factors. Results of these types of experiments would provide valuable information to sport managers and contribute to the theoretical understanding of the concepts under study.

> **CONCEPT CHECK** ✓
>
> *The challenge to sport management researchers is to understand qualitative and quantitative research designs. Knowledge derived from qualitative and quantitative inquiry and designs needs to be conveyed in useful ways to practitioners in sport management environments.*

Steps in the research process

Both qualitative and quantitative research involve a number of steps. While the seven steps outlined here are a very simplified representation of the rigors of good research (Neuman, 1997) and inquiry, they help to show the ongoing nature and key components.

1. *Choosing a General Topic.* This should be based on a strong need within sport management to know more about the topic. The topic should be of great interest to the researcher, and it is highly desirable that the topic be socially significant to improving sport and its place within society.
2. *Developing a Research Question within Related Theoretical Framework.* After much background reading and narrowing of the topic, the researcher should have a good understanding of the research question, related theory, and how the question fits with past research and will contribute to new insights.
3. *Designing the Study.* After considering the various ways the study could be conducted, the researcher will decide on a design and the details of the study. This might include the design of questionnaires, the plan for interviewing research participants, participant observation, archival searches, or the design of a controlled experiment. Ethics approval will be obtained at this stage.
4. *Collecting the Data.* The researcher collects the data, paying particular attention to appropriate protocols.
5. *Analyzing the Data.* The researcher analyzes the data, looking for patterns, significant findings, and new understandings.

6. *Interpreting Findings, Drawing Conclusions.* The results are interpreted with reasoned conclusions drawn, new questions identified, implications for future research, and changes to the management of sport, which might include new policy development or new practices.
7. *Communicating Results.* The results are shared with others in a variety of forums ranging from workshops with practitioners and scholarly conference presentations to published reports, journal articles, and books.

EVALUATING PUBLISHED RESEARCH

Good research and inquiry in sport management require accessing relevant literature. Where to locate and how to evaluate the literature are two very important aspects. Published research takes a variety of forms, including the following:

- Books written by one or more authors
- Books edited by one or more individuals, which include chapters written by a variety of contributors (of which this textbook is an example)
- Peer-reviewed journal articles by one or more authors
- Non-peer-reviewed journal articles by one or more authors
- Abstracts and proceedings of conferences
- Occasional paper series published or circulated by the agencies involved in the production, including government documents and papers from a university
- Popular magazines

There is no definitive order to this list in terms of quality of writing, scholarly rigor, or ability to make a useful contribution to the knowledge base, or to communicate to selected audiences. **Peer-reviewed** journal articles are generally considered to be regarded with greater credence in terms of scholarly writing and research. A brief description of the process by which an article is published demonstrates the nature of the peer-review process. Manuscripts submitted to the editor of the *Journal of Sport Management*, for instance, are sent to three reviewers who remain anonymous. These reviewers are from an editorial board, selected for their proven ability in research and writing, to critically yet fairly evaluate the work of their peers. It is not unusual for manuscripts to be rejected for publication (often the acceptance rate is approximately 40 percent of all manuscripts submitted for review) or to be accepted with major or minor revisions. Once manuscripts are accepted for publication, they appear as articles in the journal. The time frame for a manuscript from time of submission to a journal to its publication is often one to two years. Non-peer-reviewed writings, such as some books, do not go through the same process. The difference between the rigor exposed to manuscripts submitted to peer-reviewed journals and other journals and books should be clear. It is often easier to publish a non-peer-reviewed abstract, manuscript, or book than a peer-reviewed manuscript or book.

EVALUATING PUBLISHED SOURCES

Many types of published sources, including peer-reviewed journals, can now be found on the Internet. Given the growth of technology and the open access that allows more people to post items online without evaluation by professional experts, great care must be taken in critically evaluating the sources found.

Some questions to keep in mind when evaluating published research (including sources found on the Internet) are "What is the source of the information?" "Have the possibilities of where good information may be found been exhausted?" and "Have a variety of sources been used?"

What follows are some guiding questions that need to be answered as published research is reviewed. The published research is classified under research studies, concept pieces, and prescriptive writings.

If the work is the result of a research study:

What research question was addressed? What theoretical perspectives inform the work? Who were the subjects/respondents? How was the sample drawn and described? How were the data collected? What methodology(ies) were employed? What type of analysis was included? Were appropriate statistical applications used to analyze the data? What key results were reported? How were the results linked to previous studies or theory? Were there recommendations for future research? Were there recommendations for program change or policy development?

If the work is a "concept piece," that is, outlining a concept that is new or derived from another field of study that could be applied to sport management environments:

What issue was addressed? What theoretical perspectives informed the work? What links to sport management

were made? Was there a clear indication of how the concept is relevant to sport management and how it could be of value to the field?

If the work is prescriptive, that is, suggesting how a particular function or area of sport management should be conducted:

What was the topic under discussion? Was there support from other areas for this proposed application or use in sport management environments? Was it communicated clearly?

Questions applicable to all three types of work within inquiry and research in sport management (research studies, conceptual writing, and prescriptive) include:

Were assessments and measures of validity and reliability indicated? What is the contribution of this work to the study and understanding of sport management? Does the work make a contribution to your topic of inquiry, your position, or your line of thinking?

ETHICS IN INQUIRY AND RESEARCH

Individuals engaged in research have an obligation to conduct the research within ethical guidelines and to report the research accurately. Most institutions have human ethics committees in place that review all research proposals. Application for **human ethics** approval generally involves assurance that the project is well planned, the purpose of the research is clear, and the involvement level of subjects or respondents is detailed. How subjects or respondents are told about their involvement with the research, how they will be treated throughout the duration of their involvement with the research, and how they will be told of their right to withdraw at any time is all part of the proposal for ethics approval. The experience level of the researcher(s) is often included in submissions.

Ethics review committees work to ensure the following:

1. Subjects or respondents enter research projects voluntarily and understand the nature of the risks involved.
2. A plan for obtaining informed consent is in place.
3. If necessary, subjects or respondents will be debriefed at the end of the research project.

Cover letters for surveys and consent forms for participants in focus group research are two common areas within sport management research where good communication between the researcher and respondents or subjects is important. Johns (1992) reminds us that ethical research has a practical side as well. For good research, cooperation between the researcher and subject is necessary. Cooperation is easier to achieve and maintain when people feel ethical questions are being addressed.

The box below shows two examples of how researchers communicate with subjects as respondents in survey research (*1a*) and as key informants in focus group research (*1b*).

The interaction between researcher and respondent is much greater with qualitative methodologies. As such, it is important to ensure that the respondent feels comfortable disengaging at any time during the research and that time is taken to properly debrief after individual sessions and at the completion of the project.

The close interaction between researcher and participant often requires multiple ways of disengaging from the research process. For example, debriefing sessions involving individual and group members and continued access by the participant to the researcher are commonly used to assist both parties in moving away from the project. These are some of the challenges of qualitative methodologies and sport management research.

Ethical considerations in the publication and presentation of research include ensuring that a manuscript is submitted and under review to only one journal, identifying multiple authors in descending order based on the quality and quantity of their contribution to the research (unless noted otherwise), clearly communicating the roles of editor and contributing author to work, and providing accurate references in the writing.

Examples of informing research participants 1(a) in survey research and 1(b) as key informants in focus group research

1(a) Excerpts from cover letters in survey research

You may be assured of complete confidentiality. Your name will not be placed on the survey. Published and reported results will not identify individuals or organizations, and any discussion will be based on group data.

All individual results are confidential and will only be examined by the researchers. Your survey has an identification number for mailing purposes only so your name can be checked off the mailing list when your questionnaire is returned. Your name will not be placed on the survey.

Please do not hesitate to contact us if you have any questions. Thank you for your assistance.

1(b) Excerpt from key informant consent form in focus group research

This session is part of a research project and information will be used to help interpret results of the survey you previously completed. Tape recorders and flip charts will be used. Excerpts from the session will be used for teaching and research presentations and publications. Individual names will *NOT* be directly associated with any statements. We respect that participants have the right to withdraw at any time during the session.

Your feedback on this session, or additional comments you wish to make, are welcome. Please write. Thank you for helping.

Release and agreement by participant

I, _____, have read the above, and I am willing to participate in the session and permit use of the information gathered during the session for the purposes outlined.

Signed: _____ Date: _____

Inglis, Danylchuk and Pastore, 1996.

Based on research by Sue Inglis, 1993.

AVOIDING ACADEMIC DISHONESTY

We were going to call this section "avoiding the *P* word," or plagiarism, but chose to get your attention with the phrase "academic dishonesty." **Academic dishonesty** is the intended or unintended misrepresentation of another's work; it's cheating and is a serious offence. Each institution publishes (check your undergraduate calendar or university Website) the consequences students face in cases of academic dishonesty. Maintaining academic integrity should always be the goal. Your peers and professors will tell you to avoid plagiarizing, and in this section we will help you learn what is acceptable and unacceptable when it comes to using others' ideas or words in your writing and research assignments.

When and how to use references? (Babbie, 1999; Justice, 2003)

Reference needed when using	Reference not needed when using
• Another's exact words—use quotation marks and include the author, date, and page number(s)	• Your own ideas
• Others' ideas and interpretations—requires the author and date	• Common knowledge
• Summarizing or paraphrasing others' work—requires the author and date	

Justice's work with his students reinforces the principles of *honesty* and *clarity*. In any paper you write you will need to properly reference all the sources you use. Be honest and clear to yourself and to the reader where the ideas and words are coming from. The *Publication Manual of the American Psychology Association* (2001) is an excellent source on how to reference books, journals, interviews, newspaper, television reports, Internet sites, and others.

Have a look at this original passage from Chelladurai's 1999 *Managing Organizations for Sport*

and Physical Activity: A Systems Perspective textbook, and see if you can understand the acceptable and unacceptable uses of the passage.

In overview, the multidimensional model takes into account the characteristics of the situation, the leader, and the members, and conceptualizes three states of leader behavior—required, preferred, and actual leader behavior. (Chelladurai, 1999, p. 320)

Unacceptable:

1a. The characteristics of the situation, the leader, and the members are part of a larger argument for a systems perspective for understanding the structure and function of sport organizations. [This is blatant plagiarism, as a direct quote and ideas have been used without providing a reference—see *1b* below.]

2a. Like other multidimensional models of leadership, the sport leaders in my study identified aspects of themselves as leaders, the situation, and their followers. [This writer did not come up with the multidimensional model; therefore, a reference is required. Also, reordering and putting in one's own words the characteristics of the model are not good enough and need a reference—see *2b*.]

3a. It seems to me that how a leader behaves must be strongly dependent upon who the leader is and what they are like, who their followers are, and the type of work environment. [These are not original ideas and must include an author and date—see *3b*.]

Acceptable:

1b. Chelladurai's (1999, p. 320) "characteristics of the situation, the leader, and the members" are part of his larger argument for a systems perspective for understanding the structure and function of sport organizations. [The direct quote has been placed in quotation marks and the author, year of publication, and page number provided.]

2b. The results of my interviews with sport leaders in the sporting goods industry support Chelladurai's (1999) ideas of a multidimensional model of leadership. [Appropriate reference to the author and year of work has been provided.]

3b. Chelladurai (1999) considered three influences on leader behavior including what is necessary or required from the leader, the leader's preferred behavior, and what the leader is actually doing. [Different words have been used to convey another's work and appropriate reference to the author and year of work has been provided.]

4b. Also acceptable would be the following common knowledge statement: Leadership continues to be of interest to many sport management practitioners and researchers. [A reference is not required.]

RESEARCH SKILLS AND ABILITIES

What are the skills and abilities necessary for students (and scholars) to acquire for competence in conducting research in sport management? It is important to understand previous trails of research and how we would proceed to discover new pathways. The ideas expressed in this section serve as a self-check to see where efforts need to be made to acquire new skills.

Reading, reading, and more reading is basic to conducting good research. Reading of field-related journals as well as journals from other disciplines is essential. Reading about previous research, reading to understand methodologies that will be most appropriate to the research being conducted, and reading from sources outside of North America are important to develop our understandings and knowledge bases from broad perspectives.

Related to reading are problem-solving skills. Integration and imagination are important to extend research agendas beyond the obvious. Our present, obvious way of conducting research in sport management is to use survey design and offer a description of some phenomena. These types of scholarly activity are important, but they are not enough. There is a need to understand what sport managers identify as critical management problems, and there is a need to develop theory-based understandings to these problems. Returning, for example, to Thibault et al. (1993, 1994), we see important insight about how sport organizations develop strategies through the development of the theory and testing of the theory. The conceptual framework will have important implications for sport managers who need to understand why, given particular environmental and organizational characteristics, various types of strategies are employed. The framework is also applicable to other types of sport organizations.

We need to be able to find the links and to access various information sources to learn to make decisions about critical concepts and what is worth knowing. Included in this would be the ability to draw from a variety of literature sources and to take meaningful directions for new research that could make a contribution to sport management as well as to the parent disciplines. The research questions must, where appropriate, have relevance to the practice of management. Learning to formulate realistic research questions is a skill that requires constant refining.

Access to databases including sport management and databases from related fields and knowing how to conduct computerized searches is critical. These skills are related to other computer skills that aid the research process tremendously. Both qualitative and quantitative paradigms utilize computers in data entry and analysis.[1]

Communication skills include good writing as well as the ability to identify and deliver messages in the most effective ways. The results of our work should be communicated in ways that satisfy not only the academic journals, but also other audiences, including classroom situations and practitioners. Some of the results of our work can lead to policy development and program change.

Feeling a little overwhelmed with the idea of research and writing? Hubbuch's (1996) *Writing Research Papers Across the Curriculum* is an excellent resource to help you understand the research process involved with papers you will be writing. Two points we have found really helpful with our sport management students include Hubbuch's encouragement for each student to:

1. Be a good detective rather than a sponge when you read! Be more concerned with thinking about what the author's main argument is, synthesizing, and analyzing rather than soaking up the details by copying or underlining passages mindlessly.

2. Enter the conversation! Once you have read a few chapters and articles on a particular topic,

---

[1]For example, the SPSS/PC+ (Statistical Package for the Social Science/Personal Computer enhanced edition) is a commonly used statistical package for quantitative analysis, and the NUDIST (Nonnumerical, Unstructured Data Indexing, Searching and Theorizing) software is available for qualitative analysis.

challenge yourself to think, discuss, write, and actively participate in the issue. Students are scholars too—so get informed, join in and help the understanding, question development, and research in sport management grow.

To summarize, the skills needed to conduct and evaluate good research in sport management that have been introduced in this chapter are understanding theory development and methodologies, the ability to evaluate published research, the ability to read and develop meaningful research questions, computer skills, the ability to conduct the research, and the ability to impart new knowledge to both scholars and sport managers.

CONCEPT CHECK

A variety of sources of published research on sport management are available. Questions to evaluate the written work are helpful in assessing the merits of the work and the meaning to the individual. Individuals conducting sport management research must adhere to ethical guidelines and acceptable referencing to avoid academic dishonesty. A number of skills are necessary to conduct good research.

SUMMARY

- A framework that helps us think about sport management includes organizational behavior, organizational theory, and work-related functions such as marketing and legal issues.
- Inquiry and research in sport management are based on theory development and testing.
- Deductive and inductive reasoning are used in knowledge development.
- The foundations of sport management include sport studies and business administration. The foundation is further informed by parent disciplines such as psychology and sociology.
- Validity and reliability are important concepts in conducting research.
- Research can be viewed from qualitative and quantitative approaches. Examples of a qualitative approach include focus groups, participant observation, and social action

research. Examples of a quantitative approach include survey research, which is the most common design used in sport management research, and experimental designs.
- Of the number of published sources of sport management writing, peer-review journal articles and books have the most rigorous review process.
- Ethical considerations are important in conducting research.
- Acceptable referencing formats must be used.
- The researcher must possess a number of important skills to conduct meaningful research.
- Where appropriate, the research should be informed by theory.
- The research conducted in sport management should make a valuable contribution to understanding and improving the practice of sport management.

 ## CRITICAL THINKING EXERCISES

1. Outline a new sport management research study that would use both qualitative and quantitative methodologies. What methods would be appropriate and why? What would be the time frame for conducting the research be?
2. A sport management researcher at a highly respected university is conducting survey research involving the marketing directors of the corporations involved in the sponsorship of a major sporting event. Why would the study need to have human ethics approval? What ethical considerations should be communicated to the research participants?

 ## CASE STUDY

The marketing department of a semiprofessional baseball club approaches a sport management program. The club is interested in having research conducted to answer the following questions:

1. *Who is coming to the games?*
2. *What are the reasons the fans are coming to the games?*

3. *What aspects of the game could be changed to make the game more attractive for the fans?*

The marketing director is interested in other questions that may provide useful information. She is also interested in the various designs and research considerations that would be used to address the questions. Before contracting for this research, the baseball club needs a two-page statement by interested individuals or groups. Considering the information contained in this chapter, what would some of the important parts of the statement for the submission to the marketing director be?

 REVIEW QUESTIONS AND ISSUES

1. Outline and discuss an example of Kurt Lewin's statement, "There is nothing so practical as a good theory." The example should be from a sport management environment.
2. Select an article from the *Journal of Sport Management*. Decide if the article represents a research study or a concept piece. Use the guide questions from the section in this chapter on evaluating published sources on p. 24 to guide discussion of the article.
3. Outline an experiment that could be designed to test the hypothesis that attention to customer service factors will have an effect on customer satisfaction.
4. An athletic director at University X complains, "Every year I get requests from across the country to complete surveys. Although I am sure they are well-meaning studies, I never see any changes to the problems facing intercollegiate athletics." Discuss.

 SOLUTIONS TO CRITICAL THINKING EXERCISES

1. Have you explained the ways in which your research example is well suited to both objective (quantitative) and subjective (qualitative) measures? Is your time frame for the research reasonable?
2. Have you addressed the key considerations related to: (a) why ethics approval is important, (b) how the nature of the research would be communicated with the research participants, and (c) how confidentiality of responses would be ensured?

RELATED JOURNALS

Administrative Science Quarterly
Athletic Administration
Athletic Business
European Journal for Sport Management
Festival Management and Event Tourism
Harvard Business Review
Human Relations
International Journal of Sport Management
International Studies of Management and Organization
Journal of Business Communications
Journal of Business Research
Journal of Business Strategy
Journal of Consumer Research
Journal of HPER
Journal of Legal Aspects of Sport
Journal of Management Studies
Journal of Marketing
Journal of Marketing Research
Journal of Organizational Behavior
Journal of Sport Management
Journal of Sports Marketing Sponsorship
Managing Leisure
Organizational Behavior and Human Decision Processes
Organizational Studies
Quest
Sociology of Sport Journal
Sport Management Review
Sport Marketing Quarterly
The Academy of Management Review

 WEBSITES

www.arnova.org—ARNOVA. "The Association for Research on Nonprofit Organizations and Voluntary Action (ARNOVA) is an international, interdisciplinary network of scholars and nonprofit leaders committed to strengthening the research community in the emerging field of nonprofit and philanthropic studies." Associated with ARNOVA is an electronic forum (can be accessed through the Website) to facilitate the sharing of concerns, interests, and solutions among scholars and practitioners.

www.nassm.org—NASSM. This is the official Website for the North American Society for Sport Management (NASSM). The Website includes information concerning the membership, history and publications of NASSM, the scope of sport management, conferences, universities offering sport management programs, program review, and NASSM initiatives.

REFERENCES

American Psychological Association (2001). *Publication manual of the American Psychological Association.* 5th ed. Washington, DC: American Psychological Association.

Babbie, E. (1999). *The practice of social research.* 7th ed. Belmont, CA: Wadsworth.

Babbie, E. R. (1995). *The practice of social research.* 7th ed. Belmont, CA: Wadsworth.

Bogdan, R. C., and Biklen, S. (1992). *Qualitative research for education: An introduction to theory and methods.* 2nd ed. Boston: Allyn and Bacon.

Chelladurai, P. (1999). *Human resource management in sport and recreation.* Champaign, IL: Human Kinetics.

Chelladurai, P. (2001). *Managing organizations for sport and physical activity: A systems perspective.* Scottsdale, AZ: Holcomb Hathaway.

Daft, R. L. (1995). *Organization theory and design.* 5th ed. New York: West.

Daft, R. C. and Steers, R. M. (1986). *Organizations: A micro/macro approach.* Glenview, IL: Scott, Foresman.

Doherty, A., and Carron, A. (2003). Cohesion in volunteer sport executive committees. *Journal of Sport Management,* 17(2), 116–41.

Esterberg, K. (2002). *Qualitative methods in social research.* Boston, MA: McGraw-Hill.

Fletcher, A. D., and Bowers, T. A. (1991). *Fundamentals of advertising research.* 4th ed. Belmont, CA: Wadsworth.

Guba, E. G., and Lincoln, Y. (1981). *Effective evaluation.* San Francisco: Jossey-Bass.

Hamner, W. C., and Organ, D. (1978). *Organizational behavior: An applied psychological approach.* Dallas: BPI.

Hardy, S. (1986). Entrepreneurs, organizations, and the sport marketplace: Subjects in search of historians. *Journal of Sport History,* 13(1), 14–33.

Hardy, S. H., and Berryman, J. W. (1983). A historical view of the governance issue. In J. Frey (ed.), *The governance of intercollegiate athletics* (pp. 15–28). New York: Leisure Press.

Harris, H. A. (1967). *Greek athletes and athletics.* Bloomington, IN: Indiana University Press.

Hubbuch, S. M. (1996). *Writing research papers across the curriculum.* 4th ed. New York: Harcourt Brace.

Inglis, S. (1992). Focus groups as a useful qualitative methodology in sport management. *Journal of Sport Management,* 6(3), 173–78.

Inglis, S., Danylchuk, K. E., and Pastore, D. (1996). Understanding retention factors in coaching and athletic management positions. *Journal of Sport Management,* 10, 237–49.

Johns, G. (1992). *Organizational behavior: Understanding life at work.* 3rd ed. New York: HarperCollins.

Justice, C. (2003). *An exercise in knowing when and how to cite a source.* McMaster University. http://socserv.mcmaster.ca/justice/citationexercise.htm.

Kaplan, A. (1964). *The conduct of inquiry.* San Francisco: Chandler.

Kyle, D. G. (1987). *Athletics in ancient Athens.* Leiden: E. J. Brill.

Lambrecht, K. (1991). Research, theory and practice. In B. Parkhouse (ed.), *The management of sport: Its foundation and application* (pp. 28–29). St. Louis: Mosby.

Lather, P. (1986). Issues of validity in openly ideological research: Between a rock and a soft place. *Interchange,* 17(4), 63–84.

Morgan, D. L. (1988). *Focus groups as qualitative research.* Newbury Park, CA: Sage.

Morse, J. M. (ed.). (1994). *Critical issues in qualitative research methods.* Thousand Oaks, CA: Sage.

Mueller, D. J. (1986). *Measuring social attitudes: A handbook for researchers and practitioners.* New York: Columbia University Teachers' College Press.

Neuman, W. L. (1997). *Social research methods: Qualitative and quantitative approaches.* 3rd ed. Boston: Allyn and Bacon.

Nunnally, J. C. (1970). *Introduction to psychological measurement.* New York: McGraw-Hill.

Nunnally, J. C. (1978). *Psychometric theory.* 2nd ed. New York: McGraw-Hill.

O'Brien, D., and Slack, T. (2003). An analysis of change in an organizational field: The professionalization of English Rugby Union. *Journal of Sport Management,* 17(4), 417–48.

Parkhouse, B. (1987). Sport management curricula: Current status and design implications for future development. *Journal of Sport Management,* 1(2), 93–115.

Reason, P., and Rowan, J. (1981). Issues of validity in new paradigm research. In P. Reason and J. Rowan (eds.), *Human inquiry: A sourcebook of new paradigm research* (pp. 239–62). New York: Wiley.

Shank, Gary D. (2002). *Qualitative research—A personal skills approach.* Toronto: Pearson Canada Ltd.

Slack, T. (1997). *Understanding sport organizations: The application of organization theory.* Champaign, IL: Human Kinetics.

Steers, R. M., Porter, L. W., and Bigley, B. A. (1996). *Motivation and leadership at work.* 6th ed. New York: McGraw-Hill.

Thibault, L., Slack, T., and Hinings, B. (1993). A framework for the analysis of strategy in nonprofit sport organizations. *Journal of Sport Management,* 7(1), 25–43.

Thibault, L., Slack, T., and Hinings, B. (1994). Strategic planning for nonprofit sport organizations: Empirical verification of a framework. *Journal of Sport Management,* 8(3), 218–33.

Thomas, J., and Nelson, J. (2001). *Research methods in physical activity.* 4th ed. Champaign, IL: Human Kinetics.

CHAPTER 3

Ethics in Sport Management

Scott Branvold

In this chapter, you will become familiar with the following terms:

Absolutism	Moral norms	Teleology
Deontology	Moral principles	Theory of justice
Ethical code	Principle of proportionality	Utilitarianism
Ethics	Rationalization	Values
Morality	Relativism	

Learning Goals
By the end of this chapter, students should be able to:

- Define terms associated with the study of ethics.
- Discuss the fundamental premises of deontology and teleology.
- Identify the relevant ethical dimensions of various situations confronting sport managers.
- Apply a model of ethical analysis to the decision making process.
- Create strategies for the development of an ethical work environment.

CURRENT ETHICAL ENVIRONMENT
This chapter provides the foundation for a rational application of the principles of ethics to the ethical problems that confront the sport manager.[1] Such principles, some would argue, are not being applied systematically or with any consistency in matters of moral uncertainty. Many would suggest that the current ethical climate falls well below acceptable levels, leaving the public with serious doubts about how much trust can be placed in basic social institutions, including politics, religion, and certainly business. There are numerous examples of unethical and illegal behavior that serve as constant reinforcement of such beliefs. The Enron, Tyco, and WorldCom accounting fiascoes and the mutual fund trading scandals are just a few recent examples of the ethical problems with which the business world seems to be confronted regularly.

[1]A debt of gratitude is owed to Dr. R. Scott Kretchman, whose insightful and substantive comments greatly aided in the preparation of this chapter.

Although the "caveat emptor" or "let the buyer beware" ideology has been tempered somewhat by a variety of consumer protection measures, many consumers are still skeptical, and frequently uncovered scams and schemes have done little to ease the apprehension. White (1993) suggests that the very nature of capitalism presents a variety of ethical questions. Capitalism encourages accumulation of wealth and maximizing self-interest but can lead to materialism, greed, and callous indifference toward others. Businesses in a free market may choose to meet consumer wants by providing products that are harmful or addictive (e.g., tobacco, alcohol, gambling). Companies may choose to increase profitability by outsourcing production to less expensive labor markets, as Nike has been accused of doing. Competition in business can produce the same "win at all costs" attitude often seen on the playing field and may result in unethical actions and behaviors. Perhaps the level of cynicism and mistrust that exists in the culture should not be surprising given the amount and extent of the ethical misbehavior to which the public is regularly exposed.

The business of sport has not been immune to or isolated from the ethical problems so prevalent elsewhere. It is largely a romanticized ideal that sport is a haven for fair play, sportsmanship, and "a level playing field." That ideal has been tarnished with monotonous regularity both on and off the playing field at all levels of sport. Athletic performance is often clouded by suspicions that it may have been a product of performance-enhancing drugs. College athletics have had to confront the problems of recruiting violations, academic deceit, booster club excesses, athlete gambling, and various forms of coach misbehavior including everything from poor judgment to inaccuracies on resumés. Ethical controversy also plagues the Olympic movement, with IOC officials willing to "sell" their site selection votes while eager Olympic Organizing Committees are more than willing to engage in influence peddling by soliciting favorable votes with extravagant gifts. Professional franchise owners are accused of extorting facility subsidies from cash-strapped communities by threatening to move to another city, and athletes and agents are accused of greed and disloyalty for their "show me the money" attitude. Ethical problems have filtered down to youth sports, where coaches attempt to "stack" youth league teams and parental behavior has often gotten completely out of control.

From an ethical context, many are very concerned with the direction in which society seems to be moving. In simpler times, conduct tended to be influenced by a more unequivocal set of guidelines. This ethical **absolutism** maintains that there is an eternally true moral code that can be applied with strict impartiality. In a more complex environment, actions more often appear to be guided by a sense of **relativism**, a belief in which right and wrong are determined by the situation rather than a set of absolute rules (Robin and Reidenbach, 1989). While relativism can have a role in ethical decision making, it also results in a degree of ambiguity. Sternberg (2000) suggests that relativism may be useful as a basis for practical guidelines, but that ethical values should be based on universal principles that transcend specific interests. Consequences of a relativistic approach may include confusion regarding standards and expectations of behavior and greater latitude to rationalize one's actions. **Rationalization** of actions occurs in a variety of ways. Perhaps the chances of getting caught are slight or the penalties are minimal. In some circumstances, behavior is justified by saying "Everyone else is doing it!" or "Who's going to be hurt?" Actions may also be rationalized because the stakes are sufficiently high to be worth the risks of questionable behavior. For example, the economic incentives of successful college football and basketball programs may be enough to produce recruiting improprieties or academic shortcuts. This contingent view of what is acceptable may actually create confusion about the nature of ethics. Individuals charged with ethical misconduct frequently defend their actions by saying "I have broken no laws." Rather than viewing the law as *the floor* for acceptable behavior, many view the law as *the standard* for ethical conduct. When this is the prevailing perspective, it is common to attempt to legislate morality. The result is an increasingly regulated society that relies on laws and rules rather than on ethical standards to achieve fairness and justice. Kristol states, "It is a confession of moral bankruptcy to assert that what the law does not explicitly prohibit is therefore morally permissible" (Solomon and Hanson, 1983).

It seems that rules are too often viewed as barriers to get around rather than guidelines to live within. A monument to this perspective is the voluminous NCAA rules manual, which undergoes frequent revisions to close the loopholes that are continually sought in order to beat the system. The rules are now so complicated that many athletic departments hire a "compliance director" just to help them follow the rules. This "ethics by prescription" approach to managing behavior may actually reinforce the belief that anything is all right if there is no specific rule against it. If this represents the standard most people and organizations use to guide their actions, then concerns about the ethical climate are well justified.

FUNDAMENTAL CONCEPTS

Developing a foundation for ethical analysis first requires an understanding of the fundamental concepts of morality and ethics. These terms are often used interchangeably, and although one must not get bogged down in semantics, a brief discussion of distinctions between the two terms is appropriate.

Morality has been defined as the special set of **values** that frame the absolute limitations on behavior. It may include such basic rules as "don't steal" (**moral norms**) as well as a more general system of duties and obligations (**moral principles**) (Solomon and Hanson, 1983). Rokeach (1973) defines a value as an enduring belief that guides personal behavior and shapes personal goals. He characterizes two types of values: instrumental values (e.g., ambition, courage, honesty), which are viewed as the means to terminal values (e.g., freedom, happiness, security).

De George (1982) and Beauchamp and Bowie (1988) place emphasis on morality's concern with the "good and bad" or "right and wrong" character of actions within the context of social customs and mores of any particular culture. They also stress the idea that morality is based on impartial considerations and that individuals cannot legitimately create their own personal moral codes.

De George (1982) defines **ethics** as a systematic attempt to make sense of our moral experience to determine what rules should govern conduct. This definition suggests that ethics is the study of morality. Beauchamp and Bowie (1988) and Velasquez (1988) seem to support this idea, while stressing

that ethics involves the justification and application of moral standards and principles.

CONCEPT CHECK

Although the terms morality *and* ethics *are often used interchangeably, ethicists do note some semantic differences between them. Morality provides the set of values that limit behavior, whereas ethics involves the application of and justification for moral principles.*

PERSONAL MORAL DEVELOPMENT

Often morality is viewed as a matter of personal conscience with everyone entitled to develop their own vision of acceptable values. However, ethicists tend to take a much more objective view of morality. Moral development involves the ability to distinguish right from wrong; this ability to make moral judgments and engage in moral behavior increases with maturity (Cavanaugh, 1984).

Lawrence Kohlberg (1976) has developed perhaps the most widely accepted model of individual moral development in which he identifies three developmental levels with each level subdivided into two stages:

Level I: Preconventional—At this level, a child can respond to rules and social expectations and can apply the labels "good," "bad," "right," and "wrong." These rules, however, are seen as externally imposed (such as by parents) and in terms of pleasant and painful consequences (for example, a spanking for wrongdoing or a piece of candy for desirable behavior). The child does not have the ability to identify with others, so the motivation for action is largely one of self-interest. Stages one and two within Level I reflect largely instrumental orientations. The behavior is not motivated by a moral sensitivity but simply by the consequences of an action—at first avoiding punishment and later receiving rewards and praise.

Level II: Conventional—At this level, the expectations of family and peer groups become primary behavioral influences. The individual exhibits loyalty to the group and its norms and begins to identify with the point of view of others. This level is characterized by conformity and a willingness to subordinate individual needs to those of the group. The first stage within this level (stage 3) focuses on a "good boy/nice girl" morality, in which good behavior involves conforming to the expectations of family and friends. Actions are guided by stereotypes of what is normal behavior and are frequently judged by intention. The next stage of this level (stage 4) is termed the law-and-order stage. Right and wrong extends to conforming with societal laws, and there is a recognition of socially prescribed duties, responsibilities, and obligations. De George (1982) contends that most adults live at this conformity stage of development and that many never go beyond it.

Level III: Postconventional or Principled—At level III, there is an attempt to find a self-chosen set of moral principles that can be justified to any rational individual. Proper laws and values are those to which any reasonable people would want to commit, regardless of social position or status. The first stage (stage 5) within this level has a social contract orientation. There is an awareness of conflicting personal views and a sense that the rules should be upheld impartially because they are the social contract. A primary concern in this stage is that laws and duties be based on their overall utility as guided by "the greatest good for the greatest number." Cavanaugh (1984) points out that this stage is the "official" level of moral development of the United States government and the Constitution.

The final stage (stage 6) is based on the acceptance of universal ethical principles. At this stage, appropriate action is defined by the conscious choice of universal ethical principles that are comprehensive and consistent and deal with justice, equality, and human dignity. The motivation for adherence to these principles is a basic belief in their encompassing validity and a willingness to commit to them (Cavanaugh, 1984; Kohlberg, 1976; Velasquez, 1988).

CONCEPT CHECK

Kohlberg's model of moral development describes the progression of moral reasoning from the childlike motivations of avoiding a spanking to the mature moral reasoning of taking a principled stand based purely on the "rightness" of the principle. Kohlberg's Level III has at its roots the most widely accepted normative ethical theories, which serve as the basis for ethical analysis.

THEORIES OF ETHICS

Normally, references to ethical theories or ethical decision rules take the form of simple ethical maxims such as the following (Laczniak and Murphy, 1985):

1. The Golden Rule: Act toward others the way you would want them to act toward you.
2. The utilitarian principle: Act in a way that results in the greatest good for the greatest number.
3. Kant's categorical imperative: Act in such a way that the action taken under the circumstances could be a universal law or rule of behavior.
4. The professional ethic: Take only actions that would be viewed as proper by an impartial set of professional colleagues.
5. The TV test: Act in such a way that the actions could be defended comfortably in front a national television audience.

While these maxims may serve as handy rules for ethical conduct, complex decision making may require a more comprehensive foundation for ethical analysis. Several authors have developed theories for the ethical analysis of actions and decisions. Most of these theories are either teleological, deontological, or some combination of the two.

Theories based on **teleology** (from the Greek meaning "end") assess the morality of actions on the basis of the consequences or results of those actions; the most widely studied of these theories is **utilitarianism.** Jeremy Bentham (1748–1832) and John Stuart Mill (1806–1873) were the most influential developers of utilitarianism, which is predicated on the idea of "creating the greatest good for the greatest number." Actions are evaluated by judging their consequences and weighing the good effects and bad effects. The attempt is to achieve an optimal balance of benefits versus harms on those affected by the action. Applying utilitarianism to decision making requires selecting the action that results in the greatest net social benefit. The good of the group supersedes the good of the individual (Beauchamp and Bowie, 1988; De George, 1982; Robin and Reidenbach, 1989). The major criticisms of the utilitarian approach include (1) the difficulty in measuring utilitarian value, (2) the opportunity for unjust net consequences, and (3) the lack of concern for how results are produced (Beauchamp and Bowie, 1988).

The deontological or formalistic approach to ethical analysis was formulated primarily by Immanuel Kant (1734–1804) with more contemporary work done by William D. Ross and John Rawls. **Deontology** (derived from the Greek for "duty") is based on the idea that what makes an action right is not the consequences but the fact that the action conforms to some absolute rules of moral behavior. Kant's categorical imperative statements serve as guidelines for what would be considered moral behavior. Moral action would (1) be universalizable (i.e., it would make sense for everyone in a similar situation to take the same action), (2) demonstrate respect for the individual (i.e., others are never treated simply as means), and (3) be acceptable to all rational beings (Tuleja, 1985). Kant's vision was one of universal and consistent application of the rules of morality. His critics maintain that the theory is too vague and imprecise. There are also claims that it doesn't help resolve the issue of balancing conflicting individual rights and has too little regard for consequences (Velasquez, 1988).

Ross put forth a theory that combined certain aspects of utilitarianism with Kantian theory. He postulated that action is bound by the duties of fidelity, gratitude, justice, beneficence (generosity), self-improvement, and non-injury. These are seen as universal moral obligations above and beyond the law, but there is acknowledgment that some exceptions may exist (Laczniak and Murphy, 1985).

John Rawls has also formulated an influential ethical approach called the **theory of justice.** The major premise behind his proposals is that rules and laws of society should be constructed as if we did not know what roles we were to play in that society (what Rawls terms the "veil of ignorance"). This creates an objectivity and fairness to the ethical principles that guide actions (Cavanaugh, 1984).

CONCEPT CHECK

The most widely accepted ethical theories are either teleological or deontological in nature. Utilitarianism is the most prominent teleological theory and its focus is on consequences of actions and "creating the greatest good for the greatest number." Deontology has a more absolute orientation, suggesting that what makes an action right is not consequences but adherence to basic moral laws.

MODELS FOR ETHICAL ANALYSIS

The ethical theories in the previous section provide the foundation for numerous models that can aid in evaluating moral dilemmas. An approach suggested by Tuleja (1985) has a utilitarian orientation in which actions are evaluated on the basis of their effect on various constituent groups or stakeholders. For example, a college administrator must weigh the interests of a number of constituencies, including athletes, coaches, alumni, fans, faculty, media, and the community when making personnel decisions such as the hiring or firing of a coach.

Many of the models use a combination of the basic ethical theories to provide a multidimensional approach to dealing with ethical questions. Goodpaster (1984) summarized three avenues for ethical analysis, one based on utility (maximum benefits), one based on rights, and one based on duty or obligation. Garrett (1966) developed a theory specifically with the business manager in mind that combines concern for outcomes (utilitarianism) and process (deontology) and adds the dimension of motivation. These three components (means, ends, and intentions) are synthesized into what Garrett calls the **principle of proportionality,** which states that undesirable side effects of an action can be accepted if and only if there is some proportionate reason for doing so (Laczniak and Murphy, 1985). One might use the principle of proportionality to evaluate the process being used to provide more gender equity in interscholastic and intercollegiate sport. The means for this was federal legislation (Title IX). While Title IX was undeniably successful in its efforts to increase participation opportunities for women, several consequences (ends) such as lost opportunities for men and lower percentages of women in coaching and administrative positions could be viewed as unfortunate outcomes. The ethical analysis would involve weighing the undesirable side effects of the process against the benefits achieved.

Cavanaugh (1984) has also suggested a tridimensional approach to ethical decision making that includes characteristics of both teleological and deontological theories. He uses utility, rights, and justice as the ethical evaluation criteria. If conflicts arise among the three criteria, further analysis must be done based on the relative importance of the criteria, the freedom with which the action is taken, and the nature of the undesirable effects. Figure 3-1 provides a flowchart of steps to guide

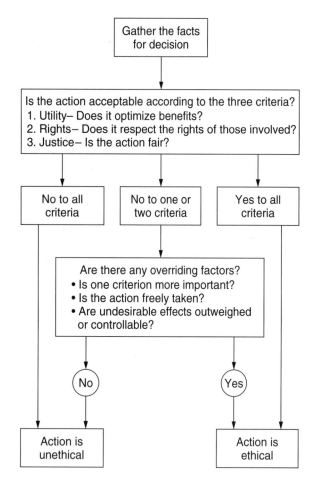

FIGURE 3-1   Flowchart for ethical decision making.
From Cavanaugh, G. (1984). *American values* (2nd Ed).
Englewood Cliffs, New Jersey: Prentice-Hall.

this ethical evaluation process. While the model may be rather simplistic, it can serve as a starting point that can be useful in ethical analysis.

PERSONAL ETHICS AND ORGANIZATIONAL RESPONSIBILITY

The distinction between personal and professional ethics is a difficult matter to address. Milton Friedman, a prominent American economist, maintains that businesses are amoral entities and the corporate executive's only responsibility is to maximize profit. Yet even this extreme proponent of free-market capitalism recognizes that this must be accomplished within the framework of basic societal rules of law and custom (DeGeorge, 1982). Ultimately organizations are collections of individuals, and decisions are made and carried out by individuals. This would seem to indicate that the ultimate responsibility for ethical behavior rests with the individual, thereby demonstrating the importance of personal ethics. If this is the case, however, how is it that people who consider themselves to be basically honest and compassionate can act so irresponsibly at times? It seems as if a different set of values is applied on the job than is applied outside the workplace. One author cites a former corporate vice president who says, "What is right in the corporation is not what is right in a man's home or in his church. What is right in a corporation is what the guy above you wants from you" (Jackall, 1988).

Circumstances may arise in which professionally defensible behavior is not always congruent with the guiding principles of ordinary norms. Honesty is a basic virtue; yet at the personal level, the "little white lie" may be a justifiable action for some situations. Are the standards of honesty at the professional level any different? Should they be any different?

Advertisers occasionally use the "white lie" as a message strategy; the term "puffery" has even been coined to describe the practice of stretching or bending the truth with inflated claims and exaggerations. Indeed, advertising is often considered one of the most ethically suspect aspects of business operations. Chonko (1995) notes that criticism of advertising practices often occurs when efforts to persuade result in inaccurate, manipulative, or deceptive messages. An advertisement for a Continental Basketball Association (CBA) franchise once encouraged people to purchase tickets to see a team whose roster was purported to be filled with future National Basketball Association (NBA) stars. Anyone familiar with professional basketball recognizes the extravagance of such a claim, yet many would not question the ethics of such an advertisement. Overtly sexual images and violence are often used in the selling of sports. Professional football and hockey leadership downplay the role of violence in their sports yet continue to allow the use of some of the most violent action footage to promote their sports. In this case, behavior is inconsistent with principles and does not adhere to the ideal societal standards of virtue. The frequency of departure from these standards and, perhaps more importantly, the willingness to routinely accept such departures are basic ethical concerns.

Values in the workplace may be developed through conscious organizational effort or they may evolve without organizational attention. When results are the primary or perhaps only organizational value supported, the consequence may be an "anything goes" ethical climate. Kristol states, "Businessmen have come to think that the conduct of business is a purely 'economic' activity to be judged only by economic criteria and that moral and religious traditions exist in a world apart, to be visited on Sunday perhaps" (Solomon and Hanson, 1983). There are likely to be situations where unethical behavior will produce greater profits, especially in the short run (Robin and Reidenbach, 1989). In a social environment in which immediate gratification is an increasingly pervasive mindset, the temptation and pressure to cut corners naturally increases.

Solomon (1999) has the notion that ethics should not consist of a set of prohibitive rules but should be "the driving force for a successful life well lived." He then provides a catalog of virtues that should be the foundation for ethical behavior. The list includes characteristics such as honesty, fairness, compassion, and trustworthiness but also includes such virtues as ambition, competitiveness, courage, and toughness. Some of these virtues run counter to the view that ethics and integrity are indications of weakness and too idealistic for the modern business world.

Organizations that ignore or even reward unethical behavior are likely to have personnel who behave unethically. Sims (1994), Cialdini (1996), and Frank (1996) are among the many authors who have addressed the costs to organizations that tolerate socially irresponsible actions and the benefits of operating ethically. All mention the internal problem of dealing with the cost of monitoring dishonest employees as well the exter-

nal problem of mending a tarnished organizational image and reputation. Situations such as the resources various sports governing bodies spend trying to detect and deter drug use or the loss of sponsorship dollars the Olympic movement experienced after corruption was uncovered in some of their business dealings are examples of the damage than can be caused by disreputable activity. Benefits such as enhanced customer loyalty, increased goodwill, and avoidance of litigation provide valuable returns for behaving ethically.

In sport, the scoreboard and the record book have become the final determinants of value and worth for many (Gibson, 1993). Stoll and Beller (1993) contend that this perspective has a tremendous influence on the moral reasoning of sport participants. Their studies indicate that a negative relationship exists between moral development and sports participation and that there is a decrease in moral reasoning the longer the athlete competes in organized sport. Such findings raise questions about the value of sport involvement in developing a sense of sportsmanship.

Sport managers are subject to some of the same pressures that athletes encounter. They are constantly making decisions that affect the financial success of their sport operations. These decisions may be related to on-the-field success or box office success (or both), and the temptation to use any means to achieve those goals can produce ethically questionable choices at times. A sample of such a choice is a Pittsburgh-based indoor lacrosse team that decided using strippers who removed articles of clothing after each score would be an effective promotional strategy. While it did draw a crowd, the promotion alienated many and ran counter to the organization's own family-oriented entertainment philosophy. (O'Neill, 2000)

The role models of an organization will set the tone for the behavior of the entire organization. The leadership will determine what the dominant perspective is toward ethical behavior. The demands, expectations, and traditions of an organization will be the behavioral guides. The organizational leaders must set clear, unambiguous expectations for the ethical conduct of their employees. When this is done, employees must then be given the authority to act and be held accountable for the ethical quality of their actions. It takes integrity and courage to act on one's values, especially when the stakes are high. An organization, through its leaders, must work diligently to create a climate in which ethical conduct is a matter of habit rather than a matter of expedience.

CONCEPT CHECK

The relationship between personal and professional ethics is difficult to determine with great precision. Individuals will bring a personal set of values to the job, but to what extent that set of values will influence job behavior depends on a number of factors, including the strength with which those values are held, the integrity and courage of the employees holding those values, the ethical environment within the organization, and the role models and leaders that influence the work environment.

ETHICS AND THE PROFESSIONALIZATION OF SPORT MANAGEMENT

Professions carry with them prestige, status, respect, and autonomy and have traditionally been allowed more control to set their own standards and to be self-regulating and self-disciplining. Standards are frequently expressed in the form of an **ethical code,** often developed and enforced by a professional organization. Many businesses and professional business organizations have also developed ethical codes and creeds. The following tables contain examples of advertising ethics and marketing ethics codes. However, many researchers question the impact some of these codes have had, contending that they lack depth or are filled with platitudes that do little to guide behavior (Robin and Reidenbach, 1989). Solomon (1999) suggests that an ethical code may be little more than a hypocritical public relations effort, but it can also be a valuable source of direction and a concrete source of guidance when developed properly. De George (1982) recommends that a code should (1) be regulative, not simply a statement of ideals, (2) protect public interests and not be self-serving, (3) be specific and relevant to the specialized concerns of the members, and (4) be enforceable and enforced. The American Psychological Association's nine principles for ethical standards can also serve as a guide to development of an ethical code: (a) responsibility,

---

TABLE 3-1 *American Advertising Federation's Code of Advertising Ethics*

---

1. Truth—advertising shall reveal the truth, and shall reveal significant facts, the omission of which would mislead the public.
2. Substantiation—advertising claims shall be substantiated by evidence in possession of the advertiser and the advertising agency prior to making such claims.
3. Comparisons—advertising shall refrain from making false, misleading, or unsubstantiated statements or claims about a competitor or his products or services.
4. Bait Advertising—advertising shall not offer products or services for sale unless such offer constitutes a bona fide effort to sell the advertised products or services and is not a device to switch consumers to other goods or services, usually higher priced.
5. Guarantees and Warranties—advertising of guarantees and warranties shall be explicit, with sufficient information to apprise consumers of their principal terms and limitations or, when space or time restrictions preclude such disclosures, the advertisement shall clearly reveal where the full text of the guarantee or warranty can be examined before purchase.
6. Price Claims—advertising shall avoid price claims which are false or misleading, or savings claims which do not offer provable savings.
7. Testimonials—advertising containing testimonials shall be limited to those of competent witnesses who are reflecting a real and honest opinion or experience.
8. Taste and Decency—advertising shall be free of statements, illustrations, or implications which are offensive to good taste or public decency.

Reprinted with permission.

TABLE 3-2 *World Marketing Contact Group Marketing Creed*

---

1. I hereby acknowledge my accountability to the organization for which I work, and to society as a whole, to improve marketing knowledge and practice, and to adhere to the highest professional standards in my work and personal relationships.
2. My concept of marketing includes as its basic principle the sovereignty of all consumers in the marketplace and the necessity for mutual benefit to both buyer and seller in all transactions.
3. I shall personally maintain the highest standards of ethical and professional conduct in all business relationships with customers, suppliers, colleagues, competitors, governmental agencies, and the public.
4. I pledge to protect, support, and promote the principles of consumer choice, competition, and innovative enterprise, consistent with relevant legislative and public policy standards.
5. I shall not knowingly participate in actions, agreements, or marketing policies or practices which may be detrimental to customers, competitors, or established community social or economic policies or standards.
6. I shall strive to insure that products and services are distributed through such channels and by such methods as will tend to optimize the distributive process by offering maximum customer value and service at minimum cost while providing fair and equitable compensation for all parties.
7. I shall support efforts to increase productivity or reduce costs of production or marketing through standardization or other methods, provided these methods do not stifle innovation or creativity.
8. I believe prices should reflect true value in use of the product or service to the customer, including the pricing of goods and services transferred among operating organizations worldwide.
9. I acknowledge that providing the best economic and social product value consistent with cost also includes: A. recognizing the customer's right to expect safe products with clear instructions for their proper use and maintenance; B. providing easily accessible channels for customer complaints; C. investigating any customer dissatisfaction objectively and taking prompt and appropriate remedial action; D. recognizing and supporting proven public policy objectives such as conserving energy and protecting the environment.
10. I pledge my efforts to assure that all marketing research, advertising, sales promotion, and sales presentations of products, services, or concepts are done clearly, truthfully, and in good taste so as not to mislead or offend customers. I further pledge to insure that all these activities are conducted in accordance with the highest standards of each profession and generally accepted principles of fair competition.
11. I pledge to cooperate fully in furthering the efforts of all institutions, media, professional associations, and other organizations to publicize this creed as widely as possible throughout the world.

Draft approved by WMCG in Verona, Italy, September, 1976.

(b) competence, (c) moral and legal standards, (d) public statements, (e) confidentiality, (f) welfare of the consumer, (g) professional relationships, (h) utilization of assessment techniques, and (i) pursuit of research activities (American Psychological Association, 1977).

Developing an encompassing code of ethics for sport managers is a problematic undertaking. The breadth of the field makes it very difficult to create a code that has much specificity. In addition, no organization fully accommodates the tremendous variety of practitioners and academicians in the field. Zeigler (1989) expressed need for those involved in sport management to develop a sound approach to ethics as it relates to their duties and

responsibilities and suggested that a comprehensive code of ethics needed to be developed. This served as the impetus for the North American Society for Sport Management (NASSM), to develop and approve an ethical creed for sport managers in 1989. The creed is one of the early efforts made to formally address the issue of professional ethics. An increasing number of sport organizations are addressing the issue of ethical conduct. Some examples include most of the major coaching associations in North America, the National Association of Academic Advisors for Athletics, the United States Olympic Committee, and the International Health, Racquet and Sportsclub Association. The National Alliance for Youth

Sports has ethics codes for athletes, parents, coaches, officials, and administrators. The National Association of Basketball Coaches met during the summer of 2003 with the specific focus of developing an ethical code in response to a number of embarrassing incidents involving coaches. (Moran, 2003)

The NCAA has implemented a certification process designed to encourage its Division I members to operate in a responsible manner. It involves a self-study and peer review that addresses four major areas that include: Governance and Rules Compliance, Fiscal Integrity, Academic Integrity, and Equity. While not exclusively an exercise in operational ethics, the process is likely to touch on a variety of ethical considerations.

As the sport industry becomes more cognizant of the need for establishing clearer ethical principles, perhaps a cooperative effort that includes various academic and professional associations in the field such as the National Association for Sport and Physical Education (NASPE), NASSM, and closely related occupational and professional groups can produce guidelines that might serve as the foundation for organizations to develop ethical codes tailored to their own operational needs.

CONCEPT CHECK

One of the characteristics of professionalization is the autonomy that provides opportunity for self-regulation. This often manifests itself in a formalized approach to ethical standards and conduct. Increasing attention is being paid to ethics in many business fields as reflected by both ethics training and the development of formal codes of ethics. Various sport and recreation organizations have also made efforts to deal with pertinent ethical concerns in more formal and proactive ways.

DEVELOPMENT OF ETHICAL SPORT MANAGERS

As the study of sport management becomes more formalized, one must examine the relationship of ethics and the future of sport management preparation and practice. With the number of academically prepared practitioners in sport management likely to increase substantially, the move toward greater professional status will probably continue. This trend has implications for the preparation of graduate and undergraduate students in sport management programs. More material dealing with ethically sensitive issues and more sport ethics and philosophy courses are being developed and included in the curriculum. (The American Assembly of Collegiate Schools of Business [AACSB] accredited business schools are required to include instruction on ethics within their curricula [Laczniak and Murphy, 1985; Robin and Reidenbach, 1989]). Petrick and Quinn (1997) identify several dimensions of management integrity that should be cultivated to produce ethical conduct. Ethical development can be viewed as a sequential process that begins with ethical awareness (perception of and sensitivity toward ethical situations). The next step can be termed assessment or reasoning to make ethical judgments. The third step progresses to ethical conduct or action. Without movement to this stage, ethics would have little practical impact. This involves the leap between talking about what is right and acting on it. Ultimately, the desire is to help prepare sport managers to exert ethical influence on those around them. Once managers begin to act in an ethical manner, it will be much easier for them to create an environment that has an impact on others.

There are ethical issues in virtually every area of sport management course-work. Topics such as honesty and accuracy in advertising and sales, price gouging, collusion, ticket scalping, and product safety have clear ethical dimensions. Ambush marketing (the effort of a company to affiliate with an event without paying a sponsorship fee) is another subject that raises very interesting ethical questions. Gender and minority equity, athlete exploitation, performance supplements, social responsibility, conflict-of-interest issues, and privacy rights are but a few of the other concerns with complex ethical considerations within the sport industry.

One response to these ethical challenges is a more concerted attempt to provide ethical training to both prospective and practicing sport management professionals. Several studies indicate that ethics committees and employee ethics training programs are becoming more prevalent in mainstream business firms (Robin and Reidenbach,

1989; Sims, 1994). This is likely to occur in sport businesses as well, and two particular reasons stand out. With the scrutiny that many sport enterprises experience, unethical actions result in negative publicity that can be very damaging to public support. A very different concern has to do with the increasingly international nature of the sporting business. The international community may have very different perspectives on what actions are ethical and unethical. Reconciling the different cultural mores will require a far more conscientious sense of ethical awareness.

CONCEPT CHECK

Attention to ethical considerations is increasingly a part of the training for sport managers. It is likely that more concerted efforts will be made to emphasize ethical training in both the educational and the job settings. The goal is to have sport managers who exhibit ethical sensitivity, sound ethical judgment, and a willingness to act and lead in an ethical manner.

SHARED RESPONSIBILITY FOR THE FUTURE

There are numerous examples of ethical misconduct in all segments of society, and certainly sport is no exception. The focus of this chapter is to encourage recognition and examination of the ethical dimensions of decision making and to provide a framework for a logical and reasoned approach for dealing with the moral and ethical choices that are certain to confront the sport management professional.

Professional behavior is grounded in personal values, but professional conduct does not always coincide with those personal values or the ideals of societal norms and virtues. To raise the level of professionalism in sport management, it is essential to take a proactive approach to ethical training. Ethical guidelines need to be carefully developed, and prospective sport managers should be schooled in the use of a systematic and analytical approach to the ethical dilemmas that they will undoubtedly encounter.

There is certainly a need for an increased awareness of and concern for the ethical issues of sport management, and this can be accomplished in a variety of ways. Incorporating ethical issues into existing academic course-work and developing courses in the ethics of sport are logical beginnings. The development of a code of ethics can begin to assist in providing a framework for ethical analysis. Beyond the classroom, practitioners must provide an environment in which a high standard of ethical conduct is the norm. Strong role models must be available and high expectations clearly outlined, and practitioners must be willing to accept that ethical behavior will not always bring the short-term, immediate benefits so demanded in this culture. The professionalization of sport management will ultimately be a cooperative venture between academics and practitioners in the field. How each partner in this endeavor deals with the issue(s) of ethics will be important in determining the status and prestige of sport management in both the academic and business communities.

SUMMARY

- Numerous examples of ethical misconduct exist in many of the basic social institutions, and sport is certainly no exception.
- The relativistic approach to ethics creates a more ambiguous behavioral environment, and action is frequently guided by legal standards rather than ethical standards.
- Ethics and morality are interrelated concepts that provide guidelines for acceptable conduct.
- Moral development starts with a very self-centered motivation, progresses to conforming with social norms, and ideally reaches the stage in which there is a reasoned belief in and commitment to universal moral principles.
- Teleology and deontology are the two primary categories of ethical theory.
- Maxims such as the Golden Rule are used as "rules of thumb" for ethical conduct, but more extensive frameworks for ethical analysis have been developed.
- Many useful models have been developed to systematize the task of ethical decision making. Several of these models incorporate characteristics of both deontology and teleology.
- Personal ethics must serve as the foundation for professional ethics, but the ethical

environment in the workplace will influence behavior.

- Ethics and integrity are not irrelevant in the modern business world but rather reflections of strength and virtue.
- Organizational and industry standards of conduct are often not congruent with personal standards, and the differences may be difficult to reconcile at times.
- There are frequently long-term consequences to unethical behavior, which outweigh the short-term gains.
- Development of a code of ethics is a step that can be taken to formalize ethical standards and expectations.
- Ethics training is becoming more prevalent in the academic setting and in the business setting.
- Ethical development should progress from ethical sensitivity to ethical judgment to ethical conduct and leadership.

 CRITICAL THINKING EXERCISES

1. As the marketing director of the athletic department at a major university, you are responsible for generating revenue through the sale of promotional opportunities, including advertising at athletic venues and in the department's printed material. Often these opportunities are sold as part of a promotional package. Recently a large beer company approached you with a proposal for a wide-ranging promotional package at a premium rate. The issue of alcohol and campus life is a particularly sensitive one at your institution, which has a reputation as a party school, and recurring incidents of binge drinking have resulted in substantial negative publicity. What are the ethical considerations that should be addressed as you weigh this proposal?

2. The annual Regatta Festival is a week-long event with substantial media coverage in your community. Your chain of Sport-o-Rama sporting goods stores in the region sells many water-related recreational products. The Regatta sales staff has discussed with you the possibility of your company

becoming an official sponsor of the event, but the price is quite steep in your judgment. You also feel you have little competition in the region and can capitalize on the event's presence without being an official sponsor. You plan a big storewide sale on Regatta week with a newspaper flyer. You are also considering the distribution of discount coupons at various sites along the race course. What ethical issues should be considered as you assess your marketing alternatives as they relate to this event?

 CASE STUDY

You are the athletic director at XYZ State University, a school of 15,000 students that is a member of NCAA Division I-AA. Your athletic program sponsors sixteen sports, but financial constraints have limited your ability to do all you would like with the program. Football has never been a primary revenue source as it is with some major Division I institutions, and attendance has dwindled over the past few years. In fact, football currently produces a larger net loss than any other sport in the program. Nevertheless, it holds a very strong traditional place on campus and in the community. The demands of gender equity have also forced resources to be reallocated and have strained the budget to the extent that either new revenue must be found to maintain the existing sports or cuts will need to be made.

One option you are considering is dropping football. Such a proposal would create a furor on campus and in the community, but it has some merit financially and minimizes gender-equity problems. Another option presented itself to you recently. The athletic director at MEGA University, a major Division I football power, called to see if you would consider playing them at their 90,000-seat stadium for a sizable guarantee. XYZ and MEGA U. played each other on a regular basis years ago, with MEGA U. routinely winning by six to eight touchdowns. There is virtually no prospect that the outcome would be much different now. The revenue produced from such a game would certainly ease some of your immediate financial problems, however.

Aside from the purely financial considerations of the scenario presented, there are some important ethical questions that must be addressed. As you weigh the options available, how would you respond to the ethical issues presented in this situation?

1. *Who are the various constituents who will be affected by your decision? How are they likely to react?*
2. *Is it appropriate to place the burden for the department's financial problems on the shoulders of an overmatched football team? What are the possible consequences?*
3. *How might either of the options be rationalized as the best decision?*
4. *What constitutes gender equity? Are there any ethical dimensions to dropping football as a method for achieving gender equity?*

ETHICAL SITUATIONS FOR DISCUSSION

The situations presented here are but a few examples of the ethical issues that can arise in sport. One or more of the following suggestions may help to make these situations more useful exercises: (a) evaluate how each situation might be dealt with at stages 4, 5, and 6 of Kohlberg's model of moral development: (b) evaluate each situation from both teleological and deontological points of view; (c) use one or more of the five maxims on page 34 to assess the appropriate actions in each situation; and (d) apply Cavanaugh's model for ethical decision making (or some other model of ethical analysis) to the situations in order to arrive at an ethically reasoned response or decision.

1. What are the ethical considerations to be addressed in the decision to use drug testing as a screening tool for prospective employees? What about the use of lie-detector tests? Would you submit to such testing? Why or why not? At what point do these tests become an invasion of privacy or a threat to basic constitutional rights?
2. Are the ethical considerations cited above the same for drug testing college and/ or professional athletes? If athletes should be randomly tested, should all students? professors? administrators? Should drug testing be only concerned with performance-enhancing substances?
3. Converse recently introduced a new basketball shoe to the marketplace with the name "Loaded Weapon." The name has been criticized by many, but the shoe has also received a great deal of preintroduction publicity (Hiestand, 2003). Does the company have any obligation to be "politically correct" in the naming of its products? If you were a college coach or administrator, would you be willing to have your players wear this shoe?
4. The Professional Golf Association (PGA) has been criticized in recent years for holding tournaments at exclusive clubs with exclusionary membership practices. While the PGA has responded to this criticism, one tournament, the Master's, has come to be the focal point for this debate. Critics contend that this major tournament is held at a club (Augusta National) with discriminatory membership practices and the PGA should do something. Others contend that, as a private club, membership decisions should be their prerogative. The club leadership has adamantly opposed being forced to change their practices simply on the basis of outside pressures. What should the PGA do? Whose rights are being infringed upon in this situation?
5. It has become common for professional franchise owners to threaten to move their teams to more supportive communities unless they are provided with a variety of benefits such as stadium funding, tax breaks, development rights, etc. Do professional franchise owners have any ethical obligations to the communities that support them? If so, what are they and are they different from those of any other business operations?
6. The difference between serving the public well (social obligations) and serving as the social conscience is sometimes difficult to determine. Several examples involving health and fitness clubs may serve to amplify this issue. Should health clubs serve alcoholic beverages in their lounge area? Should they have cigarette machines? Should they provide tanning beds for those who wish to use them? From a business standpoint, each of these may be a profitable service. From a health standpoint, there are various levels of concern about each of these services. What ethical consideration comes into play in making the decision about the

provision of such services? By not providing such services, are you playing the role of social conscience and limiting people's freedom to make their own choices?

7. Organizational image is the primary concern of the public relations effort. In many sport organizations, the media are important players in the manipulation of that image, and the ethics of this relationship may bear scrutiny on both sides. Is it appropriate to curry the attention of the media through providing free tickets, food, transportation, accommodations, and so on? Should these favors be provided only for favorable coverage? Should the media accept such favors? What are the risks to each party and to the general public with such an arrangement?

8. In many circumstances, it may be the actions of others that pose a personal ethical quandary. In such situations, the question of how you tolerate or deal with such behavior becomes the ethical dilemma. Do you report a fellow employee who is skimming small amounts of money from the cash register? Do you accept an outstanding prospective athlete's transcript that you know has been altered? Do you report a supervisor who is providing inside information to a favored supplier about competitors' bids on athletic equipment? What are the circumstances in which you tolerate these situations? Under what circumstances do you take action?

9. Employee and consumer safety are often cited as ethical problems that arise as organizations attempt to balance economic and safety concerns. There are many considerations that go into the decision on what type of playing surface to install. Are there ethical dimensions to this decision? Should artificial turf be used if the incidence of injury or the severity of injuries is higher than on natural surfaces? How much more dangerous would the surface have to be before the risks outweigh the benefits?

10. Casey Martin used the Americans with Disabilities Act (ADA) to petition for the right to use a cart while participating in profes-

sional golf tournaments. What are the ramifications of such a decision? Should the PGA have allowed such a request without court action?

11. The NFL has a rule that prohibits players from entering the NFL draft until three years after their high school class has graduated. Why does this rule exist? Is the rule legal? Is the rule ethical? In what ways does the rule make sense and in what ways does the rule seem unfair?

12. There has been a proliferation of conference realignments recently that have created a great deal of antagonism among some schools. When Miami, Boston College, and Virginia Tech left the Big East to join the Atlantic Coast Conference, there were accusations of raiding and charges of disloyalty. The Big East then invited several members of Conference USA to join the Big East. What obligations do schools have to the conferences to which they belong? What are the ethical obligations of conferences looking to expand their memberships?

REVIEW QUESTIONS AND ISSUES

1. Cite examples that depict the ethical climate that exists in society and in sport.
2. How are the concepts of ethics and morality related?
3. Discuss the contention that stage four of Kohlberg's model for moral development is the stage at which most adults tend to function ethically.
4. What are the primary characteristics of teleological and deontological theories of ethics?
5. What are the strengths and weaknesses of Cavanaugh's model for ethical decision making?
6. What is the relationship between personal and professional ethics?
7. Can ethics be taught in a college classroom or is it too late to affect or influence the ethics of college students?
8. What is the responsibility of an organization's leadership with regard to the level of ethical conduct exhibited by its employees?

9. What can an organization do to encourage high standards of ethical conduct? How can ethical codes be used in this process?
10. Is all legal behavior ethical? Is all ethical behavior legal? Defend your position.
11. Select an existing ethics code or creed from a sport organization and identify its strengths and weaknesses. Discuss how effective this code might be in practice.
12. Choose a sport organization and identify the elements you would include in the development of an ethical code.
13. Discuss what barriers you see that impede the ability of the field of sport management to develop an encompassing ethical code.

 ### SOLUTIONS TO CRITICAL THINKING EXERCISES

1. A utilitarian view would likely address the benefits versus the costs of accepting such a proposal. The financial benefits of accepting such a proposal are quite clear and could be justified or rationalized in a variety of ways. Additional revenue may provide more or higher quality opportunities for athletic participation. This proposal may also reduce the time and effort required to produce necessary resources. There are social costs to accepting this proposal, including promotion of a product that has some negative social consequences and in an environment in which many of those exposed to the promotional efforts cannot legally use the product. There are some mixed signals being sent when the institution tries discouraging underage and excessive drinking on campus while, at the same time, providing a forum for a company to encourage alcohol consumption. The inconsistency of such action poses an ethical quandary for the institution's decision makers.

2. Using Cavanaugh's model for ethical decision making, three questions need to be addressed. First, if the company decides to use the event without paying a sponsorship fee, are benefits to the parties involved optimized? The benefits to Sport-o-Rama are quite high while the benefits to the Regatta Festival are nonexistent. In fact, the Regatta Festival is damaged by such an action because it may undermine the value of sponsorship. It is unlikely that the total benefits are optimized if Sport-o-Rama takes this approach. Second, do the actions of the parties respect the rights of the other? This is a more difficult issue to assess. The Regatta has a right to sell the benefits of affiliation and to protect itself from those who may try to benefit from the event without paying for the association. Sport-o-Rama also has certain rights to communicate freely with consumers as long as it does not cross legal lines associated with using protected names, trademarks, and logos. The balance of rights is a difficult issue in this circumstance. The third question is one of justice or fairness. Is it fair for Sport-o-Rama to benefit from this event without providing any compensation? Would Sport-o-Rama feel the same way if another company were using an event sponsored by Sport-o-Rama in a similar way? Is it fair for the Regatta Festival to demand compensation from anyone who associates with this community event in any way? The response to these three issues will provide the foundation for an ethical decision.

 ### WEBSITES

www.sportsethicsinstitute.org—An excellent site that provides numerous examples of sport specific ethical dilemmas and current discussion of those issues.

www.ethics.org—The Ethics Resource Center provides a broad range of ethics information including books, articles, links, and research papers and includes issues related to general ethics, organizational ethics, global ethics, and character development.

www.ethicsweb.ca—EthicsWeb provides an excellent starting point for a broad range of ethical topics including ethical decision making and discipline-specific ethical issues and includes many interesting links.

www.cces.ca—The Canadian Centre for ethics in sport has extensive discussion of drug use in sport and educational material related to this topic.

www.nays.org—Provides examples of ethics codes for a variety of youth sport-related organizations.

www.olympic.org/ioc—The code of ethics for the International Olympic Committee is included in this site. The code addresses issues of dignity, integrity, resources, confidentiality, and relations with countries.

REFERENCES

American Psychological Association (1977). *Ethical standards of psychologists*. Washington, DC: American Psychological Association.

Beauchamp, T., and Bowie, N. (1988). *Ethical theory and business*. 3rd ed. Englewood Cliffs, NJ: Prentice Hall.

Cavanaugh, G. (1984). *American business values*. 2nd ed. Englewood Cliffs, NJ: Prentice Hall.

Chonko, L. (1995). *Ethical decision making in marketing*. Thousand Oaks, CA: Sage.

Cialdini, R. (1996). "Social influence and the triple tumor: Structure of organizational dishonesty." In D. Messick and A. TenBrunsel (Eds), *Codes of conduct: Behavioral research into business ethics (Ch. 2)*. New York: Russell Sage.

De George, R. (1982). *Business ethics*. New York: Macmillan.

Frank, R. (1996). "Can socially responsible firms survive in a competitive environment?" In D. Messick and A. TenBrunsel (Eds), *Codes of conduct: Behavioral research into business ethics (Ch. 4)*. New York: Russell Sage.

Garrett, T. (1966). *Business ethics*. Englewood Cliffs, NJ: Prentice Hall.

Gibson, J. (1993). *Performance versus results: A critique of values in contemporary sport*. Albany, NY: State University of New York Press.

Goodpaster, K. E. (1984). *Ethics in management*. Boston: Harvard Business School.

Hiestand, M. Controversial shoe name is worth shot to converse. USA Today (September 25), C2.

Jackall, R. (1988). *Moral mazes: The world of corporate managers*. New York: Oxford University Press.

Kohlberg, L. (1976). *Moral development and behavior: Theory, research, and social issues*. New York: Holt, Rinehart, & Winston.

Laczniak, G. R., and Murphy, P. E. (1985). *Marketing ethics*. Lexington, MA: D.C. Heath.

Moran, M. (2003). Coaches, NCAA agree to chart new course. USA Today (October 16), C7.

O'Neill, B. (2000). Rate it R for ridiculous. Pittsburgh Post–Gazette (March 16), C1.

Petrick, J., and Quinn, J. (1997). *Management ethics: Integrity at work*. Thousand Oaks, CA: Sage.

Rokeach, M. (1973). *The nature of human values*. New York: The Free Press.

Robin, D. P., and Reidenbach, R. E. (1989). *Business ethics: Where profits meet values systems*. Englewood Cliffs, NJ: Prentice Hall.

Sims, R. (1994). *Ethics and organizational decision making: A call for renewal*. Westport, CT: Quorum Books.

Solomon, R. C. (1999). *A better way to think about business*. New York: Oxford University Press.

Solomon, R., and Hanson, K. (1983). *Above the bottom line*. NY: Harcourt Brace Jovanovich.

Sternberg, E. (2000). *Just Business: Business ethics in action*. 2nd ed. Oxford: Oxford University Press.

Stoll, S., and Beller, J. (1993, March). The effect of a longitudinal teaching methodology and classroom environment on both cognitive and behavioral moral development. Paper presented at the American Alliance for Health, Physical Education, Recreation, and Dance. Washington, DC.

Tuleja, T. (1985). *Beyond the bottom line*. New York: Facts on File Publications.

Velasquez, M. G. (1988). *Business ethics: Concepts and cases*. 2nd ed. Englewood Cliffs, NJ: Prentice Hall.

White, T. (1993). *Business ethics*. New York: Macmillan.

Zeigler, E. F. (1989). Proposed creed and code of professional ethics for the North American Society for Sport Management. *Journal of Sport Management*, 3, 2–4.

CHAPTER 4

Managing Employee Diversity in the Sport Industry

Mark E. Moore

In this chapter, you will become familiar with the following terms:

Act diversimilarity
   strategy
Diversity
External diversity
Good-old-boy network
Internal diversity
Managing diversity

Managing of diversity by
   managing diversimilarity
   principle
Managing through
   diversimilarity strategy
People of color
Prejudices

Principle of diversity within
   diversity
Pygmalion effect
Reverse discrimination
Similarity across diversity
   principle
Stereotypes

Learning Goals

By the end of this chapter, students should be able to:

• Describe why a sport organization should effectively manage employment diversity.

• Define the dimensions of employment diversity.

• Know the benefits and costs involved with imbuing a sport organization with employment diversity.

• Understand strategies for effectively managing employment diversity within a sport organization.

• Know the phases of implementing an employment diversification strategy within a sport organization.

In the early part of the twenty-first century, opportunities within competitive sport are expanding for all population segments. Women are now provided the opportunity to compete in a variety of traditional and nontraditional sports. In addition, minorities and people with various abilities are expanding their competitive horizons within the sport domain. This is demonstrated by the diversity on the playing fields that suggests ethnic minorities no longer encounter position segregation and through the Paralympics showing that disabilities are no longer obstacles to success in competitive sport.

While competitive sport opportunities have proliferated across participant segments of society, this level of diversity has not been manifested within the managerial hierarchy of contemporary sport organizations. Lapchick (2003) reports that while women accounted for 48 percent of administrative posts within the National Basketball Association (NBA), they hold only 22 percent of these position types within Major League Baseball (MLB). With respect to race, the NBA has the highest percentage of racial or ethnic minority administrators. It classifies 21 percent of its executives as ethnic minorities. In contrast, only 13 percent of the National Football League (NFL) and 13 percent of MLB administrators are classified as ethnic minorities. Within collegiate athletics, 5 percent of athletic directors at Division I institutions are ethnic minorities, while women account for 7 percent of those leadership positions. These data are according to the *2003 Racial and Gender Report Card* complied by Lapchick. Currently, the Disability Report Card is being developed by the Center for the Study of Sport and Society at Northeastern University (Lapchick). The fact that this initiative is being undertaken suggests that people with disabilities are underrepresented within the employment realm of contemporary sport as well.

This analysis provides evidence that employment diversity is lacking within the sport industry. This lack could be very problematic for sport organizations. An existing theory hypothesizes that the diversity composition is correlated to the competitive effectiveness of an organization within its marketplace (Cox and Blake, 2002). Thus, staff diversity's impact on marketplace competitiveness will continue to augment as demographics of the workplace change. According to Kinicki and Williams (2003), workplace trends are augmenting employment diversity's importance as a determinant of competitiveness within an organization.

CONCEPT CHECK

Protected classes can be defined as ethnic minorities, women, and people with disabilities who are covered by federal equal employment opportunity laws.

TRENDS IN THE WORKPLACE

Kinicki and Williams (2003) reported that managers of contemporary organizations should be aware of

---

TABLE 4-1   *Highlights of key trends in the marketplace*

1. *Age*
   The median age of America's workforce is expected to increase to 40.6 in 2005.
2. *Gender*
   Nearly one-half of the United States' workforce is composed of women.
3. *People of color*
   Approximately 35 percent of new entries into the workforce by 2005 will be individuals of color.
4. *People of homosexual orientation*
   Based on current statistics, individuals with homosexual orientation represent from 3 percent to 10 percent of the current American workforce.
5. *People with differing abilities*
   One in six Americans has a physical or mental disability.
6. *Underemployment*
   It is estimated that 25 percent of the United States' workforce is underemployed.

Source: Kinicki, A., and Williams, B. K. (2003). *Management: A practical introduction.* New York: McGraw-Hill.

---

several workplace trends when examining the diversity composition of their entities. (See Table 4-1.)

Age

The median age of the American workforce is expected to increase to 40.6 years in 2005 compared to 34.3 years in 1980 (Kinicki and Williams, 2003). Age certainly has become more visible within the sport industry, as it is not uncommon to see coaches extending their careers past the age of seventy. Joe Paterno walks the football sidelines at Penn State in his middle 70s, while Jack McKeon and Felipe Alou recently obtained field-manager positions in Major League Baseball although both are over 65. Then there is John Gagliardi of St. John's University in Collegeville, Minnesota, who recently became the all-time winningest coach in collegiate football at the tender age of 77. While the senior segment is achieving success on the playing field, youth is also fairing well in competitive athletics. Michelle Wie is currently competing on the Ladies' Professional Golf Tour as a fourteen-year-old, and LeBron James has attained superstardom in the NBA prior to adulthood.

Gender

Ever since the passage of Title IX in 1972, there has been much debate over the status of gender within the athletic domain. Although competitive opportunities have increased for women since the enactment of this legislation, Lapchick (2003) indicated that women are in the minority when it comes to managerial appointments within the sport industry, even though the percentage of women in the aggregate workforce has increased from 27 percent in 1980 to 42 percent in 1994, according to Kinicki and Williams (2003). Despite these statistics and the presence of Title IX, there are also inequities in compensation between male and female executives across wide-ranging industries, including sport. Kinicki and Williams indicated that female executives make 60 cents to every dollar male executives earn. An analysis performed by Lapchick found that salaries of female executives were lower than those of their male counterparts within the sport industry. The data presented in this section clearly exhibit that while Title IX has broadened the participation rates of women on the playing field, this equality has not been transferred into the management of amateur and professional sport. Consequently, women still have significant progress to make before they realize full equity in the leadership hierarchy of sport organizations.

People of color

People of color are expected to contribute 34.7 percent of new entries into the workforce by 2005 (Kinicki and Williams, 2003). Despite this, there is evidence that people of color are experiencing challenges in securing managerial employment in the sport industry. As previously stated, Lapchick (2003) found that leadership positions in sport are dominated by white males. Racial discrimination is quite salient within sport, as this industry has historically erected barriers to impede the advancement of people of color. One piece of evidence is that most head coaches and field managers in professional sport are Caucasian. Additionally, players' positions in such sports as football historically have been segregated according to skin color. To rectify discriminative practices, sport organizations will have to be more aggressive in recruiting people of color to the managerial ranks. This will require a sincere commitment to employment diversity measures.

Sexual orientation

Currently, sexual orientation issues are becoming prevalent in the workplace. There is heightened attention, for instance, to issues concerning whether health benefits should be provided to same-sex partners of employees and the homophobic practices that often exclude individuals with homosexual orientations from gainful employment. Statistics show that employment discrimination is prevalent among gays and lesbians. According to Kinicki and Williams (2003), gays and lesbians comprise 3 to 10 percent of today's workforce, with 11 percent to 27 percent of those having homosexual orientation earning lower wages than their heterosexual counterparts. Although there are no known employment statistics regarding sexual orientation in the sport industry, one must provide adequate attention to this characteristic when examining workplace trends pertinent to sport. Like all groups different from the predominantly white-male heterosexual leadership, employees with homosexual orientation undoubtedly have encountered discrimination within the sport sector. If sport organizations are to become models of diversity as advocated by DeSensi (1994, 1995), they must be committed to providing equal access to people of all sexual orientations with respect to leadership opportunities.

People with differing abilities

Demographics reveal that one in six Americans has a physical or mental disability (Kinicki and Williams, 2003). There is substantial evidence that individuals with disabilities experience challenges in obtaining gainful employment. Sixty-six percent of individuals with disabilities who are willing to work are unemployed (Kinicki and Williams), while the 34 percent that have found work are primarily underemployed according to Kinicki and Williams. Within sport management, there is evidence that people with disabilities have limited opportunities to gain employment and advance up the leadership hierarchy. Moore (2002) found that collegiate and professional sport organizations only employed a small number of individuals with disabilities on their managerial staff. This suggests that sport-related entities need to have policies in place to recruit and accommodate people with disabilities more effectively. Such actions will require leadership by sport organizations to have full awareness of Title I of the Americans with Disabilities Act of 1990 (ADA), which prohibits employment discrimination against individuals with disabilities. The passage of the ADA not only conveys to sport organizations that they must abide by the law but also provides the incentive to increase their employment diversity. The valuing and proper managing of diversity have enabled individuals with disabilities to achieve an increased presence within the Olympic movement. Due to increased representation of those with varying abilities on the International Olympic Committee and affiliated governmental bodies, the Paralympics has grown into a true international athletic spectacle.

The lack of congruency between educational levels of employees and skills needed by an organization

Although educational disparity does not constitute a recognized minority class, it does impact diversity within organizations. According to Kinicki and Williams (2003), a large percentage of college graduates are currently underemployed. This trend is primarily attributed to low motivation and personal difficulties, such as single parenthood (Kinicki and Williams), and shows that the United States economy is not properly allocating human resources to meet the staffing needs of profit and nonprofit organizations. As the marketplace continues to evolve into a global arena, American enterprises of a sport and nonsport nature will be at a competitive disadvantage if educational disparity continues to increase in the workplace. Therefore, it is imperative that organizations place persons with the educational and professional credentials required in job openings. This is especially important in the sport industry, where individuals often apply for positions for which they are overqualified due to the glamour associated with working for a sport organization. Consequently, the professional qualifications of job applicants relative to the specifications of particular positions should be considered when one examines the diversity composition of an organization.

MANAGING DIVERSITY

To maintain congruency with these marketplace trends and establish a quality workforce as the representation of white male workers diminishes, organizations must learn how to effectively manage **diversity.** Kinicki and Williams (2003) stated that diversity represents all people who are alike and unlike. Allard (2002) indicated that diversity often includes varying dimensions that evoke the awareness of managers. Regardless of the particular dimension of diversity, economic and legal pressures generally shape the composition of staff diversity within a particular organizational climate. Given the salience of such forces, current and future managers should have knowledge of both **internal** and **external diversity** dimensions.

CONCEPT CHECK

Staff diversity is generally considered a function of the organizational climate. The managing of diversity, therefore, means being aware of characteristics and attitudes common to the majority of employees while valuing the differences between employees.

Dimensions of diversity

The dimensions of diversity are internal and external. Internal diversity dimensions pertain to those human characteristics with which persons are generally born. Kinicki and Williams (2003) emphasized that these dimensions typically refer to human differences that are visible throughout one's life, such as, gender, age, race, ethnicity, and physical disabilities. These factors cannot be attributed to a choice one has made in life. Conversely, external diversity dimensions manifest as a result of decisions one makes in his or her everyday life. These involve personal, educational, and career choices (Kinicki and Williams). For instance, athletes often have to decide between higher educational institutions to attend that are of equal quality. Little do they understand at decision time how such a decision will impact their professional profile as well as the diversity composition of their future employers. Also, employers often hire individuals based on the college or university they attended. This is often shown within sport organizations when executives who graduated from a prestigious sport management program hire graduates from that program. Through such hiring practices, the decision makers are shaping the degree of external diversity within their organizations.

Regardless of whether the specific dimension is external or internal, diversity is influenced by the culture of an organization (Doherty and Chelladuri, 1999). Hansen (2003) stated that diversity can improve organizational effectiveness if optimal climatic and cultural support is presented. Often, however, leadership in an organization does not understand the benefits of diversity and does not structure an appropriate climate to accommodate people with varying characteristics. This emphasizes the importance of knowing the benefits of diversity.

BENEFITS OF DIVERSITY

So what are the benefits of diversity? The benefits of diversity are many, as the following sections illustrate.

Resource allocation

By instituting diversity measures, organizations can attract better human resources who can provide an array of perspectives, skills, and experiences to serve their interests well. Bohlander and Snell (2004) identified the effective use of talent as one of the key benefits of diversity. This is of particular importance within the sport industry, which has a multimillion-dollar revenue stream. As sport organizations evolve financially, the **"good-old-boy network"** can no longer be counted upon as an effective recruitment source of human resources.

Although the good-old-boy network was once a common practice for the recruitment of personnel, it has lost its effectiveness as sport organizations adopt more formal business orientations. Further, impeding the network's effectiveness in recent times has been the depletion of the pool of qualified white males. Cox and Blake (2002) indicated that this depletion will require contemporary organizations to recruit human resources from nontraditional labor pools. This will create expanded opportunity for women, people of color, seniors, and people with differing abilities to participate in the management of sport enterprises and will ultimately broaden the diversity composition of the sport industry.

CONCEPT CHECK

The good-old-boy network is the practice of executives hiring their friends. The limited number of minority head coaches within the NFL has been attributed to the good-old-boy network.

Marketing

By effectively **managing diversity,** sport organizations can increase their marketing effectiveness. In particular, enterprises that increase and properly manage diversity will possess the staffing and expertise to understand and satisfy needs of diverse target markets (Mullin, Hardy and Sutton, 1999; Moore, 1987). Consequently, sport organizations would have the competency and expertise required to compete for the entertainment dollar. Cox and Blake (2002) communicate that effective managing of diversity helps an organization increase its marketing effectiveness by providing the knowledge and skills to reach diverse market segments.

Problem solving

When an organization has a diverse set of minds working on its behalf, employees can generally offer a thorough array of potential solutions to complex organizational problems. Cox and Blake (2002) conveyed that diverse groups have broad bases of experiences to draw upon when approaching problems. However, according to those authors, there cannot be too little heterogeneity or too little homogeneity within an organizational culture. An example of the impact of diversity on problem solving according to research, is the manner in which men and women approach problems. Cushner, McCelland, and Safford (2003) communicated that men tend to focus on modifying behavior within problem-solving tasks, while women tend to solve problems by collaboration. Through being aware of these divergent approaches, organizations can formulate a problem-solving approach to resolve the particular situation.

Systematic flexibility

When its degree of employment diversity is increased, an organization is likely to have more flexibility and greater receptiveness to change (Cox and Blake, 2002). Researchers have discovered that a culturally diverse organization can overcome resistance to change more effectively (Cox and Blake). Von Bergen, Barlow, and Foster (2002) indicated that diversity enables the workforce to be responsive to social change due to increased organizational flexibility and enhanced impersonal communications among employees. If sport organizations can effectively manage diversity, they will likely have increased flexibility that will help them survive the changing global marketplace of the twenty-first century.

Absence of employee conflict

By effectively managing staff diversity, an organization can reduce conflicts among staff members (Cox and Blake, 2002). Such situations exist because diversity helps a person to be more tolerant of individual differences on organizational issues and can provide quick conflict resolutions (Von Bergen, Barlow, and Foster, 2002). When diversity is managed properly, organizational leadership is generally in control and, therefore, able to resolve conflict when it arises (Bohlander and Snell, 2004). Furthermore, Von Bergen, Barlow, and Foster stated that a reduction in employee conflict improves organizational productivity, thereby suggesting another reason why sport organizations should pursue employment diversity measures.

COSTS OF DIVERSITY

When an organization considers such benefits, it should be aware of the costs of imbuing an organization with diversity when it is not properly managed. In the following sections, two salient costs of

diversity, identified by Kinicki and Williams (2003), are discussed with respect to sport organizations.

Stereotypes and prejudices

When organizations do not manage diversity in a proper way, ineffectiveness often appears within their work structure. Failure to properly manage diversity, according to Kinicki and Williams (2003), will result in **stereotypes** and **prejudices.** Stereotypes are negative labels and traits attributed to certain demographic groups/protected classes. Prejudice is a bias toward individuals due to their membership in a certain group that typically leads to discriminatory practices. Bias, resulting in prejudicing a society, tends to be an underpinning of stereotypes. Stereotypes and prejudices are still very pervasive in contemporary society, as they often lead to opinions that minorities do not possess the qualifications to be leaders of sport organizations. Consequently, sport enterprises must manage diversity better in the future or they will continue to be negatively impacted by stereotypes and prejudices.

CONCEPT CHECK

Historically, women have encountered the stereotype that they do not possess the physique to become skilled athletes. This stereotype has diminished with the stellar performances of female athletes in recent times.

Resistance to change

Another potential cost of diversity is resistance to diversity programs (Kinicki and Williams, 2003). Resistance to diversity in sport can result in substantial costs to organizations. The recent situation involving the Detroit Lions' decision to hire Steve Mariucci as head coach, without interviewing qualified minority candidates, caused the organization to be in violation of the National Football League's diversity employment policy. According to this directive from the league's hierarchy, each club must interview qualified minority candidates when a head coaching position vacancy occurs. The league's owners particularly felt that the Lions were indeed in violation of this policy by not interviewing minority coaching candidates Sylvester Croom of the Green

Bay Packers (assistant coach), Tim Lewis of the Pittsburgh Steelers (assistant coach) and former Minnesota Vikings' head coach Dennis Green. Sylvester Croom, parenthetically, was bypassed as well for the University of Alabama head football coaching position in the spring of 2003 in favor of nonminority candidate Mike Shula, who lacked the coaching experience of Croom. Due to their violation of the league's employment diversity policy, the Detroit Lions were fined $200,000 (http://espn.go .com/nfl/news/2003/0725/1585560.htm).

In Major League Baseball, the lack of diversity efforts appears to be costly as well. Most clubs are not able to penetrate minority consumer market segments. Given the low representation of protected group members in the front offices of MLB clubs, this should not be surprising.

These examples reveal that resistance to diversity is still very much woven into the structures of contemporary sport organizations. Consequently, if these organizations do not become more open to employment diversity, they will continue to suffer both monetary and market-share losses in the years ahead.

BARRIERS TO DIVERSITY

Since the benefits of employment diversity outweigh its costs, it is perplexing why diversity programs are not more enthusiastically accepted within sport organizations. Consequently, one would have to assume that there are barriers to employment diversity in these enterprises.

Devaluation of employees' worth

Uninformed sources within contemporary society connote employment diversity with affirmative action and similar initiatives designed to institute employee quotas. Consequently, those holding such sentiments tend to believe that diversity programs in the workplace devalue the contributions of skilled and unskilled labor. Von Bergen, Barlow, and Foster (2002) communicated that when diversity is disguised through quotas, employees classified within protected groups often develop a **Pygmalion effect.** The Pygmalion effect occurs when an employee doubts her of his self-worth because of the belief that her or his hiring is attributed to the employer's efforts to satisfy hiring quotas. When diversity is mentioned in this perspective, there is indeed a negative effect for both the employee and employer. Because of this negativity, employment diversity is often not emphasized within an organization.

Reverse discrimination

Leaders of contemporary organizations are sometimes fearful of being accused of reverse discrimination. Due to this apprehension, a rationale for instituting initiatives of workplace diversification often cannot be formulated by organizational leadership. **Reverse discrimination** occurs when an applicant from the dominant group (i.e., white males) is not selected even through that individual is the most qualified. For instance, if the Detroit Lions would have selected a less qualified minority candidate as their head coach instead of Steve Mariucci, this would have been perceived by many as reverse discrimination. Often, organizational leaders are paranoid about committing reverse discrimination because they do not have a thorough understanding of how to manage diversity within their work climates.

STRATEGIES FOR MANAGING DIVERSITY

Within contemporary organizations, there are indeed barriers to employment diversity. Such impediments were identified and delineated in the previous section. Although diversity measures under inappropriate pretenses would alarm the leadership of most organizations, such initiatives can accomplish employee diversity goals if a well-thought-out strategic framework is employed. In the following section a framework formulated by Ofori-Dankwa and Julian (2002) that proposes three specific strategies for managing and appreciating diversity will be discussed from a sport management perspective (see Table 4-2).

Managing through diversimilarity: Strategy one
Ofori-Dankwa and Julian (2002) recommended that organizations identify and appreciate individual differences while emphasizing similarities between groups of workers. A **managing through diversimilarity strategy** can enable those organizational aspirations to be realized if it is properly implemented, since it notes that all people possess similarities and differences. A strategic approach of this nature has applicability to a sport enterprise because it can reduce social distance and creates bonding between intergroup members.

In the intercollegiate athletic department at Temple University, for example, women's head

TABLE 4-2   *Description of Employment Diversity Strategies*

Managing through diversimilarity	Infusion of principles of diversimilarity	Act diversimilarity

• Recognition of demographical classifications.
• Recognition of similarities and differences across demographical classifications.
	• Five principles.
	  • Creativity and adversity.
	  • Conformity and compatibility.
	  • Diversity within diversity.
	  • The similarity across diversity principle.
	  • The managing of diversity by managing diversimilarity principles.
	• Underpinnings.
	  • There are similarities across members of demographical groups.
	  • There are differences among members within each demographical group.
		• Four components.
		  • Strive for workplace diversity according to demographical data.
		  • Identify similarities among workers of different demographical groups.
		  • Infuse the work structure with intellectual diversity.
		  • Develop an organizational culture of commonalities among workers.

Source: Ofori-Dankwa, J. C., and Julian, D. (2002). The diversimilarity approach to diversity management: A primer and strategies for future managers. In C. P. Harvey and M. J. Allard (eds.), *Understanding and managing diversity: Readings, cases and exercises* (pp. 84–94). Upper Saddle River, NJ: Prentice Hall.

basketball coach Dawn Stanley and men's basketball coach John Chaney likely possess varying coaching styles; however, both exhibit affinity for collegiate basketball and Temple athletics. Within the Temple community, there are also likely to be salient differences in coaching approaches between Coach Chaney who is of an urban background and of African-American descent, and head football coach Bobby Wallace, who is a Caucasian with roots in the rural South. Although these individuals have perceived personal and professional differences, they are bound by their commitment to intercollegiate athletics at Temple University and to the development of young athletes. These examples illustrate that proper managing of diversity within sport organizations should identify differences between individuals while simultaneously recognizing similarities as important organizational components.

Infusion of principles of diversimilarity: Strategy two

Another strategic alternative for managers seeking to imbue their enterprise with diversification is to apply principles of diversimilarity. Ofori-Dankwa and Julian (2002) indicated that to expose an organization to diversimilarity, consideration must be given to five principles. The principles will now be described in a sport context.

Creativity and adversity.   Ofori-Dankwa and Julian (2002) emphasized that both creativity and adversity are very salient within a diverse organization. While diversity often stimulates innovations and creativity, it also can bring forth various employee viewpoints. As a result, adversity in the organizational structure can be heightened. When a female athletic director is hired at a Division I university, for instance, she may provide her institution with much needed creativity in marketing the sport programs. However, the new marketing orientation may not be understood by all athletic department personnel. This lack of comprehension may cause adversity among some staff members. While this organization would be imbued with more creativity, it would likely be impacted by heightened tensions among its employees.

Conformity and Compatibility. According to Ofori-Dankwa and Julian (2002), an organization progressing toward a culturally diverse climate will generate conformity and compatibility among workers. In particular, these researchers stress that when people learn that they are similar to other workers, comparisons are often made. Returning to the athletic department at Temple University, an example of compatibility would be if women's basketball coach Dawn Staley based the perceived value of her contribution to the institution on a comparison of her salary and benefits with the compensation given to men's basketball coach John Chaney. Ofori-Dankwa and Julian believe that salary comparisons between members of different societal or work groups can strengthen an individual's conformity to the attitudes and practices of one's reference group (i.e., gender or racial class). An illustration of this proposition is shown when female college basketball coaches initiate legal action against their universities claiming they are not receiving compensation comparable to their male peers. The salary inequalities, in turn, have had a role in bonding female coaches to the advancement of their profession.

Diversity within diversity. The segmentation of workers into groups for diversification of demographic purposes does not necessarily indicate that pure similarities exist among each group's members. Ofori-Dankwa and Julian (2002) emphasize that group affiliation does not imply absence of individual differences. These authors hold the conviction that persons belonging to the same ethnic or gender classes often contrast with respect to work interests, specializations, professional experience, or educational backgrounds.

Until recently at the University of Minnesota, there was a separate department for women's athletics. One would be foolish to assume that all female coaches within this department had the same coaching style, applied the same motivational techniques, or displayed the same athletic interests. Most organizations comprise varying job functions requiring an array of experts from a multitude of disciplines. Since no work group or class can maintain exclusive homogeneity, Ofori-Dankwa and Julian stated that effective managing of diversity requires the **principle of diversity within diversity.** Based on this proposition, leadership within a sport organization cannot

assume that all members of a reference group will exhibit the same work ethic, attitudes, training and expertise when organizing and structuring work.

The similarity across diversity principle. The **similarity across diversity principle** is an approach emphasizing that while individuals may reside within one reference group, this affiliation does not exclude them from possessing the same traits, attitudes, and abilities as counterparts in other groups (Ofori-Dankwa and Julian, 2002). An example of this principle is when college students are segmented according to gender. Across the female and male student groups, there may be bonding between individuals through their affinity for sport or physical activities. Another example of this principle is Olympics spectators, who represent a wide spectrum of ethnic groups possessing common interests in sport, competition, and international camaraderie. These illustrations clearly reveal that the "similarity across diversity principle" is well manifested within the institution of sport.

The managing of diversity by managing diversimilarity principle. The **managing of diversity by managing diversimilarity principle** is a conceptualization of Ofori-Dankwa and Julian (2002), indicating that people are alike and unlike. This requires that managers must be cognizant that all employees in work groups have similar and dissimilar patterns of behavior, creating a wide range of motives, dispositions, and idiosyncrasies. For instance, both men and women may have a desire to be employed in the sport management profession for enjoyment and prestige. However, there may be more inclination among female sport managers to perform collaborative work duties, while their male counterparts may have more propensity for a competitive work situations. Given that this strategy values both similarities and differences among workers, sport managers must consider this directive when desiring to enhance workplace diversity in their respective organizations.

Act diversimilarity: Strategy three

The **act diversimilarity strategy,** according to Ofori-Dankwa and Julian (2002), is implemented in four components.

The basis of the first component is that managers should strive for workforce diversity in terms of demographics. This requires that sport-related organizations provide equal opportunity and access to all workers, including members of protected classes. Sport managers should maintain a record of demographic data to enable monitoring employee representation across protected classes. This would facilitate progress toward better workplace diversification in most sport entities and would likely lay a foundation for them to manage diversity effectively.

The second component states that managers must identify ways workers from different demographic groups are similar. This would enable managers to create bonding between various groups of employees, thus supporting the principle that all workers have similarities and differences. After assuming leadership of the newly formed Intercollegiate Athletic Department of the University of Minnesota, athletic director Joel Maturi undoubtedly had to identify similarities between male and female coaches in order solidify these entities into a coherent work unit.

Thirdly, sport managers should strive to imbue the work structure of their organizations with intellectual diversity to offer various perspectives when performing complex work tasks. Furthermore, if an organization is to achieve intellectual diversity, it must create an environment in which workers can be freethinkers and dreamers, thereby enabling creative approaches to be used when work duties are performed.

The final component of "the act diversimilarity strategy" is for managers to emphasize the common elements between segments of employees. When developing an organizational culture, sport managers must be aware of the common interests, attitudes, and values among employees. While facilitating a bonding among workers, managers must not forget the diversity efforts and aspirations of their entities. It should be stressed that the pursuit of bonding in the workplace should never transcend the overall objective of achieving employment diversity.

IMPLEMENTATION OF A STRATEGY FOR MANAGING DIVERSITY

Implementation of a strategy for managing diversity within sport organizations should be performed through adopting a multiphase approach. The following will delineate these phases.

For a sport organization to imbue diversity optimally into its work structure, there must be support from top management (Hansen, 2003). In other words, top management has to foster an appropriate climate if an organization is to be successful developing and managing diversity efforts. Without top management's leadership, diversity efforts would not likely be accepted by staff members. Research shows that the level of diversity is related to the support of top managers in collegiate and professional sport enterprises (Moore, Parkhouse, and Konrad, 2001). When top management's support has been obtained, the next step in the implementive process is enacting training programs for employees that are congruent with organizational diversity goals. Ofori-Dankwa and Julian (2002) convey that when formulating initiatives an organization should take into account both differences and similarities of the workforce. Accordingly, training programs should develop diversimilarity measures that encourage employees to respect similarities and differences among their peers. By structuring training from this perspective, an organization would strengthen employee cooperation in the workplace.

Additionally, research should be conducted to understand the organizational culture and how it will likely impact the implementation of diversity measures. Cox and Blake (2002) stresses that the culture of an organization must be assessed through research before diversity programs can be properly implemented. Further, Barbian (2003) stated that an organization's level of diversity and environment should be investigated before a directive is initiated to manage diversity efforts. Upon completion of the research phase, the organization should begin to implement the strategic approach. In this stage, management should organize programs to value and properly manage workplace diversity. These efforts, according to Cox and Blake (2002), should be implemented in a systematic manner.

A follow-up should be performed once diversity programs have been implemented (Cox and Blake, 2002). Through this evaluative procedure, managers would receive feedback on how well their diversity efforts are progressing and whether organizational expectations are being met. If the diversity initiatives are not progressing as expected, adjustments and corrective directives will have to be made. This is why a follow-up is an important phase of the implementation process.

SUMMARY

- A lack of diversity is still prevalent within the managerial hierarchy of sport organizations.
- This is perplexing as more women, ethnic minorities, and people with disabilities are participating in sport competition.
- Further adding to this complexity are statistics showing the representation of Caucasian able-bodied males is decreasing in the workforce of the industrial world.
- This has created requirements for programs and strategies designed to effectively manage diversity in contemporary organizations.
- These initiatives cannot be effective without their proper implementation.
- A multiphase approach that consists of top-management support, training, and follow-up assessment is required.

 CRITICAL THINKING EXERCISES

1. You have recently been hired as the new assistant commissioner of the West Lake League, a summer baseball league for collegiate players. During your initial week on the job, you comment to your boss, Trisha Turner, the commissioner, regarding the lack of employment diversity within the league. Commissioner Turner stated that she would be willing to discuss this issue with the board of directors at its annual meeting in St. Paul, Minnesota, during the All-Star Break this July. To assist her with this effort, Commissioner Turner requests that you write a memo offering a rationale as to why the league should manage and value employment diversity at the club and league office levels. Outline the content that you would include within the rationale.

2. Imagine that you have just recently been appointed human resource manager of the city of Schuylkill River recreation department. Schuylkill River is a community of 75,000 in southeastern Pennsylvania. The commissioner of recreation delegates to you the responsibility of developing and implementing a strategic framework for managing employment diversity within the department. Discuss the alternatives that you would consider

and the strategy that you would select for implementation.

 CASE STUDY

Dr. Cathy Stewart started her position of director of athletics at Stockholm State University, an NCAA Division II institution of 17,000 students located in Stockholm, Illinois. Stockholm has a population of 100,000, 40 percent of which is ethnic minorities. Further, 48 percent of the general student population and 50 percent of the athletes have been classified as ethnic minorities. Despite the diversity within the community and student populations, just 2 percent of the athletic department's staff members are ethnic minorities. During the past five years, Stockholm State has had an average attendance of 2,000 per game in its 18,000-seat football stadium. Basketball attendance has been even worse over this five-year span. Although the newly constructed Dover Coliseum has a seating capacity of 15,000, an average 750 fans have been attending men's and women's home games. The previous athletic director, Cody Miller, tried implementing various external marketing initiatives, including price discounts, advertising, and various unique and humorous game-day promotions to increase football and basketball attendance. By all accounts, these initiatives were not successful. Accordingly, Dr. Stewart believes internal approaches must now be implemented. She sat down to begin drafting her plan and wonders whether employment diversification would help her organization in its marketing efforts.

 REVIEW QUESTIONS AND ISSUES

1. What workplace trend do you believe will have the most negative effect on sport organizations? How can properly managing employment diversity within these organizations lessen its impact?

2. Considering the benefits and costs of employment diversification, offer reasoning for instituting a plan for managing employment diversity within a Division I athletic department.

3. What is managing of diversity? What are the dimensions of diversity? Which dimensions are

most important to sport-related organizations? Does the degree of importance of each dimension vary across organization type?

4. Distinguish between external and internal diversity dimensions.

5. Identify prospective strategies a manager can use to manage employment diversity within a sport-related organization.

6. If you were the new director of athletics at an institution of higher learning that recently merged its men's and women's departments into a coherent unit, what strategic framework would you employ for effectively managing employment diversity within the new organization?

7. Discuss an action plan a sport organization can implement to properly manage diversity within its work structure.

 ## SOLUTIONS TO CRITICAL THINKING EXERCISES

1. Your first step would be to emphasize the changing workplace trends. These would include the decline in representation of white males in the workplace and the aging of the U.S. workforce. Further, you would provide a summary of the benefits of diversification. When providing this information, you should note how employment diversity can help organizations better understand market segments. For instance, the influx of additional female managers can assist an organization in augmenting its knowledge of motives of female consumers. Thus, diversity would lead to increased marketing effectiveness within an organization. Additionally, you would mention that employment diversity would enable an organization to make better resource allocations, especially when there is a limited supply of qualified workers. As an assistant commissioner, you would also take the position that by having a diverse workforce, the league can generate a myriad of perspectives on how to eliminate persistent problems within its respective clubs. Your further rationale could be that more employee diversity is often correlated with effective organizational problem solving and more flexibility to response to unforeseen problems. Finally, you would

stress that employment diversity would help to decrease conflicts among clubs within the league as well as among the league's top leadership. In describing this position, you should convey that the proper managing of diversity provides value to a wide range of opinions.

2. As human resource manager for the Department of Recreation for the city of Schuylkill River, you would select from four major employment diversity strategies based on the degree of diversification sought by your organization. The first strategy to consider would be "managing through diversimilarity" if your organization desired minimal diversity. This strategy advocates that while individuals belonging to certain demographic groups exhibit differences, they also have similarities. A second strategic alternative would move employment diversity a step further. This strategy is titled "principles of diversimilarity." Through this strategy, you and your organization would not be placing an emphasis on memberships in demographical groups as a strategic framework but would stress tenets predicated upon "principles of diversimilarity" to communicate that all members of an organization's workforce have similarities and differences. The final strategic alternative available for your implementation is called "act diversimilarity." This strategy would imbue the City of Schuylkill River's Department of Recreation with full diversimilarity. This would require you to formulate a work structure that would enable and encourage divergent perspectives within decision-making and problem-solving tasks. By adopting this strategic alternative, your organization would need to create an organizational culture that values similarities between workers across demographical groups. Through adopting this approach, the Department of Recreation in the city of Schuylkill River would have fewer employee conflicts over the long term.

FOSTERING YOUR WORKPLACE SKILLS

1. Formulate what you would consider to be an effective diversity strategy for one of the following sport organizations: a National Football League club, an athletic department at a

university in the Southeastern Conference, a new race car circuit, or an athletic department at a traditionally all-male institution that just became coeducational.

2. Discuss how you would develop a plan for implementing an employment diversity strategy within one of the following organizations: a women's National Basketball Association club, a golf resort, or an athlete representation firm.

 WEBSITES

www.sportinsociety.org—The Center for Sport in Society Website at Northeastern University contains information relating to the Racial and Gender Report Card and the Disability Report Card.

www.bus.ucf.edu/sport/cgi-bin/site/sitew.cgi?page=/ides/ index.htx—This is the Website of the Institute for Diversity and Ethics at the University of Central Florida. Housed within the DeVos College of Business Administration, the institute offers information on managing employment diversity as well as employment statistics pertaining to various industrial segments of sport.

REFERENCES

Allard, M. J. (2002). Theoretical underpinnings of diversity. In C. Harvey and M. J. Allard (eds.), *Understanding and managing diversity: Readings, cases, and exercises* (pp. 3–32). 2nd ed. Upper Saddle River, NJ: Prentice Hall.

Barbian, J. (2003). Moving toward diversity. *Training,* 40(2), 44–48.

Bohlander, G., and Snell, S. (2004). *Managing human resources.* Mason, OH: South-Western.

Cox, T. H., and Blake, S. (2002). Managing cultural diversity: Implications for organizational competitiveness. In C. Harvey and M. J. Allard (eds.), *Understanding and managing diversity: Readings, cases, and exercises* (pp. 84–88). 2nd ed. Upper Saddle River, NJ: Prentice Hall.

Cushner, K., McClelland, A., and Safford, P. (2003). *Human diversity in education: An integrative approach.* New York: McGraw-Hill.

DeSensi, J. T. (1994). Multiculturalism as an issue in sport management. *Journal of Sport Management,* 8, 63–74.

DeSensi, J. (1995). Understanding multiculturalism and valuing diversity: A theoretical perspective. *Quest,* 47(1), 34–43.

Doherty, A. J., and Chelladurai, P. (1999). Managing cultural diversity in sport organizations: A theoretical perspective. *Journal of Sport Management,* 13(4), 280–97.

Hansen, F. (2003). Diversity's business case: Doesn't add up. *Workforce,* 82(4), 28–32.

Kinicki, A., and Williams, B. K. (2003). *Management: A practical introduction.* New York: McGraw-Hill/Irwin.

Lapchick, R. E. (2003). *2003 Racial and gender report card.* The Institute for Diversity and Ethics in Sport, University of Central Florida.

Millen fined for not interviewing minority candidates. http://espn.go.com/nfl/news/2003/0725/1585560.html.

Moore, M. E. (1987). The relationship of situational attributes and management styles to the success of marketing intercollegiate football programs. Doctoral Dissertation, University of Pittsburgh, 1987. *Dissertation Abstracts International,* 48A, 1500.

Moore, M. E. (2002, May). Examining the role of human resource management practices in increasing the representation of individuals with disabilities in sport management. Paper presented at the annual conference of the North American Society for Sport Management (NASSM). Canmore, Alberta.

Moore, M. E., Parkhouse, B. L., and Konrad, A. M. (2001). Women in sport management: Advancing the representation through HRM structures. *Women in Management Review,* 16(2), 51–61.

Mullin, B. J., Hardy, S., and Sutton, W. A. (2000). *Sport Marketing.* 2nd ed. Champaign, IL: Human Kinetics.

Ofori-Dankwa, J. C., and Julian, S. D. (2002). The diversity approach to diversity management: A primer and strategies for future managers. In C. Harvey and M. J. Allard (eds.), *Understanding and managing diversity: Readings, cases, and exercises* (pp. 84–88). 2nd ed. Upper Saddle River, NJ: Prentice Hall.

Von Bergen, C. W., Barlow, S., and Foster, T. (2002). Unintended negative effects of diversity management. *Public Personnel Management,* 31(2), 239–51.

PART II

Structure and Policy

Discussion Topic

Stanford University's Athletic Department, led by athletic director Ted Leland, consistently finishes in the top ten of the National Collegiate Athletic Association (NCAA) Division I Sears Cup competition, which measures the overall success of intercollegiate athletic departments. Stanford consistently achieves success in men's and women's revenue and non-revenue sports. Student athletes at Stanford have admirable graduation rates.

The Los Angeles Lakers basketball organization, led by team President Jerry West, made the National Basketball Association (NBA) playoffs every year and won eight NBA Championships from 1980 to 2002. The term "dynasty" has been used when referring to the Lakers organization.

Group Discussion Question: Is the success of these two organizations based on luck, or are there other factors that should be examined? How much do the leaders of these organizations have to do with the success rates?

CHAPTER 5

Functions of Management

Matthew J. Robinson and Timothy Newman

In this chapter, you will become familiar with the following terms:

Autocratic leaders
Coercive power
Conceptual skills
Democratic leaders
Demographic factors
Ecological factors
Economic factors
Environment
Environmental factors
Evaluating
Expert power
External environment
Financial resources
First-level manager
General environment

Human resources
Human skills
Internal environment
Laissez-faire leader
Leadership style
Leading
Legal factors
Legitimate power
Management by Objectives
McGregor's Theory X and Y
Mid-level manager
Organizational behaviorist
Organizational powers
Organizational theorist
Organizing

Participative leaders
Physical resources
Planning
Political factors
Power
Referent power
Reward power
Socio-cultural factors
Task environment
Technical skills
Technological factors
Top-level manager
Total Quality Management

Learning Goals
By the end of this chapter, students should be able to:

- Explain the difference between organizational behavior and theory.

- Compare and contrast the theories of viewing management in a scientific manner.

- Appreciate the importance of viewing the management of sport as a science.

- Acknowledge the importance of planning, organizing, leading, and evaluating in terms of the management of a sport organization.

- Recognize the importance of the three levels of management and the skills associated with the levels.

- Evaluate various leadership styles for the purpose of determining which is most appropriate for him or herself or the situation.

- Comprehend the sources of individual and organizational power and understand how they can be used to motivate others to do what they otherwise might not do.
- Appreciate the general, task, and internal environment and the importance of recognizing, understanding, and adapting to the various elements in order to achieve organizational goals.
- Identify those trends that will impact the sport management field in the future.

INTRODUCTION

The sport environment consists of thousands of sport organizations on several levels. These organizations can range from a Little League Baseball organization to the United States Olympic Committee (USOC) and every organization in between. At all levels, some sport organizations are more successful than others. This chapter presents an overview of management and leadership theories and concepts that an aspiring sport manager/leader must comprehend, understand, apply, evaluate, and synthesize in order to achieve the success achieved by the organizations led by Leland and West. The chapter provides a theoretical base for understanding management, and presents an overview of the functions of management, the levels of management, sources of power, the environment, and the challenges sport managers will face in the future.

There are two ways to view a sport organization. The first is an **organizational theorist** view, the second is an **organizational behaviorist** view. Organizational theory focuses on the larger organization, while organizational behavior emphasizes the small group or individual within the organization (Slack, 1997). The theorists explore concepts such as goals, systems, organizational structure, policy, and procedures. Organizational theory is discussed in detail in Chapter 6. On the other hand, organizational behaviorists focus on the individuals and small groups of people within the organization and study how their behavior impacts it. Both must be studied in order to fully understand the forces impacting management in the sport environment. This chapter is steeped in organizational behavior, specifically examining the behavior of those who lead sport organizations.

MANAGEMENT THEORY

Four major management theories influence the sport environment. This section examines the works and ideas of Frederick W. Taylor, who first viewed management as a science; Peter Drucker, who introduced **Management by Objectives** (MBO); Peter Block, who presented the theory of positive political skills; and W. Edwards Deming, who devised the model of Total Quality Management (TQM). Each theory is briefly discussed in order to provide a basic overview of management theory.

The beginnings of management theory rest with Frederick Taylor, long considered the father of scientific management. Taylor (1911) stressed that management should make efforts to secure maximum prosperity for the employer, while each employee enjoyed prosperity as well. Taylor (1911) stressed that every branch of the business should reach and sustain its highest state of excellence while every employee attains his or her maximum efficiency. In Taylor's mind, prosperity cannot exist for the employer unless the employee also prospers. To achieve maximum prosperity, Taylor's system advocates four main points: Management should (1) develop a science for each element of a man's work (thereby replacing the rule-of-thumb method); (2) scientifically select and then train, teach, and develop the workers instead of allowing the individual to choose an area and train him or herself; (3) heartily cooperate with the employees to ensure that all work is completed in accordance with the standards in the first point; and (4) equally divide the responsibility between management and workers so that management focuses on areas better suited for them rather than overextending the workers.

Drucker introduced Management by Objectives (MBO) in 1954. MBO is a management theory designed to encourage collaboration between management and employees to achieve success. According to Drucker (1954), objectives must be realistic, achievable, measurable, and motivating—otherwise they are meaningless. Drucker further postulates that objectives are inherently more realistic, achievable, measurable, and motivating when developed collaboratively with management and employees based upon open discussion and mutual agreement. Drucker also asserts that there is greater likelihood of achieving the stated objectives by using this philosophy over other methods. However, one caveat must be stated. The individual and unit objectives must align with the organization's overall objectives in order to achieve overall success.

Block's theory of management revolves around politics. When talking to most people about their organization, the discussion invariably turns to disdain of organizational politics. Politics are usually viewed in a negative light, but Block attempts to change this perception and transform it into a positive form of management. Block (1991) focuses on changing the bureaucratic mind-set that is a part of the organizational structure and emphasizing managers more effectively defining themselves and their organizational vision to create a positive environment for employees. Block believes that if employees buy into the organization's mission communicated by the leaders and are comfortable with the politics within the organization, then they will take ownership in the company and be more entrepreneurial, thereby helping the organization meet its goals.

Deming's theory of **Total Quality Management** (TQM) reached prominence at the end of World War II. Although rebuked by American businessmen who felt there was no need to change how they managed during a rapidly growing economy, Deming went to Japan in order to help rebuild businesses decimated by the war. TQM gained credibility once Japanese goods became worldwide commodities. TQM is based on 14 points that focus on management instilling a sense of purpose in the employees, developing a positive environment through consensus building and collaboration between management and employees, education and training, and understanding that the process is cyclical.

Although this section briefly discusses the works of Taylor, Drucker, Block, and Deming, entire books are devoted to each individual and their theories. A leader of a sport organization must identify which theory will be most applicable in achieving its organizational goals.

CONCEPT CHECK

The management of sport must be viewed scientifically and studied using a sound theoretical base. If this is done, sport leaders will lead more efficient and effective organizations. Aspiring sport managers need to appreciate these management theories and incorporate them when given the opportunity to lead a sport organization or one of its subunits.

THE FUNCTIONS OF MANAGEMENT

Chelladurai (2001) mentions that the functions of management have evolved from the original list of five (planning, organizing, commanding, coordinating, and controlling) presented by Fayol (1916). While recognizing Fayol's original list, Chelladurai notes that the functions that are most applicable to the sport environment are planning, organizing, leading, and evaluating.

Planning may be the most important management function. Chelladurai (2001) defined planning as "setting goals for the organization and its members and specifying the activities or programs through which to achieve those goals" (p. 95). In planning, the leader must identify the desired outcome, understand what environmental constraints are present, and establish activities that will lead to the desired outcome. Many organizations are doomed to failure because they neglect planning. Successful planning incorporates all levels of management, and leaders must clearly communicate the intended outcomes and specifically how the goals will be achieved. The leader must also recognize that he or she needs to be flexible in order to adjust to real-life situations that arise that were not addressed in the original planning.

Chelladurai (2001) describes **organizing** as the process of breaking down the different jobs that must be completed to achieve the organizational goals, and defining the relationships between the jobs and the people in the organization. This function of management requires a manager to be able to see the big picture of an organization while also assigning the smaller tasks to the right people within the organization who execute the day-to-day operations. Management is expected to align every aspect of the company with the organization's mission and objectives. A manager must be able to effectively place personnel in the right job and communicate each individual's role in fulfilling the organization's goals.

Leading is another important function of management. Chelladurai (2001) recognized that planning and organizing "set the stage for work activities" (p. 97) and states that leading deals with influencing or motivating employees to execute the responsibilities assigned in the organizing step to reach the goals developed in the planning process. A leader may have a good plan and have the employees organized well, but if he or she cannot influence the members of the organization to perform, the organization is doomed to failure. Later in the chapter, leadership styles and sources of power are discussed in terms of their importance in enabling a leader to influence the members of an organization.

Chellauduri (2001) defined **evaluating** as measuring performance and comparing that performance to standards set in the planning process. A manager must evaluate many different aspects of the organization ranging from processes to personnel and take the feedback received to either reinforce the process and/or the behavior of those in the organization, or to take corrective action.

These four functions are the foundation of managing an organization. Both Leland and West clearly planned activities, organized people effectively, led them, and used evaluation to measure their performance. Sport leaders who practice these functions increase their chances of success for the organization they lead.

CONCEPT CHECK

Planning, organizing, leading, and directing are the most applicable leadership functions to the sport management environment. Each are important as independent functions, but they also impact one another. A sport leader must be conscious of the functions and strive to master them in order to succeed.

LEVELS OF MANAGEMENT

Within a sport organization there are three levels of management: upper level, mid level and first level. The responsibilities of each level vary in both context

and importance. At each level, a different managerial skill will be of a greater or lesser importance. The general skills used throughout the levels are technical, human, and conceptual. Bridges and Roquemore (1996) defined **technical skills** as "knowledge of operations, activities, processes, inventory and the mechanics of performing particular job tasks" (p. 37). Katz (1974) saw these technical skills as being specialized to a given organization or area within an organization. Katz (1974) defined **human skills** as "the leader's ability to work effectively as a group member and to build a cooperative effort within the teams he or she leads" (p. 91). Bridges and Roquemore (1996) felt **conceptual skills** are the rarest of all skills. Katz defined these skills as "the ability to see the organization as a whole; it includes recognizing how the various functions of the organization depend on one another and how changes in any one part affect all the others" (p. 93).

First-level manager

First-level managers hold positions that are entry-level management positions. In most cases a recent college graduate would begin his or her career at this level (Figure 5-1). At this level an individual would focus more on technical aspects of the position and may have some responsibility for overseeing others.

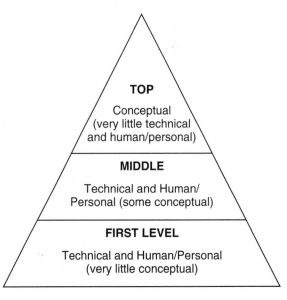

FIGURE 5-1 Levels of management and general skills needed by each in large organizations.

An example of this would be an individual who is hired as a ticket manager for an intercollegiate athletic department. In this position his or her main responsibility would be the sale of tickets for home athletic events. He or she would print the tickets, operate the box office, oversee Website sales, and reconcile the ticket sales after each contest. These would be the technical responsibilities of the position. Assisting the manager with these responsibilities may be an assistant, a graduate assistant, and two interns. The manager would set goals for the department, assign responsibilities to the individuals, develop a work schedule for each person, motivate them to achieve the goals, and evaluate their performance. Although the manager has subordinates, he or she is still very involved in the technical aspects of the position and may be working side-by-side with subordinates to ensure that all of the tickets are distributed to customers on game day. The manager alone may be working on the reconciliation at the end of the contest. First-level managers will not have a great deal of say in how the overall athletic department is run. They will do their part in achieving the overall goals of the organization by making sure they and their subordinates execute the responsibilities in the ticket area.

Mid-level manager

A **mid-level manager** is more involved with the management of individuals while also participating in the conceptual aspects of leading an organization. The technical aspect is not as significant as in a first-level management position. A person in this position is usually promoted from a first-level management position. Consider the previous example. The individual who was the ticket manager has been promoted to associate athletic director for marketing. In this position the individual now oversees the ticket manager as well as the sponsorship sales manager, the group ticket sales manager, and the advertising and promotions manager. In this position the manager oversees these areas and works with the first-level managers in achieving the subunit goals of the area. In most cases the manager will not be in the ticket office on game day selling tickets but rather has determined and communicated to the various first-level managers the number of tickets that need to be sold for each game, the number of season tickets that must be sold for a season, the amount of sponsorship revenue that needs to be generated, and

how the advertising and promotional plans for the upcoming basketball season will be executed.

Along with motivating subordinates, the manager must understand the role of his or her department in the overall achievement of organizational goals. For example, a supervisor may communicate that a certain amount of revenue must be generated to cover the expenses of the athletic department and for the individual athletic teams to be successful. In that sense, the manager must think in a broader organizational context. He or she must be able to appreciate that revenue generation is an integral part in the current state of the organization, but will also be integral if the athletic department is interested in growing.

Top-level management

The **top-level manager** sets the vision for the whole organization. He or she needs to see the big picture and how all of the individual units interact to achieve organizational goals. Again looking at the example, the former ticket manager who rose to associate athletic director for marketing has now become the athletic director. Upon ascending to the position the director has a clear vision for the department. The director wants all the teams to compete for conference championships, the athletic department to have a 90 percent graduation rate, to offer the full allotment of scholarships for all sports and endow all of those athletic scholarships, and generate 75 percent of the budget through revenue generated from ticket sales, sponsorship, and fund-raising. In the past, the athletic department only generated 40 percent of the budget while the institution supported the other 60 percent. The director has set this vision for the department: He or she needs to have mid-level managers who buy into this vision, and as athletic director needs to motivate those individuals to do their parts in achieving the organizational vision. However, the director's main focus is setting the vision while making sure middle managers are doing their part. For example, the athletic director may realize that the department is behind in regard to gender equity and it is important to address this concern. The director communicates this to a middle manager, the associate athletic director for external affairs, who the department needs to identify new revenue streams to fund this initiative. The associate AD for external affairs works with the AD in determining what those new revenue streams could be. The middle manager then communicates the plans for developing the new revenue streams to first-level managers. The first-level managers go about implementing the new initiatives to increase revenues.

CONCEPT CHECK

A successful organization will clearly delineate between the different levels of management. All three play an integral part in an organization achieving its goals. Top-level managers rise from the ranks of middle and first-level managers. All three skills are important. Managers must understand how to use each at the different levels.

LEADERSHIP STYLES

To lead an organization an individual needs to develop a **leadership style.** The selection of the style is contingent upon the person, the people he or she will lead, and the type of activity. Ultimately the individual has to select a style that will be most effective for a given situation.

Mondy, Sharplin, and Premeaux (1991) identify four general leadership styles: autocratic, democratic, participative, laissez-faire. Each will be discussed below within the context of **McGregor's Theory X and Y.** McGregor (1960) contends that there are two types of employees. In Theory Y, McGregor (1960) contends that employees view work as a source of satisfaction, are committed to achieving organizational objectives, are self-motived, are self-directed and accept responsibility, and find work as natural as play. In Theory X, McGregor (1960) contends that employees inherently dislike work and therefore must be coerced into doing it, avoid responsibility, prefer to be directed, have little ambition, and value personal security above all else.

Autocratic leaders tend to tell subordinates what to do and expect it to be done. The subordinates of an autocratic leader are not involved in decision making and have little, if any, autonomy. The autocratic leadership style is commonly practiced by individuals who view their employees as having a Theory X orientation and in situations where tasks are simple and repetitive (Mondy et al., 1991). It is believed that if the leader gives say to the subordinates, they will provide input that will lead to less work or responsibility rather than achieving organizational

goals. Autocratic leadership may be effective, but the success may be short term. Motivated subordinates eventually tire of the lack of autonomy and may seek positions with more autonomy. Also, the organization is not cultivating future leaders, for they are not given the opportunity to make even minor decisions. Legendary college basketball coach Bobby Knight has been viewed as an autocratic leader and has achieved a great deal of success using the leadership style. He has led teams to three national championships and is on target to become the coach with the most victories in college basketball history.

Democratic leaders seek input from subordinates and will do what the majority of subordinates want. It can be argued that a democratic leader is more of a facilitator than a leader. An individual who selects this leadership style views employees as having more of a Theory Y orientation. This type of leader trusts that subordinates will make decisions that will enable the organization to attain its goals. For this to happen the subordinates need to be highly motivated individuals who are looking out for the organization. This style can lead to high subordinate morale, for the subordinates feel a part of the decision-making process and in turn, buy into the vision of the organization. Some leaders have difficulty in adopting this style, for they feel they give up ultimate control as a leader. This can be especially difficult because ultimately the leader will be judged on the success and failure of a particular decision. An example of this would be a college football coach who holds a staff meeting during which the assistant coaches put forth potential game plans, and then the staff votes on which game plan will be implemented for the upcoming game.

Participative leaders tend to involve subordinates in leadership activities and decision making, but ultimately the leader retains final authority. Here again, leaders who take this approach view their subordinates as having a Theory Y orientation. Participative leaders differ from democratic in that they make the final decisions. As with democratic leadership, this style helps develop future leaders and leads to high morale because subordinates feel a part of leading the organization. An added benefit is that the leader is getting input from someone with expertise in an area. For example, an intercollegiate athletic director needs to make a decision related to marketing. His background leading to the athletic director position was in coaching. He consults his associate athletic director for marketing on the situation. He listens and may use all of the input, some of the input, or may disregard the input. Ultimately it is the athletic director's decision.

A **laissez-faire leader** takes a "hands off" approach to leadership in that he or she allows subordinates to make decisions. The mantra of a laissez-faire leader is "Hire good people and get out of their way." The laissez-faire leader will defer to the individual selected for a given position to provide the leadership in that given area. This type of leader offers incredible autonomy to his or her subordinates. So much so that it can be argued that it goes beyond a Theory Y orientation. The most important aspect of this leadership style is recruitment and hiring. This approach is common in professional sport in that a team owner or team president may hand over the sport side of an organization to an individual and remain hands off in that area. For example, when media tycoon Ted Turner first purchased the Atlanta Braves in the 1980s, he involved himself in baseball decisions such as trades and free agent signings even though he had very little experience with baseball. In turn, the Braves were not successful on the field. In the late 1980s Turner hired John Shureholtz, one of the best minds in baseball, to make baseball decisions, and the Braves were transformed into one of the dominant teams of the 1990s. Ultimately, Turner benefited from adopting a laissez-faire leadership style.

CONCEPT CHECK

Adopting an autocratic, democratic, participative or laissez-faire style of leadership is contingent upon the person, the people being led, and the activity. Each has a track record of success, so an individual must give careful consideration to which he or she will adopt before incorporating the style.

POWER

Power can be defined as the ability to get someone to do something they would not have otherwise done. Those who lead sport organizations use power to achieve organizational goals. It is important for a leader to understand the individual and organizational sources of power and determine which powers can be used.

French and Raven (1959) cited five sources of individual power. These are the powers a leader can use to influence others to do things. It is the source of power that motivates the individual to do what he or she is asked to do.

Legitimate Power—Legitimate power is power that is inherent in the position. A person will listen because the instructions come from someone who is in a position to tell them to do something. A coach will do what an athletic director tells him to do because he is the athletic director and a coach is supposed to follow the athletic director's directives.

Reward Power—Reward power is derived from a leader's ability to provide rewards to those who do what is asked of them. These rewards can come in the form of raises, promotions, recommendations, and perks. In this case, a coach will do what an athletic director asks because he knows the athletic director makes decisions on raises, and the coach would like a raise.

Coercive Power—Coercive power is based on the leader being able to punish those who do not do what is asked of them. A coach will listen, for he fears the wrath of not following an order from the athletic director. The punishment can come in the form of a demotion, the removal of certain responsibilities, suspension, or firing.

Referent Power—Referent power is the force of personality. This power comes from subordinates responding to the personal qualities of the leaders. These personality traits vary by leader. Certain people respond to certain qualities. It can be said that the subordinate does because of the leader and his or her personality. The term often associated with referent power is charisma.

Expert Power—A leader who relies on expert power has knowledge or expertise to which a subordinate wants access. It can be an assistant athletic director who works for a respected athletic director and does whatever that athletic director asks because he wants to learn from that individual. This is also very common in coaching. Many young coaches would love the opportunity to work for a Mike Krzyzewski, basketball coach at Duke University, so that they could learn from a man who is one of the great college basketball coaches of all time. Krzyzewski is able to get his assistants to do as he wishes because the coaches don't want to lose access to the knowledge of the game that Krzyzewski possesses.

Along with these individual powers a leader also needs to assess and understand the degree of power for organizational subunits and those who lead those subunits. Slack (1997) identified five sources of **organizational powers.** The first is acquisition of resources. A subunit that has the ability to secure the resources needed by the organization has more power than those that do not. For example, a football program and its head coach who generate millions of dollars in revenue for a college athletic department would wield more power than a coach of a non-revenue-producing sport like tennis. In the professional sport environment, it could be the case that the marketing department that generates the revenue for the sport organization through the sales of tickets and sponsorship would have more power than other departments that do not have revenue production as a goal.

The next source of organizational power is the ability to cope with uncertainty. The sport environment changes often, and uncertainty is associated with change. Hickson, Hinings, Lee, Schneck, and Pennings (1971) suggest that there are three ways to address uncertainty: acquiring information about future trends, absorption (or taking action after the fact), and prevention. Subunits and their leaders who are able to address or prevent uncertainty will have power. For example, in the wake of 9/11, security at athletic events has taken on increased importance. A facility manager can gain a level of power within an organization through acquisition of knowledge on the best practices that need to be taken to ensure the safety of spectators and prevent potential terrorist actions at sporting events. He or she is decreasing the uncertainty of hosting a sporting event through acquiring knowledge to make the facility and event safe. It is hoped that these preventive steps will deter any type of terrorist attack at a sporting event so that taking action after the fact would not be needed.

The more central a subunit is to the primary focus of a sport organization, the more power that subunit will have. In college athletics the central purpose of the athletic department is to offer participation opportunities for student athletes. With this in mind, it can be argued that coaches would have more power within the organization than those who hold less central positions (e.g. sports information director, facilities coordinator, etc.). In essence, there would be no need for a sports information director if there were no sports teams.

A subunit and its leader who is viewed as being irreplaceable would have more power than those that could be replaced. A football coach whose team consistently wins, fills the stadium, and generates significant revenue for the athletic department could be viewed as being irreplaceable. If that coach left, the athletic department may not be able to replace that coach with one who would be as successful. In this case, the team and coach would have more power within the organization than a coach and a sport that does not generate revenue, or a subunit that provides a service that would be viewed as nonessential or that could be switched to another subunit.

Decision making is a part of an organization's existence. Slack (1997) states that those subunits "that influence what decisions are made, when decisions are made, who is involved in the decision process, and what alternatives are presented have power." In a college athletic department the associate athletic director of external affairs who would oversee fundraising and marketing efforts may be consulted about whether it is feasible to embark on a capital campaign to renovate athletic facilities. If the individual feels there are donors willing to donate, when the campaign begins he or she will present possible alternatives in terms of potential donors and corporations who could purchase naming rights. The power is evident in this situation for athletic directors.

CONCEPT CHECK

As with leadership, each of the power sources can be used successfully. Using the various individual powers will lead to an individual being able to get people to do something they may not want to do. Understanding the sources of organizational powers and recognizing the degree of that power within an organization is important for a sport leader as well.

UNDERSTANDING THE ENVIRONMENT

Sport organizations do not operate in vacuums in that there are a number of factors outside the organization that can either contribute to or detract from a leader achieving the vision and goals he or she has established for the organization. This is the **environment.** Along with these external factors there are also internal factors that can either contribute to or detract from achieving the vision and organizational goals. A leader not cognizant of these **environmental factors** is doomed to failure.

The **external environment** consists of the general and tasks environment. Slack (1997) defined the **general environment** as those sectors that may not have a direct impact on the operations of a sport organization but can and sometimes will influence decisions made by the organization. In other words, the aspects of the general environment may impact other aspects of society of which the sport organization is a part. Slack (1997) stated that elements of the general environment are **political, demographic, economic, socio-cultural, legal, ecological,** and **technological.**

In terms of politics, in 1980 the USOC was pressured by the Carter administration, even though it did not have any jurisdiction over the USOC, not to send the U.S. Olympic team to the Moscow Olympic Games. The USOC complied with the government's wishes. From late 2000 to 2003 the United States was in a mild economic recession. The recession had an impact on sponsorship sales for sport organizations and also could have contributed to the drop in attendance at professional sport events.

Demographics weigh heavy on sport organizations' decisions to place a professional franchise whether through expansion or relocation. A city must meet a certain demographic profile in order to support a team. Socio-cultural factors can also play a part in the awarding of franchises and relocation. For example, there are certain sports that are more popular in certain parts of the United States than others. For years it was thought that a hockey franchise could not thrive in cities in warmer climates. Today there are several National Hockey League franchises in Florida, Texas, Arizona, and California.

A leader of a sport organization must be very conscious of the law, for it can impact his or her ability to lead. For example, a college athletic director needs to follow the requirements of Title IX in leading an athletic department. In terms of ecological factors, sport leaders can't fool mother nature. For example, many major athletic events take out insurance on an event in case weather would lead to the cancellation of the event.

Finally, an effective sport leader must keep abreast of technological advances to stay current and to be an effective leader. The use of the Internet, e-mail and operating systems have become standards, but an organization must keep abreast of changes within specific areas like ticket sales, media relations, facility management, and the like in order to meet their organizational goals.

In terms of the **task environment,** Slack (1997) defined this environment as being more directly tied to the sport organization than the general environment. This means that the elements of the task environment directly impact the organization and whether it achieves its organizational goals. Slack (1997) cites competitors, customers/members/fans, suppliers, legislative agencies, and athlete groups as aspects of this environment. In terms of competitors, an aspect of sport that is unique is that although two National Basketball Association (NBA) teams may be competitors on the court, off the court they are not. The off-court competitors are the other sport and entertainment options in a geographic location. For example, in Miami, the Heat may compete with the Philadelphia 76ers in the standings of the Atlantic Division of the Eastern Conference of the NBA, but their marketing staffs will share ideas on promotions that have worked in their respective markets. On the other hand, the Heat marketing staff is competing with the marketing staffs of the Marlins of Major League Baseball (MLB), the Panthers of the National Hockey League (NHL), and Dolphins of the National Football League (NFL) in selling tickets, sponsorship, and luxury seating.

Along with competitors a leader of an organization must be conscious of the customer. This can be best summed up with the cliché "The customer is always right." A sport organization that has a $500,000 sponsor better underpromise and overdeliver in order to keep that customer satisfied and willing to renew when the contract with the sport organization expires. The marketing aspect of an organization is very conscious of maintaining positive customer relationships.

In terms of legislative agencies, every sport organization must follow guidelines and rules established by a governing agency (see the chapter on governance). For example, college athletic departments must adhere to rules established by the NCAA, and national teams must adhere to rules established by international federations and the International Olympic Committee (IOC). The agencies establish rules ranging from eligibility to which substances are banned as performance-enhancing drugs. The actions of a sport organization and its members are limited by the guidelines and rules established by the agency. Not following those rules can lead to suspensions of athletes and punishment of the organization. In college athletics a player can lose eligibility for accepting payment associated with his or her athletic abilities, and a university's athletic department can be placed on probation for a coach breaking recruiting rules. In terms of professional sport, athlete groups/unions play a prominent role. A sport organization must recognize the terms addressed in a collective-bargaining agreement between a league and the collective bargaining unit. There also have been work stoppages in all four major U.S. professional sport leagues associated with negotiating a collective-bargaining agreement between the leagues and the players unions. (See the chapter on collective bargaining).

Finally, suppliers of products or services are essential to an organization achieving its goals. For example, it is common for sport organizations to contract out their concession services to concessionaire businesses. If this company does not do an effective job of preparing and selling the concessions, the sport organization may suffer because the customers may not attend because of poor products or service. There are numerous other suppliers with whom a sport organization will interact. The degree to which they supply the product or service impacts a sport organization.

Along with those factors outside an organization, there are also factors from within that impact the sport organization. These aspects create the **internal environments.** An individual leading a sport organization must be cognizant of any official documents that lay out the guidelines, polices, and procedures for how the organization is to be run. For example, the NCAA has a constitution and bylaws that explain how the organization will operate. The leaders and staff of the NCAA must adhere to this constitution. An athletic department will have a policy and procedure manual that spells out how to do things. These policies can range from explaining how a coach is to secure reimbursement for travel expenses to how an

employee is to call in sick. These documents are an extension of the mission and vision of the organization and provide the organization's framework. These documents ensure that all involved with the organization understand how it runs and ensures that everyone is doing things the same way.

Along with documents that create the framework for the organization, a leader of a sport organization must also be conscious of what resources are at his or her disposal. The three common resources are human, financial and physical.

An athletic director may want to have a successful athletic department, but half of his head coaches are part-time coaches and he does not have a marketing director to sell sponsorship and or tickets. These limited **human resources** will prevent him from achieving his goals of winning teams and generating more revenue.

Limited **financial resources** is often the most common complaint of organizational leaders. This limitation prevents an organization from achieving its goals. In Major League Baseball, several organizations are identified as being in small markets. They are deemed as such because they cannot negotiate a significant local broadcast contract because of the market size. Because of the lack of that financial resource, they do not have the revenue to keep their most talented players when they are eligible for free agency nor to bid on other available free agents. A general manager with a small-market team is contending with this internal environmental factor in trying to do his job. Billy Beane, general manager of the Oakland Athletics, has gained notoriety for his ability to overcome the internal constraint of lack of financial resources to field competitive teams on a regular basis. Other small-market teams have not had the success that large market teams like the New York Yankees, Boston Red Sox, and Atlanta Braves have had.

Finally, a sport leader must be conscious of **physical resources.** In recent years many new arenas and stadiums have been built for professional sport organizations. The rationale behind the building was that the current facility did not afford the opportunity to generate revenue through the sale of personal seat licensees (PSLs) and luxury boxes and that free agents were not interested in playing in outdated facilities. In college athletics, there is an "arms race" between universities seeking to have the most modern facilities to attract the best recruits. Those without modern facilities are at a disadvantage in the recruiting process.

The last internal factor is culture and/or tradition. A leader must be conscious of the organization's culture and the traditions that have been established within the organization. Ignoring the culture and those traditions could be detrimental to the leader. For example, an individual hired as athletic director at the University of Michigan may face resistance if he or she decides to do away with the unique Wolverine-style decal on the football helmet. There are certain aspects of a culture that may be negative and need to be eliminated, but the individual must recognize the aspects of the culture that cannot be changed and those that need to be changed for the good of the organization.

A leader of a sport organization must be conscious of the environment and adapt where needed so that the organization can succeed.

CONCEPT CHECK

Environmental factors impact a manager's ability to lead a sport organization. Recognizing, understanding the significance of, and adapting to the aspects of the general and task environment and internal environmental factors are vital to the manager and the organization being successful.

FUTURE TRENDS

As we progress rapidly through the first decade of the new millennium, sport managers face a variety of challenges. How managers deal with these challenges will shape the sport industry for future generations. These challenges include the increased scrutiny under which sport organizations are placed, financial challenges, and gender equity.

According to Pitts and Stotlar (2002), the sport industry ranks as the sixth largest industry in terms of dollars spent and the largest industry in terms of participants. In 1996, according to Mullin, Hardy, and Sutton (2000), sport programming on the four major networks alone consisted of 2,100 hours, and this did not include cable networks, pay-per-view, radio, or the Internet. Millions of Americans are involved in sport in one way or another; many are participating in sports, self-proclaimed fans of sport, spending money in the sport industry, or working in a sport-related field. With such high

visibility among Americans, it seems as if all decisions and actions of sport organizations are scrutinized. These actions can range from Washington Redskins owner Daniel Snyder rehiring coaching legend Joe Gibbs to the Cleveland Browns' decision to relocate to Baltimore during the 1990s.

Although sport is a billion-dollar industry, Howard and Crompton (2004) state that financial challenges are affecting every segment of the sport industry. For example, in terms of collegiate athletics, the most competitive athletic teams operate on a break-even basis while lower ranked programs lose money on a yearly basis. With more and more choices available to consumers in terms of how discretionary or recreational dollars are spent, organizations must always remain cognizant of the fact that the consumer is the lifeblood of every organization. Whether the economy is robust or faltering, people will spend money on recreation—the issue becomes how and where the consumer chooses to spend that money. For many fans, the decision is based not only on personal interests in the sport or the team, but also on the degree to which the organization appreciates the fan. As a result, managers of sport organizations must not take fans for granted and must consistently make decisions that encourage the consumer to spend money within their organization.

Americans are bombarded with choices every day through a variety of media. The emergence of extreme sports in the last ten years is an example of what can be done with the power of television. With all of the sports programming in electronic media and the increased number of teams/sports, advertisers have their choice of sponsoring the teams or sports that best fit their needs. The market has gone from being sport organization driven to the sponsoring organization being in control. Outside of the four major sports, sponsorships are one of the top reasons an organization is profitable. In fact, for many, sporting events cannot occur without revenue generated through sponsorship. With this in mind, sport managers need to find creative ways to help these organizations meet their marketing objectives.

Gender equity is another issue that sport managers must face head-on in the upcoming years. Although Title IX has been in existence for over thirty years, the last twenty years have recorded the most outstanding growth in women's participation. According to the NCAA (2003), women's participation in NCAA-sponsored sports has risen from 74,239 in 1981–1982 to 155,513 in the 2001–2002 academic year, an increase of over 100 percent. During the same time period, participation at the high school level has jumped from 1,810,671 to 2,806,998, or a 55 percent increase, and, in the 2002–2003 academic year, numbers rose to 2,856,358 (NFHS, 2003). Sport leaders face concerns related to funding the increased interest and the need to meet those interests. Tough decisions need to be made in terms of whether or not women's sports programs will be added at the expense of male funding. Once again, the complicated nature of the sport environment is requiring creativity on the part of its leaders.

Sport managers must also address the constantly changing issues of technology. With rapid technological advances, management often faces the unenviable dilemma of how to remain on the cutting edge without investing money in areas that quickly become outdated. Whether it be video boards in the stadium, Web hosting, online stores, or the next newest thing, decisions must be made to determine the best ways to use technology in order to produce a superior product or service and to enhance the consumer experience. In an overall sense, regardless of the issue, successful management depends on critical examination of the organization's ability to effectively manage its resources to meet and exceed the expectations of the consumer in the ever-changing sport environment.

It is not an accident that certain sport organizations are more successful than others. Successful organizations have leaders who understand and appreciate management theory; plan, organize, lead and evaluate effectively; hire members in the organization with strong technical, human, and conceptual skills; demonstrate appropriate leadership styles; utilize personal and organizational power effectively; understand the environment; and are aware of the future challenges in the sport industry.

SUMMARY

- There are two ways to view a sport organization. The first is an organizational theorist view; the second is an organizational behaviorist view. Both must be studied in order to fully understand the forces impacting management in the sport environment.
- Four major management theories influence the sport environment: Frederick W. Taylor's, who first viewed management as a science; Peter Drucker, who introduced Management by Objectives (MBO); Peter Block, who presented the theory of positive political skills; and W. Edwards Deming, who devised the model of Total Quality Management (TQM).
- The management functions that are most applicable to the sport environment are planning, organizing, leading, and evaluating.
- In planning, the leader must identify the desired outcome, understand what environmental constraints are present, and establish activities that will lead to the desired outcome.
- Organizing requires a manager to be able to see the big picture of an organization while also assigning the smaller tasks to the right people within the organization who execute the day-to-day operations of the company.
- Leading deals with influencing or motivating the employees to execute the responsibilities assigned in the organizing step to reach the goals developed in the planning process.
- A manager must evaluate many different aspects of the organization ranging from processes to personnel and take the feedback received to either reinforce the process and/or the behavior of those in the organization or to take corrective action.
- Within a sport organization there are three levels of management: upper level, mid level and first level. A first-level manager primarily uses technical skills but will use some human skills. A mid-level manager will use human skills and some conceptual skills. An upper-level manager will use conceptual skills and some human skills.
- There are four general leadership styles: autocratic, democratic, participative, laissez-faire. Autocratic leaders tell subordinates what to do; democratic leaders seek a consensus of the subordinates; participative leaders seek input from subordinates in making decisions; and laissez-faire leaders give subordinates a great deal of autonomy.
- Power can be defined as the ability to get someone to do something they would not have otherwise done. It is important for a leader to understand the individual and organizational sources of power and determine which powers can be used.

REVIEW QUESTIONS AND ISSUES

1. Identify a leader of a prominent sport organization (e.g. coach, athletic director, team president, general manager). Determine which type of leadership style he or she practices, and what sources of individual and organization powers he or she uses.

   Answer: The student should listen to the responses of the subject to determine the leadership style. If the responses focus on setting policy and telling subordinates what to do, he or she would be autocratic. If the person seeks consensus from his or her employees he is a democratic leader. If a person seeks advice from subordinates, but ultimately makes the decision, he is participative leader. If he gives free reign to employees, he is laissez faire.

   In terms of individual powers, if a person relies on their position to get subordinates to work, he or she relies on legitimate power. One that uses his or her knowledge and the access to that knowledge as a motivator uses expert power. One that uses incentives such as raises, promotions or fringe benefits relies on reward power. One that use threats of punishment relies on coercive power. Finally, an individual who uses the force of his or her personality to motivate employees toward organizational goals uses referent power.

   In assessing response of the individual interviewed in regards to his or her subunit's organizational power, the student should refer to the sources of organizational power. A subunit and its leader that generate revenue for an organization will have more power than one that does not. A subunit that is more close to the central purpose of the organization will have more power than one farther away. A subunit that is viewed as irreplaceable has more power than one that is replaceable. Those subunits and leaders who are more involved than others will have more power than the others.

2. Compare and contrast the theories of Taylor, Drucker, Block, and Deming.

   Answer: The student should look for similarities between the theorists' works as well as differences. Taylor focused on specializing work and on employee productivity, Drucker focused on employees aspiring to achieve stated objectives, Block emphasized the political nature of management, while Deming focused on empowering employees.

3. Choose a sport organization, evaluate the environment in which it operates and determine how the external and internal environmental factors impact the organization's ability to achieve its goals.

   Answer: The student must consider the general and task elements of the external environment as well as the aspects of the internal environment in responding to the answer. Those general factors are political, demographic, economic, socio-cultural, legal, ecological and technological. The task factors are competitors; customers/members/fans; suppliers, legislative agencies and athletes groups. In terms of internal factors the student needs to recognize internal documents as well as human, financial and physical resources.

FOSTERING YOUR WORKPLACE SKILLS

1. As an aspiring sport manager, what sources of power do you see yourself using? What management style do you see yourself adopting?

   Answer: The student needs to refer to the types of power and determine if they are a match for the person, the situation, and those that will be led. These three areas should be considered in the student's response. For example, what would be the most appropriate source of power for an individual who wants to be an athletic director at an NCAA Division III college and this person is not comfortable punishing people and does not feel he or she has a charismatic personality?

2. Interview a first-level, mid-level and first-level manager in a sport organization. Inquire about their job responsibilities and determine which general management skills they utilize (technical, human, conceptual).

   Answer: The student should determine the level of the individual within his or her organization. Once that is determined the student should focus on which of the three general management skills they utilize the most, and which are secondary. The student should evaluate whether the management skills are consistent with what was presented in the text. The student should assess if the individual is more involved with performing technical tasks, motivating individuals, or developing long range plans for the organization.

REFERENCES

Amis, J., and O'Brien, D. (2001). Organizational theory and the study of sport. In B. Parkhouse (ed.), *The Management of Sport: Its Foundation and Application*. 3rd ed. Boston: McGraw-Hill.

Barr, C. A., and Hums, M. A. (1998). Management principles applied to sport management. In L. P. Masteralexis, C. A. Barr, and M. A. Hums (eds.), *Principles and Practice of Sport Management* (pp. 1–19). Gaithersburg, MD: Aspen.

Block, P. (1987). *The empowered manager: Positive political skills at work*. San Francisco: Jossey Bass.

Bridges, F., and Roquemore, L. (1998). *Management for athletic/sport administration: Theory and practice*. 2nd ed. Decatur, IL: ESM.

Chelladurai, P. (2001). *Managing organizations for sport and physical activity: A systems perspective*. Scottsdale, AZ: Holcomb Hathaway.

Drucker, P. (1954). *The practice of management*. New York: Harper & Rowe.

Fayol, H. (1949). *General and industrial management*. London: Pitman. (First published in French in 1916.)

French, J. R. P., and Raven, B. (1959). The bases of social power. In D. Cartwright (ed.) *Studies in social power* (pp. 150–67). Ann Arbor: University of Michigan Press.

Hickson, D. J., Hinings, C. R., Lee, C. A., Schneck, R. E., and Pennings, J. M. (1971). A "strategic" contingencies theory of interorganizational power. *Administrative Science Quarterly*, 14, 378–97.

Howard, D., and Crompton, J. (2004). *Financing sport*. 2nd ed. Morgantown: Fitness Information Technology.

Inglis, S. (2001). Research and inquiry. In B. Parkhouse (ed.), *The Management of Sport: Its Foundation and Application*. 3rd ed. Boston: McGraw-Hill.

Katz, R. L. (1974). Skills of an effective administrator. *Harvard Business Review*, 52, 90–102.

McGregor, D. (1960). *The human side of enterprise*. New York: McGraw-Hill.

Mondy, R. W., Sharplin, A., and Premeaux, S. R. (1991). Management: Concepts, practices and skills. 5th ed. Needham Heights, MA: Allyn & Bacon.

Mullin, B., Hardy, S., and Sutton, W. (2000). *Sport marketing*. 2nd ed. Champaign, IL: Human Kinetics.

Napier, R., and Gershenfeld, M. (1999). *Groups theory and experience*. 6th ed. Boston: Houghton Mifflin.

National Collegiate Athletic Association (2003, April). 1981–82, 2001–02 NCAA Sports Sponsorship and Participation Rates Report. Indianapolis, IN.

National Federation of State High School Associations (2003, September 2). Participation Summary. Retrieved January 1, 2004, from http://www.nfhs.org/Participation/2003/2002_2003_Participation_Summary.pdf.

Pitts, B., and Stotlar, D. (2002). *Fundamentals of sport marketing*. 2nd ed. Morgantown: Fitness Information Technology.

Slack, T. (1997). *Understanding sport organizations: The application of organization theory*. Champaign, IL: Human Kinetics.

Taylor, F. W. (1911). *The principles of scientific management*. The American Society of Mechanical Engineers. New York: Harper & Brothers.

Walton, M. (1986). *The Deming management method*. New York: Perigee Books.

CHAPTER 6

Organizational Theory and the Study of Sport

John Amis and Danny O'Brien

In this chapter, you will become familiar with the following terms:

Archetypes
Bounded rationality
Centralization
Coalitions
Complexity
Configurations
Decentralization
Decision making
Departmentalization

Differentiation
Formalization
General environment
Globalization
Organizational change
Organizational effectiveness
Organizational structure
Political behavior
Power

Reengineering
Resource-based approach
Span of control
Specialization
Strategy
Sustainable competitive
  advantage
Task environment

Learning Goals
By the end of this chapter, students should be able to:

- Understand why sport organizations are structured and designed in different ways.
- Know why organizational effectiveness is a contested term, and how it may be differentially determined by different stakeholders.
- Be able to describe different factors that impact the development of organizational strategy.
- Appreciate the various ways in which the external environment can affect sport organizations.
- Understand the ways in which power and political behavior are used extensively within organizations.
- Be able to critique the rational approach to decision making.
- Appreciate some of the key issues involved in organizational change.

THE STRUCTURE AND DESIGN OF SPORT ORGANIZATIONS

As we start exploring how and why sport organizations function in particular ways, the ways in which they are structured and designed are of primary consideration. The **organizational structure** is important because it plays an important role in determining how information flows, how decisions are made, and who has power. While there are a number of ways in which we could break down organizational structure, the three most commonly used dimensions in the literature are **complexity, formalization,** and **centralization.** These have been theoretically and empirically established as measures of organizational structure in both the sport and non-sport-related literature (e.g., Amis, Slack, and Hinings, 2004a, 2004b; Kikulis, Slack, and Hinings, 1995a, 1995b; Miller and Dröge, 1986; Pugh, Hickson, Hinings, and Turner, 1968; Slack and Hinings, 1992, 1994).

Complexity

The level of complexity of an organization refers to the degree to which various operations are broken down, or **differentiated.** We can consider differentiation in three separate ways: horizontal, vertical, and spatial. Figure 6-1 provides a diagrammatic representation of complexity and its various elements.

Carried out to improve organization efficiency, *horizontal differentiation* refers to either the creation of separate departments, **departmentalization,** or the employment of specialist workers, **specialization.** In functional or task specialization, the total work to be performed in the organization may be divided into separate, discrete, and narrow tasks. Social specialization involves the employment of specifically trained individuals to perform equally specific organizational activities. Departmentalization refers to the ways the various products and services, functions, and geographic locations that the sport organization operates in lead to the formation of discrete departments. Obviously, the more the sport organization is specialized or departmentalized, the more complex it becomes to operate because communication and coordination of activities tend to become increasingly problematic.

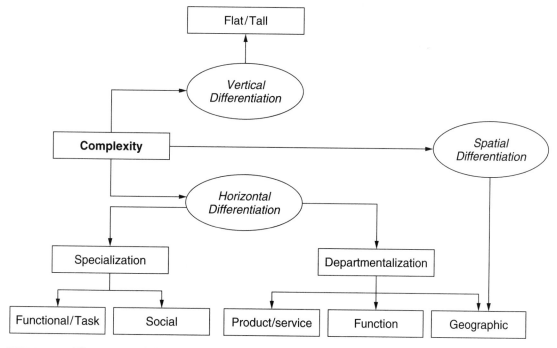

FIGURE 6-1   The structural dimension of complexity and its various elements.

Vertical differentiation refers to the number of hierarchical levels in a sport organization. Organizations with a high level of vertical differentiation are referred to as "tall," while those that do not display many vertical layers of management are referred to as "flat." As horizontal differentiation increases and the organization increases in size, so vertical differentiation also tends to increase (Blau and Schoenherr, 1971). This is primarily because the difficulties associated with direct supervision limits the number of individuals that any one person can directly monitor. This is known as **span of control.** Those organizations that employ highly trained professional workers tend to have flat structures, with one manager able to effectively supervise a large number of workers. The extensive professional training that workers have received acts as an effective control and coordination mechanism. For example, the chairman of the Department of Human Movement Sciences and Education at the University of Memphis supervises thirty full-time and up to thirty part-time staff, a large span of control. By contrast, Archer and Amis (2001) reported that the Running Company, a specialist running-shoe retailer located in eastern England, had an owner/manager and three staff members, resulting in a span-of-control of only three, allowing much more direct supervision as a method of control.

Spatial differentiation refers to the degree of geographical separation of the various divisions of the same organization. An organization based entirely on one site, such as the Running Company referred to above, has a very low degree of spatial differentiation. On the other hand, a large organization such as the National Football League (NFL) can be considered highly spatially differentiated because its franchises are distributed throughout the United States. In addition, the NFL has part ownership of the European-based NFL-Europe. This makes the NFL's operation much more difficult to coordinate and much more complex than the running-shoe retailer.

As technological advances have collapsed the time and space (Harvey, 1990) in which sport organizations operate, **globalization** has become a recurrent and dominant managerial consideration. Satellite television, the Internet, and cheaper travel are among the technological advances that have fundamentally changed the nature of business for many sport organizations. Rather than simply competing in local markets, it has become incumbent upon managers of transnational corporations (TNCs), those that operate across national borders, to consider how their operations should be altered to service multiple international markets simultaneously. Most commentators agree that while it is important to benefit from the efficiencies that a global operation can provide, it is necessary to customize products, services, and/or marketing in some way to resonate with local populations (Bartlett and Ghoshal, 1989; Robins, 1997). Amis (2003) showed how Guinness used sport to achieve this local resonance while still maintaining a common global position that would not be diluted by the wide penetration of satellite television and increased travel opportunities that were resulting in individuals being increasingly exposed to marketing messages from multiple national sources. Silk and Andrews (2001) have also highlighted the ways in which sport is used by managers of TNCs to articulate particular advertising messages in locally resonant ways. Of course, such considerations significantly add to the spatial complexity of the organization.

In sum, the more horizontally, vertically, and spatially differentiated an organization is, the more complex it becomes. Increased complexity results in an organization in which coordination and communication are more difficult and management more demanding.

Formalization

One way to manage complexity is through the use of policies, rules, and regulations, known as formalization. In a highly formalized organization, such as one that uses production-line techniques to manufacture sports equipment, employees will have little discretion over how and when they carry out their tasks. Because of the high levels of interdependence and required uniformity, all roles and responsibilities must be clearly defined. By contrast, workers who are faced with more novel situations and have to rely on individual assessment and decision making will be less constrained. Thus, a player on the Washington Redskins football team will have an extensive playbook to learn, and will find that his on- and off-season professional activities are highly prescribed. By contrast, the head coach of the team will find his job far less formalized, with the freedom to set his own and others' day-to-day activities.

As is clear in the Washington Redskins' case, formalization may vary not just among organizations but also among departments and hierarchical levels within the same organization. For example, Nike's research and development department in Oregon operates under much less formalized conditions than do its subcontracted manufacturing facilities in Southeast Asia or its distribution plants in cities such as Memphis, Tennessee (personal communication, Ken Griffin, Nike's Memphis Warehouse and Distribution Manager, 16 September 2003). This is a direct result of the research and development department employing highly trained professionals who require a far greater degree of flexibility in their day-to-day activities than do the less skilled production or distribution line workers whose activities must be more rigidly coordinated. Likewise, because of their need to operate quickly and in the best interests of the entire organization, senior managers are usually subject to less formalization than are lower level managers.

Formalization allows strict worker control without the necessity for expensive close supervision. It also permits the standardization of outputs, allowing items such as athletic shoes to be designed on one continent, manufactured on another, and sold on a third.

Centralization/decentralization

Centralization refers to the locus of decision making. More specifically, it refers to the hierarchical level of the organization at which decisions are made (Amis and Slack, 1996). In centralized organizations, decisions are made by upper levels of management; in more **decentralized** organizations, similar decisions would be delegated to a lower hierarchical level. As an organization grows, it quickly reaches a point whereby it becomes impossible for a single individual to make all decisions necessary for day-to-day operation. In addition to not possessing sufficient expertise in all areas of the operation (e.g., research, manufacturing, marketing, and finance), if one person were to attempt to take responsibility for all decisions, it would take an intolerably long time to make even minor decisions. Consequently, decisions that are regarded as less crucial are delegated to lower levels, allowing senior management to concentrate on strategic decisions affecting the entire organization. At the University of Memphis Athletic Department, for

example, there are departments that are concerned with fund-raising, media relations, marketing, National Collegiate Athletic Association (NCAA) compliance, and various other internal and external operations. The athletic director (AD), while overseeing all departments, is not involved with minor details, such as ensuring that the local newspaper has the statistics on the men's basketball team, or that the women's soccer team has a balance of home and away fixtures. The AD is more concerned with securing corporate sponsorship agreements, arranging television schedules, changes to Conference-USA regulations, and the potential ramifications of conference realignments. By delegating authority in what is a relatively decentralized department, the AD can maintain control of the athletic department while ensuring that it functions effectively. At a smaller athletic department, many more of the day-to-day functions are handled by the AD, and thus we can consider it to be more centralized.

The design of sport organizations

It is something of a truism to say that all sport organizations are different. Organizations do, however, exhibit various common characteristics. For example, sport organizations may be complex or simple, they may be highly formalized or flexible, they may have centralized or decentralized decision-making mechanisms. When organizations are regarded along such dimensions, it becomes possible to classify various combinations of these characteristics to produce design-types or **configurations.**

In one of the more traditional configurations, a functional design (see Figure 6-2), organizational activities are grouped together according to their particular function or specialization (e.g., Mintzberg, 1979, 2003). For example, in a national governing body of a particular sport, the marketers may be grouped together in a department responsible for marketing the organization's products and/or services. Similarly, the legal, financial, and community development departments may have specialists employed to provide in-depth knowledge and expertise germane to their respective fields. This type of design configuration is most appropriate in stable organizational environments where efficiency through economies of scale is the overriding imperative, and where control and coordination needs to be exercised through the vertical

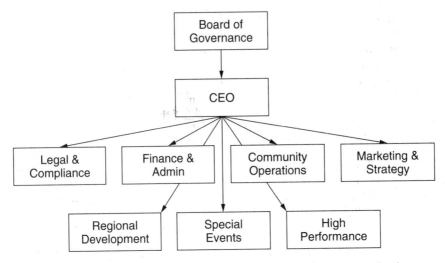

FIGURE 6-2   A functional organization design in a national sport organization.

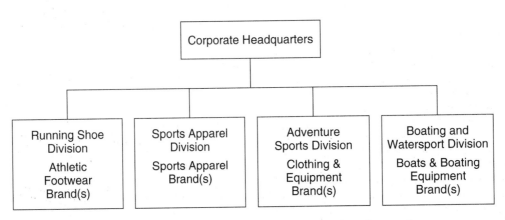

FIGURE 6-3   A divisional organization design in a sporting goods and apparel company.

hierarchy (Draft, 2001). The main problem with the functional structure is that it can make responses to environmental change notoriously slow. The emphasis on the vertical hierarchy may cause decisions to pile up, potentially resulting in lost opportunities. In addition, if horizontal coordination among departments is poor, individuals in departments may lose sight of organizational goals and thus decrease the sport organization's overall effectiveness.

An alternative configuration is a divisional design (e.g., Mintzberg, 1979, 2003). This design features the organization of divisions according to their outputs such as products, services, programs or businesses. For example, when Billabong International, the giant surf, skate, and snow equipment and apparel corporation, purchased both Von Zipper (sunglasses and ski goggles) and Element (skate wear) in 2001, it added new product divisions (Hoovers Online, 2003). The divisional design, shown in Figure 6-3, works best in larger organizations operating in unstable environments with numerous products, services, or businesses. It features a decentralization of decision making that enhances responsiveness to environmental change. However, without adequate coordination across product lines, integration and standardization of outputs can become difficult. In addition, the economies of scale that are a feature of the functional design are lost in the divisional grouping as each separate division has to replicate organizational functions such as research design, marketing, or production.

When a sport organization needs to emphasize product innovation, functional expertise, and environmental responsiveness simultaneously, the matrix design (Mintzberg, 2003) can meet these multifocused requirements. In the matrix design, illustrated in Figure 6-4, strong horizontal and vertical linkages result in both product and functional managers having dual authority. Daft (2001)

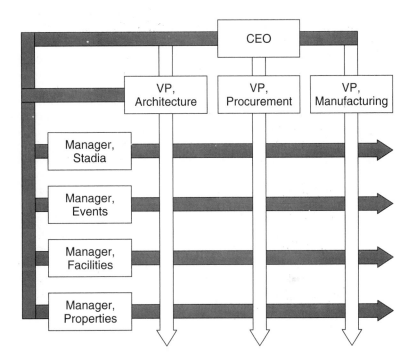

FIGURE 6-4   A matrix organization design in a company specializing in sport facility architecture and construction.

suggested that there are three conditions that make the matrix design appropriate: first, where there is pressure to share scarce resources such as people or equipment across products or programs; second, if there is dual pressure for in-depth technical knowledge (functional design), and innovative new products (divisional design), the dual-authority of the matrix design can help maintain an effective balance; third, when a sport organization's environment is complex and uncertain, the matrix design can help facilitate a large amount of vertical and horizontal coordination and information processing. The main disadvantage of the matrix design is that the dual authority structure can be confusing and frustrating for organizational members. The matrix also requires managers to spend a great deal of time in meetings. Thus, without adequate training in conflict resolution and human relations skills, the information and power-sharing characteristics of the matrix may simply not work.

Whatever the design characteristics of a sport organization, there is still a need for coordination of the processes and activities within it. Mintzberg

(1979, 2003) proposed six alternative ways by which coordination can be achieved. *Direct supervision* is the most basic type and consists of one individual giving instruction to others. An executive director, who manages a small national sport organization's head office, will generally operate in this manner, directly supervising all other individuals within the office, such as technical director, marketing director, secretary, and receptionist.

Standardization of work occurs when the way work is to be carried out is determined by someone other than the person doing the actual work. At Nike's athletic shoe division, the standardization of work is the role of the design specialists and production engineers; the actual work of making the shoe is done by unskilled production workers. The *standardization of outputs* occurs when it is the results of the work that are specified, not the way in which these results are to be achieved. For example, managers at the forty-six David Lloyd Leisure clubs in the United Kingdom must provide experiences that are broadly similar, irrespective of the club in which a consumer chooses to join (Amis and Slack, 2003).

The fourth way coordination can be achieved is through the *standardization of skills.* Sport law firms, for example, employ lawyers whose skills have been standardized through training programs. These skills are further regulated by the professional organizations to which these people must belong. Fifth, coordination can be achieved through *mutual adjustment* whereby processes and procedures are modified through informal communication among parties. The Nike Category Product Teams—made up of individuals from different departments such as research and development, marketing, sales, and production—that are responsible for moving a new athletic shoe from the initial design through production and marketing of the final product are a good example of this method of informal coordination. Finally, coordination can take place through a *standardization of norms.* In this case, shared values and beliefs provide parameters on how to act in particular situations. For example, crowds at a sporting event act in concerted ways to support their team based on common understandings.

Mintzberg's (1979, 2003) work also focuses attention on a number of structural configurations that go beyond the three outlined above. While the reader is directed to Mintzberg's work for more insight into these designs, it is important to note that they are ideal types. It is highly unlikely that organizations that exhibit pure forms of these design types could be found. What these configurations allow, however, is a comparison and contrast of sport organizations along a number of dimensions. As well as providing information regarding what type of sport organization design works best in different situations, these design types also provide a frame of reference for examining other organizational phenomena. For example, do functional, divisional, and matrix forms formulate strategies in different ways? What about the way in which decision making is carried out? Do different configurations better facilitate innovation or cost control? It is this type of insight that increases our theoretical understanding of sport organizations and improves the practical performance of sport managers.

It is also worth pointing out that an alternative to the creation of ideal typologies is to collect data on real-world sport organizations and construct a taxonomy. This was the approach taken by Lisa Kikulis and her colleagues in the creation of Kitchen Table, Boardroom, and Executive Office **archetypes** as

means to classify Canadian National Sport Organizations (NSOs) (Kikulis, Slack, and Hinings, 1992, 1995a). The Kitchen Table archetype defines an organization operated by a group of dedicated volunteers that rely on membership fees and fund-raising for their financing. There are generally low levels of complexity and formalization with decision making centralized with the volunteer board of directors, with the overall objective of the organization the provision of participation opportunities. The Boardroom archetype has an increased emphasis on the performances of elite-level athletes, while still providing domestic participation opportunities. Although decision making is still centralized with the volunteer board of directors, professional staff make day-to-day operational decisions; thus complexity is increased. Sport organizations that adhere to an Executive Office design focus almost exclusively on the preparation of elite-level athletes for international competition. This necessitates the employment of greater numbers of specialist staff, the operation of high-performance centers, and increased international events. As a consequence, levels of complexity and formalization are much increased; these organizations also tend to be more decentralized with more authority devolved to professional staff members.

CONCEPT CHECK

Three primary concepts are used to examine the structure of an organization: complexity, formalization, and centralization. Organizational design refers to the patterning of structural dimensions.

SPORT ORGANIZATION EFFECTIVENESS

The concept of effectiveness is one that is fundamental to any organization. Understanding how and what makes an organization effective is something that is, or should be, central to the role of any manager. As Wolfe, Hoeber, and Babiak (2002) noted, **organizational effectiveness** received much scholarly attention up until the mid-1980s (e.g., Cameron, 1980, 1986; Cameron and Whetten, 1983; Connolly, Conlon, and Deutsch, 1980; Yuchtman and Seashore, 1967) before attention on the subject waned. Within the sport field, effectiveness also enjoyed a period of sustained scholarly interest (e.g., Chelladurai, 1987; Chelladurai and Haggerty, 1991; Frisby, 1986), although again, attention subsided. A major reason for the decline in research on organizational effectiveness, despite its obvious importance, was probably the inherent difficulties in operationalizing and studying the central dynamics. Within any organization, determining what constitutes effectiveness, who should decide what it is, and over what time period it should be assessed are frequently contested. As a result, researchers have come up with various approaches in an attempt to explain this aspect of organizations. Four of these, the goal attainment, systems resource, internal process, and strategic constituents approaches, are briefly discussed here.

Goal attainment approach

One of the most logical, and often apparently straightforward, ways in which to determine effectiveness is by assessing how well an organization achieves particular goals. Thus, we could compare the relative effectiveness of the New York Yankees and the New York Mets by how many World Series they have won or how many tickets they have sold over the last five seasons. Frisby (1986) and Chelladurai (1987) both employed this approach in assessing the relative effectiveness of sport organizations. For this approach to be workable there must be a consensus among members of the organization on the goals that are to be pursued. In addition, there must be a small enough number of goals to be manageable. Unfortunately, this is often not the case. As Wolfe et al. (2002) noted, organization goals tend to be multiple, occasionally contradictory, and often difficult to identify. Thus, seeking to establish agreed upon goals, such as maximizing revenue, keeping ticket prices affordable for the local community, building a championship winning team, constructing a new stadium or arena, or even deciding upon a city to which to relocate can all generate disagreement as to how effectiveness should be defined.

Systems resource approach

A central problem for most organization managers is the ability to secure the necessary raw materials in order to function effectively. These may include capital, fans, raw materials, skilled or unskilled labor, or land. Thus, one potential way in which to determine effectiveness is to assess how well managers are able to secure those resources that are highly valued, but difficult to acquire (Yuchtman and Seashore, 1967). While it does have apparent utility, care must be taken when using this approach with public-sector sport organizations. Because much of the funding distributed to these organizations is often guaranteed, or at least subject to only minor yearly fluctuations, the securing of these types of resources is not an appropriate measure of effectiveness. Second, an organization can be effective even when it does not obtain what are apparently the most desirable resources. For example, the Florida Marlins' $54 million official payroll ranked twenty-first of all Major League Baseball teams. Yet, they were able to win 91 games, and made up a $110 million payroll difference to defeat the New York Yankees in the 2003 World Series (http://www.baseballamerica.com/today/features/03top-10s/marlins.html, accessed 14 December 2003). Thus, despite not apparently having the best players, a key resource, the Marlins were still, by one measure at least, highly effective.

Internal process approach

Rather than assessing how well goals are attained or scarce resources secured, the internal process approach instead provides a focus on the activities that are carried within the organization. Here, indicators of effectiveness can include things such as a supervisor's concern for her or his workers, feelings of group loyalty, good communication, and the personal development of subordinates (Daft, 2001). The difficulties in measuring internal cohesiveness and of ascribing particular outcomes to certain processes can make this approach problematic, but it may have utility in allowing the comparison of organizations with different inputs and/or outputs.

Strategic constituents approach

At the start of this section we noted the rise and then fall in popularity of organizational effectiveness as an area of study. In fact, there has been a resurgence of interest in the effectiveness of sport organizations, notably in the work of Richard Wolfe and his colleagues (e.g., Putler and Wolfe, 1999; Trail and Chelladurai, 2000; Wolfe et al., 2002). A key feature of each of these studies is the recognition of the need to adopt a broader, more inclusive approach to the study of organizational effectiveness that takes into account the fact that organizations consist of a number of different stakeholders with varying objectives and priorities (see Connolly et al., 1980). For example, as Wolfe et al. (2002) suggested, while an intercollegiate coach might perceive winning to be the most important determinant of a university athletic program's effectiveness, the athletic department's compliance officer might perceive the number of NCAA infractions to be the most critical determinant, while a faculty member might cite graduation rates as the key indicator of an effective program. The utility of this approach stems from the ways in which multiple stakeholder groups are acknowledged and their relative demands assessed. A clear difficulty comes with trying to accurately identify the relative importance of the different constituent groups. Despite this, in its more realistic portrayal of the inherently multidimensional and highly contested nature of organizations in general and effectiveness in particular, the strategic constituents approach can be considered to be a useful tool in trying to ascertain the effectiveness of sport organizations.

THE STRATEGIC MANAGEMENT OF SPORT ORGANIZATIONS

In order for a sport organization to function effectively, managers must come up with an appropriate **strategy,** a game plan that addresses issues such as what services to provide, how to best allocate resources, and how to counter moves of competitors. Most commentators agree that strategies are normally long-term, concern a significant proportion of the organization's activities, and help an organization "fit" with the environment in which it operates (e.g., Johnson and Scholes, 1999).

Of course, it is not possible in the space available to cover all of the strategic options available to the manager of a sport organization, or the multitude of models and explanatory devices that have been created to assist managers in their strategic decision making. Consequently, we focus here on two of the more widely used approaches to strategy analysis and formulation. The first features some of the classic work of Harvard Business School industrial economist Michael Porter; the second, a more recent development in the strategic management literature, known as the resource-based view of the firm that is starting to be utilized in the study of sport organizations.

Porter's (1980) "five-force model," outlined in Figure 6-5, is intended to direct strategic attention to those five aspects of an organization's environment that have the potential to most significantly affect the organization, whether that organization is an active competitor within the industry or a new player considering involvement. As such, it can help in strategy formulation. The first key force that we consider is that of *suppliers*. The power of suppliers is predominantly determined by their concentration. If there are a small number of suppliers for a particular resource compared to its demand, and little opportunity for purchasers to shift to a substitute product or another supplier, then power shifts toward the supplier. Television rights fees for both the NFL and English Premier League soccer soared during the 1990s and 2000s as consumer demand for both products grew. With only a single legitimate supplier of the product in each case, and several television companies that wished to carry the games, bargaining power was heavily shifted in favour of the sport organizations.

Conversely, the power of *buyers* depends on the concentration of

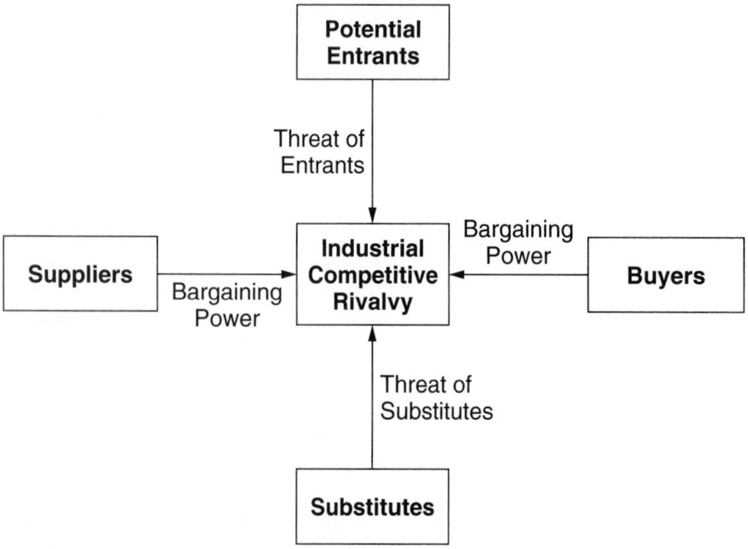

FIGURE 6-5   Porter's (1980) Five-Force Model for strategic analysis.

potential purchasers for a particular product. The broadcasting landscape in the UK has changed radically over recent years. The collapse of ITV Digital, the unwillingness of the quasi-government-controlled British Broadcasting Company (BBC) to invest a large portion of public money on rights for professional soccer, and the limited resources of Channel 5 and other potential purchasers, have shifted bargaining power back toward BSkyB in its negotiations with the Premier League. Indeed, the European Commission is, at the time of writing, investigating the agreement between the Premier League and BSkyB because of the perceived monopolistic power of BSkyB (see Gibson, 2003).

The threat of *new entrants* largely depends upon the financial, technical, and regulatory barriers to entry into a particular industry or market. Such barriers may make it impossible or unprofitable to engage in competition. Thus, in the example above, no competitor to BSkyB has been able to match the financial or technical capital that BSkyB can utilize in its battle to secure Premier League soccer rights, thus erecting barriers to entry that have thus far proven insurmountable. However, the intervention of a key regulator, the European Commission, may effectively remove that barrier to entry and open up the market to other competitors.

The threat of *substitutes* stems from the availability of alternative products that can provide a comparable service or experience. Thus, while the English Premier League has control over its own product, broadcasters can secure their own access to professional soccer by buying the rights for other domestic, European, or international competitions. Other sports and alternate forms of programming, most notably films, can and do serve as substitute products for those media outlets unable to secure Premier League rights. Of course, the relative power of substitutes depends on how closely they can match the experience provided by BSkyB and its coverage of the Premier League.

Finally, competitive rivalry stems from the willingness of competitors to pursue aggressive strategies against their rivals in a particular business. This can take the form of various measures, such as aggressive price reductions or the willingness to pay a premium to secure long-term exclusive agreements with important suppliers of scarce resources. Competitive rivalry will be most intense when there are a number of similarly sized organizations competing for scarce resources. At the moment,

competitive rivalry for BSkyB's Premier League rights is not too intense because of its overwhelming dominance in the market, but that could change depending on the findings of the European Commission investigation.

Depending on the outcome of this analysis, a manager can decide on the strategic approach that would best position his/her organization with respect to the major forces in the environment. It may even convince him/her that the organization would be more successful in a different market or industry.

The resource-based view of the firm

Rather than the external focus that Porter's five-force analysis provides, the resource-based view brings an internal consideration with its emphasis on viewing organizations as bundles of resources that can be utilized to provide a position of **sustainable competitive advantage** (Barney, 1991, 2001; Peteraf, 1993; Wernerfelt, 1984). This approach has begun to receive notice by those doing research on sport organizations, and we briefly examine some of this work. In one of the first applications of the **resource-based approach** to the sport industry, Amis, Pant and Slack (1997) showed how sponsorship agreements need to be considered as strategic investment, and as such, should be tested against certain preconditions. First, the value of different sponsorships should be distributed unevenly, or heterogeneously, across the industry. This is of overriding importance: if all firms have access to equivalent resources, in this case sponsorship agreements, then no advantage can accrue to any individual organization. Second, any sponsorship that is capable of providing a competitive advantage must be imperfectly imitable. That is, there should be no ready substitute available that a rival firm can use to nullify the advantage. Third, the resource, once secured, should be imperfectly mobile: it should not be possible for a competitor to simply acquire the sponsorship once it is seen as valuable. This is achieved in the first instance by the use of contracts, but over time, an image builds up that ties the sponsor and the sport together, thus reducing the effectiveness of the sponsorship elsewhere. Finally, there must be *ex ante* limits to competition—there must be some risk in entering into any sponsorship agreement. If such an investment was risk free, in other words if its true value was clearly apparent in advance to all firms, there would be no opportunity for accruing any sustainable competitive advantage.

Of course, the resource-based approach has much wider application than sport sponsorship. Smart and Wolfe (2000) used this theoretical framework to underpin their investigation of Penn State University's football program, arguing that the trust, relationships, and organizational culture that had been established over time were central to the sustainability of Penn State's success. A recent special issue of *European Sport Management Quarterly* should also be of interest to those interested in the ways in which this theoretical approach can inform our understanding of the strategic management of sport organizations. In this issue, Mauws, Mason, and Foster (2003) use Porter's five-force analysis outlined above and the resource-based view to present a holistic examination of the potential economic worth of professional sport franchises. Smart and Wolfe (2003) then provide an analysis of professional baseball that suggests that while player resources explained approximately 67 percent of the variance in winning percentage, leadership accounted for only 1 percent. Finally, Amis (2003) used the resource-based approach to investigate the use of sport in the development, management, and utilization of the key intangible resources of image and reputation by Guinness. Clearly, from our admittedly biased perspective, the resource-based view has a lot to offer managers of all types of sport organization.

ENVIRONMENTAL INFLUENCES

While resources are clearly important to the development of organizational strategy and structure, managers must also take into account the environment within which their sport organization exists. The **general,** or **distal, environment** comprises all those factors that in some way influence the organization, or sport industry in general, but over which managers can exert little direct control. The nature of these factors will vary depending on the particular facet of the sport industry in which the organization operates, but most commentators agree that they will likely include some or all of the following (e.g., Daft, 2001; Robins and Stuart-Kotze, 1994; Slack, 1997).

The *political landscape* in a particular region or country will directly influence the actions of sport managers. Houlihan's (1997) comparative analyses of sport policy in the UK, Australia, the Republic of Ireland, Canada, and the United States graphically illustrate the effects of different political systems. The 2003 tax credit issued by the Republican government in the United States had the effect of placing $400 of what was frequently viewed as disposable income in the hands of millions of consumers, and thus increased their power to spend money on sporting and leisure activities. The general *economic framework* in which sport organizations operate will also have a pronounced affect on managerial decision making. Bank rates, exchange rates, and the general economic climate are among those economic factors that sport managers have to consider in their decision making. For example, during times of economic recession, most people have less money to spend on leisure activities, such as attending sporting events, which may in turn force professional sport franchises to reduce the price of admission or increase targeted marketing initiatives. *Legal regulations* have become prominent in the sport and leisure industry in recent years. Legislation to protect children from abuse from coaches and officials (Brackenridge and Kirby, 1997) and improve safety of fans at sporting events (see the Taylor Report [1990] for details on this in the United Kingdom) have become much more pronounced in resent years. Similarly, environmental protection laws have affected manufacturers of sporting goods, constructors of new stadia and arenas, and hosts of major events.

Socio-cultural factors, such as the class structure of the social system within which the sport organization operates, trends in consumer taste, and local sporting traditions, can all dramatically affect the success of sport organizations. For example, the Women's United Soccer Association, a professional women's soccer league, folded in 2003 despite the overwhelming popularity of soccer as a children's activity, because the management of the league could not convince enough American consumers to watch the sport either in person or on television. *Technological advancements* must be constantly monitored because they may change the nature of the industry in which the sport organization operates. The use of carbon-fiber composites in the manufacture of tennis rackets and golf club shafts revolutionized both industries, immediately rendering many previous techniques obsolete. Further, Amis (2003) notes how the widespread penetration of satellite television and cheaper travel opportunities radically altered the global marketing strategy of

Guinness. *Ecological issues* regarding physical surroundings can play an important role in a sport organization's success. For example, many ski resorts in Europe were disastrously affected by the brutal avalanches in the devastating winter of 1998–99.

While a broad understanding and appreciation of those factors in the general environment is important, most of a manager's attention will be directed to those parts of the environment that s/he can more directly affect on a day-to-day basis. Depending on the organization, these facets of what is variously known as the **task, proximal** or **specific environment** may comprise customers, employees, suppliers, members, fans, shareholders, or competitors. These components of the task environment have the facility to cause great uncertainty for management, which makes strategic decisions such as the allocation of resources, the hiring of personnel, or the level at which to set ticket prices much more difficult. Thus, managers try to control uncertainty through the use of devices such as long-term contracts with suppliers and key employees, marketing campaigns, and even informal (and sometimes illegal) agreements as to how to act in competitive situations, such as not dropping prices below a particular level.

POWER AND POLITICS

Any attempt at understanding how and why sport organizations function in particular ways would be incomplete without an examination of the utilization of **power** and **political behavior.** Because of the differentiation, discussed above, which characterizes virtually all organizations, we can think of (sport) organizations as being comprised of mutually interdependent subunits located within an identifiable social system (Hickson et al., 1971). Because some of these subunits are more important to the functioning of the organization than others, some groups of individuals will have more power than others. Thus, built into any organization is an embedded structure of advantage and disadvantage (Hardy and Clegg, 1999; Walsh et al., 1981). Power can therefore be defined as a capacity to determine outcomes. As Zaleznick and Kets de Vries (1975, p. 109) suggested, "power transforms individual interests into coordinated activities that accomplish valuable ends."

Typically linked to the control of scarce resources, the accomplishment of tasks central to the effective operation of the organization, and/or the reduction of organization uncertainty, power represents the ability of what are political units to constitute and recreate the structure of the organization according to their own preferences (Amis et al., 2004b; Hickson et al., 1971; Pettigrew, 1973). Hinings and Greenwood (1988) suggested that the ability to mobilize power in large part depends on the degree to which power is concentrated in the hands of a small number of individuals or dispersed more widely across the organization. Amis et al. (2004b) built on Hinings and Greenwood's (1988) conception of power to show that a key determinant in the propensity of a voluntary sport organization to change is likely to be the willingness of the volunteer board of directors to relinquish some power. Those organizations that retained a concentrated power structure and were resistant to change were, in the examples cited by Amis and his colleagues, almost certainly able to prevent any meaningful change taking place.

In addition to power distribution being an inherent function of the social nature of organizations, a highly influential essay by French and Raven (1960) highlighted five bases of power that are more individually located. We finish this section with a brief consideration of French and Raven's work and its application to sport organizations. First, a sport manager can exhibit *legitimate power* because of his or her position in the organization. For example, the owner of the Running Room, cited above, has the power to set working hours for his staff members. He is not required to discuss the decision with his staff, although he may wish to do so, and his decisions will tend to be accepted without question (though not always necessarily agreed with!). Often with legitimate power comes *reward power*, the power to allocate benefits and favors to those who conform to the power holder's demands. The decision of a newly appointed chief executive officer of a ski hill to promote those who have loyally supported his or her rise to the top is a clear example of reward power. *Coercive power* is in some ways the opposite of reward power and can be employed by those who have the power to punish or impose sanctions on others. The threat to fire workers who are consistently late is an example of coercive power. *Referent power* arises from the charismatic appeal that some individuals have. Michael Jordan and David Beckham have been able to sign lucrative contracts to endorse products as much because of their perceived idiosyncratic personal appeal as for their sporting ability. Finally, *expert power* is based on demonstrated knowledge of a particular area. Bill Parcells is able to draw on this base of power because he is widely perceived as an expert football coach. Of course, these bases of power are not mutually exclusive; in fact their cumulative effect renders the individual ever more powerful.

The utilization of organizational and personal bases of power is termed political behavior (Pettigrew, 1973). Building **coalitions** with individual actors and groups, employing supposedly neutral outside experts, and controlling the flow of information are all political activities in which sport managers may engage to mobilize their power and realize desired outcomes. Sack and Johnson (1996) showed how such bases of power were effectively mobilized through intensive political behavior by "a small group of business elites" to bring the Volvo International Tennis Tournament to New Haven, Connecticut, despite opposition from local residents.

CONCEPT CHECK

Strategy and environment are contingency factors that affect the structure of an organization. Sport managers may also mobilize the power that they have and engage in political activity to additionally influence the structure of the organization.

DECISION MAKING IN SPORT ORGANIZATIONS

Our discussion of power and politics will, we hope, have raised awareness as to the importance of understanding the ways in which decisions are made within sport organizations. Beyer (1981) in fact suggested that **decision making** constitutes the most important managerial function. However, despite increased recognition as to the pervasive influence of political activity within organizations, the dominant approach to decision making has been the so-called rational model in which decision making is viewed as a linear series of steps consisting of a recognition of the need for action, diagnosis of the problem, a search for possible solutions, evaluation of various alternatives, choice of a perceived opti-

mal solution, and implementation of a particular choice (Miller et al., 1999). The associated belief that such a process can be based on a quantitative evaluative approach has underpinned numerous research streams. Within the sport literature, for example, Boronico and Newbert (1999) used this logical rational approach to develop a stochastic model that outperformed a college football coach in determining the most effective plays in particular settings.

Despite the inherent appeal of the rational approach, and its apparent effectiveness in settings such as that outlined above, there are a number of procedural and organizational limitations that tend to flaw the rational decision-making process. Herbert Simon (1945) has provided the most compelling critique of the rational decision-making process. Noting the limitations imposed by organizational complexity, individual cognitive capacity, the inherent biases that predispose decision makers to favour certain alternatives over others, and the time and resources available to determine a particular outcome, Simon (1945) argued that individuals are simply incapable of the logical, objective decision making that the rational model calls for. Thus, problems often lack clarity, outcomes cannot be precisely defined, and organization stakeholders often disagree about what constitutes a successful outcome (see the discussion on effectiveness above). Thus, rather than seeking an optimal solution, decision makers operate under conditions of **"bounded rationality"** and thus "satisfice" (Simon, 1945) by selecting the first available option that achieves predetermined minimum standards. Thus, while some simple, recurring—programmed—decisions may lend themselves to a more rational approach, most strategic decisions made in conditions of some uncertainty certainly do not. Instead, decision making can be more accurately described as a struggle in which different groups compete for the allocation and control of scarce resource (Miller et al., 1999). Amis and Burton (1996) provided a critique of the rational process in their analysis of sport policy formulation in Canada, arguing instead for a more pragmatic approach that recognizes the inherently messy ways in which decisions are made. Similarly, Hill and Kikulis (1999) found that decision making in western Canadian university athletic departments was characterized by political behavior, actions that promoted self-interests, and a variety of issues that varied the pace and sequencing of the decision process. Thus, rather than seek to follow the rational model, students are urged to become familiar with the inherently political nature of organizations, and the uses (and abuses) of power by those who seek to promote their own self-interests through the decision-making process.

CHANGE IN SPORT ORGANIZATIONS

In recent years, dealing with **organizational change** has become an increasingly important managerial role. As Amis, Slack, and Hinings (2004a) have noted, increasing commercialization, alterations to geopolitical boundaries, technological advancements, and greater competition in the marketplace have resulted in pronounced changes to many sport organizations, often over very short periods of time. Consequently, the study of transitions in sport organizations has become a popular topic for academic research (e.g., Amis, Slack, and Hinings, 2002, 2004a, 2004b; Hinings, Thibault, Kikulis, and Slack, 1996; Kikulis, 2000; Kikulis, Slack, and Hinings, 1992, 1995a, 1995b; Macintosh and Whitson, 1990; O'Brien and Slack, 1999, 2003, 2004; Slack and Hinings, 1992, 1994; Stevens and Slack, 1998).

Much of the work on organizational change cited above has focused on Canadian National Sport Organizations (NSOs). These organizations were a useful research cite because, between, 1984 and 1996, they underwent fundamental alterations to their structures, systems, and values. As we noted above, of particular importance in this body of work was Kikulis et al.'s (1992, 1995a) identification of the Kitchen Table, Boardroom and Executive Office archetypes. The ways these organizations changed in response to the varying pressures exerted primarily by the Canadian government over this twelve-year period are apparent in the work by Amis and his colleagues. Three things perhaps stand out from this body of work. First, large-scale, or radical, change does not proceed in an orderly linear manner. Because of the inherent discomfort that people feel when faced with change, resistance is likely and thus change tends to take place in a messy way, characterised by changes in the sequence and speed in which different parts of the organization are altered (Amis et al., 2004a). Second, managers responsible for implementing change must take time to build trust with key groups within the sport organization being changed. Individuals at different levels of the organization who hold values that are

opposed to the changes being proposed are often able to block the transformation process relatively easily (Amis et al., 2002). Third, as we noted above, organizations are inherently political and thus managers wishing to implement widescale change must take account of the varying interests held by different groups, understand where and how power is distributed within the organization, and be able to create a vision as to how the organization needs to change that people within the organization will accept (Amis et al., 2004b). Thus, organizational change is an intensely personal experience.

Recently, it has become popular to address the radical changes of the type investigated by the researchers listed above through a process of **reengineering.** As Rigby (2001, p. 156) explains, "Business Process Reengineering involves the radical redesign of core business processes to achieve dramatic improvements in productivity, cycle times, and quality. Companies start with a blank sheet of paper and rethink existing processes, typically placing increased emphasis on customer needs. They reduce organizational layers and unproductive activities in two ways: they redesign functional organizations into cross-functional teams, and they use technology to improve data dissemination and decision making." The emphasis in periods of reengineering is thus on process rather than function, which requires a shift from a vertical organization structure to a more horizontal or matrix structure. Such a shift in the span of control of the organization and the ways in which people relate to one another entails concomitant changes in culture and the overall management philosophy of the sport organization. Typically, such widespread changes in organizational operations produce fear, uncertainty, and the potential for organizational conflict. Therefore, the role of management in periods of reengineering is to communicate to organization members the vision and goals of the change process, and to encourage an acceptance of teamwork, communication, cooperation, and empowerment (Daft, 2001). Inevitably, however, resistance to change may persist.

The importance of understanding the origins, and consequences, of resistance cannot be overstated. Heracleous and Barrett (2001, p. 770), for example, found that proposed changes in the London insurance market were only possible after those introducing a new business system consulted closely with the key workers who were central to the effective functioning of the market. Market leaders realized over time, after sustained communicative actions to this effect by brokers and underwriters, that implementation of the electronic placing system would fail unless its design recognized and embodied more traditional insurance practices. Amis et al. (2004b) similarly demonstrated the importance of incorporating influential sub-units into the change process in order to prevent their resistance from stifling the transformation.

As should be apparent, resistance will take place if different parties feel that the benefits of change do not outweigh the associated costs. This was demonstrated by O'Brien and Slack's (2003, 2004) examination of the changes that took place in English Rugby Union as a result of the sport turning professional in the mid-1990s. Stakeholders were confronted with environmental pressures to reengineer their clubs from amateur, volunteer-led organizations into corporate entities with professional management, players, and coaching staffs. Despite increases in funding from new broadcast deals, gate takings, and sponsorship arrangements, in many cases the volunteers who had traditionally controlled "the clubs" resented the loss of power from the required organizational changes.

In both the work on Canadian NSOs and English rugby, it is apparent that change is best managed through a process of open communication. Affected parties should ideally be involved in the process as much as possible and provided with sufficient information to prevent them from encountering the uncertainty that frequently causes fear, resentment, and disaffection with the transformation process. In this way, the changes that managers of all sport organizations have to implement at times will be more likely to succeed.

CONCEPT CHECK

There are many processes that take place in sport organizations. Because of space we have only looked at two of the most important, the process of decision making and the process of change. Others include the process of human resources management, the process of managing organizational culture, and the process of leadership.

SUMMARY

- A sport organization must be structured to fit with the demands of the contextual situation within which it operates. The three most common dimensions used to describe the structure of a sport organization are complexity, formalization, and centralization. The way in which the dimensions of organizational structure are patterned is referred to as the design of the organization. Sport organizations may exhibit many different organizational design types. Mintzberg's (1979, 2003) configurations have been very influential in the wider management literature; Kikulis et al.'s (1992, 1995a) archetypes, the Kitchen Table, Boardroom, and Executive Office, have enjoyed much prominence in the sport management literature.

- For most sport managers, the main objective is to develop an effective sport organization. Effectiveness can be looked at from a number of different perspectives. The strategic constituents approach, which takes into account the political nature of organizations and the influence this has on effectiveness, is the most useful of these perspectives.

- A sport organization's strategy and environment will influence the type of structure it exhibits. These variables are called *contingencies* because a sport organization's structure is contingent upon them.

- Structure will also likely be heavily influenced by the distribution of power within a sport organization, and the political behaviour in which influential actors engage. Senior individuals and the members of dominant coalitions within a sport organization may attempt to preserve the structure of an organization to preserve power and privileged positions. The emphasis that some organizational theorists place on power and politics stands in contrast to the rationality of the contingency approach.

- Many different processes occur within a sport organization. We looked briefly at two of these, the process of decision making and that of change. Some people see decision making as a rational process, but many organizational theorists challenge this position and suggest that decision makers operate with bounded rationality. That is to say that decision choices are limited by factors such as expertise, cognitive capabilities, organizational politics, and time. Change is also an important process in sport organizations. It is somewhat paradoxical because although sport managers seek stability and predictability, if the organizations they manage are to remain competitive, they must change to meet the demands of their respective markets.

 CRITICAL THINKING EXERCISES

1. The Association of Professional Surfing (ASP) is the world governing body for professional surfing, and runs a twelve-event World Championship Tour (WCT). The WCT is held at the world's premier surf locations in Australia, the United States, Brazil, Europe, South Africa, and Tahiti. The format for each WCT event is a one-on-one competition that, if conditions permit, takes four days to complete. In August 2003, for the first time, the U.S. cable television sport network ESPN included surfing in its annual "X-Games." Using eight of the WCT's top surfers, this was an innovative, made-for-TV surfing event held at Huntington Beach, California. The format pitted two teams of four surfers representing the West and East Coasts of the United States over four quarters of twenty-minute heats. A worldwide audience of 100 million viewed the event (Webster, 2003). However, Boost Mobile, the $1.2 million sponsor of a WCT event to be held one month later at nearby San Clemente, protested to ASP CEO Wayne "Rabbit" Bartholomew, arguing that the ESPN event would dilute the impact of its WCT event sponsorship. ESPN had also recently refused to pay a $35,000 sanctioning fee to the ASP for the appearance of WCT competitors. Rabbit Bartholomew proceeded to tell the eight WCT competitors that if they took part in the ESPN event, they would be banned from the 2003 WCT. In response, the WCT competitors defied the ban and took part anyway. Clearly, Rabbit Bartholomew had a decision to make. Should he now ban eight of the WCT's top drawcards from the rest of the 2003 tour?

What are some of the issues that might have influenced his decision?

2. In the late 1980s, a multinational consumer electronics firm was trying to establish itself across North America. Prior to June 1991, the firm annually committed about 20 percent of its marketing budget to sponsoring a wide range of sporting events, teams, and individuals. Over a short period of time, money was invested in sponsoring Indy Car racing, golf tournaments, tennis competitions, an NFL quarterback, and various Canadian Olympic athletes. However, by 1994, a rigid policy of not pursuing any new sponsorship agreements was in place, despite the fact that the medium was proving very popular with the firm's competitors. Why do you think that the firm had this sudden change in strategy?

 CASE STUDY

In the late 1960s, a young blacksmith and rock climber, Yvon Chouinard, noticed while climbing on the big walls of Yosemite and the spires of Wyoming's Grand Tetons the damage that was being caused by the equipment that climbers were using. Using his skill as a blacksmith, he designed a piece of hardware that provided the same kind of protection on the rock face but could be removed with no damage to the wall. It was a durable, high-quality piece of equipment that could be used repeatedly with no unnecessary harm to the environment.

Yvon's interest in climbing and the environment, and also in function and quality, led him to research the clothing people used while climbing. He was intrigued by the heavy canvas shorts and pants he saw in Europe, and the thick cotton rugby shirts from Scotland. Calling his business The Chouinard Equipment Co., Yvon brought the clothes back from Europe and sold those and his climbing hardware out of the trunk of his car in the parking lots of Yosemite National Park. The quality of Yvon's products was of paramount importance, since his life was on the line just like his customers'. As the business grew, Yvon changed its name to Patagonia and became an early advocate for, and a manufacturer of, innovative products for "clean climbing," a style of climbing that did not deface the rock. By the early

1980s, the company was becoming financially successful, and Yvon immediately began giving money to environmental activities. He also adopted the mission statement: "to make the best quality products with no unnecessary harm." The natural progression from there was to look at the environmental impacts of Patagonia's products and corporate activities.

In the late 1980s, Yvon thought that Patagonia had achieved a breakthrough by using the tagua nut to make buttons, thus replacing a plastic resin-based material with one that was sustainably harvested from the Brazilian rainforest. To his horror, however, he discovered that the tagua nut buttons, after several washings, began to break by the thousands. As all Patagonia products come with a lifetime guarantee, they were forced to sew new buttons onto all shirts returned to them. As Jill Zilligen, Patagonia Director of Environmental Programs, stated, "We learned that, in a business built on quality and environmental ethic, we had to be strategic in our environmental improvements" (Zilligen, 1996, p. 2).

So in 1991, the company turned their attention inwards, and set about research and development to learn more about the impacts their products had on the environment. They commissioned a study on the four main fibers used in their lines: polyester, nylon, cotton, and wool. They studied the full life cycle of the products and concluded that there were parts of the process they could control and change and others that they could not immediately impact. Out of this, they were able to introduce a line of products made from recycled polyester and soda bottles—a warm, quick drying fleecy fabric called PCR (post consumer recycled) Synchilla. They also concluded that, due to the insecticides used in its production, the most environmentally harmful fiber used in their clothing was in fact cotton. This led to Patagonia's spring 1996 commitment to using only organically produced cotton in its products.

To make such a radical change in production processes involved every member of the company. Senior management took employees on trips through the Californian Central Valley cotton fields and sent out educational materials to their associates around the world. They also directly sourced their own raw materials, and then worked at educating their distributors to make sure that the products actually

sold. In addition, they changed their organization from functional work groups to product development teams, and held conferences to bring vendors, contractors, and Patagonia staff together to explore new ways of improving quality and environmental performance. Finally, all staff were given paid time off to field-test new products.

Yvon Chouinard's company today employs around 950 people, makes in excess of 300 lines of clothing and accessories each season, and in 2002, had sales in excess of $220 million (Hoovers Online, 2003). Patagonia has also recently diversified into the surfboard and surfwear industry, applying the same principles of quality and environmental awareness in their production methods. The firm has come a long way since Chouinard's days of selling products from the trunk of his car. They're now sold in specialty stores throughout the world.

 REVIEW QUESTIONS AND ISSUES

1. Describe the changes that Patagonia has experienced over the last thirty years.
2. Following the reengineering process as a result of the tagua nut problem, what changes do you think took place in Patagonia's structure and processes?
3. With wholesale changes to production processes, and a strong emphasis on research and development, what implications would this have for the division of labor, authority structure, and control systems at Patagonia?
4. A possible source of resistance to the changes stemming from Patagonia's environmental initiatives is the increased cost of organic and heavily researched raw materials. What steps has the company taken to reduce this resistance? What other problems might there be for companies taking an environmental stance in their product development?

 SOLUTIONS TO CRITICAL THINKING EXERCISES

1. The mass exposure provided by ESPN and the X-Games' innovative, made-for-television teams format presented the opportunity to advance the sport of surfing by taking it to a

potentially new and broader audience. Success could result in additional sponsors being attracted to the sport, as well as potentially lucrative broadcast contracts. In turn, events such as the X-Games have the potential to undermine the ASP's core product, the World Championship Tour, and may alienate current long-standing tour sponsors. In addition, the current pinnacle for professional surfers is to be crowned World Champion, a prize the X-Games teams format does not provide for. Ultimately, when ESPN relented and paid the $35,000 sanctioning fee to the ASP, Bartholomew conceded and allowed the eight WCT competitors to take part in the X-Games without penalty. Nonetheless, further critical strategic decisions remain ahead for Bartholomew and the ASP, where the precarious path between growth and stability must continue to be navigated.

2. Although initially viewed as a useful marketing technique, the sponsorships that the firm was involved in lacked any strategic coherence. All of the agreements had been initiated by groups looking for support. There was no attempt to secure sponsorship agreements as part of a preconceived marketing strategy. Consequently, the agreements did little to help the firm build a recognizable marketing presence. Further, because of the rapidity with which new agreements were entered into, there is little likelihood that any of the agreements across the firm were leveraged to, for example, help build corporate culture, further relationships with key clients, or help in brand development. Sponsorship investments were simply viewed as securing walking billboards, and thus were the first things to be curtailed when funds became less available. See Amis, Pant, and Slack (1997) for more details on this case.

FOSTERING YOUR WORKPLACE SKILLS

Consider a sport organization in which you have worked, or have intimate knowledge. Address the following questions:

1. Describe the organization in terms of its levels of complexity, formalization and centralization/decentralization.

2. Identify the key stakeholders, and how they would determine the effectiveness of the organization.

3. What examples of political behavior can you identify? How was this linked to the use of power and attempts to protect particular subunit interests?

4. Describe the ways in which some specific decisions were made. Are they exemplary of a rational process, or characterized by the use of power and political behavior?

5. What changes has the organization recently experienced? Describe whether the change was successful, and why you feel this outcome was realized.

 WEBSITE

http://www.patagonia.com—Students interested in how organizations in the sport industry can integrate values such as environmental awareness into their structure and operation can review the evolution and efforts of this manufacturer of climbing, hiking and surfing equipment.

REFERENCES

Amis, J. (2003). "Good things come to those who wait": The strategic management of image and reputation at Guinness. *European Sport Management Quarterly*, 189–214.

Amis, J., and Burton, T. B. (1996). Beyond reason: National sport policy in Canada. *Avanté*, 2(2), 17–36.

Amis, J., Pant, N., and Slack, T. (1997). Achieving a sustainable competitive advantage: A resource-based view of sport sponsorship. *Journal of Sport Management*, 11, 80–96.

Amis, J., and Slack, T. (2003). Analysing sport organizations: Theory and practice. In B. Houlihan (ed.), *Sport and Society* (pp. 201–217). London: Sage.

Amis, J., and Slack, T. (1996). The size-structure relationship in voluntary sport organizations. *Journal of Sport Management*, 10, 76–86.

Amis, J., Slack, T., and Hinings, C. R. (2004a, forthcoming). The pace, sequence and linearity of radical change. *Academy of Management Journal*.

Amis, J., Slack, T., and Hinings, C. R. (2004b, forthcoming). The role of interests, power and capacity in strategic change. *Journal of Sport Management*.

Amis, J., Slack, T., and Hinings, C. R. (2002). Values and organizational change. *Journal of Applied Behavioral Science*, 38, 356–385.

Archer, C., and Amis, J. (2001). Examining sustainable competitive advantage in a specialist sport retail outlet: A resource-based perspective. Paper presented at the Ninth Congress of the European Association for Sport Management in Vitoria, Spain, September 20–22.

Bartlett, C. A., and Ghoshal, S. (1989). *Managing across borders: The transnational solution.* Boston: Harvard Business School Press.

Barney, J. B. (1991). Firm resources and sustained competitive advantage. *Journal of Management, 17,* 88–120.

Barney, J. B. (2001b). Resource-based theories of competitive advantage: A ten-year retrospective on the resource-based view. *Journal of Management, 27,* 643–650.

Beyer, J. M. (1981). Ideologies, values, and decision making in organizations. In P. C. Nystrom and W. H. Starbuck (eds.) *Handbook of Organizational Design* (pp. 166–202). London: Oxford University Press.

Blau, P. M., and Schoenherr, R. A. (1971). *The structure of organizations.* New York: Basic Books.

Boronico, J., and Newbert, S. (1999). Play calling strategy in American football: A game-theoretic stochastic dynamic programming approach. *Journal of Sport Management, 13,* 114–138.

Brackenridge, C., and Kirby, S. (1997). Playing safe. *International Review for the Sociology of Sport, 32,* 407–420.

Cameron, K. S. (1986). Effectiveness as paradox: Consensus and conflict in conceptions of organizational effectiveness. *Management Science, 32,* 539–553.

Cameron, K. S. (1980). Critical questions in assessing organizational effectiveness. *Organizational Dynamics, 9,* 66–80.

Cameron, K. S., and Whetten, D. A. (1983). *Organizational effectiveness: A comparison of multiple models.* New York: Academic Press.

Chelladurai, P. (1987). Multidimensionality and multiple perspectives of organizational effectiveness. *Journal of Sport Management, 1,* 37–47.

Chelladurai, P., and Haggerty, T. (1991). Measures of organizational effectiveness of Canadian national sport organizations. *Canadian Journal of Applied Sport Sciences, 16,* 126–133.

Clegg, S. R., and Hardy, C. (eds.) (1999). *Studying organization: Theory and method.* Thousand Oaks, CA: Sage.

Clegg, S. R., Hardy, C., and Nord, W. R. (eds.) (1999). *Managing organizations: Current issues* (pp. 26–42). Thousand Oaks, CA: Sage.

Connolly, T., Conlon, E. M., and Deutsch, S. J. (1980). Organizational effectiveness: A multiple constituency approach. *Academy of Management Review, 5,* 211–218.

Daft, R. L. (2001). *Organizational theory and design.* 7th ed. Cincinnati, OH: South-Western.

French, J. P. R. Jr., and Raven, B. (1960). The bases of social power. In D. Cartwright and A. Zander (eds.), *Group dynamics* (pp. 607–623). New York: Harper and Row.

Frisby, W. (1986). Measuring the organizational effectiveness of national sport governing bodies. *Canadian Journal of Applied Sport Science, 11,* 94–99.

Gibson, O. (2003, 1 December). Brussels promises football rights decision. *The Guardian* (http://media.guardian.co.uk, accessed 15 December 2003).

Hardy, C., and Clegg, S. R. (1999). Some dare call it power . In S. R. Clegg and C. Hardy (eds.), *Studying organization: Theory and method* (pp. 368–387). Thousand Oaks, CA: Sage.

Harvey, D. (1990). *The condition of postmodernity: An enquiry into the origins of cultural change.* Oxford: Blackwell.

Heracleous, L., and Barrett, M. (2001). Organizational change as discourse: Communicative actions and deep structures in the context of information technology implementation. *Academy of Management Journal, 44,* 755–778.

Hickson, D. J., Hinings, C. R., Lee, C. A., Schneck, R. E., and Pennings, J. M. (1971). A strategic contingencies theory of intraorganizational power. *Administrative Science Quarterly, 16,* 216–229.

Hill, L., and Kikulis, L. (1999). Contemplating restructuring: A case study of strategic decision making in interuniversity athletic conferences. *Journal of Sport Management, 13,* 18–44.

Hinings, C. R., and Greenwood, R. (1988). *The dynamics of strategic change.* Oxford: Basil Blackwell Ltd.

Hinings, C. R., Thibault, L., Slack, T., and Kikulis, L. M. (1996). Values and organizational structure. *Human Relations, 49,* 885–916.

Hoovers Online. http://www.hoovers.com/free/. Retrieved December 11, 2003.

Houlihan, B. (1997). *Sport, policy and politics: A comparative analysis.* London: Routledge.

Johnson, G., and Scholes, K. (1999). *Exploring corporate strategy.* 5th ed. Hemel Hempsted, UK: Prentice Hall Europe.

Kikulis, L. M. (2000). Continuity and change in governance and decision making in National Sport Organizations: Institutional explanations. *Journal of Sport Management, 14,* 293–320.

Kikulis, L. M., Slack, T., and Hinings, C. R. (1995a). Sector-specific patterns of organizational design change. *Journal of Management Studies, 32,* 67–100.

Kikulis, L. M., Slack, T., and Hinings, C. R. (1995b). Does decision making make a difference? An analysis of patterns of change within Canadian national sport organizations. *Journal of Sport Management, 9,* 273–299.

Kikulis, L. M., Slack, T., and Hinings, B. (1992). Institutionally specific design archetypes: A framework for understanding change in national sport organizations. *International Review for the Sociology of Sport, 27,* 343–370.

Macintosh, D., and Whitson, D. (1990). *The game planners: Transforming Canada's sport system.* Montreal and Kingston: McGill-Queen's University Press.

Mauws, M. K., Mason, D. S., and Foster, W. M. (2003). Thinking strategically about professional sports. *European Sport Management Quarterly, 3,* 145–164.

Miller, S. J., Hickson, D. J., and Wilson, D. C. (1999). Decision-making in organizations. In S. R. Clegg, C. Hardy, and W. R. Nord (eds.), *Managing organizations: Current issues* (pp. 26–42). Thousand Oaks, CA: Sage.

Mintzberg, H. (2003). The structuring of organizations. In H. Mintzberg, J. Lampel, J. B. Quinn, and S. Ghoshal (eds.), *The strategy process: Concepts, contexts, cases* (pp. 209–226). Upper Saddle River, NJ: Prentice Hall.

Mintzberg, H. (1979). *The structuring of organizations.* Englewood Cliffs, NJ: Prentice Hall.

Morgan, G. (1997). *Images of organisation.* 2nd ed. London: Sage.

O'Brien, D., and Slack, T. (2004). The emergence of a professional logic in English rugby union: The role of isomorphic and diffusion processes. *Journal of Sport Management, 18* (in press).

O'Brien, D., and Slack, T. (2003). An analysis of change in an organizational field: The professionalization of English rugby union. *Journal of Sport Management, 17,* 417–448.

O'Brien, D., and Slack, T. (1999). Deinstitutionalising the amateur ethic: An empirical examination of change in a rugby union football club. *Sport Management Review, 2,* 24–42.

Peteraf, M. A. (1993). The cornerstones of competitive advantage: A resource-based view. *Strategic Management Journal, 14,* 179–191.

Porter, M. E. (1980). *Competitive strategy: Techniques for analyzing industries and competitors.* New York: Free Press.

Pettigrew, A. M. (1973). *The politics of organizational decision-making.* London: Tavistock.

Pugh, D. S., Hickson, D. J., and Hinings, C. R. (1969). An empirical taxonomy of work organizations. *Administrative Science Quarterly, 14,* 115–126.

Putler, D. S., and Wolfe, R. (1999). Perceptions of intercollegiate athletic programs: Priorities and trade-offs. *Sociology of Sport Journal, 16,* 301–325.

Rigby, D. (2001). Management tools and techniques: A survey. *California Management Review, 43*(2, Winter), 139–156.

Robbins, S. P., and Stuart-Kotze, R. (1994). *Management.* Canadian 4th ed. Scarborough, ON: Prentice Hall Canada.

Robins, K. (1997). What in the world's going on? In P. du Gay (ed.), *Production of Culture/Cultures of Production* (pp. 11–66). London: The Open University.

Sack, A., and Johnson, A. (1996). Politics, economic development and the Volvo International Tennis Tournament. *Journal of Sport Management, 10,* 1–14.

Silk, M., and Andrews, D. L. (2001). Beyond a boundary? Sport, transnational advertising, and the reimagining of national culture. *Journal of Sport & Social Issues, 25,* 180–201.

Simon, H. A., (1945). *Administrative behavior.* New York: Macmillan.

Slack, T. (1997). *Understanding sport organizations: The application of organization theory.* Champaign, IL: Human Kinetics.

Slack, T., and Hinings, B. (1994). Institutional pressures and isomorphic change: An empirical test. *Organizational Studies, 15,* 803–827.

Slack, T., and Hinings, C. R. (1992). Understanding change in national sport organizations: An integration of theoretical perspectives. *Journal of Sport Management, 6,* 114–132.

Smart, D. L., and Wolfe, R. A. (2003). The contribution of leadership and human resources to organizational success: An empirical assessment of performance in Major League Baseball. *European Sport Management Quarterly, 3,* 165–188.

Smart, D. L., and Wolfe, R. A. (2000). Examining sustainable competitive advantage in intercollegiate athletics: A resource-based view. *Journal of Sport Management, 14,* 133–153.

Stevens, J. A., and Slack T. (1998). Integrating social action and structural constraints. *International Review for the Sociology of Sport, 33,* 143–154.

Taylor, Rt. Hon. Lord Justice. (1990). *The Hillsborough Stadium Disaster: Final Report.* London: Her Majesty's Stationery Office.

Trail, G., and Chelladurai, P. (2000). Perceptions of goals and processes on intercollegiate athletics: A case study. *Journal of Sport Management, 2,* 154–178.

Walsh, K., Hinings, B., Greenwood, R., and Ranson, S. (1981). Power and advantage in organizations. *Organization Studies, 2,* 131–152.

Webster, A. (2003, October). Surfapalooza. *Inside Sport, 142,* 118–125.

Wernerfelt, B. (1984). A resource-based view of the firm. *Strategic Management Journal, 5,* 171–180.

Wolfe, R., Hoeber, L., and Babiak, K. (2002). Perceptions of the effectiveness of sport organisations: The case of intercollegiate athletics. *European Sport Management Quarterly, 2,* 135–156.

Yuchtman, E., and Seashore, S. E. (1967). A systems resource approach to organizational effectiveness. *American Sociological Review, 32,* 891–903.

Zaleznick, A., and Kets de Vries, M. F. R. (1975). *Power and the corporate mind.* Boston: Houghton Mifflin.

Zilligen, J. (1996, August 11). The role of business organizations on ecological sustainability: A reality check. Speech given at Academy of Management Conference, Cincinnati, Ohio.

CHAPTER 7

Sport Governance

Matthew J. Robinson

In this chapter, you will become familiar with the following terms:

Administrative articles
Articles
Associationwide committee
Athletic board
Barnstorming
Board of directors
Broadcast Act of 1960
Collective-bargaining
  agreement
Commissioner
Common committee
Common provision
Constitution
Division dominant provision
Dominant provision
Executive committee

Executive director
Faculty athletics representative
Federated committee
Federated provision
Intercollegiate athletic
  conference
Interscholastic athletic
  conferences
Interscholastic competition
Intramural programs
Inter-university governance
  structure
National Collegiate Athletic
  Association
National Federation of State
  High School Associations

NCAA Division I
NCAA Division II
NCAA Division III
NCAA National Office
Operating bylaws
Owner-controlled league
Player-controlled league
Reserve clause
Salary cap
Sanity Code
School board or board of
  education
State athletic associations
Student-athlete advisory
  committee

Learning Goals
By the end of this chapter, students should be able to:

- Appreciate the importance of governance in the sport industry.

- Comprehend the difference in governance structures between interscholastic, intercollegiate, and professional sport in the United States.

- Know the structure of sport governance for interscholastic sport in the United States.

- Appreciate the importance of the NCAA in the governance of intercollegiate athletics in the United States.

- Recognize how professional sport governance is owner controlled, but that players have gained more say in the governance structure through collective bargaining.

- Understand the governance structure for national governing bodies and international sport.
- Evaluate the decisions made by sport governance bodies in relation to the knowledge presented in the chapter.

OVERVIEW

Sport at all levels continues to grow in scope, recognition, and importance in the United States. As this growth continues, governance takes on increased importance at all levels of athletic competition. Interscholastic sport is as popular as ever with both fans and participants. Its governing rules and powers are challenged in court by its member institutions and athletes on a regular basis. Within the last ten years, the National Collegiate Athletic Association restructured its governance structure to grant more autonomy to its membership divisions. In professional sport, although the owners have the most say in governance issues, the players have gained more power in the governance of their respective sports through collective bargaining. The increased recognition and national emphasis given to international competition and the financial benefits associated with hosting the Olympic games has led to increased scrutiny of National Governing Bodies, National Olympic Committees, Olympic Organizing Committees, and the International Olympic Committee. These governance structures are instrumental in creating the rules and policies that promote fairness and safety in competition. They enforce those rules to enhance the credibility of sport at all levels.

This chapter examines the governance of sport in three different environments: interscholastic, intercollegiate, and professional.

INTERSCHOLASTIC ATHLETICS GOVERNANCE

Sport and athletic competition in American high schools has a long and distinguished history. The inclusion of physical activities in the academic curriculum can be traced to the Turner Societies in Germany during the nineteenth century as well as English private schools that promoted individual physical activities as well as cooperation through rugby football (Baker, 1988). In America, where the public school system made obtaining an education possible for all citizens, school sports were touted as a potentially powerful tool for formulating the kinds of attitudes and behaviors associated with

effective citizenship. Athletic participation provided the practical lessons in cooperation and social discipline required for those living in an industrial society (O'Hanlon, 1982).

Interscholastic competition is athletic contests pitting athletes representing different academic institutions against each other on the high school level. The earliest form of interscholastic competition at the turn of the twentieth century was student initiated. A 1907 study of high school athletic programs discovered that students ran one out of six programs. This changed dramatically as faculty and administration expressed concerns over commercialism, poor sportsmanship, and cheating (O'Hanlon, 1982). The faculty took the position that varsity sports could promote sound values if they were properly regulated. This position has been the rationale for the creation of sport leagues and **state athletic associations.** State high school athletic associations strive to regulate and standardize competition between schools through the enforcement of eligibility rules and other rules governing competition between schools. This movement was successful. By 1924 all but three states had established a state athletic association (O'Hanlon, 1982). The faculty had taken the control of athletics away from the students and placed it in the hands of educators.

As society saw the varied benefits of varsity athletic competition, emphasis on interscholastic competition grew, as did the number of sports offered. Early interscholastic competition included football, basketball, and baseball for males, but through the twentieth century, varsity athletic programs included other sports as well as opportunities for females to compete. By the latter part of the twentieth century, high school sport programs became the single most significant dimension in the entire sport enterprise (VanderZwag, 1998). Over 17,000 high schools are members of the **National Federation of State High School Associations,** and approximately 10 million male and female athletes compete in interscholastic competition (www.nfhs.org). This number does not include the millions that participate in high school **intramural programs** or sport instruction offered through physical education classes. Intramural programs are athletic programs housed within academic institutions and promote competition among the students from a particular academic institution.

The governance of interscholastic athletic competition involves four dimensions: the individual school district of which the school is located, the athletic conference in which a school's athletic program competes, the state athletic association that governs sport in a particular state, and The National Federation of State High School Associations that oversees high school athletics in the country (see Figure 7-1).

The NFSHS, located in Indianapolis, Indiana, is the national service and administrative organization for high school athletics. The NFSHS's role is to provide leadership and national coordination for interscholastic athletic competition in the United States by publishing playing rules for sixteen boys

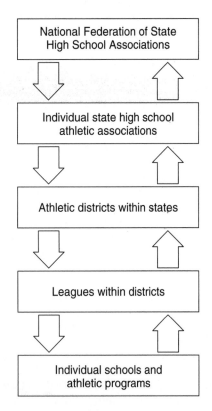

FIGURE 7-1 Governance structure for interscholastic athletics in the United States.

and girls sports, and providing educational services and programs for the members for fifty-one state associations whose members make up the NFSHS. The organization has a board of directors consisting of representatives from eight geographic districts as well as individuals who hold several at-large positions. The board of directors oversees the activities of the organization and establishes its policies and procedures. The NFSHS does not possess any enforcement powers. The rules established by the NFSHS are not mandatory or enforceable.

The state associations govern athletics in each given state. These state associations have the power to establish rules and in most cases possess enforcement powers. The extent of these powers varies from state to state. The majority of the state associations exist for the purpose of providing uniform standards for athletic competition within the state, offering state championships, ensuring that athletic competition is fair, safe and sportsmanlike, and providing an environment that emphasizes the overall development of the participants. To learn more about individual state associations, visit www.nfhs.org. The site includes links to individual state sites.

A state association will have an **executive director** and a staff that runs the day-to-day operations of the state association. The executive director is a hired employee who oversees the direction of the state association and implements policies and procedures. Although the executive director implements the rules, the rules that govern athletic competition come from the members. Most states act as a representative democracy where authority lies within the member institutions.

A state association will also have a **board of directors.** A board of directors is a governance body consisting of representatives from various districts within the state. The board is empowered to make policy decisions on behalf of the members. These individuals represent the interest of their respective districts.

At the district level, there is a district committee with representatives from each of the conferences or leagues that compete within the district. There will also be various district committees that will ensure the operations of the state association.

Membership in **interscholastic athletic conferences** is usually based on geographic location. In some instances, school size and whether a school is private or public are considered when forming conferences. At the conference or league level, there is a board or committee that consists of representatives from each member institution. The representatives who serve in the governance structure are usually the principals or athletic directors from the member institutions. The representatives at the various levels elect them. Therefore, each member institution has a say in creating the legislation it will have to follow.

Even with a comprehensive governance structure in place, the actual administration of high school athletics is primarily conducted on the local level. Most policy and procedural decisions are made at the school district or school level (Covell, 1998). The local schools must be cognizant of and operate within the rules established by the state association. A **school board** or **board of education** is a body made up of individuals living within the boundaries of a school district; it has the authority to establish the policies and procedures and allocate resources for all school district programs, including athletics. The school board approves budgets, determines the feasibility and allocation of resources for the building of athletic facilities, votes on the hiring and firing of athletic department personnel, and votes to establish policies for the school district's athletic programs.

Within the individual school district, the athletic director has the responsibility of implementing those policies established by the school board for the athletic programs within the district. These programs usually include interscholastic athletic teams on the high school or secondary level as well as the middle school level. The most extensive athletic programs exist at the high school level, with the middle school programs serving as feeder programs for the high school programs.

In larger school districts where there may be more than one high school, there will be a districtwide athletic director as well as an athletic director at each individual high school. The district athletic director oversees the athletic program for the entire district while the school athletic director oversees the athletic program at the particular high school. The districtwide athletic director will be supervised either by the superintendent of the school district or an assistant superintendent for extracurricular programs. In the case of the high school athletic director, he or she is supervised by the high school principal.

> ## CONCEPT CHECK
>
> *The governance of interscholastic athletic competition involves cooperative efforts among the individual schools, athletic conferences, state athletic associations, and The National Federation of State High School Associations. Each level has its own governance structure and plays an integral role in the overall governance of interscholastic competition in the United States.*

INTERCOLLEGIATE ATHLETICS

Intercollegiate athletics have played an integral and visible role in sport and society during the twentieth century and will continue into the twenty-first century. The **National Collegiate Athletic Association** (NCAA) is the largest and most influential governing body in intercollegiate athletics. The NCAA had operating revenue of over $357 million for the 2001–2002 year, and $273 million of that revenue came from the broadcast rights to the NCAA Men's Division I Basketball championships as well as several other championships (2000–01 NCAA Financial Report). The NCAA offers championships in 16 male sports, 14 female sports, and 3 coed sports. Over 367,000 male and female student athletes competed in NCAA-sanctioned sports in the year 2001–02. (Participation: 1982–2002 Sponsorship and Participation Report).

The first documented intercollegiate athletic event was a crew race pitting Harvard against Yale in 1852 (Sack and Staurowsky, 1998) in which Harvard was the victor. A rematch occurred in 1855. Athletic competition between institutions of higher learning expanded to include baseball in 1859, and in 1869 Princeton and Rutgers competed in the first intercollegiate football game (Davenport, 1985).

In its earliest stages, students administered intercollegiate athletics, but athletics claimed an integral role in an institution. Important athletic contests generated large gate receipts, and success, especially in football, brought prestige to a college. This arrangement was satisfactory with administrators until the athletic operation on campuses became so large that the students could no longer control them (Nelson, 1982). The hiring of professional athletes to play was a common practice, athletes moved from school to school at will, enticements were offered to gifted athletes, and athletes only attended classes during their respective seasons.

Faculties at institutions expressed concern over the student-run programs and took action to address the problems. In the early 1880s Princeton's faculty took action with the creation of the first athletic committee, which was formed to settle questions related to the athletic program (Smith, 1983). By the end of the nineteenth century, most institutions had created some type of faculty body to oversee athletics, but the rules established by the individual institutions often led to either competitive advantages or disadvantages for individual institutions. These conflicts led to discussions of an **inter-university governance structure** to develop consistent rules that all institutions would follow.

Early attempts at inter-institutional governance were not successful. Resolutions passed by a conference of faculty members from East Coast institutions in 1882 were not accepted by other institutions because of a lack of consensus on the various individual resolutions (Smith, 1983). In 1898 faculty, alumni, and student representatives from seven of the eight current Ivy league institutions met at Brown University to address the reform of intercollegiate athletics (Sack and Staurowsky, 1998). Issues addressed at the Brown Conference included athlete eligibility, pay for play, and the faculty role in the governance structure. This meeting did not present any enforceable rules for the governance of intercollegiate athletics, but it did offer a model for the governance of athletics within the university environment. Institutions, conferences, and national governing bodies adopted many of the recommendations later.

The first athletic conference, the Intercollegiate Conference of Faculty Representatives, was established in 1895. Better known as the Western Conference or Big Ten Conference, it provided a blueprint for the control and administration of athletics by faculty representatives from the member institutions. Many of the rules the Big Ten established in regard to eligibility and payment of players were later adopted by the national regulatory body, the National Collegiate Athletic Association, that came into existence at the turn of the century.

The impetus behind the creation of a national regulatory body was an alarming number of deaths in college football in 1905. President Theodore Roosevelt intervened from the White House and called for changes that would debrutalize the game (Lewis, 1969; Michner, 1976; Savage, 1929). Roosevelt's decree led to the formation of the Intercollegiate Athletic Association of the United States in 1906. The purpose of the organization was stated in its chief objective: "The regulation and supervision of college athletics throughout the United States, in order that athletic activities in the colleges and universities may be maintained on an ethical plane in keeping with the dignity and high purpose of education" (Lewis, 1969, p. 721).

The organization, which started with 39 members, took on its current name in 1910. In the NCAA's early stages, it was primarily a regulatory body, and its annual convention served as a forum for open discussion of problems in intercollegiate athletics. The organization's power grew because of the increased belief in faculty control of athletics. The NCAA promoted the formation of conferences in the model of the Big Ten, and in turn these conferences encouraged its member institutions to follow the NCAA's lead (Davenport, 1985).

The scope of the NCAA's responsibilities grew as more institutions and conferences became members. Stern (1979) noted that from its origins in 1906 to 1948, the NCAA increased its influence by mandating rules of play, offering educational material and meetings, offering administrative recommendations for athletic programs, instituting championship play in 1921, awarding financial incentives, and encouraging U.S. Olympic team participation.

In 1948 the NCAA membership established the **Sanity Code** for the purpose of developing guidelines for recruiting and financial aid and enforcing those guidelines. The Sanity Code was ineffective as abuses in the aforementioned areas increased in number and seriousness. Ultimately it was abandoned by the membership (Tow, 1982). The ineffectiveness of the Sanity Code led to binding legislation in 1952 that delegated enforcement powers to the policy-making body of the NCAA, the NCAA Council. The NCAA also hired its first full-time executive director, Walter Byers. The NCAA had become a regulatory body with the power to investigate abuses of and enforce the NCAA rules, and to punish offenders (Byers, 1995; Stern, 1979; Tow, 1982).

The NCAA is the definitive governance organization in intercollegiate athletics. It is a voluntary organization of over 1,200 institutions, conferences, and organizations devoted to the sound administration of intercollegiate athletics (2002–03 NCAA

Manual, 2002). The member institutions of the NCAA are diverse, with different educational missions, enrollments, and athletic philosophies. To address the diverse interests of its members, in 1974 the NCAA adopted Article 11 of the NCAA constitution. Article 11 established criteria and philosophies for the three NCAA Divisions.

NCAA Division I institutions strive for regional and national excellence, recognize the dual objective of serving both the university and general public, and strive to finance their athletic programs through funds generated by the athletic enterprise. It also should be noted that those institutions that are classified as Division I must offer a minimum number of scholarships (NCAA Manual, 2002–03). **NCAA Division II** institutions offer financial incentives on a more modest scale, place an emphasis on scheduling fellow Division II institutions within a geographic region, and accept the dual objective of their athletic programs serving the general public and campus (NCAA Manual 2002–03). **NCAA Division III** institutions, on the other hand, strive to place the emphasis on the student-athlete instead of the spectator, award no financial aid, and give primary emphasis to in-season competition. Athletic participants are not treated differently than the other members of the student body (NCAA Manual 2002–03).

The NCAA constitution has 33 **articles** that serve as its basis for governance. The NCAA's **constitution** consists of six articles that address the purpose of the association, the principles for conduct of intercollegiate athletics, its structure, its membership, its legislative process, and the role of institutional control. The organization also has thirteen articles that serve as its **operating bylaws.** These bylaws address: Ethical Conduct, Conduct and Employment of Athletics Personnel, Amateurism, Recruiting, Eligibility, Financial Aid, Awards and Benefits for Student-athletes, Playing and Practice Season, Championship and Post-season Football, Enforcement, Division Membership, Committees, and Athletics Certification.

These bylaws are the product of the legislation adopted by the membership. There are four types of legislative provisions or bylaws. A **dominant provision** is a rule that applies to all members of the association. A **division dominant provision** is specific to a division and must receive a two-thirds majority vote by the membership to pass. A **common provision** is one that applies to more than one of the three

divisions of the association. A **federated provision** is a rule that is adopted by one of the divisions and only needs a simple majority vote of the membership present to pass (NCAA Division III Manual, 2002–03).

The division dominant and federated rules are each division's interpretation of articles based on each division's philosophy. A classic example is that Division I is allowed to award financial aid based on athletic ability while Division III is not. Also Division I recruiting rules are much more stringent than the recruiting rules in place for Division III.

Finally the NCAA has four **administrative articles** that set forth the policies for administrative regulations, executive regulations, enforcement policies and procedures, and athletics certification policies and procedures. All of this information is made available to the membership in the form of the NCAA Manual. This publication is found in every NCAA member institution's athletics department and can be viewed at www.NCAA.org. Athletic directors, compliance coordinators, and coaches use the manual to ensure they are operating within the framework of the NCAA bylaws and to understand the operations of the NCAA as a governing body.

In the past, the NCAA was structured so that each institution had one vote, so that a Division III institution had the same power as a Division I institution when voting on legislation that impacted the NCAA. In 1996, the NCAA was restructured to give more autonomy to the three divisions. In the restructured NCAA, there is an **executive committee** that has representation from all three divisions, but with the majority of the board coming from Division I institutions (see Figure 7-2). Division I has a board of directors consisting of institutional chief executive officers (CEOs), while Division II and III have Presidents Councils consisting of institutional CEOs. Below this level, each division has a Management Council consisting of athletics administrators and faculty athletics representatives, and in the case of Division III, institutional CEOs also.

Divisions II and III still meet at an annual convention where members vote on legislation that will impact the respective divisions. Division I's structure is based on conference representation. Legislation is approved by a fifteen-member Board of Directors who represent the various Division I conferences rather than by a vote of the 305 Division I members at an annual convention. At all three levels there is a committee structure that assists in the governance of

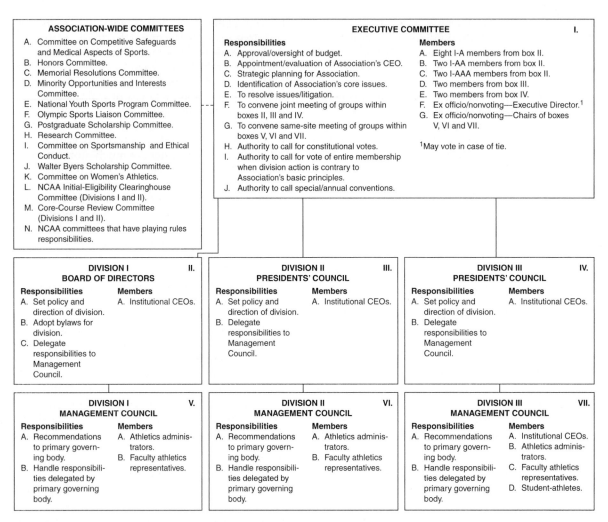

FIGURE 7-2   Association governance structure.
© National College Athletics Association.

each division. The committees consist of presidents, athletics directors, faculty athletic representatives, coaches, and student athletes.

Within the organization there are **association-wide committees** that deal with issues impacting all of the members of the association and consist of members from all three divisions; **common committees** that deal with issues impacting more than one of the divisions and have members from those divisions impacted by the committee; and **federated committees** that deal with issues directly related to a specific division and have members

from the respective division. There are thirty standing general committees that are appointed by the NCAA Council or the executive committee to perform those duties necessary to the operation of the NCAA. There are also rules committees without championship administration responsibilities, sports committees with playing rules and championship administration responsibilities, and sports committees with only championship administration responsibilities. These committees are responsible for formulating the rules of play for the respective sports and hosting the championships in each sport.

Finally, there are special committees established by the association to address specific issues or concerns. More information on NCAA committees can be found at www.NCAA.org and by viewing the NCAA Manual.

The **NCAA National Office** is not involved in the legislative process but rather works for the membership. The office does so by providing services, hosting championships, conducting educational workshops, educating the membership on rules, and investigating rules violations. The NCAA national office receives the most recognition in the area of investigating violations. In this capacity the members of the NCAA staff investigate institutions and their staffs for violating rules that the members created. The National Office is headed by an executive director and is divided into the following departments: Championships, Education Services, Enforcement, and Eligibility Appeals, Finance and Business Services, Membership Services, and Public Affairs.

Along with belonging to the NCAA, most institutions belong to an athletic conference. In most cases, an **intercollegiate athletic conference** consists of institutions with the same institutional and academic missions and level of commitment to athletics, and geographic region. In recent years at the major-college level, institutions have either joined conferences or switched conferences, and geography has not been as major a factor as in the past. Air travel has made it possible for institutions to belong to conferences outside of a geographic region. This is best demonstrated by Penn State University being a member of the Midwest-dominated Big Ten Conference, and Notre Dame, a midwestern university, being a member of the Big East Conference. Barr (1998) cited four reasons for a school to change conference affiliation or to join one: (1) exposure from television contracts with existing conferences; (2) potential revenues from television and corporate sponsorship through conference revenue-sharing; (3) difficulty for independent schools in scheduling games and generating revenue; and (4) the ability of a conference to hold a conference championship game in football, which has the potential of generating millions of dollars for the members of a conference with twelve members.

Institutions belonging to the conference must adhere to the rules established by the conference. At times the rules that the conference establishes may be more stringent than those established by the

NCAA, but they cannot be less stringent. The conferences have an executive director and a conference office, which handles the day-to-day operations of the conference and is responsible for organizing the conference championships for its members as well as enforcing conference rules and offering interpretations of both conference and, when necessary, NCAA rules. The members of the conference establish the rules for the conference members. The governance structure of each conference differs in that in some conferences, the control rests in the hands of the presidents of the institutions, while in others it may rest in the hands of the athletic directors.

The NCAA states that the control and responsibility for the conduct of intercollegiate athletics should be placed in the hands of the individual institutions. The chief executive officer of each institution is responsible for how an institution conducts its intercollegiate athletic program (NCAA Division III Manual, 1998). Each institution must appoint a **faculty athletics representative.** The duties of the faculty athletics representative are defined by each institution, but it must be a person who holds faculty rank at the institution. An institution must also establish a **student-athlete advisory committee** consisting of current student-athletes so that they have a voice in how athletics are conducted on a particular campus. Some institutions choose to establish an **athletic board** consisting of athletic administrators, institutional administrators, alumni, faculty, and student-athletes to establish policies for the athletic programs.

In 1993 the NCAA membership approved a certification process that entails a self-study and external review to be conducted once every ten years. The self-study is conducted by members of the institution's administration, athletic department, faculty, students, and board members. Once the self-study is complete, the external review team receives the report and then visits the campus of the institution. The areas addressed in the certification review are governance and commitment to rule compliance; academic integrity; fiscal integrity; and equity, welfare, and sportsmanship. After the visit, this external review team prepares a report based on the self-study and visit. The content of the report includes an evaluation of the cooperation of the institution to the process; an evaluation of the institution's adherence to the process; a summary of perceived strengths and weaknesses, and a recommendation on the certification status (NCAA

Manual 2002–03). The three possible certification classifications are certified, certified with conditions, or not certified. The process encourages institutions to operate in the appropriate manner as determined by the NCAA and its governance structure.

CONCEPT CHECK

The NCAA is a membership-driven organization. The members of the association created the legislation that is enforced by the NCAA executive director and national office. The NCAA addresses the diversity of its membership by offering three divisions from which an institution may choose. Each division has established its own governance structure through the restructuring of the NCAA in 1996, but still all three divisions are involved in the overall governance of the NCAA.

GOVERNANCE OF PROFESSIONAL SPORT

Professional sport has been a part of the sport landscape in America since the early part of the nineteenth century. Professional sport participants are financially compensated for their talents and services. There are four major sport leagues in the United States: football, basketball, baseball, and hockey. There are professional tours in men's and women's golf, tennis, ice skating, beach volleyball, bowling, and skiing. Several auto-racing circuits exist, and professional boxing and horseracing have been fixtures on the American sport scene since the 1700s. Professional sport leagues also exist in indoor and outdoor soccer, women's basketball, lacrosse, and roller hockey. Minor leagues in baseball, basketball, hockey, and soccer exist for the purpose of player development for the major sport leagues.

The four major team sport leagues are the most recognizable and profitable entities in professional sport. The National Football League has thirty-two teams with some teams' estimated value being greater than $700 million. The league has an average annual broadcast rights fee deal valued at $1.1 billion (By the Numbers, 2003). The National Basketball Association has 30 teams and the league drew over 20 million fans during the 2001–02 NBA season. ("By the Numbers," 2003). The National Hockey League has twenty-six teams, and the average team will generate over $25 million through attendance (Ozanian,

1998). Major League Baseball, the oldest professional team sport league, has thirty teams divided into two leagues. In 2002 the New York Yankees drew over 3 million fans and paid over $171 million in player salaries ("By the Numbers," 2003).

The first all professional sports team in America was the Cincinnati Red Stockings baseball team formed in 1869. The team's manager, Harry Wright, raided other clubs for their best players and paid them to play. The ten-man team had a payroll of $9,300 (Baker, 1988). In 1871 the National Association of Professional Baseball Players was formed. It was a ten-team **player-controlled league** where the players organized the teams, determined player salaries, and developed the schedule. The league existed for five turbulent years during which twenty-five different clubs came and went, gambling ran rampant, players changed teams on a regular basis, and teams would not appear for scheduled games in order to save travel money (Baker, 1988; Helyar, 1994).

In 1876 William Hulbert initiated the creation of the eight-team National League to replace the troubled player-controlled league. The National League set a precedent for all professional sport leagues that would follow in other sports because it was an **owner-controlled league** and the players would be employees. Many of the governing practices set forth by the National League are still in effect in all professional sport leagues today. The constitution of the National League provided for a central office and a five-man board of directors selected by the owners with one serving as the president of the league. There was no player representation within the governance structure. The league constructed a seventy-game schedule, and teams could be expelled for not finishing a season. It also hired umpires who worked for the league and not for the teams in individual cities, forbade gambling within ballparks, and did not allow Sunday play to improve the credibility of the league (Baker, 1988).

Two key elements of the governance of early professional baseball were the **salary cap** and the **reserve clause.** The owners viewed these as means of ensuring the financial viability of the league and its member teams. The salary cap instituted in 1889 placed a limit of $2,500 on a player's salary (Helyar, 1994). The reserve clause restricted the movement of players. The rule stated that once a player signed a contract with a club, he was the club's property unless he was traded to another team, or released. These two measures ensured that the owners would keep salary costs down, therefore leaving more profit for the owner. The National League thrived under the owner-controlled format, but the players did not have much say in the governance of the game and had little control over their careers (Miller, 1991).

The National League was the lone professional team sport league at the turn of the twentieth century. Eventually a minor league circuit named the Western League moved east, renamed itself the American League, and did battle with the National League for players and spectators (Helyar, 1994). The American League did not have a salary cap and did not recognize the National League's reserve clause, and began to offer the National League's best players higher salaries. The two leagues sued for peace in 1903 and combined to create the major leagues, where each league would recognize the reserve clause. A National Commission was established, with the president of each league and membership agreed upon by both. The body oversaw professional baseball for seventeen years.

In the wake of the Black Sox scandal of 1919, the National Commission was viewed as ineffective in governing baseball. It was decided that only an outsider of impeccable integrity could do the job of restoring baseball's good name after the gambling scandal at the 1919 World Series (Heylar, 1994). Judge Kenesaw Mountain Landis accepted the position as the **commissioner** of baseball under the condition that he had absolute authority to act in the best interest of the game. Landis held the position of commissioner of baseball for twenty-four years. There have been eight commissioners who have since followed Landis.

Professional football, hockey, and basketball followed baseball's path as a professional sport league. Professional football's origins were in small industrial towns in the Midwest. The National Football League was formed in 1920 when men from town teams in Ohio met in Canton, Ohio, to discuss cooperation in scheduling and player salaries and to agree on not stealing one another's players (Fox, 1994). Eventually there were fourteen charter teams from Ohio, Indiana, Illinois, and western New York. The league's first president was football legend Jim Thorpe, and he was followed by Joe Carr a year later. Carr would serve as president of the NFL until his death in 1939.

Carr took a league of small-town teams and led its transformation into a thriving big-city league. Under Carr's leadership teams were prohibited from paying college players to turn professional by not allowing a player to join the league until his class graduated, and Carr was responsible for introducing the player draft to professional sport (King, 1996). He also introduced a standard player contract to ensure continuity on teams and established Sunday as game day.

Early professional basketball consisted of teams **barnstorming** across the country with no set season or schedule. A stable national league for pro basketball started in 1946. Two years later it would become the National Basketball Association. The league's first commissioner also served as commissioner of the American Hockey League. The early owners of professional basketball teams were also the owners of arenas as well as the hockey teams that played in the arenas. This was the case for many years in Boston and New York (Gorman and Calhoun, 1994). These owners viewed basketball as a way to increase the usage of the arenas. Professional hockey was played primarily in Canada; in fact, a team from the United States was not able to complete for the Stanley Cup until 1916 (Gorman and Calhoun, 1994). The league had only six teams until it expanded to twelve teams in the 1960s.

Each of these sports followed the owner-controlled governance structure created by baseball. The governance structures for the four major sport leagues are very similar. Each league has a commissioner, a board of governance or committee structure consisting of the owners and front-office personnel of the franchises, and a league office. The owners hire the commissioner of each league. The owners also decide and pay the commissioner's compensation and determine the commissioner's duties and responsibilities (Miller, 1991). The owners also have the power to remove the commissioner. A commissioner will serve a term, and at the end of the term the owners will vote whether or not to renew the term. The commissioner has the responsibility of protecting the best interest of the respective sports, but it can be argued that since the owners pay the commissioner's salary, he represents the owners' interest. This was demonstrated by the role David Stern, the NBA's commissioner, played in representing the owners against the players in negotiations related to the owners' lockout of the players during the 1998–99 NBA season.

Professional sport commissioners have had a significant impact on the growth of sport leagues. Pete Rozelle, the commissioner of the National Football League from 1960 to 1989, helped shape the modern professional sport landscape. Rozelle saw the benefits of televised sport and was instrumental in the U.S. Congress passing the **Broadcast Act of 1960.** This law enabled the NFL to negotiate a television contract with a network. Rozelle recognized that the success of professional football was tied to the success of the league. Revenue from network television contracts would be divided equally among all of the teams in the league, thus ensuring the viability of all of the franchises. He was instrumental in the merger of the AFL and NFL and proposed the idea of the AFL and NFL championship game known as the Super Bowl. He initiated NFL Properties, which sells NFL-licensed products and generates millions of dollars for NFL teams each year. He also participated in negotiations for television contracts that provided large financial rewards for the NFL teams. The other sport leagues followed the NFL's lead set by Rozelle.

Stern is credited with saving the NBA as it struggled with low attendance, low television ratings, high salaries, and a poor public image in the early 1980s. Stern became commissioner in 1984 and was able to negotiate with the players association a salary cap to limit a player's salary. But the salaries would be tied to the success of the league. The players would receive 53 percent of the projected gross revenue of the league each year (Gorman and Calhoun 1994; Halberstam, 1998). Stern also was successful in using the league's marquee players Magic Johnson, Larry Bird, Julius Erving, and Michael Jordan to market the NBA in the United States as well as globally.

Even though the commissioner is the most visible individual in the governance structure of professional sport, the owners do have the final say on the governance of their leagues. Through a committee structure, the owners propose rules and rule changes, vote on expansion and franchise relocation, negotiate the league's network broadcast contracts, and represent management in contract negotiations with the player's unions.

It has been through the players' unions that players have had a voice in the governance of their respective sports. Through **collective-bargaining agreements** players have a say in areas such as compensation in terms of minimum salary, fringe benefits, and pension; rules for use of labor, such as games per week, and starting times related to travel; terms of free agency; individual job rights; methods of enforcing the collective-bargaining agreement; discipline; injury protection; economic issues such as meal money and travel expenses; and rules for agent certification (Greenberg, 1992). Collective bargaining led to the end of the reserve clause in baseball in 1975. This led to free agency in baseball and set precedent for free agency in other sports (Miller, 1991). For more on collective bargaining in sport, refer to Chapter 18, Labor Relations in Professional Sports.

The commissioner and the league office are responsible for running the day-to-day operations of the league. The league office handles scheduling of contests, oversees the umpires and referees, administers special events like all-star games and championships, fines and suspends players for breaking league rules, conducts public relations, advertising and marketing for the league as a whole, and implements licensing agreements.

CONCEPT CHECK

The governance structures for the four major sport leagues are similar in that each professional league has a commissioner, a board of governance or committee structure, and a league office. The owners still have ultimate say in the policies that are developed, but the commissioner, an employee of the owners, is very influential. The players have gained more influence in the governance of professional sport through the rise of players associations and collective bargaining.

SUMMARY

- The public school system in the United States made obtaining an education possible for all citizens, and school sports were viewed as a powerful tool for formulating the kinds of attitudes and behaviors associated with effective citizenship.
- State high school athletic associations strive to regulate and standardize competition between schools through the enforcement of

eligibility rules and other rules governing competition between schools.

- High school sport programs are the largest dimension in the entire sport enterprise, with over 17,000 high schools being members of the National Federation of State High School Associations and over 6 million male and female athletes competing in interscholastic competition.
- The governance of interscholastic athletic competition involves individual schools, athletic conference, state athletic associations, and the National Federation of State High School Associations cooperating to ensure effective governance of interscholastic competition.
- The majority of the state associations exist for the purpose of providing uniform standards for athletic competition within their states; offering state championships; ensuring that athletic competition is fair, safe, and sportsmanlike; and providing an environment that emphasizes the overall development of the participants.
- Even with a comprehensive governance structure in place, the administration of high school athletics is primarily conducted on the local level. The local schools must recognize and operate within the rules established by the state association.
- A school board is a body made up of individuals living within the boundaries of a school district that has the authority to approve budgets, determines the feasibility and allocation of resources for the building of athletic facilities, votes on the hiring and firing of athletic department personnel, and votes to establish policies for the school district's athletic programs.
- In its earliest stages, students administered intercollegiate athletics, and this arrangement was satisfactory with administrators until the athletic operations on campuses became so large that the students could no longer control them. Faculties expressed concern and took action with the creation of the faculty athletic committees that oversaw athletics at institutions.
- Early attempts at inter-institutional governance were not successful, but ultimately

a national inter-institutional body was created in the form of the NCAA. The NCAA increased its influence by mandating rules of play, offering educational material and meetings, offering administrative recommendations for athletic programs, instituting championship play in 1921, awarding financial incentives, and encouraging United States Olympic team participation.

- The NCAA became a regulatory body with the power to investigate abuses of and enforce the NCAA rules and punish offenders in 1952.
- The member institutions of the NCAA are diverse, with different educational missions, enrollments, and athletic philosophies. To address the diverse interests, the NCAA created three divisions, each with its own philosophy, criteria for membership, and governance structure.
- The NCAA constitution has thirty-three articles that serve as its basis for governance.
- Fourteen of the articles serve as the organization's operating bylaws. A bylaw can either be a dominant, a division-dominant, a common, or a federated provision.
- In 1996, the NCAA was restructured to give more autonomy to the three divisions.
- In all three NCAA divisions, there is a committee structure that assists in the governance of the division. The committees consist of presidents, athletic directors, faculty athletic representatives, coaches, and student athletes.
- The NCAA national office is not involved in the creation of legislation, but rather serves the members of the organization. The national office is headed by an executive director and is divided into the following departments: Championships, Education Services, Enforcement and Eligibility Appeals, Finance and Business Services, Membership Services, and Public Affairs.
- An intercollegiate athletic conference usually consists of institutions with the same institutional and academic missions and the same level of commitment to athletics that are located in the same geographic region.
- Institutions belonging to a conference must adhere to the rules established by the

conference. The rules that the conference establishes may be more stringent than those established by the NCAA, but they cannot be less stringent.

- Due to financial considerations, it has been commonplace for institutions to change conferences or to decide to join one. It has also been commonplace for institutions to overlook the geographic considerations when joining a conference.
- The NCAA placed the responsibility for the conduct of the athletic program in the hands of the president of each institution. Governance on campus must include a faculty athletics representative and a student athlete advisory board. An institution may choose to create an athletic board to be involved in governance.
- The National League established a precedent for all professional sport leagues because it was an owner-controlled league and the players were employees.
- Two key elements of the governance of early professional baseball were the salary cap and the reserve clause. The owners viewed these as means to ensuring the financial viability of the league and its member teams.
- The governance structures for the four major professional sport leagues are very similar. Each league has a commissioner, a board of governance or committee structure consisting of the owners and front office personnel of the franchises, and a league office.
- The commissioner and the league office are responsible for running the day-to-day operations of the league. The commissioner, who is an employee of the owners, and the league office handle the scheduling of contests, oversee the umpires and referees, administer special events like All-Star games and championships, fine and suspend players for breaking league rules, conduct public relations, advertising and marketing for the league as a whole, and implement licensing agreements.
- Through a committee structure, the owners propose rules and rule changes, vote on expansion and franchise relocation, negotiate the league's network broadcast contracts, and represent management in contract negotiations with the players' unions.

CRITICAL THINKING EXERCISE

1. What are the major similarities and differences between the governance of interscholastic athletics and intercollegiate athletics?

CASE STUDY

East State University, an NCAA Division I institution, has been a member of the Large Eastern Athletic Conference since its inception in 1950. East State, which annually fields an outstanding football team, also fields twenty-one intercollegiate athletic teams and has a reputation of being an outstanding academic institution. ESU annually wins the LEAC football championship, because the fellow LEAC institutions field weak football teams. Only four times in the past ten years has a LEAC institution besides ESU gone to a bowl game. The LEAC is better known for the academic reputation of its members than their athletic reputation. ESU has been successful in several other male and female sports, but is not known for competitive men's or women's basketball programs.

The Middle West Athletic Conference is interested in having ESU join its conference so it can have two six-team divisions and have a conference championship football game. The MWAC is perennially the strongest football and basketball conference in the country, often sending four or five teams to bowl games as well as six or seven teams to both the NCAA men's and women's basketball tournaments. If ESU joined the MWAC, the closest conference school would be 400 miles away and the farthest 1,000 miles. The MWAC consists of large universities with strong commitments to athletics, but with less than reputable academic traditions.

As a member of the ESU athletic board, you have a vote on whether ESU joins the MWCA or not. How would you vote? Please weigh the pros and cons of the decision and offer the rationale for why you would vote the way you would.

REVIEW QUESTIONS AND ISSUES

1. For what reasons do state interscholastic athletic associations exist?
2. What is the role of a school board in the governance of interscholastic competition?

3. How did the NCAA increase its influence over the governance of intercollegiate athletics between 1906 and 1948, and what steps were taken to make the NCAA a regulatory body in 1952?
4. Compare and contrast the philosophies of NCAA Divisions I, II, and III.
5. Define a dominant provision, a division-dominant provision, a common provision, and a federated provision.
6. With the restructuring that occurred in the NCAA in 1996, discuss the differences in the governance structures among the three NCAA divisions.
7. What are the criteria for intercollegiate athletic conference membership, and what have been the potential rationales for institutions joining or switching conference affiliation in the 1990s?
8. Define the role of the NCAA membership and the national office in the governance of intercollegiate athletics.
9. What are the components of governance within an NCAA institution?
10. What impact did Pete Rozelle as NFL commissioner have on the modern professional sport landscape?
11. For what innovation is David Stern, commissioner of the NBA, responsible? How did it help save the NBA from financial difficulties?

SOLUTIONS TO CRITICAL THINKING EXERCISES

1. Similarities: Both governance structures are set up to be representative democracies. The members have a voice in the rules that are created, adopted, and enforced by governing bodies.

   Differences: At the intercollegiate level, a great deal of governance power is at the national level with the NCAA. The bylaws created by the NCAA membership are practiced and enforced by a national governing body. In the case of interscholastic governance, the national governing body is not a legislative body. The state athletic associations have a greater influence over the governance of athletics in individual states.
2. Government departments and agencies fund organizations that provide services and do things that the government wants done. Often,

these are services that the government feels are important but which it cannot deliver, so it delegates the job to voluntary organizations. The not-for-profit sport organization receives public funds with strict funding guidelines attached. This often puts the sport organization at the mercy of changes in government policies and programs, leaving it in a very precarious financial position.

The government may even try to interfere in the sport organization's management on the grounds that the money comes from the public purse and the government therefore has a duty to be involved in the organization's day-to-day administration. Sport leaders ought not to accept such interference. For while it is natural that they should be accountable to their members, they should not be accountable to the state, which is not a member.

On the other hand, sport is an important part of the cultural fabric of our society and pivotal in maintaining our national identity. It is government's responsibility to support those organizations that contribute to these areas. Government funding provides the seed, the starting point, from which sport organizations can reach out and gain wider individual and business support.

WEBSITES

The National Collegiate Athletic Association
www.ncaa.org—This site is where the nation's colleges and universities speak and act on athletic matters at the national level.
The National Federation of State High School Associations
www.nfhs.org—This site provides information about individual state associations.

REFERENCES

Baker, W. J. (1988). *Sports in the western world* (Rev. ed.). Urbana, IL.: University of Illinois Press.

Barr, C. A. (1998). Collegiate sport. In *Principles and practices of sport management*. Gaithersburg, MD: Aspen.

Byers, W. (1995). *Unsportsmanlike conduct: Exploiting college athletes*. Ann Arbor, MI: The University of Michigan Press.

Covell, D. (1998). High school and youth sports. In *Principles and practices of sport management*. Gaithersburg, MD: Aspen.

Davenport, J. (1985). From crew to commercialism—The paradox of sport in higher education. In d. Chu, J. Seagrave, and B. Becker (eds.), *Sport in higher education* (pp. 5–14). Champaign, IL: Human Kinetics.

Fox, S. (1994). *Big leagues: Professional baseball, football, and basketball in national memory*. New York: William Morrow.

Gorman, J., and Calhoun, K. (1994). *The name of the game*. New York: Ernst and Young.

Greenberg, M. J. (1992). *Sport law practice*. Charlotteville, VA: Michie.

Halberstam, D. (1999). *Playing for keeps: Michael Jordan and the world he made*. New York: Random House.

Helyar, J. (1994). *The lords of the realm: The real history of baseball*. New York: Villiard.

King, P. (1996). *Football: A history of the professional game*. New York: Sports Illustrated.

Lewis, G. (1969). Teddy Roosevelt's role in the 1905 football controversy. *Research Quarterly*, 40, 717–724.

Michner, J. (1976). *Sports in America*. Greenwich, CT: Fawcett Crest Books.

Miller, M. (1991). *A whole different ballgame*. New York: Fireside.

National Collegiate Athletic Association (2002). *1998 NCAA Financial Report*. Indianapolis, IN.

National Collegiate Athletic Association. (2002). *1997–98 NCAA Annual Reports*. Indianapolis, IN.

National Collegiate Athletic Association. (2002). *1997–98 NCAA Manual*. Indianapolis, IN.

National Collegiate Athletic Association. (2002). *1998–99 NCAA Division III Manual*. Indianapolis, IN.

National Collegiate Athletic Association. (2002). *Participation: 1982–2002 sponsorship and participation report*. Indianapolis, IN.

Nelson, D. (1982). Administrators' views of athletic governance. In J. Frey (ed.), *The governance of intercollegiate athletics*. (pp. 49–57). West Point, NY: Leisure Press.

O'Hanlon, T. P. (1995). School sports as social training: The case of athletics and the crisis of World War I. In D. K. Wiggins (ed.), *Sport in America: From wicked amusement to national obsession* (pp. 189–206). Champaign, IL.: Human Kinetics.

Ozanian, M. K. (1998). Selective accounting. *Forbes*, December 14, 124.

Sack, A. L., and Staurowsky, E. J. (1998). *College athletes for hire: The evolution and legacy of the NCAA's amateur myth*. Westport, CT: Praeger.

Savage, H. J. (1929). *American college athletics*. New York: The Carnegie Foundation for the Advancement of Teaching.

Smith, R. A. (1995). Preludes to the NCAA: Early failures of faculty intercollegiate athletic control. In D. K. Wiggins (ed.), *Sport in America: From wicked amusement to national obsession* (pp. 151–162). Champaign, IL.: Human Kinetics.

Sport Business Journal (2003). *By the Numbers: 2003*. Street and Smith. Charlotte, NC: Author.

Stern, R. (1979). The development of an intercollegiate central network: The case of intercollegiate athletics. *Administrative Science Quarterly*, 24, 242–266.

Sutton, W., and Gladden, J. (1998). Professional sport. In J. B. Parks, B. R. K. Zanger, and J. Quarterman (eds.), *Contemporary sport management* (pp. 243–262). Champaign, IL.: Human Kinetics.

Tow, T. C. (1982). The governance role of the NCAA. In J. Frey (ed.). *The governance of intercollegiate athletics* (pp. 108–116). West Point, NY: Leisure Press.

VanderZwaag, H. J. (1998). *Policy development in sport management*. 2nd ed. Westport, CT: Praeger.

CHAPTER **8**

International Sport Governance

Mireia Lizandra and Sue Vail

In this chapter, you will become familiar with the following terms:

Amateur Sports Act of 1978
Association of National Olympic
  Committees (ANOC)
Bill C-54
Bill C-131
Calgary Olympic Development
  Association (CODA)
Canadian Olympic Committee
Canadian Sport Policy
Candidate Cities
Coaching Association of Canada
Coaching Association of Canada
  (CAC)
Executive board
Football

International Federations (IFs)
International marketplace
International Olympic Committee
National Basketball League
  (NBA)
National Coaching Certification
  Program
National federations (NFs)
National Football League (NFL)
National Governing Bodies
  (NGBs)
National Olympic Committees
  (NOCs)
National Sport Organizations
  (NSOs)

Olympic Charter
Olympic Games
Olympic Movement
Olympism
Organizing Committees of the
  Olympic Games (OCOGs)
President
Session
Sport Canada
The Olympic Partner Program
  (TOP)
United States Olympic
  Committee (USOC)

Learning Goals

By the end of this chapter, students should be able to:

- Understand why sport as an institution will continue its growth in scope, recognition, and importance in the global community.
- Know why governance takes on an increased importance at all levels of sport.
- Understand why the increased recognition and national emphasis given to international competition and the financial benefits associated with hosting the Olympics have led to increased scrutiny of the role of the International Olympic Committee.
- Be able to describe the international sport federations.
- Appreciate that these governance structures are instrumental in creating the rules and policies that promote fairness and safety in competition.

Football[1] is the most popular sport around the world. It has crossed all boundaries. In the summer of 2003, for the opening of the new stadium for the Philadelphia Eagles, the Lincoln Financial Field, Manchester United and the F.C. Barcelona, two European football teams, played the first match in front of a sold-out crowd. All the tickets were sold in a few hours, weeks before the game. One has to wonder what made this event so successful.

In this global economy, sport, like other businesses, is playing a major role in the **international marketplace.** Television has been a vehicle for this global expansion. It has created a global viewership. Along with sport merchandise consumption and a wider sport fan attendance, major sport leagues and sporting events have reached millions of people in hundreds of countries. Sporting events have crossed domestic boundaries. In 1999 we could already see this global approach when the opening day game of the Major League Baseball season was played in Monterrey, Mexico, between the San Diego Padres and the Colorado Rockies in front of 26,000 fans. Almost 200 countries watched the game (Wissot, 1999). The 2002 Salt Lake City Winter Olympic Games were televised in 160 countries with 2.1 billion viewers (International Olympic Committee, 2002). Super Bowl XXXIV was telecast in more than 185 nations. In addition, the advent of cyberspace has influenced all aspects of the global economy, including sport. Every day, millions of people around the world access a vast wealth of sports information by simply logging onto their computer. ESPN.com was accessed by 1,241,652 people in September 2003. CBS SportsLine.com had 530,766 visitors the same month (http://espn.go .com/mediakit/research/competitive.html).

To this end, it is obvious that the scope of knowledge for the future sport manager goes beyond the domestic domain. Understanding sport at the international level will help you become a better sport manager no matter what field you pursue in sport management. This chapter will address the governance and management of sport at the international level. We will focus on the Olympic movement since the Olympic Games, as the single largest international sporting event, is the pinnacle of event management (Thoma and Chalip, 1996). We will discuss the role of the most relevant North American professional sports leagues in the global market as well as the development of the most popular sport in the world, football, and its role in the United States. We will also analyze how sport is governed in a particular country, Canada, to become familiar with a sport system that differs so much from the one in the United States.

OLYMPIC MOVEMENT AND OLYMPISM

Before explaining the governance and management of Olympic sport, we need to become familiar with two concepts: **Olympic Movement** and **Olympism.** Historically, Pierre de Coubertin is considered the founder of modern Olympism. The **Olympic Charter** (International Olympic Committee, 2003) states:

Olympism is a philosophy of life, exalting and combining in a balanced whole the qualities of body, will and mind. Blending sport with culture and education, Olympism seeks to create a way of life based on the joy found in effort, the educational value of good example and respect for universal fundamental ethical principles. (International Olympic Committee, 2003, p. 9)

Under Coubertin's initiative the International Athletic Congress of Paris was held in June 1894. During the Congress the **International Olympic Committee** was constituted on June 23, 1894.

The Olympic Charter continues, stating:

The Olympic Movement led by the International Olympic Committee, stems from Modern Olympism.

The goal of the Olympic Movement is to contribute to building a peaceful and better world by educating youth through sport practiced without discrimination of any kind and in the Olympic spirit, which requires mutual understanding with a spirit of friendship, solidarity and fair play. (International Olympic Committee, 2003, p. 9)

The Olympic movement includes the International Olympic Committee, the **International Federations (IFs),** the **National Olympic Committees (NOCs),** the **Organizing Committees of the Olympic Games (OCOGs),** the national associations, clubs, and the persons belonging to them, particularly the athletes. It also includes other organizations and institutions as recognized by the International Olympic Committee (International Olympic Committee, 2003).

---

[1]In the United States, football is referred to as soccer to differentiate it from American football.

THE INTERNATIONAL OLYMPIC COMMITTEE

The International Olympic Committee (IOC) is a nongovernmental, nonprofit organization with headquarters in Lausanne, Switzerland. It is considered the supreme authority of the Olympic Movement.

The Olympic Charter is the codification of the fundamental principles, rules, and bylaws adopted by the International Olympic Committee. It governs the organization and operation of the Olympic Movement and stipulates the conditions for the celebration of the **Olympic Games.**

The International Olympic Committee owns exclusive rights to:

- The Olympic symbol—Represented by five interlocked rings. It represents the union of the five continents and the meeting of athletes from all over the world at the Olympic Games. The Olympic symbol can be used alone, in one or in several colors (blue, yellow, black, green, and red).
- The Olympic flag—It has white background, and the Olympic symbol in its five colors is located in the center.
- The Olympic motto—"Citius, Altius, Fortius" or "Swifter, Higher, Stronger."
- The Olympic anthem.
- The Olympic Games—The Olympic Games consist of the Games of the Olympiad and the Olympic Winter Games. The term "Olympiad" is frequently misused. It does not refer to the games themselves but rather to the four-year period following the games. The games of the Olympiad are held during the first year of the Olympiad, which they celebrate. Beginning in 1994, the year of the XVII Olympic Winter Games, the Olympic Winter Games are held during the second calendar year following that during which an Olympiad begins. (International Olympic Committee, 2003)

These Olympic marks become very important because they are the trading tools of the International Olympic Committee (Thoma and Chalip, 1996).

The International Olympic Committee is governed by its members, chosen and elected from among persons its nominations committee considers qualified. All Olympic Movement members have the right to submit nominations. Some of the rules that apply to the IOC members are:

- All IOC members are natural persons and can be active athletes and presidents or senior leaders of IFs, organizations recognized by the IOC and NOCs.
- IOC members are representatives of the International Olympic Committee in their countries and not delegates of their countries within the International Olympic Committee. For example, an IOC member from Mexico represents the International Olympic Committee in Mexico and not Mexico in the International Olympic Committee.
- IOC members are not personally liable for the debts and obligations of the IOC.

When the International Olympic Committee was founded, there were 14 members. Currently there are 125 IOC members, 21 honorary members and 4 honor members, and one honorary president for life. An IOC member who retires after having served the IOC for at least ten years and having rendered exceptional services to it may be proposed by the IOC Executive Board to be elected as honorary member. The IOC Executive Board may elect as honorary president for life an IOC member who has rendered exceptional services as president of the IOC. IOC members retire at the end of the calendar year when they turn 70 years old, unless they were elected before 1966, in which case they are members for life.

IOC governance

The organs of the IOC are:

- The **Session**
- The **Executive Board**
- The **President**

The general assembly of the members of the International Olympic Committee is called a Session. The Session is the supreme body of the IOC. It is held at least once a year. The President can request an extraordinary session. The main function of the Session is to adopt, modify, and interpret the Olympic Charter. Its decisions are final. The Session may delegate powers to the Executive Board. The official languages of the session are French, English, German, Arabic, Spanish, and Russian.

The Executive Board consists of the IOC President, four Vice Presidents, and ten additional members. All the members of the Executive Board are elected by the Session, by secret ballot, by a majority of votes cast. The Executive Board is responsible for managing IOC finances, preparing the annual report, submitting the names of persons it recommends for IOC membership, establishing the agenda for IOC Sessions, and other duties. The Vice Presidents and the additional ten members are elected for a period of four years. The Vice Presidents may not be reelected to the Executive Board for four years after their mandate expires, except if elected as President. The members may not be reelected to the Executive Board for four years after their mandate expires, except if elected Vice President or President.

A President heads the International Olympic Committee. The IOC President is elected by secret ballot from among its members, for a period of eight years. The President may be reelected for successive four-year terms. He supervises all the activities of the International Olympic Committee.

The President nominates special commissions or working groups to study certain specific subjects and formulate recommendations to the Executive Board. These commissions have a significant role, and they can propose recommendations to the International Olympic Committee. The members appointed in these commissions are a mix of IOC members, IF, and NOC representatives, consultants, and technicians in specific areas. Examples of these special commissions are the Finance Commission, the Medical Commission, the Press Commission, and the two latest commissions, the IOC 2000 Reform Commission and IOC Ethics Commission.

IOC finance

To generate support for the Olympic Movement and the Olympic Games, the IOC manages a marketing program. This program has become the driving force behind the promotion, financial security, and stability of the Olympic Movement. The IOC, as the holder of the rights to the Olympic Games and the Olympic marks, is responsible for the overall direction and management of the Olympic marketing program. This includes television broadcast partnerships, corporate sponsorship, ticketing, and licensing. The Olympic marketing revenue is distributed among the organizing committees for the Olympic Games, the National Olympic Committees, Olympic Solidarity, International Olympic Sports Federations, miscellaneous organizations, and the IOC. The main source of revenue for the IOC is TV rights and sponsorship. Broadcasting contributes 50 percent of the Olympic marketing revenue; sponsorship contributes 40 percent; ticketing contributes 8 percent, and licensing contributes 2 percent.

Olympic sponsorship is the relationship between the Olympic movement and corporations intended to generate support for the Olympic Movement and the Olympic Games and, in return, benefit the sponsor (International Olympic Committee, 2003). After the great success of the 1984 Los Angeles Games, the IOC established in 1985 **The Olympic Partner Program (TOP)** under which corporations pay millions of dollars for status as an official Olympic sponsor for a minimum of four years. The idea behind TOP was to sell a limited number of worldwide sponsorships, thus increasing the benefits received by each of the companies. As such, each TOP sponsor was granted exclusivity in a sponsorhip category. This meant that the IOC would not sell any advertising rights to the competitors of TOP sponsors, thus supposedly providing exclusive rights to the sponsor. For example, when Coca-Cola signed the TOP program under the category of soft drinks, it was guaranteed that Pepsi could not be associated with the Olympic Movement at all.

TOP I was in effect from 1985 to 1988 and included the Calgary Winter Olympics and Seoul Summer Olympics. Nine companies, paying a minimum of $10 million each, participated. In TOP II, between 1989 and 1992, covering the 1992 Albertville Winter Olympic Games and 1992 Barcelona Summer Olympic Games, 12 companies paid approximately $20 million each. In TOP III, which included the 1994 Lillehammer Winter Olympics and 1996 Atlanta Summer Olympics, the sponsorship fees were $40 million, and 10 companies paid this amount for category exclusivity. For TOP IV, which included the 1998 Nagano Winter Olympic Games and 2000 Sydney Olympic Games, the sponsorship was $45 million, and 11 companies signed. In TOP V, which included the 2002 Salt Lake City Winter Games and 2004 Athens Summer Games, 10 companies have signed and are estimated to generate $600 million in financial and technical support. TOP VI (2005–2008), which encompasses sponsorship of the 2006 Olympic Winter Games in Torino and the 2008 Olympic Games in Beijing, has already signed some companies: John Hancock, Coca-Cola, Kodak, SchlumbergerSema, and Swatch (International Olympic Committee, 2002).

CONCEPT CHECK

The Olympic Movement comprises the International Olympic Committee, the International Federations, the National Olympic Committees, the Organizing Committees of the Olympic Games, the national associations, clubs, and the persons belonging to them, particularly the athletes.

The International Olympic Committee (IOC) is the supreme authority of the Olympic Movement. It is governed by three bodies: the Session, the Executive Board, and the President.

The IOC Olympic marketing program includes the television broadcast partnership (50 percent), corporate sponsorship (40 percent), Olympic Games ticketing (8 percent) and Olympic licensing (2 percent). The IOC established in 1985 The Olympic Partner Program (TOP) under which corporations signed exclusive sponsorship agreements for a minimum period of four years.

The National Olympic Committees

The National Olympic Committees are the organizations responsible for the development and protection of the Olympic Movement in their respective countries. The Olympic Charter (International Olympic Committee, 2003) specifies in Rule 31 the NOCs' requirements:

- Propagate the fundamental principles of Olympism at the national level within the framework of sports activity and otherwise contribute, among other things, to the diffusion of Olympism in the teaching programs of physical education and sport in schools and university establishments.
- Ensure the observance of the Olympic Charter in their countries.
- Encourage the development of high-performance sport as well as sport for all.
- Help in the training of sports administrators by organizing courses and ensure that such

courses contribute to the propagation of the Fundamental Principles of Olympism.
- Commit themselves to taking action against any form of discrimination and violence in sport.
- Fight against the use of substances and procedures prohibited by the IOC or their IFs, in particular by approaching the competent authorities of their country so that all medical controls may be performed in optimum conditions.

The National Olympic Committees are responsible for the representation of their respective countries at the Olympic Games and at the regional, continental, or world competitions patronized by the IOC. They also supervise the preliminary selection of potential bid cities. Before a candidate city can compete against those in other countries, it first must win the selection process by the NOC in its own country. Then, the NOC can name the city to the IOC as a candidate to host the Olympic Games (International Olympic Committee, 2003).

The NOCs are grouped into regional organizations as follows:

- Association of National Olympic Committees of Africa (ANOCA) based in Cameroon. ANOCA organizes the African Games. There have been eight editions of the African Games.
- Olympic Council of Asia (OCA) based in Kuwait. OCA organizes the Asian Games every four years. There have been fourteen editions of the Asian games.
- The European Olympic Committees (EOC) based in Italy.
- Oceania National Olympic Committees (ONOC) based in the Fiji Islands.
- Pan American Sports Organization, which encompasses the National Olympic Committees of North, South, and Central America (PASO) based in Mexico. PASO organizes the Pan American Games. The games have taken place every four years since 1951. (Association of National Olympic Committees, 1998)

The common objective of these regional associations is to uphold the Olympic Charter and promote sport in their regional area. The umbrella organization for all the National Olympic Committees is the

Association of National Olympic Committees (ANOC). There are currently 201 NOCs.

The United States Olympic Committee

The **United States Olympic Committee** is the organization that provides leadership and guidance for the Olympic Movement in the United States and around the world (United States Olympic Committee, 1997).

The **Amateur Sports Act of 1978** appointed the USOC as the coordinating body for all Olympic-related athletic activity in the United States. It designated the USOC as the sole authority for supervision and development of sports contested in the Olympics and Pan American Games. The USOC was also given the responsibility of promoting and supporting physical fitness and public participation in athletic activities by encouraging developmental programs in its member organizations. The USOC member organizations include Olympic and Pan American sport organizations (the National Governing Bodies), affiliated sport organizations, community-based and education-based multisport organizations, athletes' representatives, the Armed Forces, Disabled in Sports, state fund-raising organizations, associate members, and representatives of the public sector.

The Amateur Sports Act granted the USOC exclusive rights to the symbol of the International Olympic Committee, the USOC emblem, and the words "Olympic," "Olympiad," and "Citius, Altius, Fortius" in the United States.

The Amateur Sports Act also included provisions for recognizing **National Governing Bodies (NGBs)** for the sports on the Olympic (winter and summer) and Pan American Games programs. It gave the USOC the general authority, on a continu-ing basis, to review matters related to the recognition of NGBs in the act.

The federal government has no direct authority over the USOC. In turn, the USOC obtains almost no funding from federal sources. The majority of USOC revenue is derived from private fund-raising, licensing, and sponsorship agreements. Sports outside the Olympic Movement and Pan American Games (including professional teams and leagues) are subject to neither USOC nor federal oversight.

The USOC also supports the bid of U.S. cities to host the Winter or Summer Olympic Games, or Pan American Games. After reviewing the bids, the USOC may endorse one city per event as the U.S. candidate city. The USOC developed an internal bid process to choose a U.S. candidate city for the 2007 Pan American Games. San Antonio, Texas, was chosen by the USOC to bid against other Pan American cities. PASO elected Rio de Janeiro to be the host city for the 2007 Pan American Games. The same process has been put in place for a U.S. bid city for the 2012 Olympic Games. Eight cities were bidding to become the U.S. candidate city for the 2012 Olympic Games (United States Olympic Committee, 1999). New York City won the bid and is currently bidding at the international level to host the 2012 Summer Olympic Games.

USOC's organizational structure

The organizational structure of the USOC includes volunteer leadership consisting of the officers, an Executive Committee, a Board of Directors, standing and special committees, and an executive director and paid staff. There is also an Athletes' Advisory Council to serve as a source of opinion and advice to the board and all other USOC committees.

- The officers of the USOC consist of a president, three vice presidents, a secretary, and a treasurer.
- The executive committee has the responsibility for supervising the conduct of the business affairs of the USOC according to the policy guidelines prescribed by the board of directors.
- The board of directors establishes the policies to be followed in carrying out the purposes and objectives of the USOC. It meets twice a year, unless otherwise decided by the members. It has the authority to amend the USOC constitution and bylaws, admit

new members or terminate membership of current members, and receive and review reports of the Executive Committee, Executive Director, and all committees or other persons, concerning USOC activities.

- The standing and special committees are part of the USOC structure for the purpose of making recommendations to and reporting to the board of directors and Executive Committee and carrying out other functions assigned to them.
- The Athletes' Advisory Council helps to improve communications between the USOC and currently active athletes, and to serve as a source of opinion and advice to the board of directors.

However, the USOC approved a new organizational structure in October 18, 2003, during its board meeting in Cleveland. The tentative timeline to have the new structure in place is the fall of 2004. The new structure will consist of reducing the board of directors to 11 members (four independent directors, two NGB Council representatives, two athlete representatives, and three IOC members). However the size of the board could change as IOC members are added. The IOC members are automatically on the board. It will also eliminate the Executive Committee and create an Olympic Assembly, which will provide input to the board (United States Olympic Committee, 2003).

CONCEPT CHECK

The United States Olympic Committee is the organization that provides leadership and guidance for the Olympic Movement in the United States. It is the sole authority for supervision and development of sports contested in the Olympics and Pan American Games.

The organizational structure of the USOC includes volunteer leadership consisting of the officers, an Executive Committee, a board of directors, standing and special committees, and an executive director and paid staff. There is also an Athletes' Advisory Council. The USOC will implement a new organizational structure in the near future, reducing the board of directors to eleven or thirteen members and creating on Olympic Assembly to provide input to the Board.

International Federations

The International Federations are international nongovernmental organizations recognized by the International Olympic Committee administering one or more sports at the world level and encompassing organizations administering such sports at the national level (International Olympic Committee, 2003). In the United States, the **national federations (NFs)** are known as national governing bodies (NGBs). For example, for the sport of baseball, the International Baseball Federation (IBA) is the International Federation and USA Baseball is the national governing body of the sport of baseball in the United States. Another example would be for the sport of basketball. The Fédération Internationale de Basketball (FIBA) is the international federation, USA Basketball is the national governing body for basketball in the United States, and the Federación Española de Baloncesto is the national federation for basketball in Spain.

The role of the International Federations is to establish and enforce the rules concerning the practice of their respective sports and ensure the development of their sports throughout the world.

We can categorize the International Federations as follows:

- Recognized International Federations whose sports appear on the Olympic program have the status of International Olympic Federations. There are two categories: the International Olympic Summer Federations (see Table 8-1) and the International Olympic Winter Federations (see Table 8-2). As such, they participate in annual meetings of the IOC Executive Board.
- Recognized International Federations whose sports are not part of the Olympic program (see Table 8-3).

In order to discuss common problems and decide on their events calendars, the summer Olympic Federations, the Winter Olympic Federations and the recognized federations have formed associations:

- The Association of Summer Olympic International Federations (ASOIF).
- The Assembly of International Winter Sports Federations (AIWF).
- The Assembly of IOC Recognized International Sports Federations (ARISF).

TABLE 8-1   *International Olympic Summer Federations*

International Amateur Athletic Federation (IAAF)
International Rowing Federation (FISA)
International Badminton Federation (IBF)
International Baseball Federation (IBA)
International Basketball Federation (FIBA)
International Amateur Boxing Federation (AIBA)
International Canoe Federation (FIC)
International Cycling Union (UCI)
International Equestrian Federation (FEI)
Fédération Internationale d'Escrime (FIE)
Fédération Internationale de Football Association (FIFA)
International Gymnastics Federation (FIG)
International Weightlifting Federation (IWF)
International Handball Federation (IHF)
International Hockey Federation (FIH)
International Judo Federation (IJF)
International Federation of Associated Wrestling Styles (FILA)
Fédération Internationale de Natation Amateur (FINA)
Union Internationale de Pentathlon Moderne et Biathlon (UIPMB)
International Softball Federation (ISF)
The World Taekwondo Federation (WTF)
International Tennis Federation (ITF)
The International Table Tennis Federation (ITTF)
Union Internationale de Tir (UIT)
International Archery Federation (FITA)
International Triathlon Union (ITU)
International Sailing Federation (ISAF)
International Volleyball Federation (FIVB)

TABLE 8-2   *International Olympic Winter Federations*

Union Internationale de Pentathlon Moderne et Biathlon (UIPMB)
International Bobsleigh and Tobogganing Federation (UIPMB)
World Curling Federation (WCF)
International Ice Hockey Federation (IIHF)
International Luge Federation (FIL)
International Skating Union (ISU)
International Ski Federation (ISU)

TABLE 8-3   *Recognized International Federations*

International Federation of Sports Acrobatics (IFSA)
Fédération Aéronautique Internationale (FAI)
The International Mountaineering and Climbing Federation (UIAA)
World Confederation of Billiards Sports (WCBS)
Confédération Mondiale Sports Boules (CMSB)
International Dance Sport Federation (IDSF)
Word Amateur Golf Council (WAGC)
World Karate Federation (FMK)
International Korfball Federation (IKF)
International Federation of Netball Associations (IFNA)
International Orienteering Federation (IOF)
International Roller Skating Federation (FIRS)
International Federation of Basque Pelota (FIPV)
Federation of International Polo (FIP)
Fédération Internationale des Quilleurs (FIQ)
International Racquetball Federation (IRF)
International Rugby Football Board (IRFB)
International Life Saving Federation (ILS)
International Water Ski Federation (IWSF)
World Squash Federation (WSF)
World Underwater Federation (CMAS)
International Surfing Association (ISA)
International Trampoline Federation (FIT)

- The General Association of International Federations (AGFIS/GAISF), which also includes other sports federations.

All of the sports included on the Olympic program have an International Federation. After each Olympic Games, the International Olympic Committee reviews the program and determines whether new sports and/or new events can be added. At this time, International Federations that are recognized by the International Olympic Committee but are not included on the Olympic program can petition to be included. We need to take a step back and realize that an International Federation needs to request its recognition to the International Olympic Committee. The IOC will grant two years of provisional recognition, and after these two years, the IOC grants final recognition in writing.

So, when an International Federation petitions to be included in the Olympic program, it has to comply with some requisites. To be included on the summer Olympic program a sport must be practiced by men in at least 75 countries on four continents and women in at least 40 countries on three continents. To be included on the Winter Olympic program, it must be practiced in at least 25 countries on three continents. The sport is admitted to the program of the Olympic Games at least seven years before the Olympic Games. A discipline (a branch of an Olympic sport comprising one or several events) must have a recognized international standing to be included in the program of the Olympic Games. The standards of admissions for disciplines are the same as those required for sports. An example of a discipline would be beach volleyball. An event (a competition in an Olympic sport or in one of its disciplines and resulting in a ranking) must have a recognized international standing both numerically and geographically, and have been included at least twice in world or continental championships. Only events practiced by men in at least 50 countries and on three continents may be included in the program of the Olympic Games.

No International Federation is obligated to keep the sport it governs on the Olympic program. Each IF establishes its own eligibility rules for its sport. An International Federation can have a set of eligibility rules for the Olympic Games, which must be approved by the International Olympic Committee, and another set of rules for other international competitions (i.e., world championships).

CONCEPT CHECK

The International Federations are international nongovernmental organizations recognized by the International Olympic Committee that administer one or more sports at world level and encompass organizations administering such sports at national level.

Bidding process

The bid process to host the Olympic Games is a long and scrutinized process that can last many years. The 1998 crisis in Salt Lake City was a turning point in changing this process. Salt Lake City was heavily criticized for influencing IOC members to vote in favor of Salt Lake City. As a result of this crisis a

Reform Commission was formed to find solutions. At the 110th IOC Session in December 1999, a new procedure for the selection of the host city for the Games of the XXIX Olympiad in 2008 was approved. This procedure was to be applied from then on. The procedure consists in the following: In a preliminary phase, the cities communicate to the IOC their interest in hosting the Olympic Games. At this time, these cities are considered "Applicant Cities." Their applications are assessed by the IOC administration and experts under the authority of the Executive Board. They will have to complete a dossier. At the end of their process, the IOC Executive Board will determine which five cities should pass the preliminary phase and be accepted as "Candidate Cities." At this point, those cities accepted as "Candidate Cities" will proceed to a second phase, during which their candidatures will be examined by an Evaluation Committee. These Candidate Cities have to present a Candidature File to the IOC, followed by a visit by the IOC Evaluation Commission to each of them. The Candidature File consists of several questions about the city, venues, infrastructure, transportation, and the like. The Evaluation Commission will submit a report on all candidatures to the IOC two months prior to the Session. The host city will be chosen at that session. For the 2012 Olympic Games, nine cities are bidding: Paris, London, Moscow, New York, Leipzig, Istanbul, Rio de Janeiro, Madrid, and La Havana. Since the quality of all the bids is so strong, the IOC is considering having the nine Applicant Cities become Candidate Cities and continue the process until election, which will be in July 2005 in Singapore (Novo, 2003).

CONCEPT CHECK

The bid process to host the Olympic Games is completely regulated by the IOC. Any city interested in hosting Olympics Games must communicate this decision to the IOC. The Executive Board of the IOC will recognize such cities and will nominate them as Applicant Cities. From the original pool of all the applicant cities, the IOC will choose five and they will become Candidate Cities. Although this rule may not apply all the time if the bids are strong enough to continue the process. The candidate cities must prepare a Candidature File and present it to the IOC.

Organizing committees of the Olympic Games

Finally, when a city is selected to host the Olympic Games, an organizing committee of the Olympic Games (OCOG) has to be formed. The International Olympic Committee entrusts the organization of the Olympic Games to the National Olympic Committee of the country of the host city as well as to the host city itself. The International Olympic Committee has entrusted the Hellenic Olympic Committee and the city of Athens to organize the 2004 Games. For this purpose, an organizing committee has been formed, *Athens 2004*.

The International Olympic Committee has entrusted the Italian Olympic Committee and the city of Torino to organize the 2006 Winter Olympic Games. In this case the organizing committee has been called *Torino Organizing Committee*. The IOC has entrusted the Chinese Olympic Committee and the city of Beijing to organize the 2008 Games. The *2008 Beijing Organizing Committee* was formed for this purpose. The IOC has entrusted the Canadian Olympic Committee and the city of Vancouver to organize the 2010 Winter Olympic Games. For this purpose, an organizing committee of the Olympic Games has been formed, *Organizing Committee for Vancouver 2010*.

From the time of its constitution to the end of its liquidation, the organizing committee must comply with the Olympic Charter, the contract entered into between the IOC, the National Olympic Committee, and the host city, and the instructions of the IOC Executive Board. The Organizing Committee starts its work with a period of planning followed by a period of organization, which culminates in the implementation or operational phase. As an organizing committee of the Olympic Games, it will have to address many areas, including operations, accommodations, accreditation, logistics, host broadcasting, television rights, medical need, the Olympic Village, security, technology, tickets, transportation, sport competitions, and others (Thoma and Chalip, 1996). The IOC will provide to the organizing committee the majority of the budget up front due to the long-term broadcast and sponsorship revenue. In the case of the Salt Lake 2002 Winter Olympic Games, the budget was provided entirely through the support of Olympic marketing and broadcast program. It received approximately $1,390.5 million from the Olympic marketing program, including $443 million from broadcast revenue (International Olympic Committee, 2003).

A final report on the celebration of the Games in English and French has to be completed within two years after the end of the Games (International Olympic Committee, 2003).

CONCEPT CHECK

When a city is selected to host the Olympic Games, it has to form an organizing committee. The IOC, the city, and its respective NOC will have to sign an agreement. The organizing committee for the Olympic Games will be responsible for staging the Games. A final report will have to be presented to the IOC in English and French two years after the end of the Games.

THE NORTH AMERICAN PROFESSIONAL SPORTS LEAGUES IN THE GLOBAL COMMUNITY

The most popular professional sports in the United States are American football, baseball, basketball, and ice hockey. More than the others, American football and basketball have ventured into the international marketplace to look for opportunities. These opportunities have come in different ways. For example, Reebok International Ltd. saw an opportunity to penetrate the Chinese market by signing Yao Ming to a multiyear marketing deal. Until recently, Yao Ming, the 7-foot 6-inch Houston Rockets center, had an endorsement deal with Nike. When the deal expired, Reebok came with full force to sign the Chinese player. Yao Ming will help market Reebok in his native China through print and television ads, promotional appearances, and his signature collection of athletic footwear and apparel (Associated Press, 2003).

The leagues have used television to expose and export their sport. More than 60 broadcasters from 223 countries and territories are receiving **National Football League (NFL)** programming for the 2003 NFL season. Thanks to an agreement with China's only national terrestrial broadcaster (CCTV), the NFL has been available in more than 300 million households with a potential audience of over 1 billion. NFL fans in Japan have also been enjoying two new shows this season. Other local TV stations from Canada, Finland, Turkey, Israel, and other countries have either signed or renewed agreements to bring American football to their households (National Football League International, 2003). As a result, most of these professional leagues have opened offices oversees. Playing preseason games or exhibition games in other countries has proven to be very effective. The **National Basketball League (NBA)** started the 2003 preseason with four international games played in Mexico City, Mexico, featuring the Dallas Mavericks and the Utah Jazz; in Puerto Rico featuring the Philadelphia 76ers and the Miami Heat; in Paris, with the San Antonio Spurs playing the Memphis Grizzlies; and in Barcelona, Spain, featuring the 2003 Euroleague Champions F.C. Barcelona against the Memphis Grizzlies. Another preseason highlight included a game between the Toronto Raptors and Panathinaikos (Greece)—a first-division club from the Hellenic Basketball Federation—in Toronto (National Basketball League, 2003). All these games were televised.

The NFL has also been playing preseason games overseas since 1986. In fact, the NFL is the only one that started an international professional football league. Formerly known as the World League, the NFL European League has helped export American football to Europe. The league has been relatively successful, especially in Germany, where three of the six teams come from. The league played its eleventh World Bowl in Glasgow in June 2003.

The NBA has done a great job trying to reach different markets. With Websites in Spain, France, Germany, Japan, Taiwan, and the UK, the NBA has been able to reach thousands of people in many countries. It has also capitalized on other programs such Africa Camp 2003, in which a contingent of NBA players, coaches, and legends served as coaches and educators for the inaugural Africa 100 Camp attended by young players. Another success has been the Latinos Unidos Tour, in which international players traveled to Brazil and Argentina as part of the NBA Latinos Unidos Tour 2003 and coaches offered clinics to other coaches (National Basketball League, 2003).

The NFL has also used the talent of its players to promote the sport in other regions. Kansas City Chiefs tight end Tony Gonzalez helped to promote a different kind of football to sports fans in South America when he was joined by Damian Vaughn, the NFL's first Brazilian player, in a trip to Brazil in April 2003. The popularity of American football

in Brazil has been on the rise. It is estimated that 36 million Brazilians watched Super Bowl XXXVII highlights and the halftime show live on Globo Television, Brazil's number one network (National Football League International, 2003).

The fact that all these leagues have international players has helped to promote the sport. The NFL has foreign-born players from at least 28 different countries. The NBA also has an international flavor. A great number of baseball players are from Dominican Republic, Cuba, or other Latin American countries. Ice hockey has numerous players from Europe.

It is obvious that the positioning of these leagues in the global market has brought them brand recognition and, ultimately, benefits.

CONCEPT CHECK

The North American professional sports leagues, mostly the National Football League and the National Basketball Association, have entered the global community, using television and the Internet. Preseason games played overseas by these professional leagues have been a good investment for brand recognition. International players have joined these leagues, helping the leagues in their international endeavor.

Football

Football is the most popular sport on the planet. The Football World Cup is a very popular sporting event played every four years and watched around the world. However, football has not always been welcomed in the United States because of the strong presence of other professional sports and a lack of understanding of the game itself. However, the 1994 World Cup played in the United States proved the opposite. The United States welcomed soccer, and fans filled the stadiums during the tournament. With this great success, a professional football league was started in 1996 called Major League Soccer (MLS). Fans came out in full force during Major League Soccer's inaugural season. Nearly 3.1 million fans attended the first Division I professional soccer league on American soil in 12 years. In 1998, two teams were added to the league, making a total of 12 teams. The 1999 season featured the first major league stadium built specifically for soccer in the United States. In 2000, the impact of young American players was seen when the U.S. Olympic Team finished fourth at the Sydney Olympic Games. World-class international players also brought global exposure for the league. In 2001, the impact of MLS became notorious when the U.S. Men's National Team captured their fourth consecutive berth in the World Cup. While, the league had to cease operations in two cities in 2002, MLS continued its success and led the U.S. to the quarterfinals of World Cup Korea/Japan (Major League Soccer, 2003). The league stills struggles but it is finding acceptance.

Women's football has also become successful after the 1999 Women's World Cup played in the United States and won by the United States for the second time. It was considered the best-attended women's sporting event ever. Tickets sales totaled 650,000, many more than the 112,000 sold for the last World Cup in Sweden in 1995. This reflected the enthusiasm for the world's most popular sport in a nation many people had regarded as a soccer desert (Reuters, 1999). As a result, a women's professional soccer league (WUSA) was launched in April 14, 2001. It started with eight teams featuring the best players from the 1999 U.S. World Cup Championship Team and top-flight international players.

In May 23, 2000, the WUSA and MLS announced a cooperative agreement that allowed the two leagues to grow and work together. WUSA signed 32 international players. By May 2001, WUSA announced regional TV coverage of every game (Women's United Soccer Association, 2003). The eight teams played two more seasons, but, unfortunately, the league suspended operations in September 2003. One of the reasons for this decision was that not enough women attended the games or watched on television. In the opinion of Neal Pilson, a consultant and former president of CBS Sports, there were three major reasons for women's sports struggling on television: TV outlets, timing, and advertising (Fleischman, 2003). The league spent $40 million from investors in its first year, although that money was supposed to last five years. It spent about $110 million in its three seasons. Its total losses were close to $90 million. The league founder and chairman, John Hendricks, said that the principal problem was a lack of national sponsors. It had hoped to find eight sponsors willing to invest $2.5 million each but ended up with just two (Jensen, 2003). However, there have been continued efforts to resurrect a WUSA presence in 2004 and beyond. Among other efforts, the league is developing various grassroots outreach programs that would involve the nationwide network of clubs across the country as well as individuals not affiliated with a club (Women's United Soccer Association, 2003).

CONCEPT CHECK

Football is the most popular sport in the planet. It entered the U.S. market after the great success of the 1994 World Cup. The professional football league (MLS) started in 1996. Women's soccer also became successful after the 1999 World Cup played in the United States. A professional women's soccer league started in 2001. It suspended operations at the end of the 2003 season because of a lack of sponsors.

THE CANADIAN AMATEUR SPORT SYSTEM

Around the rinks and the playing fields, the pools, the ski hills and trails in Canada, emulating their heroes, are thousands of young Canadians of all backgrounds, learning together. Cheering them on, coaching them, and enduring the endless rounds of car pools and early morning ice times are the parents who through their countless hours of "parent duty" experience the positives of sport as well. Sharing a cup of coffee at five A.M. in a cold rink can be an incredible stimulus to conversation and the beginning of a better understanding among Canadians. It's cold out there at five A.M. whether you are French, English, male or female.

For the Love of Sport (1992)

Introduction

Although Canada and the United States are similar in many ways, the ways in which our respective amateur sport systems have developed over the past 30 years are distinctly different. This section has three purposes:

- To assist the student in understanding the evolution of the Canadian amateur sport system.

- To assist the student in understanding the current structure and governance of the Canadian amateur sport system.
- To assist the student in understanding what future changes are needed in the Canadian system.

Sport management as a profession and a discipline was first recognized in the early 1970s when the federal government, under then Prime Minister Pierre Trudeau, responded to a task force report on sport, which moved the management of sport from the proverbial kitchen table to the boardroom. **National Sport Organizations (NSOs)** were formally recognized by the federal government and received funds to support athlete and organizational development. At the same time, universities began to offer programs to train physical educators, and the research and practice of sport-related subjects, including sport administration/management, was recognized as a discipline.

Since the birth of the formalized sport system in Canada, federal, provincial, and municipal governments have played a major funding and policy role. To this day, the system is largely dependent on public funds to provide athletes, coaches, and recreational participants with ongoing programs and services. Throughout the 1990s, all levels of government implemented major cutbacks in their sport budgets, and this had a crippling effect on many aspects of the system.

In essence, the high level of government involvement in sport over the years has been a two-edged sword. On one hand, the foundation for the Canadian sport system would not have developed as rapidly or as uniformly without government support. On the other hand, a financial overreliance on government leadership and funding has evolved, leaving sport vulnerable to political whimsy and the financial constraints and priorities of the government in power.

As we move into the 21st century, the Canadian sport system is floundering. From a high performance perspective, Canada has not produced the number of medals that many politicians feel is critical for continued financial support. From a health perspective, sport is not yet seen as an essential contributor to a healthy lifestyle, although more cause–effect research supports this position as each year passes. Generally speaking, sport in Canada is not viewed as an integral part of the culture, as it is in many European countries.

CONCEPT CHECK

The high level of government involvement in the development and maintenance of the Canadian sport system has been a two-edged sword. On one hand the system could not have developed so rapidly or uniformly; on the other hand, an overreliance on government leadership and funding has evolved.

The evolution of the amateur sport system in Canada

In 1959 the Duke of Edinburgh, Prince Philip, made a speech to the Canadian Medical Association decrying the state of fitness of Canadians and challenging the medical profession to take steps to rectify this deficiency (Macintosh et al., 1987). At the same time, Canada's weak performance at the Olympics and other international games did not go unnoticed by members of Parliament.

As a result, in September 1961 **Bill C-131,** an Act to Encourage Fitness and Amateur Sport, was unanimously passed in the House of Commons. The purpose of the act was to provide access to sport and fitness for all Canadians. The act had a $5 million budget attached to it, which initially allowed for the establishment of the base of the Canadian sport system as it exists today. A sport presence was also established within the federal government bureaucracy, "Fitness and Amateur Sport," a branch within the then Department of Health and Welfare. This government branch was to assist in shaping the development of the amateur sport system in Canada.

It took the best part of 10 years to plan for the implementation of the Canadian sport system, and then around 1970 the system started to take shape. In 1971 Hockey Canada was formed to address Canada's poor showings at international competitions. ParticipACTION came into being with a mandate to make Canadians more aware of the importance of physical activity, and ultimately to become more physically active. The **Coaching Association of Canada** was born, and from that the **National Coaching Certification Program** was developed and implemented. University programs were established to do research and educate students about the value of sport and physical activity. Finally a National Sport and Recreation Center was created in Ottawa that housed the offices of all of the newly formed National Sport Organizations (e.g., Basketball Canada, Canadian Figure Skating Association). Provinces followed suit with the creation of provincial sport centers to house the offices of provincial sport organizations.

Over the next few years, a number of federal-provincial cost-sharing agreements were set up for sport program development across the country. Problems arose when Quebec refused to participate and many of the smaller provinces were unable to fund their share of the cost-sharing agreements. These agreements were discontinued in the late 1960s and deemed to be unsuccessful in encouraging mass participation sport. At that point the 10 provinces independently developed their sport systems based upon the resources and priorities of each. Interestingly, in spite of the independent development, each provincial sport system parallels the national system in large measure.

Through the 1970s and 1980s the federal government developed a number of other policy papers and reports, which attempted to further define the roles of governments and to develop the sport delivery system. In 1976 the Fitness and Amateur Sport Branch of the Department of Health and Welfare received its own Minister of State, the Honourable Iona Campagnolo. This was viewed by the sport community as a stronger commitment by the federal government to supporting the growth of fitness and amateur sport in Canada. Unfortunately, it turned out to be just a "stopover" for junior ministers to gain some experience before receiving more prestigious posts. Between 1976 and 1984, the Branch had eight different ministers, each with different priorities and different policy thrusts that were imposed on the sport community. These were challenging times.

In spite of many policy changes, federal and provincial monies allocated to the sport system continued to grow through the 1980s, allowing the sport bureaucracy to flourish and expand. Canada was the envy of most other governments in the Western industrialized nations that were striving for international supremacy (Macintosh and Bedecki, 1987, p. 180). Over that time period the federal government provided grant support for over 60 National Sport Organizations, which covered everything from the rental of office space and staff salaries to athlete assistance stipends and travel expenses.

In the mid-1980s, then Minister Otto Jelinek, a former world-class figure skater, challenged the National Sport Organizations to obtain 50 percent of their funding from private sources and established a Sport Marketing Council to encourage all NSOs to become more financially self-reliant. Unfortunately, the amateur sport bureaucracy had become very dependent on public funding over the previous 20 years, and many of the NSOs felt that the federal government would and should continue to support amateur sport at the same level. Because the government had always provided for sport, most were not motivated to search out other sources of funding beyond membership fees and government grants. However, much to the disbelief of many sport leaders, government funding for sport in the 1990s reached an all-time low.

It has only been in recent years that many sport leaders are beginning to understand that the government's priorities are not necessarily those of sport and that the monies received by sport must be used to address the government's priorities, which are generally less to do with athlete and infrastructure development and more to do with national identity and international prestige.

Structure and roles within the current Canadian sport system

The Canadian sport system was built by government in the image of government and is in every way a bureaucracy, with all of the strengths and limitations of that type of an organizational structure.

In the late 1980s and early 1990s many members of the sport community felt that too great a portion of the federal monies were being used to support the development of the infrastructure and not enough funds were reaching the athletes and being used for athlete development. In 1992, Fitness and Amateur Sport released a task force report entitled *Sport: The Way Ahead*. This report was prepared in response to several broader policy implications documented in the *Report of the Commission of Inquiry into the Use of Drugs and Other Banned Practices Intended to Increase Athletic Performance* (Dubin Report) which was released in 1990. Specifically, the task force was asked to examine the purpose and place of sport in society, the underlying values and ethics that should shape its conduct, the roles and responsibilities of the Canadian NSOs, and the federal government's future role in sport policy and programs (Fitness and Amateur Sport, 1992, p. 8). Among the many recommendations included in this report was an emphasis on the need to design and implement new community-centered models for the development of sport, to be created in partnership with provincial government and other stakeholders (Fitness and Amateur Sport, 1992) (see Figure 8-1).

The emphasis on the development of community-centered sport has remained a central theme within the Canadian sport community; however, there has been little success in recreating the system, in the way that the task force report was suggesting. Large gaps still exist between what is happening at the community level, at the provincial level, and at the level of national sport programming. Part of this issue relates to the complex sport bureaucracy that has

evolved in Canada. Each NSO has its own delivery system for its programs and services, and it is rare for sports to work together to address the common sport needs of participants and athletes in a province or a community. Additionally, there is often a competitive attitude by the sport leaders within one sport organization, where the provincial sport members refuse to cooperate or share information with their national counterparts. The same problem often applies to the relationship between PSOs and their respective community clubs. Unfortunately, the situation has worsened in recent years, as public funding for sport has been reduced and competition for new resources has become more intense.

The harsh reality of reduced funds to amateur sport appeared in the mid-1990s as the federal government began to act on redefining and streamlining its role in funding amateur sport. Drastic cuts were made across the board, crippling many sport organizations. The number of NSOs receiving federal support was cut in half. When federal and provincial governments decided that it was time to

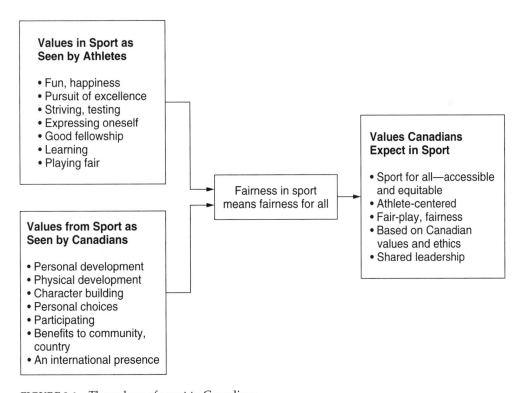

FIGURE 8-1 The values of sport to Canadians.

reduce the deficit, sport was seen as a "frill" that could be done without.

New sport policy for Canada

In 2003 the Fitness and Amateur Sport Act (1961) was replaced by the Physical Activity and Sport Act **(Bill C-54)** in order to better respond to the complexities of the modern world of sport. The purpose of the bill is to encourage, promote, and develop sport and physical activity. Further, "its intent is to reflect and strengthen the important role that the Government of Canada plays with respect to physical activity and sport" (Sport Canada Website).

In conjunction with the tabling and approval of the new act, **Sport Canada** spearheaded a consultative process that resulted in a new **Canadian Sport Policy.** The stated Vision of the Canadian Sport Policy is to have, by 2012, a dynamic and leading-edge sport environment that enables all Canadians to experience and enjoy involvement in sport to the extent of their abilities and, for increasing numbers, to perform consistently and successfully at the highest competitive levels (Canadian Sport Policy, 2002). The four goals of the policy are: enhanced participation, enhanced excellence, enhanced capacity, and enhanced interaction. It is hoped that the vision and goals of the new policy will be achieved by the development and implementation of four action plans: a federal government action plan; individual action plans by specific provincial/territorial governments; a collaborative federal-provincial/territorial government action plan; and action plans undertaken by sport communities.

This new focus on physical activity (along with the continuing focus on sport) is a departure from previous sport policy. Some sport leaders see this as a strong government mandate and significant opportunity to address needed work at the grass roots to increase sport participation in communities. Others feel that this goal of "enhanced participa-tion" will not be fully addressed by governments or the sport community because the time and resources needed to make a difference will not be committed. Some believe that many sport leaders do not really understand the larger roles that sport has to play in society, roles that relate to health issues, socio-cultural issues, and community capacity building.

The current role of Canadian governments in sport and physical activity

The federal government supports sport through Sport Canada, a branch within the Department of Canadian Heritage. Sport Canada's mission is to support the achievement of high-performance excellence and the development of the Canadian sport system to strengthen the unique contribution that sport makes to Canadian identity, culture, and society (Sport Canada Website). It funds amateur sport at the national level through national sport, multi-sport and multiservice organizations. The annual support varies from year to year. Generally, the more successful its athletes are internationally, the greater the funding support to a National Sport Organization (see Figure 8-2).

The federal government supports sport to the extent that sport allows it to meet such objectives as assisting Canada in having a strong international presence or contributing to the country's sense of heritage. These funds are used to provide athlete assistance (e.g., living expense money while the athlete is training), administrative assistance for the national office (e.g., staff salaries, board of directors meetings), coaches training, and travel and monies in support of travel to or the hosting of major national or international games. Each sport organization must submit complete documentation and meet stringent funding guidelines to receive financial support from the federal government.

The federal government has supported, to a limited extent, physical activity through the Department of Health. As the implementation of the various action plans for the implementation of the Canadian Sport Policy unfold, it will be interesting to observe the extent to which Sport Canada and Health Canada are able to successfully collaborate to address common areas of increasing participation in physical activity.

At the provincial/territorial government level, the 10 provinces and three territories have different priorities for funding their sport organizations and provide differing amounts of grant monies on an annual basis. In Ontario, for example, the provincial government recognizes and values sport's contributions to profiling Ontario nationally and internationally. Currently, given the government's desire to reduce health care costs, it recognizes physical activity as a vehicle to a healthier lifestyle for Ontarians and is supporting sport to play a bigger role in health promotion.

Municipal governments provide funding to support community sport across towns and cities in Canada, primarily through their respective Departments of Parks and Recreation or Departments of Community Services. Municipal governments, up until the last five years, delivered many sport programs directly to community members. Recently, more and more are working in partnership with community sport groups, which then deliver such activities as tennis lessons, figure skating lessons, or swimming lessons.

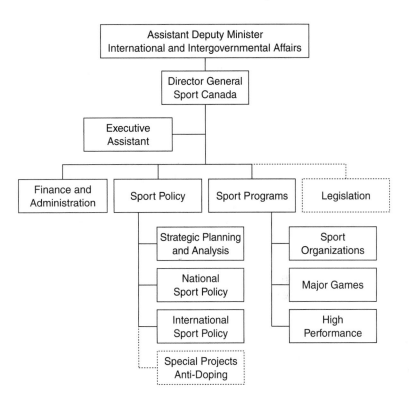

FIGURE 8-2   Sport Canada's organizational structure.

The role of the Canadian Olympic Committee (COC)

The **Canadian Olympic Committee** (previously the Canadian Olympic Association) is a not-for-profit, nongovernmental organization and the second largest contributor of financial assistance to Canadian athletes, coaches, and sport organizations (next to the federal government). It is responsible for all aspects of Canada's involvement in the Olympic movement, including Canada's participation in the Olympic and Pan American Games and a wide variety of programs that promote the Olympic Movement in Canada through cultural and educational means. The COC is governed by a volunteer board of directors and has 33 employees located in regional offices across Canada. In 1997, the COC generated over $7 million, primarily from marketing initiatives in sponsorship, licensing, and special events, and expended over $11 million on athletes, national sport organizations, and sporting events (COA Annual

Report, 1997, p. 8). It is also responsible for the Canadian Olympic Foundation, which manages several segregated funds in excess of $100 million.

The role of the Calgary Olympic Development Association

"CODA is Canada's leader in developing Olympic winter sport excellence" (CODA Website). As indicated in its mission statement, the primary responsibility of the **Calgary Olympic Development Association (CODA)** is to winter sport athletes and organizations. The CODA board of directors has grown the 1988 Olympic Games legacy from $80 million to $200 million in a decade and will contribute to the support of winter sport athletes and facilities even more substantially for the coming decade (1998 CODA Annual Report).

The role of the Coaching Association of Canada

Established in 1971, the **Coaching Association of Canada (CAC)** has the mission to "enhance the experience of all Canadian athletes through quality coaching" (CAC Website). Its four core strategies are: coach education and training; professionalization and membership; promotion and communications; and resource and organizational development.

The 3M National Coaching Certification Program (NCCP), one of the major programs of the CAC, provides information and training to promote coaching excellence and establishes minimum behavioral standards for active coaches. The program is designed to increase knowledge about general theory, provide technical information, and transfer knowledge to practice through experiential learning. Levels 1 through 3 of the NCCP teach fundamentals for coaches at the community, regional, and provincial sport levels. Levels 4 and 5 are aimed at coaches developing athletes for national and international competition.

Through the NCCP, coaches have been certified in every province and territory. Since its inception, more than 875,000 coaches have taken part in the program, which has helped them to develop the skills, knowledge, and attitudes required to coach effectively (CAC Website).

Currently the NCCP is undergoing a transition to a competency-based approach. A coach is trained and may achieve certification to coach a specific type of participant in a particular coaching environment. It will be up to each sport to determine which streams and contexts apply to its development system. The abilities deemed important to coach in a given context determine the scope of training required. It is anticipated that some aspects of the new NCCP will be in place by 2004.

The roles of National and Provincial Sport Organizations

There are approximately 60 National Sport Organizations (NSOs) in Canada, each serving a different sport (e.g., Basketball Canada, Tennis Canada). Each of these not-for-profit organizations has a twofold mandate: to provide Canadians with opportunities to participate (participation development) and to support the development of high-performance athletes (high-performance development). High performance means that the athlete is skilled enough to be able to compete at a national or an international level. Almost all of these organizations received financial support from the federal government in the 1970s and 1980s; however, less

than half are now eligible. Generally, those NSOs able to produce athletes that bring home medals from international competitions are supported by Sport Canada funding. Now, under the new Canadian Sport Policy, funds are also available to those NSOs that are making efforts to increase ongoing participation, recruit new participants, and reduce drop-out rates.

Each NSO is governed by a volunteer board of directors, generally comprising people who represent each province or region across the country, and often the board will have representation from members of the business community who are well connected and can assist with revenue generation. The role of these governing boards is to make policy decisions that will provide a framework for those within the organization to work toward common goals. In reality, what often happens is that boards become tangled up in the technical aspects of the sport (e.g., who should be on the national team) and lose sight of their mandate as "trustees of the game." The memberships of NSOs generally comprise each province, and each pays a membership fee based on population size. Some NSO memberships are based on "regional" boundaries rather than provincial boundaries, and still others have individual or club-based memberships at the national level.

NSOs have differing sizes of staff complements. Generally all have an executive director, general manager, or chief executive officer who reports directly to the board and who is responsible for carrying out the policy decisions of the board through his/her staff. Other staff positions in a national office could include: national coach, technical director, program coordinators (e.g., coaching, competitions). Staff sizes range from less than 5 to greater than 50 for organizations such as Skate Canada and Tennis Canada.

CONCEPT CHECK

It is the role of each National Sport Organization to address both the development of high-performance athletes and to increase participation. Often the organization's role in high performance takes precedence, sometimes at the expense of growing the sport and making it accessible for all Canadians.

Each NSO in Canada is governed by an International Sport Federation, which establishes the rules of the sport and, among other things, determines where its respective international competitions will be held. There are also a number of other national sport organizations with which each NSO needs to communicate (see Figure 8-3).

Each NSO has a provincial counterpart, and some have organizations in the Northwest Territories and the Yukon. It is the mandate of each Provincial Sport Organization to provide participation opportunities and athlete development opportunities for the people in its respective province. Just as the national mandate of the NSO is often skewed more toward high-performance

development (sometimes at the expense of participation development), so are the activities of the PSOs (e.g., Ontario Tennis Association, Athletics Ontario). A strong focus on participation or grass roots development is a difficult, time-consuming, and resource-consuming commitment, and the results are not immediate, which discourages many PSO boards from fully realizing their mandates in this area.

The memberships of PSOs most often comprise community sport clubs, be they private or public. Each club pays a fee to access the programs and services of the PSO, and this fee is usually based on the number of members in that club. Ironically, in some provinces, the relationship between the PSO and its

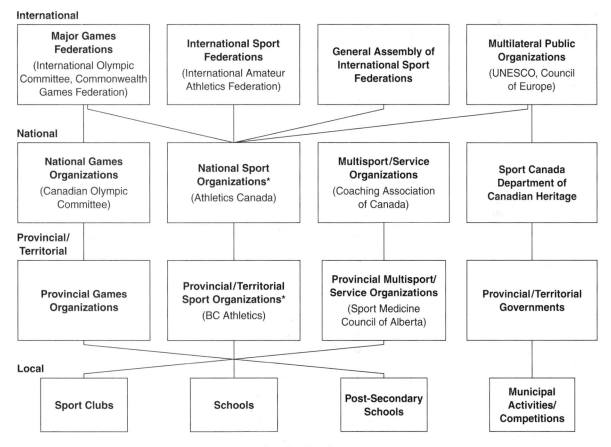

*Also includes associations for athletes with disabilities (e.g., Canadian Blind Sport Association)

FIGURE 8-3   The Canadian sport community infrastructure. Organizations in parentheses are cited as examples.

member clubs is competitive rather than collaborative. This is an issue that can have many negative ramifications for that sport.

Community sport organizations

There are hundreds of thousands of community sport clubs across Canada, and they comprise the heart of the amateur sport system. Without community sport, there would be no sport. It is here that children are exposed to the sport experience for the first time, and the extent to which that experience is positive will have an impact on that child for the rest of his or her life. Community sport organizations are generally volunteer-driven, usually by a small group of dedicated people or sometimes by one community champion. Interestingly, although there are often several sport clubs or minor sport organizations in one small town, seldom do they join forces to advocate or to generate revenue.

Further, seldom is there collaboration with the parks and recreation department in that town, although both are providing sport programs and services. School sport is the other major sport delivery partner at the community level, and too often schools have parallel sport systems that do not communicate with sport clubs or parks and recreation. The impact that this is having on the system is huge. Many precious resources and programs are being duplicated.

Sport participation in Canada

Sport participation is on a decline in Canada. In 1998, 34 percent of Canadians 15 years of age or more (8.3 million) participated regularly in one or more sports. This number is down by 11 percent from the 45 percent (9.6 million) that reported participating in 1992 (Statistics Canada, 2000). The Canadian sport system supports 3,000,000 registered athletes of national and provincial sport organizations, 850 carded high-performance athletes, 400,000 coaches, and 1,000,000 volunteers (Coaches Report, 1998, p. 23).

It was also found that more men (43 percent) than women (26 percent) were active sport participants. Twice as many men participated through clubs, leagues, recreation programs, and provincial sport organizations (Coaches Report, ibid.).

Sport participation levels decrease dramatically as Canadians age. The younger the individual, the more likely he/she is to participate in sport. Unfortunately, this active lifestyle does not seem to continue beyond our 20s. Statistics Canada (2000) also reported that the higher the education and household income, the higher the sport participation rate.

There are some regional and provincial differences in participation rates across the country. In 1998, residents of Atlantic Canada and Ontario were reported to have the lowest levels of participation, while Quebec, Alberta, and British Columbia report the highest.

Golf, hockey, baseball, and swimming were by far the sports most frequently reported as most popular by adult Canadians (Statistics Canada, 1998). Golf has replaced hockey as the number one sport activity reported. Over 1.8 million Canadians reported playing golf on a regular basis in 1998, compared to 1.3 million in 1992. Hockey ranked second with 1.5 million adult Canadians playing hockey.

Swimming, golf, baseball, and volleyball (in descending order) were the sports of choice for women 15 years or older, while men preferred hockey, golf, baseball, or basketball. Just over half (54 percent) of Canadian children aged 5–14 were actively involved in sport. Girls (48 percent) tend to be less active in sport than boys (61 percent).

There are many factors that influence sport participation. Research on Canadian children has found that the following factors have a positive influence on children's participation: fun, learning and skill improvement, being with friends, success and winning, and physical fitness and health. Children drop out of sport due to: competitive stress, parental pressure, lack of fun, lack of playing time, limited opportunities for improvement, and/or dislike of the coach (Coaching Report, 1998, p. 24).

A TIME FOR CHANGE IN THE CANADIAN SPORT SYSTEM

The Canadian sport system has matured over the past 30 years. Its stability over that period of time, due to a steady flow of government dollars, made it the envy of most other countries. The achievements of organizations like the Canadian Figure Skating Association and Hockey Canada attested to the success of the system. More recently, Bill C-54 and the Canadian Sport Policy would seem to indicate a renewed commitment by government to provide new resources that will both increase the number of Canadians who are physically active and support our high-performance athletes more fully.

However, the results of these new policy actions will not be seen overnight. Many issues still plague the Canadian sport system. From a high-performance perspective, Canadian athletes and teams have not been dominating the national and international scene, even in hockey, which has always been used as a barometer of success. Funding reductions to sport through the 1990s have taken their toll. The sport community has not been able to replace these funds through other sources, and consequently it has had less money to support athlete development as well as grass-roots development.

The chart below indicates some of the paradigm shifts that need to take place if the Canadian sport system is to continue to grow and prosper.

Paradigm Shifts Needed in the Canadian Amateur Sport System

Element	From	To
Structure	centralized	decentralized
Funding	single funding source (public)	diversified funding sources (public and private)
Leadership	government-directed	sport-directed
Policy-Making	government-centered	sport-centered
Delivery System	vertical and duplicative	partnered and cost-efficient

So what can be done to improve the Canadian sport system?

Certainly the full implementation of the Canadian Sport Policy will help, but we do not yet know the extent to which major stakeholders (governments and not-for-profit sport organizations) will develop and implement their respective action plans. If Sport Canada does not lead by example over the coming years, providing new resources and innovative thinking to address excellence, participation, capacity, and interaction, it is unlikely that the other stakeholders at the national, provincial/territorial, and community levels will follow through with their plans.

Even with the new policy, many feel that important systemic needs have not been fully addressed, needs such as:

- Educating sport leaders about how to build community capacity through sport and for sport (thereby increasing participation).
- Creating and maintaining lasting partnerships between and among sport and government interest groups.
- Overhauling the current ineffective sport delivery system.
- Filling the national sport leadership void.

Too often sport participation is seen only as an end in itself rather than as a means to an end. Community leaders need to understand the benefits of physical activity participation to their towns or cities, and sport leaders must be proactive in working with community leaders to provide sport and physical activity opportunities for all residents, thereby creating more sport participants and healthy, active communities.

Canada's high-performance athletes and their coaches have pointed to facility access as a primary need. Sport Canada in partnership with such organizations as the Canadian Olympic Committee, the Coaching Association of Canada, the Calgary Olympic Development Association, and the respective provincial governments have joined forces to create six multisport training centers across Canada. The creation of these centers is one of the most promising consequences of the growing acceptance by Canada's sport leadership that the key to survival is partnership.

The sport delivery system overall is still structured in a very redundant and isolated fashion. NSOs and PSOs, as well as many community sport clubs, are trying to operate within the delivery system of their own sport exclusively rather than collaborating with other sport organizations or community groups to reduce costs and improve service.

Sport Canada, the federal agency responsible for providing funds to NSOs, now restricts its funding to 38 organizations (from 63 organizations in the late 1980s), leaving almost half of Canada's national sport organizations in financial limbo with no link to the national system. Sport Canada's budget of approximately $60 million is a minor investment in a system that addresses so many of the government's priority issues. If the new Canadian Sport Policy is to have teeth, significantly greater financial support from Sport Canada must be forthcoming, as well as support from nongovernment sources.

CONCEPT CHECK

The amateur sport delivery system in Canada is in need of a major overhaul. Each NSO and PSO, as well as many community sport clubs, deliver their sport programs to the same target populations and often end up competing with each other, rather than looking at ways to work collaboratively toward common goals, saving time and money.

Many sport organizations are still overly dependent on government support and look to government officials to provide leadership and policy direction, still not understanding that sport's priorities are not necessarily the government's priorities. The Canadian sport system needs to become self-led. The current leadership has become too dependent on government to define its future. This is not to say that governments should not continue as funding partners for NSOs and PSOs, but the sport system needs to establish its own leadership structure, make policy decisions, and decide what the best use of its collective resources is. Although some organizations have surfaced in the last few years (e.g., Athletes Can, Active Living Coalition), it is too soon to know if they will be seen as leaders by the sport and physical activity community.

The health of the Canadian amateur sport system will depend upon the willingness of sport organizations and their potential partners to let go of the past and grab hold of the future, collectively growing sport for athletes and participants alike.

SUMMARY

- This chapter addressed the Olympic Movement as a model of international sport management. Sport is a global business. In becoming a better sport manager, one must not limit one's knowledge to the domestic arena. Because we are involved in a global economy, it is important for the sport manager of the future to understand the globalization of sport. The Olympic Movement is probably the best example of this globalization. Specifically, the focus has been on the Olympic Movement, since the Olympic Games are often used as a model of international sporting event. It is important to understand the structure of the Olympic Movement, including the International Olympic Committee, the National Olympic Committees, the International Federations, the National Governing Bodies or National Federations, and the organizing committees of the Olympic Games. Specifically, we have described the United States Olympic Committee for its role in the Olympic Movement and as it is considered one of the most developed NOCs in the world.

- We have also addressed the role of professional sport leagues in the global community. Especially the National Football League and the National Basketball Association have focused their interest in exporting their sport and their brand to other countries. Using television and the Internet as their major vehicles has been very successful. Preseason games played overseas have helped tremendously, positioning their brands in these foreign territories and increasing their popularity.

- Football is a very popular sport played on the six continents but it has had a hard time in the United States. However, after the success of the 1994 World Cup, football seemed to have a better acceptance in the United States. As a result, a professional league started in 1996. The league has had its struggles but overall has been successful. Women's soccer also acquired big popularity when the 1999 World Cup was played in the United States. An international professional women's soccer league started in 2001. The league has not been that successful and it had to cease operations at the end of the 2003 season.

- Some sports have a harder time than others gaining popularity and recognition. Sometimes it is a lack of financial support, but many times it is a cultural barrier that needs to be crossed.

- The Canadian sport system was created by the federal government in the early 1960s.
- After 1970 a number of national sport and multisport organizations came into being, including the Coaching Association of Canada, Hockey Canada, and ParticipACTION.
- Although Canadian government funding of sport increased steadily through the 1970s and 1980s, drastic cuts took place in the 1990s when the government was questioning the significance of sport's contributions to its objectives and in light of the focus on reducing the deficit.
- In 2003 sport legislation was changed with the passing of Bill C-54 and the implementation of the Canadian Sport Policy.
- The sport system in Canada is based on a bureaucratic structure that is duplicative and competitive, often not providing the best service to athletes or participants.
- Changes need to be made in the Canadian system to rebuild the delivery system, educate sport leaders about how to develop physical activity and sport capacity in communities, and establish nongovernment sport leadership.

 CRITICAL THINKING EXERCISES

1. If Paris and Lyon, two French cities, are interested in bidding to host the 2012 Olympic Games, what National Olympic Committee will be responsible for appointing one of the two as the bid city?
2. If New York is elected to host the 2012 Olympic Games, what NOC will be responsible for signing agreement along with the city and the IOC?
3. Should government subsidize not-for-profit sport organizations? Many people think that government should continue to fund, but others disagree, feeling the public dollars would best be spent in other areas. What do you think and why?
4. How does the Canadian sport system need to change to reduce duplication of resources and to better serve both high-performance athletes and recreational participants?

 CASE STUDY I

The board members of the Fédération Internationale des Quilleurs (International Bowling Federation) have decided in their last meeting to pursue the inclusion of bowling in the Olympic program. They understand that such effort will take some years. You, as the executive director of the Fédération Internationale des Quilleurs, have been asked to put together a long-term plan with the objective of having the sport of bowling be included in the Olympic program. What steps will you need to follow? What are the International Olympic Committee requirements for a sport to be included in the Olympic program? When will you present the request to the International Olympic Committee? What would be the first Games that bowling could be included as an Olympic sport?

 CASE STUDY II

"To lead the growth of tennis and foster the pursuit of excellence for all players." This is the mission statement of Tennis Canada. As the chief executive officer of this National Sport Organization, you have been concerned about participation in the sport. Club membership numbers have stayed much the same over the past several years, and although they are serving their members well, it is important for Tennis Canada to play a role in growing the game.

You commissioned a study to find out how many people were playing tennis in Canada and where they were playing. Upon completion of this market research, it became clear that a significant number of people were playing tennis but that most of them were being introduced to the sport on public courts provided by parks and recreation departments outside of the tennis club "family." In fact, about two-thirds of the adults and half of the children that had played tennis at least once in the past year had played in the summer on public courts. You know that the tennis club system has little communication with the municipal parks and recreation system, and that in some communities, due to funding cuts, parks and recreation

*departments are not maintaining some public tennis
courts or continuing their tennis programming.
Also, some municipalities do not offer tennis because
they do not have qualified instructors in the
community.*

*Given this information, and your knowledge of the
sport system in Canada, what actions might you take
to ensure that Tennis Canada fulfills its role in
stimulating participation and growing the club
system?*

REVIEW QUESTIONS AND ISSUES

1. Define the Olympic Movement.
2. Discuss the relationship among the International Olympic Committee, International Federations, National Olympic Committees, and Organizing Committees of the Olympic Games.
3. Name your National Olympic Committee and define its organizational structure.
4. Name the two international sport competitions the United States Olympic Committee is responsible to send U.S. athletes to as stated in the 1978 Amateur Sport Act.
5. Not all the International Federations are part of the Olympic program. Do you see it as an advantage or disadvantage to be part of the Olympic program?
6. What has the NBA done to make its brand popular overseas? What other activities would you propose to help in this international recognition?
7. Why do you think a women's professional football league has not been completely successful in the United States?
8. Why did the Canadian federal government decide to use public funds to support sport?
9. What year was Bill C-131 enacted to encourage both fitness and amateur sport development? What new bill has recently been passed?
10. When did the Canadian government decide to reduce funding to sport organizations and why?
11. What are the goals of the Canadian Sport Policy and how will this policy be implemented across the country?

12. In addition to the federal government, what other organizations play a role in funding athlete development?
13. For what program is the Coaching Association of Canada known internationally? What does this program provide?
14. How does a National Sport Organization link with its community clubs to deliver its programs?
15. What types of paradigm shifts need to be made in the Canadian sport system and why?

SOLUTIONS TO CRITICAL THINKING EXERCISES

1. Since Paris and Lyon are in France, the French Olympic Committee, Comité National Olympique at Sportif Français, will have the authority to designate the city as a candidate to host the 2012 Olympic Games.
2. New York as the host city will have to sign the agreement with the IOC and the United States Olympic Committee, its NOC.
3. Government departments and agencies fund organizations that provide services and do things that the government wants done. Often, these are services that the government feels are important but that it itself cannot deliver, so it delegates the job to voluntary organizations. The not-for-profit sport organization receives public funds with strict funding guidelines attached. This often puts the sport organization at the mercy of changes in government policies and programs, leaving it in a very precarious financial position.

   The government may even try to interfere in the sport organization's management on the grounds that the money comes from the public purse and the government therefore has a duty to be involved in the organization's day-to-day administration. Sport leaders ought not to accept such interference. For while it is natural that they should be accountable to their members, they should not be accountable to the state, which is not a member.

   On the other hand, sport is an important part of the cultural fabric of our society and pivotal in maintaining our national identity. It is government's responsibility to support those organizations that contribute to these areas. Government funding provides the seed, the starting point, from which sport organizations can reach out and gain wider individual and business support.

Governments should be involved in supporting the sport system in Canada. However, sport organizations have been overly dependent on government funding for too long. Sport leaders need to diversify their sources of income and their services and find ways to increase their self-financing in order to be less dependent on government funding and less vulnerable to the changing political winds.

4. The structure of the sport system in Canada is very bureaucratic, and as such it is subject to many layers of administration and duplication. Each National Sport Organization has its own delivery system for its programs and services, and more often than not, all are trying to reach the same target markets at the same time. From a high-performance perspective, each NSO has independently trained its own national-level athletes. From a participation development perspective, a single high school or elementary school might have at least a dozen sport organizations that want to access children with their programs. It is difficult for a school principal or physical education teacher to respond to all of these requests or to make decisions about what is best to offer the child. Sometimes the education leader will just reject all requests because it is too time-consuming to sort out the advantages and disadvantages of each proposal.

It is a similar situation between the sport system and the municipal recreation system in Canada. Both offer sport programs, but often there is very little communication between sport leaders and recreation leaders, so both often end up offering the same services in a community when resources and energies could be combined.

How can this duplication of services and resources be minimized? From a high-performance-athlete-development perspective, multisport training centers are a good start. Athletes share support services and re-

ceive top-notch coaching. From a participation-development perspective, one solution involves the building of partnerships among sport leaders, so that, for example, a number of sports might work in collaboration on introductory programs for kids or for adults. Sport leaders also need to work more closely with the recreation leaders and school leaders in communities to ensure that they are collectively offering the best range of services that are accessible and affordable.

FOSTERING YOUR WORKPLACE SKILLS

1. Analyze the feasibility of starting a Basketball World League.
2. Develop a strategic plan to convince public and private companies and organizations that your city has potential as a future host of the Olympic Games.
3. Develop a manual to assist those cities that are thinking of bidding to host the Olympic Games in your country.
4. Analyze the role of the Canadian government in supporting the development of sport and physical education at the grassroots level.
5. As executive director of the Canadian Figure Skating Association, develop a business plan to run your organization.

 WEBSITES

Canadian Olympic Committee
http://www.coc.ca—This site describes the mission and governance structure of the COC, as well as providing up-to-date information on major games and Canadian athletes.
Coaching Association of Canada
http://www.coach.ca—This site describes the mission and major programs of the CAC, including the 3M National Coaching Certification Program and other related programs. There is a link to the Canadian professional Coaches Association, as well as information about coaching tips, conferences and seminars.
International Olympic Committee
www.olympic.org—Students planning to pursue a career in the international sport marketplace can use the information available in this Website to become more knowledgeable about the governance of international sport.

Sport Canada, Department of Canadian Heritage
http://www.pch.gc.ca/sportcanada/—This site describes Sport Canada's mandate, structure, programs and policies. It also overviews the sport system in Canada, major games and sporting events, and selected sport facts. For information on specific Canadian Sport Organizations, there is a link with the majority of sport and multisport organizations in the country.

United States Olympic Committee
www.olympic-usa.org—Students planning to pursue a career in the Olympics can look at this Website and find out more about the United States Olympic Committee, considered the most developed NOC in the world.

REFERENCES

Associated Press. (2003). Reebok signs Yao with eye toward China. *Philadelphia Inquirer*. October 24.

Association of National Olympic Committees. (1998). *Yearbook 1998*.

Calgary Olympic Development Association. (1998). *Annual Report*. Calgary, Alberta, Canada.

Canadian Olympic Association. (1997). *Annual Report*. Toronto, Ontario, Canada.

The Contribution of Coaching in Canada. (1998). *Coaches Report*, 5(2), 18–24.

Fleischman, Bill. (2003). Women's sports can't get women to watch. *Philadelphia Daily News*, September 19.

International Olympic Committee. (2002). Unprecedented Winter Games Marketing Success. *Olympic Marketing Matters*, June 1.

International Olympic Committee. (2003). *The Olympic Charter*. Lausanne, Switzerland: IOC.

International Olympic Committee. (2003). The International Olympic Committee. htpp://www.olympic.org.

Jensen, Mike. (2003). WUSA players looking to find a new avenue. *Philadelphia Inquirer*, September 19.

Liberman, Noah. (1999). TV partners provide juice to Net sites. *Street @ Smith's Sport Business Journal*, 2, no. 3, 21.

Macintosh, D., and Bedecki, T. (1987). *Sport and politics in Canada*. Kingston: McGill-Queens University Press.

Macintosh, D., and Whitson, D. (1990). *The Game Planners*. Kingston: McGill-Queens University Press.

Major League Soccer. (2003). MLS Year-by-year season overview. http://www.mlsnet.com/archive/year-by-year.html.

Minister of State, Fitness and Amateur Sport. (1992). *Sport the Way Ahead*. Ottawa, Ministry of Supply and Services Canada.

National Basketball League. (2003). NBA Preseason 2003 Tips Off. October 5. http://www.nba.com/schedules/preseason_030807.html.

National Basketball League. (2003). NBA. http://www.nba.com/global/index.html.

National Football League International. (2003). Foreign-born players in the NFL. http://www.nfl.com/international/foreignborn010822.html.

National Football League International. (2003). Tight end Tony Gonzalez to promote American football in Brazil. http://www.nfl.com/international/story/6302149.

National Football League International. (2003). NFL coverage spans the globe—agreements bring football to Japan, China. http://www.nfl.com/international/story/6633757.

Novo, Carlos. (2003). Jacques Rogge: "Barcelona '92 avala a Madrid." *La Vanguardia*, December 17.

Reuters. (1999). History in the making. Women's soccer conquers the U.S. *Sports Illustrated*. http://www.sportsillustrated.cnn.com/soccer/world/1999/women's_worldcup/news/1999.

Sport Canada. (2002). *Canadian Sport Policy*. Ottawa.

Sport Ontario. (1992). *For the love of sport*. Toronto, Ontario Ministry of Tourism and Recreation.

Statistics Canada. (2000). *Sport participation in Canada*. Ottawa: Minister of Public Works and Government Services Canada.

Strengthening the Canadian Sport System. (1998). *Coaches Report*, 5(2), 4–11.

Thoma, James, and Chalip, Laurence. (1996). *Sport governance in the global community*. Morgantown, WV: Fitness Information Technology.

United States Olympic Committee. (1997). *97/98 Fact Book*. Colorado Springs, CO.

United States Olympic Committee. (1999). *Olympic beat*. Colorado Springs, CO. May, 14(4).

United States Olympic Committee. (2003). http://www.olympic-usa.org.

Wissot, Michael. (1999). Swinging for foreign fences is new "international pastime." *Street @ Smith's Sport Business Journal*, 2, no. 2, 40.

Women's United Soccer Association. (2003). History. http://www.wusa.com/about_us/history/.

Women's United Soccer Association. (2003). Update on the WUSA. http://www.wusa.com/.

CHAPTER 9

Managing the Facility

Aaron Mulrooney and Alvy Styles

In this chapter, you will become familiar with the following terms:

Attest function
Boilerplate contract
Booking
Bootleggers
Budget cycle
Contracted reservation
Convenience foods
Earned media
Event coordinator
Event settlement
External audit
Generally accepted accounting
  practices (GAAP)

Hawkers
Housekeeping
House expenses
In-house
Internal auditing process
Mission statement
Performance scale
Point of sale
Private seat license (PSL)
Promoter
Request for proposals (RFP)

Respondeat superior
Setup and breakdown
Standard operating procedures
  (SOPs)
Stocking
TEAM
Tentative-hold reservations
Walk-up sales
Will-call location
Vendors

Learning Goals
By the end of this chapter, students should be able to:

- Describe the various types of management that are prevalent in today's sport facilities.
- Identify the various types of organizational areas that are crucial to the successful operation of a facility.
- Describe some of the unique aspects of financial management and revenue generation that exist in facilities.
- Identify and describe some of the liability and safety concerns that a facility manager needs to address.

TYPES OF MANAGEMENT
There are a number of management alternatives. Facilities can be operated by their owners, by the primary or anchor tenants, by not-for-profit entities, or by private management companies.

Owner
This management organization may be public or private (Laventhol and Horwath, 1989). If the facility is owned or operated by a government agency, operational efficiency is constrained or reduced by

the regulations and procedures that are often associated with governmental bureaucracy. Such items as purchasing procedures; contract approval processes (often by the legislative body); hiring, promotion, and dismissal of personnel; and other government policies (including just plain politics, such as patronage) are just a few of the operational performance areas of the building that are affected by bureaucracy. To alleviate this situation, many publicly owned facilities have moved toward independent authorities, such as not-for-profit operations and private management companies (Laventhol and Horwath, 1989).

The main problems facing privately owned and managed facilities are enormous costs and human resources. Because of these burdens, many privately owned facilities have opted to move toward not-for-profit operations and private management companies.

Not-for-profit operations

These entities generally involve a commission or a board of directors, appointed by a governmental body to act as an agent of the local government (Laventhol and Horwath, 1989). This board is exempted from numerous government regulations and procedures in order to run an efficient facility. Over time, however, the quality of the board may deteriorate as political patronage and reputation become standard operating procedure.

Private management: The future alternative

Although sport facilities have traditionally been owned and governed by public authorities, the situation appears to be changing. Sport facilities were originally designed as a community economic-impact entity, but many facilities have become a drain on community resources. In difficult economic times, this burden on the taxpayer can be significant.

If a facility has significant problems or is unable to realize its managers' expectations, alternative management organizations, other than an **in-house** group, should be considered. One of these alternatives is private management. This type of management enables the governmental or institutional entity to maintain control over the facility, but with the opportunity to:

- Reduce or eliminate an operating deficit.
- Offer patrons improved service.

- Increase the quantity and quality of the events booked.
- Become part of a larger facility network, which would facilitate greater opportunities.
- Provide greater operational flexibility concerning policies and overall operational structure.

These advantages have enabled this facility management alternative to experience dramatic growth over the past decade. It is interesting to note that a number of different types of management groups—ranging from hotels, to food service groups, to specialty facility management groups—have entered this competitive arena. Each of these management groups evaluates a facility's needs based on its current financial picture, staffing requirements, marketing needs, event scheduling, and the political situation.

PRIVATE-MANAGEMENT SELECTION PROCESS

After resolving any obvious internal problems and disagreements, the facility's governing body will initiate the private-management selection process. The first step is the issuance of a **request for proposals (RFP)** (IAAM, 1990). This formal process begins with the issuance of statements outlining what is expected from a contracted management organization. Materials should be attached to provide the responding management organization with an overall picture of the facility's present situation. Such items as long- and short-term plans and projections, actual and projected budget and income, annual and usage reports, and existing contracts should be included.

The second step is dispatching the RFP document to all major management groups, as well as prominently displaying it in all appropriate trade and professional publications. The RFP bid response period varies from 30 to 90 days, depending upon conditions. The RFP also should indicate whether the bid will be a public process, open to the press, and whether bid proposals will be available to competitors (IAAM, 1990).

Third, all interested participants/bidders will be provided with a facility tour and an in-depth examination of the RFP. Addenda will be prepared as a result of the meeting between bidders and the facility's governing body.

Fourth, all proposals that are received before the deadline are reviewed by a designated body and finalists are determined. All bidders will be notified as to their success or failure in the bidding process. The finalists are provided with an opportunity to give a personal presentation to the review body. At this stage, the bidders have the right to know about their competition and the stage of the decision process. It is important that flexibility be part of the process, because bidders sometimes need to change their proposals as new information becomes available.

Fifth, following the personal presentations, one bidder should be selected to proceed into the negotiation stage, which involves representatives from both groups as well as legal assistance. Negotiations are initiated through a written document based on the RFP and the proposal. An agreement is apparent when there is resolution of the differences between these two documents.

The final (approval) stage comes at the end of the negotiation phase, when the final authority (e.g., the commission or state legislature) approves the contract (IAAM, 1990).

CONCEPT CHECK

Although many facilities are managed by their owners or by not-for-profit governmental agencies, the current trend is toward contracting with private management companies. These companies should be required to submit competitive bids through the request-for-proposals (RFP) process.

OPERATIONS

Operations are the most complex and comprehensive function in all of sport facility management. Facility operations managers have a wide variety of departmental responsibilities, including event coordinating, engineering, security, maintenance, and housekeeping. They must possess an adequate knowledge of budgeting, cost control, methodology, and negotiation skills to effectively complete their job responsibilities.

Operations of a sport facility vary significantly from the operations management of most businesses, although the underlying principles are similar. Operations management in a major sport facility focuses on how services are produced rather than

the production of those services, which is the traditional definition of operations management.

Management teams

A sport facility is operated by a management team. This team, depending upon the facility's size and function, is headed by an individual titled general manager, CEO, or executive director. Other members of this team oversee marketing, public relations, advertising, and operations. This section focuses on management functions, especially those associated with the general manager's office. These functions include philosophy, mission, policies and procedures, organizational elements, booking and scheduling, contracts, the management manual, and evaluation procedures.

Policies

A policy is a definitive course of action selected from various alternatives, in light of given conditions, to guide and determine present and future decisions. Policies are developed from the **mission statement,** which should be the basis for establishing all aspects of the operational procedures (Thompson and Strickland, 1990). A policy is the reason—the why—behind management's decision to function in a particular manner.

Procedures

Procedures are the "how" of accomplishing policies. They are the established, traditional way of doing something, and they include a series of steps to be followed by facility staff members to accomplish their assigned duties. From the outset, the manager will encounter numerous problems, from change orders to equipment purchases to overseeing the entire project to ensure that the final product is what was intended. Prior to the facility's opening, the building manager should establish a philosophy and tone, as well as appropriate building policies and operational procedures. These general policies and procedures should then be effectively communicated to staff, tenants, and the general public in a manner that clearly reflects the parameters under which the facility is to be used.

Philosophy

The philosophy of the facility manager should provide a basis for establishing guidelines and a proper orientation to operations. This philosophy may be based on the attitude that the facility should either serve the community without concern for profit and proper management control or exhibit fiscal responsibility through the control of appropriations and revenues, with the goal of breaking even or earning profit. A combination of the two approaches might be preferable to the either/or philosophy, but local circumstances might dictate the final choice.

Mission statement and goals and objectives

The operation of all facilities is guided by a mission statement or an operational direction. While many facility organizations, especially those tied to government agencies or large corporations, have formal mission statements, others operate with general and wide-ranging guidelines. It is these mission guidelines that provide the parameters for developing an organization's budget.

Goals and objectives that support and justify the facility's mission, or statement of purpose, need to be developed. They should be developed by competent management and compiled from input from all operational personnel (Hitt, 1985).

Goals are the achievable statements of purpose, or expectations, provided by management personnel. If fulfilled, they justify the fiscal resources requested in the budget document. Generally, sport facility goals are not as formalized as in other industries (e.g., increase sales by 18 percent and open new markets in the South).

Objectives are the supporting qualifications of the specified goals, not the goals themselves. All objectives should be measurable, quantifiable, and subjective. Most facilities, depending on their size, are departmentalized, but management should involve all personnel, regardless of their duties. This participative-management approach (a bottom-up rather than top-down approach) is vital if all personnel are expected to support the mission, goals, and objectives of the facility.

CONCEPT CHECK

To be successful as an entertainment complex, a sport facility must define its mission, philosophy, procedures, and policies, as well as establish specific goals and objectives.

ORGANIZATIONAL AREAS

Within a facility, there are important operational areas that need to be considered in order for the facility to operate smoothly and effectively, including:

- Booking and scheduling
- Marketing, public relations, and advertising
- Security
- Safety and medical services
- Housekeeping and maintenance
- Box office
- Concessions and novelties
- Traffic and parking
- Financial management
- Risk management

BOOKING AND SCHEDULING

Event booking and scheduling is one of the most important areas of concern in maintaining a facility. A facility without events has little or no purpose. Events are the primary source of revenue and the lifeblood of any facility. In addition, booking and scheduling and public relations are the departments most responsible for molding the facility's image by direct association with the sponsor and by their ability to coordinate the facility's schedule.

To comprehend the different approaches to scheduling, a facility's mandate must be understood. Facilities differ not only in their public/private management approach but also in their mission. A public facility is obligated to provide for the scheduling of community events, whereas a private facility, depending upon its formation agreement, may limit charitable and nonprofit activities.

A privately operated facility has the ability to promote its own events, although many do not because of legal ramifications. A privately managed facility can actively court business and aggressively seek to attract events by bidding or presenting comprehensive proposals to promoters.

Whatever the facility's purpose and mission is, the general approach to booking is reserving a specific space, within a specific facility, for a specific date, at a specific time, for an agreed-upon amount of money. **Booking** is the act of engaging and contracting an event or attraction.

Attracting an event

The first step in securing an event is the development of a positive public image. One key to developing a positive image is the production of a facility brochure, detailing the specifications of the building, staff, types of events, and event suitability. A well-planned and -produced informational brochure should be directed to all individuals who might be interested in securing the facility for a planned event. Events that are successful should be featured prominently in future facility publications, which should be revised annually.

Other elements in attracting events are maintaining visibility with local and national promoters, visiting appropriate trade fairs and conventions, and networking with other facilities. Success in booking an event is much more likely to result not from walk-in trade but from whom you know.

Scheduling

Scheduling is the reservation process and coordination of all events to fit the facility's available time. This reservation process involves scheduling a series of like events (e.g., football games or symphony concerts) and providing the best possible event mix to fit the facility's usage. Event dates must be properly spaced (not overlap). Individuals responsible for scheduling must have an in-depth knowledge of operational functions and be able to secure the appropriate number of events for the facility while not overtaxing the staff, overworking the building, overspending the budget, or saturating the marketplace.

For the scheduling process to maintain its cohesiveness, it is imperative that the record of scheduled events be solely under the control of a single individual who writes and erases information from the scheduling book. Changes in arrangements and notification of event alterations are the designated individual's unique responsibility.

Reservation process

There are two categories of reservations for space in a public facility, tentative and confirmed.

Tentative-hold reservations are made when an organization requests a specific date and time on the facility calendar but no actual contract has been prepared. If another organization desires the same date and time and can provide the necessary earnest money, the facility scheduler will contact the original tentatively scheduled organization and inquire about its intention to book the facility. It is not uncommon to have a succession of first, second, and

third tentative holds on a given date or set of dates because they are often requested a year or more in advance.

After notification, confirmation will be requested and a contract readied. Customarily, the facility notifies the scheduled organization of its placement and any resultant changes in the schedule.

A confirmed reservation, or **contracted reservation**, refers to an organization that has placed a deposit for the agreed-upon date and time and contract negotiations have commenced. A facility should establish guidelines concerning the length of the time a tentative hold may remain on record. At the same time, the facility should be as flexible as possible about the confirmation period. Different types of events require different confirmation and condition deadlines, depending on circumstances and the promoter's reputation. Any facility that hopes to maintain its integrity must adopt a reservation system that is fair and reasonable.

Contracting

After an organization confirms a tentative hold, the next step is to negotiate the contract. A contract consists of an offer, an acceptance, and consideration. The concluded agreement creates obligations for all parties involved. After negotiations are finished, there are five requirements to complete a contract:

1. Consideration: legal value (money) and mutual obligation of both parties.
2. A valid offer and a valid acceptance.
3. The substance of the contract must be legal.
4. A specific duration (time) for the contract.
5. A written and/or verbal contract.

It is necessary that qualified individuals design, prepare, and understand the contents of the contract, which should consist of mutually agreed-upon terms. This will ensure that the facility is not bound to terms in an agreement that it cannot meet.

Most facilities do not retain a full-time attorney to create a contract for each new facility event. Instead, a boilerplate contract containing a standard form is used. The **boilerplate contract** is similar to an apartment lease, with language in a standard form and with appropriate "fill-in-blanks" to address specifically agreed-upon terms.

Boilerplate contracts provide consistency and generally reflect a situation favorable to all parties. Variations in language concerning events provide a more streamlined contractual device. Addenda may be used to create a more customized form, modify or eliminate contract clauses, or clarify changes that have been agreed upon by both parties.

Contracts should be kept as simple as possible to avoid confusion and to expedite the contractual process. Large facilities that host a variety of events use three basic boilerplate contract forms, each addressing different event types:

- Ticketed events, open to the public, require language addressing ticket sales, gate proceeds, ushers, and ticket takers. Addenda usually refer to elements concerned with insurance, special financial arrangements, and promotions. Public events require more precise contractual procedures because the facility attempts to preserve the security of patrons and maintain building control.
- A nonticketed or closed event, such as a convention or trade show, deals with display booths and banquets but not invitations or ticketing. Contracts for these events are less complex because the event is not open to the public, thus reducing liabilities.
- A small event held in a facility's meeting room, such as a prom or a seminar, eliminates the need for the manpower of a large event that uses the arena. The contract in this case is simple and straightforward.

CONCEPT CHECK

The booking and scheduling process is an important aspect of achieving success in a facility. Events must be properly scheduled and contracted so that all parties know their rights and responsibilities. Formal policies and procedures will make this phase of facility management operate more smoothly.

MARKETING AND PROMOTIONAL-STRATEGY DEVELOPMENT

During the negotiation stage, the **promoter(s)** and facility marketing organization should be in contact to determine the type and extent of facility involvement with the proposed event. The level of facility involvement will hinge on the event type and the promoter's approach to marketing its event.

In some cases, the client(s) will undertake the entire marketing operation, from contact with the local media (radio, television, and newspapers) to promotions being run in the facility on the day of the event. This type of control will depend upon the experience and expertise of the promoters in the development of their events. Client-controlled promotion will limit the cost of the event to the facility but also lower the amount of revenue due to the facility at the time of settlement.

In most cases, promoters will not have developed ties with the local community and media. If this is true, they will often want the event's entire marketing campaign to be organized by the facility marketing organization. This marketing responsibility requires the development of a marketing plan.

Initial marketing efforts

After the establishment of the initial marketing assumptions (based on research) and the marketing plan and budget, the real work begins. The first phase, depending upon the event and the results of market research initiatives, begins with the establishment of contact with the local media. This initial contact includes discussion of the purchase of media time or space, and sets up some form of trade/promotion with these media. It is imperative that this media advertising be targeted at the appropriate audience (O'Shaughnessy, 1988).

At the same time, the group sales department attempts to contact corporations and service groups in an attempt to book groups for the upcoming event. Such promotional activities as press conferences and star athletes visiting key "publics," commonly known as **earned media,** should be planned and carried out. According to Will Peneguy of the New Orleans Super Dome, these public-awareness activities should be scheduled in close proximity to the actual event, while the initial media contact could be as much as a year in advance.

CONCEPT CHECK

Awareness and information are the keys to a successful marketing campaign. Once these are achieved, the job of attracting people to a facility becomes easier.

SECURITY

Security functions usually fall under the jurisdiction of the operations department in most facilities. In large facilities a full-time, in-house security staff is employed. This compounds the responsibilities of the operations manager, because in-house security officers are employees of the facility and it assumes liability for any negligent actions on their part under the legal doctrine of *respondeat superior.*

Therefore, it is vitally important that proper rules and procedures be established, written, and made accessible to all members of the security department (Jewel, 1992). These rules and procedures should provide security personnel with a clearly delineated picture of restrictions and limitations, and what specific behaviors are expected of the staff within the scope of their employment. This area is a constant source of legal headaches for a facility.

It is vital that all employees, from administration to ticket takers, understand facility policies and required responses. Any problem that arises must be resolved quickly, with limited public knowledge of the incident. A facility that has stringent policies and procedures that are developed for the protection of patrons will help reduce liability.

Since September 11, 2001, numerous changes have taken place in stadiums and arenas in terms of security. The NFL released stadium security guidelines. The following is an example of some of the security measures at the Cleveland Browns Stadium.

- No bags larger than a small purse will be permitted inside the stadium.
- Bags, backpacks, fanny packs, large purses, and large camera cases will not be allowed inside the stadium.
- Binoculars, diaper bags, and small cameras will be permitted subject to inspection.
- All credentialed individuals must show a photo ID and submit their birth date and Social Security numbers. (Cleveland Browns Newsroom, 2003)

In addition, parking has become more restricted at most venues and facilities, and the number of uniformed police officers has increased. It is important for the image of a facility that patrons see extra security precautions being taken. In today's climate patrons are more than willing to tolerate delays for the sake of their personal security.

Finally, technology has enabled facility managers to better monitor patrons and protect them from injury, as well as monitor the actions of employees. Camera technology has reached the point where a camera could be in the button of a security guard and no one would know it. Digital imagery and recorders allow security officers to monitor and review any situation that might arise within the facility during an event. Computer systems have also enhanced security through the use of digital scanners and photo ID cards. These cards monitor the holder's movements as well as deny access to those who do not possess the proper credentials. Future technological advances (using biometrics) include fingerprint and hand geometry readers, eye scans, and voice and facial recognition.

ALCOHOL MANAGEMENT

The majority of patron problems involve the excessive consumption of alcohol. However, most of today's facilities have minimized this problem by adopting strict policy guidelines pertaining to alcohol distribution during events. The essence of this policy is that there are specified times within a game, concert, or other event when alcohol will not be available for sale. To ensure that this policy is adhered to strictly, beverage sellers should be educated to recognize signs of unacceptable intoxication or purchases attempted by underage patrons. Even with strict policies concerning alcohol consumption, problems are inevitable.

At the sportsmanship and fan behavior summit in Dallas in February 2003, issues related to alcohol consumption and its effect on fan behavior were discussed with leaders in intercollegiate athletics. Of particular concern was the impact that alcohol has on the postgame activities of fans. After Ohio State's victory over Michigan on November 23, 2002, fans stormed the field. It wasn't an isolated incident. On the same day, alcohol consumption contributed to each of the following incidents:

- Ohio St. 14, Michigan 9 (Columbus, Ohio): Police used pepper spray to disperse the crowd.
- Oklahoma St. 38, Oklahoma 28 (Stillwater, Okla.): OSU fans tear down goalposts after beating Oklahoma for the second year in a row.

- Oregon St. 45, Oregon 24 (Corvallis, Ore.): Security guards surrounded the goal posts as fans rushed the field.
- N.C. State 17, Florida St. 10 (Raleigh, N.C.): Fans rushed the field before the game ended.
- California 30, Stanford 7 (Berkeley, Calif.): Cal fans threw QB Kyle Boller around, mosh-pit style.
- Utah 13, BYU 6 (Salt Lake City): Fans carried Utah coach Ron McBride around the field chanting, "Keep Coach Mac!"
- Hawaii 20, Cincinnati 19 (Honolulu): After players brawled, policy used pepper spray on fans in the stands (*The NCAA News*, 2003).

The **TEAM** (Techniques for Effective Alcohol Management) coalition recommends the following for all venues and facilities.

Sports and entertainment facilities in the United States (both professional and university) should:

- Train both concessions and operations employees in an alcohol management training program.
- Set an employee policy to always use safety belts when driving.
- Post signs in their parking facilities reminding guests to always buckle up.

TEAM venues should provide at least one designated driver booth.

- Fans that sign up to be designated drivers must present a valid driver's license providing their age.
- Designated drivers should sign an agreement pledging to:
  Not drink alcohol while at the stadium.
  Take responsibility for driving home their friends and family who have been drinking.
  Ensure that everyone wear's safety belt.

TEAM venues should set policies regarding the purchase and consumption of alcohol that represent the average of all sports venues participating in TEAM.

- Alcohol sales cut-off time:
  MLB: end of 7th inning
  NFL: end of 3rd quarter

  NBA: end of 3rd period
  NHL: end of 2nd period
- ID policy: 30 and younger
- Maximum number of beers per purchase: 2 beers
- Maximum serving size per beer: 20 oz.
- Denial of outside beverages into the facility (TEAM Coalition, 2003).

SAFETY AND MEDICAL SERVICES

An emergency is any incident or situation that has resulted in, or could cause, the injury of employees, patrons, or visitors. Examples of potential emergency situations are bad weather, fires, bomb threats, medical emergencies, airplane crashes, utility losses, and hazardous materials. These situations can occur in a facility at any time, but how prepared are facilities to handle them when the situation arises?

Authority

It is important that a definitive chain of command be established to maximize coordination and direction in emergency situations and to quickly deal with such emergencies. During any event in a public facility, a staff member should be empowered to take charge and make decisions when a problem arises. This staff member is usually the **event coordinator** or the operations manager, whose responsibility is to ensure that every facet of the event goes according to schedule and that problems are resolved in a professional and timely manner.

Emergency response training

Response to an emergency situation by the facility staff must be prompt and professional. The difference between a well-trained response and an erratic, poorly trained response could be the difference between life and death. An emergency response plan should be devised for all perceivable emergency situations. It is vital to thoroughly train all personnel who will most likely be involved in these response procedures.

Emergency response procedures

Each facility is unique, so it is necessary for each facility to develop its own emergency response procedures. A detailed plan covers facility staffing, physical attributes, event type and classification, and type and numbers of appropriate emergency medical personnel per event. Constant communication with emergency medical staff, strategically positioned with the necessary response equipment and supplies, is required for immediate and appropriate reaction.

Emergency procedures are vital in large-scale situations, such as a bomb threat, a fire, or a mechanical failure (Figure 9-1 provides a bomb threat procedure). In each instance, a specific procedure should be followed to ensure maximum safety. An evacuation plan must be understood and implemented correctly by the entire facility staff. Safe evacuation of patrons, in a professional and orderly manner, will minimize panic and resultant injuries. In most large facilities, ramps and other nonmechanical exit devices are employed in

---

Date _____

Time _____

Keep caller talking. Give excuses (can't hear, bad connection, etc.)

Caller's message (exact) _____
_____
_____

Where is the bomb? _____

What time will it go off? _____

What does it look like? _____

What kind of bomb is it? _____

Why are you doing this? _____

Who are you? _____

Details of caller

Man/ Woman/ Child   Old/ Young

Voice: loud – soft – raspy – high pitch – pleasant – deep – intoxicated

Manner: calm – angry – rational – irrational – coherent – incoherent – emotional – righteous – laughing

Speech: fast – slow – distinct – distorted – stutter – nasal – slurred – lisp

Background noises: Factory – trains – planes – bedlam – animals – music – quiet – office machines – voices – street – party – kids

Language: excellent – good – fair – poor – foul

Accent: local – foreign – race

DO NOT DISCUSS THE CALL WITH ANYONE ELSE!

FIGURE 9-1   Bomb threat procedure.

emergency situations; elevators or escalators should not be used under any circumstances. When an unusual situation develops, where no specific plan has been established, management must select the most appropriate and efficient response choice.

CONCEPT CHECK

Establishing security, alcohol management, and emergency procedures is of the utmost importance when managing a facility. Improper security and/or alcohol management procedures can result in the injury of patrons and lawsuits against the facility. Providing emergency services also has legal ramifications, but the facility is ethically bound to provide a safe and enjoyable environment.

HOUSEKEEPING AND MAINTENANCE

Housekeeping and maintenance are functions designed to keep a facility clean and prepared for patrons. The task of cleaning a facility is one that cannot be underestimated.

Housekeeping in a facility is not like cleaning a house, because the areas to be cleaned and maintained are vast and varying: bleacher seats, portable seats, large restrooms, loges, carpets, tile and concrete floors, and numerous stairwells, elevators, and upholstered seats, to name just a few.

Maintenance and housekeeping duties consist of many different functions and responsibilities. Maintenance components include structural maintenance, equipment maintenance, **setup** and **breakdown** of events, and custodial functions (Jewel, 1992). Maintenance management also requires awareness of and adherence to federal and state regulations, as well as the ability to implement preventive maintenance and safety plans within the facility. Housekeeping is the physical cleaning and arrangement of the facility and its furnishings. (Figure 9-2 can be used as a guide for a maintenance schedule.)

Once the general mission statement has been developed, a plan for housekeeping and maintenance should be established. Management should consider the facility type, location, relationship to other facilities in the community, traffic access, usage level, types of groups using the facility, available labor, sources of revenues, and financial bottom-line responsiveness. This plan should establish guidelines concerning purpose, operation, storage, staffing, inventory, repair, and safety.

- Purpose: A facility should provide clean, well-organized, and safe spaces and equipment for events, lessees, and audiences.
- Operation: To operate effectively, a facility should have space and equipment set according to event requirements before the lessee's move-in time. It should operate the event efficiently by answering all late requests in a timely manner and maintaining an acceptable level of cleanliness in all areas during the event. Every attempt should be made to prevent safety violations. At the close of any event, all equipment should be secured, all refuse should be disposed of, spaces and equipment should be cleaned and returned to their original status, and all deficiencies should be reported and corrected in a timely manner.
- Storage: The storage of equipment should allow for quick identification and inventory; maximum space utilization; convenience to using area; protection against tearing, bending, scarring, water or dust accumulation, broken parts, and/or damage of any other kind; proper spacing; and safe handling.
- Operations staff: The operations staff should be organized into two or three departments, such as housekeeping/arrangements, engineering, or technical. These areas may be further subdivided. The housekeeping/arrangements section could be subdivided into such groups as (1) setup crew(s), providing for setup and striking events; and (2) deep-cleaning crew, which would be scheduled to complete major cleaning tasks, such as carpet shampooing, tile stripping and waxing, and glass washing.
- Housekeeping/arrangements: All setup crews should be composed of a foreman, one or more leadmen, and part-time workers as required. These crews will operate eight hours per shift, three shifts per day, seven days per week.

```
Concourse Restroom Maintenance

Condition of restrooms at the start of shift

MEN EAST _____    WOMEN EAST _____
MEN NORTH _____    WOMEN NORTH (2) _____
MEN WEST _____    WOMEN WEST _____
MEN S.E. _____    WOMEN S.E. (2) _____
MEN S.W. _____    WOMEN S.W. _____

Record of maintenance during shift
```

Restrooms — Time (maintained and/ or checked)

Restrooms							
MEN EAST							
WOMEN EAST							
MEN NORTH							
WOMEN NORTH (2)							
MEN WEST							
WOMEN WEST							
MEN S.E.							
WOMEN S.E. (2)							
MEN S.W.							
WOMEN S.W.							

Maintenance needed or repairs to be made: _____

Attendants on duty: _____ Date: _____

FIGURE 9-2   A sample maintenance schedule.

CONCEPT CHECK ✔

A clean and well-maintained environment does much to improve the mood of the patrons. Housekeeping and maintenance should have high priority when managing a facility.

BOX OFFICE

The box office is probably one of the most important areas in sport facilities today. The box office, although not a complicated operation, is the public's initial contact with the facility and the entity that financially drives the operation, collecting the majority of revenue for all events.

Too often the box office area is the least-thought-about area in facility planning. It is assumed that people will tolerate confusion and discomfort to buy a ticket for a desirable event. This may be true, but to make patrons feel good about spending their money, the box office should be organized and easily accessible to the customer.

The size of the box office area should accommodate the sale and distribution of tickets. An adequate number of windows should be available to handle an unexpected number of **walk-up sales.** Sales windows should be located on all sides of the facility rather than just at the main entrance (Jewel, 1992).

To adequately serve the public, each sales window should be capable of selling the entire price range of tickets and generate sales of 400 to 700 tickets during the night. This figure will vary depending on the type of ticket-selling machines that are being used and the speed of the machines' operators. Therefore, it is safe to assume that if you have an 18,000-seat facility, it should have 18 to 24 windows available for ticket sales. Although this is an optimum number of windows, most sport facilities will not have enough space for this many windows. The previously mentioned ration of windows to projected sales is a useful rule of thumb, and with good record keeping and the use of historical data, one can gauge the number of ticket windows needed for a particular event. Nothing will turn a patron off faster than having to wait in line for a ticket and miss part of an event because of poor planning by the facility.

The main entrance to the facility should contain about 40 percent of the ticket-selling windows, with the other 60 percent distributed among the other entry areas of the arena. Box office lobbies should be of sufficient size to allow patrons to line up in front of the windows. (Remember, few people stand in line alone; the entire family or groups of friends stand in line together.)

Under normal circumstances, a covered area 30- to 50-feet deep should be provided in front of the selling windows. If possible, some ticket windows should be located on the outside of the building. This will allow for ticket sales in several locations and prevent lines from backing up against the turnstiles, which are generally adjacent to the ticket-selling windows. An outside ticket-selling window is also a good idea for the sale of tickets for future events, which would permit the sales without the need to open the building.

All box office windows should be located outside the turnstiles in an area that is easily accessible to the public. Specific windows should be designated for will-call and reservations, preferably in a separate area away from the main entrance. These windows tend to cater to the repeat business patron, and a separate window and entrance seem to promote future sales.

Box office personnel

Depending upon the size and mission of a facility, personnel number and designation vary considerably. As an important operational part of a facility, the box office requires a minimum number of full-time staff. Normally, the box office manager and two or three assistants are the only full-time staff members, with the remaining employees hired as part-time personnel.

The box office manager has the sole responsibility for the box office operation and supervision of all personnel. This individual is responsible for ordering, selling, and distributing event tickets, as well as for the final box office statement. Policy development, personnel selection and placement, safety, and discipline of box office personnel are additional responsibilities. The box office manager and his/her assistants work closely with promoters and all facility operations personnel.

Box office policies

Box office policies are relatively uncomplicated, with the ultimate goal to provide an efficient and secure service-oriented operation. Employees should be instructed in appropriate dress and attitude. Areas of policy should include

- Courtesy toward patrons
- Familiarity with event seating
- Efficient ticket processing

Working conditions

The box office generally operates from 8:30 A.M. to 4:30 P.M. on nonevent days and until intermission on event days, depending on ticket demand.

Public relations

All personnel should be instructed about the appropriate techniques for meeting and greeting the ticket-purchasing public and about proper dress and etiquette.

Equipment operations

Equipment operations include ticket counters (tickets divided into numerical sequence, by price breaks, or by rows and sections according to the seating plan); cash drawers for cash placement and stub count at the end of the day; computer terminals and printers for printing computerized tickets; cash registers; and telephones and answering machines to provide messages and record ticket orders.

Sales policies

When tickets are sold, all transactions involving the sale are final for the specific event. When an event has concluded, it is vital that all ticket sales, after accounting for unsold and complimentary tickets, equal the revenue generated. In other words, capacity minus total tickets sold equals unsold tickets plus appropriate evidence for all transactions.

Refunds and exchanges

The general rule is that no refunds or exchanges should take place. All sales are final. This rule results from the fact that the facility and its personnel are agents for the promoter and do not make the rules. Any refund or exchange policy must be approved in writing by the facility contractor or promoter.

Telephone orders

Procuring tickets by telephone is usually acceptable as long as certain restrictions are in place:

- A ticket for a seat should be held for only three days.
- Telephone ticket orders should be accepted only if the promoter and facility management agree that this would be an appropriate sales method to be employed for a specific event. Telephone sales should be event-specific.
- All telephone orders should be recorded as cash transactions.

Mail orders

For convenience, patrons should be permitted to order tickets through the mail. This not only creates another avenue to sell tickets for that specific event but permits the facility to provide information concerning future events when the tickets are returned to the patron.

Will call

Every facility should establish a **will-call location**. It is imperative that when a patron arrives for ticket pick-up, proper identification is produced before the tickets are provided to the patron.

Lost tickets

Refunds and exchanges are subject to the agreement of the promoter. However, in the case of a ticket lost prior to the event, the ticket manager should have the discretion to issue a duplicate ticket and void the original ticket. If the ticket manager decides that the patron should purchase a new ticket, then the original ticket can be returned to the box office for a full refund prior to the performance. This lost-ticket policy affects the facility's image, and every effort to resolve the situation should be encouraged without exceeding the limitations of prescribed authority.

Ticket purchases

The number of tickets purchased by a patron is up to the discretion of the box office manager and subject to the agreement of the promoter. There is usually no set limit to the number of tickets purchased.

Scalping

Scalping can be a serious problem, and although the facility and box office can do little to combat scalping, there are usually local laws that address the problem. In fact, most authorities arrest and fine scalpers.

Ticketing variables

There are a number of elements concerned with ticket sales and operations, such as the following:

- Capacity: The box office should strive to maximize revenue by selling every seat in the facility. It should be remembered that the configuration and capacity of each event is different, depending on the event type and requirements.
- Seating: There are two types of seating arrangement in a facility, regardless of configuration: (1) reserved, where a specific seat is designated for each patron. This type of seating arrangement is prevalent at events such as athletic contests and concerts. This arrangement provides the patron with "first come, best seat" when buying tickets. (2) General admission is a seating arrangement used primarily at lower quality, egalitarian productions. This arrangement implies that all patrons purchasing tickets will

receive the same quality seating opportunity as those who purchase tickets in advance. Although both methods appear to have inherent inequities, a compromise arrangement is to provide tiered seating prices (e.g., ground floor: $30; 2nd floor: $15, etc.), which all professional sport facilities use.

- Ticket type: The ticket is a contract (agreement) between the management/promoter and the purchaser of the seat. The box office manager should deal only with a reputable, bonded ticket company when ordering well in advance of an event, to minimize the chance of error. This policy should be in place regardless of the ticket type (i.e., ticket roll or computerized tickets). Computerized tickets, although much more expensive than the traditional ticket stock, have certain advantages, such as event information printed on them: name of sponsoring organization, ticket price, program name, performance date and time, facility name, and seat location. Also, appropriate advertising can be included on ticket stock.

Ticket sales strategy

Although ticket sales strategy and policy will be codirected by the marketing department, it falls under the purview of the box office. Elements of this strategy are

- Pricing: The box office, the marketing department, and the promoter jointly develop a ticket sales strategy. A decision needs to be made regarding whether tickets will be sold on a house scale (i.e., pricing established by the box office) or by a **performance scale** (i.e., pricing established by the event promoter).
- Incentives: Many traditional types of sales incentives have been used, including discounted tickets or tickets that make use of unusual seating areas (e.g., standing room) or special circumstances. These are determined by the promoter and/or the box office. Group sales are made to groups for a price reduction, which is beneficial when an event has a lower ticket demand or corporate involvement is required. Season tickets predominate at athletic or theatrical events presented on a seasonal basis.

Daily reporting

A daily transaction or report form—which provides the facility with a record of daily transactions—should be completed for all ticket sales, mail orders, and anything else deemed important by management.

Event summary

Although the event summary is prepared by the business office, the box office must initiate the process by providing event information at the conclusion of each event. The information should cover ticket prices; ticket categories, including complimentary or other special ticket classifications; and the number of tickets sold and unsold.

Computer ticket management

As facilities investigate various options to minimize personnel costs, eliminate cumbersome operational procedures, and become "auditor-friendly," a computerized ticket system combined with an overhead counting system and/or ticket scanners provide an ideal solution. This computer-operated system is dependent on software options. It provides the box office with patron information at the **point of sale,** organized either alphabetically, by postal code, or by subscriber number; a computerized mailing list, updated daily, which can be used for notification of upcoming events or to solicit patron response for a specified performance; and the ability to monitor ticket sales versus marketing efforts. If money is spent on advertising or direct-mail solicitations, these promotional efforts need to be compared to ticket sales.

Private seat licenses (PSLs)

Although some of these alternate revenue sources have been mentioned previously, **private seat licenses (PSLs)** are becoming important in ensuring profitability or that the "bottom line" is achieved. A PSL, in its truest form, is a one-time fee that gives an individual the right to will or pass on the tickets and the right to buy tickets for as long as the purchaser and the designee desire. Some facilities, however, have PSLs that have a limited duration. For example, Texas Tech University PSLs allow for a seat to be purchased for a period of 10 years. The price of PSLs varies from $500 to $10,000, depending upon seat location and venue. For example, Pittsburgh Steelers PSLs cost between $250 and $2,500, the Carolina

Panthers up to $5,400, St. Louis and Nashville up to $4,500, and Cincinnati and Cleveland up to $1,500. The monies generated from PSLs, in most cases, go directly to the teams and do not have to be split with other teams or the leagues.

> ## CONCEPT CHECK
>
> *The box office of a facility has enormous responsibilities. It must make sure that patrons can purchase tickets and enter the facility in a timely fashion. And because large quantities of cash are handled by the box office, reliable staffing is a must. Finally, the staff must be courteous, because the box office is the first contact the patron will have with the facility's personnel.*

CONCESSIONS AND NOVELTIES

A facility's food service is the business operation that prepares, delivers, and sells food and beverages to customers. There are three forms of food service operations: concessions, catering, and novelties (which includes programs). In this presentation, catering will be included in the area of concessions.

Concessions

Concessions play a vital role in the success of a facility. A well-operated concessions department is often a major determining factor in the financial success of any sport facility. It is an accepted fact that food and drink go hand-in-hand with sports and recreation.

For example, during 1989–1990, the Superdome in New Orleans reported that concessions revenue amounted to $7.5 million, or 60 percent of its operating revenue. At a smaller sport facility, Fogelman Basketball Arena at Tulane University, a 72 percent net profit was reported on concessions operations in the facility in 1990.

In order for a concessions operation in a facility to survive, much more than serving good food at a reasonable price is required. It demands that management has a knowledge of marketing, financial management, business planning, purchasing, inventory management, business law, insurance, advertising, and personnel.

Stocking

Stocking is an important component of the concessions operation. The manager must initially decide which products to purchase based upon quality, price, service, and customer acceptance. The staff of a facility often taste-tests items to determine the best products. Today, the most popular foods appear to be hot dogs, nachos, popcorn, peanuts, soft drinks, and beer.

When deciding on the quality of products, one should scrutinize past records carefully. Nonperishable items (e.g., cups, napkins, and other paper goods) should be purchased in large quantities for the whole season. Perishable or time-sensitive items (e.g., hot dogs and buns) must be ordered fresh for every event. In large facilities, restocking takes about one week, while in smaller facilities it takes approximately five hours. Some interesting facts about concessions are:

- Beer and alcohol account for a high percentage of concession profits.
- Popcorn is probably the largest revenue producer in terms of margin. The cost of a box of popcorn is about five cents, while patrons pay $2.00 to $2.50 a serving.
- Concessions sales are constant one hour before a game; 80 percent of sales take place at halftime, while only about 20 percent of sales take place after halftime.

Convenience foods

All the foods in concession stands are called convenience foods. There are three types of **convenience foods** that facilities stock: frozen, powdered, and dehydrated. Frozen foods include a large selection of fruit juices and meat, in a variety of sizes from individual servings to amounts sufficient for volume feeding. Dehydrated and powdered foods are appropriate for facilities because they can be stored for long periods of time without spoilage and are often packaged in bulk. They require only water or a short period of cooking for reconstitution. Some of the dehydrated and powdered foods on the market today are seasonings, soups of many varieties, milk, pastry mixes, sauces, gravies, and beverages.

The wide variety of convenience foods available enables concession stands to present a varied menu to the public and permits employees with limited knowledge and little training to prepare appetizing "fail-proof" dishes. Convenience foods enable operators to save money, time, and labor, especially in the areas of cleaning, trimming, packaging, string, cooking, and serving.

The development of convenience foods and disposable packaging, containers, and utensils has enabled food service operations to become efficient and practical. Disposable products in common use are semirigid foil pans, plastic pouches, foil and plastic packets, foam containers, cardboard containers, and other disposable items, such as plates, cups, eating utensils, doilies, aprons, and uniforms. Boil-in-a-bag pouch and chemically generated foods have been developed to reduce both cooking time and cost.

Other developments involve foil and plastic packets that encase individual servings of condiments (e.g., tomato sauces, mayonnaise, salt, pepper, etc.) and foam or cardboard containers preshaped for specific carryout items. These disposable products enable minimally trained labor, with minimal equipment, to serve a variety of well-prepared convenience foods and other products that are easy to stock and dispense. These products also reduce sanitation problems.

The concessions operation should not only stock good food but also have adequate storage space and appropriate location(s) for the spectators. In large facilities, service elevators are located near the various storage areas and near all seats. There should be enough concession stands to serve the total number of seats, and any patron should be able to reach the nearest food stand in about 40 to 60 seconds.

Concessions advertising

Concessions operations should be bright, colorful, well lit, and decorated with attractive pictures of the food and beverages being served. Menu boards should be installed to clearly indicate products and prices. Signage should be in neon that is not the same color as the building. At large facilities, pictures of food should be displayed on the menu board. Pictures of brand-name products, easily recognized by customers, eliminate questions about the quality of the merchandise. Further, to keep lines moving, most menus should list all prices in increments of 25 cents. Simple combinations should be listed on the menu in large, readable print to provide direction for the customer and to eliminate complex orders that can result in lost sales or patrons missing a portion of the event while waiting in line for food.

Concessions should be well organized, with clear indications of where patrons should line up for service. Equipment, food, and cash registers should be conveniently located so that customers can be quickly served by a single person in each selling section. It is important that employees be trained to manage large crowds and keep lines moving. At the same time, they should be encouraged to increase sales through suggestive selling techniques. They should attempt to convince the customer that all items are reasonably priced and that buying a larger size actually results in saving money.

Alcoholic beverages

In a facility operation, alcoholic beverages are the most profitable segment of the concessions operation. In fact, alcohol and beer manufacturers sponsor facilities and events to promote their products. There is a downside to this situation, of course, especially when there is community opposition to the sale of alcohol in the facility, particularly to the underaged and individuals who may drive an automobile after the event has concluded.

Another element that needs to be considered is the liability that the facility can incur if an accident occurs involving a patron who indulged in alcohol while attending a facility event. Lawsuits have been won by patrons where the facility, event, and concessionaire all have been held liable for fights or injuries due to the consumption of alcohol. Dram-shop laws as well as social-host liability statutes have a definitive impact on facilities when they serve alcohol. Dram-shop laws allow plaintiffs injured by intoxicated defendants to bring lawsuits against not only the intoxicated defendant but also the establishment that served the alcohol. Social-host liability statutes primarily deal with liability of an individual or establishment that serves alcohol to minors.

Concession maintenance

Employees should keep themselves well groomed and their workplace clean because customers may have a negative reaction to employees or concession stands that appear to be unclean. Large facilities usually employ a supervisor for every concession stand, and no employee is allowed to leave until the stands are spotless. At some large facilities (e.g., the Superdome, with 10,000 to 12,000 employees working concessions annually), most of the employees belong to nonprofit groups, such as softball leagues, Girl Scouts, Boy Scouts, or church groups, who volunteer their labor, with each group receiving a percentage of sales. To ensure cleanliness and compliance with health guidelines, floor drains and adequate ventilation and exhaust systems must be installed in stand and kitchen areas.

At the end of an event, employees must cope with a significant volume of refuse from disposable products. This debris should be removed through incineration, which requires a minimal amount of space because the paper items and some plastics are reduced to ash. A second method is to use a shredding machine that converts plastics and paper into a pulp by removing excess water and shredding the fiber. A third method, compression, packs refuse under pressure to reduce its size for ease of removal.

Hawkers/vendors

Another highly profitable aspect of the concessions operation is **vendors,** or **hawkers,** who take food or beverages to the patrons in their seats. Hawkers generate substantial sales because many patrons want food and beverage service but do not want to miss any of the event.

Trends

Concessions operations now provide name-brand products (e.g., Popeye's Chicken and Domino's Pizza), for which the facility receives a percentage of sales. In the near future, many of the items served at concession stands will be more healthful foods, such as soup and salads. There will probably also be specialty operations, such as a sweet shop with a large assortment of candies or a hot dog shop with several combinations (e.g., cheese dog, chili dog, onion dog, or turkey dog). In the beverage area, there is often a demand during rush periods at sporting events for fast bar service. To satisfy this demand, computers have been used to control the mixing and pouring of any one of 1,000 beverages in four seconds, with the liquor content in each being uniform.

Another recent innovation is to place frozen foods in an oven drawer and set a timer. After the correct time has elapsed, the oven automatically turns off and the door opens. The advantages of this innovative cooking equipment are that it saves time and requires much less space than conventional equipment.

Along with the recent trends of serving brand-name products, more healthful foods, specialty shops, and new equipment for bartending and cooking, new packaging has been developed. For example, the package of the future may be a rigid aluminum foil dish and cover with a pull tab, containing a hamburger, French fries, condiments, and wipe-and-dry towels. Pulling the tab before opening the cover will break a heat capsule that after 30 seconds will bring the contents to eating temperature. The ultimate development would be self-destruction of the container when the cover is replaced.

Food safety and sanitation practices

To control food contamination and the spread of disease, every employee must have knowledge of basic food safety and sanitation practices. Food services attract all types of bacteria, insects, and animal pests because they provide them with the three basic ingredients necessary to sustain life: food, water, and warmth.

To eliminate contamination, food service management needs to inspect delivery vehicles to ensure that they are properly refrigerated and sanitary. All products should be accredited and inspected by the appropriate government agencies. Upon delivery, crates or boxes should never be stored outside when unloading because insects can infest them and be introduced into the concessions operation. In addition, all spills should be cleaned up as soon as they occur, and food should be refrigerated until needed and cooked as soon as possible.

Another important way to inhibit food contamination is personal hygiene. Every employee must be aware that hands are a primary source of contamination. Every time employees scratch their heads or sneeze, they are exposing their hands to bacteria that will spread to anything they touch. All employees should practice basic hygiene. For example, they should have short or controlled hair, clean hands and short nails, a daily shower or bath, clean clothes, and no unnecessary jewelry; be clean shaven; and not smoke in the proximity of the food and beverages. In addition, ill employees should not attend work, because they can expose the food preparation and service areas to bacterial contamination.

In most communities, there are regulations that affect food service operations. In fact, most employees are mandated to pass some form of medical examination (e.g., tuberculosis test) and complete a written examination concerning the handling of food.

Novelties

The success of novelty sales depends upon applying the appropriate formula to each situation. The following are four different novelty formulas that have been traditionally used:

- Flat fee: This negotiated fee is paid directly to the facility, usually for a nonticketed event (e.g., meetings, school graduations, or religious services). This fee should be collected in advance or be part of the deposit.
- Percentage of vendor sales: This is a common fee arrangement wherein the vendor pays the facility a percentage of the sales, ranging from 5 to 20 percent, depending upon the parties involved, facility, and event.
- Percentage of facility sales: In this arrangement, the facility, which is responsible for inventory and all sales, receives a percentage of total sales. This is a profitable method for the facility operation and is preferred because the facility knows the amount of inventory on hand and controls its flow. At the close of an event, with the final inventory completed, the vendor will receive a percentage of sales, ranging between 55 and 75 percent. The facility will then pay the sellers out of the facility's percentage of sales, which could range from 5 to 20 percent.
- Fee per person: This method is profitable for the facility and the easiest to handle by all parties. The vendor agrees to pay the facility a set amount per person in attendance, including complimentary tickets. The fee will vary from event to event, depending upon the attraction and vendor items and may range from 1 cent to 25 cents per person. This fee should be collected in advance or by the first intermission, based on anticipated attendance or house capacity.

Sales personnel

Training can make a difference in the simple areas, such as appearance, uniforms, and the attitude of the vendors. However, training how to sell is extremely important if the operation is to generate profit. Another factor is the employment of experienced novelty-sales personnel. Although anyone can sell T-shirts or novelties, it takes a special ability, developed by experience, to generate the type of sales desired in a novelty operation.

Shoplifting is not limited to retail outlets. Novelty personnel should be trained to control their stock so

that the only items that leave the stands are those that are sold. This is extremely important at such events as concerts, where a large number of people will want to purchase T-shirts and other items.

Splits and deals

If an event threatens to bypass the market and facility because of a better novelty deal in another facility, reworking the deal and split should be considered. There is no accepted standard formula to follow, because competition between facilities will dictate the requirements and generate the business.

Bootlegging

It is common practice for most major events, where novelties are sold, to obtain a federal injunction regarding copyright law infringement. This provides police with the authority to confiscate unauthorized merchandise and/or arrest its vendors. Local ordinances that govern the sale of items on the street can be most beneficial in eliminating **bootleggers.**

CONCEPT CHECK

Most patrons know that they will be paying more for food and other items within a facility. It is important that the sales staff and the products be of the highest quality. Patrons are becoming more and more demanding of concessions, and the facility must rise to meet these expectations.

TRAFFIC AND PARKING

Traffic flow is an extremely important part of a patron's visit to a major facility. There are two main components of traffic flow: the flow on the public streets to the facility and the flow within the parking lot if there is on-site parking. Figure 9-3 is a sample organizational roster that can be used to ensure that personnel are properly assigned to assist the flow of traffic in a facility's parking lot.

Although public streets are controlled by either the local police or the state highway patrol, the facility should make every effort to coordinate traffic flow in its lots with that of the public streets. One of the most common complaints at events that draw very large audiences is the time it takes to get into and leave the facility's parking lots. A trend in some of the newer facilities being built in urban areas is to

Parking Personnel Posting Sheet

Event: _____   Date: _____

Supervisors: _____   Supervisors: _____

_____   _____

Cashiers: **Attendants:**

West: (1) _____   East#1: (1) _____   (5) _____

        (2) _____ _____   (2) _____   (6) _____

        (3) _____ Leader   (3) _____   (7) _____

Center: (4) _____   (4) _____   (8) _____

        (5) _____ _____   East#2: (1) _____   (5) _____

        (6) _____ Leader   (2) _____   (6) _____

East#1 (7) _____   (3) _____   (7) _____

        (8) _____ _____   (4) _____   (8) _____

East#2 (9) _____ Leader   West: (1) _____   (5) _____

     (10)_____ _____   (2) _____   (6) _____

     (11)_____ Leader   (3) _____   (7) _____

North   (12)_____   (4) _____   (8) _____

     (13)_____   North: (1) _____   (5) _____

     (14)_____ _____   (2) _____   (6) _____

     (15)_____ Leader   (3) _____   (7) _____

Time out: (4) _____   (8) _____

East#1: (1)_____ (2)_____ (3)_____   Center   (1) _____   (5) _____

East#2: (1)_____ (2)_____ (3)_____   Lot: (2) _____   (6) _____

West : (1)_____ (2)_____ (3)_____   (3) _____   (7) _____

North: (1)_____ (2)_____ (3)_____   North   (4) _____   (8) _____

Center: (1)_____ (2)_____ (3)_____   Reserve: (1) _____   (2) _____

Misc Info: _____

_____   Loge: (1) _____   (2) _____

_____   Point: (1) _____   (2) _____

FIGURE 9-3   Parking personnel posting sheet.

take advantage of public transportation (trains and buses).

There are three common revenue-generating methods appropriate for a facility: a direct collection on a per-car basis; a dollar charge per ticket issued; and a flat rate for specific events. Additional sources of parking revenue can be generated from selling preferred, personalized parking spaces; per-event, all-event, season, or annual parking passes; valet parking for VIP parking at a standard fee per automobile; and marketing parking lots for new or antique cars, motor homes, ski or boat shows, carni-

vals, food festivals, grand prix races, driver safety school, and swap meets.

FINANCIAL MANAGEMENT

Every sport facility operation should have a business operations unit. In small facility operations, much of this function is delegated to one individual and the remainder, especially the tedious, time-consuming tasks, is contracted to an outside organization.

General accounting and finance concepts, for the most part, will be left to other courses that deal in depth with these functions. Discussion in this chapter will focus on the essential elements of the facility business operation: type and process, white papers, event settlement, auditing, payroll, risk management, and bad debts.

Budget

Although a sports facility operates on a day-to-day basis, the most important element of business operations is the development of the budget document. A budget is simply an estimate of receipts and payments for a period of time, usually one or two years. It is also important as a predictive tool, for it can anticipate the flow of revenues and expenditures and be used as a tool of control. A budget is a guide to the financial expectations of a facility and an expression of management's plans (Garrison, 1982).

Political: Government budget process

Most sport facilities today are involved one way or another with government. It is critical for a general manager to have some knowledge of the political process and methodology pertaining to the public budgeting process.

Most state and local governments operate on periods longer than one year—in many cases, a biennium (two years). Therefore, budget requests for public sport facilities may have to be submitted 1½ years prior to actual budget appropriation. By necessity, this projected budget is limited in scope and detail and is often inaccurate. Often, expenses are inflated and income deflated because of the numerous hearings, volatile economies, and political nature of the budget process. Even though the final approved budget may seem to be "carved in stone," if the desired bottom line is not reached, political advocates can lobby for an adjustment to the budget.

Operational budget process

The submission of a budget request to a government agency does not hinder internal budget operations. Operational budget submissions are usually prepared up to 60 days before actual implementation. This time limitation provides limited flexibility when compared to the governmental product.

Budget cycle

There are four phases in the **budget cycle:** preparation, presentation and adoption, execution and postexecution, and audit.

The preparation of the budget begins with the establishment of the facility's mission, goals, and objectives. The overall objective of the entire process of preparing the budget is to end up with a budget that is coordinated into a well-balanced program. The program impact is the heart of any budget justification enabling the facility to achieve the stated mission if provided the requested resources (IAAM, 1990).

The next step is the actual preparation of financial data, which requires a review of past budget items. After review, the new financial data and their justifications are submitted as a draft that, hopefully, is acceptable to management. These materials provide information concerning the levels of personnel services, wages, benefits, materials, supplies, utilities, and services for the facility operation.

The presentation of a draft or revised budget document is a political process, particularly in large facilities. Initially, the budget document is circulated among proactive supporters for their input and approval. This document should be clear and precise and include any supporting documentation (e.g., letters, charts, comparison statistics, etc.) that may provide the reader with insight and understanding. After the supporters review the document and suggest changes, the revised document is circulated to the entire audience. At this time, the budget preparers must be ready to defend the document in an open forum. As soon as the document is approved and adopted by the assemblage, it is ready for interpretation and execution.

Once the budget is adopted, senior management (especially the general manager) is charged with its dissemination among the various facility departments. All budgeted groups, such as operations or engineering and maintenance, are obligated to maintain control over spending, using techniques such as monthly statements to maintain control of expenditures. Monthly meetings are recommended to ascertain whether budget goals and objectives are on target or need adjustment. It is important to remember that while certain budget limits are carved in stone, the budget document is flexible enough for some accommodation. Any substantial shift in facility goals and objectives will require a budget review and revision. The budget document and resulting implementation then must be altered accordingly. However, the prime directive, regardless of potential alterations, is to achieve the mission, goals, and objectives established at the outset of the process.

Simply put, this procedure evaluates whether all the budget assumptions were achieved, and it is critical that fiscal budget limitations be adhered to. Overspending in any budget situation, private or public, is unacceptable. The evaluation process determines the level of success and is employed in the development of the next budget document.

Facility accounting

Accounting within a sport facility is similar to that of any other business operation. The only exception is that the operations involved with government demands are simpler and need not be responsive to stockholders, unlike a private facility operation. However, accounting procedures generally involve three fundamental accounting disclosures:

1. Managerial (internal) accounting is based on projections resulting from income and financial data. This information will be used to guide management's decision-making efforts.
2. Financial (external) account reports primarily involve an income statement, a balance sheet, and a cash flow statement. These reports are subject to auditing and must conform to the **generally accepted accounting procedures (GAAP)** that are used by accountants in preparing such reports (Walgenbach, Dittrick, and Hansen, 1980). External reports are not tax reports.
3. Tax accounting reports that are compiled in accordance with the guidelines of the taxation authority (e.g., the Internal Revenue Service).

All external communications are subject to an annual audit by an independent auditing firm, to report the financial status of the organization. It is important that these audits be objective and unbiased because the confidence of the public, as well as the stockholders or bondholders, is important to the future financial health of the facility management organization.

Event settlement

The **event settlement** process uses procedures normally involved in cost accounting or managerial accounting. This procedure is used to compute the operational costs of producing an event. Evaluation of this data guides management decisions, which in turn affect future events.

Two costing systems are employed in this event settlement procedure. The first is process costing, which is primarily used in industry and costs the entire operational process. The second is job order costing, where costs or expenses, such as labor and overhead, are identified by the job. The job order costing method is better suited to the special-order production needs of a sport facility (Davidson et al., 1988).

Sport facilities should analyze cost data both before and after an event settlement because they will (1) provide an operational measure in terms of dollars generated, (2) assist management in economic and negotiating decisions, (3) justify the need for greater funding, resources, and reimbursement, and (4) provide accountability. If an item is overlooked in the development of a settlement estimate at the end of an event, the facility or management group will have to suffer the loss, because recuperation will be impossible.

Any services associated with the production of an event are channeled into the costing of that event. These sources, known as **house expenses,** include such things as a plumber retained to unstop toilets and prevent a potential flood; stagehands and light operators; a specific facility setup configuration, such as a basketball floor; and the security guard assigned to the box office to protect the facility's deposits against theft. These services cannot be charged to the event promoter because they are the responsibility of the facility and are not recoverable cost items.

A cost accounting system enables the facility business office to itemize detailed contractual elements of the event/promotion and those that define the responsibilities of the facility's management (Garrison, 1982). Expenses must be collated and recorded; otherwise, the facility management will absorb these expenses rather than pass them on to the promoter. The event settlement process, especially at a concert, usually begins about midway through the performance and may conclude before the end of the show. The only real concern after settlement is completed is that the show does not run over the projected time allotment; in that case, additional costs accrue to the facility management.

If the event settlement process has not been completed before the event has ended and the promoter has left, the likelihood of recapturing one's investment is probably "slim to none." Groups that have a good reputation and have been dealt with successfully over the years build up a level of trust and are considered stable operations. Their events are usually resolved within 10 days of the event closure. With all other events, a facility would normally require a hefty deposit. In fact, it would be expected that in the majority of cases the rent would be paid 30 days in advance rather than after the event.

Policies covering event settlement procedures are event-specific and part of the facility management philosophy. The bottom line is that every penny the facility spends for an event that is caused by the event must be accounted for and, hopefully, fully recovered by the facility.

Auditing

Regardless of business classification or location, safeguarding management's operating and financial controls is the objective of the audit process. There are two segments of the auditing process: the internal audit and the external audit (Walgenbach, Dittrick and Hansen, 1980).

Internal audit. The internal audit is a management tool that ensures that the company's assets are used properly and safeguarded at all levels. It is vital that all employees adhere to company policy and follow established procedures. There are two crucial elements within this **internal auditing process:** asset security and personnel compliance. Asset security involves the internal accounting control procedures. Substantial losses sometimes occur due to the theft of products or funds or the misuse of funds or equipment. It is important to realize that every employee is a *potential* thief. Personnel compliance attempts to provide personnel with operational guidelines to protect both the employee and the organization from potential future litigation. Appropriate supervision of employees should include random visitations to a facility—at night, on the weekend, or at unusual times. Management should attempt to vary its visits and not be predictable.

It is prudent to establish a paper trail, which is a collection of documents that can be used in an audit to substantiate any transactions involving the exchange of goods. Cash register tapes, purchase orders, requisitions, checks, contracts, ticket sale reports, and concession reports are often part of this paper trail. This information should be retained in the event of litigation arising out of employee dishonesty.

External audit. An **external audit** examines the organizational accounting records and financial statements to make certain that they are appropriately prepared and not misleading. The external auditor, usually a certified public accountant (CPA), tests and checks the accounting system underlying the financial statements, using the accepted American Institute of Certified Public Accountants (AICPA) auditing standards. This external audit is known as the **attest function,** which provides independent assurance as to whether appropriate procedures have been used.

Problem resolution

The internal auditing process should be an ongoing practice by management throughout the year, while the required external audit can be quarterly, although it is usually annual. Both of these audit processes are necessary to maintain the financial health and credibility of an organization. If an individual or group that is trusted and holds security clearance is involved in a facility problem, the penalty should be quick and should fit the crime. It is important that an example be set for all personnel. Management must have extremely tight control, because its credibility is on the line. If there is any infraction or other problem, swift action must be initiated to resolve the situation, keeping in mind any potential fallout.

Payroll

Payroll in a facility denotes, as in any other business, the compensation paid to employees on a regular basis. In a sport facility operation, the majority of employees are seasonal and part-time (employed no more that 37 hours per week). These employees are usually paid on a weekly basis at an hourly rate. Full-time employees (employed at least 40 hours a week) are paid biweekly or monthly. Overtime pay begins when an employee works more than 40 hours a week. The rate of pay for this overtime is 1½ times the regular rate. Unionized employees are sometimes reimbursed at higher rates. Full-time employment is classified as either staff or management. The staff (line) classification usually includes hourly employees, while management is paid a salary, regardless of the time spent on the job.

The employee remuneration package consists of both wages/salary and deductions. Examples of some of these deductions are Social Security, federal income taxes withheld, state and local income taxes, state disability insurance, unemployment compensation, and any voluntary employee deductions. The employee's net (take-home) pay is calculated by taking the employee's gross pay (wages earned) and subtracting all the appropriate taxes and other deductions. At the end of the financial year, every employee, regardless of employment status, will receive a W-4 form prepared by the accounting division of the operation.

Payroll represents the largest portion of the total cost of any operation. All records pertaining to payroll must be maintained by the employer to prepare annual tax calculations and support the audit process. To satisfy government, union, and employee expectations, it is important to use a payroll method that is facility-specific and that satisfies all the conditions established. Instead of using a manual payroll operation, a facility can use on of several computer software applications available for calculating payrolls. These can be customized for a facility's special needs.

CONCEPT CHECK

Financial management is an extremely important aspect of facility management. Budget payroll and event settlement are probably the main features of financial management. To successfully manage this area, the facility manager must know something about accounting terminology and procedures.

RISK MANAGEMENT

Risk is defined as a hazard or the possibility of danger or harm. Risk management focuses on limiting exposure to harm in the facility (Berlonghi, 1990). The most common danger that a sport facility manager tries to minimize is injuries to patrons at the facility, which create the potential for lawsuits. These lawsuits can cause substantial monetary losses to the sport facility. The obvious goal of minimizing injuries and avoiding lawsuits and monetary losses may sound easy, but in fact it is a very complicated and difficult task to do correctly.

In order to be efficient at this task, the risk manager should identify the possible risks, assess their likelihood, calculate how to respond to the risks, and create standards and procedures (a strategic plan) for decreasing the risks.

Identification stage

At the risk identification stage, the facility manager must discover the various risks that may cause losses during any given event. There are primary and secondary factors that must be addressed in order to reduce the likelihood of losses to the sport facility. Primary factors are the base of operations at every sport facility, and each sport facility manager must consider them when trying to reduce risk. These factors are within almost complete control of the sport facility manager. It should be noted that while a well-trained staff is the risk manager's best tool for identifying risks, staff members can also be risks themselves.

Risk assessment

The assessment of risks should be systematic, using amount and frequency of loss as the two criteria. A matrix can be created that allows a consistent approach to the assessing process. Figure 9-4 gives the sport facility manager nine categories in which to classify any identified risk.

Risk treatment

The next stage, risk treatment, can also be accomplished with the use of a matrix. As you can see from Figure 9-5, the matrix is now filled with various treatments for risks based on three frequencies of occurrence and the three amounts of loss.

	High Frequency	Moderate Frequency	Low Frequency
High Loss			
Moderate Loss			
Low Loss			

FIGURE 9-4 Risk assessment matrix.

	High Frequency	Moderate Frequency	Low Frequency
High Loss	Avoid	Shift	Shift
Moderate Loss	Shift	Shift or keep & decrease	Shift or keep & decrease
Low Loss	Keep & decrease	Keep & decrease	Keep & decrease

FIGURE 9-5   Risk treatment matrix.

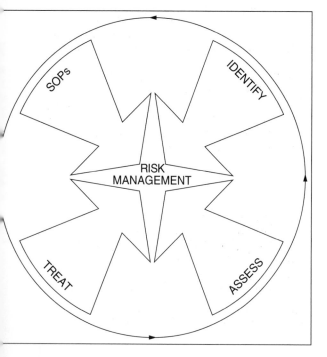

FIGURE 9-6   The risk management process.

Avoidance

Clearly, one should avoid risks that cause a great amount of loss or occur often. For example, a sport facility should never hold an event that has caused great damage to sport facilities elsewhere or that has equipment that is inherently dangerous, such as diving boards in swimming pools. Holding an event that has caused extensive property damage at

other facilities and/or led to lawsuits would not be prudent. This type of event should be avoided altogether. The sport facility manager is an effective risk manager if he or she does not allow such an event to take place in the interest of eliminating all potential losses that might occur.

Transferring risks

This treatment of identified and assessed risks focuses on the sport facility manager's knowledge that certain losses will occur but it is difficult to determine the approximate losses involved and the frequency of occurrence. The matrix has identified these risks more or less as middle-of-the-road risks. Looking at the matrix, however, does reveal that some very high losses are included. We do not wish to avoid these risks, because the frequency of their occurrence is moderate or below. Also, the risks that occur very frequently are moderate and therefore should not be avoided.

Keeping and decreasing risks

The final option for treating risks is to keep the risk and attempt to decrease the amount of loss the risk can cause. We can see in the matrix that risks that are to be kept and decreased are those that have low or very low potential for loss. A sport facility can accept these risks because there is very little chance of suffering substantial losses. Of course, this assumes that once the sport facility manager decides to keep the risk, proper precautions are taken to decrease the occurrence of and the monetary loss associated with the risk. This is accomplished by developing standard operating procedures, which is the final step in the risk management process.

Standard operating procedures

Under **standard operating procedures (SOPs),** the sport facility manager develops a strategic plan that will provide the most efficient and effective way to decrease the occurrence of risks. The strategic plan is basically a step-by-step set of instructions that give detailed directions for the appropriate courses of action, given the event and the risks associated with it. SOPs should be developed for both risks that are transferred and risks that are kept and decreased. (See Figure 9-6 for an illustration of the risk management process.)

CONCEPT ✔**HECK**

It is extremely important to realize that risk management is a dynamic process that must continually be analyzed and modified. By following the risk management process, the facility manager can make the facility safer for patrons while reducing potential liability situations.

SUMMARY

- The trend in facility management is toward private management companies rather than in-house operations. Private management companies are solicited through the request-for-proposals (RFP) process.
- In order to effectively manage a facility, a mission statement—along with policies, procedures, goals, and objectives—must be established.
- Booking and scheduling deals with obtaining events and contracting with the promoters of the events. It is important to have a good fit between the facility and the event in order for operations to be effective.
- Marketing and promotions attempt to publicize events and attract patrons to them. Exposure is the key element in the success of the marketing campaign.
- Proper security and emergency procedures must be developed in order to minimize lawsuits and provide a safe environment for patrons to enjoy the events.
- The box office is in charge of ticket sales and admissions. It is an extremely important aspect of the facility because it handles a great deal of money and it is the first part of the facility the patrons deal with.
- Concessions and novelties have become an increasingly important aspect of facility management. Expectations of patrons have increased to the point where concessions need to provide a higher level of food products and other items to meet these expectations.
- Financial management deals with budgeting, event settlement, and auditing. These aspects of facility management require knowledge of the practices and principles of accounting and finance. Because many crucial decisions are based upon budget, event settlement, and auditing documents, it is extremely important that all of them be professionally prepared.
- Risk management's purpose is to provide a structure to alleviate liability problems that could lead to significant financial losses. Also, the process of developing standard operating procedures for a facility provides a safe environment.

 ## CRITICAL THINKING EXERCISES

1. As a facility manager, what are the steps you would follow in a risk audit, and what are some things you would be looking for?
2. As a facility manager, how would you market a new facility? How does this differ from marketing events?

 ## CASE STUDY

You have just been hired as the facility manager for the Coliseum. The president of the Coliseum wants you to create an operations manual that will help the building run more efficiently while making your job easier to perform. The following is a list of priorities given to you by the president of the Coliseum:

1. *Operations management: Describe and diagram the optimal organizational structure. This structure should include position description and projected salaries.*
2. *Risk management: Describe the overall function of risk management within your arena. Give five potential risk management scenarios and explain in detail their resolution using risk management principles.*
3. *Alcohol management: What is TEAM and describe how it can be used to protect a facility from liability.*
4. *Marketing: Develop a marketing plan for your facility, including projected costs and benefits and two advertising campaigns for your facility.*
5. *Event management: Describe this process in your facility, including a chain of command for personnel (parking, security, ticket takers, ushers, etc.). Choose a special event that could be held at your facility, and describe what special-event management needs this event might create.*

6. *Concessions/food service: Describe the function of concessions in your facility. Give reasons why you would or would not own the concessions, have an agreement to get a percentage of concessions, or simply lease the space for concessions.*

REVIEW QUESTIONS AND ISSUES

1. Describe the advantages of contracting with private management companies.
2. What is RFP? Describe this selection process.
3. Define booking and scheduling.
4. Describe the reservation process. Comment on the statement that this process is not fair.
5. How does the mission of the facility influence its reservations and priorities?
6. How would you resolve a problem of two sport promoters desiring the same date and time?
7. Identify the four components of operations management.
8. List the operations manager's responsibilities.
9. When coordinating an event, what are the elements considered important from an operational perspective?
10. List the important elements concerned with the development of an emergency manual.
11. How has technology helped to make security more effective?
12. Discuss the TEAM process in terms of its strengths and weaknesses.
13. What measures need to be taken to ensure prompt and professional emergency response training for facility staff?
14. Define the terms *housekeeping, maintenance, engineering,* and *structural and equipment maintenance.*
15. List the elements of a maintenance and housekeeping plan.
16. Explain the following terms: *in-house food service management, concessions, stocking, convenience foods,* and *hawkers.*
17. Under what circumstances would you let an in-house food service management operation contract?
18. Explain the following terms: *novelties, bootlegging,* and *merchandising deals* with sport teams and athletes.

19. Why is the box office an important segment of the facility operation?
20. Identify the important components of box office operations.
21. What is a budget?
22. How does the political/government budget process differ from the private/operational budget?
23. Identify and comment on the phases of the budget cycle.
24. Describe the various budget types that can be involved in a facility budget.
25. Identify and describe the phases of a white paper. How does this apply to a sport facility?
26. Describe how event settlement works in a sport facility.
27. List internal auditing procedures that could be used in the various segments of the facility operations.
28. Why is it important to develop collections procedures?
29. Identify traditional revenue sources and operational segments in a facility.
30. List additional revenue sources.
31. Identify the essential elements of the risk management process, and describe the function of each.

SOLUTIONS TO CRITICAL THINKING EXERCISES

1. Identify, assess, treat, and develop standard operating procedures. Torn carpet, protruding objects, wet spots, lighting, access points, proper food preparation, etc.
2. Marketing a new facility is a fairly simple task. Marketers usually focus on the new amenities and try to build an exciting image to entice the patrons to come and see the new facility. The target market in event marketing is usually much narrower than when marketing a facility. So in promoting an event, a marketer can use much more specific enticements to draw patrons to the facility.

FOSTERING YOUR WORKPLACE SKILLS

1. Assume that you are the facility manager at the Coliseum. Develop a standard operating procedure (SOP) for spills (something omitted

from the operations manual). In this procedure, you need to describe what role, if any, the various departments would play in reporting, monitoring, and/or cleaning up spills.

2. After you have written your SOP, discuss the following problem. (Assume that the SOP has been put into effect and that it is reasonable in terms of implementation.) A spill has just taken place, and the following events occur: (1) Three ticket takers see the spill and do nothing; (2) two security guards see the spill, but they are called to a fight and do not report the spill until 15 minutes after they spotted it; (3) an usher immediately reports the spill but does not keep patrons from walking in the area; (4) the cleaning crew cleans the spill 40 minutes after it was notified of it (45 minutes after it occurred); and (5) a patron slipped and fell because of the spill, broke an ankle, and is suing the Coliseum for $45,000.

 WEBSITES

FacilitiesNet

www.facilitiesnet.com/—This site for facility professionals includes industry news; an online bookstore; bulletin boards; *Building Operating Management, Maintenance Solutions, Energy Decisions,* and *Education* magazines; and information on products and equipment.

International Facility Management Association (IFMA)

www.ifma.org—Site includes publications, job opportunities, online library, product information, publishing opportunities in the *Facility Management Journal,* training seminars, and World Workplace conference. IFMA focuses on management and administration needs of facility managers.

REFERENCES

Associated Press (2003). Available: http//www.teamcoalition.com.

Berlonghi, A. (1990). *The special event risk management manual.* Dana Point, CA: Self-Published.

Cleveland Browns-News Room (2003). Available at http//www.clevelandbrowns.com/news.

Davidson, S., Maher, M., Stickney, C., and Weil, R. (1988). *Managerial accounting: An introduction to concepts, methods and uses.* Chicago: Dryden Press.

Garrison, R. (1982). *Managerial accounting.* Plano, TX: Business Publications.

Hitt, W. (1985). *Management in action.* Columbus, OH: Battelle Press.

International Association of Auditorium Managers (1990). Unpublished proceedings, Ogelbay, Virginia, School for Public Assembly Facility Management.

Jewel, D. (1992). *Public assembly facilities.* Malabar, FL: Krieger.

Laventhol and Horwath. (1989). *Convention centers, stadiums, and arenas.* Washington, DC: Urban Land Institutes.

O'Shaughnessy, J. (1988). *Competitive marketing: A strategic approach.* Boston: Unwin Hyman.

TEAM Coalition (2003). Available at http//www.teamcoalition.com/about/policies.

The NCAA News (2003). Available at http//www.ncaa.org/news.

Thompson, A., and Strickland, A. (1990). *Strategic management, concepts and cases.* Homewood, IL: BPI Irwin.

Walgenbach, P., Dittrick, N., and Hansen, E. (1980). *Principles of accounting.* New York: Harcourt Brace Jovanovich.

CHAPTER 10

Basic Law Applied to Sport

Annie Clement

In this chapter, you will become familiar with the following terms.

Acceptance
Assault
Assumption of risk
Battery
Civil Rights Act (1991)
Civil Rights Restoration Act
 (1987)
Clayton Act (1914)
Comparative fault
Compensatory damages
Consent
Consideration
Contract
Contributory negligence

Disclaimers
Equal protection clause
Equity in Athletics Disclosure
 Act
False imprisonment
First Amendment
Fourth Amendment
Fourteenth Amendment
Freedom of the press
Freedom of religion
Freedom of speech
Injunctive relief
Intentional tort
Invasion of privacy

Negligence
National Labor Relations Act
Norris-LaGuardia Act (1932)
Offer
Procedural due process
Product liability
Punitive damages
Reckless misconduct
Reserve clause
Rozelle Rule
Self-defense
Sherman Act (1890)
Standard of care
Title IX

Learning Goals
By the end of this chapter, students should be able to:

- Define and identify negligence and its elements—duty, breach, cause, and damage.

- Understand an intentional tort and how it differs from negligence.

- Define product liability and understand the responsibilities of the manufacturers and retailers.

- Understand how constitutional and statutory laws, including the First, Fourth, and Fourteenth constitutional amendments, apply to the management of sport.

- Explain the basic concepts of equal protection under the Fourteenth Amendment and why it is important to sport and sport management.

OVERVIEW

The law applied to sport, often referred to as sport law, has experienced tremendous growth in the past 10 to 15 years. This is a result of the industry's recognition of the importance of law to the daily concerns in sport and physical activity. Law provides the unique knowledge that enables sport, recreation, and physical activity specialists to analyze the professional standards of care and design risk management protocols. Another element in the success of law in sport is the magnitude of sport literature produced by legal researchers. This interest and accommodation from the legal profession reinforces sport's presence as a rapidly growing and important business. This chapter will provide an overview of legal theories of significance to the entry-level sport management professional. It will include the torts of negligence, intentional tort, and product liability. Contracts will be mentioned as well as the constitutional and statutory areas of the First, Fourth, and Fourteenth Amendments to the U.S. Constitution, labor law, and antitrust law.

NEGLIGENCE

Negligence, a tort often found in sport and physical activity, usually results from injuries suffered while participating in risky endeavors. Negligence is defined as something that a reasonable person would not be expected to do or failing to do something that a reasonable person would be expected to do. It is conduct that falls below the standard, established by law, for the protection of others from unreasonable harm (Restatement, Second Torts, 282). Elements of negligence are:

Duty
Breach of duty
Breach of the duty the cause of the injury
Damages

For negligence to be found by a court of law, all four elements must exist. Legal duty is the responsibility of the defendant to the plaintiff. It may be the duty of an ordinary person or a member of society in general, or it may be the higher duty of a professional acting in his or her professional capacity. The legal duty of a professional is the same as the professional's **standard of care.** The plaintiff must prove that the legal duty existed and that it was breached or not carried out. Further, the plaintiff has to demonstrate that the breach of the legal duty was the cause of the injury. Damages must exist. Damages may be physical or psychological; most sport injuries tend to be physical.

Defenses

Defenses to torts include contributory negligence and assumption of risk. **Contributory negligence** exists when the injured party did or did not do something that contributed to his or her injuries. A person who fails to wear a life jacket in a boat, assembles equipment incorrectly, or ignores safety recommendations may have contributed to his or her injuries. **Assumption of risk,** another defense found in sport incidents, requires that the plaintiff knew of the danger or was given facts sufficient to enable a reasonable person to comprehend the danger involved. The user must be aware of the danger, recognize and appreciate the risk involved in the danger, and voluntarily take the risk. **Comparative fault** is a system in which the relative fault of each party is assessed and is used in awarding damages. If the victim were to be found 40 percent responsible for his or her injuries and the person in charge of the activity found 60 percent responsible, a $100,000 damage award would result in only $60,000 for the injured party.

Damages

Damages, or relief from the court, may be compensatory, punitive, or injunctive. **Compensatory damages** are medical bills, lost wages, rehabilitation, and other expenses associated with the injuries. **Punitive damages,** in contrast, are damage awards fashioned by the court in an effort to stop agencies and persons from causing serious harm to the public. They are based on the assets of the agency or person causing the harm and the perceived amount of money necessary to stop the agency or individual from continuing to engage in the harmful activity. The third type of damage is **injunctive relief,** or the stopping of the harm.

Cases

The following are cases in negligence, one in golf and one in football. Shirley Alters and Elizabeth Wolinski were playing golf together (*Alters v. Wolinski,* 2002). Wolinski was driving a golf cart. An incident occurred and Alters ended up with a broken ankle. Two different stories were told to the court. Alters said that Wolinski drove over her ankle and leg with her golf cart. Wolinski said that Alters was riding in the cart and decided to get out of it while the cart was moving. She saw Alters fall from the cart, but she did not think that she had hit Alters. The jury returned a unanimous verdict finding that Wolinski, the driver of the golf cart, was not negligent. The court of appeals confirmed the trial court's decision.

In *Southwest Key Program v. Gil-Perez* (2002), Gil-Perez sued a home for boys stating that the home was negligent in permitting the young men to play tackle football without protective equipment. Gil-Perez sustained a severe knee injury. In his suit, he alleged negligence supervision and negligent instruction and organization of the game. The jury found for the victim. The program appealed. The court of appeals reversed the earlier court's decision and found for the program. Also, they found that the evidence was insufficient to show the element of cause in negligence.

INTENTIONAL TORTS

Intentional torts differ from negligence in that negligence pertains to an incident that one did not expect. An intentional tort is an intentional act. The person engaging in the act may or may not have intended to harm another. In intentional torts the court will ask if there was an intent merely to do the act, or an intent to do the act and to harm the plaintiff. An act executed with intent to harm another is not only an intentional tort but could become a criminal offense (Clement, 2004). Intentional torts include battery, assault, false imprisonment, and reckless misconduct.

Battery is an intentional physical contact with another person without the person's consent. Many batteries occur in sport. If the battery is a strategy used in the sport, the courts will assume that the participants consented to the battery when they chose to participate in the sport. When the battery is outlawed by the rules of the sport, automatic consent no longer exists and the offense could become actionable. Assault is the threat of harm or the belief by the person experiencing the assault that he or she is in great danger. The threat must be physical; words, as threatening as they may be, do not constitute assault.

False imprisonment is intentionally restraining or confining another. This is a popular legal theory in shoplifting. **Reckless misconduct** is conduct creating "an unreasonable risk of physical harm to another"(Restatement, Second, Torts, 500).

Defenses

Defenses to an intentional tort are consent, self-defense, and defense of others. Consent occurs when the person involved does not object to the act or accepts the act as part of game play. **Self-defense** and defense of others permits a person who has been attacked to protect themselves and others from harm. The person may take whatever actions are reasonable for that protection and until professional assistance can be obtained.

Case

Christensen was found guilty of aggravated battery following an incident in a pick-up soccer game when he punched a player in the face fracturing the player's eye socket (*Christensen v. The State*, 2000). The trial court held Christensen to a criminal conviction for aggravated battery. This means that the intentional tort (hitting the player) was so severe that it was close to being a crime. Christensen appealed. One of his claims was self defense; he believed that he was about to be hit by the injured player. The Court of Appeals of Georgia did not accept Christensen's claim and affirmed the trial court's decision.

PRODUCT LIABILITY

Sport managers may be manufacturers, wholesalers, retailers, owners, or users of sport-related products. Sport equipment is a major retail business. Persons who invest money in sport equipment expect that the equipment or product will be safe and will meet his or her needs.

Whether the sport administrator is the chief executive officer of a large sporting goods manufacturer, purchasing agent for a National Football League team, or a person about to purchase a first set of golf clubs, product liability is important. **Product liability** becomes an issue when a product is defective. For the product to be considered defective, the defect must have existed when the product left the manufacturer's or retailer's contact, and the defect must have caused the injury.

The three primary types of product defects are defective manufacturing, defective design, and inadequate or faulty instructions or warnings. A manufacturer's defect means that the product does not perform or was not built as the manufacturer planned or that an unsafe product has been created in the construction process. A defective design means that the product, built according to the manufacturer's plan, contains a design flaw or fault that will expose the user to unreasonable harm.

Inadequate or faulty instructions or warnings means that the manufacturer, wholesaler, and retailer have a duty to provide instructions on the proper use of the product and to warn of risks of dangers. Instructions should be provided in such a way that the purchaser would eagerly pass them on to the users of the product.

Duty to warn

A manufacturer and a retailer have a duty to warn when the product danger is not apparent to the purchaser. Many courts have ruled that there is no duty to warn if the danger is obvious. Some courts have said that even though the danger might be considered obvious to some people, the manufacturer retains a duty to warn. When the user, as a result of expertise and experience, knows of the product's danger, there is no duty to warn. When a profession generally knows a product's dangers, there is no duty to warn.

Misrepresentation

Misrepresentation is an untrue statement of fact that leads a person to believe something that is not true. When the seller has misrepresented facts about a product or made misleading statements about its use, an injured plaintiff may sue for misrepresentation. The product need not be defective or unreasonably dangerous; however, a physical injury is required for a claim to be brought.

Advertisements, brochures, and salespeoples' statements should be examined for misrepresentation. In the retail industry, the comments of salespeople should be monitored to ensure that the purchaser is aware of potential hazards and risks of using the equipment.

Consumer Product Safety Act

In 1968 Congress established the National Commission on Product Safety to explore the need for federal regulation of consumer products. Congress had found many unacceptable products, including ones from which people were unable to protect themselves (15 USCA 2051[a]). The commission proposed the Consumer Product Safety Act (CPSA) to reduce the unreasonable risk of injury and death that comes with the use of products available to the public. The legislation helps consumers evaluate products, helps develop safety standards, promotes research, and supports investigations into the causes of injuries and death (15USCA 2051[b]). The CPSA also requires manufacturers to inform the commission of substantial product hazards that can cause serious harm to users. An individual injured by a product whose manufacturer is in violation of a consumer product safety rule may bring an action in federal court.

Defenses

Defenses to product liability are contributory negligence, assumption of risk, misuse, and disclaimers. Contributory negligence and assumption of risk were discussed earlier. A major defense in breach of warranty is the **disclaimer.** This is a statement in which the manufacturer and retailer explain how the product is to be used and state that they will not be responsible if the product is used in ways other than that recommended.

CONCEPT CHECK

Product liability is the responsibility of the manufacturer, wholesaler, and retailer of sport equipment. For the product to be considered defective, the defect must have existed when the product left the manufacturer or retailer and the defect must be the cause of the injury. The Consumer Product Safety Act was created to reduce injury and death resulting from the use of products. State law also exists in this area.

CONTRACTS

A **contract** is a legally enforceable agreement between two or more people in which one of them has made an **offer,** the party to whom the offer was made has **accepted** the offer, and **consideration** has been determined. Consideration is usually money; however, it can be something meaningful other than money. Contracts may be oral or in writing. Only adults can be held to a contract; minors are not permitted to enter into contracts. A number of state and federal codes, including the Uniform Commercial Code, dictate the types of agreement that are required to be in writing. Agreements with merchants, for example, are under the Uniform Commercial Code.

A contract is breached when one of the parties fails to live up to the agreement. When this occurs the nonbreaching party may ask the courts to settle the dispute. The court will determine the validity of the contract. If the contract is valid, the court may direct the parties to carry out the promises or provide a damage award to the person harmed by the breach. Some contracts are drafted with liquidation damages to be paid in the event of a breach. There are many types of contract, including employment agreements, warranties, leases, and releases.

CONSTITUTIONAL AND STATUTORY LAW

The U.S. Constitution is the primary law of the nation. In addition, each state has its own constitution. Federal and state statutes, executive orders, and city ordinances are laws enacted by legislative bodies to ensure efficient management at all levels of government. The U.S. Constitution and respective state constitutions bind state courts. Constitutional and statutory laws may be litigated in state and federal civil courts; statutory laws may be enforced by agencies designed to carry out the particular laws.

The First, Fourth, and Fourteenth Amendments to and Article 1 of the U.S. Constitution play an important role in the interaction between sport management professionals and their clients. Historically, the First and Fourteenth Amendments applied only to actions of federal agencies. Today, state agencies (such as recreation commissions and schools) are covered.

FIRST AMENDMENT

The **First Amendment** states, "Congress shall make no law respecting an establishment of religion, or prohibiting the free exercise thereof; or abridging the freedom of speech, or of the press; or the right of the people peaceably to assemble, and to petition the Government for a redress of grievances." First Amendment rights are the freedoms of religion, speech (including symbolic protest), and press. In making decisions about the freedoms of religion, speech, and press, the courts balance the needs of the public against the rights of the individual.

Freedom of religion

Under the First Amendment's **freedom of religion,** the government may not enact laws that aid a particular church or religion. Also, the First Amendment guarantees the right of religious belief and the freedom to practice that belief. The amendment separates church and state, and protects people in their religious beliefs. The establishment clause of the First Amendment allows, for example, free bus transportation and textbooks to parochial schools.

The 2000 Supreme Court decision in *Santa Fe v. Jane Doe,* the current controlling decision on prayer in school athletic events, was that the Texas "school district's policy authorizing high school student's delivery of invocation and/or message before home varsity football games was held to violate the establishment of religion clause of the federal Constitution's First Amendment. . . ." The district had permitted students to read Christian prayers at graduation ceremonies and home football games. Also, the students had voted on how the situation would be handled and elected the students that were to give the invocations.

Freedom of speech

Freedom of speech is the freedom to speak, to remain silent, to discuss with others, and to advocate and communicate ideas. Ideas can be conveyed, but language that is obscene, libelous, or slanderous is not protected. Verbal and expressive speech in public is not to be suppressed unless it interferes with the normal course of mainstream society or causes harm to others. The courts will examine the following points to determine whether speech should be protected.

1. Subject of the speech
2. To whom the speech is directed
3. Location of the speech
4. Manner of delivery

Freedom of the press

Freedom of the press is freedom to write and draw, which is similar to freedom of speech.

Invasion of privacy

Invasion of privacy, closely related to the Fourth Amendment search-and-seizure clause, is often an issue in drug testing and the reporting of a suspicion of drug use. The right has been challenged among amateur and professional athletes. The state's interest with reference to drug testing is the health of athletes, particularly that of minors, and the establishment and maintenance of the natural competitive qualities of the performers. The athletes' interest is privacy. Details of invasion of privacy will be discussed under the Fourth Amendment.

CONCEPT CHECK

The First Amendment to the U.S. Constitution provides for freedom of religion, speech, and the press. Freedom of religion guarantees all persons the right of belief and the freedom to practice their beliefs. The First Amendment separates church and state and protects people in their religious beliefs. An area of First Amendment of concern to sport managers is prayer in public sport events.

FOURTH AMENDMENT

"The right of the people to be secure in their persons, houses, papers, and effects, against unreasonable searches and seizures, shall not be violated, and no warrants shall issue, but upon probable cause, supported by oath or affirmation, and particularly describing the place to be searched, and the persons or things to be seized." The system for analyzing facts under the **Fourth Amendment** is the same as that used in First Amendment analysis: balancing the needs of the state against the needs of the individual.

Drug testing

Cases having to do with testing for drugs in academic institutions include *University of Colorado v. Derdeyn* (1991, 1993, 1994[a], 1994[b]); *Hill v. National Collegiate Athletic Association* (1994); *Acton v. Vernonia School District* (1995, 1994, 1992) and *Vernonia School District 47 v. Acton* (1995); *Board of Education of Independent School District No. 92 of Pottawatomie County, et al. v. Lindsay Earls, et al.* (2002); and *Todd v. Rush County Schools* (1998). Leaders in athletics believe that drug testing is necessary for the safety and health of the athletes and to assure fair competition.

Challenges to drug testing have focused on league rules, university policies, and standards employed in the drug-testing industry. *University of Colorado v. Derdeyn* involved the constitutionality of the university drug-testing program instituted to prepare athletes for the mandatory NCAA drug-testing policies. The tests ranged from random testing of athletes' urine samples obtained under direct visual observation to a system that depended on "reasonable suspicion" based, in part, on a random rapid-eye-movement examination.

A trial court determined that the program violated the students' Fourth Amendment rights and their rights under the Colorado constitution. Also, the consent given by the students for the tests was found to be coerced. The Colorado Supreme Court affirmed this decision. The court stressed that when student consent was not voluntary, it could not be used to validate an unconstitutional search. The University of Colorado's petition to the U.S. Supreme Court for a writ of certiorari was denied, as was the petition to the same court for rehearing was denied.

In January 1994, the Supreme Court of California ruled in *Hill v. National Collegiate Athletic Association (NCAA)* that the NCAA drug-testing program did not violate the plaintiff's California constitutional right to privacy. Individual student privacy was balanced against the NCAA's need to maintain an equitable form of competition and a safe playing environment.

Acton v. Vernonia (1995, 1994, and 1992) and *Vernonia School District 47 v. Acton* resulted in a U.S. Supreme Court decision that upheld the right of public schools to randomly test athletes for drugs. Wayne Acton's parents refused to consent to the drug-testing policy and brought a suit against the school system for violating their son's Fourth and Fourteenth Amendment and Oregon Constitution rights. The district court found for the school; the Ninth Circuit Court of Appeals reversed. The Supreme Court accepted the case. The Supreme Court reversed the Ninth Circuit and found for the school, affirming the district court's decision. The reasoning of the Court was the same as the reasoning found in *Hill*.

In 2002, in *Board of Education of Independent School District No. 92 of Pottawatomie County, et al., v. Lindsay Earls, et al.*, the U.S. Supreme Court again ruled on this issue, stating that "Public school district's subjection of all students participating in district's competitive extracurricular activities to urinalysis drug testing held not to violate Federal Constitution's Fourth Amendment" (822).

Todd v. Rush County Schools found the Seventh Circuit Court of Appeals upholding a school policy that required all students engaging in extracurricular activities to submit to random drug testing. At the same time the Colorado Supreme Court ruled that a random drug test of members of a school marching band was unconstitutional (*Trinidad School District No. 1 v. Lopez*, 1998).

CONCEPT CHECK

The Fourth Amendment provides a right for persons to be secure against unreasonable searches, including drug testing. Drug testing is important to ensure the safety and health of athletes and to maintain equitable competition. Court decisions show that random drug testing has been prohibited in universities when permission for the tests was coerced but accepted when the NCAA took the leadership in obtaining permission.

FOURTEENTH AMENDMENT

The **Fourteenth Amendment** states, in part, "No State shall make or enforce any law which shall abridge the privileges or immunities of citizens of the United States; nor shall any State deprive any person of life, liberty, or property, without due process of law; nor deny to any person within its jurisdiction the equal protection of the laws". State actions are covered under the Fourteenth Amendment to the Constitution; private actions, unless explicitly stated, are not covered. Analysis under these laws is the balancing of the interests of the state against the rights of the individual. Procedural due process and equal protection are the areas of greatest significance to the sport manager.

Procedural due process

Procedural due process is a system that enables members of society to be assured of fair treatment. It provides an opportunity for an individual to be heard, to defend personal actions, and to be assured of fair treatment before a right or privilege is taken

away. The following are basic concepts to consider in creating a due process system:

1. Knowledge of the charge and complaint.
2. A right to a hearing in which one may choose to use an attorney or other counsel.
3. Opportunity to respond to charges with adequate time to prepare the response.
4. Opportunity to present witnesses and to question witnesses presented by others.

Employers and administrators have a number of well-defined responsibilities to their employees. Procedural due process is used in hiring, evaluating, and terminating an employee.

CONCEPT CHECK

The due process clause of the Fourteenth Amendment is a system for assuring fair treatment of a person when a right or privilege is taken from them.

Equal protection

The Fourteenth Amendment's **equal protection clause** states, "No state shall make or enforce any law which shall . . . deny to any person within its jurisdiction the equal protection of the laws." An equal protection challenge in scholastic or collegiate sport could be a complaint by a group of people, such as women, that they are being treated different from men in athletics and that no justification exists to warrant the difference is treatment.

Among the cases that prompted the creation of Title IX of the Educational Amendments of 1972 and influenced their operating guidelines were *Brenden v. Independent School District* (1972, 1973), *Hollander v. Connecticut Interscholastic Athletic Association, Inc.* (1971, 1972), *Reed v. Nebraska Athletic Association* (1972), and *Haas v. South Bend Community School Corporation* (1972). *Brenden, Hollander, Reed,* and *Haas* were complaints in which high school women requested the opportunity to participate on men's teams when no team was available to women. *Brenden, Reed,* and *Haas* succeeded; *Hollander* failed. Requests were granted in Nebraska, Minnesota, and Indiana, and denied in Connecticut.

Title IX of the Education Amendments of 1972

Title IX states that "No person in the United States shall, on the basis of sex, be excluded from participation in, be denied the benefit of, or be subject to discrimination under any education program or activity receiving Federal financial assistance." Title IX extended the principles articulated under the Fourteenth Amendment to all schools, public and private, that rely on federal and state funds. Title IX is enforced by the Department of Education, which can withhold federal funds for violation of the statute.

Many of the complaints in the early days of Title IX were resolved within the school districts, by other agencies, or by the Office of Civil Rights. Among the few complaints that went to court were *Yellow Springs Exempted Village School District v. Ohio High School Athletic Association* (1981), *Gomes v. Rhode Island Interscholastic League* (1979), and *Petrie v. Illinois High School Association* (1979).

The equal protection clause of the Fourteenth Amendment, Title IX of the Education Amendments, and various state equal rights statutes provide protection against and have been used as avenues of redress for discrimination. Generally, female high school athletes have employed the Fourteenth Amendment to gain entry to sports; college athletes have used Title IX for the same purpose.

Examples of leading gender equity court decisions

Ridgeway (1988, 1986), *Haffer* (1987), and *Blair* (1989) are the classic cases that charted the course in discrimination issues.

Ridgeway v. Montana High School Association, the most comprehensive decision on athletics at the secondary level, was a class action suit brought on behalf of all Montana high school girls against the Montana High School Athletic Association alleging violation of Title IX, the Fourteenth Amendment to the U.S. Constitution, and the Montana Constitution. The plaintiffs claimed that discrimination existed in the number of sports, the seasons of play, the length of seasons, practice and game schedules, and access to facilities, equipment, coaching, trainers, transportation, the school band, uniforms, publicity, and general support. The parties accepted an agreement that provided for equal opportunity and placed a court-appointed facilitator in charge.

Haffer v. Temple University concerned Temple University women currently participating in athletics and those who had been deterred from participating because of sex discrimination. Their claims focused on three basic areas: the extent to which Temple University afforded women students fewer "opportunities to compete" in intercollegiate athletic, the alleged disparity in resources allocated to the men's and women's intercollegiate athletic programs, and the alleged disparity in the allocation of financial aid to male and female students. The complaint alleged discrimination in opportunities to compete, expenditures, recruiting, coaching, travel and per diem allowances, uniforms, equipment, supplies, training facilities and services, housing and dining facilities, academic tutoring, and publicity. These actions were in violation of the Fourteenth Amendment and the Pennsylvania Equal Rights Amendment. The court ruled for the plaintiff in all areas except meals, tutoring, facilities, and scheduling.

Blair v. Washington State University was similar to the foregoing decisions, except that the trial court chose to exclude football in the equity calculation. The plaintiff appealed the football decision, and the Washington Supreme Court reversed the decision, requiring that football be included in all calculations for finance and participation. Although this decision is precedent only for the state of Washington, it serves as an example in other states.

Civil Rights Restoration Act (1987)

The **Civil Rights Restoration Act (1987)** restored Title IX to it original strength and removed the program-specific status. Title IX was once again applied to an entire institution and to the institution's entire program.

Civil Rights Act (1991)

The **Civil Rights Act (1991)** placed the burden of proof on those who practiced discrimination, not on those who suffered discrimination. For example, when discrimination is alleged in a university athletic department, the athletic department and the university have the burden of proof. They must show evidence of equitable participation in intercollegiate athletics and in intramural and club sports and must demonstrate that no discrimination occurred or currently exists.

Further, the 1991 Civil Rights Act provided the victims of intentional discrimination with the right to recover damages. Punitive damages are based on reckless indifference.

Equity in Athletics Disclosure and Fair Play Acts
Within the 1994 reauthorization of the Elementary and Secondary Education Act is a provision requiring schools to publish male/female enrollment and athletic participation ratios. Schools are to list varsity team membership; operating and recruiting expenses; number, gender, and salary of coaches; student aid; and revenue generated by sports. The Fair Play Act requires that the information obtained in the **Equity in Athletics Disclosure Act** be published and available to the student consumer who wishes to make an informed decision in selecting a school.

The following are examples of a few cases settled in recent years. *Roberts v. Colorado State Board of Agriculture* (1993[1], 1993[2], 1993[3]) saw current students and former members of the women's varsity fast-pitch softball team bring suit challenging the elimination of Colorado State University's softball and baseball teams in response to budget cuts. The district court and the U.S. Court of Appeals, Tenth Circuit, required the university to hire a coach and put softball back into its program.

In *Cohen v. Brown University* (1977, 1996, 1995, 1993, 1992), women gymnastics and volleyball team members brought a class-action suit against Brown University, a private college, following the demotion of their teams from varsity to club status. The U.S. District Court for the District of Rhode Island issued a preliminary injunction restoring the teams to varsity status (1992). The U.S. Court of Appeals, First Circuit, affirmed. The district court, after a lengthy trial, found Brown University to be in violation of Title IX and ordered the institution to submit a plan of compliance in 120 days (1995). Brown failed to meet the requirement and appealed. The U.S. Court of Appeals upheld the district court's ruling that Brown University had violated Title IX; Brown University's petition to the United States Supreme Court was denied (*Brown University et al. v. Cohen, et al.*, 1997).

Pederson et al. v. Louisiana State University et al. (1996), a case consolidated with a complaint by Pineda, claimed unequal treatment of female varsity athletes. Intent had become important to

contemporary cases because the courts have to find intent before they award punitive damages. The court found the university in violation of Title IX; however, the court stated that the university did not intend to harm the women. The "Court holds that the violations are not intentional. Rather, they are a result of arrogant ignorance, confusion regarding the practical requirements of the law, and a remarkably outdated view of women and athletics which created the byproduct of resistance to change" (918). (Cases submitted by Peterson and Pineda were combined by the courts.)

Horner et al. v. Kentucky High School Athletic Association et al. (2000, 1994) was a class action suit in which the claim was that the association's failure to sanction fast-pitch softball violated the Equal Protection clause of the Fourteenth Amendment, Title IX, and the Constitution of the Commonwealth of Kentucky. The district court granted defendant's motion for summary judgment, holding that, "(1) Defendants had complied with Title IX because they had offered equal opportunities in accordance with the interests and abilities of students; and (2) Defendants had complied with the Equal Protection Clause because they permitted students to participate in sanctioned sports without gender restriction." The plaintiff appealed. The court of appeals affirmed the judgment for the defendants on the equal protection claim because plaintiff failed to prove intentional discrimination. They reversed the decision with reference to Title IX. The Kentucky High School Athletic Association changed its rules, permitting fast-pitch softball and thus eliminating the Title IX claim. Horner appealed. The U.S. Court of Appeals for the Sixth Circuit affirmed the equal protection and other claims. The women accomplished their goal but they did not win the lawsuit.

National Wrestling Coaches Association et al. v. United States Department of Education (2003) was an action requesting that the U.S. Department of Education stop enforcing Title IX, a statute prohibiting sex discrimination in education. The National Wrestling Coaches Association also challenged the Department of Education's enforcement of their 1979 Policy Interpretation and 1996 Clarification of Title IX, and the enforcement of its regulations. Plaintiffs contend that both of these policy statements violate the Equal Protection component of the Due Process of the Fifth Amendment, and exceed the agency's regulatory authority under the statute by requiring the very discrimination the statute prohibits." Defendants moved to dismiss the action. The courts granted the defendant's motion to dismiss the case.

CONCEPT CHECK

Equal protection and Title IX are the leading legal theories of sex integration in athletics. They were strengthened by the Civil Rights Act of 1987 and 1991. The Civil Rights Act of 1991 authorized money damages, compensatory and punitive, in Title IX decisions.

ARTICLE 1 OF THE U.S. CONSTITUTION

Article 1, Section 8, Number 3 states that Congress shall have the power "to regulate commerce with foreign nations, and among the several States, and with the Indian tribes"; Number 18 gives Congress the power "to make all laws which shall be necessary and proper for carrying into execution the foregoing powers, and all other powers vested by this Constitution in the Government of the United States, or in any department or officer thereof." This congressional authority has been further expanded by the **Sherman Act (1890),** the **Clayton Act (1914),** the **Norris LaGuardia Act (1932),** and the **National Labor Relations Act.** Antitrust and labor relations theories in these laws influence the rights of players and team owners in professional sports.

Labor laws

The Sherman Act (1890) set the stage for the evolution of antitrust law. Its purpose was to promote competition in the business sector through regulations designed to control private economic power. Professional sport, a private business operated to make a profit, comes under the laws. The Sherman Act regulates interstate commerce, including goods, land, and services. Violations of the act are examined by the courts using a rule-of-reason test that balances the illegal practice against the anticompetitive effect. Procompetitive and anticompetitive goals are examined in an effort to find the least restrictive means to reach a legitimate procompetitive goal. For example, is the restraint of a

professional player's movement from one team to another the least restrictive method of maintaining equity in competition? Is the restraint of a professional player to a one-year contract commitment to a particular team a viable method of maintaining equity in competition?

Sections 4 and 6 of the Clayton Act (1914) are significant to professional athletes as they negotiate individual contract components and collective-bargaining agreements. "The courts may award under this section . . . simple interest in actual damages for the period beginning on the date of service of such person's pleadings."

Section 6 states that "the labor of a human being is not a commodity or article of commerce." The Clayton Act strengthened and defined the Sherman Act. The act gives direction to athletes seeking redress for violations of antitrust and labor laws. Unfortunately, baseball's exemption from antitrust laws, discussed later, has denied baseball professionals a means of redress for many years.

The Norris-LaGuardia Act (1932) defines, and in some authors' opinion, restricts the incidents in which federal courts can grant an injunction in labor disputes. The Norris-LaGuardia Act (1932), and the sections of the Clayton Act that it reinforces, protects union activity from antitrust scrutiny. Union–management agreements that are a product of "good-faith" negotiations receive protection from antitrust law.

Under the National Labor Relations Act, "Employees shall have the right to self-organization, to form, join, or assist labor organization, to bargain collectively through representatives of their own choosing, and to engage in other concerted activities for the purpose of collective bargaining or other mutual aid or protection."

It is an unfair labor practice for either an employer or a labor organization to restrain or coerce an employee in the exercise of his or her rights. It is also an unfair labor practice for a labor organization to refuse to bargain collectively with an employer that is the official representative of its employees. The National Labor Relations Board (NLRB) is authorized by the act to hear and render decisions on unfair labor practices. It also has the power to petition the U.S. District Court for appropriate temporary relief or a restraining order. The National Labor Relations Act guides businesses and members of unions, including athletic-player unions, in negotiations and in implementing collective-bargaining agreements in sport.

Antitrust cases

Through the years, sport has presented some unique issues to the courts for antitrust examination. The sport industry differs from other businesses in many ways. A consumer who is unhappy with the goods or services of a typical business can seek another source of supply, while in sport there is no real substitute for the college and professional sport market.

Another unique characteristic of sport is that its product or service is the competition between teams. Equity (a level playing field) must be maintained to enable live spectators and television audiences to observe close, exciting, and competitive encounters. League owners are forced to work together to secure the league while at the same time engaging in fierce competition with the other members of the league.

Only in sport does a player join a collective-bargaining unit and then negotiate individually for additional resources. In business and industry, the employee is either a member of a union, accepting the results of a collective-bargaining agreement, or an independent worker, negotiating an individual employment contract. Athletes, upon employment, automatically become members of players' union, which negotiates basic elements of the work, economic, and fringe benefits package. All athletes accept the results of this agreement, and outstanding athletes then bargain, usually through their agents, for additional economic and work-related privileges.

Unique among sports are the three U.S. Supreme Court decisions that exempted baseball, prior to 1998, from all antitrust laws. In *Federal Baseball Club of Baltimore v. National League of Baseball Clubs* (1922), the Supreme Court held that baseball was exempt from the Sherman Act because it did not meet the definition of "interest commerce."

In 1953, the Supreme Court had a chance in *Toolson v. New York Yankees* to reverse its earlier decision and deny baseball the antitrust exemption awarded in 1922. The issue was that the **reserve clause** was an alleged violation of the Sherman and Clayton Acts. The plaintiff focused the complaint on television in an effort to demonstrate interstate commerce. The court reaffirmed *Federal Baseball,*

saying that the business of baseball had operated successfully for 30 years and the antitrust exemption should stand. *Flood v. Kuhn* (1972) involved the professional player Curt Flood, who was traded to another club without his knowledge. The Supreme Court, in maintaining baseball's antitrust exemption, noted that professional baseball's long-standing exemption from antitrust law was an established aberration not held by other sports but that it should be allowed to stand.

Curt Flood Act of 1998

The Curt Flood Act of 1998 provides: "that major league baseball players are covered under the antitrust laws (i.e., that major league baseball players will have the same rights under the antitrust laws as do other professional athletes, e.g., football and basketball players), along with a provision that makes it clear that the passage of this Act does not change the application of the antitrust laws in any other context or with respect to any other person or entity" (P. L. 105-297).

Although other sports profit from minor antitrust exemptions, baseball's exemption has not been extended to all sports. Television network pools, blackouts of nonlocal telecasts when the home team is playing at home, and blackouts of home team games when it is playing in home territory constitute antitrust exemptions. These exemptions exist in a number of sports, but football appears to profit most from them.

In 1974, football players decided to challenge the Rozelle Rule under antitrust law (*Mackey v. National Football League,* 1992). The **Rozelle Rule** was a practice started in the 1960s that required a team signing a veteran free agent to compensate the team that lost the player. Compensation was usually a player or draft-choice trade. Although different from baseball's reserve clause, a system football players had previously worked under, the new Rozelle Rule was viewed as equally offensive. Even more difficult for football players to understand was the fact that football was subject to antitrust law, which should have given them greater freedom.

The district court found that the Rozelle Rule violated the Sherman Act. The Eighth Circuit Court of Appeals affirmed the district court. Following the *Mackey* decision, a right-of-first-refusal compensation was developed through the collective-bargaining system. Under this rule, owners were permitted to match outside players' offers and by so doing, retain a player's service. The right of first refusal was not popular with players; they believed that it gave too much control to the owners. In light of the fact that the first-refusal system of compensation was negotiated by the players' union and that unions usually have limited antitrust exemptions, the players had a difficult challenge in their many trips to court to attempt to change the first-refusal system (*Powell v. National Football League,* 1991). Finally, in *McNeil,* judge Doty played a major role in crafting contract provisions that have become the current standard. Teams now have exclusive rights over players for their first three years in the league; in years four and five, players remain under a limited right of first refusal; and at the end of year five, players become unrestricted free agents. Salary cap implementation is accompanied by free agency in the fourth year. A number of categories such as "franchise player" and "designated transition player," have been established to accommodate the needs of outstanding talent.

CONCEPT CHECK

Article I of the Constitution and the Sherman, Clayton, Norris-LaGuardia, and National Labor Relations Acts established the antitrust and labor law theories and that influence the rights of players and team owners in professional sports. The Sherman and Clayton Acts promote competition and prohibit monopolies, the Norris-LaGuardia Act address the needs of the individual, and the National Labor Relations Act provides a road map for collective bargaining.

Professional athletes have used the courts to gain freedom from contract restraints imposed by team owners.

SUMMARY

- Negligence is something that a reasonable person would not be expected to do or failing to do something that a reasonable person would be expected to do. Elements of negligence are duty, breach, cause, and damage.

- Comparative fault assesses the relative fault of each party and is used in the damage award. Damages are compensatory, punitive, and injunctive.
- In intentional torts, the plaintiff intended the act.
- Managers who are manufacturers, wholesalers, retailers, or owners of sport products play a role in product liability. The three primary types of product defects are manufacturing defects, design defect, and lack of proper instruction or warnings.
- Consumer Product Safety Commission statutes have been created to reduce society's risk of injury and death from the use of products.
- A contract is a legally enforceable agreement between two or more people or agencies.
- The U.S. Constitution is the primary law of the country, and each state has a constitution or primary set of laws. In addition, federal and state statutes have been enacted by legislative bodes to ensure efficient management of the federal and state governments.
- The First Amendment to the U.S. Constitution includes the rights of religion, speech, and press.
- The Fourth Amendment to the U.S. Constitution involves privacy rights.
- Under the First and Fourth Amendments, the courts balance the needs of the state against the needs of the individual.
- Primary elements of the Fourteenth Amendment are due process and equal protection. Procedural due process enables an individual to be heard, to defend his or her action, and to be assured of fair treatment before a right or privilege is taken away. An equal-protection challenge must show that groups of people are being treated differently, without justification, than the general public.
- Title IX states that "No person in the United States shall, on the basis of sex, be excluded from participation in, be denied the benefit from participation in, be denied the benefit of, or be subject to discrimination under any of, or be subject to discrimination under any education program or activity receiving Federal financial assistance."

- The Civil Rights Act (1991) placed the burden of proof on those who practice discrimination and provided for both punitive and compensatory damage recovery.
- Article 1 of the U.S. Constitution and the Sherman, Clayton, Norris-LaGuardia, and National Labor Relations Acts identify the rights of players and team owners in professional sports.
- The Sherman and Clayton Acts promote competition and prohibit monopolies.
- Sports differ from business and industry in market, product definition, and employment agreements.

 CRITICAL THINKING EXERCISES

1. Create a secondary or collegiate sports program that will meet the requirements for equity under the Fourteenth Amendment to the U.S. Constitution. Be sure to identify the school enrollment.

 REVIEW QUESTIONS AND ISSUES

1. Obtain a printed court decision and locate the elements of negligence in the decision.
2. Obtain a printed agreement and identify the components of a contract in the document.
3. The duty to warn includes a duty to inform the purchaser about the proper use of the product and to warn of potential dangers in the use of the product. Using a product you know, write a warning statement for that product that satisfies both the duty to inform and the duty to warn.
4. Using the results of court decisions, explain the U.S. Constitution's First Amendment freedoms of religion, speech, and press.
5. Explain the balancing system used by the courts in First and Fourth Amendment decisions.
6. Explain procedural due process, identifying when and how it is used.
7. Explain the relationship between the Fourteenth Amendment's equal-protection clause and Title IX of the Education Amendments (1972) in athletics.

8. How do labor laws define antitrust relationships?
9. Identify and explain the unique characteristics of sport as a business.
10. Contrast baseball's antitrust exemption with the treatment of other sports under antitrust law.

 SOLUTIONS TO CRITICAL THINKING EXERCISES

1. Student responses will be individualized.
   You are employed as a clerk selling fishing boats in a sporting goods store. As you finalize a boat sale it becomes apparent that the new owners do not know how to swim. Under product liability, duty to warn, do you have an obligation to tell the new owners that they should be able to sustain their bodies in deep water should an accident occur?

FOSTERING YOUR WORKPLACE SKILLS

1. You are a college athletic director. An administrator, who has authority over your department, complains to you about a football player who drops to one knee and silently says a quick prayer after scoring touchdowns. The administrator does not feel this is appropriate during a game, even though it causes no delays. How do you handle this situation in regards to the First Amendment's protection of freedom of religion?

 WEBSITES

Women's Equity Resource Center
http://www.edc.org/WomensEquity—The Women's Educational Equity Act (WEEA) Equity Resource Center was established more than 20 years ago to bring support and resources to the many exceptional efforts that are improving the education of girls and women in the United States. The WEEA Center is a national project that promotes bias-free education, believing that gender equity works for everyone—for girls and women, men and boys.

Legal Information Institute
http://www.law.cornell.edu/topics/sports.html—Provides an overview of sports law, including links to federal and state resources.

The Sports Lawyers Association
http://www.sportslaw.org—The Sports Lawyers Association (SLA) is a nonprofit, international, professional organization

whose common goal is the understanding, advancement, and ethical practice of sports law. There are over 1,000 current members: practicing lawyers, law educators, law students, and other professionals with an interest in law relating to professional and amateur sports.

Lexis Nexis Universe

http://www.lexis.com—Contains most state and federal cases at the appeals level or higher. Also contains law reviews and other legal periodicals.

REFERENCES

Acton v. *Vernonia School District*, 66 F. 3d 217 (1995) and 23 F. 3d 1514 (1994) and 796 F. Supp. 1354 (1992).

Alters v. Wolinski, DO37596, 2002 Cal. App. Unpub. LEXIS 5490.

Blair v. Washington State University, 740 P. 2d 1379 (Washington, 1989).

Board of Education of Independent School District No 92 of Pottawatomie County, et al. v. Earls, 536 U. S. 822, 122 S. Ct. 2559 (2002).

Brenden v. Independent School District, 342 F. Supp. 1224 (1972), affirmed 477 F. 2d 1292 (1973).

Civil Rights Restoration Act (1987), Public Law 100-259, 102 (1987).

Civil Rights Act (1991), Public Law 102-166 (1991).

Clayton Act (1914), 15 USC 15, 4 and 6 (1914).

Clement, A. (2004). *Law in sport and physical activity*. Cape Canaveral, FL: Sport and Law Press.

Cohen et al. v. Brown University, et al., 101 F. 3d 155 (1996); 879 F. Supp. 185 (1995); 991 F. 2d 888 (1993); 809 F. Supp. 978 (1992); and *Brown University v. Cohen*, 117 S. Ct. 1469 (1997).

Consumer Product Safety, 15 USCA Section 2051 to 2083. St. Paul, MN: West pp. 209–294.

Curt Flood Act of 1998, Public Law 105-297, Sect. 2, 112 Stat. 2824.

Federal Baseball Club of Baltimore v. National League of Baseball Clubs, 259 U. S. 200 (1922).

Flood v. Kuhn, 407 U. S. 258 (1972).

Gomes v. Rhode Island Interscholastic League, 441 U. S. 958; 99 S. Ct. 2401 (1979); 469 F. Supp. 659 (1979) vacated as moot, 604 F. 2d 733 (1979).

Haas v. South Bend Community School Corporation, 289 NE 2d 495 (1972).

Haffer v. Temple University, 524 F. Supp. 531 (Ed Pa. 1981), affirmed 688 F. 2d 14 (3rd Cir. 1982) and 678 F. Supp. 517 (Ed. Pa. 1987) and 115 FRD 506 (Ed. Pa. 1987).

Hill v. National Collegiate Athletic Association, 865 P. 2d 633 (1994).

Hollander v. Connecticut Interscholastic Athletic Association, Inc., Civil No 12-49-27 (Super. Ct., New Haven, Conn., March 1971); appeal dismissed 295 A. 2d 671 (1972).

Horner v. Kentucky High School Athletic Association, 206 F. 3d 685 (2000), 43 F. 3d 265 (6th Cir. 1994).

Kama v. California State University, CO33757, 2001 Cal. App. Unpub. LEXIS 2476.

Mackey v. National Football League, 543 F. 2d 606 (1976) and cert. Dismissed 434 U. S. 801 (1977).

McNeil v. National Football League, 790 F. Supp. 871 (1992).

National Labor Relations Act, 29 USC 157.

National Wrestling Coaches Association, et al. v. United Sates Department of Education, Civ. No. 02-0072 (EGS), 2003 U. S. Dist. LEXIS 9677.

Norris LaGuardia Act (1932), 29 USC 102 (1932).

Pederson, et al. v. Louisiana State University, 912 F. Supp. 892 (1996).

Petrie v. Illinois High School Association, 75 Ill. App. 980, 394 N. E. 2d 855 (1979).

Powell v. National Football League, 764 F. Supp. 1351 (1991); 930 F. 2d 1293 (1989); 690 F. Supp. 812 (1988); 678 F. Supp. 777 (1988).

Reed v. Nebraska Athletic Association, 341 F. Supp. 258 D. Neb. 1972).

Restatement, Second, Tort, St. Paul, West.

Ridgeway v. Montana High School Association, 858 F. 2d 579 (9th Cir. 1988); 633 F. Supp. 1564 (1986); 638 F. Supp. 326 (1986).

Roberts v. Colorado State Board of Agriculture, 998 F. 2d 824 (1993[1]); 814 F. Supp. 1507 (D. Colo. 1993[2]); and *Colorado Board of Agriculture v. Roberts*, 510 US 1004; 114 S. Ct. 580 (1993[3]).

Santa Fe v. John Does, 530 U.S. 290 (2000).

Sherman Act (1890), 15 USC 1 and 2 (1890).

Southwest Key Program v. Gil-Perez, 81 S. W. 3d 269 (Tex. 2002).

Title IX of the Education Amendments of 1972, 20 USC 1681 (1976).

Todd v. Rush County Schools, 133 F. 3d 984 (1998).

Toolson v. New York Yankees, 346 US 356 (1953).

Trinidad School District No. 1 v. Lopez, 963 P. 2d 1095 (1998).

University of Colorado v. Derdeyn, 832 P. 2d 1031 (1991); 863 P. 2d 929 (Colo. 1993); 114 S. Ct. 1646 (1994[a]); petition for writ of certiorari denied; 62 USLW 3843 (June 20, 1994[b]); petition to U. S. Supreme Court for rehearing denied.

Vernonia School District 47J v. Acton, 515 U. S. 646; 115 S. Ct. 2386 (1995).

Yellow Springs Exempted Village School District v. Ohio High School Athletic Association, 647 F. 2d 651 (1981).

PART III

Economics and Finance

Discussion Topic

James Madison University renovated their athletic program in 2000 because of a possible Title IX lawsuit demanding a women's softball team, and because of a reduced budget caused by an economic crisis in Virginia. The Athletic Director (AD) had to decide how to maintain the sports being offered, add another sport, and still balance the reduced budget. The AD had to make some unpopular decisions regarding scholarships for particular sports. The AD directed some of the revenue saved from the restructuring to programs with better revenue potential—football and men's basketball.

Group Discussion Question: As the AD, what resources and information would you use to determine: (a) the revenue possibilities of each sport; (b) the annual expenditures of each sport; (c) which teams should have scholarships eliminated and why; (d) the increases that should be given to football and basketball and why; and (e) the narrative needed to gain support for your decisions?

CHAPTER 11

Economics and Sport

Michael A. Leeds

In this chapter, you will become familiar with the following terms:

Absolute advantage	Marginal revenue	Price ceiling
Comparative advantage	Marginal utility	Profits
Complements	Monopoly	Purchasing power effect
Demand	Monopsony	Substitutes
Equilibrium	Multiplier effect	Substitution effect
Excess demand	Negative externality	Sunk costs
Excess supply	Normal goods	Supply
Inferior goods	Opportunity costs	
Marginal cost	Positive externality	

Learning Goals
By the end of this chapter, students should be able to:

- Recognize how the basic economic forces of maximization, constraint, and cost—particularly opportunity cost—apply to the sports industry.

- Use supply and demand to explain movements in prices and salaries in the sports industry.

- Identify and apply the different types of cost.

- Appreciate the importance of reasoning "on the margin."

- Grasp the concept of comparative advantage and how it applies to sports.

WHAT IS ECONOMICS?
Economics is unlike any other discipline one encounters in college. It is not a set of facts to memorize or dates to remember. Instead, it is a way to interpret everyday events. It is little wonder that one finds economics departments in both colleges of liberal arts and colleges of business, since economics applies equally well to discussions of Microsoft's marketing policy and the status of women in developing countries. One economist has even used economic theory to divine the true meaning of *The Wizard of Oz*.[1]

---

[1]Rockoff, 1990.

The word *economics* comes from the Greek word *oikonomikos,* which literally means "household management." While it seems a long way from running a household to running a multinational corporation, economists point out that successful management of both boils down to putting the resources at hand to their best possible use. Economists have also established basic principles of behavior that characterize how people decide what to do. These principles apply whether one is a stockbroker on Wall Street, an auto mechanic in Havana, or a Bedouin in Yemen. All that differs is the setting within which one applies these principles. This chapter will introduce several basic principles of economic behavior and show how they apply to the world of sports. While each economist may come up with his or her own set of basic rules, some variation of the following will be at the core of anyone's list of economic principles:

- All our actions involve costs and benefits.
- Decisions are typically made on the margin.
- Freely functioning markets are typically the best way to allocate resources.
- People should specialize and trade with one another according to their comparative advantage.
- Under some circumstances markets fail, and government can increase social well-being.

The remainder of this chapter will explain each of these principles and show how each applies to the realm of sports.

COSTS AND THE NEED TO CHOOSE

Economists believe that individuals and groups base their decisions on comparisons of the costs and benefits of their actions. These costs often take the form of an explicit price tag. For example, if you spend $100 on tickets to a Philadelphia Flyers hockey game on Saturday night, then you have $100 less to spend on tickets to a Philadelphia Eagles football game on Sunday afternoon.

One need not spend money to suffer a cost. For example, if one friend offers to take you to an Eagles game while another offers to take you to a Flyers game that same night, you spend no money. However, since you cannot be in both places at once, you still endure a cost. Here the cost is the happiness you would have experienced if you had gone to the game you chose to miss. Economists call these missed chances **opportunity costs.** Opportunity

costs can occur because of explicit expenditures (spending your money on the Flyers instead of the Eagles) or because of implicit expenditures (spending your *time* with the Flyers instead of the Eagles).

Opportunity costs also play a role in the decisions made by producers. In fact, they account for the difference between how economists and accountants view **profits.** To an accountant, profits are the difference between the revenues a firm takes in and the expenditures it must make in order to produce. Economists consider this picture incomplete, because it does not take into account the profits the firm could have made had it decided to produce something else. A firm could thus make sizable *accounting profits* but—because it could have made even higher profits doing something else—endure an *economic loss* (negative *economic profits*) at the same time.

The main advantage to using accounting profits as a measuring stick is the fact that one can readily observe them. One cannot really compute economic profits, because they involve opportunity costs and hence rely on a counterfactual question: how well could the firm have done if it had produced something else? One can, however, infer the existence of economic profits or losses by looking at the behavior of firms. If the firms in an industry are making an economic profit, then the accounting profits in that industry exceed the opportunity costs, which are the profits that could be made elsewhere. Other firms thus have an incentive to enter the industry. If the firms in the industry are making an economic loss, then the accounting profits do not exceed the opportunity costs, and the firms in the industry have an incentive to leave. One can tell if firms in an industry are making economic profits by observing whether firms are entering or exiting the industry.

An example of how opportunity costs affect producers can be found in the move of the Brooklyn Dodgers to Los Angeles in 1958.[2] From 1903 to 1953, the so-called Golden Era of Baseball, no major league baseball teams entered, left, or changed cities. In the early to mid-1950s, several teams changed cities: the Braves moved from Boston to Milwaukee, the Athletics from Philadelphia to Kansas City, and the Browns from St. Louis to Baltimore, where they were

---

[2]The New York Giants also left for the West Coast after the 1957 season, but they were clearly following the Dodgers' lead.

rechristened the Orioles. All these teams, however, were losing money in cities that had other, more profitable teams (the Boston Red Sox, Philadelphia Phillies, and St. Louis Cardinals). The Dodgers' departure from Brooklyn was another matter entirely. When they moved, the Dodgers were the most profitable team in baseball.

At first glance, it seems incongruous that such a prosperous team should seek to leave while other, less profitable teams—like the Washington Senators, whom the city of Los Angeles initially sought to attract[3]—stayed put. The key to the move can be found in the notion of opportunity cost. While the Dodgers made considerable profits in Brooklyn, their owner, Walter O'Malley, recognized that having the Southern California market all to himself would bring untold riches. Thus, despite making considerable accounting profits in Brooklyn, the Dodgers were operating at an economic loss.

OPERATING ON THE MARGIN

In this era of multimillion-dollar contracts, team owners routinely complain that the high salaries they pay to their players force them to raise ticket prices. Such reasoning sounds plausible. After all, if a firm's costs go up, it seems perfectly reasonable for the firm to try to recoup the cost, and the only way to do so is to pass the higher costs along to customers in the form of higher prices. However, applying such reasoning to free agents and ticket prices ignores one of the basic rules of economic behavior: people consider the *marginal* impact of their actions.

To see what marginal thinking is and to appreciate its importance, suppose that you are the lucky student who purchased the millionth copy of this textbook. As a prize, the publisher offers you a choice: it will send you either a one-carat diamond or a glass of water.[4] The choice seems absurdly easy; presumably everyone would take the diamond. Choosing the diamond, however, raises a serious problem. A diamond, after all, is a luxury item that has little practical use for most of us, while we all need water to survive. It seems absurd that someone would choose a glittery trinket over something that would keep her alive, yet that is what we would all do.

The key to the paradox lies in the need to distinguish between the total happiness, total utility, that we gain from a good with the *marginal* happiness—or **marginal utility**—that it brings. The total value of water to us dwarfs the total value of diamonds, but none of us considered total values when choosing the diamonds. We were concerned only with how much extra happiness or utility we would get from *one more* glass of water or *one more* diamond. The fact that water is readily available reduces the happiness one gains from one more glass of it—its marginal utility—almost to zero. Unless you are dripping in diamonds, the marginal utility of one more diamond will be very high, despite the fact that you realize that water is, on the whole, more important. (See Figure 11-1.) Similarly, people and firms typically worry about what they have to pay to get a little more of something rather than what they have spent overall. When buying diamonds or water, for example, we ask ourselves how much we would have to spend to get a few more diamonds or a little more water rather than how much we have ever spent on these two items. **Marginal costs** are the reason why we may choose to buy a little more water rather than another diamond even though the additional diamond brings us much more additional happiness. A little more water may mean less

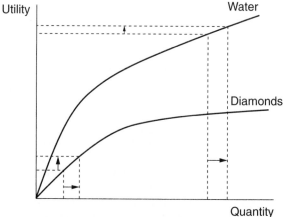

FIGURE 11-1   The total utility of water is much higher than the total utility of diamonds, but an extra diamond adds more utility than an extra glass of water. As a result, moving to the right along the utility curve for water causes utility to rise only slightly. Moving to the right along the utility curve for diamonds causes utility to rise by a greater amount.

[3]Sullivan, 1987, p. 42.
[4]This is one example of the classic "diamond-water paradox."

than another diamond to us, but it costs so much less than a diamond that we may still prefer buying it.

This simple insight has enormous implications. It tells us that we can predict human behavior by looking only at the benefits and costs of doing a little more. The benefits and costs of what came before do not matter. Firms and people become as happy as they possibly can when they equate the marginal benefits with the marginal costs of their actions. Think of a firm's profits as a large pile of money. Additional revenues take the form of more dollar bills on top of the pile, while additional costs mean that the firm takes some bills off the top. The firm's profits rise with an additional sale, as long as it can put more bills on top of the pile than it removes. Profits fall when an additional sale removes more bills from the top than it adds. The firm will thus expand its sales as long as it can add to the height of the pile. The height of the pile is maximized when the amount it adds and the amount it removes are equal, that is, when **marginal revenue,** the extra revenue the firm receives for selling one more unit of output, equals marginal cost, the cost to the firm of producing and selling one more unit of output. (See Figure 11-2.)

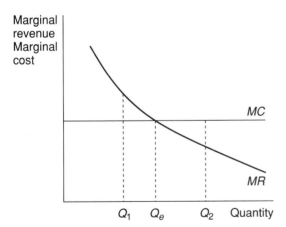

FIGURE 11-2   At Q_1 marginal revenue exceeds marginal cost, so the firm can add more to revenue than to costs by producing more. At Q_2, marginal cost exceeds marginal revenue, so the firm can reduce its costs more than its revenues by producing less. At Q_e, the firm cannot increase its profits by changing its level of output. A small change in output causes costs and revenue to rise or fall by the same amount.

Now suppose that a fire breaks out and burns away half the pile. Economic theory tells us that since the fire does not affect anything the firm will do in the future—it simply burned away profits from previous actions—the firm should not do anything differently. Setting marginal revenue equal to marginal cost still maximizes the height of the pile; the pile just is not as high as it once was. In effect, the economic principle of thinking marginally teaches us that we should ignore past costs—what economists call **sunk costs**—and let "bygones be bygones."

Consider now the impact of signing a free agent to a huge contract, such as the Philadelphia Phillies' signing of Jim Thome for $85 million. The contract adds greatly to the Phillies' total costs. However, it has no impact on the Phillies' marginal costs. To see why, one must first recognize that the Phillies' are not selling Jim Thome. Rather, they are selling *tickets* that enable people to watch Thome (and others) play. Jim Thome will cost the Phillies' $85 million whether they sell three million or three hundred tickets. Since they must pay him his salary no matter what, his salary represents a sunk cost and is irrelevant to any decision about tickets or ticket prices.

Still, teams do raise their ticket prices when they sign expensive free agents. They do so, however, not because they must but because they can. Signing a new star player excites the team's fans and makes them more eager to see the team play. This, in turn, makes them willing to pay a higher price to see the team play.

SUPPLY AND DEMAND

When people ask economists why it costs hundreds of dollars for a family of four to see a basketball game or why a highly educated social worker earns a small fraction of the salary of a minimally educated linebacker, the response invariably contains the phrase "supply and demand."

Understanding the forces of supply and demand reveals the solution to several puzzles. Specifically, it shows

- why championship teams frequently raise ticket prices the next season.
- why it is so hard to get a ticket to a Duke University basketball game.
- why salaries in the NBA are so much higher than in the WNBA.

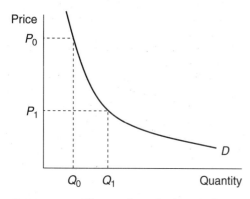

FIGURE 11-3   The number of tickets Duke fans are willing and able to buy rises from Q_0 to Q_1 as the price of tickets falls from P_0 to P_1.

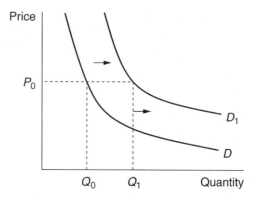

FIGURE 11-4   The increased demand for Duke basketball makes fans willing to buy more tickets at any given price. At price P_0, fans are now willing to by Q_1 tickets to Duke games.

The **demand** for tickets to a Duke basketball game at the Cameron Arena (or for any good or service) is the relationship between the price of those tickets and the number of tickets that consumers are willing *and able* to buy. As seen in Figure 11-3, this relationship is invariably negative: as the price of tickets falls, the number of tickets that consumers are willing and able to buy rises. The *demand curve,* which illustrates the relationship between the price of tickets and the number of tickets that consumers buy, slopes down.

The relationship is negative for two reasons. First, if the price of tickets to Duke games falls, consumers buy more tickets and fewer other goods (such as tickets to UNC games, textbooks, or pizzas). We call this displacement of other goods the **substitution effect,** because consumers substitute tickets to a Duke basketball game for other items they could buy.

The lower price of tickets also allows consumers to buy more tickets and *more* of other items as well. Because consumers' money goes farther than it did, we call this impact the **purchasing power** (or *income*) **effect.** Increases in purchasing power will normally lead consumers to buy more of an item, so we call such goods **normal goods.** Sometimes, however, consumers will buy less of an item as their purchasing power rises. We call such items **inferior goods.** While many low-quality items (such as generic napkins, or poor cuts of meat) are inferior goods, the term need not imply that a good is bad. For example, as one's income rises to extremely high levels, one may buy fewer diamonds and more

rubies. All "inferiority" means in this context is that one buys less of something as one's purchasing power rises. A good can be inferior for a given person at a given income level yet be normal for a different person with the same income or the same person with a different income level.

The willingness or ability of consumers to buy tickets to Duke games—and hence the position of the demand curve—may rise or fall for a number of reasons. For example, as the desire to consume a particular item increases, consumers become willing to spend more for that item. As teams become more successful, their fan base expands beyond a set of hard-core fans. The added interest of fans causes the demand for tickets to increase, pushing the demand curve out to the right (see Figure 11-4).

As long as tickets to Duke games are normal goods, changes in income increase the number of people willing and able to buy them. As a result, the demand for tickets should be higher among relatively wealthier groups[5] (again, see Figure 11-4). This also means that the demand for tickets should be *pro-cyclical,* rising in good economic times and falling in bad times.

A decline in the price of another good will cause the demand for Duke tickets to rise or fall, depending upon whether the other good is a **complement** or a **substitute** for tickets. For example, a decline in

---

[5]This helps to explain why most sports—even those for which a majority of the participants are black—have primarily white fans.

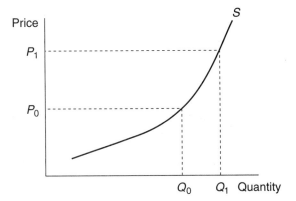

FIGURE 11-5   As the price of tickets rises from P_0 to P_1 the number of tickets Duke is willing and able to sell rises from Q_0 to Q_1.

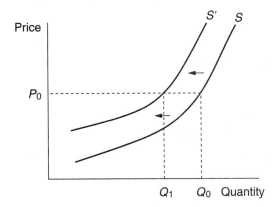

FIGURE 11-6   The higher costs of inputs makes Duke willing to supply fewer tickets at any given price.

the price of tickets for a Duke women's game will cause some fans to switch from going to men's games to going to Duke women's games. Tickets to women's games are substitutes for tickets to men's games. On the other hand, a decline in the price of Duke paraphernalia or parking fees around Cameron Arena will cause attendance at men's games to rise, since many fans also spend money on parking, T-shirts, or pom-poms (complementary items) as part of a trip to a game (see Figure 11-3).

The **supply** of a good is also a relationship between price and quantity. This example relates the price of tickets to the number of tickets that Duke is willing and able to provide. Duke can increase the number of tickets it sells either by increasing the number of tickets it sells per game or by increasing the number of home games that it plays. As the price of tickets rises, the marginal benefit of admitting another person to a game rises, and Duke has an incentive to sell additional tickets. The supply relationship is thus positive, and the *supply curve* slopes up, as seen in Figure 11-5.

The position of supply curves also depends upon a variety of factors. If the cost of *inputs* to staging a ball game rises, then at any price the marginal cost of admitting another fan rises. This reduces the incentive for Duke to provide seats, and the supply curve shifts to the left (see Figure 11-6).

Similarly, technological or institutional changes may affect the position of the supply curve. Changes in travel technology have enabled teams to get to

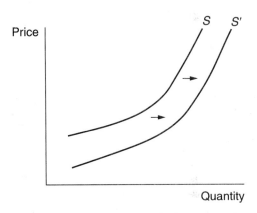

FIGURE 11-7A   Technological advances push out the supply curve.

and from away games more quickly and easily, allowing them to schedule more games, pushing the supply curve to the right (see Figure 11-7a). The limits placed by the NCAA on the number of games that basketball teams may play shifts a portion of the supply curve back (see Figure 11-7b).

Finally, the rewards to alternative activities may affect how much of a product a firm will want to provide for any given reward. If the price Duke could charge for admission to a women's basketball game rose high enough, it may inspire Duke to schedule more women's games and to decrease the number of men's games it stages, shifting the supply curve to the left (see Figure 11-7b).

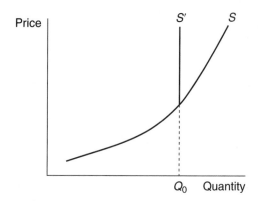

FIGURE 11-7B   A limit on the number of games shifts back a portion of the supply curve. In this case, a limit of Q_0 games per season causes the supply curve to become vertical at Q_0.

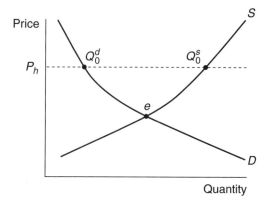

FIGURE 11-9A   Excess supply ($Q_0^s - Q_0^d$) occurs when price is above equilibrium. Producers are willing and able to sell Q_0^s, but consumers are willing and able to buy only Q_0^d.

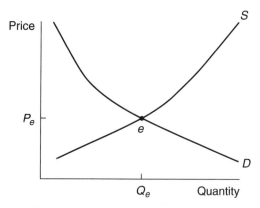

FIGURE 11-8   The equilibrium price and quantity occurs where supply and demand meet. Everyone willing and able to buy the item at the price P_e can do so, and everyone willing and able to sell the item at the price P_e can do so.

Taken alone, supply and demand simply express a series of "if/then" statements: if the price of a ticket to a Duke basketball game is P_0, then fans want to buy Q_0^d, tickets, while the university wants to sell Q_0^s. Neither one says how many tickets fans buy, how many tickets Duke sells, or what the price of a ticket is. To determine what actually happens, economists combine the concepts of supply and demand by literally combining the supply and demand curves into a single picture. Figure 11-8 shows that the two curves cross at the point

labeled e. Economists call e the **equilibrium** point, because at that point the actions of consumers and producers are in balance. In this case the balance is between the quantity of tickets that Duke fans are willing and able to buy at the price P_e and the quantity that Duke is willing and able to sell at P_e. As a result, neither fans nor the university have any desire to alter either the price that is charged (the equilibrium price) or the quantity that is bought and sold (the equilibrium quantity).

The meaning of equilibrium becomes clearer when one sees what happens at prices other than the equilibrium price. If producers charge a price above the equilibrium price (P_h in Figure 11-9a), **excess supply** (also known as a *surplus*) results, because customers are willing and able to buy only Q^d while producers are willing and able to sell Q^s. Frustrated because they cannot sell all that they are willing and able to sell at the price P_h, producers will lower the price they charge in order to attract more customers. As the price of Duke tickets falls, more fans are willing and able to buy the tickets. A lower price of tickets, however, reduces the incentive Duke has to stage games for its fans, decreasing the supply of tickets to Duke games. The larger quantity demanded and the smaller quantity supplied reduce the excess demand until the price reaches P_e, and the excess supply vanishes.

If producers charge a price below equilibrium (P_1 in Figure 11-9b), **excess demand** (or a shortage) results, because producers are not willing and able to

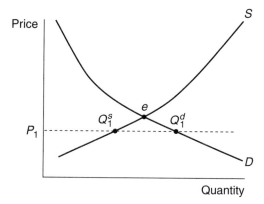

FIGURE 11-9B   Excess demand ($Q_1^d - Q_1^s$) occurs when price is below equilibrium. Here consumers are willing and able to buy Q_1^d, but producers are willing and able to sell only Q_1^s.

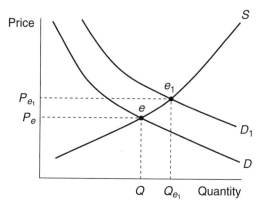

FIGURE 11-10   When demand rises the equilibrium changes from e to e_1 and equilibrium price and quantity rise.

sell as much as consumers are willing and able to buy. In this example, frustrated Duke fans bid the price of tickets up, causing some fans to stop trying to buy tickets and increasing the incentive for Duke to increase the number of seats it can provide. Again, the price moves in the direction of P_e until the excess demand vanishes.

When demand or supply curves move, the equilibrium price and quantity also change. For example, if Duke were to win the NCAA championship this year, the demand for tickets next year would increase, because people would be more

willing to buy tickets at any given price to see a champion play (Figure 11-10). As a result, the equilibrium price and quantity of tickets to Duke games rise to P_{e_1} and Q_{e_1}. Similarly, if rising fuel prices sufficiently increase the cost of travel to Durham, NC, and thus increase the cost of staging a game, the supply curve would shift back, and the equilibrium price would rise to P_{e_2} while the equilibrium quantity would fall to Q_{e_2}.

Sometimes governments or other authorities decide that the market does not distribute goods or services appropriately. They feel the need to protect low-income residents from the high cost of housing by imposing rent controls. They try to protect the incomes of family farmers with price supports designed to keep the prices they receive high. In the sports world, governments try to protect fans from high admission prices with anti-scalping laws, while schools charge ticket prices to students that are well below the equilibrium price of tickets. Unfortunately, such policies often have unanticipated and undesirable consequences.

Universities often allow their students to purchase tickets at far below the equilibrium price. Their rationale is the desire to be "fair" to students who cannot afford to pay the equilibrium price. It is not clear, however, that a lower price is fair to the students, either. At an artificially low price, excess demand results, since students will be willing and able to buy more tickets than the university makes available (as was true for P_1 in Figure 11-9b).

With price no longer determining who buys a ticket and who does not, Duke must come up with a new method of allocating tickets. The "method"—such as it is—can be found in the crowds of students that camp out for days as they wait for season tickets to go on sale. The students who show up first—and who wait the longest—are the ones who can buy the tickets. Such an allocation "mechanism" fails to lower the price of tickets. It simply replaces the explicit cost of a market price with the opportunity cost of the students' time. A first-come, first-served policy may be more "fair" to students who cannot afford to spend much money on basketball tickets, but it is less "fair" to students who cannot afford to spend much time waiting. Students with demanding classes or jobs will not be able to afford the "cheap" tickets.

The fact that a first-come, first-served policy tends to exclude students who prefer to spend their time doing other things may explain why schools adopt it as an allocation mechanism. Schools may reason that losing money on tickets sold to students who are willing to skip class or miss work to wait for a ticket actually increases their revenue overall. This policy is likely to attract students who are more rabid fans than would a price-based allocation mechanism.[6] The presence of rabid fans is likely to improve the performance of the home team. A more successful team will generate more publicity for the school and will increase the demand for tickets among nonstudents, allowing the school to charge an even higher ticket price to its alumni and outside supporters.

Some schools try to be even more "fair" by distributing the discounted student tickets according to a random lottery. Economists, however, would question whether such a system is fair at all. Under such a system a student who is only mildly interested in basketball (perhaps willing to pay only P_1 in Figure 11-9b) may win the lottery, while a student who desperately wants to see Duke play (and is willing to pay P_h in Figure 11-9a) loses out. Such a system may still work if the students could resell their tickets to those who place a higher value on their tickets.[7] Unfortunately, anti-scalping laws—again erected in the name of "fairness"—prevent such transactions from taking place. Anti-scalping laws prohibit the sale of tickets at prices above the official price listed on the ticket.

Economists call an official price that is set below the equilibrium price a **price ceiling.** Just as a ceiling prevents a helium-filled balloon from rising any farther, a price ceiling prevents the price from rising to its equilibrium level. Two problems result from a price ceiling. First, because the price is held below equilibrium, excess demand results (as in Figure 11-9b), and some consumers who are willing and able to buy the tickets will be unable to do so. Second, if the excess demand for tickets is met randomly, some people who place a high value on the tickets will not receive them, while others who place a relatively low value on the tickets do. For example, a consumer who is willing and able to pay P_h may not win the lottery, while one who is willing

and able to pay P_1 is. In the absence of anti-scalping laws the person who has the ticket can sell it to the person who wants it at an intermediate price, say P_e. This secondary transaction benefits everyone. The buyer pays only P_e for a ticket she values at P_h, while the seller receives P_e for a ticket he values at only P_1. Anti-scalping laws prevent such transactions from taking place, however, as the official price of the ticket is set at P_1.

CONCEPT CHECK

Markets are in equilibrium at the price at which consumers are willing and able to buy the same amount that producers are willing and able to sell. At equilibrium there is no excess demand or excess supply. This occurs where the supply curve and the demand curve intersect. Price ceilings keep the price from rising to the equilibrium level. Excess demand results, frustrating consumers, and misallocating resources. Price floors keep the price from falling to equilibrium, frustrating producers, and again misallocating resources.

COMPARATIVE ADVANTAGE AND THE GAINS FROM SPECIALIZATION

While supply and demand tell us a great deal about what people do, they do not tell us everything. We know, for example, that no individual, household, or nation is completely self-sufficient. We all produce only a small amount of what we need in the course of a day. Think of the breakfast you had this morning or of the clothes you are wearing. Imagine how much time and effort it would have taken to provide all of that from scratch. Relying on others to produce most of the goods and services we consume has vastly increased our standard of living. The same principle has been played out on an international scale by trade between nations that specialize in producing relatively few of their needs. Economists are almost universal in their advocacy of "free trade" among nations.[8]

The principle that people become better off by specializing in relatively few activities can also be found in the sports world. While it was once normal

---

[6]Duke fans, the "Cameron Crazies," are renowned for rowdiness unexpected at an expensive, private university.

[7]College athletes' reselling tickets at highly inflated prices has landed more than one college program in hot water with the NCAA.

[8]Frey et al., 1984.

for football players to play both offense and defense, such players are now rare, and they typically play only one position full-time. The last player in the NFL to play both offense and defense full-time was "Concrete Charlie" Bednarik of the Philadelphia Eagles in 1962. At the college level, players routinely played both offense and defense until the mid-1960s.

The idea that we gain from specialization seems simple enough, but the principle behind it—the theory of **comparative advantage**—has been called "perhaps the most complex and counterintuitive principle of economics."[9] The basic message of comparative advantage is that specialization makes one better off only if one specializes in the correct activity. Initially, one might believe that people should specialize in what they are best at. This idea underlies the thinking of many politicians who oppose free trade. They fear that without protective legislation we shall soon not be able to produce anything, because developing countries will produce everything much more cheaply. This fear is unfounded. Even if a country produces everything more efficiently than we can—that is, if it enjoys an **absolute advantage** in producing the goods—it will still pay for that country to import some goods from us. That is, the other nation may be able to produce some goods slightly better than we can, but it can produce other goods much better than we can. The other nation will be best off if it specializes in the areas where its absolute advantage is greatest, where it enjoys a comparative advantage.

One can find a perfect illustration of the principle of comparative advantage in the career of Babe Ruth with the Boston Red Sox and New York Yankees. From 1915 through 1917, Babe Ruth was one of the best pitchers in baseball. During that period he won 65 games for the Red Sox and lost only 33 with an earned run average of 2.02. As late as 1919 he started 17 games for the Red Sox (and completed 12) and had an earned run average of 2.97. After that year, however, Ruth was sent to the Yankees, for whom he pitched in only five games in 15 years.[10] Instead, Ruth played right field, while the Yankees used pitchers who were clearly his inferiors.

Ordinarily, one would question the sanity of a manager who starts a lesser player in place of a star. In this case, the management of the Yankees recognized that Ruth enjoyed an absolute advantage over the Yankee pitching staff, since he would have done a better job than most of his team's pitchers. Using pitchers other than Babe Ruth probably cost the Yankees an extra run or two every fourth game because the other pitchers were not as good. However, the Yankees also recognized that they would score several additional runs every game if Ruth could concentrate on his hitting. The fact that Babe Ruth was an excellent pitcher but became a towering figure as an everyday player meant that he had an absolute advantage at both positions but had a comparative advantage as an everyday player. Because he specialized at what he was relatively best at, Babe Ruth—and the teams that he played for—are now acknowledged as among the best that ever played the game.[11]

CONCEPT CHECK

People should not try to be self-sufficient. They are better off when they specialize in one activity and buy what they lack from others. They should specialize in the activity at which they have a comparative advantage. One has a comparative advantage in the activity in which one is relatively best. One can be better than others at many different activities, but one has a comparative advantage only in that activity at which one's superiority is greatest.

WHEN MARKETS FAIL

Markets generally do a good job of allocating resources to their most desired use. Government intervention intended to improve the market outcome—such as the price ceilings previously discussed—actually produce a worse outcome. Under certain conditions, however, markets fail to perform properly. When markets fail, government intervention can lead to a socially preferred outcome. Three common sources of market failure, *monopoly* power, *monopsony* power, and *externalities*, play a

---

[9]Buchholz, 1989, pp. 64–65.
[10]Data were taken from "Babe Ruth's Lifetime Stats" online at http://www.baberuth.com/stats.html.

[11]For a more complete treatment see Scahill, 1990.

major role in the sports marketplace. In learning about each source of failure you will also learn

- The monopoly power of the NFL in negotiating media contracts played a major role in an $18 billion television deal.
- The monopsony power that leagues used to exert allowed them to keep the salaries they paid well below what the players were worth. The loss of this power led to an explosion of salaries.
- The positive externalities that cities see in having a professional franchise have led them to provide massive subsidies to millionaire owners.

A firm has **monopoly** power when it dominates a market enough to be able to set the price it wants for a product. When a firm operates in a *competitive* market, it has so many rivals selling the same product that it would lose all its business if it tried to charge more than the prevailing market price. A souvenir vendor selling a Cleveland Indians pennant for $6 will quickly go out of business if he is surrounded by vendors who are selling the same pennant for $5. Firms with monopoly power—a "monopolist" holds the greatest such power by being the only firm in the marketplace—can set the price that they deem best. Monopoly markets are thus marked by higher prices and—since demand curves slope down—lower output than competitive markets.

Firms that compete with each other in a market sometimes try to join together and exercise monopoly power that no one of them could exercise alone. They *collude* with one another by setting a common price and coordinating their sales policies. The U.S. government effectively outlawed most monopolies and collusive organizations, known as *trusts*, with the 1890 Sherman Act. The act and most of the legislation based on it covers two basic types of activities. It prohibits "every contract, combination, . . . or conspiracy in restraint of trade or commerce." It also makes it illegal for firms to "monopolize or attempt to monopolize, or combine, or conspire . . . to monopolize" trade or commerce.[12]

The government can deal with a monopoly by breaking it up into many smaller, competing firms, as the government sought to do with Bell Telephone

in the 1980s. When the government feels that many small firms will operate far less efficiently than one large firm, it may allow the monopoly to remain intact but closely *regulate* its actions.

Professional sports and amateur sports have enjoyed a number of exemptions from our nation's antitrust laws. Baseball enjoys the most extensive exemption of any sport thanks to a 1922 Supreme Court decision that declared that baseball "was not within the scope of federal antitrust laws."[13] None of the other major sports, and no other industry, shares this blanket exemption from antitrust laws. The courts quickly recognized the illogic of baseball's exemption. Though they steadfastly refused to reverse their ruling on baseball, they did hand down repeated decisions that denied similar exemptions to other sports.

The other major sports have exemptions that are limited to specific activities, such as merchandise marketing and media contracts. Even these *limited exemptions* from the antitrust laws have played a major role in the development of several sports. The lifeblood of the National Football League, for example, is its national television contracts with CBS, Fox, and several cable channels.[14] In 1960, the NFL remained a distant second to baseball in popularity. Its games were typically played in baseball stadia and were televised (if at all) under low-paying, locally negotiated agreements.[15] All this began to change when Pete Rozelle was named commissioner of the NFL in 1960. Rozelle immediately sought to replace the collection of local TV markets with a single, centrally negotiated contract. Such a single, networkwide contract meant that stations that wanted to televise a football game had to deal with a single provider, giving the NFL monopoly power over the supply of games to television. The prospect of monopoly power meant that Rozelle first had to obtain exemption from the antitrust laws. In 1961 Congress did extend a limited exemption to the sports not covered by baseball's

---

[12]Quoted in Roberts, 1991, p. 135.

[13]Decision of Chief Justice Oliver Wendell Holmes quoted in Zimbalist, 1992.
[14]Sheehan (1996) claims that if it were not for its lucrative national TV deals, the NFL would be no more profitable than the NHL.
[15]The reliance of football on baseball can even be found in the names of the older teams. The Detroit Lions, Chicago Bears, and New York Giants played off the popularity of the Detroit Tigers, Chicago Cubs, and New York Giants.

exemption, allowing them to negotiate contracts as leagues rather than on a team-by-team basis (Leifer, 1995).

The monopoly power conveyed by the limited exemption gave football the power to restrict the number of games carried on television and to increase the broadcast fees it could charge many times over. Prior to being granted exemption from antitrust legislation, the New York Giants made $200,000 per year from their television contract, while the Green Bay Packers made only $30,000 (Leifer, 1995, p. 130). A recent contract that the NFL signed with ABC, CBS, and ESPN will pay the NFL $18 billion over eight years. When that sum is split evenly among the 30 teams, that works out to approximately $75 million per team per year. Inflation and the growing popularity of football (due in no small part to television) do not come close to explaining such astonishing growth in revenue.

The fact that the revenue goes to the league, not individual teams, and is then split evenly also helps to explain how the NFL can field competitive teams in cities as different as New York and Green Bay. Because the NFL gets so much of its revenue from a common source, the distribution of revenue is the most equal of all the major sports. As a result, football does not have a gulf between teams from "large markets" and teams from "small markets."

While monopolies typically operate in the market for goods and services, one generally finds **monopsonies** in the market for inputs like labor. For much of their history, the major sports teams held extensive monopsony power. Teams were able to limit their players' ability to sell their services to the highest bidder. One powerful tool at their disposal was the reserve clause, which effectively bound a player to his team for as long as the team wanted him.[16] With players unable to seek higher pay elsewhere, owners used this monopsony power to depress wages well below those that would prevail in an open market.

While the reserve clause no longer exists in any major sport, teams still seek to limit player mobility and salaries. Hockey retains the greatest restrictions on mobility, as relatively few players become unrestricted free agents. Baseball has the fewest restrictions, though it has recently introduced a "luxury tax." The luxury tax forces teams that spend more than a specified amount to pay an additional sum into a central pool. This pool is then divided among teams with smaller revenues.

Football and basketball lie between hockey and baseball: Players have relatively easy access to free agency, but *salary caps* impose direct limits on the amounts teams can pay. Salary caps specify that players get a given share of the league's revenues.[17] This share of overall revenues is then split evenly among the teams. Thus, if a league with 30 teams has agreed to pay its players 60 percent of its $1 billion revenue, then each team has a "cap" of $20 million. To allow some room for negotiation, the cap is actually a band of possible amounts centering around the official cap. Teams have become so expert at exploiting loopholes in the salary cap regulations, however, that very few teams actually pay less than the amount specified by the salary cap. During the 1997–1998 season, Michael Jordan alone made more than the official salary cap of the Chicago Bulls. The NBA owners locked out players in 1998 in a successful effort to strengthen the team salary cap by placing limits on how much individual players can earn.

A third cause of market failure is the fact that an individual's or firm's decisions may affect innocent bystanders who have no say in that decision. Economists call such spillover effects *externalities.* An externality that has a deleterious impact on bystanders is called a **negative externality.** The best-known example of a negative externality is pollution. Pollution is a by-product of the production process that affects the health and well-being of individuals who have no say in what the firm does. Because the firm has no reason to account for the costs it imposes on innocent bystanders (it may not even be aware that it is imposing such costs), it does not build these costs into its production decisions, and therefore it overproduces. For example, a chemical factory may have production costs of $15 per gallon for the chemicals that it produces, while the pollution it discards into a nearby stream imposes costs of $10 per gallon on a nearby community. If

---

[16]Professional soccer also placed restrictions on player movement through the use of "transfer fees." These fees force teams to provide monetary compensation to teams whose players they have signed.

[17]The definition of "revenue" has been the source of contentious bargaining between the leagues and the players' unions.

the firm can charge $20 per gallon, it sees that its marginal benefits ($20) outweigh its marginal costs ($15) and will try to expand. The marginal cost to society as a whole, however, includes the pollution ($15 + $10 = $25). This means that society would be better off if the firm produced less.

The conflict between the private decision and the public desire lies at the heart of the market failure from externalities. Governments try to eliminate the conflict by getting the firm to "internalize" the externality. In this example that means getting the firm to account for the damage its pollution causes when it makes its production decision. This often takes the form of fines, taxes, or fees for "pollution permits."[18]

Not all externalities cause harm. A firm's production may convey unintended benefits on the surrounding community, creating a **positive externality**. A firm that creates a positive externality does not take account of the full benefits that it provides to society and produces too little as a result.

Governments try to encourage firms that provide positive externalities to produce more. This sometimes takes the form of patents or copyright laws that give the creator monopoly power over her creation. In other cases, the government provides direct subsidies, such as the grants it provides to individuals and companies that perform basic research.

In recent decades, state and local governments have become increasingly involved in subsidizing sports teams. For example, in 1950 only one major league baseball team (the Cleveland Indians) played in a publicly built stadium. By 1985, seventeen teams were playing in publicly built stadia. In football, the Los Angeles Rams, Los Angeles Raiders, Cleveland Browns, and Houston Oilers all moved to smaller markets (St. Louis, Oakland, Baltimore, and Nashville) to occupy publicly funded stadia. Cities justify such subsidies for team owners who can often be found on *Forbes* magazine's list of America's 400 wealthiest individuals by citing the positive externalities associated with a professional franchise.

Proponents of subsidies claim that the expenditures by fans who attend a sporting event create a ripple effect, not unlike the ripples one sees after throwing a pebble into a still pond. The initial impact is the spending by fans at the stadium and at area hotels and restaurants. The expenditure adds to the incomes of people associated with the team and with the city's hospitality industry in general. These people then spend some of their extra income on a variety of goods and services, adding to the incomes of yet another group of people, starting another round of expenditure. The initial expenditure thus generates additional income for a wide variety of people who have nothing at all to do with the team or stadium, so the initial expenditure might be multiplied many times over. Cities see this indirect **multiplier effect** as a way to stimulate economic growth and to generate tax dollars.

The debate over sports subsidies hinges on the size of the direct impact of the stadium and of the multiplier effect of the initial impact.[19] Most economists agree that the direct impact of a stadium is far smaller than one might believe. A stadium induces growth in a city's economy only if it generates new expenditure within the city's bounds. If a sports franchise draws fans away from some other form of entertainment—if, for example, fans stop going to a local college basketball game in order to attend a professional game—the franchise is rearranging existing expenditure, not generating new expenditure.

Multiplier effects can be similarly overstated. The size of a multiplier depends upon how much induced expenditure remains within the city. Smaller cities are especially likely to see "leakages" into surrounding communities, as people spend money in nearby towns. Regardless of the size of the city, most of the income accrues to a relatively small number of people earning unusually high incomes. These people generally live outside the team's "home" city and spend their time and money elsewhere. They are also likely to spend less of their additional income than are people of more modest means. Smaller induced expenditure further reduces the overall multiplier effect.

As a result of the confusion over direct impacts and multiplier effects, estimates of the value of franchises to cities vary widely. In one particularly egregious example, two studies of the impact that

---

[18]One can buy such permits on the Chicago Mercantile Exchange.

[19]Noll and Zimbalist (1997) have an excellent discussion of the problems involved in measuring the benefits a franchise brings to a city.

the loss of the Colts had on Baltimore's economy varied by a factor of 150.[20]

SUMMARY

- Economics explains why people behave the way they do. It states that people follow certain rules of behavior regardless of the social and institutional setting.
- All our actions involve costs and benefits. Many costs do not involve explicit expenditures. Opportunity costs are the value of actions we could have undertaken but chose not to. Opportunity costs distinguish an economist's view of profits from an accountant's view of profits. Opportunity costs explain why a highly profitable team like the Brooklyn Dodgers would choose to move to Los Angeles.
- Decisions are typically made on the margin. People choose how much of a good to consume by weighing the marginal benefits and marginal costs. Firms base their production decisions on marginal revenues and marginal costs. Sunk costs, expenditures that have already been made, have no role in our decisions.
- Freely functioning markets are typically the best way to allocate resources. The forces of supply and demand naturally push the market toward equilibrium with no central authority.

- Demand curves show the quantity of an item that consumers are willing and able to buy at a given set of prices. Supply curves show the quantity of an item that producers are willing and able to sell at a given set of prices. The equilibrium price and quantity can be found at the intersection of the supply and demand curves.
- Price ceilings impose artificial upper bounds to the price. Keeping the price below the equilibrium creates shortages and may prevent the people who most value the item from being able to obtain it. Anti-scalping laws often exacerbate the problem.
- People should specialize and trade with one another according to their comparative advantage. The best pitcher on the great Yankee teams of the 1920s hardly ever pitched for them. Babe Ruth had an *absolute* advantage as a pitcher, since he was better than the other pitchers on his team. The other pitchers, however, had a *comparative* advantage over Ruth as pitchers because the cost to them of concentrating on their pitching was far less. They did not have Ruth's potential as an everyday player.
- Under some circumstances, markets fail, and government can increase social well-being. Monopoly, monopsony, and externalities are three forms of "market failure."
- Monopoly, a market in which there is only one firm, occurs when there is only one seller in a market. Sports leagues exert monopoly power by colluding, agreeing on common pricing and output strategies. Monopoly power gives league members the power to charge higher prices than if they competed with one another. All the major sports leagues exert monopoly power over national TV contracts. The monopoly power of the NFL helps to explain its recent $18 billion agreement.
- Sports teams used to be able to hold salaries below the equilibrium level by exerting monopsony power over their players. Monopsony exists when there is only one buyer in a market. Leagues owed their monopsony power to the reserve clause, which prevented players from selling their services on an open market.

---

[20]One cited a cost of $200,000 per year, while another said the cost would be $30 million per year (see Quirk and Fort [1992], p. 173).

- Externalities consist of "innocent bystander effects," in which people who are not involved in the market decisions of producers and consumers are affected by those decisions. A negative impact results in a negative externality, and a positive impact results in a positive externality. Professional franchises often use positive externalities to justify the subsidies they demand from cities. They claim that the dollars spent on sporting events have multiplier effects on the local economy.

 CRITICAL THINKING EXERCISES

1. You are a city official in Oakhurst, NJ. A minor league baseball team approaches you and offers to locate in Oakhurst if you will subsidize a new ballpark. What factors should you consider before responding?
2. You are the owner of a franchise that has just been fined $10 million for violation of antitrust laws. What should you do to ticket prices as a result?

 CASE STUDY

Free agency caused salaries in major league baseball to explode. In the first decade of free agency, the average salary rose approximately 700 percent, from about $51,500 in 1976 to over $370,000 in 1985. Owners grew increasingly alarmed as salaries rose to unprecedented levels. In an effort to control salaries, owners replaced Commissioner Bowie Kuhn with Peter Ueberroth, the man responsible for staging the highly profitable 1984 Olympic Games in Los Angeles.

Almost immediately, Ueberroth set out to discourage the owners from spending so freely for free agents. He delivered blistering lectures to them denouncing their free-spending ways and urged them to let each other know which free agents they wished to retain. His arguments had an immediate impact on the owners. Between the 1985 and 1986 seasons, roughly two-thirds of all free agents re-signed with their original teams without a single offer from another team. Salaries rose an anemic 5 percent.

Between 1986 and 1987, average salaries actually fell by 2 percent. Andre Dawson, one of the few stars to sign with a new team, did so only by presenting a signed contract to the Chicago Cubs and telling them to fill in whatever salary they wanted to pay.

The Major League Baseball Players' Association (MLBPA) immediately began to suspect that the owners were conspiring with one another. It responded by filing two separate grievances with independent arbitrators, charging that the owners were colluding with one another in violation of the terms of the collective bargaining agreement. Both arbitrators ruled in favor of the MLBPA. As a result, the owners were forced to stop their collusive behavior and to pay $280 million in damages.

 REVIEW QUESTIONS AND ISSUES

1. Teams that win championships often raise their prices the following season. Use supply and demand to explain why.
2. A student on a full athletic scholarship at Temple University claims that her education costs her nothing. Explain the error of her reasoning.
3. Why did the Texas Rangers raise ticket prices when they first signed Alex Rodriguez?
4. Neighborhoods with sports facilities often complain about traffic tie-ups, loud noises late at night, and increased crime rates. Explain how this shows that sports franchises can produce negative externalities as well as positive externalities.
5. Why did Deion Sanders give up a lucrative career as an outfielder to play football full-time?
6. Professional sports teams have "territorial rights" that prevent other teams in their league from moving close by. Explain how this gives teams monopoly power.

 SOLUTIONS TO CRITICAL THINKING EXERCISES

1. You will want to weigh the costs and the benefits of the franchise. The largest benefit will be the increased spending that occurs in town. You must be careful to count only additional spending in town. You do not want to count

expenditures that people make when going to a baseball game that they would have made on some other activity in town (e.g., going to the local cinema). You will want to apply the appropriate multiplier to the added expenditure to account for the ripple effects of the added expenditure. Since Oakhurst is a small town and much of the economic impact is likely to spill over, the multiplier effect is likely to be small. You may want to account for intangible benefits like increased visibility and civic pride, although these are hard to quantify. Against these benefits you will want to measure the costs that a stadium will impose on Oakhurst. You will want to count explicit costs, like expenditures or subsidies, as well as implicit costs, like tax breaks or the value of land donated for the stadium.

2. The fine is a sunk cost. You will have to pay $10 million regardless of how many games you play or tickets you sell. If you want to maximize your profits, you should operate where marginal revenue equals marginal cost. The fine does not affect the profit-maximizing decision. It just means that the profits you make will be lower than before.

FOSTERING YOUR WORKPLACE SKILLS

1. In order to combat terrorism, the football team you work for installs metal detectors. These detectors cost $5 million each but essentially cost nothing to operate. The team asks you to analyze what it should do to ticket prices as a result. Write a one-page analysis for the team. Suppose it costs $2 per customer to operate the machine. Does your answer change? If so, why and how? If not, why not?

2. Your baseball team is trying to decide what to do about ticket prices for the coming year. What sort of factors would cause you to raise or lower the price of the tickets you charge to see your team play?

3. Your college is trying to decide how to distribute basketball tickets for the coming season. Two methods that are being considered are a first-come-first-served method and a price increase designed to "clear the market." Which

policy would you choose? Write a position paper that justifies your choice. (Hint: There is no single correct answer here.)

 ## WEBSITES

"Sherman Takes the Field" at *http://userwww.service.emory.edu/~tyavero/antitrust/*
Examines the legal ramifications of the monopoly and monopsony power exercised by sports leagues. It also provides links to related sites.

"New Park Financing" at *http://www.wcco.com/sports/stadiums.html*
Examines several recent stadium deals, paying particular attention to the contributions made by states and municipalities. The link to *http://www.ballparks.com* lets you read about current and old stadia and arenas.

REFERENCES

Buchholz, T. (1989). *New ideas from dead economists*. New York: New American Library.

Frey, B., Pommerehne, W., Schneider, F., and Gilbert, G. (1984, December). Consensus and dissension among economists: An empirical inquiry. *American Economic Review* 74(5), 986–94.

Leifer, E. (1995). *Making the majors: The transformation of team sports in America*. Cambridge, MA: Harvard University Press.

Noll, R., and Zimbalist, A. (1997). The economic impact of sports teams and facilities. In R. Noll and A. Zimbalist (eds.), *Sports, jobs, and taxes: The economic impact of sports teams and stadiums*. Washington, DC: Brookings Institution Press.

O'Sullivan, A., and Sheffrin, S. (1998). *Microeconomics: Principles and tools*. Upper Saddle River, NJ: Prentice Hall.

Quirk, J., and Fort, R. (1992). *Paydirt: The business of professional team sports*. Princeton, NJ: Princeton University Press.

Roberts, G. (1991). Professional sports and the anti-trust laws. In P. Staudohar and J. Mangan (eds.), *The business of professional sports*. Urbana, IL: University of Illinois Press.

Rockoff, H. (1990, August). The Wizard of Oz as a monetary allegory. *Journal of Political Economy* 98(4), 739–60.

Scahill, E. (1990, Fall). Did Babe Ruth have a comparative advantage as a pitcher? *Journal of Economic Education*, 402–10.

Sheehan, R. (1996). *Keeping score: The economics of big time sports*. South Bend, IN: Diamond Communications.

Sullivan, N. (1987). *The Dodgers move west*. New York: Oxford University Press.

Zimbalist, A. (1992). *Baseball and billions*. New York: Basic Books.

CHAPTER 12

Accounting and Budgeting

Lawrence Ham

In this chapter, you will become familiar with the following terms:

Accounting
Assets
Balance sheet
Budget
Capital budget
Cash flow analysis
Cost of goods sold
Cost tracking
Current assets
Current liabilities
Depreciation
Enterprise fund system

Equity
Fund accounting
Gross margin
Gross profit
Gross sales
Income statement
Increment-decrement budget
Journals
Liabilities
Line item budget
Long-term investments
Long-term liabilities

Net income
Net loss
Net profit
Net sales
Object classification budget
Operating expenses
Percentage column
Performance budget
Planning programming budget
  system (PPBS)
Program budget
Zero-based budgeting

Learning Goals

By the end of this chapter, students should be able to:

- Discuss the causal connection between good fiscal policy and effective organizations.

- Read and interpret budgets and financial statements.

- Identify methods for preparing and controlling a budget.

- Prepare an expenditure and revenue budget.

- Prepare a budget narrative to justify expenses and revenue projections.

- Identify the types of budgets used by sport managers.

- Identify the three financial statements used by sport managers in private business.

- Identify the requirements for sound fiscal management for the public and the private enterprise.

- Identify and describe the steps of the budget process.

- Identify and define the budgeting, accounting, and financial terminology required of sport managers.

FISCAL MANAGEMENT

Sport managers of the future have a much greater responsibility to make sure that the organization is fiscally sound than they have had in the past. Many managers were good at budgeting, which required the manager to assess, predict, and administer the budget, but that was as far as the responsibility went. Today's manager must be familiar with accounting, budgeting, investing, and managing the organization's funds to ensure success. Although professional sport managers usually hire a financial advisor to handle the fiscal management of the organization, the competent sport manager of the future must be able to accomplish many of the same tasks as the financial advisor. The sport managers who accumulate knowledge regarding fiscal management decision making will be more successful in leading their organizations in the future. Bucher and Krotee (2002) have suggested that fiscal management and control have become increasingly important responsibilities for management in light of current financial problems, issues, and constraints.

The effective fiscal manager must ensure there is an economy of resources. This is accomplished by analyzing the operations of the agency to determine if the right things are being done to ensure the efficient use of resources. After determining what the organization's procedures are in relation to fiscal management, the sport manager develops a fiscal plan that includes mechanisms such as:

- Financial records
- Financial planning
- Maximizing profits
- Cost tracking issues
- Customer service and accountability issues

The fiscal plan considers each of these mechanisms as a means of strategically ensuring success. The plan is developed utilizing the organization's mission statement, vision statement, and established goals and objectives. In addition to the organization's overall goals and objectives, annual goals and objectives that are developed are analyzed to determine if any adjustment needs to be made to the fiscal plan. Goals and objectives should also be considered for each component of the fiscal plan, since the organization's monetary condition could be dependent on any one mechanism, or all of the mechanisms used for an organization's financial success.

Fiscal management is based on three conditions: The first is that top management set the goals and objectives for the fiscal plan and appropriate the funds necessary to provide the program or service. Second, the sport manager has a responsibility to certify that funds have been expended appropriately. The third condition requires the sport manager to establish technical and mechanical procedures for accounting and for security of the fiscal structure and the budgetary process (Horine, 1995). An awareness of good fiscal management requires the sport manager to become an accountant, controller, record keeper, collector, inventory specialist, investor, legal representative, and an administrator. All of these abilities are important to the successful sport manager. Each responsibility requires managers to complete the tasks themselves or be able to review and understand the work of other professionals hired for the tasks. Although the responsibility of fiscal management falls predominantly on the sport manager, efficient budgets and good fiscal management require involvement of the entire staff. An organization's budget development, as well as the establishing of fiscal management policies, must be a cooperative venture if the organization is to be successful. Sport managers depend on staff members for budgetary support in the preparation stage and the administration stage. To demonstrate a comprehension of fiscal awareness, sport managers should develop expertise or knowledge of the following:

- Financial records—Records the sport manager should keep include data such as a daily analysis of time, materials, and equipment used on any task. Any record that may assist the manager during the budget preparation stage should be reviewed to determine if it should be filed for budget use or as historical information for future research use.
- Accounting—Sport managers will be required to keep financial records to be used by the accountant or for the manager to use when estimating costs affiliated with the use of time, materials, and equipment. Whether the manager is in a public agency or a commercial business, simple accounting principles will be used.

- Collections—Managers have the responsibility of collecting data and keeping records of financial transactions, which will be used during budget preparation. It is extremely important for the manager to develop a system of record keeping and for collection of receipts and other information as this material will have to be utilized to complete budget calculations. Examples of receipts the sport manager will want to collect include items such as rentals, concessions, donations, gifts, cash payments, day-to-day expenses, etc.
- Controls—The sport manager must establish policies and procedures for controlling operations such as purchasing, cash collections, and distribution of petty cash, as these are all areas where ethics can be temporarily forgotten. The manager should establish safeguards and controls over who handles these potential problem areas.
- Administrative directives—As the leader of an organization, the sport manager must develop policies for the fiscal management of an organization. These policies should be reviewed with all administrative staff that will be responsible for directing the organization's operations so that the organization will have an effective and efficient fiscal policy.
- Investments—Sport managers in the 21st century are going to be asked to advise on investments made possible by competent fiscal management. Although this has become a fairly new responsibility for sport managers, there is a trend developing that encourages the sport manager to utilize revenue produced from programs, activities, and services to produce alternative funding possibilities through investing.
- Conformance to laws—Sport managers must ensure proper administration of the agency according to local, regional, or federal law. This responsibility requires sport managers to be knowledgeable about the legal aspects required of organizations. All employees should be made aware of those laws that may affect their day-to-day operations and the future security of the organization.
- Property inventories—It is impossible for a sport manager to prepare an accurate budget without doing an analysis of all, equipment, supplies and materials needed to perform the tasks assigned to the department, division, or budget unit. This analysis should also include an estimation of future needs based on previous use.

Another important concept (and responsibility for the sport manager) involves the ability of the fiscal manager to forecast revenue possibilities for the year. Many organizations require managers to prove that enough revenue will be made during the year to offset expenses before they will approve the budget request. Conceptually, a fiscally sound organization would be able to justify requested expenses with anticipated revenues. An important consideration during this part of the process involves the methodology used to determine the expenses. The sport manager must be sure that budget expenditures have included both direct and indirect costs. Many budgets are prepared without determining what the indirect costs are and how that might affect the final budget calculations. For a true comparison to be made, indirect costs must be calculated. Otherwise, costs for any activity, program, or service cannot be accurately determined. Commercial agencies require the sport manager to recover all costs associated with any one program, whereas public agencies "encourage" the sport manager to at least break even. Preparing a cost comparison such as this allows the sport manager to identify specific expenses and revenues attributed to any single program, activity, or service. Costs that are overlooked many times when trying to determine the monetary needs for specific events are simple things like the secretaries' time to send out mailings or the hour that you spent in the boss's office going over figures. Good fiscal managers include this time as part of the total cost of the program, activity, or service. That way an accurate estimate can be made of an event's costs and then compared to the revenues to be made.

OPTIONS IN FISCAL MANAGEMENT

Various options in fiscal management have been used by sport managers to ensure fiscal responsibility. As the fiscal manager of the organization, you have responsibilities for recording, monitoring, and controlling the financial consequences of past and current operations while acquiring funds to meet current and future needs. To accomplish these responsibilities, the efficient sport manager needs to acquire knowledge in various methods used to perform these tasks. Some recommendations for sport managers in fiscal management include: (a) using effective accounting methods, (b) using accounting tools such as the balance sheet, the income statement, and the cash-flow statement, (c) using accounting journals and ledgers, (d) developing successful budgeting habits and skills, and (e) cost tracking.

DEFINITION AND ROLE OF ACCOUNTING

Accounting can be defined as the collection of financial data about an organization (Bendit and Koehler, 1991). The process includes gathering, recording, classifying, summarizing, and interpreting data. Accounting examines an enterprise's profit or loss, determines how it occurred, and determines assets and liabilities, all in relationship to the form of business ownership. These entities can be related to one another to provide information about the financial status of the business. This information helps the sport manager in the planning process and in making crucial financial decisions. Gaining knowledge regarding accounting is a necessity for good fiscal management.

Cash versus accrual accounting

A manager who uses *cash-accounting* methods records revenues and expenses *only* when cash is actually received. For example, charge sales are not reported until the charge is paid or when the charge account has a zero balance. The same is true of charged purchases. When a business receives merchandise and the bill is not payable for 30 days, then the reporting of the expense only occurs when the bill is paid.

Accrual-accounting methods record revenues and expenditures as they occur—that is, a charged sale or a charged purchase is recorded on the same day it takes place under the accrual method.

Professionally speaking, the accrual method is the most often used because it is believed to show the most accurate picture of the revenue and expenditures of the business.

FINANCIAL STATEMENTS

A manager's primary task in financial management involves ensuring a profit for the enter-

prise, having current information on the financial condition of the business, and knowing the cash flow of the operation to prevent shortages. With this in mind, the following financial statements become the working tools of the sport manager. Financial statements are documents or reports that bring together all the data in the accounting process. These statements are generally calculated annually, quarterly, and monthly in order to describe the financial condition of the organization (Crossley and Jamieson, 1997). These financial statements are normally used by private (for-profit) business enterprises, but in some cases of public/nonprofit ownership, a manager could be expected to use them. This is especially true of the balance sheet.

Balance sheet

The **balance sheet** is considered one of the most important financial statements. The four main uses of the balance sheet are that it (1) shows changes in the business over a period of time, (2) shows growth or decline in various phases of the business, (3) shows the business's ability to pay debts, and (4) through ratios, shows financial position. An organization's financial condition may be determined at any given time by reviewing the balance sheet.

Assets. The balance sheet is exactly what the name implies. It shows a balance in a business's assets as compared to the liabilities and owner's equity. On the left side of the balance sheet, one will find a listing of the assets (see Table 12-1). **Assets** are considered to be what a business owns. The listing of assets is considered individual accounts. For example, the value that coincides with the asset called inventory would be backed up with an inventory account record. Assets can be divided into (1) current assets, (2) long-term investments, and (3) fixed assets.

Current assets are considered cash on hand and any asset that can be converted to cash within 12 months from the date on the balance sheet. Examples of current assets include accounts receivable (charges owed by customers), inventory (wholesale cost), temporary investments (e.g., interest-bearing bank accounts), certificates of deposits (CDs), stock in another business that will be converted within one year, and prepaid expenses (e.g., rent, insurance).

Long-term investments are any investments made by the business that have a maturity date beyond one year. One example would be a CD purchased with a five-year payoff date. *Fixed assets* are the items a business owns that cannot be sold without changing the business operations. Examples of fixed assets are real estate (land and buildings), furniture, equipment, and automobiles.

Depreciation is a legal term used by businesses to lower the value of an asset as it gets older. After an asset is purchased and begins to be used in daily operations, the value of that item diminishes. The straight-line method of depreciation estimates the "life" of an asset, the amount of time one would expect this asset to last. For example, what is the life expectancy of a car? If it's estimated to be seven years and the original cost of the car was $14,000, then every year $2,000 would be deducted from the book value of the car listed on the balance sheet. This is not to say that in seven years the car does not have any *market value*, but rather, for the purpose of calculating the assets of this business, the car has been totally depreciated for income tax purposes because depreciation is tax-deductible (Table 12-1).

TABLE 12-1   *Balance Sheet: ABC Sporting Goods Yearly Report*

Assets		Liabilities	
Current assets		**Current liabilities**	
Cash	$20,000	Accounts payable	$7,200
Accounts receivable	8,000	Short-term loans	0
Inventory	50,000	Interest payable	6,000
Short-term investments	5,000	Current portion of	12,000
Prepaid expenses	3,720	long-term loan	
Total current assets	86,720		
Long-term investment	0	**Taxes payable**	
		Accrued payroll	2,300
Fixed assets		Total current	
Land	0	Long-term liabilities	27,500
Building: $48,000 cost	46,080	Loans payable	72,000
accumulated (50 yr.)		Total liabilities	$99,500
depreciation of			
$1920, book value			
Fixtures: $35,000 cost	28,000	**Equity**	
accumulated (10 yr.)		Montague's investment	20,000
depreciation of $7,000,		Hicklin's investment	20,000
book value		Plus net income	81,000
Furniture: $10,000 costs	8,000	Less total partner	41,000
accumulated (10 yr.)		withdrawal	
depreciation of $2,000,		Total partner equity	$80,000
book value		Total liabilities and equity	$179,500
Automobiles: $15,000 cost	10,700		
accumulated (7 yr.)			
depreciation of $4,300,			
book value			
Total fixed assets	85,100		
Total assets	$179,500		

The total amount of assets will be found at the bottom of the asset side of the balance sheet. It is computed by adding together the total current assets, long-term assets, and fixed assets.

Liabilities. **Liabilities** are considered a business's debt, how much money the business owes to other parties. Liabilities are found in the right-hand column of the balance sheet and are divided into current liabilities and long-term liabilities.

Similar to current assets, **current liabilities** are those debts that must be repaid within one year. Examples of current liability accounts include accounts payable (goods and services purchased on credit, usually payable within 30 days), short-term notes (amount of principal owed to a lender, totally payable within one year), the current portion of long-term notes (current principal amount due), interest payable (interest due on either short-term or long-term notes), taxes payable (only applicable to a corporation that owes corporate taxes), and accrued payroll (salaries or wages due).

Long-term liabilities include all the loans a business may have that are not currently payable. These are usually larger loans that were acquired to purchase large items (fixed assets), such as real estate, automobiles, and fixtures needed to open a business for operations.

All the current liabilities and long-term liabilities are added together to come up with the total for liabilities owed.

Equity. Owner's **equity** is the amount of money invested by owners. In a sole proprietorship, the business begins with the amount of money the owner invested from personal funds. In a partnership, it is the amount of money each partner invested individually. Earned income is added to the owner's investment. Subtracted from this amount are any withdrawals made by the owner. This amount would now be considered the total owner's equity. Equity is found underneath liabilities on the balance sheet (see the following box). This should be defined individually for each owner.

In a corporation, the equity would include all the stockholders' purchased shares of stock.

Once the total liabilities and the total equity are calculated, these two figures are added together. The combined values should equal (be balanced

---

Equity equation

Owner's investment
+ Income earned
− Withdrawals made
Owner's equity

---

with) the total assets found in the column on the left in Table 12-1.

Income statement

Another extremely important financial document is the income statement. The income statement and the balance sheet are often used by bankers or interested investors when it comes to making decisions about lending to or investing in a business. The importance of these two documents cannot be overstated.

The purpose of the **income statement** is to analyze the success of a business. The profit (or loss) of a business is found in the income statement. This allows a manager to compare the cost of running a business with the sales generated. The purchases and distributions made to the owners rely on the income statement. An income statement is read from the top down. The top line is the gross proceeds, with the bottom line reflecting the net income (see Table 12-2). The exact items found on the income statement will depend on the nature of business. The following information discusses typical items listed on many businesses' income statements.

Examples of sport-related revenue to be entered on the income statement can be revenue received from rental of luxury boxes at the coliseum, membership fees for participants that belong to the players' clubs, retail shops such as pro shops or for selling of team memorabilia, food and beverage locations throughout sports facilities, vending machines, and concessions. These are but a few of the many revenue possibilities found in sport management career positions.

Sales. *Sales* figures always appear first on an income statement. **Gross sales** are the total amount of revenue (excluding sales tax) that is generated. Revenue that is obtained through ticket sales, merchandise purchased, food service, memberships, etc., is considered gross sales. If a

TABLE 12-2   Income Statement: ABC Sporting Goods, Yearly Report

	Amount ($)	% of net sales
Revenue		
Gross sales	273,200	101
Less sales returns and allowances	3,200	1
Net sales	270,000	100
Cost of sales		
Beginning inventory	50,000	18.5
Plus purchases	135,000	50
Total goods available	185,000	69
Less ending inventory	50,000	18.5
Total cost of goods sold	135,000	50
Gross profit	135,000	50
Operating expenses		
Salaries and wages	22,000	8
Commissions	2,300	1
Advertising	1,500	0.5
Insurance	2,500	1
Depreciation	9,300	3
Interest	6,000	2
Office supplies	800	0.02
Utilities	2,200	1
Miscellaneous	7,400	2.7
Total operating expenses	54,000	20
Total operating income	81,000	30
Pretax income	81,000	30
Tax on income (corporation only)	0	
Net income (net profit)	81,000	30

Cost of goods sold

Beginning inventory
+ Purchases
Total goods
− Ending inventory
Total cost of goods sold

beginning inventory's value is based on the wholesale cost of the merchandise. The value should be calculated on the first date of the income statement, usually the beginning of the year. The addition of the purchased inventory should include all purchases throughout the entire period (usually one year). From the total amount of merchandise, the ending inventory is subtracted. Ending inventory is the cost of the "remaining in inventory" on the last day of the year.

When the cost of goods sold is subtracted from net sales, the resulting value is called the **gross profit** or **gross margin.**

Operating expenses. **Operating expenses** include all other expenses a business accrues during day-to-day operations. Examples of operating expenses include salaries, insurance, rent or loan payments, advertising, and utilities. The income statement is used by most business owners to complete income tax forms. For that purpose, you will find such deductions as depreciation, even though it is not considered actual cash paid out by the business. Depreciation is used to replace fixed assets that have been used during normal business operations; in other words, it is considered the cost of doing business (Ellis and Norton, 1998).

Earnings before taxes and taxes due. A business owned as a sole proprietorship or a partnership is not responsible for paying federal income taxes. The owners of the business are required to declare the percentage of the business profit that is attributable to their specific percentage of ownership on their individual income tax. Only the corporation is required to pay corporate income tax on the business's profits. State or local municipalities may have separate laws that govern a specific location.

business has a return policy—where money is given back to dissatisfied customers—this amount should be subtracted from the gross sales figure. Other values that should be subtracted are called *allowances* (e.g., discounted sale price, cost of stolen or shoplifted merchandise, losses incurred from damages, and prompt-payment discounts). The resultant figure is called **net sales.**

The **cost of goods sold** (sales) must be calculated (see the equation in the following box). The

The business owner should be aware of this; but if this isn't the case, this section of the income statement can be omitted.

Net income or net profit. **Net income** or **net profit** is the amount of money remaining after all expenses (liabilities) have been paid. This amount can be used for retained earnings for the business, divided among partners, or used to pay dividends to stockholders in the corporation. If the business accrues a **net loss** over the year, the amount of the loss will be shown in parentheses—e.g., (4800) represents a $4,800 loss.

Percentage column. The **percentage column** is a very useful management tool. It can show a manager what percentage of the net sales is being spent in specific areas of the business. If a particular percentage appears to be too high (higher than last year's income statement or higher than the standards set in this type of business operation), the manager will know that the expense should be lowered. For example, if the cost of goods sold in a retail operation is 75 percent of the net sales, most managers would consider this percentage too high. To remedy this situation, one could either raise the retail price so that net sales would increase or search for other wholesale vendors that would sell merchandise to the business at a lower cost, which would decrease the cost of goods sold.

Cash flow analysis

Cash flow financial statements serve a third purpose for the sport manager. The information found in the cash flow document is a detailed accounting of receipts (revenue) and disbursements (expenses). Cash flow does *not* tell the manager the business's financial condition (balance sheet), nor does it show the profit or loss (income statement) of the business. It only shows the manager "cash in" and "cash out." Cash flow is normally documented monthly. This gives the manager the ability to analyze the financial situation over a period of time. Also, after several years of business operations, the manager is able to see patterns of cash flow that might indicate the need for a short-term loan or, just the opposite, periods of time when cash is abundant and should be invested for maximum profit opportunities.

TABLE 12-3   *Cash Flow Analysis: ABC Sporting Goods, 1st Quarter 20XX*

	January	February	March
Sales			
Inventory			
Clothing	2,300	2,700	3,400
Equipment	10,540	1,500	9,900
Layaway paid	1,320	1,000	4,000
Total sales	14,160	5,200	17,300
Less cost of sales	7,300	7,000	7,200
Gross margin	6,860	(1,800)	10,100
Less expenses			
Salaries	1,200	1,200	1,200
Commission	800	300	0
Advertising	100	300	100
Insurance	0	1,250	0
Loan payment	700	700	700
Office supplies	150	70	50
Utilities	250	250	200
Miscellaneous	300	200	540
Total	3,500	4,270	2,250
Cash Flow			
A − B = C Surplus (or deficit)	3,360	(6,070)	8,850
Cash balance			
Cash at start	0	3,360	290
Cash flow	3,360	(6,070)	8,850
Bank loan (L) or rent (R)		3,000L	3,000R

Table 12-3 shows an example of a **cash flow analysis**.

Journals

Journals (sometimes referred to as *ledgers*) are the financial documents that the sport manager uses for recording all financial transactions during day-to-day operations. Most businesses use two basic record books: sales journals and disbursement journals (Pickle and Abrahamson, 1986).

TABLE 12-4 *Sales Journal*

Date	Account or description	Greens fees ($)	Pro shop ($)	Food and beverages ($)	Lessons or tournaments ($)	Member fees ($)
June 1	Daily sales	366	127.43	100.20	55	1,500
June 2	Daily sales	824	447.60	275.75	110	9,000
June 3	Daily sales	455	235.75	155.45	0	500
June 4	Daily sales	875	455.00	325.40	330	2,500
June 5	Daily sales	1,225	347.25	466.65	220	0
June 6	Daily sales	665	348.50	207.65	55	0
June 7	Daily sales	235	473.90	768.45	2,300	0
Week total		4,645	2,435.43	2,299.55	3,070	13,500

Sales journals. *Sales journals* record cash sales and receipts of daily income. The journal headings are based on the exact specifications for the business. For example, a stadium operation might define its journal headings as ticket sales, concession sales, group sales, and Skybox sales. See Table 12-4 for an example of a sales journal from a golf club.

A more detailed look at the sales receipts is warranted if the manager wants more specific information. In the case of the golf course's greens fees and pro shop sales, it might be appropriate to divide sales into cash and charge categories. Or membership dues could be divided into new memberships and renewals. The options are virtually unlimited, the point being that every business should design its sales journal in the manner deemed appropriate.

The sales journal can also be used to verify the amount of cash that is deposited in the bank daily. By adding the columns, it is easy for a manager to see if discrepancies exist. The totals are also used for the income statement and cash flow analysis. All the financial statements should be used to cross-check one another.

Disbursement journal. The *disbursement journal* is similar to the sales journal in its format. The column headers are changed to reflect expenditures specifically defined by the individual business. Examples of disbursement category headings are payroll, all types of vendor purchases (e.g., merchandise, food, beverages), advertising, and

insurance. The income statement and cash flow analysis documents should use the same terminology (see Table 12-5).

The columns of the disbursement journal are usually totaled at the end of the month, although some businesses choose to do it more often. The uses of this information are numerous. For example, the columns that coincide to the items on the income statement can be used to formulate that financial document, and the total amount for checks written can help the manager check bank statements.

A more detailed explanation of how to set up journals can be found in many small-business management courses and textbooks.

SUMMARY OF ACCOUNTING
Accounting practices vary with the form of business ownership, but the three most commonly used financial statements are the balance sheet, the income statement, and the cash flow analysis. All three financial statements serve a different purpose and should be used together. Journals are used to record all sales and disbursements, whether either cash or accrual accounting methods are used.

The intention of the previous section was to prepare the sport management student with a working knowledge of accounting practices. More in-depth knowledge should be obtained in a small-business management or accounting and finance course.

TABLE 12-5 *Disbursement Journal*

Date	Payee or account	Check no.	Amount of check ($)	Vendor inventory ($)	Advertising ($)	Payroll ($)	Food and beverages ($)
June 1	T. Jones, Mgr.	1010	987.43	0	0	987.43	0
June 1	A. Stone, Mgr.	1011	632.76	0	0	632.76	0
June 1	Philadelphia Beverage	1012	98.10	0	0	0	148.10
June 2	Spalding Golf Distribution	1013	887.66	887.66	0	0	0
June 2	WMMR Radio	1014	350.00	0	350.00	0	0
June 4	MaxFli Golf Supplies	1015	544.78	544.78	0	0	0
June 5	Pennsylvania Liquor Authority	1016	99.75	0	0	0	249.75
	Total distribution	—	3,603.48	1,432.44	350.00	1620.19	397.85

A successful budgeting habit required of all sport managers is obtaining an understanding of budgeting terminology, which fiscal managers are accustomed to using.

ACCOUNTING FOR PUBLIC/NONPROFIT ORGANIZATIONS—BUDGETING

Most organizations that operate as a nonprofit enterprise (e.g., private universities or nonprofit clubs that are supported by voluntary contributions and other sources) or that are organized as a part of a governmental agency (municipalities and state-owned universities that are tax supported) receive allocations from the general fund of the overall unit. These entities are established under specific regulations and restrictions, by law, to operate on a nonprofit basis. Therefore, they are not subject to income tax laws. In sport management, examples of these types of operations are school athletic programs, community youth sport programs, club sport programs, and municipal golf courses.

Each year, a public/nonprofit organization submits a budget request to its superior body (e.g., city council budget review committee, university financial officer, board of directors). A sport manager will be competing for funds with many other groups within the organization (unless it is an athletic department that is expected to be self-sufficient). Over the past decade, traditional sources of revenue, including tax support, broadcast revenues, and gate receipts, have not kept up with rapidly escalating costs (Masteralexis, Barr, and Hums, 1998, p. 67). The way in which the budget is presented, the selection process for the items included on the budget, and the related justifications are three extremely important tasks required of a management team. Remember that a sport or athletic program is only one part of a large picture, and the preparation and administration of an effective budget is probably one of the best public relations tools a manager can use, internally and externally. On the other hand, the mishandling of funds, when other constituencies are vying for a "share of the same pot," can be professional suicide. The purpose of the budgetary process is to facilitate the realization of the organization's goals and objectives through fiscal responsibility, sound business practices, effective decision-making, and prudent financial management (Stier, 1999 p. 158). This can be accomplished by the sport manager by understanding the terminology associated with budgeting, the types of budgets available for use, the process of budgeting, and suggestions for successful budgeting.

Budgeting deferred

By definition, a **budget** is a statement of financial position based on estimates of expenditures and suggested proposals for financing them—in other words, a management plan for revenue and expenses of an organization for a period of time (usually one year). Some of the criteria to consider when establishing a budget are past revenues generated, changes in prices or fees, marketing research predictions, the current promotion and advertising strategies, and the economic environment of the general public and the institution (Bendit and Koehler, 1991). The following list includes practical advantages of budgeting:

1. It substitutes a plan for "chance" in fiscal operations; foresees expenditure needs; and organizes staff, along with the work that needs to be accomplished.
2. It requires a review of the entire operation (all divisions and subdivisions) in terms of funds available and revenue needs; it prevents overbudgeting (padding).
3. It promotes standardization and simplification of operation by establishing priorities and objectives, and it eliminates inefficient operations.
4. It provides guidelines for a staff to follow.
5. It provides the governing body with factual data for evaluating the efficiency of the operation.
6. It helps the taxpaying public (contributors) to see where revenues are coming from and what expenditures are for.
7. It acts as an instrument for fiscal control.

BUDGET PROCESS

It is important to follow a systematic process when it comes to developing or reviewing a budget. Ten steps have been identified as a comprehensive approach to the budget process. Keep in mind that the budget should be completed and approved months in advance of the organization's financial calender year.

Step one—Examine the organization's mission, goals, and objectives.

Step two—Research the organization's strengths and resources relative to the future needs.

Step three—Include all key players in the budget process. The knowledge and expertise of others should be included in the data-gathering step, as well as the actual construction of the budget.

Step four—Review the information and data gathered. Include a past, present, and future analysis.

Step five—Prepare the budget by using the budget type, as well as the criteria set forth by the organization's executives.

Step six—Examine the budget for accuracy, feasibility, and reality.

Step seven—Submit the budget to a few key people for additional critical analyses.

Step eight—Prepare and execute a formal budget presentation. Anticipate questions and timely responses.

Step nine—Implement the budget.

Step ten—Audit the budget. This should be done as the cyclical budget process begins for the next year (modified from Stier, 1999).

Types of budget

Organizations affiliated with the sport industry use many different budget styles. The budget types being reviewed are those methods that sport managers will most convincingly be responsible for.

Object classification budget. The **object classification budget** is one of the most traditional types of budgets and one of the easiest to understand. To conceptualize an object classification budget, one must understand the basic premise of structure that the budget uses: It is established using an object classification that defines the areas of expense in a uniform grouping of categories. The following is a typical classification system:

1000 Services: Personnel
    1100 Salaries, regular
    1200 Salaries, temporary
    1300 Wages, regular
    1400 Wages, temporary
    1500 Other compensations
2000 Services: Contractual
    2100 Communication and transportation
    2200 Subsistence, care, and support
    2300 Printing, binding, and advertising
    2400 Utilities
    2500 Repairs
    2600 Janitorial
3000 Commodities
    3100 Supplies
    3200 Materials
4000 Current charges
    4100 Rents
    4200 Insurance
    4300 Refunds, awards, and indemnities
    4400 Registrations and memberships
5000 Current obligations
    5100 Interest
    5200 Pensions and retirement
    5300 Grants and subsidies
    5400 Taxes
6000 Properties
    6100 Equipment
    6200 Buildings and improvements
    6300 Land
7000 Debt obligations

The advantage of this budget's classification is the uniformity of the numbering system and the ease in setting up the budget. The clarity among similar organizations can be very helpful to the sport manager for the purpose of making comparisons.

Line item budget. The **line item budget** is very similar to the object classification budget, and these two budgeting systems are the most often used in the public sector. The term *line* refers to the listing of each item on a line in the budget; the items are not defined by a numbering system, they are simply listed by name. This allows for more flexibility than the object classification bud-

TABLE 12-6 *Line Item Budget for XYZ Swim Pool and Club*

	Current budget	Proposed budget
Personnel		
Manager	$4,000	$4,500
Guards	6,300	6,700
Instructors	2,800	3,000
Coaches	1,200	1,500
Maintenance	1,000	1,200
	15,300	16,900
Supplies		
Office supplies	350	450
Operating supplies	4,600	5,000
Repair and maintenance supplies	3,500	3,900
Miscellaneous	500	600
	8,950	9,950
Operations		
Utilities	4,200	4,500
Telephone	400	500
Insurance	1,300	1,400
Printing and advertising	600	700
Security	500	650
	7,000	7,750
Capital expenditure		
Equipment	3,500	4,000
	3,500	4,000
	$34,750	$38,600

get. See Table 12-6 for more details on setting up a line item budget.

In the early 1900s, line item budgets listed every single cost item—for example, each employee's name was listed under the salary/wage category. The complexity of this method is obvious. Now a budget includes expenditure categories in an effort to simplify the system (Deppe, 1993).

Increment-decrement budgeting. The **increment budget** is used with both the line item and the object classification budget systems. The principle of the increment budget is based on the assignment of a set percentage of budget increase or decease and revolves around the importance of the budget message, given by the governing authority. Even during those lean years when the sport manager is told to reduce the budget request by a set percentage from the previous year, a good fiscally conscious sport manager will adjusts reductions based on revenue capabilities and need for specific programs. The programs capable of producing significant revenue will be budgeted differently from those that do not have that capability. This does not mean that programs will always be cut from the sports agenda, but that they may have to operate on minimal funding. This type of process is a change over previous increment budgets in that the effective sport manager utilizing a good fiscal policy has now been given the privilege of deciding on where the percentages are reduced, whereas previously the same percentage was taken from all cost centers regardless of their effectiveness to the organization. This budgeting methodology is usually used where an established long-range planning effort is being required and a strategic plan for growth and development is being used. Whether short-term or long-range planning, the increment budget provides a predictable growth over a period of time, whereas the **decrement budget** provides a predictable decline.

Program budget. The **program budget,** unlike the three previous budgets, separates an organization by unique units. A program budget could easily be adopted by an athletic department. Each sport would develop a separate budget, with a narrative description of the sport's goals and those features of its program that are deemed to be the most important. This allows the athletic director to compare the various budget requests and make decisions based on a fuller understanding of their needs instead of simply looking at lines and numbers. The three components of a program budget are (1) agency goals, (2) program goals, and (3) unique features of the program. This process is then followed by a line item or object classification budget.

Performance budget. The difference between a program budget and a performance budget is

minute. The purpose of a **performance budget** is to explain what services are being provided by the institution rather than just how much money is being spent. The budget is broken into categories or service activities. Each category is defined by the amount of time that is involved to perform the activity. Then a cost can be attributed to each activity. The manager has a great deal of financial control and can be precise when using this type of budget (Kelsey and Gray, 1986).

Planning programming budget system (PPBS). The focus of this type of budget is on the end product of the service provided rather than the actual cost. One of the purposes of the **planning programming budget system (PPBS)** is to provide a rationale for each of the competing budget units within an agency or department. The budget provides a narrative picture of the expenditures rather than simply listing the amount of money spent. When resources are scarce, this budget type can be a useful management tool (Kelsey and Gray, 1986).

Zero-based budget. A **zero-based budget** is based on the premise that an organization begins each year with no money. This type of budget was designed to stop basing the current budget on last year's budget (Rue and Byars, 1995). From that point, a budget is prepared by justifying each expenditure as if it were a new expense. The purpose of this type of budget is to control over-budgeting and waste. The manager has to scrutinize the reasonableness of every budget request in relationship to the whole department.

This method is a radical departure from traditional methods that look at past costs, add an increment for projected expenses, and continue to operate in the same manner year after year (Deppe, 1993).

Capital budget. A **capital budget** describes capital expenses that include long-range budget items. A capital budget usually covers a number of years—as many as ten years. It includes major purchases, such as new buildings and equipment, that are not found in operating budgets that only cover one year. Capital budgets, like program budgets, require a narrative explanation or justification for each expense.

Enterprise funds

A newer method of financial management that is being implemented in many public/nonprofit organizations is called the **enterprise fund system.** The premise that this system works on is that every individual program of operation is viewed as a separate enterprise. The revenue generated by the enterprise is then used to finance the enterprise's operation. Originally, the enterprise fund system expected the operation to break even, which meant that the enterprise needed to generate at least as much income as was budgeted for expenses. But it is more common today to expect a profit. In a municipal setting, this could mean that the profit generated by a financially successful enterprise, such as the community golf course, could be used to fund another program, such as the "latch-key program" for underprivileged youth, which is known to lose money.

Fund accounting

Fund accounting is a standard method of accounting used by many government operations (Rossman, 1984). A fund is defined as a fiscal and accounting entity with a self-balancing set of accounts recording cash and financial resources, with liabilities and equity. The format of the financial document is very similar to the balance sheet. The accounts are separate operations (programs or activities) within the organization, and they include funds that aren't necessarily reflected in day-to-day operations, such as capital funds, benefits funds, or retirement funds. The segregation of the fund accounts usually has been specified by external sources, such as the board of directors (Rossman, 1984). Sometimes these funds are referred to as cost or revenue centers.

Annual reviews of the accounts will be used to evaluate the activities that took place within the segregated fund. Decisions will be made on the fund account's future, based on the growth or decline in the financial picture of the account. Getz (1997) describes cost-revenue management as an important process of reviewing and identifying all cost and revenue centers to ensure financial health.

Another option to ensure fiscal responsibility involves the preparation, submission, and administration of the budget. It is extremely important for sport managers to develop successful budgeting habits. Some suggestions for successful

budgeting have been developed that may help the sport manager make the budgeting process less cumbersome and threatening. By completing these tasks, the manager reduces the chances of budgetary problems developing during the budget process.

Budget development

During the budget development and preparation stage, sport managers should:

- Collect past budgets (five years of past budgets gives a more accurate forecast for the upcoming year) to prepare for analysis of expected or possible costs.
- Collect the statements from the past year for all expenditures and analyze areas of expected increase.
- Thoroughly check out the budget message (budget requirements/guidelines, expectations, limitations for increases, etc.) to address what parameters need be established for preparation.
- Determine where the preview steps are and who will be completing these reviews so you can prepare to address the steps where you expect the most trouble (cuts).
- Inform all key staff of required date for budgetary needs for their specialty areas, i.e., maintenance, facilities, etc., for the next budget year.
- Divide organizational budget into operating and capital activities.
- Adhere to time limitations. (Ideally give your administrator/reviewer time to analyze and ask you questions about the budget and also to request justifications from you on the questionable areas.)
- Prioritize budget requests according to necessity. Since, historically, all budgets go through some of kind of a reduction or budget cut, priorities should be established to take into consideration the downhill effect where anything cut at the top of a budget may affect something else in the budget.
- Include budget requests even if you think (know) they will be cut. This is especially important for capital outlay items as they can then be included in the organization's capital improvement plan (CIP) or the

business's marketing plan for future consideration.

- Review budget instructions for clarity, practicability of dates, etc.
- Remember that the budget preparation step is cyclic, goes on all year, so the process should not stop. As soon as you have submitted this year's budget, start on next year's the next day. If you are considering fiscal management and budgeting throughout the year then during budget time, you might not be as overwhelmed.
- Prepare your budget carefully with all justifications included. It is especially important to include justification on new items, items that indicate an increase or reduction, and items that you feel your clientele will need or want. Explain each item in enough detail to ensure that the budget presentation will go smoothly. This eliminates confusion during the budget review by a higher authority and gives you additional confidence in your budget presentation.

Budget presentation. The budget presentation can be the most important part of the budget process. This is your chance to reiterate the importance of the items that you have included in the budget that may be questioned. Suggestions for the presentation include:

- Develop an opening statement describing some past accomplishments, especially during lean years.
- Clarify budget direction for the upcoming year according to the tasks that may be accomplished with the proper funding.
- Deliver the opening statement in a relaxed, confident demeanor.
- Answer questions in short, precise, factual responses.
- Answer only what you are asked. Don't give more information than requested. If more clarification is needed, they will ask you for it.
- Remain controlled and confident even in the face of adversity. Even when you see reductions that you know will have an effect on your delivery of services, give the reviewer the facts and figures for the

effects the cuts will have, tell them what the cuts will mean in programming, and then move to the next item. Heated arguments are seldom won during a budget defense.
- Know your budget. It has been suggested that any disorganization during the review can have a very negative effect. You should have the budget rehearsed to the point that any question can receive an answer without looking for it in the pages of the budget. If you have to search for the answer, there is a good chance that item will be cut.
- Make your own cuts if possible. When you are asked to revise the budget and reduce the requested amount, realize that at least they are giving you the power to cut where you think it is best, so don't get too upset. The worst case scenario is working for an organization that makes your cuts for you and then tells you to accomplish the assigned tasks with what you are being given.

Budget administration

It is during the administration of the budget that sport managers become good fiscal managers. This is where you can save money and increase revenues. Although some organizations may give directions on administering the budget, many will let you develop your own administrative policies for budget management. It is extremely important to keep your staff apprised as to budget conditions. You will have to depend on them to keep the records that will make next year's budget preparation easier. As you will learn from your first budget defense, keep all records during the budget calendar year that will allow you to improve next year's budget request. The staff's record keeping ability will determine how much additional work you will have to do during budget preparation trying to retrieve lost data. Employees can help solve the problems if they are involved in crafting the solutions. You might consider using teams of employees.

Some additional considerations or suggestions for improving fiscal management include:

- Consider the investment perspective. The more discretionary revenue you produce the more capital you will have to invest to produce additional revenue to offset expenses.

- Don't necessarily just try to save money in budgets; make money.
- Focus on both sides of the balance sheet—spending and earnings, debits and credits.
- Spend that which is necessary to maximize returns—not just minimizing expenses.
- Develop economic impact statements on everything you do—will it make money in the long run or lose money?
- If you operate with different funds within the budget, it is not advisable to move monies from one fund to another. This usually indicates that the sport manager is not staying informed about the fiscal management of the organization or the manager did not do a competent assessment of the organization's needs during the budget development.

Tracking cost for successful budgeting

One of the most successful fiscal management methods is **cost tracking.** Benefits that have been identified as a result of cost tracking include:

- Improving management decision making.
- Providing system for cost effectiveness of an organization.
- Making available past operations for review before establishing current operations.
- Letting you know the costs affiliated with specific activities, projects, or facilities.
- Allowing for competent budget requests by providing reliable facts and figures during budget negotiations. This is supported through good record keeping.

It addresses concerns regarding the:

- Efficient allocation and use of resources.
- Effective performance of management.
- Compliance with applicable laws, rules, and standards.
- Cost-effectiveness of alternative methods of task completion and goal attainment.
- Reliability of information provided by management.
- Results of programs, activities, and facilities and their impact on recipients.

- Achievement of organizational goals and objectives.

Cost tracking requires the sport manager to develop a system that will allow for the competent recording of all costs associated with any cost center. These costs include personnel time, equipment used, materials used, and supplies used. It also must include the indirect costs associated with that specific event, project, activity, or service. An integral component of successful cost tracking is the involvement of the employees. No sport manager can be everywhere all the time. The most accurate systems for cost tracking have the employees trained in the record-keeping procedures required to track costs. If you are the facility manager of the home of a professional sports team and you are asked what it costs to maintain the facility, you should be able to determine this figure through the use of trained employees and an effective cost-tracking system.

SUMMARY OF ACCOUNTING FOR PUBLIC/NONPROFIT ORGANIZATIONS

Separate budgets can be written for expenditures and revenues, or the projected revenue should be included in the expense budget. Most departments or programs have some method for generating income. Projected revenues should be estimated in the same way expected expenses are. Whether it be in ticket sales, user fees, or memberships, the amount of income required to operate the programs should be projected. This can be very useful in getting approval of the budget from the financial director, because it shows potential. In the book *The Ultimate Guide to Sport Event Management & Marketing,* the authors describe the "Elements of a Successful Sport Event Business." One of those elements states that a successful plan will explain how you will amortize this capital investment and repay the loan or provide profits for your shareholders (Graham, Goldblatt, and Delpy, 1995, p. 193). The type of budget chosen will be decided upon by the institution or the department, so the sport manager should become familiar with a variety of methods.

The sport manager will have two important functions when it comes to dealing with the financial affairs of the department. The first is to oversee disbursements made by each unit, making sure that budgets are not overspent. The second is to develop a budget that will make it possible for the institution to realize the highest possible return on its investment (Lewis and Appenzeller, 1985).

Enterprise funds and fund accounting are two terms the sport manager should be familiar with because of their implications for public/nonprofit financial accounting.

CONCEPT CHECK

The two most important tasks a sport manager will have to master when it comes to budgets is to (1) prepare and justify the annual budget and (2) control the expenses and disbursements once the budget has been approved.

SUMMARY

- Sport managers, regardless of their specific job function within the organization, will have a critical role in the management of capital revenue and expenditures. The importance of understanding of accounting and finance cannot be overstated. Every sport business needs to be concerned with fiscal responsibility and sound business practices. This is true for both profit and nonprofit businesses and organizations. The need to develop and follow a sound budget and to make effective and efficient fiscal decisions is essential for every business and organization (Steir, 1999).
- The $152 billion estimate of sport product and services spending based strictly on spectator sport and sport participation ranks the industry as the eleventh largest industry in the United States (Hiestand, 1997). This figure should have all potential sport managers extremely sensitive to financial issues. This chapter is truly the first education in a series of educational experiences that sport management students should encounter during their academic curriculum.

CRITICAL THINKING EXERCISES

1. You are the new athletic director of an athletic department that has a national reputation as a financial success story. What part will you play in financial decisions?
2. As the executive director of a major sport event that is seeking corporate sponsorship, which financial statements will you prepare for potential sponsors? This event has been estimated to bring 30,000 visitors and $10 million to your community.

CASE STUDY I: PREPARING THE INCOME AND EXPENSE STATEMENT

The statement of income and expense (profit and loss statement) covering the past fiscal year for the athletic department must be submitted to the university accounting office in one month. As the director of athletics, you are responsible for several programs. One is varsity sports, which include football, women's basketball, men's basketball, women's volleyball, and men's baseball as revenue-producing sports. Non-revenue-producing sports in your program are track, wrestling, swimming, tennis, and field hockey. In addition, there are several club sports under your direction. These are soccer, rugby, lacrosse, water polo, and crew. Finally, your department oversees a fitness program offered to faculty, their partners, retirees, and students.

1. *What are some typical accounts you would use for each program?*
2. *What special income and expense accounts are you likely to encounter for each program?*
3. *Into what major categories would the income and expense statement be divided?*
4. *What types of indirect overhead would you have for each program?*
5. *How would indirect overhead expenses affect your figures?*

CASE STUDY II: PREPARING THE BUDGET

As manager of a corporate fitness program, it is your responsibility to submit a budget for the next fiscal year to the director of human resources and development. The fitness program, which employs two fitness specialists and you, has operated for three years and has consistently lost money. The director of human resources and development has agreed to subsidize the program with an additional $10,000 with the understanding that a portion of the funds will be allocated to a marketing and advertising campaign.

1. What steps would you take in planning and preparing your budget?
2. From whom would you solicit information?
3. What options do you have when allocating funds?
4. What changes in the budget would you propose?
5. Would the process of forecasting be helpful to you? If so, how?
6. How might asking "what if" questions be useful?

 REVIEW QUESTIONS AND ISSUES

1. What is accounting, and what is the difference between cash accounting and accrual accounting?
2. What are the three financial statements most often used in business, and what is the major purpose of each?
3. What are assets, liabilities, and equity in reference to a business? How is each used on a balance sheet? What is depreciation?
4. What is the difference between gross sales, net sales, gross profit, and net profit?
5. How does one calculate the cost of goods sold?
6. What are some examples of operating expenses?
7. What are sales and disbursement journals, and how are they used?
8. How does accounting differ in a private business operation versus a public/nonprofit organization? Give examples of each type of business operation.
9. What are the most commonly used types of budgets? Describe how each type is set up.
10. What are enterprise funds, and how are they being used in public operations?
11. What is fund accounting, and who would be most likely to use it?

 SOLUTIONS TO CRITICAL THINKING EXERCISES

1. All financial decisions ultimately rest on your shoulders. Never take the position that, "if it isn't broken, don't fix it." The type of budget used will be a university decision, but the budgetary process, the contents of the budget, and the implementation of the budget will be your responsibility. So include all the steps of the budget process and surround yourself by the key individuals who will give you the best advice and support before you make the required presentation to the board of trustees.
2. Most communities are frantically looking for ways to bring outside revenue into their cities. Sport events have been identified as attractive ways to do this. Before corporate sponsors are going to support your efforts, they will expect to see all of your financial statements. This is especially true if this event has been produced in the past. If other communities have sponsored this event in the past, if available, their financial records would be a tremendous help. In any event be prepared to distribute a complete event plan, which among other things must have a detailed and clear financial report. Even if the event has the status as a nonprofit, a pro forma balance sheet and income statement are essential.

FOSTERING YOUR WORKPLACE SKILLS

1. Prepare an expenditure budget for a collegiate volleyball team for one season.
2. Prepare a budget presentation for a departmental budget where you are the athletic coordinator.
3. As general manager of the Yakima Suns, you are interested in forming a partnership with the city government, since they own the building where the team plays. The present agreement expires on July 1. Prepare a partnership proposal, identifying the benefits of the partnership for your team and for the city, including an estimate of revenue possibilities.
4. Prepare an annual fiscal plan for a 10,000-seat arena, outlining expenditures and revenue possibilities. The arena hosts musical events and shows, and is home of the Rock Island Renegades, a minor league ice hockey team.

5. As executive director of the Sun Belt Conference, you have the responsibility for fiscal management. Prepare a final budget (to be submitted and defended) including both the expenditure and revenue budgets with justifications.

 WEBSITES

www.ral-cpa.com/ralsports.htm—Resnick, Amersterdam, Leshner P.C. CPA, Building Sports and Entertainment Businesses. The accounting/consulting firm Resnick, Amersterdam, Leshner P.C. has served over 30 professional sports franchises or entertainment businesses since 1986. The firm helps organizations grow their revenues, control cash flow, and manage investments. They also provide tax and financial planning for professional athletes and entertainers.

www.teammarketing.com/io.htm—Team Marketing Report Inc. Team Marketing Report Inc. specializes in developing a complete directory of the ownership and financial structure of pro sports. TMR has joined forces with Houlihan Lokey Howard & Zukin, (www.hlhz.com), the specialty banking firm and advisor to over thirty sport franchises. The result is the most complete source of sports business data and analysis around, including inside details on every MLB, NBA, NFL, and NHL franchise, broadcast deals, revenue figures, lease arrangements, sponsorships, and more.

REFERENCES

Bendit, O. G., and Koehler, L. S. (1991). Accounting and budgeting. In B. L. Parkhouse (ed.), *The management of sport: Its foundation and application.* St. Louis: Mosby Year Book.

Crossley, J. C., and Jamieson, L. M. (1997). *Introduction to commercial and entrepreneurial recreation.* Champaign, IL: Sagamore.

Deppe, T. R. (1993). *Management strategies in financing parks and recreation.* New York: Wiley.

Ellis, T., and Norton, R. L. (1998). *Commercial recreation.* St. Louis: Times Mirror/Mosby.

Getz, D. (1997). *Event management and event tourism.* Elmsford, NY: Cognizant Communication Offices.

Graham, S., Goldblatt, J. J., and Delpy, L. (1995). *The ultimate guide to sport event management & marketing.* Chicago: Irwin.

Hiestand, M. (1997). How big's the big? *USA Today,* February 14, 2C.

Kelsey, C., and Gray, H. (1986). *The budget process in parks and recreation.* Reston, VA: AAHPERD.

Langley, Thomas D., and Hawkins, Jerald D. (2002). *Administration for exercise related professions.* Belmont, CA: Thomson-Wadsworth.

Lewis, G., and Appenzeller, H. (1985). *Successful sport management.* Charlottesville, VA: Miche.

Masteralexis, L. P., Barr, C. A., and Hums, M. A. (1998). *Principles and practice of sport management.* Gaithersburg, MD: Aspen.

Pickle, H. B., and Abrahamson, R. L. (1986). *Small business management.* New York: Wiley.

Rossman, J. R. (1984). Fund accounting: A management accounting strategy. In J. J. Bannon (ed.), *Administrative practice of park, recreation and leisure services.* Champaign, IL: Management Learning Laboratories.

Rue, L. W., and Byars, L. L. (1995). *Management skills and application.* 7th ed. Chicago: Irwin.

Siropolis, N. (1984). *Small business management: A guide to entrepreneurship.* Boston: Houghton Mifflin.

Stier, W. F. (1999). *Managing sport, fitness and recreation programs.* Needham Heights, NJ: Allyn & Bacon.

CHAPTER 13

Financing Sport

Tom H. Regan

In this chapter, you will become familiar with the following terms:

Cash flow
Cash inflows
Cash outflows
Financing activities
Financing sport

General obligation bonds
Investing activities
Municipal securities (munis)
Operating activities
Revenue bonds

Revenue streams
Tax exemption
Tax increment financing bonds

Learning Goals
By the end of this chapter, students should be able to:

- Explain various types of financing needed for different sport organizations
- Establish the need for cash flow management.
- Identify the sources of different financing options.
- Display a knowledge of financing, accounting, and basic business principles such as the *time value of money* and *discounted cash flow*.

OVERVIEW

Professional, collegiate and interscholastic organizations require financing options and opportunities to compete in the business of sport. Leagues, teams, and communities are challenged to maintain and support adequate facilities and teams for sport organizations.

Financing sport-related facilities often requires public, private, and joint public/private financing. The financial arrangements surrounding sport may be the most creative area of business outside the playing field. Financing sport business is a simple enough concept: You must have adequate funds to enable the landlord, tenant, and team owner to start, expand, and continue operations.

The purpose of this chapter on **financing sport** is to explain a few of the various types of financing needed for different sport organizations and establish the need for cash flow management. The fact that funds are needed is the simple part. Where they come from is another matter. We will identify the sources of different financing options. *Cash flow* is essential to a successful sports enterprise. Sport is seasonal in nature; the teams play specific schedules during assigned times. The management of cash flow requires a knowledge of finance, accounting, and basic business principles such as the *time value of money* and *discounted cash flow.* The list is by no means exhaustive, but a strong foundation for the sport business manager.

THE PUBLIC NEED

It is important for government leaders to attract professional teams to their region or city. In the United States, cities compete to attract and retain professional sports franchises. Federal, state, and local government subsidizes the financing of sports facilities. Financing arrangements are a key element to attract teams and investors. A key element of the funding plans is the **exemption** from federal and most state and local income tax on the interest earned on qualified **municipal securities (munis)** that could be issued to finance these stadiums. The borrower can then sell bonds at a lower interest rate than if the interest was taxed.

Government authorities are usually proponents of stadiums. They claim that without the necessary local support, teams might choose to relocate and the cities would lose employment, tax revenues, and other indirect benefits. Government opponents claim that benefits are probably overstated and likely future costs understated, making probable the need for even more public support in the future.

Sport facility financing

"Build it, and they will come" is a familiar passage from the hit movie *Field of Dreams.* Professional, collegiate, interscholastic, and touring sports require adequate facilities to practice and play the game in addition to attracting fans. The United States has great athletic facilities throughout the country. Often stadiums become a source of regional community pride, for example, Oriole Park at Camden Yards in Baltimore, Maryland, and The Ballpark, in Arlington, Texas.

The majority of professional and university sport facilities have traditionally been financed by municipal debt with annual debt service funded from the municipality's general fund or from one of several other revenue sources. In recent years, the recession, increase in construction costs, and municipalities' budget constraints have resulted in various private-sector financial participation. Private-sector participation in financing facilities is

primarily due to the increase in available revenues generated by the facility. These public, private, and joint public/private financing arrangements are necessary for sport facility construction today.

Public facility financing

Sport arenas, stadiums, and multipurpose facilities are large capital projects for municipalities. Several mechanisms are used in structuring public-sector participation in sports facility development, expansion, and renovation. Among the most common public-financing instruments are bond issues backed by general obligations and/or dedicated revenues, lease appropriations bonds (certificates of participation), and tax increment bond financing (see Table 13-1).

State and local governments issue bonds in the capital market to finance their capital spending programs—construction of arenas, stadiums, parking lots, and infrastructure upgrades. Infrastructure improvements include roads, water/sewer, and other utility needs. Investors call these bond issues *municipals* because they are issued by municipalities, subdivisions of states; they are also called *tax-exempts* because the interest investors receive is exempt from federal taxation. Most states exempt state income tax as well on the interest earned from their bonds. Each state differs on how interest earned on bonds is taxed on a state basis. For example, in South Carolina state citizens do not pay state income tax on bonds issued by a state municipality; however, bond interest earned from out-of-state bonds is subject to South Carolina state income tax.

General obligation bonds. **General obligation bonds,** backed by the full faith and credit of the issuing body (state, local, or regional government), generally require the use of ad valorem taxes. *Ad valorem* taxes are property taxes. This means taxes

---

TABLE 13-1 *Public financing instruments*

Public	• General Obligation Bonds
Financing	• Revenue Bonds
	• Certificates of Participation
Instruments	• Tax Increment Bonds

are levied according to the value of one's property; the more valuable the property, the higher the tax, and vice versa. The underlying theory of ad valorem taxation is that those owning the more valuable properties are wealthier and hence able to pay more taxes. General obligation (GO) bonds typically result in a lower cost of issuance and higher credit rating, and the bond size is often reduced because a debt reserve fund is not always required. However, in some cases the bonding capacity of the municipal unit for other capital needs can be reduced.

Revenue bonds are special obligations in public financing that are payable solely from a particular source of funds, which may include tax/surcharge revenues from hotel/motel, restaurant, sales, liquor/ beer, cigarettes, rental cars, and other sources (see Table 13-2).

No pledge of state, regional, or local ad valorem tax revenues is required; however, the typical revenue bond does carry a higher interest rate and requires a higher debt services coverage ratio as well as debt service reserve.

Certificates of participation (COPS). This public-financing mechanism involves the governmental entity creating a corporation to buy (build) a public facility, such as an arena or convention and visitors' center. The corporation then issues certificates of participation to raise money to buy (build) the public facility. The government leases back the building, and the lease payments are supposed to pay back the bonds. All this happens without a public vote.

Though certificates of participation (COPS) seem like traditional bonds, they are *not* backed by the full faith and credit of the government entity that issues them. In a recession-hammered environment, certificates of participation and lease appropriation financing become popular with local governments looking to fund projects as real estate values decline, and with them property tax collections. These securities are not backed by the full faith and credit of a municipality; therefore, they are a greater risk than a general obligation bond and rated a full step lower.

Tax increment financing (TIF). Tax increment financing transactions are based on the incremental property tax value of the ancillary economic development projects that are triggered by a major new facility. The tax base of a defined area identified as the tax increment financial (TIF) district surrounding the capital project is frozen, and any increases in the tax base are used to repay **tax increment financing bonds.** The area surrounding the facility may be one county/parish or several counties/parishes.

The economics of any tax increment financing district are highly dependent on the development potential of a chosen site and its surrounding land. It is essential to anticipate future revenues on increases in ad valorem taxes or funding sources described in Table 13-2.

Other public sector contributions. The general public indirectly subsidizes sport organizations in other ways. There are a number of ways facilities have obtained additional public funding or government has directly reduced interest costs or borrowing requirements. A few of these mechanisms include the purchase or donation of land; funding of site improvements, parking garages, or surrounding infrastructure; direct equity investments or construction of related facilities, either directly or through an independent authority and lending the government's credit by guaranteeing payment on new debt. Public-sector financing is extensive in professional sport franchises. Cities, states, and regional communities have financed the construction of major arenas, stadiums, and related convention centers for the benefit of the economic community.

TABLE 13-2 *Public Facility Funding Sources*

Public Facility Funding Sources	• Hotel Tax
	• Meals Tax
	• Liquor Tax
	• Sales Tax
	• Auto Rental Tax
	• Property Tax
	• TIFF Districts
	• Business License Tax
	• Utility Tax
	• Road Tax
	• Public & Private Grants
	• State Appropriation
	• Taxi Tax
	• Team Tax

A recent trend is a joint financial arrangement described in the next section.

CONCEPT CHECK

Facility construction often requires public-financing instruments. General obligation bonds, revenue bonds, certificates of participation, and tax increment bonds are the primary financial mechanisms used by municipalities to develop, expand, and renovate facilities. Each public-financing instrument has advantages and disadvantages depending on the financial situation of the community and the issuer.

Private and joint public/private financing

The trend seems to be leaning toward joint public/private partnerships. Public/private partnerships have been utilized for the financing of major public assembly projects, particularly sports facilities. Typically, the public sector utilizes its authority to implement project funding mechanisms, with the private sector contributing project-related or other venue sources. The expanded revenues generated by the facilities and their tenants have resulted in increases in the level of private participation in facility financing. Several of the private-sector revenue streams, which have been utilized in structuring facility financing, include the items in Table 13-3.

Recent examples of joint public/private participation are illustrated in Table 13-4. It is clear that

---

TABLE 13-3 *Private-Sector Revenue Streams*

- Premium seating
- Building rent
- Corporate sponsorship
- Lease payments
- Vendor/contractor equity
- Parking fees
- Merchandise revenues
- Advertising rights
- Concessions revenue
- Naming rights
- Food and beverage serving rights

---

there has been extensive state and local government interest in the development of sports and other public assemble facilities in recent years, and there are a variety of ways to structure the financing for those facilities. Expanding building operating and tenant revenue streams have encouraged a public/private partnership whereby public-sector financing vehicles (various bonding techniques) are supplemented with private-sector revenue streams. Creative financial arrangements allow communities to benefit economically and create a lifestyle conducive to public opinion. Table 13-4 provides examples of how communities created a financial vehicle to build sport and entertainment facilities.

Examples of financing new stadiums include the following: The Alamodome in San Antonio, Texas, is a 77,000-seat domed arena. The Alamodome was completely funded by an additional 0.5 percent sales tax on all retail sales. The $170 million project was completed in 1993 and is now debt free. Therefore, the facility only has to cover operational expenses, not bond premium and interest expense.

Another example concerns the Colorado Rockies, the newest member of the National League and Major League Baseball. The Rockies attracted over 4,600,000 fans during the 1993 season. Coors Stadium was completed for the 1995 season opener in Denver. The new stadium cost $179,803,016 to complete. Financing the stadium required a vote by the public to collect 0.1 percent sales tax upon all taxable retail sales within the jurisdiction of a special tax district. The special tax district includes six Colorado counties: Adams, Arapahoe, Denver, Jefferson, Boulder, and Douglas. Colorado state legislators allowed the special tax district to be created in H.B. No. 90-1172, creating a financial mechanism to provide a sales tax revenue stream to finance the $158 million in revenue bonds necessary to build Coors Stadium.

A key element in financing sport-related facilities is the relationship between government and entrepreneurial sport owners. A public/private partnership exists between the parties to create an entertainment and economic opportunity for the regional economy. Without this relationship, few professional or collegiate programs could financially exist. Financing facilities and the revenue streams shared between the tenant and the municipality are essential for retaining and attracting sport franchises, special events, and fans.

TABLE 13-4   *Financing Participation for Public/Private Facilities*

	Public	Private
Alamodome	— City revenue bond backed by 0.5% sales tax	— Arena revenues
America West Arena	— City revenue bonds backed by excise taxes	— Naming rights — Arena revenues
Bradley Center Arena	— Land donation purchased with general bond issue	— Local family donation
Charlotte Stadium (proposed)	— Land donation	— Naming rights — Arena revenue — Premium seating deposits — Luxury suite revenue
Coors Stadium	— Special tax district revenue bond secured by Sales tax increase, 1/10 of 1%	— Naming rights — Arena revenues
Delta Center Arena	— City tax increment financing bonds	— Private loan secured by building revenue — Naming rights
Cleveland Cavaliers Arena	— County general obligation bonds — Luxury tax allocation	— Private donations and foundation contributions — Premium seat deposits and revenue
Target Center Arena	— Tax increment financing bonds	— Loan secured by arena and health club revenues — Naming rights
Ballpark in Arlington	— City revenue bond secured by sales tax increase — Infrastructure improvements	— Luxury suite revenues — Ticket surcharge — Seat options — Concessionaire payment

The proper financial team needs to be assembled in order to design, organize, and finance a public, private, or public/private facility. Components of a successful team should include the following members:

- Issuer/owner
- Facility management
- Feasibility consultant
- Examination accountant
- Business plan consultant
- Financial advisor
- Architect
- Cost estimator
- Design builder
- Construction manager
- Senior underwriter
- Co-underwriter
- Bond council
- Issuer's council

The financing team must work together to obtain the goal and objective of the community or owner. Each facility's scenario is different and requires study and analysis. Successful facility financing is a partnership between the regional community, the owner/tenant, government, and the financial institutions (Figure 13-1).

The next section focuses on the revenue streams in sport and the importance of cash flow management.

CASH FLOW IN SPORT

All good business requires proper utilization of cash. Sport is a seasonal business that requires cash management. Professional sport franchises

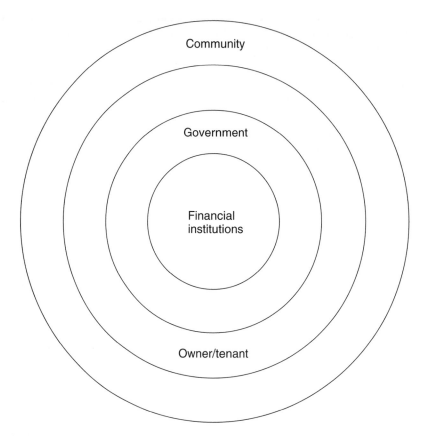

FIGURE 13-1 Community partnership for facility success.

cost hundreds of millions to purchase existing teams, and expansion franchises require tens of millions. For example, the Baltimore Orioles were purchased for an estimated $173 million, and the Philadelphia Eagles received approximately $185 million. Major League Baseball expansion teams in 1993 were required to pay $95 million for the privilege of joining the league. National Football League owners required a franchise fee projected at $700 million for the Houston Texans and the National Hockey League expansion franchise fee was $50–$70 million.

Major collegiate athletic departments have budgets in excess of $30 million. The athletic director must be a fund-raiser, budget director, and professional manager. The college athletic department requires proper use of cash flow to help finance and schedule stadium maintenance, sport expansion, or postseason play.

CONCEPT CHECK

A trend toward public/private partnerships for the financing of major sport facilities is becoming more common. The private sector realizes the potential benefit of programming the facility for additional revenue streams. Public/private partnerships are decreasing the municipality's involvement in operating the stadium.

Revenue streams

Sports create **revenue streams** and produce cash very quickly. The major revenue producers are ticket sales, concessions, advertising, broadcasting (local radio, local television, and national media), parking, preferred seating, and licensing agreements, along with other miscellaneous revenue.

Professional sport organizations negotiate a contract with the municipalities. For example, the Colorado Rockies lease is a standard for the profession and includes the following terms with the special tax district and the city and county of Denver. Table 13-5 identifies the sharing of revenue in a publicly financed stadium.

The Colorado Rockies stadium agreement is beneficial to the team, as Table 13-5 indicates. The public officials must consider the overall business relationship between the owners, other Major League Baseball owners, and the subsidizing public. Each must feel the new franchise in Colorado has a reasonable opportunity to be economically successful. Leagues, teams, cities, and business need cash flow to successfully operate.

Cash flow is defined as reported net income plus amounts charged off for depreciation, depletion, amortization, and extraordinary charges to reserves that are bookkeeping deductions and not paid out in actual dollars and cents. The primary purpose of the cash flows statement is to provide relevant information about cash receipts and cash disbursements of an enterprise during a particular period. This will help investors (partners), creditors and others to:

1. Assess the team's ability to generate positive future net cash flows.
2. Assess the sport enterprise's ability to meet its obligations.
3. Assess the difference between net income and cash receipts and disbursements.
4. Assess the effects of both cash and noncash investing and financing during a period.

The term cash in FASB #95 refers to cash in the bank and all short-term liquid investments that can be readily converted to cash. Examples of items considered to be cash equivalents are marketable securities with less than three months' maturity, treasury bills, commercial paper, and money market funds.

Cash receipts and cash disbursements are classified as operating, investing, or financing activities. In sport organizations it is often difficult to compare teams, and the statement of cash flows provides an opportunity to compare like-kind enterprises. **Investing activities** include the purchase or sale of securities or other entities, the sale or purchase of fixed assets, and loans made or payments on loans received. **Financing activities** include issuing securities, borrowing, paying of dividends, buying

TABLE 13-5   *Colorado Rockies Stadium Agreement Summary*

Date of Agreement	March 14, 1991
Term	17 years, with option to renew for 5-year term.

Sharing of revenue

Admissions	Starting in 2000, Team pays 2½% of net taxable income, provided partners of Team have received distributions equal to 5% of contributions.
Concessions	Team keeps all revenue.
Parking	Team keeps all revenue.
Advertising	Team keeps all revenue.
Other events	Team keeps all revenue.
Television Revenue	Team keeps all revenue.
Stadium Club	Team keeps all revenue.
Set Fees	—
Reimbursements	Starting in 1995, Team pays City up to $150,000 a year for operating costs if City's costs exceed revenues.
Miscellaneous	—

SHARING OF COSTS

Field Maintenance	Team
Stadium Maintenance	Team

GAME DAY

Ushers, etc.	Team
Security	Team
Cleaning	Team
Utilities	Team
Field Equipment	Team
Concession Equipment	Team

Treasury stock (the company's own stock), and repaying debt.

The cash flows from the investing and financing activities are usually balance sheet items. The final section of the statement of cash flows is the

operating-activities section. This activities section covers everything that is not investing or financing activities. Daily sport business activity generates operating funds as do most business organizations on interest or dividends earned. Accounts receivable and accounts payable are generally operating activities. Cash flow derived from operating activities typically applies to the cash effects of transactions entering into profit computations. **Cash inflows** from operating activities include:

1. Cash sales or collections on ticket receivables.
2. Cash sales or collections on licensed merchandise.
3. Cash receipts from returns on loans (interest income) or dividend income.
4. Cash received from licensees and lessees.

5. Receipt of a litigation settlement (i.e., between city, team, owner, and players).
6. Reimbursement under an insurance policy (strike insurance, etc.)

Cash outflows for operating activities include:

1. Cash paid for raw material and merchandise for resale.
2. Principal payments on accounts payable arising from purchase of goods.
3. Payments to suppliers of operating expense items (insurance, advertising, supplies).
4. Player and personnel salaries/wages.
5. Payment of taxes.
6. Payment of interest expense (bonds or loans).
7. Lawsuit payment (collusion settlement).

TABLE 13-6   *Sports Enterprises, Inc. Balance Sheet Years Ending 20X3 and 20X4 (Thousands of Dollars)*

Assets	20X3	20X4	Cash (Ind. Dec)
Current Assets			
Cash	$280	$230	ignore
Accounts receivable	340	380	(40)
Inventory	210	260	(50)
Total Current Assets	$830	$870	
Property, plant and equipment	500	525	(25)
Less: Accumulated depreciation	(110)	(125)	15
Net Fixed Assets	$390	$400	
Total Assets	$1,220	$1,270	
Liabilities & stockholders' equity			
Current Liabilities			
Accounts payable	$220	$220	−0−
Taxes payable	80	110	30
Total Current Liabilities	$300	$330	
Long-term liabilities—bonds	432	240	(192)
Total Liabilities	$732	$570	
Stockholders' Equity:			
Common stock	280	290	10
Paid-in-capital	40	50	10
Retained earnings	168	360	192
Total Shareholders' Equity	$488	$700	
Total Liabilities and Equity	$1,220	$1,270	

8. Charitable contributions.
9. Cash refunds to customers for merchandise, ticket sales or service.

Current profitability is only one important factor for success in sport. It is essential that current and future cash flows are positive. In fact, a profitable sport franchise may have a cash crisis. Inadequate cash flow has possible serious implications, since it may lead to declining profitability, greater financial risk, and even bankruptcy. Teams are sold because of franchise market value increases and cash flow decreases. To demonstrate how important cash flow is to a sport manager, review the financial statements in Table 13-6.

CONCEPT CHECK

Major professional and collegiate sport organizations produce cash very quickly. The revenue streams include ticket sales, concessions, advertising, sponsorship, broadcasting, parking, preferred seating, licensing agreements, and other miscellaneous revenues. Cash flow provides relevant information about cash receipts and disbursements of a sport enterprise. The statement of cash flows includes an operating, financing, and investing section. Cash flow is an essential management tool for analysis of financial information.

The balance sheet indicates all the information needed to calculate the statement of cash flows for Sport Enterprises, Inc., for the year ended 20X4. Additional information is helpful to clearly understand the cash flow statement. Earnings after taxes (net income) was $202,000, depreciation expense was $15,000, and common stock was issued.

Table 13-6 enables us to prepare a statement of cash flows as seen in Table 13-7. It is important to note that preparing a statement of cash flows involves calculating the dollar change in each of the balance sheet items *other than cash.*

It is important to note that Sport Enterprises, Inc., had $202,000 in earnings after taxes; however, it produced a $50,000 decrease in cash flow for the year ended 20X4.

The sport manager needs to understand why cash decreased by $50,000. This is accomplished by careful examination of the statement of cash flows

TABLE 13-7 *Sports Enterprises, Inc. Statement of Cash Flows for Period Ended 20X4*

Operating Activities	
Earnings after tax	$202,000
Add: Depreciation expense	15,000
Increase in accounts receivable	(40,000)
Increase in inventories	(50,000)
Increase in taxes payable	30,000
Net cash flow from operating activities	**$157,000**
Investing Activities	
Increase in plant and equipment	($25,000)
Other	−0−
Net cash used by investing activities	**($25,000)**
Financing Activities	
Payment of dividends	($10,000)
Issue of common stock	20,000
Retirement of bonds	(192,000)
Net cash used by financing activities	**($182,000)**
Net increase (decrease) in cash	**($50,000)**

in Table 13-7. Cash was primarily decreased by the retirement of $192,000 in bonds. The answer to a cash flow problem is always the change in cash. The difference between 20X3 cash of $280,000 and 19X9 cash of $230,000 equals a ($50,000) decrease in cash for the period ending 20X4.

Managing cash flow is essential for the sport administration professional. Cash flow will assist in determining future expansion of facilities, players' salaries, bonuses, and investment opportunities, to mention only a few essential components. The sport business game is managing cash flow. *You must win!!!*

SUMMARY

- Financing sport-related facilities usually requires public, private, and joint public/private financing. New construction, expansion, and maintenance of stadiums, arenas, and practice facilities are assets needed to attract and retain professional teams.
- Professional, collegiate, and interscholastic sport facilities are usually built using public financing instruments such as general

obligation bonds, revenue bonds, certificates of participation, and tax increment bonds.

- Investors call these bond issues municipals or munis because they are issued by municipalities, subdivisions of states; they are tax exempt investment instruments and appeal to high income investors.
- Private-sector sport organizations are creating public/private partnerships to finance a few major sport facilities. The financing arrangement must be negotiated between the governmental unit and team ownership. Financing a public/private sport facility provides opportunity for creative financial agreements between communities and sport owners.
- The proper financial team should be assembled in order to design, organize, and finance a public, private, or public/private facility. A successful financial team should include: owner, facility manager, feasibility consultant, accountant, financial advisor, underwriters, bond council, and issuer's council.
- Sport is seasonal and requires proper cash flow analysis. Season tickets may be sold six to eight months before the season opens, and the business manager or controller needs to utilize proper cash flow techniques.
- Cash flow involves knowledge of the balance sheet and income statement. FASB #95 requires a statement of cash flow to be a required financial statement for organizations. Cash flow involves inflows and outflows of cash related to operating activities.
- Sport business managers must be aware of financial arrangements available for facility construction and how to analyze and manage cash flow.

 CRITICAL THINKING EXERCISES

1. The Houston NFL franchise required a record $700 million franchise fee from Robert McNair. Houston was able to outbid the Los Angeles ownership group for the new franchise. You are the chief financial officer (CFO) for the Houston Texans franchise. What other financial issues must be considered for football to begin in the 2002 NFL football season and to operate a new NFL team and stadium for the next decade?

2. The Philips Arena in Atlanta, Georgia, cost an estimated $213 million to build. It was a public/private partnership between the area taxpayers ($62.5 million) and private ownership. The new arena is home to the Atlanta Thrashers and the Atlanta Hawks and has 90 luxury suites and 1,800 club seats. Philips Corporation paid a record $185 million over 20 years for naming rights at the facility. What financial information is necessary to negotiate a naming rights deal of this magnitude? Consider tangible and intangible benefits from the perspective of Philips Corporation and the potential trend this may create for other new arenas.

 REVIEW QUESTIONS AND ISSUES

1. Identify and discuss facilities recently constructed for sport organizations in the United States.
2. What public financing options are available for constructing a stadium or arena?
3. Describe and identify public/private and private financing options available for construction of major sport facilities.
4. What is the difference between cash flow and cash?
5. Describe how sport is seasonal and the effect this has on cash inflows and outflows.
6. Public financing instruments are usually tax free. What is the benefit to the investor? Benefit to the community?
7. Why do communities build stadiums for sport organizations?
8. Give examples of private financing of sport facilities.
9. Cash flow requires revenues streams. Discuss and identify the major revenue streams produced by sport enterprises.

CASE STUDY I

You are interested in purchasing a minor league AAA baseball team. The team is located in Colorado and requires an infusion of capital. In order to consider the purchase price you need to create financial statements and amortization and depreciation schedules. The financial information is very poor, but what is available follows:

1. *No balance sheet, income statement, or cash flow statement exists.*
2. *The team was created in 2003 and uses the accrual basis of accounting.*
3. *The Colorado team was capitalized as follows: (in 2003)*
   a. *Sold 100,000 shares of common stock for $10.0 per share.*
   b. *Borrowed $1,000,000 @ 8 percent for seven years.*
4. *The team incurred certain costs and expenditures in 2003.*

a. *Equipment*	$ 250,000
b. *Building*	1,000,000
c. *Land*	100,000
d. *Inventory (year end)*	20,000
e. *Player salaries*	3,000,000
f. *Baseball operations expense*	820,000
g. *General and admin. expense*	310,000
h. *Utilities*	100,000
i. *Maintenance*	125,000
j. *Bad debt expense*	12,000
k. *Insurance expense*	100,000
l. *Miscellaneous*	115,000

5. *The team generated revenue in 2003 as follows:*
   a. *Ticket sales 1,000,000 fans @ $5.00/ticket.*
   b. *Stadium concessions 1,000,000 fans @ $1.00 per fan.*
   c. *Parking $100,000 per year.*
6. *Depreciation information:*
   a. *Building—thirty-year life using straight line method.*
   b. *All other long-term assets over a five-year life and straight line method of depreciation.*
7. *Other information:*
   a. *The Baseball team must pay the City 10 percent for each ticket sold. This is called a license fee.*
   b. *The team invested in a Certificate of Deposit (C.D.) on January 1, 1999 for 24 months @ 10 percent compounded daily. The C.D. had a face value of $200,000 and interest income is recorded at year end.*
   c. *Prepaid insurance was $20,000.*
   d. *Accounts receivable balance is $80,000 at year end.*
   e. *Accounts payable $75,000 at year end.*
8. *Accrual basis of accounting is observed.*
9. *Income tax rate is 34 percent.*

10. *Dividend paid—$5 per share of common stock at year end December 31. Dividend is paid each year.*
11. *2004 INFORMATION: DECEMBER 31, 2004.*

	Balances
a. *Inventory*	$ 40,000
b. *Prepaid insurance*	20,000
c. *Accounts receivable*	60,000
d. *Equipment*	300,000
e. *Accounts payable*	100,000

12. *Revenue: 2004*
   Tickets, concessions and parking same as previous year. Don't forget interest income.
   Expenses: 2004
   All 2004 expenses are the same except Depreciation expense.

Requirements for Case Study

1. *Prepare financial statements for Sports Properties, Inc.*
   a. *Balance sheets for 2003 and 2004.*
   b. *Income statements 2003 and 2004.*
   c. *Statements of cash flows 2004.*
2. *Prepare: corresponding schedules:*
   a. *Loan amortization schedule.*
   b. *Depreciation schedule.*
   c. *Cash balance "T" account schedule for 2003 and 2004.*
3. *Do an analysis of the financial statements and indicate strengths and weaknesses of Sports Properties, Inc. (Be specific.)*

 CASE STUDY II

The University of the South wants to increase revenue streams inside the stadium. They have decided to build luxury boxes in the stadium. They are in the process of evaluating alternative financing arrangements to fund the construction of the boxes. They need $2.5 million for construction and operation. The project includes building 28 corporate boxes with 24 seats per box. Compare financing arrangements and discuss the advantages and disadvantages of each.

 SOLUTIONS TO CRITICAL THINKING EXERCISES

1. The franchise must pay $700 million in cash to the NFL owners. This fee will have to be borrowed or paid from earnings from the McNair

ownership group. The ownership group must now obtain a stadium to play the football schedule at an estimated cost of $300 million. The ownership group must organize an administrative staff and coaches at an estimated cost of $5 million, and then draft players to compete in the NFL at an estimated cost of $50–$70 million. This must be completed before one fan has entered the proposed new facility to watch an NFL game.

The essential element to plan for an expansion franchise is cash flow. The Houston organization must formulate a plan to borrow money though bank loans, public or private bonds, and equity investors to accomplish this task. The task will involve partnerships with interested corporate investors, public governmental support, and community taxpayers. The business plan has to include an anticipated rate of return for the ownership group.

2. The financial information necessary to negotiate a naming rights deal of this magnitude must include the tangible monetary benefits for Philips Corporation. You must be able to demonstrate that the naming of Philips Arena will provide $185 million of tangible and intangible exposure. The Atlanta Hawks and Thrashers will be the major tenants promoting fan attendance. However the concerts, road shows, and other touring entertainment will provide potentially greater attendance than the team sports. A breakdown of naming rights costs per fan per year and over the life of the 20 year contract should be developed.

A recall survey should be developed to highlight the media exposure for the Philips Arena. The number of times the arena's name is used on national television, newspapers, and other media outlets should be recorded. The media exposure has a monetary value that can be determined by developing a schedule indicating what it would cost to advertise the brand name in the various media. The Philips Arena will be the site of future NBA and NHL all-star games and hopefully playoff games. These events will focus national and international attention on the Philips Arena.

The naming rights deal is a trendsetter for new arenas looking to subsidize public facilities that host private sport enterprises. Philips

Arena's naming rights will now be the baseline for larger media markets to negotiate new naming rights agreements. It appears like a great marketing scheme, but it is really a financial arrangement between the arena and private corporations to build new multipurpose facilities throughout the nation.

FOSTERING YOUR WORKPLACE SKILLS

1. As a manager of a corporate fitness center, you are responsible for submitting a budget for the next fiscal year to the director of development. The fitness program, which employs two fitness specialists and you, has operated for three years and consistently lost money. The director of development has agreed to subsidize the program with an additional $10,000 with the understanding that a portion of the funds will be allocated to a marketing and advertising compaign:
   a. What steps would you take in planning and preparing your budget?
   b. From whom would you solicit information?
   c. What options do you have when allocating funds?
   d. What changes in the budget would you propose?
   e. How might asking "what if" questions be useful?

 WEBSITES

http://www.wwcd.com/stadiums/home.html—This Website is for dealers in the collectibles community. It contains links to live sport scores and has a listing of stadium and arena seating charts.

http://www.sun-sentinel.com/money/details.htm—This Website contains information about sports, entertainment, and news covering southern Florida.

REFERENCES

Cooley, P., and Roden, P. (1998). *Business financial management.* 3rd ed. Hinsdale, IL: The Dryden Press.

Hurt, Richardson, Garner, and Cadenhead, T. (1993). *Stadium lease arrangements.* San Antonio, TX. International City Managers Association, Sports and special events conference.

Regan, T. (1993). *Financing stadiums and arenas in the United States and Europe.* Paris, France. 4th Annual International Conference on Sports Business.

PART IV

Marketing

Discussion Topic

The National Basketball Association has been one of the most successful professional leagues in sport marketing. However, in the past few years, there has been considerable discussion about the "urban" image (music, clothing, tattoos, player antics) of the game and its association with an urban culture. While this association has been popular with many teens and specific segments of the consumer market, it has also alienated many of the upper-class market segments that represent the suite and season ticket holders that, along with sponsors, provide vital revenues to the teams.

Group Discussion Question: What are the issues surrounding this phenomenon and the impact that it may have on team marketing, merchandising and sponsor acquisition?

CHAPTER **14**

Sport Marketing: Strategies and Tactics

Dianna P. Gray and Chad D. McEvoy

In this chapter, you will become familiar with the following terms:

Advertising	Marketing plan	Product usage
Bartering	Niche	Promotion
Core product	Personal selling	Public relations
Demographics	Place	Sales promotion
Distribution	Positioning	Strategic planning
Market	Price	Target market
Market segmentation	Product extensions	Telemarketing

Learning Goals
By the end of this chapter, students should be able to:

• Demonstrate comprehension of the basic principles of sport marketing and the ability to apply these principles to actual problems in sport.

• Define, distinguish, and apply the principles of pricing; promotion, publicity and advertising; sales and distribution; and sponsorship, to a sport team or organization.

• Demonstrate the ability to analyze and problem solve via the case study approach to marketing problems and apply these skills to the specific problems found in the Nike case study at the end of the chapter.

• Demonstrate the ability to gather and analyze relevant sport marketing information using secondary (Internet, marketing databases, and published research) and primary sources (interviews and surveys), and apply the findings to a specific sport marketing problem.

• Develop a marketing plan using the outline at the end of the chapter as a guide.

The purpose of this chapter is to present concepts relative to sport marketing and discuss the application of these concepts as practiced in sport organizations. This will be achieved by defining sport marketing and illustrating sports' unique characteristics; explaining the marketing management process; identifying and analyzing consumers; introducing the concept of marketing communication and the marketing mix; and developing a strategic marketing plan. The student who is cognizant of the strategic marketing management process will more fully understand the role of marketing in the sport organization.

WHAT IS SPORT MARKETING?

A definition of *sport marketing* must be preceded by a definition and examination of marketing. Perreault and McCarthy (2002) define *marketing* as the performance of activities that direct the flow of goods and services from producer to user to satisfy the customer and accomplish the organization's objectives. Kotler (2003) defines *marketing* as the human activity directed at satisfying needs and wants through exchange processes. The American Marketing Association defines *marketing* as the "process of planning and executing the conception, pricing, promotion, and distribution of ideas, goods and services to create exchanges that satisfy individual and organization objectives" ("AMA Dictionary," 2004). An emphasis on satisfying consumers' want and needs is everywhere in today's marketplace; successful organizations are those that realize their objectives by satisfying customers' needs. Marketing is as much a way of conducting business as it is a theoretical concept.

The term *sport marketing* is said to have been coined by *Advertising Age* in 1978 to describe the activities of consumer and industrial product and service marketers who were increasingly using sport as a promotional vehicle. This is commonly referred to as marketing *through* sport; that is, *using sport* as a promotional vehicle or sponsorship platform for companies that market consumer and, to a lesser extent, industrial products. What is absent from this description is the marketing *of* sport. This aspect of sport marketing involves the specific application of marketing principles and processes to market goods and services directly to sports participants and spectators, or end-users.

Many authors have developed definitions for the concept and practice of sport marketing (see, for example, Brooks, 1994; Milne and McDonald, 1999; Mullin, Hardy, and Sutton, 2000; Pitts and Stotlar, 2002; Shank, 1999), all of which encompass the essential elements of marketing. For our purposes, *sport marketing* will be defined as the anticipation, management, and satisfaction of sport consumers' wants and needs through the application of marketing principles and practice. Sport marketing begins and ends with the customer—whether an individual or organization—in mind. The successful sport marketer will focus on understanding sport consumers and providing them with sports products and services that meet their needs.

A commonly asked question is whether sport as a product differs significantly from other goods and services. Virtually all sport marketers maintain that sport has certain characteristics in its core, extensions, and presentation that make the sport product unique, requiring an approach that may, at times, vary from the approaches of mainstream business marketing. What follows is a brief examination of sports' unique qualities that alter traditional marketing approaches and dictate the "locus of control" of the sport marketer.

Intangibility and subjectivity

Simply put, the consumer takes nothing away from attending a sport event but impressions and memories. The wide variety of possible impressions and interpretations of the event pose a challenge for the sports marketer, namely to achieve a probability of consumer satisfaction. For example, consider a group of five people attending a Major League Baseball game. One member of the group might remember that parking was time-consuming and expensive; another might have been disappointed with the outcome of the game because the home team lost; a third may have been impressed by the quality of the pitching matchups, while the fourth member of the group may have been disappointed in the lack of scoring; and the fifth person may remember enjoying the event because of social interaction with the other members of the group. Each member of the group had an opinion that—although not necessarily related to the core product, or game itself—will influence future purchasing decisions regarding that product. In describing baseball, Bill Veeck, the former Chicago White Sox owner who is best known for putting players' names on the back of uniforms and setting off fireworks after home runs, illustrates the intangibility of the sport product by stating, "The customer comes out to the park with nothing except the illusion that he is going to have a good time. He leaves with nothing except a memory" (Veeck and Linn, 1965).

Inconsistency/unpredictability

One of the great attractions of sport, for both participants and spectators alike, is the belief that on any given day, any team or individual, regardless of past performance, can win. This attitude would certainly describe die-hard Cubs fans and more recently, Florida Marlin fans (the unlikely World Series champions in 2003). Many factors can affect the outcome of a game or contest. Such factors include players' motivation, injuries, trades, momentum shifts, and environmental conditions such as weather and time of year. These factors and the lack of a game script interact to guarantee that each game, event, or contest will be unique and the outcome uncertain . . . often until the last out or "heave-ho" desperation pass.

Product perishability

The sport product can be sold no later than the day of the event. In reality, it should be sold well before game day to help ensure franchise stability, consumer interest, and product credibility. There is virtually no consumer market for yesterday's football, baseball, or basketball game. In professional sport, as well as for basketball and football at many NCAA Division I schools, tickets should be presold to guarantee stable revenue and to generate profits. If tickets are not presold, and the team does not perform up to the fans' expectations, gate receipts will likely drop and revenue from ticket sales will decline.

Emotional attachment and identification

Numerous studies have been conducted to measure the attitudes and behavior patterns of Americans regarding sport participation and attendance, as well as the effect of sport on the lives of Americans. The ESPN Sports Poll reveals, among other findings, the tremendous popularity of sport in America, not only in terms of sport participation, but also game attendance and media consumption of sport. And avid fans are not limited to adults; children ages 7–11 identified the National Basketball Association (NBA) as their favorite sport (79 percent of children polled), and teens (ages 12–18) prefer the National Football League (NFL) (ESPN Sportspoll.com).

Evidence of the prevalence of sport can also be seen by examining the growth of the sports industry. In 1987 sport was a $47.2 billion-a-year enterprise (Sandomir, 1988); by 1995 that figure had risen to $152 billion (Meek, 1997). The most recent research on the economic impact of sport identifies it as a $213 billion-a-year industry, making it the sixth largest industry in the United States ("The answer is," 1999, p. 23). Sport is not simply another big business; it is one of the fastest-growing industries in the United States, and it is intertwined with practically every aspect of the economy—from advertising and apparel, to computer technology and video games, to travel and tourism.

The development of properties divisions and merchandising departments in all professional and major college athletic programs has contributed to this sport frenzy by giving interested fans an opportunity to purchase a variety of apparel, uniform replicas, or related team items. This aspect of sport management is known as licensing, as sport organizations license, or allow, other companies the right to produce merchandise with the sport organizations' logo or likeness, called a trademark. As part of such an agreement, the manufacturer of the merchandise, the licensee, pays a royalty fee to the sport organization, the licensor, for the use of their trademark. Royalty fees typically range from 6 to 10 percent of the wholesale price for each item sold. The sales of caps, T-shirts, sweatshirts, jackets and other clothing emblazoned with Olympic marks, NFL individual and Super Bowl teams, college and professional basketball teams, and the like, has increased dramatically in recent years, becoming a major revenue source for sport organizations. Table 14-1

TABLE 14-1   *Annual Merchandise Sales Figures*

Sport league/organization	Merchandise sales
National Football League	$ 2.5 billion
All Colleges	$ 2.5 billion
Major League Baseball	$ 2.3 billion
NASCAR	$ 1.2 billion
National Basketball Association	$ 1.0 billion
National Hockey League	$900 million

Source: *SportsBusiness Journal.*

identifies annual merchandise sales for different sports leagues and organizations.

Focus and "locus of control"

In mainstream business marketing, marketers play a critical role in determining the composition of their organization's marketing mix (how the four P's will be blended and used) and product positioning. However, in sport marketing the marketer's input is inappropriate and thus, is not actively sought. Players are acquired, traded, platooned, placed on injured reserve, and used with no input from the marketer, whose responsibility is to market the game to a variety of market segments regardless of the team's current status. Although the trade or acquisition of a particular player may help or hurt attendance, these decisions are not the purview of the sport marketer. The scheduling of the opposition is another factor that is outside the scope of the sport marketer's responsibility, yet it has a significant effect on attendance in team sports (Rudman and Sutton, 1989).

For example, in college football, one season after winning the 2002 Bowl Championship Series (BCS) national championship game, the Ohio State football program found itself embroiled in controversy when sophomore sensation Maurice Clarett was ruled ineligible and suspended for the entire season. Any marketing strategy that focused on the return of Clarett, the Big Ten player-of-the-year the previous season, had to be abandoned. On the other hand, marketers with the NBA Cleveland Cavaliers and Denver Nuggets were ecstatic following the 2003 NBA lottery draft because LeBron James and Carmello Anthony would suit up the following season. Early into the 2003 NBA season both Cleveland and Denver were enjoying increased ticket sales and higher attendance figures; but these increases could disappear should either James or Anthony be injured.

Similarly, in participant sports, crucial factors such as weather, this week's gasoline prices, or the presence of road construction are outside the locus of control of sport marketers but have significant effects on demand at golf, tennis, and ski facilities. Thus, the focus of the marketer is largely on the **product extensions** that are within (the locus of) his or her control. Table 14-2 summarizes the unique characteristics of sport, examining the market as well as the four P's of the marketing mix.

TABLE 14-2	*Unique Sport Characteristics*
Market	Sport organizations compete and cooperate simultaneously
	Sport consumers consider themselves experts
	Wide fluctuation in consumer demand (seasonal, weekly, and daily demand differences)
Product	Intangible
	Subjective
	Produced and consumed on same site
	Inconsistent
	Perishable/no shelf life (must presell)
	Publicly consumed; affected by social facilitation
	Sport marketer has no control over core product
Price	Difficult to price using conventional methods
	Small percentage of total money spent by consumer goes to sport organization
	More money obtained from product extensions, TV, etc. (indirect revenues)
Promotion	Tremendous media exposure
	Businesses want association with sport
Place/ distribution	Produced and consumed in same place
	Atmosphere contributes to enjoyment
	Sport marketer should focus efforts here
	TV and media; tickets

CONCEPT CHECK

Sport marketing has unique characteristics and considerations not found in most areas of product marketing. Intangibility, subjectivity, inconsistency, unpredictability, perishability, emotional attachment and identification, social facilitation, public consumption, and focus and locus of control are factors that interact to form a series of challenges for the sport marketer.

STRATEGIC SPORTS MARKETING

Strategic sport marketing is a system designed to help management make better marketing decisions. A strategic decision is the creation, change, or retention of a strategy (Aaker, 1998). Philip Kotler (2003) defines the strategic market planning process as the managerial process of developing and maintaining a strategic fit between the organization's goals and resources and its changing market opportunities. The tangible result of this planning process is a marketing plan. Later in the chapter, the development of a marketing plan will be covered. The strategic marketing process is essentially a three-step progression: planning, implementation and evaluation.

Strategic planning

Sport marketers must realize that they work in an environment that changes regularly. As previously discussed, the sport marketer cannot predict or control what happens over the course of a season. Therefore, an essential component of the **strategic planning** process is conducting an environmental analysis (Aaker, 1998; Kotler, 2003). An environmental analysis is an ongoing assessment of the "climate," including internal and external factors that may or may not affect marketing efforts. For example, in intercollegiate athletics the environment would include the university itself, the athletic department, the local business community, citizens and alumni, state government, media, boosters, and corporate sponsors. Consider for a moment what would happen if the most visible and highly ranked football teams in your conference decided to join another conference. What impact would this decision have on the remaining conference schools? This scenario is not hypothetical; in 2003, Big East football powers Miami University, Virginia Tech, and Boston College decided to leave the conference and join the Atlantic Coast Conference (ACC). You might recall how contentious this decision was, particularly for the remaining Big East conference schools. On the other hand, the ACC welcomed three new schools with competitive and highly ranked football programs, thus changing the position of the ACC from a basketball conference to one that was competitive in both basketball and football.

As you can see, sport marketers must be prepared for both positive and negative changes in the environment. A useful framework for analyzing the environment and preparing plans to deal with various situations is known as a SWOT analysis. This planning tool allows marketers to evaluate the sport organization's strengths and weaknesses, and estimate the opportunities and threats present in the competitive environment. Another way to view strategic planning is to think of it as preparation for unforeseen events or contingencies. External contingencies (the OT aspect of a SWOT analysis), such as a depressed economy and new NCAA or league regulations, are factors outside of the organization's control. Internal contingencies (the SW aspect of a SWOT analysis) are factors that are within the organization's control and include such things as the organization's mission and goals, financial resources, and human resources.

Another important benefit of strategic planning is its use in identifying potential customers and then classifying market segments. Once the segments are identified, the sport marketer then targets the appropriate market segment(s) and develops the core marketing strategy. This includes the selection of target market(s), the choice of a competitive position, and the development of an effective marketing mix to reach and serve the chosen consumers (Kotler, 1997).

Identifying and targeting sport consumers

To be successful in the highly competitive sport and entertainment business, the sport marketer must know something about the people who will be the ultimate consumers. This learning process consists of examining the characteristics and needs of the target market, including the consumer's lifestyle and purchase decisions, so that product, **distribution** (place), promotion, and pricing decisions are made accordingly. By knowing as much as possible about the consumer, the sport marketer can satisfy the target markets, keep consumer dissatisfaction to a minimum, and remain competitive by maintaining or increasing market share.

Before beginning to plan ways of marketing a sport product or service, the sport marketer should answer some general questions about the consumer. First, who is the consumer of the product or service? Here the marketer is trying to obtain information about the *final consumer,* the person who actually decides to purchase the produce or service. Where does the consumer live? How does the consumer learn about the available sport and entertainment opportunities? To what forms of media is the consumer exposed? How far in advance of the event does the consumer decide to attend or participate? When does the consumer purchase the ticket to the event? What does the consumer do before the game (pre-event) and after the game (post-event)?

After getting general information about the sport consumer, the marketer seeks answers to more specific questions. At this stage, the marketer begins to compose a profile of the sport consumer by examining demographic and lifestyle information. Consumer **demographics** are the statistical descriptions of the attributes or characteristics of the population. By looking at demographic information, both individual characteristics and overall descriptions, the sport marketer can begin to develop consumer profiles that may pinpoint both attractive and declining market opportunities. Table 14-3 (on the next page) provides a demographic comparison of NBA and NASCAR fans.

One of the best ways to obtain demographic information is to conduct primary research, usually by means of a survey. This is not always feasible because of financial or time limits; however, there are also several secondary sources of information marketers can use. These sources give the sport marketer not only information about the general population but also specific information about sport consumers. The federal government collects a wealth of data on its citizens. U.S. government sources include the *U.S. Census, American Statistics Index,* and *ASI Abstracts*. Population statistics from other sources such as chambers of commerce, convention and visitors' bureaus (CVBs), public utility companies, and marketing firms can supplement the census data. Published sport-specific demographic data can be obtained from individual sport franchises, the national offices of the major sport leagues, sport marketing firms, institutions and private corporations that have commissioned studies, or university libraries.

There are also a variety of serial publications and electronic databases (LexisNexis Statistical is an excellent source) that offer the marketer demographic information. *American Demographics* and *Brandweek* are magazines that report demographic data. Other secondary sources of demographic information include the Women's Sport Foundation, *The Sports Business Journal, Athletic Business, American Sports Analysis* (by American Sports Data, Inc.), *USA Today,* and local newspapers.

Zeroing in on your customer base

Although the information gathered from secondary sources can help the sport marketer identify potential consumers, it is at best general information.

Specific information about current consumers should be collected directly if possible. The tools available for this purpose—the survey, the exit poll, and the focus group—have proven to be effective. However, for the sport marketer the most feasible way of gathering information on current consumers is to conduct an in-arena or club members survey. The results of such marketing research will allow the sport marketer to make more informed market selection decisions.

Grouping consumers based on common wants and needs is called market segmentation. Theodore Levitt, in his classic book *Marketing Imagination* (1986), said that if marketers were not thinking about market segmentation, then they were not thinking. **Market segmentation** is the process of dividing the overall market into groups with relatively similar product needs or purchase behaviors so that a specific marketing approach can be developed to match those needs. The following box identifies common approaches to segmentation and lists typical variables that, singly or in combination, may be used to determine market segments.

Basis of Segmentation: Approaches Used Alone or in Combination to Segment Markets

Segment descriptors	Examples
Demographic	Gender, age, marital status, number of children, ethnic background
Geographic	Location/region, size and density of where people live
Socioeconomic	Income, education, occupation
Psychographic	How people live and what interests them; dividing markets into segments on the basis of consumer life styles. Activities, interests, and opinions.
Behavioral	Frequency of product consumption and usage; brand loyalty
Benefits	Grouping consumers into market segments on the basis of the product features and the desirable consequences sought from the product

TABLE 14-3   *Comparison of NBA and NASCAR Fan Demographics*

NBA Fan Demographics

	1998	1999	2000	2001	2002	Change from 1998
GENDER	n = 13,132	12,179	13,006	9,102	11,073	
Male	52.9	53.4	53.6	53.2	54.3	2.7%
Female	47.1	46.6	46.4	46.8	45.7	−3.0%
ETHNICITY	n = 12,817	11,851	12,699	8,862	10,761	
White	65.4	64.5	64.4	63.2	61.8	−5.6%
African-American	17.1	17.5	17.5	17.9	18.3	7.0%
Hispanic	12.8	13.2	13.1	13.7	14.5	13.6%
Asian	1.4	1.1	1.1	1.3	1.3	−4.5%
Other	3.3	3.6	3.9	4	4.1	23.0%
HOUSEHOLD INCOME	n = 9,202	8,430	3,593	6,295	7,637	
Under $20,000	16.8	17.1	16.8	18.4	17.9	6.7%
$20,000–$29,999	17	16.4	17.1	16.2	16.4	−3.8%
$30,000–$49,999	28.9	28.3	28.8	28	27.7	−4.1%
$50,000–$99,999	29.2	28.8	27.6	27.7	27.9	−4.5%
$100,000–$149,999	5.2	6.1	6.5	6.2	6.3	20.8%
$150,000+	2.9	3.3	3.2	3.6	3.8	32.6%

NASCAR Fan Demographics

	1998	1999	2000	2001	2002	Change from 1998
GENDER	n = 10,504	9,649	9,925	7,917	9,804	
Male	61.4	61.5	59.5	58.9	58.8	−4.2%
Female	38.6	38.5	40.5	41.1	41.2	6.7%
ETHNICITY	n = 10,265	9,412	9,673	7,715	9,497	
White	79.5	79.3	77.5	76.6	74.9	−5.7%
African-American	8.2	7.8	8.6	8.4	9.6	17.2%
Hispanic	8.3	8.7	9.3	10.2	10.6	27.6%
Asian	0.8	0.5	0.5	0.6	0.7	−6.5%
Other	3.2	3.8	4.1	4.1	4.1	28.4%
HOUSEHOLD INCOME	n = 7,847	7,127	2,987	5,800	7,182	
Under $20,000	16	15.9	17.9	17.9	18.9	18.3%
$20,000–$29,999	17.2	16.7	16.8	16.9	16.5	−4.3%
$30,000–$49,999	30.6	30.2	31.1	29	29.1	−4.9%
$50,000–$99,999	29.3	29.5	27.3	28.4	27.6	−5.7%
$100,000–$149,999	4.6	5.3	4.6	5.2	5.3	15.9%
$150,000+	2.4	2.4	2.3	2.7	2.5	6.1%

From: *Sports Business Journal* (2004), "By the Numbers."

Although demographics are valuable in giving the marketer an understanding of large-scale similarities and trends about the consumer and the market segments, the data do not reflect the cultural or social factors that influence consumers. Demographic profiling is a popular approach to segmenting sports consumers because of the straightforwardness of collecting and analyzing demographic data. However, the sport marketer also needs to identify consumers' interests. What are the customers' preferences in music, entertainment, and television? What are the consumers' political, religious, or environmental concerns? One solution to this dilemma is to understand the market segment's values, attitudes, and lifestyles. Consumers' activities, interests, and opinions (AIOs) can be inventoried by asking respondents various questions about their work, sport activities, family, social life, education, and political preferences. Although more difficult to obtain than demographic data, such analysis is important to sport marketers because it presents a fuller picture of the consumer and helps sport marketers refine their demographic screening.

Another valuable segmentation approach focuses on **product usage,** an important dimension for sport marketers. Key to the success of any sport organization is its ability to attract and retain fans. Behavioral segmentation groups consumers by *how much* of a product they use, *how often* they purchase, and *how loyal* they are to the team or a brand. Product usage is traditionally divided into light, medium, and heavy users. As shown in Table 14-4, Mullin (1983) identifies four more sport-specific categories.

College, professional, and private sport and leisure organizations pay considerable attention to the heavy user, that is, the season ticket holder or the club participant who has a yearly rather than a three-month membership. The percentage of consumers who are heavy users varies from sport to sport, franchise to franchise, and club to club. Some baseball organizations rely heavily on the light user, the person who purchases a ticket one hour before the game. Other baseball organizations rely more on season ticket sales. Some football organizations sell out the stadium every week and have long waiting lists of loyal fans that want to purchase season tickets, whereas others have difficulty selling out one game. In a similar fashion, fitness and health clubs put a great deal of effort into the renewal of annual

memberships, usually at the end of the "indoor" season, since the late spring and summer months are low usage months, even among heavy users, at most clubs.

Sport marketers should realize the importance of classifying consumer markets by product usage rate. The differing needs of light, medium, and heavy consumers must be satisfied as much as possible. Furthermore, the marketer should consider the light consumer's needs as much as the heavy user's, since today's light consumer could be tomorrow's medium or heavy consumer. An example of this strategy is currently practiced by the Colorado Rockies, the MLB team headquartered in Denver.

TABLE 14-4   *Consumption Rate Groupings*

Usage segment	Identification pattern
Heavy user	Season ticket holders
	Club members and/or contract-time holders
Medium user	Miniseason plan users
	Heavy single-game/event ticket purchasers
Light user	Infrequent single-game/event ticket purchasers
Defector*	Individuals who have used the sport product in the last 12 months but who have not made a repeat purchase since that time
Media consumer	Individuals who do not go to the stadium or coliseum but rather "follow" the team or sport via the media
Unaware consumer	Individuals who are unaware of the sport product and its benefits
Uninterested consumer	Individuals who are aware of the sport product but choose not to try it

From: Mullin, B. (1983). *Sport marketing, promotion and public relations,* Amherst, Massachusetts, National Sport Management. *Levin defines *defectors* as people who have attended an organization's event at least once but have not returned within the last 12 months. In many cases, disenchanted heavy users become defectors; in other cases, defectors are individuals who did not gain sufficient satisfaction on the initial purchase or trial.

The Rockies typically sell out the majority of the stadium well before opening day. However, there is a section of the ballpark—the Rockpile—where the $4 tickets go on sale two hours prior to the start of the game, thus allowing Rockies' fans who don't have season tickets a chance to attend home games. With more and more MLB teams selling out the entire stadium in the preseason, teams that provide an opportunity to purchase tickets for the occasional fan are assuring themselves of future customers as well as providing the team with tremendous public goodwill.

CONCEPT CHECK

Strategic market management is a systematic process by which managers evaluate the sport organization's strengths and weaknesses, measure the competition and external environment, and then develop a marketing strategy that matches the team's goals with the opportunities in the marketplace. Steps in this process include planning, consumer identification, market segmentation, the selection of target market(s), the choice of competitive position, and the development of an effective marketing mix to satisfy sport consumers. Developing a profile of current consumers, including demographic and psychographic information, is an important component of strategic planning.

TARGET MARKETING: EFFECTIVELY REACHING MARKETING GOALS

Once a clear picture of just who the customers are has been determined and segments identified, the marketer selects a **target market**(s) to which an appeal will be made. Target marketing is the process of focusing a marketing strategy on a particular segment(s) in order to better accomplish the organization's marketing and profit objectives. The strategy of target marketing is based on the concept that it is more profitable to zero in on a specific and often narrow market segment using a focused approach than it is to use the shotgun approach of attempting to appeal to every consumer.

What are markets?

We have already used the word market frequently in this chapter. What exactly do we mean by the term *market?* Marketers define a **market** as an aggregate of people who, as individuals or as organizations, have needs for products in a product class and have the ability, willingness, and authority to purchase these products (Kotler, 1997; Perreault and McCarthy, 2002; Pride and Ferrell, 1997). You will often hear people refer to a market as the total population of people in a particular geographic area. However, our definition is more specific as it includes people seeking *specific products* in a specific product category. For example, weekend athletes are part of the market for athletic footwear and apparel, as well as the market for sports equipment, training aids, nutritional supplements, instructional guides, magazines, video games, and other sport related products. As you can see, many different markets exist within the sport industry.

Market segmentation strategies and target market selection

Market targeting consists of the decision processes and activities conducted to find a market to serve. Once the market segments are identified, the marketer must determine which segment shows the most promise and develop a plan to reach the targeted segment or segments and initiate the exchange process. The marketer can adopt one of three strategies: (1) undifferentiated marketing—in which the organization attempts to go after the whole market with a product and marketing strategy intended to have mass appeal; (2) differentiated marketing—in which the sport business operates in several segments of the market with offerings and market strategies tailored to each segment; and (3) concentrated marketing—in which the organization focuses on only one or a few segments with the intention of capturing a large share of these segments. Table 14-5 compares marketing strategies for three target markets.

Undifferentiated or mass marketing strategy. In the past, millions of dollars were spent marketing a product to some "typical" or "average" consumer. However, no company or organization can survive in today's competitive marketplace by selling to a mythical average customer. The mass-marketing or undifferentiated approach does not recognize different lifestyles or market segments; the focus of this marketing strategy is on the

TABLE 14-5   *Marketing Strategies*

Marketing approach	Mass marketing	Market segmentation/ Concentrated marketing	Multiple segmentation/ Differentiated marketing
Target market	Broad range of consumers	One well-defined consumer group	Two or more well-defined consumer groups
Product	Limited number of products under one brand for many types of consumers	One brand tailored to one consumer group	Distinct brand for each consumer group
Price	One "popular" price range	One price range tailored to the consumer group	Distinct price range for each consumer group
Distribution	All possible outlets	All suitable outlets	All suitable outlets—differs by segment
Promotion	Mass media	All suitable media	All suitable media—differs by segment
Strategy emphasis	Appeal to many types of consumers through a uniform, broad-based marketing program	Appeal to one specific consumer group through a highly specialized, but uniform, marketing program	Appeal to two or more distinct market segments through different marketing plans catering to each segment

From Evans, J., and Berman, B. (1994). *Principles of marketing.* New York: Macmillan.

common needs of consumers, rather than on their differences. Within a mass-marketing approach, different consumer groups are not identified or sought. Although a mass-marketing approach is not the sport marketer's principal method of reaching consumers, it does have a place in the marketing of the sport product. For example, the Colorado Eagles of the Central Hockey League use mass mailings as a low-cost way of getting ticket and game information to Northern Colorado Front Range residents.

The Eagles, working with area merchants and retailers use statement, stuffers[1] and schedule cards as its primary mass-marketing approach. Any entity that mails bills or statements, such as banks, utility companies, and department stores, or stores that will allow the display of pocket schedules, can be approached for this cooperative venture.

Concentrated or market segmentation strategy. Nearly all businesses and organizations serve a multitude of market segments, and future market share will be won by the sport organizations that do a better job of identifying and targeting different market segments. A market segmentation or concentrated approach identifies and approaches a specific consumer market through one ideal marketing mix that caters to the specific needs of the chosen segment. Market segmentation is an efficient way to achieve a strong following in a particular market segment. One caution should be noted, however. After identifying two or more potential market segments, the segment with the *greatest opportunity* should be selected as the target market, not necessarily the segment with the most consumers. The largest segment may not provide the greatest opportunity because of heavy competition or high consumer satisfaction with

---

[1]Statement stuffers are coupons or advertisements that are sent to consumers with a bill or invoice. The company sending the bill absorbs the mailing costs, which usually does not entail cost beyond what was already involved in mailing the bill or invoice. The sport organization assumes the cost of developing and printing the coupon or advertisement. In addition to the obvious publicity for the sport organization, the company sending the bill or invoice engages in positive public relations, as well as association with a sport franchise.

2004 FULL 8 GAME SEASON TICKETS — ONLY - $ 100/FURY FAN/Season!

- ONLY-$100 Per Person/Season Ticket
- Guaranteed VIP Seating — No Waiting - Center Court — 8 FURY Home Games
- FREE — FURY T-Shirt -
- FREE — FURY Souvenir Program
- FREE — FURY Email Newsletters and Updates!
- 20% Discount off of all FURY Merchandise with your FURY VIP Card
- Access to FURY practice sessions at anytime with FURY VIP Card
- ½ Price Off — NWBL Playoff and Pro Cup Championship Tickets
- Season Ticket Appreciation night where you can meet the team!
- Have a chance to be chosen to join the "Shoot Out Contest" at each game

2004 "4 PACK" - 4 GAME SEASON TICKETS — ONLY - $ 65/FURY FAN/Season!

- ONLY - $65 Per Person/Season Ticket
- Guaranteed VIP Seating — No Waiting - Center Court — 4 FURY Home Games
- FREE — FURY T-Shirt
- FREE — FURY Souvenir Program
- FREE — FURY Email Newsletters and Updates!
- 20% Discount off of all FURY Merchandise with your FURY VIP Card
- Access to FURY practice sessions at anytime with FURY VIP Card
- ½ Price Off — NWBL Playoff and Pro Cup Championship Tickets
- Season Ticket Appreciation night where you can meet the team!
- Have a chance to be chosen to join the "Shoot Out Contest" at each game

2004 INDIVIDUAL GAME DAY TICKETS

- Adults — General Admission - $12.00
- Children Under Age 12 — General Admission - $10.00
- Children Under Age 5 — General Admission — FREE

FIGURE 14-1   Ticket packages targeting different market segments.

acompetitor. Finding a **niche**[2] is a key to successful marketing.

Differentiated or multiple segmentation strategy. A multiple-segmentation approach combines the best aspects of the mass-marketing and segmented-marketing approaches. It is similar to the segmented-marketing approach except that the sport organization markets to two or more distinct segments of the market with a specialized plan for each segment. Sometimes a sport organization will market to consumers through a mass marketing strategy to reach a very broad audience and *also* use a segmented approach geared to specific segments. The more unique segments there are, the better a multiple-segmentation approach will be.

For example, as part of their marketing strategy, the Colorado Chill of the National Women's Basketball League (NWBL) uses an approach targeting two distinct groups. Seniors and families were targeted and eligible for discounted season tickets. The NWBL Dallas Fury's strategy was similar as they developed season ticket packages (see Figure 14-1) to match three different market segments: heavy users, light-medium users, and families with young children. Brochures describing the appropriate offer were sent to the identified segments, followed by individual telephone calls. This approach is also common in college programs as a strategy to attract various fan segments and generate interest for sports other than football and basketball.

---

[2]Sport marketers attempt to find a unique position in the marketplace by distinguishing their sport product from competing products. This unique position is called a niche.

CONCEPT CHECK

For best results, the sport marketer should develop a campaign that is highly focused and directed to a specific group of people. This practice is target marketing. The three methods of reaching the target market(s) are mass marketing, market segmentation, and multiple segmentation. The sport marketer must identify and target different market segments to succeed in today's competitive marketplace.

FACTORS INVOLVED IN THE MARKETING OF SPORT: PLANNING THE MARKETING MIX

As has previously been defined, marketing is a complex process and its success (to culminate in an exchange) requires the formulation of a strategy to attract and reach the potential consumer. That formula is composed of the traditional elements of the marketing mix—product, price, promotion, and place (distribution). Additionally, an examination of positioning and packaging will aid in understanding the complexities of planning the *marketing mix.*

PRICE

What is price?

Let's start the discussion of this element of the marketing mix with an example: the money you pay for a ticket to a sporting event, concert, or movie is its price. The amount you pay for a tennis clinic in Hilton Head with Dennis Vandermeer, a new pair of Nike running shoes, or a pair of inline skates is also an example of price. **Price** is an expression of the *value* of a sports product or event. What you are willing to pay for any of the items just mentioned—the price—is a function of how much you value the product or service.

Price is very visible and intricately related to the other major elements of the marketing mix—product, promotion, and place (distribution). In addition, because of discounts, rebates, coupons, and promotional incentives, it is considered controllable and flexible. Price involves the determination of goods and services and the calculation of value of the exchange that can be used by all parties involved in the transaction (Kotler, 2003). In mainstream marketing, price tends to be an important strategic consideration and, in some cases, the most important component of the marketing mix. Sport,

and in particular spectator sport, does not give price the same strategic importance as does mainstream business. In a study of 3,009 fan responses in two selected NBA cities, Rudman and Sutton (1989) found that cost of tickets ranked fourth in importance in one city and fifth in another city, behind such considerations as opponent, team record, presence of superstars, and effect of the game on league standings.

We know that consumers equate price with value. A product that is deeply discounted or even free may be perceived as having little or no value. Bill Veeck would never give away tickets, no matter how poorly his team was performing. According to Veeck, "Tickets are the one thing I have to sell. To give them away is to cheapen the product I am selling" (Veeck and Linn, 1962). Similarly, when new sports leagues launch franchises in cities with existing professional sports teams, the new product usually is priced nearly the same as the existing product. To offer the new sports ticket at a lower price would tell the public that, in some way or another, the new product must be inferior to the existing product.

Pricing strategies

Early in the planning process, the sport marketer will have to choose a pricing strategy. Price is most commonly considered as an amount of money; however, it can be more broadly defined as anything of value that is exchanged. **Bartering,** also known as trading-out, is a common practice in sport marketing and consists of an exchange that does not involve money. Tickets, program ads, scoreboard space, and arena signage are valuable commodities to some companies. Sport organizations should use these commodities to trade for goods and services that are needed to execute the campaign.

The Ohio State University's director of marketing and sponsorships, David Brown, uses this strategy to trade women's volleyball and basketball tickets for radio advertising. The university gives tickets to selected local radio stations in exchange for advertising equal to the fact value of the tickets. For example, if the face value of the ticket were $5, the amount of advertising traded would be $5,000 for 1,000 tickets. The radio station gives tickets away in pairs over the air, resulting in a minimum of 500 "mentions." An additional feature of this trade-out agreement is that three additional "mentions" per giveaway are required, resulting in 15,000 advertising slots over the course of the season.

A new school of thought related to the pricing of tickets is variable ticket pricing—setting a different price for the same seat for different games. The variable price depends on such factors as the quality of the opponent, time of year (early, mid- or postseason), home team's record, or extra entertainment (e.g., live music concert or fireworks) (Breul, 2003). There are positive and negative attributes of this approach, but on balance, the positive aspects seem to prevail. Among MLB teams that have experimented with this pricing strategy are the Arizona Diamonbacks, St. Louis Cardinals, and the New York Mets (King, 2003). Table 14-6 summarizes some of the variable ticket pricing strategies used in Major League Baseball.

The key to successful pricing strategies is to react to market demand and the elasticity or inelasticity (how price changes affect or do not affect the consumer and hence demand for the product) of consumer demand. In other words, does a price increase or decrease affect demand? In most cases, pricing strategies do not stand alone at all times. Promotional strategies and product positioning may alter perceived value and in some cases, actual price (for a time). Such strategies combined with pricing usually temporarily increase consumer demand for the product.

CONCEPT CHECK

Price is a very visible element of the marketing mix and, although most often thought of as a dollar amount, can include anything of value that is exchanged. Exchanging tickets for services, especially advertising, is a form of bartering or trading-out, and is a common practice in sport marketing.

Positioning

Before we go further and discuss promotion and advertising, it is important to understand the concept of **positioning**. One of the classics in the marketing literature is the book *Positioning: The Battle for Your Mind* (1986) by Ries and Trout. According to Ries and Trout, positioning "starts with a product, a piece of merchandise, a service, an institution, a company, or even a person. However, positioning is not what you

do to a product. Positioning is what you do to the mind of the prospect. That is, you position the product in the mind of the prospect."

With so many sport products and services available today, each accompanied by countless advertisement, consumers have become immune to the plethora of traditional marketing communications. They do this in self-defense; there just isn't enough room in their heads to store every piece of information about every product. The result is that consumers either put products into neat little categories, or they ignore them.

The concept underlying positioning is relatively simple: find a hole (or niche) and fill it. People generally pick one or two product attributes to associate with a product, then file the information. When they need said attributes, the product associated with them comes to mind.

7-Up found a niche in the soft drink industry and outpositioned Coke. Even though Coke's marketing budget was many times larger, 7-Up was able to turn Coke's bigness (and their caramel coloring) against them. How? By positioning themselves as the Un-Cola. 7-Up represented an alternative beverage choice for those consumers who wanted a noncola soft drink.

Positioning can use factors such as price, age, distribution, use, benefits, size, time, and technology to communicate its message (Ries and Trout, 1986). A classic example of the use of a positioning strategy in sport involved the Stowe, Vermont, ski resort area. A column in *Harper's Bazaar* by travel writer Abby Rand listed what she perceived to be the top ski resorts in the world. Stowe was one of the top 10. The complete list was Stowe; Aspen, Colorado; Courcheval, France; Jackson Hole, Wyoming; Kitbuhel, Austria; Portillo, Chile; St. Christopher, Austria; St. Moritz, Switzerland; Sun Valley, Idaho; and Vail, Colorado. Seizing the opportunity to position itself as simultaneously elite and accessible, Stowe developed advertisements that showed the shoulder patches of the "top 10" ski resorts, with the caption, "Of the world's top ten ski resorts, only one is in the East. You don't have to go to the Alps or the Andes or even the Rockies to experience the ski vacation of a lifetime. You need only head for the Ski Capital of the East: Stowe, Vermont" (Ries and Trout, 1986). By mentioning the top 10 ski resorts in the world, the advertisement created a list of elites in

TABLE 14-6 *Variable Ticket Price Strategies*

Variable Pricing Based on Opponent

Club	No. of affected games (identifier)	Games/opponents (no. of games)	Details of pricing variance
Anaheim Angels	20 (Premium)	Opening Day, Boston (1), Los Angeles (3), N.Y. Mets (3), N.Y. Yankees (6), Oakland (2), Seattle (1), Texas (2), Toronto (1)	$5 increase
Cleveland Indians	10 (Showcase)	Opening Day, Cincinnati (3), Los Angeles (3), N.Y. Yankees (3)	$5 increase
Colorado Rockies	3 (Classic)	Arizona (including one as Opening Day)	NA
	49 (Premium)	Arizona (2), Atlanta (3), Cleveland (3), Chicago Cubs (3), Detroit (3), Florida (3), Kansas City (3), Los Angeles (3), Milwaukee (3), Philadelphia (3), Pittsburgh (3), San Diego (5), San Francisco (9), St. Louis (3)	NA
	29 (Value)	Arizona (5), Cincinnati (3), Houston (3), Los Angeles (6), Montreal (4), N.Y. Mets (3), San Diego (5)	NA
New York Mets	17 (Gold)	Opening Day (Chicago Cubs), Atlanta (3), Montreal (1), N.Y. Yankees (3), San Francisco (3), Seattle (3), St. Louis (3)	NA
	21 (Silver)	Arizona (3), Atlanta (6), Cincinnati (3), Colorado (3), Philadelphia (6)	NA
	27 (Bronze)	Chicago Cubs (2), Colorado (1), Florida (6), Los Angeles (3), Milwaukee (3), Montreal (8), Philadelphia (1), San Diego (3)	NA
	16 (Value)	Florida (3), Houston (3), Milwaukee (3), Montreal (1), Philadelphia (3), Pittsburgh (3)	NA
Tampa Bay Devil Rays	13 (Prime)	Atlanta (3), New York Yankees (10)	$1–$10 increase
	13 (Value)	Anaheim (2), Baltimore (3), Boston (1), Kansas City (1), Texas (2), Toronto (4)	$4–$10 decrease
Toronto Blue Jays	7 (Premium)	Opening Day, Chicago Cubs (2), N.Y. Yankees (2), Oakland (2)	Increase of several dollars
	26 (Value)	Anaheim (1), Baltimore (4), Boston (4), Chicago White Sox (4), Kansas City (1), Minnesota (1), N.Y. Yankees (2), Pittsburgh (3), Tampa Bay (3), Texas (3)	Decrease of several dollars

Variable Pricing Based on Date

Club	No. of affected games	Days/dates	Details of pricing variance
Atlanta Braves	21	Fridays from May–August and all Saturdays	$3 increase
Chicago Cubs	19	Opening Day and all Fridays, Saturdays and Sundays from June 6–Aug 17	25 percent increase
	8	Monday–Thursday afternoon games from April 9–May 7	50 percent decrease
San Francisco Giants	39	Friday–Sunday	$1–$5 increase
St. Louis Cardinals	50	May 16–Aug. 28	$2 increase

NA: Not applicable; see introductory information.
Source: MLB.com, the teams. From *Sports Business Journal* (March 31, 2003). Variable pricing in Major League Baseball, p. 33.

the consumer's mind, forming the basis for comparison of all resorts not on the list. Professional sports have been positioned as having the most talented athletes in the world, and this positioning has been the downfall of new sport leagues as they have attempted to compete with the established leagues.

Another popular form of positioning, this time used in spectator sports, is to position a sporting event as more than the activity itself. This is done primarily through such promotions as "fireworks night," appearance by the Famous Chicken (formerly known as the San Diego Chicken), and so on. The positioning is that you are receiving something more for your money, a bonus. Family nights involve both promotion and pricing strategies that help position the sporting event as a "family affair," something wholesome and traditional that gives the family an opportunity to share an event. It is important for a marketer to know that not all spectators attend a sporting event simply to watch the game. Others may attend for the atmosphere, socializing with friends or family, entertainment, such as aforementioned "fireworks night," or some combination of the reasons.

Marketing research, and in particular consumer feedback and reactions, is the key to successful positioning. Marketing research is the key because your marketing solution is not inside the product or even inside your own mind, but inside the mind of the prospective consumer (Ries and Trout, 1986). The accompanying box shows how K-Swiss, a small athletic footwear company, positioned its shoe against Nike, Reebok, and other footwear manufacturers' shoes.

PROMOTION

Promotion, another of the P's in the marketing mix, is a process in which various techniques are used to communicate with consumers. Sport promotions are most successful when the message the marketer wants to convey is directed toward one or more target markets. An organization can communicate to its target markets in a variety of ways, including advertising, personal selling, publicity, sales promotions, and sponsorship. Before implementing any promotion, however, the sport marketer should map out the goals of the campaign. A key to the effective use of promotional strategies and activities is determining what you wish to accomplish and designing a specific promotion activity to reach this identified outcome. The following steps can serve as a general outline for planning a promotion:

1. *Define your target market.*
2. *Set measurable objectives.* What action do you want the target market(s) to take? What is your goal for this promotion?
3. *Determine the strategy.* How will you motivate the target market(s) to take the desired action?
4. *Research various promotional ideas.* Talk to other sport marketers, at both the professional and institutional (high schools and colleges) levels for ideas. Visit health and fitness clubs in your locale. Other sources for ideas include the library (for books that catalog promotions), marketing organizations, and local business.
5. *Select the promotional approach.* Choose one that is the most likely to be successful with your target market(s).
6. *Develop a theme for the promotion.* Devise a short, catchy slogan to attract the attention of the target market.
7. *Create support material.* This material should be in the form of advertising, sales promotions, and publicity.

Using spectator sport as an example and having a goal of increasing attendance, the marketer would need to know who attends and who does not attend,

---

> *Product: Tennis shoes*
>
> **TARGET MARKET:** Upscale buyers of athletic wear and suburban casual wear
> **COMPETITION:** Nike, Reebok, Adidas, Converse, Prince, Diadora, Fila, New Balance
> **PRODUCT'S BENEFITS:** Wearer will look and feel better in the classic K-Swiss design; K-Swiss tennis shoes wear longer due to thicker, more durable sole
> **HOW DIFFERENTIATED FROM COMPETITION:** K-Swiss uses a 25-year old, classic, mainly-white design; focus is on performance, not frills and gimmicks. Shoppers keep coming back to the K-Swiss Classic, the all-white, all-weather, all-leather tennis shoe that was introduced in 1966.

what promotional efforts have been used in the past, and how successful they were. Similarly, the marketer needs to identify variables that attract fans or affect a fan's decision to attend or not attend a game. Marcum and Greenstein (1985) in a season-long analysis of selected professional baseball teams, identified day of the week, opponent, and type of promotion as factors affecting attendance. McDonald and Rascher (2000) found that using promotions resulted in an average of a 14 percent increase in game attendance for Major League Baseball teams.

Keep in mind that the promotional mix used for one product, event, or service may not be appropriate for another. Sometimes the emphasis will be on personal selling, and at other times, advertising will be the primary need.

Advertising. Because of the tremendous role of media in sport, **advertising** is probably the most crucial element of the promotional mix. Advertising, that is, presenting a paid message about the sport organization's product or service, is possibly the most readily identifiable form of communication in this country. Billions of dollars are spent annually on advertising, involving the following traditional and sport-specific media:

Newspapers	Painted transit
Magazines	advertisements
Television	Ticket backs
Radio	Scoreboards
Athlete endorsements	In-arena signage
Internet	Outfield fences
Direct mail	Pocket schedule cards
Posters	Game programs
Outdoor advertising	

One of the most popular forms of advertising used in sport marketing is endorsement. Endorsements feature a well-known or noteworthy athlete who endorses the benefits of a particular product or service. Coors Brewing Company uses former athletes and well-known sports broadcasters to endorse the qualities of its beer. Nike has used a number of athletes to introduce and endorse its products, including Michael Jordan, Andre Agassi, Mia Hamm, and LeBron James. Endorsement contracts sometimes contain performance and morality clauses to protect the sponsor from damages resulting from association with a "tainted" athlete. Such contracts may require

drug testing, restrict the athlete's lifestyle, and require that the athlete use the product.

Selecting the advertising medium is the first step. The key element in selecting the medium to carry the advertising message is determining which medium will best reach the target market. All of the media—newspaper, radio and television stations, magazines, and now the Internet—have conducted their own studies to describe the audiences they reach. The sport marketer should match the demographics and lifestyles of the sport audience with those of the advertising medium.

Another factor to be considered in selecting the medium is the cost of each. It is much more expensive to advertise on a national network affiliate than on a local cable network. Advertising via television may be the best way to reach the target market, but a limited budget may mean that other outlets, such as radio or outdoor advertising, have to be used. The sport marketer should also consider other creative advertising outlets, such as shopping cart placards, grocery bags, bus posters, banners on street light poles, or electronic messages such as marquees, in an attempt to convey a message to prospective consumers.

The Internet. One of the fastest growing and influential advertising media of the past decade is the Internet. The advent of the Internet is unparalleled in the history of communications and advertising. The Internet surpassed 50 million users in just four years; it took radio 38 years and television 13 years to reach the 50-million-user milestone!

The Internet has already become a valuable source for sports-related information and it is rapidly becoming a popular medium for sport marketers who wish to use its features to promote products, services, and events. As a communications and selling vehicle, it has immense and dynamic potential for sport marketing. Possibly the most attractive reason to market online is the demographic similarity of sports fans and Internet users. The typical Internet user can be described as entertainment-minded, college-educated males between the ages of 18 and 34 (Gladden, 1996)—a very close match to the demographic profile of traditional sports fans. Other reasons for utilizing the Internet as a communications and promotions medium are its flexibility and interactive nature, ability to reach a focused target market, and relative cost effectiveness (cost per thousand hits). However, similar to other promotional tools, the risk of clutter and incorrect targeting of market segments can compromise the Internet's effectiveness. And it goes without saying that technology problems can undo an otherwise outstanding Internet promotion.

Nearly all sport organizations have aggressively developed a Web presence in recent years. Many colleges and universities have partnered with the FANSonly network (www.fansonly.com), an Atlanta-based company that creates and manages a network of athletic Websites, to develop interactive sites and Internet promotions. The schools' Websites allow them to conduct promotions, post news and information, provide Webcasts of special events such as press conferences (during which the event can be watched in real time as well as be archived on the Internet site for later viewing), market and sell products and special events, and numerous other functions ("The FANSonly," 1999; Yow, 1999). Internet promotions can—and should—be supplemented with print, media (TV, radio, newspaper, and outdoor) and game-day promotions.

Sales promotion. Another aspect of the promotional mix, a **sales promotion** is any activity that cannot be called advertising, personal selling, or publicity. Sales promotions are various short-term activities that are designed to stimulate the purchase of a sports product or service. Sales promotions include many strategies, with the promotions in Table 14-7 being the most common.

Using a "theme" as part of a promotional strategy can be very effective. The theme should enable the intended audience to form a mental image, impression, or association with the product. Such was the case with the very successful promotion of the Oakland Athletics, titled "Year of the Uniform." This promotion was targeted at youth 14 years of age and under and was designed to "guarantee" that the youth attended multiple games, because an individual needed to attend at least six games to receive the entire clothing set, and an additional two games for gifts such as balls and mugs. Attendance at "Year of the Uniform" games, which were strategically scheduled against quality opponents to maximize attendance and related nongate revenues, was 40 percent to 60 percent higher than on other days.

Personal selling. **Personal selling** is another form of promotion that can be very successful if the marketer capitalizes on its unique strengths and uses it in the right situations. Personal selling is direct interpersonal communication to inform and persuade. The advantage of personal selling in persuading and informing is that it enables the salesperson to interact with the prospect by explaining, questioning, and refuting objections. A common form of sport-related personal selling takes place in the health and fitness club industry. The personal selling usually takes place after the prospect samples the product through a free visit, and at the conclusion of the visit the prospect is briefed about the benefits of membership and may or may not be offered a financial incentive to joint the club immediately. If the prospect has objections or reservations, the salesman has a list of responses to refute the objection and break down resistance. Although the methodology of personal selling does not include coercion, in some cases it is used in the hope of closing the sale.

Personal selling can take place face to face or through **telemarketing,** a form of personal selling using the telephone to inform and persuade and to offer the consumer an opportunity to purchase goods or services. Telemarketing has been a very effective sales tool for spectator sports. Telemarketing companies that specialize in the management of telemarketing campaigns and that train salespeople often contract to sell season tickets, group tickets, game plans, or selected individual tickets for professional teams, as well as for colleges and universities that face difficult marketing tasks or limited resources. The team or organization usually contracts to pay the telemarketing company's expenses and a percentage of income generated. The contract may or may not include a minimum payment regardless of success. Sport managers should pay close attention to legal developments related to telemarketing and the legality of "do not call" lists compiled by federal and state governments.

Publicity and public relations. Publicity differs from advertising in that it is *nonpaid*, nonpersonal communication about a product or organization. Often the sponsor is not identified, and the message reaches the public because of its newsworthiness. Nonprofit agencies involved in recreation, such as

TABLE 14-7 *Sales Promotion*

Sales promotion tools	Examples
Coupons Redeemable certificates that offer a reduced price or voucher for an additional item with purchase. **Caveat:** Overuse can undermine the perceived value of the product	Certificates found in the newspaper, direct mail coupon packets, or inserted in the product's package; some coupons can now also be found online and printed for future use. • The Colorado Rapids (MLS) target families by offering a 4 for 4 coupon in the Denver papers, selling four game tickets, hotdogs, soft drinks, and chips for $40.
Premiums, gifts, and giveaways Various promotional items given away to fans by a sponsor or the team; items usually exhibit both the team's and sponsor's marks/logo. **Caveat:** Although premiums and giveaways may increase attendance, careful planning is needed to make certain that you have sufficient items to distribute and/or that the promotional item cannot be used in a manner that might injure patrons or athletes (for example, baseball or hockey puck nights).	Caps, balls and pucks, water bottles, sports cards, schedule magnets, pennants, posters, umbrellas, tote bags, mugs, uniform shirts, etc. • *Sports Illustrated* and *ESPN The Magazine* give away various promotional items when they receive a paid subscription (windbreaker or sweatshirt, watch, video, championship album, etc.). • Sears, a NCAA Corporate Partner, gave away seat cushions to all ticket holders at the Women's Final Four.
Sampling A smaller portion or sample of the product is given to customers; a product is displayed/exhibited for the purpose of introducing fans to it.	Lip balm, sunscreen, nutrition bars, sports beverages, Band-Aids, analgesic creams, etc. • Exhibitions are a common way of introducing prospective fans to a new or unfamiliar sport.
Point-of-purchase displays (POPs) Eye-catching cardboard cutouts, banners, or retail displays that call attention to the product and/or communicate special offers or price reductions to consumers.	Brochures, special packaging, eye-catching product arrangements, bottle tags, etc. • Anheuser-Busch develops unique POP displays for its Bud Light Super Bowl promotion.
Contests Contests and sweepstakes are used to create interest or awareness of a product. Contests pit contestants again each other; sweepstakes promotions are games of chance (no skill is necessary to play).	• United Airlines is sponsoring a sweepstakes to win 2 tickets to the 2004 U.S. Open tennis tournament; interested contestants may enter online or by mail • The NFL sponsors the punt, pass and kick competition. (The NHL has a similar contest modeled after the PPK, the dribble, pass, and shoot competition.)

the YMCA, YWCA, or YMHA, or national governing bodies (NGBs), such as those for USA Swimming or gymnastics, depend on publicity as a primary tool to communicate with the public. A great deal of publicity comes through news releases. A news release tells about an event or activity that is newsworthy and that merits publicity through the appropriate media. A news release should tell the "who, what, where, when, why, and how" in a concise format and should be electronically sent to the appropriate media personnel by the agency or organization. Most nonprofit agencies and organizations depend on publicity as the prime way of generating awareness of their missions and programs. To assist local YMCAs, the National YMCA office issues press kits for specific programs. For example, a press kit for youth soccer may provide a release containing information about soccer participation in the United States, and quotes from physicians or soccer players about the benefits of play and competition. Often the local program director merely inserts the information about registration, place, and time for the local program.

A unique form of publicity in professional sport involves the United Way and the National Football League. Television messages, paid for by the National Football League, promote and publicize various United Way agencies and services within the home cities of each National Football League franchise. These publicity sports are unique in that they also serve as advertisements for the National Football League by promoting the activities of its players and the charitable activities and functions of the league.

Public relations is a sport organization's overall effort to create a positive image for itself with its target public(s) and the community in which it operates. Public relations is the overall plan for conveying this positive message, but publicity is the tool that communicates the message.

CONCEPT CHECK

Promotion is the process of communicating with the consumer about the sport product. The sport marketer must be aware that interference or noise in the communication process may prevent the consumer from receiving or understanding the intended message. This knowledge is useful in planning and implementing the promotional mix. Elements of the promotional mix are advertising, sales promotions, publicity/public relations, and personal selling. The marketer develops promotional strategies to get the consumer's attention, arouse interest in the product, create a desire, and ultimately, motivate the consumer to purchase.

PLACE

Place in the marketing mix is the geographic location of the product, such as the stadium, arena, or club and the target market, as well as the point of

origin for distribution of the product or service. **Distribution** is the transfer or products, goods, and services from the producer to the consumer. Products move from the producer to consumer through channels of distribution—any series of firms or people who participate in the flow of the product or service to the consumer (Perreault and McCarthy, 2002). The length of distribution channel varies; it may be direct or may require wholesalers, retailers, and assorted "middlemen." Probably the most unique aspect of this distribution process in the case of spectator sports is that the product does not move from the production site to a consumer outlet. The production and consumption occur at the same site—the stadium or arena. Thus, the consumption site in sport is perceived to be more critical than the distribution channels of traditional marketing. This same perception accounts for the emphasis on color and product extensions such as juice bars, lounges, and child care facilities in the construction of new health and fitness clubs. Several factors associated with the location may affect the success of the enterprise. Among these factors are accessibility, attractiveness, and the actual location.

Accessibility has been described as a variable that affects fan attendance at professional sport (Marcum and Greenstein, 1985). Accessibility, or the relationship between the location of the product presentation and the location of the target market or consumer, is an important aspect of sport marketing. Accessibility is a convenience factor, and the consumer's perception of this convenience may significantly affect the success of the enterprise. Access factors such as highways, public transportation, transportation costs, route (direct or indirect), and length of time required to get to the facility all could significantly affect consumer traffic and success in reaching the target market.

Another function of the place concept is attractiveness. Is the place (area, facility, and so on) attractive (both inside and outside)? How does the attractiveness element function in attracting potential consumers? Do all of the qualities of the "place" combine to form a pleasing venue, or do some elements conflict with other aspects, weakening the total attractiveness? For example, consider 3Com Park (at Candlestick Point), home to the San Francisco 49ers. A location at the mouth of the San Francisco Bay sounds very attractive, but there are times when the location brings fog, wind, and cold, and the combined meteorological effects make the place less hospitable. The construction of a new facility, especially a unique facility such as the Baseball Grounds of Jacksonville (home of the Class AA Jacksonville Suns), can serve as an attraction and become a marketing tool in itself. To protect fans from the intense summer heat, the new ballpark has what HOK officials say is the largest minor league rooftop their sports architectural firm has ever designed. With the opening of the new ballpark the Suns sold 1,000 season tickets, a team record (*By the Numbers*, 2004).

Although the technological innovations of facilities such as the Sky Dome (with its retractable roof) helped to ensure fan comfort, the new trend in facility design, especially in baseball, is to take the nostalgia and intimacy of the old ball parks' architecture but outfit them with all the modern amenities. New stadia are built with cup holders at every seat (some seats even sport an attached LED screen for ordering food and drinks, or for playing video games), premium seat-holder concourses, game rooms, specialty restaurants, hot tubs, and more. Thus, the stadium becomes a permanent marketing tool that helps bring people to the ballpark. The success and attractiveness of Camden Yards (home of the Baltimore Orioles), Jacobs Field (home of the Cleveland Indians), Coors Field (home of the Colorado Rockies), Bank One Ballpark (home of the Arizona Diamondbacks), and most recently, the Great American Ball Park in Cincinnati (home of the Cincinnati Reds) supports this type of facility design and construction.

The issue of location is also complicated by the location's appropriateness for the activity. The prestige of the facility or the public's opinion of the facility also affects its success. At The Ohio State University, arguably home to some of the finest athletic facilities in the country, soccer and lacrosse are played in the Jessie Owens Memorial Stadium, a facility that seats 10,000. Although the matches in these sports are rarely viewed at full capacity, the prestige of playing in one of the finest multisport facilities in the country helps recruit athletes and also implies that the sport is more important than it would be if it were played on a field in another part of the campus.

Establishing the distribution network

Another form or channel of distribution is the sport media. Given the effect of the media on sport and the fact that most sport products cannot be physically delivered to the consumer, sport marketers use the media to develop their market. Marketing one's event through a wide broadcast and cable network not only generates widespread interest in and awareness of the product, but it can also have a direct effect on sales by creating media consumers. Broadcast rights agreements also provide a lucrative revenue stream for sport franchises, particularly at the professional level. There is a considerable reliance on media revenues in major league football, baseball and basketball (college and NBA). In fact, only the National Hockey League (NHL) relies more on gate receipts than media revenues. In all likelihood, media revenues will continue to increase if the NFL eight year, $17.6 billion agreement (with ABC, CBS, and Fox), and the NCAA Men's Basketball Tournament 11-year, $6 billion contract with CBS are any indication (*By the Numbers*, 2004).

Ticket distribution

Even with a growing dependence on broadcast revenues, the physical distribution of game or event tickets is an important part of the place aspect of the marketing mix. The goal of the ticket distribution system is to encourage consumer purchases by making the system as convenient and accessible as possible. Moreover, the ticket distribution system also serves to market and advertise the game. Strategies used by sport organizations include the following.

All sport organizations should have a comprehensive in-house ticket office that sells individual game and season tickets. The ticket office would also be involved in working with selling group tickets and the corporate sales program. Maintaining customer-oriented in-house ticket operations is a necessary tactic. This includes expanding the hours of operation so that consumers can come to the ticket office before or after work as well as during the lunch hour. The ticket office should be open late at least one evening a week. Telephone numbers, including toll-free numbers, should be available for the convenience of consumers who wish to charge their tickets to credit cards. Tickets should also be available for pickup by consumers just before the game at the will-call window.

Assuming there is availability, tickets can also be sold online. Customized Web ticket areas can be developed on the team's Website, including off-line ordering forms and offering full online transactions. Web-based ticket sales is a rapidly growing sales outlet that will likely continue to grow in the coming years. Tickets can also be franchised to be sold by a third-party company such as Ticketmaster. Ticketmaster, one of the largest e-commerce sites on the Internet, is the world's leading ticketing company, and in 2002 sold more than 95 million sports and entertainment event tickets (ticketmaster.com). The advantage of such a contract for the sport marketer is the connection with a well-established, highly visible network of ticket outlets. A consumer can go to any of these ticket outlets, and thanks to the computerized ticket system, buy the desired seat from the pool of available seats for a particular event. After the consumer selects the seat, the computer prints the event ticket. This system enables the consumer to choose a seat from all the unsold seats rather than having to select from a limited allotment of tickets. However, a disadvantage of this system is the sport marketer's loss of control over the operation and loss of ability to monitor consumer satisfaction. Franchised ticket outlets sell tickets for many organizations and do not promote any game or event. They also charge consumers a service fee, often as much as $10 per ticket sold.

Concept Check

The place element of the marketing mix is both the physical sport facility and the physical distribution of the product by means of tickets. The transfer of the product to the consumer is made through channels, that is, ticket outlets. Other ways of distributing the sport product include telemarketing, providing fans with toll-free numbers, and through the network and cable media.

Packaging

Packaging, or product presentation, is also a key factor in successful sport marketing. The importance of packaging in traditional marketing is underscored by the following quote: "Packaging as a medium of persuasion is an island of neglect" (Heller, 1989). In other words, too much is assumed about the consumer's point-of-purchase decision. The package should function as an advertisement and should make its promise loud and clear. Obviously, this philosophy has a great deal of merit for traditional products, but what does it

mean for the sport product? Is there an effective packaging methodology for the sport product? With sporting goods and related sports products, the package can explain benefits, such as Nike's "air system" or Asics "gel system." Packaging also can explain the benefits of a "larger sweet spot" on a tennis racket or the strength and control of graphite skis. Is there a similar package concept for spectator sport?

The factors that make packaging spectator sport different are the same factors that make spectator sport different from more traditional products. That is, the intangibility of the spectator sport product requires the packaging to be composed mainly of expectations. Second, the packaging, because of the nature of the spectator sport product, is not used at the point of purchase, but must be informational and is used before the actual event. Brochures, pamphlets, and "imagery-related" advertising are the essential packaging forms used for spectator sports. Highlight films, depicting the high points of the past season, are also integral to the packaging function, in that they illustrate the "ingredients" contained in the product.

Some packaging techniques used in professional sports are selling groups of tickets for games held on weekends; "Super Saturday," a variation of the weekend package containing only Saturdays; or mini-vans, a group of games from the entire season combining strong and weak attractions. Other offers including promotional events, weekend and weekday games, limited game packages such as the Six Pack or Baker's Dozen, whereby the fan or the organization selects specific games. The benefits are the low initial cost of a limited number of games, the fact that seats are guaranteed, and usually a "free" or bonus game, that is, 13 games for the price of 12.

Another form of ticket packaging is the flex book: a series of coupons that may be redeemed at the box office for games of the customer's choice. The flex book is attractive because it enables the consumer to choose any games with no date restriction, and it usually offers the benefit of one "free" or bonus game. The limitation of the flex book from the consumer's perspective is that the seats are limited by availability, and consumers are cautioned to redeem their coupons as soon as possible to guarantee a seat for the games of their choice. In most cases, flex coupons are not redeemable at the gate on game day, forcing some planning by the consumer. On the other hand, the consumer may use all coupons for one game or elect to attend a variety of games, giving the consumer a degree of discretion. The flex book is usually used in cases where supply (seats) exceeds demand and often is confined to general admission tickets.

Another packaging technique is to combine the primary product with product extensions. An excellent example was devised by the Peoria Chiefs, a baseball club of the Class A Midwest League. The Chiefs designed packages for groups that include game tickets and concession or souvenir items for a discounted price. For example, an $8.50 group ticket (available to groups of 20 or more) includes a general-admission ticket, popcorn or peanuts, a 22-ounce soda in a souvenir plastic cup, and a team yearbook (purchased separately the items would cost $10.50). Such packages have been shown to be effective in luring groups to the park for the first time. Figure 14-2 illustrates how product extensions, such as a team mascot, adds to the "sport package" by providing entertainment at the game. Some mascots are so popular that they have their own Web pages and line of merchandise.

FIGURE 14-2   Product extensions—such as mascots, contests, halftime shows, and special events—add to the "sport package" by providing entertainment in addition to the core, or the game itself.

CONCEPT CHECK

The 4 P's (product, promotion, price, and place) are a formula that helps the marketer reach and satisfy potential consumers. These facets may be manipulated, emphasized, combined, and integrated to help achieve a successful sports marketing formula.

MARKETING PLAN

The tangible result of the strategic planning process and development of the marketing mix (four P's) is the **marketing plan,** a document that becomes the framework for the marketing efforts of the sport organization. The sport marketer's research becomes most effective when it is incorporated into a systematic and formal marketing plan. The marketing plan enables a sport organization to establish strategies, objectives and priori-

ties, develop schedules and budgets, identify tactics, and initiate checkpoints to measure performance. Developing a marketing plan also helps the sport organization in recognizing potential problems, opportunities, and threats that may emerge in the future. This section introduces the components of a marketing plan and outlines its most important elements. See the box on the next page for a list of important questions that should be considered in putting together a marketing plan.

Marketing plans generally fall into two primary categories: (1) new product plans and (2) annual plans. The *new product plan* is developed for a product, service, or brand that is new to the market. You can be certain that Nike, Wilson, Callaway, and others develop complete new product marketing plans before committing resources to manufacture and distribution. Although the new product marketing plan may be sketchy in some areas, it is necessary to try to think through all contingencies before embarking on a fully developed campaign. The new product marketing plan will have more unknowns than the annual marketing plan. The time frame for new product plans is from the introduction of the product through to its establishment in the marketplace.

> **Your marketing plan should provide answers to the following questions:**
>
> 1. What is your product and how does it benefit your customers?
> 2. Who, exactly, are your customers?
> 3. What business are you in and what is your position relative to your competitors?
> 4. What barriers exist to keep competitors from taking your customers?
> 5. Who is/are your target market(s)?
> 6. How will you communicate with your customers? What is your positioning and advertising strategy? Do you have a creative theme?
> 7. What are the various promotional techniques and media channels you will use to reach your audience?
> 8. How much will it cost to market your product or service?
> 9. What month will you implement the various promotional techniques and media messages?

The *annual marketing plan* is for products, events, services, programs, and brands that are already established. It is wise to formally review the organization's marketing agenda at least one a year—hence, the term annual marketing plan. Keep in mind that the marketing plan is a road map for *future* marketing activities (both the new product and annual plans). Therefore, even with the annual plan there will be some unknowns.

Every marketing plan should be organized so that all important information is included. There are a variety of marketing plan outlines that will allow you to accomplish this. The outline that follows represents the typical plan. What is most important, however, is that your marketing ideas are presented in a logical and organized manner.

MARKETING PLAN OUTLINE

EXECUTIVE SUMMARY: (The executive summary is an aspect of the final report and is written last, even though it appears at the beginning of the plan.) The executive summary presents an overview of the entire marketing plan, followed by the detailed marketing plan.

I. INTRODUCTION

A. Identify the organization's *mission statement.* The mission clarifies the basic values underlying management's marketing goals, decisions, and practices; it is, essentially, the organization's *reason for being.* Analyze relevant past and current marketing data; the development of a marketing plan begins with a clear understanding of "where we are."

B. Background: Include history of the organization, previous target markets, and the organization's philosophy (written or unwritten) that may have an impact on their marketing approach.

II. SITUATIONAL or SWOT ANALYSIS

A. *Internal organizational (company) analysis:* identify *strengths and weaknesses* of the organization (program/team/department). If available, include in your report a copy of the organizational chart. Use the following categories to assist you in completing your STRENGTHS and WEAKNESSES analysis:
   1. Product
   2. Management and Employees
   3. Budget and Finances
   4. Customers

B. *External environmental analysis:* Identify *opportunities and threats.* Review the economic indicators that are relevant to your product or service. Governmental agencies, trade association, library sources, and business publications are excellent sources of data concerning the economic conditions relative to sport. Use the following categories to assist you in completing your OPPORTUNITIES and THREATS analysis:
   1. Demographics
   2. Economic Climate and Demand Trends
   3. Technological Trends
   4. Government and Public Policy Trends

C. *Competitive analysis:* Knowledge of competitors and their affiliated brands is critical in designing effective marketing strategies. It is important to understand what the competition is doing even if you believe they are wrong. What are the competitors' doing differently from this organization.

III. CUSTOMER ANALYSIS AND TARGET MARKET IDENTIFICATION

A. Customer Analysis
1. List customers you serve.
2. Include customer demographics.
3. If available, include lifestyle information in this section.
   a. Examples include purchase frequency, brand or team loyalty, where tickets purchased or where service is enjoyed, activities, interests, opinions, etc.
B. Target Market(s)
1. Identify and select market segments that represent the most likely customers for your product or service.
2. Describe your target market segment in detail, segmenting it however appropriate (e.g., demographics, psychograhics, geography, product usage, lifestyle, etc.).

IV. MARKETING GOALS AND OBJECTIVES:
Marketing objectives should be established to help the sport organization achieve its goals. These predict market share, sales volume, and position in relation to price and quality. State them precisely. Objectives must be stated in such a way that results can be *measured.* Marketing objectives generally are stated in terms of achieving X percent market share for a particular product or service, achieving X percent market penetration within certain market segments, and achieving X percent sales growth for all or selected product lines or tickets.

V. MARKETING STRATEGY:
How do you plan to achieve your objectives? In this section describe what is to be done to achieve the marketing goals and objectives identified in section IV. Your strategy may be trying to differentiate your product from the competition, or segmenting the marketing differently, or positioning (or repositioning) the product relative to competitors, etc. This section explains what you are planning to do strategically, given the current position of your product in the product life cycle. Be sure to consider how your main competitor(s) will likely respond to your marketing strategy (if applicable) and what you will do to counter this (avoid threats and exploit opportunities).

VI. MARKETING TACTICS:
How will you implement the marketing strategy(ies) identified above? Tactics explain *how* to carry out strategy. Tactics in this section are built around the elements of the *marketing mix:* Product or Service; Position; Price; and Distribution (Place).

A. Describe the PRODUCT. How will you POSITION or REPOSITION your event or product? Which of the three basic product tactics, introduction, change, or withdrawal, will you use to support your strategy and achieve your marketing goals?
B. PRICES must be established for each product line or service. Pricing objectives must match objectives for product lines. Describe the PRICING OBJECTIVE for each product line or service. Identify which pricing tactics—penetration pricing, meet-the-competition, skim pricing, promotional, etc.—you will use.
C. Describe the DISTRIBUTION for each product line or service. The use of new channels of distribution often offers opportunities to gain a competitive edge (differential advantage). Examples of distribution channels include direct mail, door-to-door sales, electronic shopping, site flexibility etc.
D. PROMOTION (include ADVERTISING, PUBLICITY AND SALES). Prior to developing your budget it is imperative that you determine what is desired of your promotions and advertising. Keep in mind that in every sport organization there are limited resources. Therefore, resources should be employed where they will have the greatest "bang for the buck."

VII. IMPLEMENTATION AND CONTROL

A. ACTION PLAN: present a calendar or chart showing what promotions, ads, etc., will be used, and the month the activity is due to be completed.

B. BUDGET: the proposed budget should reflect the projected costs associated with the marketing plan.

C. EVALUATION: how are you going to measure if your goals and objectives are met?

Sources of information that are helpful for this project include the following: *Predicasts Forecasts; US Industrial Outlook; Infotrac Business File; Survey of Buying Power; American Sports Analysis; Predicasts Basebook; Study of Media and Markets; Valueline; Standard and Poor's Stock Reports; Moody's manuals; SEC File; Market Share Reporter; Lifestyle Market Analyst; 1995 United States Census; Thomas Reporter; Rand McNally Commercial Atlas and Market Guide; SRDS Sports Advantage* or other Standard Rate and Data Service sources; journal articles; newspaper articles; and government publications. Two excellent texts on marketing plans are Cohen's (1998) *The Marketing Plan,* and Stotlar's (2001) *Developing Successful Sport Marketing Plans.*

SUMMARY

- Sport marketing has its roots in traditional marketing but is also distinct in a variety of ways.
- Sports are consumed for a variety of reasons, some of which may have little or no relation to the intent of the producer of the product. The sport marketer must be aware of these motivations for consumption of the product.
- The marketing of the sport product should be strategically and systematically planned. The strategic plan gives a framework to the entire marketing process.
- Because of the unpredictability of the sport product, the sport marketer must market both the core product and the product extensions.
- The focus of sport marketing is on identifying and segmenting the market(s) and then developing a marketing mix that will appeal to the selected target(s). To learn the needs of sport consumers, the marketer must conduct demographic, psychographic, and behavioral analyses.
- Sport marketing concepts act as a formula (the four P's) and function in an interrelated

manner to produce the effect that the marketer planned to achieve. Each of these factors can be manipulated to reach a target market, create awareness, provide information, or force a reaction.

- Product usage information is crucial to sport marketing. Because product usage varies by strata, the marketer must develop strategies that address the needs of light, medium, and heavy users. Overemphasizing strategies targeted to the heavy users, particularly if it means neglecting light and medium users, could cost the sport organization in the future.
- Positioning a product is necessary today because of the overwhelming volume of advertising. The concept of positioning is to differentiate, or position in the mind of the consumer, your product from your competitors' product. Positioning is the same as niche marketing.
- The sport marketer must select a pricing strategy early in the marketing planning process. Price is the most visible and flexible component of the marketing mix, and it contributes to the consumer's perception of the value of the sport product.
- Before launching any promotion, the sport marketer should set the goals of the promotional campaign. The promotional mix includes advertising, sales promotions, publicity, and personal selling.
- Advertising, because of its vast reach and high cost, and sales promotions, because of their flexibility, are important aspects of the promotional mix.
- The marketing plan is a written document, resulting from the strategic planning process that guides the sport marketer throughout the season.

 CRITICAL THINKING EXERCISES

1. If you were the marketing manager for an NBA team, say the New York Knicks or the Denver Nuggets, how would you customize the elements of the marketing mix to try to increase attendance? How would you adjust the elements of the marketing mix if you worked

for the Los Angeles Lakers or the Chicago Bulls? As an alternative, complete the exercise using the following WNBA teams: Indiana Fever or Washington Mystics; Los Angeles Sparks or the Houston Comets.

2. As the Associate athletic director of marketing for a NCAA Division I or II school, how would you price tickets for sports *other* than football? What factors would you consider when making your ticket pricing decisions?

 CASE STUDY

Nike: A Company for the Ages[3]

Nike founder Philip Knight created the sports footwear and apparel empire now known as Nike in 1962, when he started the company Blue Ribbon Sports. Nike was once an upstart company, loud, brash, and fearless. While these traits still characterize Nike, the company is different today than it was 30 years ago. Always regarded as a leader in product innovation, Nike is now looked upon as a leader in corporate innovation as well. More than the authority on what is "cool," Nike is at the forefront of an ever-growing global mix of sports, technology, and consumer culture. The company, which midway through 2003 had generated revenues of $10.7 billion (an 8 percent increase over the previous year and the highest annual revenues in the company's history), is the largest seller of athletic footwear and athletic equipment in the world. And for the first time in its history in 2002, Nike's international business exceeded that of the United States. Knight's passion and drive for excellence influence the company's corporate culture and have been passed on to Nike's employees.

The athletic footwear, apparel, and equipment industry is keenly competitive in the United States and internationally. Nike competes with an increasing number of athletic and leisure shoe companies, athletic and leisure apparel companies, sports equipment companies, and large companies having diversified lines of athletic and leisure shoes, apparel, and equipment, including Reebok, Adidas, and others. The

company's success is largely due to its ability to adapt its structure, management, and marketing processes to meet the demands of its competitive environment, both domestically and abroad. Nike has dominated the athletic footwear market for over two decades. However, like other global companies, Nike has faced some challenges, both in the United States and abroad, including global economic recession, West Coast port closures, and the SARS virus that temporarily paralyzed Asian markets. These and other world events gave every global business an indication as to just how quickly markets could be depressed by unexpected circumstances.

For Nike, continued global expansion centers largely around soccer, providing footwear, apparel, and equipment sponsorships to Manchester United and Juventus, the Brazilian and Mexican National Teams, and the Turkish Football Federation. In most countries, soccer is the premier sport, and basketball and football are viewed as characteristically American. Adidas-Salomon has been the dominant footwear and apparel supplier for soccer worldwide; however, Brazil's victory over Germany in the 2002 World Cup should serve to fuel Nike's momentum in its global soccer efforts.

Reebok, Adidas, and other athletic footwear companies are also interested in selling their products globally, and the competition between these athletic footwear heavyweights is constant. But given that international revenue outpaced U.S. revenue for the first time in Nike's history, the company may want to refocus its marketing efforts stateside.

1. Why are athletic footwear and apparel ideal products for global marketing?
2. How should Nike position itself in United States, Europe, and Asia Pacific markets?
3. Other than in soccer, what global opportunities exist for Nike now? Five years from now?
4. What threats do competing companies pose for Nike in the United States, Europe, Asia, and other global markets?
5. Compare Nike's domestic marketing and athlete endorsement strategies with those of Adidas and Reebok.
6. What advantages does Nike have in its competition with Reebok, Adidas, and other athletic footwear companies for leadership in United States, Europe and other Asia Pacific markets?

[3]Sources: Holmes, B. (2003, July 21). "The real Nike news is happening abroad." *Business Week*, 30; Holmes, S. (2002, June 10). "Nike's vision of soccer greatness." *Business Week*, 12; http://www.nike.com/nikebiz.

7. *What are the environmental factors that could affect Nike's market position in the United States and abroad?*

REVIEW QUESTIONS AND ISSUES

1. What are the unique characteristics of sport and how do these differences affect the marketing of sport?
2. Using the Simmons or Mediamark marketing reports (or similar marketing research database), identify the demographic and, if available, lifestyle profile of a sport's participant and spectating audience (e.g., NBA, NFL, NASCAR, World Cup Soccer, etc.).
3. What does the term *market segmentation* mean? What are the types of segmentation that are commonly used, and how does segmentation help the sport marketer identify a target market?
4. What is a target market? Discuss the steps in identifying and selecting a target market when marketing "official clothing" of a professional franchise. How might this target differ from that of a market for "official clothing" of a college or university?
5. What are the differences between core product and product extensions? Which of these concepts is more important to the sport marketer? Why?
6. What does the term *positioning* mean? How would you attempt to position a three-on-three-basketball tournament (to be held for the first time on your campus) to students? To alumni? To the community?
7. What techniques and strategies would you use to promote your three-on-three-campus basketball tournament? Justify your choices.

SOLUTIONS TO CRITICAL THINKING EXERCISES

1. The sport marketer cannot change the product; therefore, the price and promotion elements of the marketing mix would be the first choice for manipulation. Price could be changed to temporarily increase demand for tickets by developing a sales promotion, for example, a four-for-four coupon. Other, non-price-related promotions could also be developed to increase interest in the games, for example, a frequent fan series of promotions that encourage repeat attendance, or frequent purchaser reward programs. Be careful, however, not to rely too heavily on sales promotions to increase demand.
2. The first step would be to determine the school's philosophy regarding charging for nonrevenue sports. Some schools do not charge for any sports except football, men's and women's basketball, and volleyball or hockey. However, if you do charge for nonrevenue sports events, a value must be placed on the worth of the event. Be careful not to charge too little for the event, as it could result in a low perceived quality by potential fans. Another option for nonrevenue sports would be to develop a ticket package that would allow fans to choose various events.

WEBSITES

www.nba.com; www.wnba.com
www.nfl.com
http://mlb.mlb.com
www.nhl.com
www.mls.com
www.NASCAR.com
www.pga.com; www.lpga.com
www.atptennis.com; www.wtatour.com—Official sites for major leagues; each team has a link on the league page so that each team can be reached.
www.usolympicteam.com
www.paralympic.org—Information on the Olympics and Paralympics.
http://msn.espn.go.com/
http://cbs.sportsline.com/
http://sportsillustrated.cnn.com/
www.collegesports.com/
www.SportingNews.com
www.FoxSports.com—Sites that report on both the spectator and business aspects of sports.
www.sgma.com/index.html
www.nsga.org/public/pages/index.cfm?pageid=1z—SGMA's and National Sporting Goods Association sites.
www.teammarketing.com
http://www.sportsbussinessjournal.com/—General sports marketing information.

REFERENCES

Aaker, D. (1998). *Strategic market management*, 5th ed. New York: John Wiley & Sons.

American Marketing Association (n.d.). *Dictionary of marketing terms.* Retrieved December 14, 2003 from http://www.marketingpower.com/live/mg-dictionary.php.

Brooks, C. (1994). *Sports marketing: Competitive business strategies for sports.* Englewood Cliffs, NJ: Prentice Hall.

Bruel, J. (2003, January 27). Find hidden revenue under the seat cushions. *Street & Smith's Sport Business Journal, 5,* 23.

Cohen, W. A. (1998). *The marketing plan,* 2nd ed. New York: John Wiley & Sons.

ESPN Sports Poll (n.d.). Retrieved December 30, 2003 from http://www.sportspoll.com/home.asp.

Gladden, J. (1996). Sports market bytes: The ever expanding impact of technology on sport marketing, Part I. *Sport Marketing Quarterly, 5*(3), 13–14.

Heller, R. (1989). *The supermarketers.* New York: E. P. Dutton.

King, B. (2003, Dec. 1). More teams catch on to variable ticket pricing. *Street & Smith's Sport Business Journal, 5,* 33.

Kotler, P. (1997). *Marketing management: Analysis, implementation, planning and control,* 9th ed. Upper Saddle River, NJ: Prentice Hall.

Kotler, P. (2003). *Marketing management: Analysis, implementation, planning and control,* 15th ed. Upper Saddle River, NJ: Prentice Hall.

Levitt, T. (1986). *Marketing imagination.* New York: The Free Press.

Marcum, J., and Greenstein, T. (1985). Factors affecting attendance at major league baseball, Part II. A within-season analysis. *Sociology of Sport Journal, 2,* 314–22.

McDonald, M., and Rascher, D. (2000). Does bat day make cents? The effect of promotions on the demand for major league baseball. *Journal of Sport Management, 14*(1), 8–27.

Meek, A. (1997). An estimate of the size and supported economics of the sports industry in the United States. *Sport Marketing Quarterly, 6*(4), 15–21.

Milne, G., and McDonald, M. (1999). *Sport marketing: Managing the exchange process.* Sudbury, MA: Jones and Bartlett.

Mullin, B. (1983). *Sport marketing, promotion and public relations.* Amherst, Massachusetts: National Sport Management.

Mullin, B., Hardy, S., and Sutton, W. (2000). *Sport marketing,* 2nd ed. Champaign, IL: Human Kinetics.

Perreault, W., and McCarthy, E. J. (2002). *Basic marketing: A global-managerial approach,* 13th edition. Boston: Irwin/McGraw-Hill.

Pitts, B., and Stotlar, D. (2002). *Fundamentals of sport marketing* (2nd ed.). Morgantown, VW: Fitness Information Technology.

Pride, W., and Ferrell, O. (1997). *Marketing concepts and strategies,* 10th ed. New York: Houghton Mifflin Co.

Ries, A., and Trout, J. (1986). *Positioning: The battle for your mind.* New York: McGraw-Hill.

Rudman, W., and Sutton, W. (1989). The selling of the NBA: Market characteristics and sport consumption. Presentation at the National Basketball Association's Annual meeting, Palm Springs, California: September.

Sandomir, R. (1988, November 14). The $50 billion sport industry. *Sports Inc.,* 14–23.

Shank, M. (1999). *Sports marketing: A strategic perspective.* Upper Saddle River, NJ: Prentice Hall.

Stotlar, D. (2001). *Developing successful sport marketing plans.* Morgantown, VW: Fitness Information Technology.

Street & Smith's. (2004). *By the numbers: The authoritative annual research guide and fact book.*

Street & Smith's. (1999, December 20–26). The answer is. *SportsBusiness Journal, 1,* 23–29.

The FANSonly. (1999, March). *The FANSonly network: Your ticket to college sports!* Atlanta, Georgia: Author.

Ticket Master (n.d.). Retrieved January 5, 2004, from http://www.aboutticketmaster.com/sell.html.

Veeck, W., and Linn, E. (1965). *The hustler's handbook.* New York: Putnam.

Yow, D. (1999, March). New directions on the 'net. *Athletic Management,* 14–17.

CHAPTER 15

Sponsorship

Dave Stotlar

In this chapter, you will become familiar with the following terms:

Advertising	Leveraging	Sampling
Ambush marketing	Market research	Sponsorship
Competitive-market strategy	Media exposure	Sponsorship agreement
Cost-plus method	Philanthropy	Target markets
Demographics	Pricing	Valuation
Exchange theory	Relative-value method	
Legal counsel	Return on investment	

Learning Goals
By the end of this chapter, students should be able to:

- Understand the basic theories and terminology pertinent to sport sponsorship.

- Identify corporate and organizational goals and objectives associated with sport sponsorship.

- Understand specific sport sponsorship strategies which exist in the sport industry.

- Be able to develop a sport sponsorship proposal including a specific presentation.

OVERVIEW

On a worldwide basis, sport organizations and corporations have entered into partnerships wherein each agrees to assist the other in forwarding their own objectives. One such partnership is sport **sponsorship.** For sports organizations, it's an effort to obtain funds from sponsors to operate their sports events and programs. For corporations, it's a chance to get their products in the minds of consumers. This relationship originated decades ago, but it has increased in popularity and sophistication over the last 15 years (Wilkinson, 1986; Ensor, 1987; Asimakopoulos, 1993; Graham, 1993; Irwin, 1993). It has been estimated that more than 4,800 U.S. companies involved in sports marketing and sponsorship spent $10.5 billion, up 3.7 percent over 2002. Contributing to this total were several companies that spent over $100 million each on sponsorship programs (IEG, 2002a). Worldwide spending was $26.2 billion for 2003 with a growth rate of 7 percent.

PHILOSOPHICAL BASIS FOR SPONSORSHIP

Initially, sports professionals must develop an understanding of sponsorship from a philosophical view. Sport sponsorships are based on the **exchange theory:** "If you give me something, I'll give you something." Therefore the definition of a sport sponsorship is a situation wherein a sport organization grants the right of association to another company or organization. As we will see, the right of association can take many forms.

A determination must be made early in discussions between the parties involved regarding whether the exchange can be equal—*can* be equal as opposed to *will* be equal. Some sponsorship arrangements cannot provide equal value to both parties—for instance, the junior high school sports program that is asking for money to print its sports program. Any corporation that provides these funds is actually doing it for **philanthropy** rather than for financial reasons. However, a company that pays a fee to put its corporate logo on the side of a race car in the Indianapolis 500 may be able to generate an advertising value that substantially exceeds the amount paid. Irwin (1993) noted that "in years past, corporations provided financial assistance to sporting events and athletic programs for philanthropic purposes, [but] today's corporate interests are strictly promotionally motivated."

CONCEPT CHECK

Those who desire to obtain a sport sponsorship must make an initial determination with respect to their ability to deliver commensurate economic value in the exchange. If this criterion cannot be met, a philanthropic approach is mandated.

A key step in making a sponsorship proposal that appeals to a sponsor is to provide a comparison of the requested amount to competitive **advertising** costs and value. Each potential sponsor is engaged in other marketing activities, each of which has a price and a value. You must study and prepare data that show the benefit of sport sponsorship in terms that the corporation can evaluate. Remember, the person who agrees to give you the sponsorship must be able to defend her or his decision to the corporate management or stockholders.

A key component in the sponsorship process is the measurement of **return on investment** (ROI). Is there an equivalent increase in sales attributable to the sponsorship? Conventional data on the advertising and promotions conducted by corporations show that only about 16 percent of the promotions produced sales that were greater than the costs of the promotion (Abraham and Lodish, 1990). These authors also believe that if a promotion is not effective in increasing sales within a six-month period, it will never produce sales. With this in mind, it becomes essential for those entering a sport sponsorship to accurately and quickly measure the impact and success of the partnership. Data on VISA International's Olympic sponsorship produced data that measured a 3 percent increase in customer preference from before the Olympic games to after their completion. Although that may not seem like a large increase, 3 percent of a multibillion-dollar industry is a considerable amount of money. Since VISA began its Olympic sponsorship in 1988, its market share has improved from 40 percent to 65 percent. During the same period, American Express share has slipped from 21 percent to 9 percent.

Sport managers must be fully cognizant of the data with which to demonstrate the accomplishment of specified corporate objectives. This should be provided by the sport organization or event owner, but it is occasionally collected by the sponsor. Motorola conducted its own market research to investigate the effectiveness of its motorcycle team sponsorship in Europe and found that it received a six-to-one return (IEG, 1993b).

CONCEPT CHECK

Sport organizations that use sponsorship as a marketing tool must be prepared to evaluate sponsorship in the same manner as other marketing efforts.

According to research data, "sponsorship may send a more convincing message than traditional advertising" (Performance Research, 1991). The study found that 70 percent of golf enthusiasts could recall the sponsors of events, whereas only 40 percent could remember the television commercials aired during the events. However, one should not underestimate the power of broadcasting commercial advertising during sports programs. Only about 8 percent of television viewers can recall commercials aired during nonsports programs.

During the 1990s, Princeton Video Images introduced a new advertising concept for sport events: virtual signage. Their technology "allows a broadcaster to electronically insert an image—generally an advertisement—onto any one-color surface, including a playing field or boundary" (Bernstein, 1998, p. 24). The National Basketball Association has not allowed virtual signage, but Major League Baseball and the National Hockey League have used the technology on several national telecasts. The X Games and various professional tennis tournaments employed this technology extensively during the late 1990s. Considerable controversy exists concerning control of the images that are presented during the event. Facility owners protested these applications because they had often promised stadium advertisers that their signs would be seen by television audiences during events telecast from the facility.

The San Diego Padres encountered a problem when their TV broadcaster sold virtual signage during telecasts of home contests. The following year, the Padres specified in their broadcast contract that the team, not the broadcaster, would have the rights to any virtual signage inserted into Padres games (Bernstein, 1998).

One can also have professional **market research** firms collect data for you. One such company is Performance Research, which conducts research in the area of sponsor exposure for companies involved in the trade. It conducts field-based research in such areas as aided and unaided recall, advertising awareness, responses to promotions, product usage, and brand loyalty.

During the 2000 Olympic games, Performance Research studied the recognition by consumers of Olympic sponsors. Their data found that the recall rate for Olympic sponsors was higher than in Atlanta (Performance Research, 2003; Stotlar, 2001a).

In another independent study, people were asked to identify, from memory, sponsors of the Olympic Games (TOP) and the USOC. An analysis of the data indicated that only a small portion were able to recall Olympic (TOP) sponsors. Coca-Cola had the highest recall at 26 percent followed by VISA at 21 percent, Kodak at 19 percent, and McDonald's at 16 percent. USOC sponsors achieved

lower recall with Coca-Cola leading all other sponsors with 17 percent, McDonald's with 12 percent, General Motors and Kodak with 11 percent. Nike, not a USOC sponsor, was cited as sponsor by 12 percent of subjects.

Aided recall measures (recognition) yielded higher success rates for all sponsors. This method provided a list of possible sponsors, actual and foils, from which to subjects were asked to identify actual sponsors. VISA was correctly identified as a TOP sponsor by 73 percent of the subjects, followed closely by Coca-Cola with 72 percent. Other TOP sponsors recognized included: Kodak at 54 percent, McDonald's at 54 percent, IBM with 49 percent, Xerox at 39 percent, UPS at 31 percent, Panasonic with 25 percent, and Time/SI and Samsung at 24 percent. Other TOP members were noted by less than 20 percent of subjects. United Airlines and Seiko, USOC but not TOP sponsors, were noted as TOP sponsors by 38 percent and 28 percent of the subjects respectively (Stotlar, 2001b).

Sports organizations have a variety of objectives, but two of the most prominent are finance and media exposure. Interestingly, these are the same objectives that sponsoring corporations seek.

CONCEPT CHECK

Establishing a base for a sponsorship relationship is paramount to its success. The sport organization and the sponsor must work together in all facets of the relationship. According to Wilkinson (1988), "in an ideal relationship between the organization and the sponsor, each helps the other meet its objectives."

Because sponsorship is "playing a more central role in corporate thinking, it becomes more important to understand consumer reaction to sponsorship efforts and to research the influence of sponsorship on attitudes" (Sandler and Shani, 1993). In general, only a few people feel that sport sponsorship is a "bad thing" (IEG, 1993b). At the same time, however, some consumers think that sports are becoming too commercialized.

Market research has found that the Olympic rings are the most recognized logo in the world, with 93 percent of the population able to correctly recognize the rings. Therefore, sponsors may desire to associate with the Olympic rings to enhance their recognition value. In addition, sponsors of the winter Olympics could benefit from the estimated worldwide TV audience of 4 billion viewers (*Olympic Marketing Fact File,* 2002).

Probably the most revealing data indicated that 69 percent of consumers felt that "the fact that a company is an official sponsor has no impact on my purchase habits" (Sandler and Shani, 1993). Although the research data are mixed in their summary of consumer reaction to sponsorship, you could argue that if the companies didn't think that it was a good investment, the billions of dollars now committed to sport sponsorship would disappear.

According to Irwin (1993), "without the support of corporations, the world of sport, as we know it, would collapse." This may seem dramatic, but the world of sport has become increasingly dependent on corporate sponsorships for operating revenues. For example, 50 percent of the U.S. Olympic Committee's 2001–2004 budget came from sponsorship and licensing revenue. Similarly, between 50 and 60 percent of the budgets for the Athens and Salt Lake Olympic Games were based on sponsorship dollars (Olympic Marketing Fact File, 2002). In addition, almost all of the top NCAA universities have corporate sponsorship programs in place. For example Ohio State University collects $2.5 million per year from the 15 sponsors in the Schottenstein Center (Cordova, 2003). Thus the relationship between sport organizations and sponsors must include advantages to all parties involved.

RESEARCHING SPONSORSHIP PROSPECTS

Many sports marketers fail to adequately prepare themselves to enter the sponsorship business. The key to success is the ability to research prospective companies. Probably the best place to start is to obtain a thorough understanding of the corporate sponsorship environment. The International Events Group (IEG) in Chicago has organized a corporation around the sponsorship industry, and its publication, *IEG Sponsorship Report,* is an important tool in researching prospective sponsors. In 2001, the International Events Group reported that the most active categories of sponsorship were soft drinks, banks, automotive, telecommunications, and beer (IEG, 2001).

Sponsorship proposals are considerably more effective if they tie sponsorship elements specifically to objectives of the sponsoring corporation (Irwin, 1993). One of the more effective steps in investigating corporations' objectives and goals is gaining access to their corporate literature, such as the annual report. This document will tell you a lot about the inner workings of a company.

All publicly traded companies with over 500 shareholders and $10 million in assets must file an annual report with the SEC (Securities and Exchange Commission). This report details profits and losses and typically gives a forecast for the coming year. These can be accessed at www.sec.gov or through a stock broker. Another point of access is through a public domain group called the Public Register's Annual Report Service (www.prars.com). Many sport organizations are not-for-profit organizations which the Internal Revenue Search classifies as 501(c) (3) organizations. While they are not required to file an annual report they are required to file an IRS 990 Form. The larger organizations' 990 forms such as the Rose Bowl and United States Olympic Committee can be located through www.guidestar.com. There are, however, many things that a company doesn't want its shareholders to know that you need to know. From this perspective, you can read clippings from area papers or talk to people who do business with the company. Just knowing who holds what office is not enough; you have to know who the power brokers are in the organization.

One good example is the Coca-Cola Company. The best point of access for a sponsorship with Coke is the local bottler. More than 90 percent of the proposals funded by Coke come through to corporate headquarters with support from the local bottling company. The corporate belief is that if the local bottlers are in favor of an event and believe that it will have a positive impact on sales, then it's worth doing. However, the local distributor for other corporations may not have the money, the interest, or the authority to enter into this type of arrangement (Cordova, 2003).

Additional research must be done on a corporation's prior sponsorship experiences. If it has had good experiences, your chances will be better; if it has had one or more bad experiences, you will have a difficult time demonstrating that your results will differ.

EXAMINING SPONSORSHIP OBJECTIVES

Irwin (1993) identified **media exposure** as one of the three most highly rated factors by sponsors in judging sponsorship proposals. *Telling* sponsors that they will get media attention is valuable, but *measuring* it provides data for legitimizing the corporation's involvement in sports marketing. Sponsors are increasingly demanding more sophisticated measurement of value. These measures typically parallel measures used to evaluate all corporate marketing elements. Spoelstra remarked: "prove it to the decision-makers' boss" (Spoelstra, 1997, p. 172). In short, it helps them to help you. In a service-related business, it's your responsibility to provide them with these data.

Another consideration is **leveraging** media coverage through sponsorship. You are going to be spending money on advertising anyway, so why not seek a media sponsor and arrange for a four-to-one arrangement (for $4 worth of media space or air time, you give them $1 credit toward sponsorship). For instance, Digital Computer was approached by a minor league baseball team as sponsor. Digital Computer's goal was to produce a five-to-one return on their sponsorship investment. To assist digital in meeting their objectives, the team assembled all available sponsorship and media inventory including, field signage, program ads, and TV tags to parallel Digital's objectives. In the end, Digital provided $500,000 in sponsorship (50 percent product, 50 percent cash) and received an ROI of nine to one. This will give you more advertising for your dollar, your sponsors more media benefit, and the media source special-event associations (Spoelstra, 1997).

Irrespective of the validity of calculating the value of camera/action shots on an equal basis with actual ads, it gives the sponsors (or marketing managers) data with which to defend their decisions to use sport as a marketing vehicle. One company, Joyce Julius and Associates, provides support data to help event owners justify return on investment to sponsors. They calculate the total time that a sponsor's logo appears on the televised coverage of major events. Based on the cost of airing a 30-second commercial during the event, they can determine the value of the sponsor's exposure. For example, midway through the 2003 NHRA drag-racing season General Motors had achived $19.1 million in television exposure (www.joycejulius.com).

The ability of sponsors to receive positive visibility and increase sales with favorable publicity has been shown to be an attractive mechanism for sponsors. Yet many sport organizations have experienced high levels of conflict between event management decisions and sponsors' satisfaction. During the 2002 Winter Olympic Games, conflict occurred in many of the cities where the Olympic Torch Relay was run. The relay was co-sponsored by Coca-Cola and Chevy trucks, yet managed by the Olympic Organizing Committee. The sponsors wanted the relay to always pass the local Chevy dealership, whereas the planning committee often had other routes planned. Be careful not to jeopardize the integrity of your event for the desires of sponsors.

Before undertaking a sponsorship, most corporations develop a set of criteria for evaluating possible opportunities. This process has been discussed extensively (*IEG's Complete Guide to Sponsorship,* 1995; Irwin and Asimakopoulos, 1992; Irwin, 1993). To follow are typical factors to be considered beyond the media aspects previously discussed.

Target markets

There has to be a careful match between the **demographics** of the sponsor's consumers and the audience/participants of the sports event. In discussing their sponsorship of a golf tournament, one Acura (automobile) executive said the golfing market was its most desirable demographic target. An IEG study reinforced the importance of this when they found that demographics and attendance were the two most often cited factors for event sponsorship (IEG, 2002b). The sport organization has several avenues through which this information can be provided. The organization can collect its own data, or it can use secondary data collected by a commercial firm.

At many universities, turnstile operators use Universal Product Code (UPC) scanners to record students' ID cards when they enter the stadium. With this information, the university can identify exactly who came to the game. Although only 50 percent of colleges collect this type of information, it is essential for sponsors. Consumer research firms such as Simmons Market Research Bureau also collect similar data on a nationwide basis. Their data can be used to relate to sponsors the "typical audience" for specific sports events. Their study of media and markets also provides data on television viewership of sports events. These will provide a rough idea of the audience profile for sports events.

The geographical reach of the sponsorship is also important. While once relegated to the southeastern part of the United States, stock car racing now has a national reach and has recently conducted races in Japan. Research commissioned by NASCAR indicated that its fans had the following characteristics: 60 percent male, 68 percent married, 58 percent between 18 and 44 years old, 81 percent home owners, with 3.4 cars per household, and 42 percent earning over $50,000 per year (Scott, 2002). These data are imperative when attempting to select sponsors who have these people as their primary consumers. You simply cannot make a good match without good data.

Product sampling opportunities

"Qualitative research shows that **sampling** is the single best way to convert people" (*IEG's Complete Guide to Sponsorship*, 1995). To calculate the benefit for the sponsor, one can compare the cost of the sampling to the anticipated return. Sampling can convert about 10 percent of product users to the company's product. Assume that the typical consumer purchases $20 of the company's product per year, with a profit of $15. If the company spent $100,000 ($50,000 each for the sponsorship and for the cost of labor and products) for the sampling, there would need to be almost 7,000 conversions, which could only be realized if the event drew a crowd of about 70,000. Events can be both cheaper and more effective than other avenues of sampling. For example, many road races assemble "goodie bags" for participants, with product samples supplied by sponsors. For many years, U.S. Swimming also used this technique to provide a sponsor's sunscreen products for its members. In another example, Kodak uses its Olympic sponsorship to connect with the thousands of professional photographers who spend considerably more (on image processing) than normal consumers (*Olympic Marketing Fact File*, 2002).

It is your responsibility to control sampling. Sponsors generally do not want consumers to take multiple samples, which would detract from product sales. Depending on the type of product, the timing of distribution is critical. You would certainly want to hand out the above-mentioned sunscreen to people on their way into the event on a sunny day. However, you may not want to provide cookie samples to incoming consumers because it could hurt your concession sales. For large or perishable products, it may also be wise to distribute them as people exit the venue. If you do any post-event research, it is also a good idea to ask about the samples provided.

OTHER CONSIDERATIONS
Client entertainment

People will pay incredibly large sums of money for the opportunity to play in a "pro-am" golf event with a top golfer. The power to invite business associates to a skybox still carries substantial weight in many sponsorship decisions. VIP parking and seating, hospitality suites (or tents), and specially designed event apparel are other perquisites that accompany sport sponsorships. The activities are called business-to-business (B2B) opportunities and are becoming an important component of sponsorship proposals.

The management of an event is also a consideration for sponsors. In 1999, the scandal surrounding the award of the 2002 Olympic Winter Games to Salt Lake City caused great concern among sponsors. Several sponsors withdrew and the USOC executive responsible for overseeing sponsor recruitment and service, John Krimsky, resigned. The past history of the organizing committee and the professional reputation of the staff are critically important because the image of the corporate sponsor is being placed in the hands of the sport organization.

The image of the products and services offered must also result in a good match. Because sport is associated with a healthy lifestyle, many sponsors may seek to relate their products to that image.

Sponsorship options

Brooks (1994) suggests that sponsorship provides a variety of "athletic platforms" that can serve as the basis for sponsorship: individual athletes, facilities, or an event. Each of these must be selected in reference to corporate goals and objectives. A single platform will be a good fit for all companies. Individual athletes can give a corporation a personal touch.

Michael Jordan was the all-time leader in endorsements. His service as a spokesperson for Nike was arguably the most successful endorsement arrangement ever to occur in sport. However, few of the current athletes have experienced the marketing success of Jordan. As a result, many of the major corporations began to curtail their endorsement programs in the late 1990s. At one point, Reebok had over 130 NBA players under contract; they decreased their stable of NBA endorsees to fewer than 10 during the 1999 season. Similar strategies were employed by Nike and Fila (Bernstein, 1998).

Tiger Woods, arguably the heir apparent to Jordan, signed a contract with Nike immediately following his final amateur match. The five-year, $40 million contract was one of the highest in the history of sport. Other sponsors to sign Woods included Buick, Rolex, and American Express. Electronic Arts secured Tiger to endorse a video game after his victory at the 1997 Master's. In total, Woods' endorsement earnings amount to about $50 million per year (Stone, Joseph, and Jones, 2003).

Women have not been successful in securing levels of individual endorsements equal to men. The leading female endorsers were identified in 2003 as Serena Williams, Annika Sorenstam, Mia Hamm, Venus Williams, and Lisa Leslie (Glase, 2003). However, several marketing executives see women's sport as a growth area for endorsements.

Each component in the platform that is made available for sponsors has its strengths and weaknesses. The task for sport managers is to find an appropriate fit between the company and the sport organization.

Sponsorship models

Conceptual models for managing sport sponsorships have been derived from field-based applications. The model presented (Irwin and Asimakopoulos, 1992; Figure 15-1) has been derived from existing sponsorship proposals and agreements. By examining this model, administrators can gain the skills necessary to effectively work with sponsorship partners. Specific examples and procedures are presented for you to use as models in building sponsorships for your sport organization.

One aspect of sport sponsorships that has been difficult to foresee for many managers is that corporations often would rather deal with large projects than be burdened by a multitude of small ones. One specific recommendation for sport sponsorship is that high-cost deals are more profitable and less work than numerous small ventures (Stotlar, 2001). Therefore, it is important to offer the company several options in its sponsorship agreement, ranging

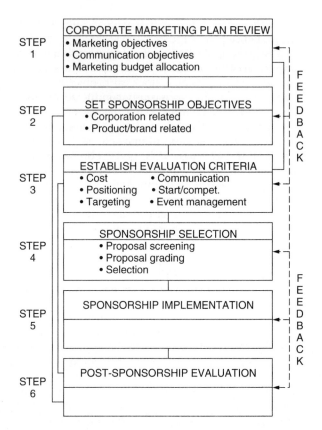

FIGURE 15-1   Six-step approach to sponsorship management.
(From Irwin, R. L. and Asimakopoulos, M. (1992). An approach to the evaluation and selection of sport sponsorship proposals, *Sport Marketing Quarterly,* pp. 43–51, December.)

from exclusive ownership of all events and opportunities to smaller and less expensive options, such as in-kind donations or program advertising.

The framework for this, like any business relationship, is established through the **sponsorship agreement.**

SPONSORSHIP AGREEMENT

The laws pertaining to sports sponsorship are not well defined. The contracts between the sponsor and the event/property holder should be carefully constructed. Remember, consult your **legal counsel** so that all matters are included in the contract in clear language with mutual understanding. The most critical points to be addressed in the contract include the following (IEG's *Complete Guide to Sponsorship*, 1995).

Terms like *title sponsor* and *official supplier* have no standard meaning in the industry. Therefore, you must clarify the rights the sponsor is getting and the rights the promoter is retaining. You also need to preserve the value of the sponsor's exclusivity. Avoiding competitors is only part of the problem. Developing an appropriate sponsor mix is also a consideration. You should carefully match each sponsor with other sponsors, products, and corporate image. For instance, based on the 2002 Olympic Winter Games, the U.S. Figure Skating Association may not want to offer the category "official legal counsel." Pizza Hut may not want an "official antacid" for an event if it were a title sponsor. McDonald's would not want to have Pepsi as the official soft drink because of its ties with Coca-Cola. If a soft drink company is secured, be sure to give attention to the contracts at the venue and any conflicts that might arise.

Each partner should strive to protect each other's trademarks and logos. Cooperation is always intended, but abuse can occur if the issue is not addressed. Typically, any use of an event logo or corporate trademark requires the owners' approval unless it is specially covered in the contract. Both parties need to be protected from liability through insurance. A sponsor does not want to be sued by an injured spectator or participant. Most events arrange for special coverage for all parties involved in an event. You might even have "insurance coverage" as a sponsorable category.

The agreement must include details on the use of the sponsors and event logos, including facilities and uniforms. Most sport organizations—including the IOC, USOC, NCAA, NFL, MLB, and NBA—have rules regarding the size of corporate logos that can be displayed on team uniforms. The primary catalyst in the logo issue was ski racers who, at the end of a race, immediately raised their skis in the air, with the logo facing toward the TV camera. In many cases the skis raised on the poduim are not the actual skis used in the race, but are the latest product the manufacturer is trying to market.

NASCAR strikes deals with sponsors and requires all drivers to place NASCAR's sponsors' logos on its cars for each race. Specific rules exist for the placement of the logos on the race cars (Figure 15-2). The winning drivers of NASCAR races engage in a furious practice in victory lane: They constantly change hats sporting various sponsor logos. Not only does this give each sponsor its moment in the sun (and camera lens), but it's in the contract. Even the sequence is prescribed.

The NCAA published guidelines for all corporations involved in sponsoring its championships. In this document, the NCAA maintains absolute control over the sponsors' signs, advertisements, and even their specific wording. The NCAA document requires that "all advertising copy and promotional activities by NCAA national corporate partners utilizing the NCAA's name or registered marks must have prior approval of the NCAA" (National Collegiate Athletic Association, 2003).

Protection against unfulfilled promises should be addressed in the contract. If an event promises to deliver a designated number of spectators or TV audience share, it should be written into the contract and possibly backed financially through a letter of credit (*IEG's Complete Guide to Sponsorship*, 1995). The penalties (or bonuses) should be preset in

FIGURE 15-2   Sponsors pay up to $10 million per year for primary sponsorship of NASCAR teams.

writing so that all parties clearly understand the stipulations.

The types of event signage that will be available and the number, location, and responsibility for making and hanging them are all important matters to be covered in a contract. The actual production, installation labor, and postevent procedures are also essential points. Most sponsors do not want to risk their corporate image with the presentation of their logos on banners and signs (IEG's *Complete Guide to Sponsorship*, 1995). Therefore, most sponsors will oversee the production of an event's signage. However, organizers should be careful and supervise the installation. In one situation, at the Denver Grand Prix, one sponsor put up more than its allotted signs and erected them in places that had not been agreed to by event organizers. Only on the morning of the race did the organizers notice the problem, and it was too late to correct the situation. It's debatable whether it was an error or a strategic move by the sponsor to gain more exposure.

Most agreements control a sponsor's signs, advertisements, and even their specific wording. The difference between using the terms "official sponsor" and "official supplier" may mean thousands of dollars from a company, and one would not want to allow a minor sponsor to detract from the value sold to a major contributor.

Sometimes the selection and control of signage precludes existing signage in a local facility or secured by participating teams. Is your agreement enforceable regardless of the venue's or the team's previous sponsorship commitments? In constructing the sponsorship contract, remember the recent advent of virtual signage technology. You must make sure to include clauses that prohibit the modification of existing stadium advertising in the broadcast image. Without proper attention to these details, controversies are sure to surface. One Major Soccer League executive said that "the stadium takes a position that they have some proprietary interest in [virtual signage], our position is that they don't" (Bernstein, 1998, p. 24).

An organization's mailing lists and the use of individual athletes are often key factors in sponsorship. Many sponsors would like to use both for their benefit. You have probably kept records from advance ticket orders, season ticket holders, or association members. Corporations can use these to strengthen ties to consumers. Direct-marketing campaigns are more effective if they come through an organization with which the consumer already has an association. Some sponsors like to use participants in their promotions. Be careful if you promise to provide them because they may not allow you to make agreements for their appearance with sponsors. If you have a participation contract with the athletes, this stipulation should be part of the contract. All participant agreements should also contain a clause that allows for photographs to be taken at the event that may contain an athlete's likeness and provide a release for that photograph's use by the event and sponsors.

There is a concern about the length of sponsorship agreements. There has been a steady increase in contract coverage over the past few years. Data have shown that long-term agreements (a minimum of three years) provide better results for both partners. Industry data indicated that the average length of a sponsorship agreement was five years (*IEG's Complete Guide to Sponsorship*, 1995). Therefore, the right of first refusal is always an element of interest. Sponsors generally like to have the right to future options for an event. They have placed their reputation on the line with you and should be accorded this consideration. Remember, this is a partnership that can benefit all of the participants.

Corporations occasionally enlist an agency to assist them with securing sport sponsorships. According to the industry leader, International Events Group (IEG, 1999), only 8 percent of sponsorship proposals resulted from contact through a sponsor's PR/ad agency. Fifty-seven percent of the successful sponsorship proposals came through a "cold call" (the property approaches the sponsor without previous contact).

Interestingly, 15 percent of agreements resulted from sponsors contacting a property directly. In 8 percent of the cases, the sponsorship came about through contact with a member of the sponsoring company's board. Seven percent of the time, the property used an outside agency to secure a sponsor (IEG, 1999).

There has been considerable confusion over the most successful approach strategy for sponsorship acquisition (IEG, 1999). The decision about entry channels, whom to contact at a particular company, varies considerably from one corporation to the next. All sponsors handle proposals differently. Some give a local distributor the authority to make decisions related to sponsorship, while others centralize sponsorship decisions at the corporate headquarters. You must evaluate point of access carefully for each of your potential sponsors.

According to Gearson (1994), if you want to use an agency to secure a sponsorship for your company, there are several factors to consider. Although many agencies create advertising campaigns and sponsorship proposals, some have little or no knowledge of the corporation's marketing plan. Sponsorship activities must be directly tied to the company's marketing plan, with significant measurement of resulting sales and revenue. Only as a partnership, where the company and the agency work together, can the end product be successful.

PRICING SPONSORSHIPS

The prices for sport sponsorship can range from a few hundred dollars to the $65 million each Olympic sponsor pays for World-Wide Partner status. Brooks (1994) details three different approaches to sponsorship **pricing.** The **cost-plus method** involves calculating the actual expenses incurred in providing the sponsorship package with an inclusion for profit for the organization. Expenses include all items included in the package, such as tickets, parking, dinners, souvenirs, and signage. A reasonable profit margin can be added, and the package ensures that the sponsorship will generate a profit.

The second method described by Brooks is the **competitive-market strategy.** The competitive market has changed since the 1990s. Early in the development of sport sponsorships, leverage was on the side of the event holder. Major events like the Indianapolis 500 would have many companies that wanted to sign sponsorship deals, and sometimes a bidding war erupted between potential sponsors. However, as more sport organizations and events entered the field, leverage shifted to the companies, which could then choose their options from a broad field of opportunities. As with any product pricing strategy, one must be competitive with alternative sponsorship options. The problem is trying to discover their price. With retail products, you can go to a store, pick up a company's product, and see how much is being asked. In the sponsorship business, it is difficult to know the pricing structure of competitors' packages.

Probably the most widely used method of sponsorship pricing is the **relative-value method.**

Brooks (1994) reported that this strategy is based on the market value of each sponsorship component. For example, program ads could be compared to ads in the newspaper, scoreboard signage to billboards, and public-address announcements to radio advertising. The issue here is whether the comparison is legitimate. Is the same impact achieved? Is one message more powerful than another? Media impressions from event coverage are considerably less effective than a direct advertising message. If the event places the sponsor's logo in its media purchases, the value is about 10 percent of the media cost; however, if the event is given real advertising spots and space from a media sponsor, the value would be equal to the full rate offered to other advertisers.

Valuation is the most critical aspect of pricing. What is the *real* value of anything? You can offer a rental car company seats in the VIP section for the event as part of its package, but how much are those tickets worth: $50, $100, or what? Those seats will not be sold, anyway. They will all be distributed to sponsors, so just print $100 on the ticket (the ink doesn't cost anything!). It's perfectly legitimate because the rental car company is going to calculate its provision of cars at $75 per day, even though it could never get that on the open market. One should also accept in *trade-out* only those items that one would have had to purchase.

The type of value exchanged is an important element in price negotiations. Industry data indicate that 50 percent of the sponsorships are cash payments from the sponsor to the event owner (sport organization). Twenty-two percent of the deals are in-kind (product donations), with another 29 percent of the arrangements combining the two forms of exchange (IEG, 2001). In all of these negotiations, one shouldn't forget to include the associated labor costs for producing the sponsor's services.

IMPLEMENTATION

The execution of each detail prescribed in the sponsorship agreement is the implementation goal. Most sports administrators have developed highly successful planning and implementation strategies. Some of those used in the business world are also beneficial. Systems such as the Harvard project review, critical-path method (CPM), and project evaluation and review technique (PERT) provide a viable framework for sponsorship management.

The task of implementation does not fall only on the shoulders of the sport organization. A sponsor must clearly understand that purchasing a sponsorship is only part of its commitment. It must leverage its association across all of its marketing elements. A generally accepted ratio suggests that a sponsor must spend at least as much money promoting its association with the event (or sportsperson) as it paid for the rights. Many sponsors exceed the ratio and spend as much as five times their sponsorship fee supporting and promoting that sponsorship through consumer tie-ins, advertising, and public relations (Stotlar, 2001).

CONTROVERSIES

In a 1998 settlement with major tobacco companies, 46 states signed an agreement that restricted all tobacco sponsorship of sporting events by 2001. The accord specified that any sponsorship agreement in place prior to August 2, 1998, could be retained, but not renewed. The interpretation of the settlement "allows tobacco companies to tie into one series, event or team sanctioned by a single organization ("Landmark settlement," 1998, 1). Ultimately, sponsorship of NASCAR's Winston Cup series would not continue. The title sponsorship was purchased by cell phone giant Nextel for $750 million over a 10-year contract. Many sport properties continue to avoid tobacco sponsorships because of the controversy.

Another controversial issue in the sponsorship setting is **ambush marketing.** Ambush marketing has been defined as "a promotional strategy whereby a non-sponsor attempts to capitalize on the popularity/prestige of property by giving the false impression that it is a sponsor. [This tactic is] often employed by the competitors of a property's official sponsors" (IEG's *Complete Guide to Sponsorship,* 1995, 42). Several prominent examples of ambush marketing have developed within the sport industry.

During the 1994 Soccer World Cup, Nike cleverly distributed free hats during one of the final matches with Brazil. The hats were adorned with the Nike "swoosh" and the word "Brazil" in gold colors on a green background (Brazil's colors). Inside the stadium, Nike was assured a major "on-camera" presence even though Adidas was the official sponsor of the event.

To reduce ambush marketing during the Olympics, the IOC established a fund to publicize the names of ambush marketers in national news-papers. The advertising copy stated that "Deceptive advertising is not an Olympic sport," and "Every time a company runs an ad like this, our Olympic team loses" (Myerson, 1996, D1). This tactic had the desired effect, as very few cases of ambush (or parasite marketing as the IOC calls it) occurred. In addition, the IOC reported that the 2002 Winter Olympics were relatively free from ambush marketing activities (*Olympic Marketing Fact File,* 2002).

Controversy has also surrounded high schools that have engaged in the sponsorship frenzy. While many high schools have traditionally had soft drink sponsor score boards, the late 1990s brought into play the concept of schoolwide sponsorship wherein the school allowed sponsoring soft drink companies exclusive sales rights in exchange for sizable rights fees. Pepsi negotiated a deal with the Jefferson County school district in Colorado for signage and exclusive product sales at 59 schools and advertisements on 10 school buses. Each high school received $25,000, each junior high got $15,000, and each elementary school collected $3,000. However, in 2002 the school board of Los Angeles public schools voted to stop the sale of soft drinks on campus beginning in 2005.

Venue sponsorship and naming rights have also migrated to the high school level. A Spartensburg, North Carolina, school district sold naming rights to its football field for $100,000 and is seeking additional rights fees for all athletic and performing arts venues. Grapevine High School, in Texas, signed a 10-year agreement for between $3 and $4 million with Dr Pepper for roof-top signage because it is near a major airport (Popke, 2002).

> ### CONCEPT CHECK
>
> *Sport marketers should be aware that not all members of the community will embrace their involvement with all corporate sponsors. Many will see the association as counterproductive to the interests of sport.*

TRENDS

In Stotlar's 1999 research, sport executives and sponsors were surveyed about the future direction of the industry. The study asked respondents to indicate where sponsorship dollars would be directed over the next three years. Participants on the team/property side provided the following data:

- 18.3 percent believed that local levels of competition would attract more dollars.
- 24.2 percent felt that the regional competitions would be more successful.
- 57.6 percent reported that national-level sport competition would receive the majority of sponsorship dollars over the next three years.

Sponsors responded in very similar ways:

- 13 percent believed that local competitions would attract more dollars.
- 21.7 percent felt that the regional level would be more successful.
- 56.5 percent reported that national-level sport competition would receive the majority of sponsorship dollars over the next three years.

In addition, 8.6 percent of the corporate sponsors thought that international sponsorships would begin to attract dollars away from the North American market for multinational corporations (Stotlar, 1999, 89).

Extreme sports is certain to be a category that will receive increased attention in the near future. This will enable sponsors to reach the much-sought-after youth market.

Another significant trend is the advancement of "grassroots" (community-based) sponsorship. Greenwald and Fernandez-Balboa's 1998 research reported significant increases in the implementation of this strategy. They found that the factors similar to those cited for national-level sport sponsorship selection were identified for companies engaged in sponsoring grassroots sport. Most notably they discovered that increasing corporate exposure and consumer awareness were highly rated corporate objectives. Another advantage of grassroots sport sponsorship was that these situations provided an increased potential for product sampling and prototype testing. The authors noted that in grassroots sport sponsorship "corporations are increasingly pumping money into grassroots sports organizations, and in turn, grassroots sports organizations are better able to pro-

vide corporations with substantial returns on their investments (Greenwald and Fernandez-Balboa, 1998, p. 42).

Reebok and legendary basketball promoter Sonny Vaccaro joined forces to create a grassroots basketball event to influence the youth basketball market. According to Reebok's CEO, "Grassroots basketball is one of the most exciting and relevant elements of youth culture. With Sonny on our team we can develop this initiative to a level of significance that firmly positions Reebok for long term and sustainable growth in this critical area" ("Sonny Vaccaro," 2003). In the future, more companies will realize that speaking to consumers in a local environment is more persuasive than through nationwide involvement.

LITTLE THINGS MEAN A LOT

Attention to little details can have a major effect on one's success. In this section, a few experiences, both positive and negative, are offered for review. During one event, where one of the major sponsors was a brewing company, a reception for sponsors was scheduled in a hotel executive suite. The person who planned the reception thought all of the details for the reception had been covered. The invitations had been sent out, the room decorations were assembled, name tags had been made, and the bar and bartender had been arranged with the hotel. However, when the bar was set up by the hotel, the sponsoring brewing company's beer was not available; only their competitor's product had been stocked by the hotel. Although the sponsor understood the problem, event organizers were monumentally embarrassed.

When the managers of a series of surfing events were searching for sponsors, they kept their staff busy switching the Coke and Pepsi in the corporate board room's refrigerator during negotiations between their two most promising sponsor candidates. Although it may seem trivial, one doesn't want to be pushing hard to secure Coca-Cola as a million-dollar partner and pull a Pepsi out of the refrigerator!

In another case, the event organizers were working hard to get all of their sponsorable categories filled. They were extremely happy when they secured Budget as their car rental company. The problem was that General Motors had been the primary title sponsor for several months. As they soon found out, Budget's rental fleet consisted primarily of Fords.

Often the presentation of ideas is just as important as the concept itself. For the Pepsi Center in Denver, city officials and team owners used computer-generated graphics to show the actual stadium with sponsor signs in place. Although one may not be able to commission state-of-the-art computer graphics, sample program ads, banners, and gift items adorned with the sponsor candidate's logo can certainly be provided. This will not only show the sponsor what its money will buy, but show that you care about how the corporation is represented.

SUMMARY

- With industry leaders projecting a future growth rate in sports sponsorships of 7 percent per year, it is apparent that sport sponsorships will continue into the next century. It is essential for the sport manager to fully comprehend this marketing element.
- The relationship between a sport organization and event owners involved with sponsorship must include advantages to both parties. A well-developed sponsorship can provide market value and increased profits for corporations, scarce operating revenues for sport organizations and events, and a full spectrum of sports events for participants and spectators.
- Through a properly structured sponsorship agreement, one can ensure that benefits for both the sport organization and the sponsor(s) are achieved.
- With models derived from existing sponsorship proposals and agreements, one can develop the skills necessary to succeed in the exciting world of sport sponsorships.

 CRITICAL THINKING EXERCISES

1. As the coach of a college basketball team, you encounter a situation where your institution has signed an all-school agreement with Nike to supply shoes and uniforms for the team. Your star player tries to wear the Nikes, but complains that her feet hurt. The player insists on wearing Reeboks. How would you resolve this issue?

2. As the event manager of a rodeo in Colorado, you have secured Coors Brewing Company as title sponsor of your event. Everything seems to be going well—the banners are up, the beer for the concession stand has been ordered, and the local Coors distributor will be on hand to award trophies to the winners. However, opening day of the rodeo at your final staff meeting, you learn that your volunteer who coordinates event entertainment arranged for the Budweiser Clydesdales to perform between shows. The Coors people are furious. How would you handle the problem?

 CASE STUDY

As the organizer of an event, you entered into a television agreement with a national cable network to televise the finals of your national swimming championship to ensure that your sponsors would have a platform for their message. In the agreement, you guaranteed the television appearance of Olympic 100 m freestyle gold medalist Chris Nathan. In your negotiations with Chris, you agreed to pay an appearance fee and all expenses to the meet, and Chris signed the contract. However, when the event began, it was clear that Chris was out of shape and was not swimming well. Chris did not qualify for the finals in the 100 m freestyle or any other event. On the morning of the finals, a network executive came to you with questions about your contract guaranteeing the television appearance of Chris. The network is demanding that unless Chris appears in a race, no broadcast rights fees will be paid and the event will not be aired. The major sponsors begin calling because they have heard that the event may be canceled from television. In the sponsorship contract, you guaranteed that the event would be televised nationally and that the sponsors' venue signs would have on-camera air time. How would you work to resolve this situation?

REVIEW QUESTIONS AND ISSUES

1. What are the essential elements for a well-written sponsorship contract?
2. What issues would need to be addressed if you were offered a considerable amount of

sponsorship money by a local brewing company for your college?

3. Discuss the pros and cons of selecting an individual athlete as a representative for a company's products. In a group, select a product and athlete spokesperson.

SOLUTIONS TO CRITICAL THINKING EXERCISES

1. While there is no right or wrong answer, the students should cover several points. First they should consider reviewing the contract to determine if any provisions exist for solving the problem. In many of the contracts there is a provision that stipulates that the company will send a representative to customize shoes for any player who experiences difficulties with fit or comfort. Another solution could be to allow the player to wear the Reeboks, but cover or black out the logo. If the coaches think that the problem is not really an issue and choose to allow the player to wear the Reeboks without modification, the institution may risk losing the contract.

2. Perhaps the best solution would be to cancel the Budweiser performance. If they have already arrived and incurred travel expenses, your event should reimburse them and write it off as a loss. Another approach would be to visit with the Coors representatives and request suggestions from them to resolve the problem. One idea would be to make an announcement that the title sponsor, Coors, has graciously allowed their primary competitor, Budweiser, to perform for the enjoyment of the audience. Ultimately, as the event manager, you have the authority to decide what occurs in the arena.

FOSTERING YOUR WORKPLACE SKILLS

The United States Taekwondo Union (USTU) is a national governing body (NGB) for the sport of taekwondo. Taekwondo is an Olympic sport, but one in which the US has not won many medals. For most NBGs, sponsorship funding is critical for development and athlete training. For many years, the USTU has struggled to maximize sponsorship revenues. Using the World Wide Web or

any other sources of information, gather information to be included in a sponsorship proposal. Using the outline below, construct a sample sponsorship proposal. It should not be longer than 5 pages and should cover the points on the outline. You might need to think of creating new and exciting opportunities for the sponsorship menu beyond those that might exist.

Sponsorship proposal

Introduction—a description of USTU and their events and property (i.e., membership base, mission, history, and structure of the organization).

Benefits for the sponsor—matches between the corporate marketing strategies and your benefits (i.e., target market demographics, psychographics, image, awareness, sales increases).

Menu—a detailed list of the individual elements that could be presented to the sponsor (i.e., event signage, product donations, event ceremonies, newsletters).

Pricing—what is the value represented by the components of sponsorship. Try to avoid "Gold, Silver, Bronze" type packages because they are not tailored to the needs of a sponsor.

Summary—a brief overview of the rationale for the sponsor.

WEBSITES

www.sponsorship.com—The International Events Group provides the most accurate and timely information on the sponsorship industry from sports and entertainment to events and fairs. This site offers information, news, and current events. It also has a job bank where candidates and properties can exchange employment-related information.

www.olympic.org—This is the Website for the International Olympic Committee. It has news and information on Olympic-related matters in French and English. It also contains profiles on IOC sponsors and links visitors to Websites for upcoming Olympic Games.

REFERENCES

Abraham, M. M., and Lodish, L. M. (1990). Getting the most out of advertising and promotion. *Harvard Business Review* (May–June), 50–60.

Ambush marketing: Under control in Nagano. (1998, Summer). *Olympic Marketing Matters*, 9.

Asimakopoulos, M. K. (1993). Sport marketing and sponsoring: The experience of Greece. *Sport Marketing Quarterly* (September), 2(3), 44–48.

Bernstein, A. (1998b, June 22–28). High tech a [virtual] sign of the times. *SportBusiness Journal*, 24, 36.

Brooks, C. M. (1994). *Sports marketing.* Englewood Cliffs, NJ: Prentice Hall.

Conklin, A. (1999, July). Dollar signs. *Athletic Business*, 45–51.

Cordova, J. (2003). Executives outline sponsorship strategies for Coke and Miller. *Team Marketing Report*, 15(4), 8.

Ensor, R. J. (1987). The corporate view of sports sponsorships, *Athletic Business* (September), 40–43.

Gearson, R. F. (1994). What to expect from your ad agency. *Fitness Management* (January), 22–23.

Glase, T. (2003). Serena Williams voted the most marketable female athlete. *Sport Business Journal*, 6(22), 10.

Graham, P. J. (1993). Obstacles and opportunities for the marketing and sponsoring of sport in Russia. *Sport Marketing Quarterly*, 2(2), 9–11.

Greenwald, L., and Fernandez-Balboa, J. M. (1998). Trends in the sport marketing industry and in the demographics of the United States: Their effect on the strategic role of grassroots sport sponsorship in corporate America. *Sport Marketing Quarterly*, 7(4), 35–48.

IEG's Complete Guide to Sponsorship (1995). Chicago: International Events Group.

IEG Sponsorship Training Supplement: National Association of Sports Commissions. (1999, April 15). Chicago: International Events Group.

IEG (2001, October 15). IEG survey finds sponsor pool growing more diverse. *IEG Sponsorship Report*, 20(19), 1, 4–5.

IEG (2002a, December 23). 2003 spending to rise as sponsors ask for, receive more for their money. *IEG Sponsorship Report*, 21(24), 1, 4–5.

IEG (2002b, March 11). IEG/Performance Research survey reveals what matters to sponsors. *IEG Sponsorship Report*, 21(5), 1, 4–5.

International Events Group. (1993a). 1994 sponsorship spending will exceed $4 billion. *Sponsorship Report* (December 20), 1–2.

International Events Group. (1993b). Sponsorship report, assertions. *Sponsorship Report* (February 14), 45.

International Events Group. (1994). Crediting sponsors. *Sponsorship Report* (March 14), 4–5.

International Olympic Committee. (1993). Ambush marketing. Lausanne, Switzerland: International Olympic Committee.

Irwin, R. L. (1993). In search of sponsors. *Athletic management* (May), 11–16.

Irwin, R. L., and Asimakopoulos, M. (1992). An approach to the evaluation and selection of sport sponsorship proposals, *Sport Marketing Quarterly* (December), 43–51.

Irwin, R. L., and Stotlar, D. K. (1993). Operational protocol analysis of sport and collegiate licensing programs. *Sport Marketing Quarterly*, 2(5), 7–16.

http://www.joycejulius.com/Newsletters/a_second_look__sept_2003.htm. Retrieved 10/15/03.

McManus, J. (1989, February 13). Embarassment of riches. *Sports, Inc.*, p. 52.

Myerson, A. R. (1996, May 31). Olympic sponsors battling to defend turf. *New York Times*, D1, D17.

National Collegiate Athletic Association. (2003). *1982–01 Sports Sponsorship Participation Report.* Indianapolis, IN: National Collegiate Athletic Association.

Olympic Fact Book. (2002). Colorado Springs, CO: United States Olympic Committee.

Olympic Marketing Fact File. (2002). Lusanne: International Olympic Committee.

Performance Research (1991, May 14). *Economic slump.* Newport, RI: Performance Research.

Popke, M. (2002, October). Your name here. *Athletic Business*, 13–14.

Sandler, D. M., and Shani, D. (1993). Sponsorship and the Olympic games: The consumer perspective. *Sport Marketing Quarterly* (September), 2(3), 38–43.

Scott, D. (2002). "What drives NASCAR?" International sport and entertainment conference, University of South Carolina.

"Sonny Vaccaro Joins Reebok." Retrieved from www.sponsorship.com/new/content/4559 on October 9, 2003.

Spoelstra, J. (1997). *Ice to the Eskimos.* New York: Harper Business.

Stone, G., Joseph, M., and Jones, M. (2003). An exploratory study on the use of sports celebrities in advertising: A content analysis. *Sport Marketing Quarterly*, 12(2), 94–102.

Stotlar, D. K. (1999). Sponsorship in North America: A survey of sport executives. *International Journal of Sports Marketing and Sponsorship*, 1(1), 87–100.

Stotlar, D. (2001a). *Developing successful sport sponsorship plans.* Morgantown, WV: Fitness Information Technology.

Stotlar, D. (2001b). "Sponsorship and the Sydney Olympic Games." 2001 Conference of the North American Society for Sport Management, Virginia Beach, VA.

Wilkinson, D. G. (1986). *Sport marketing institute.* Willowdale, Ontario: Sport Marketing Institute.

Wilkinson, D. G. (1988). *Event management and marketing institute.* Willowdale, Ontario: Sport Marketing Institute.

Part V

Professional Relations

Discussion Topic

According to NCAA statistics, Division I revenue distributed to the major college basketball conferences exceeded $97 million in the 2002–2003 season. *Sports Illustrated* has reported that salaries of Division I college basketball coaches are now approaching the top salaries for CEOs, led by Tubby Smith's $20 million, eight-year deal at Kentucky. Yet, in accordance with NCAA rules, college athletes receive no compensation other than their scholarships.

Group Discussion Question: Is it fair that these athletes, many of whom will never even graduate from college or play professionally, aren't paid any more than their scholarships?

CHAPTER **16**

Group Decision Making and Problem Solving

Laurence Chalip—Revised by Judith A. Switzer

In this chapter, you will become familiar with the following terms:

Brainstorming	Divergent thinking	Nominal group technique
Convergent thinking	Facilitator	Plunging in
Delphi panel	Free rider problem	Social loafing
Delphi technique	Groupthink	Status influence
Dialectical decision making	Limited creative flexibility	

Learning Goals
By the end of this chapter, students should be able to:

- Explain why group decision making and problem solving are pivotal tasks for sport managers.
- Describe typical decisions that are made by collegiate athletic coaching staffs.
- Identify four benefits of utilizing groups in the problem-solving process.
- Identify four pitfalls that endanger the efficacy of group decisions. Provide examples.

THE SCOPE OF GROUP DECISION MAKING AND PROBLEM SOLVING

Whether managing a unit, a task force, or an entire organization, managers work with and through groups. During the course of a career, groups may help the manager to create plans, generate ideas, solve problems, make decisions, set agendas, establish policies, and govern. Consider the following examples.

Planning

Organizers of the Sydney Olympic Games in 2000 needed to develop plans to enhance the tourism that would be generated by the Games. The degree to which the Games would foster tourism into Australia and beyond Sydney would depend on what various tourism managers did to leverage the Olympic Games. In order to begin a coordinated planning process, consultants to the Tourism

Forecasting Council (of Australia) convened groups of tourism managers and policy makers from throughout Australia to discuss possible strategies and potential outcomes that might be associated with Olympic tourism. The ideas that were generated in these discussions were then fed back to the managers and policy makers for comment and further consideration. Finally, the comments of the group were used as a basis for planning the tourism development component of the 2000 Olympic Games. (The outcomes of this work are discussed in Tourism Forecasting Council, 1998.)

Generating ideas

Early in 1994, a company, Playmakers, was created to provide sport services to organizations in Maryland, Virginia, and Washington, D.C. Playmakers's services were based on ideas generated during day-long creative sessions several months before. At those sessions, four managers with experience in the sports industry met to discuss new services that might be well received by athletes, parents, coaches, and administrators. Problems with existing sports programs were discussed, and successful nonsport businesses were scrutinized for concepts that might be applicable to the sports industry. The resulting ideas for solving problems and borrowing concepts were then aggregated into a comprehensive service plan. That plan established the conceptual foundation for the new sports enterprise.

Problem solving

Problems crop up throughout the normal course of doing business. Solutions to these problems may require input from several departments or experts. For example, in the university's athletic department, concerns about athlete eligibility can precipitate meetings among representatives from the compliance, coaching, and academic support units. Similarly, problems that might accrue when moving a team franchise from one city to another might need to be identified and resolved through meetings of various front-office staff.

Decision making

Each year, athletes leaving college sport are drafted onto professional teams. The process requires that decisions be made about who should be drafted and in what order. Those decisions require input from scouts, coaches, and management. These are not individual decisions: they are group decisions (cf. Whittingham, 1992). Similarly, when designing or redesigning a sport facility, architects often like to meet with groups of future users in order to determine core needs and design criteria that must be taken into account in facility design.

Agenda setting

When the Clinton administration took office in 1993, it made health care reform a leading priority. Since the health benefits of regular exercise are well established, it concerned some sports leaders that sport was not incorporated into the Clinton health agenda. In response, the President's Council on Physical Fitness and Sports called a two-day "strategic planning forum" in November 1993. Experts from government, medicine, recreation, sport service organizations, and the sporting goods industry were brought together to discuss ways in which to add sport to the national health agenda.

Policy making

In 1974, President Ford created the President's Commission on Olympic Sports. That commission formulated the recommendations that served as the basis for the Amateur Sports Act. As part of the commission's work, it formed groups of experts, one for each Olympic sport. Each group met to discuss the needs for its sport and policies that might address those needs.

Governance

Many sports organizations are responsible to boards or committees elected from the membership or assigned to represent specific constituencies. Local recreation leagues, regional sports associations, and the United States Olympic Committee are all governed on the basis of decisions made by groups.

We see that *group decision making* and *problem solving* can become significant elements of the sports manager's work. A substantial body of research has been devoted to understanding the methods and pitfalls of group decision making (e.g., Davis, 1992; Goodwin and Wright, 1998, pp. 295–314; Hollenbeck et al., 1998). To be effective, the manager must address three issues (1) When should a group be used? (2) Who should be included? (3) What methods will optimize the group's efforts and provide appropriate decision support? Each of these tasks is discussed in the next section.

WHEN TO USE A GROUP

Groups can be advantageous when solving problems or making decisions (Kerr et al., 1996; Koopman and Pool, 1991). Consider the following four benefits:

1. More ideas are possible as increasing numbers of persons are included. For example, the four sport managers who met to plan Playmakers were able to identify more existing problems, more potential solutions, and more useful concepts than any one, two, or three of them could have generated alone.
2. More information is available. For example, at successive stages of developing the analysis of tourism strategies for the 2000 Olympic Games, the many tourism managers and policy makers were able to share their experiences, as well as results from consultations and marketing research already carried out. Consequently, a more complete analysis was obtained, and better planning was enabled.
3. Alternative perspectives become accessible. For example, coaches, compliance officers, and academic support personnel can each contribute different reflections about athlete eligibility and the resources available to address athletes' needs.
4. The fairness of a decision is judged, in part, by who had input. Thus the President's Commission on Olympic Sports in the United States and the Sport Development Inquiry Committee in New Zealand each sought legitimacy for their recommendations by obtaining testimony from representatives of as many sport organizations as could be invited to the many hearings that were held (Chalip, 1995, 1996).

However, these benefits are not without cost. It is more time-consuming to engage in group decisions than to simply make a decision independently. This is particularly true if the matter to be addressed is one over which there is likely to be some conflict (Janis and Mann, 1977). Yet conflict can be beneficial. Although conflict over sensitive decisions can challenge group cohesion, conflict can also aid decision making, by prompting the search for information and requiring consideration of alternative views (Dooley and Fryxell, 1999; Putnam, 1986).

These factors suggest the following three criteria for determining whether or not to seek group input into a decision: (1) How important is the quality of the decision? (2) How much do others have to accept or commit to the decision for it to be implemented? (3) How much time is reasonable to make the decision?

Logical analysis suggests that the manager has five alternatives (Vroom and Yetton, 1973): (1) Solve the problem independently, using information available at the time; (2) obtain information from others, but make the decision independently; (3) collect suggestions (as well as information) from others individually, then make the decision independently; (4) collect suggestions and information from others as a group, but make the decision independently; or (5) meet with the group to formulate alternatives, and make the final decision as a group.

Which of these five alternatives the manager should choose depends on the requisite quality, commitment, and time for decision. The first alternative should be chosen in cases when the decision is relatively trivial (i.e., the concern for quality is negligible), particularly if subordinates are likely to accept the decision. It is also chosen when urgency prohibits consultation with others. The second alternative is appropriate when decision quality is important, but subordinates are likely to accept the decision. As the need for information and subordinate support rises, the manager will move to the third and fourth alternatives. Finally, when decision quality is important and subordinate support is critical, alternative five is appropriate.

Figure 16-1 illustrates the relationship between situational factors and the choice of decision strategy.

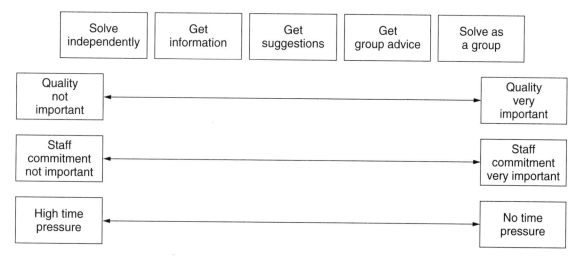

FIGURE 16-1 The relationship between situational factors and choice of decision strategy.

CONCEPT CHECK

The advantages of group problem solving and decision making include more available ideas, more available information, alternative perspectives, and enhanced fairness. Disadvantages of working with a group are time consumption and potential for conflict. However, conflict can also be beneficial if it furthers the group's exploration of ideas. Decision quality, support, and time constraints determine whether or not a manager should seek group input into a decision.

WHOM TO INCLUDE

Groups tend to be most effective when they include from 5 to 12 members (cf. Moore, 1987). The preceding discussion suggests two criteria for selecting group members: (1) persons who have requisite information, and (2) persons affected by the decision or who may have to cooperate in implementing the group's decision. Research into effective group decision making also suggests the value of including persons simply because they add diverse viewpoints, beliefs, or inclinations (Janis, 1982; Lamm, 1988). This can be particularly important if the decision is relatively risky.

Janis (1982) studied decision processes in four policy failures (the Bay of Pigs invasion, the invasion of North Korea, Pearl Harbor, and the Vietnam War) and two policy successes (the Cuban missile crisis and the Marshall Plan). He concludes that groups whose members readily agree make poorer policy choices than do groups whose members dispute options and values. The problem, he argues, is that groups prizing harmony will avoid contentious evaluation of policy alternatives. Consequently, the group will censor the input of information or values that are inconsistent with dominant preferences. Since this prevents the group from learning from its decision failures, it can cause the group to persist with policies even after they have become overtly detrimental. Janis calls these phenomena **groupthink.** He describes them this way:

The more amiability and esprit de corps among the members of a policy-making in-group, the greater is the danger that independent critical thinking will be replaced by groupthink, which is likely to result in irrational and dehumanizing actions directed against out-groups.

The groupthink formulation has generated substantial research. Findings from field studies and laboratory experiments are generally supportive (e.g., Choi and Kim, 1999; Mulcahy, 1995; Schafer and Crichlow, 1996).

TECHNIQUES FOR GROUP DECISION

Even if the manager is careful to minimize group vulnerability to groupthink, other pitfalls endanger the efficacy of group decision. Four of these are particularly important: *social loafing, status influence, limited creative flexibility,* and *plunging in*. A number of techniques for group decision making have been reported to aid groups in circumventing these pitfalls. To clarify the circumstances under which each technique becomes advantageous, it is first necessary to describe the four pitfalls.

Since the product of a group's activities is typically a joint product, the rewards to individual group members are rarely contingent on their individual performance in the group. If the decision or problem solution is truly a result of group interaction, it becomes impossible to specify accurately what percentage of the outcome is attributable to each member. In the best group decisions, the products of interaction among group members may be more significant than the discrete bits contributed by individual members. Consequently, it is rarely possible to apportion credit or benefits to each member in proportion to the member's unique contribution. This makes it possible for group members to reduce their individual efforts, allowing others to sustain the group's work. This problem of **social loafing,** sometimes called the **free rider problem,** can impede the group's performance (Hardin, 1982).

Social loafing is not the sole cause of differences in individual contributions to the group's activity. Higher-status individuals are likely to wield more influence than persons of lower status (Hollander, 1964). **Status influence** manifests itself both in terms of group process and the outcome of the group's work. Higher-status individuals are more likely to speak and be spoken to. Their input is likely to be deemed more credible. The group is most likely to choose an alternative preferred by high-status members.

The search for alternatives is itself guided by the *mental models* of group members (Cannon-Bowers et al., 1993; Carroll et al., 1998). Each member of the group understands the problem on which the group is working by constructing working models of it in their minds (Johnson-Laird, 1983). A substantial body of work has shown that members will make considerable use of *analogies* to construct their mental models. Collins and Gentner (1987) describe the phenomenon this way:

Analogies are powerful ways to understand how things work in a new domain. We think this is because they enable people to construct a structure mapping that carries across the way the components in a system interact. This allows people to create new mental models that they can run to generate predictions about what should happen in various situations in the real world.

There is, however, a limitation that can become particularly acute as the group works together. Research shows that people often fail to search through an adequate array of analogies when problem solving (Gick and Holyoak, 1980; 1983). This **limited creative flexibility** may be exacerbated in the group situation because the group will communicate most effectively if members share a common mental model (Cannon-Bowers et al., 1993; Carroll et al., 1998). The utility of a common mental model may cause the group to anchor on a single model or a limited subset of analogies. In so doing, the group loses a proportion of its creative flexibility.

Creative flexibility requires a balance of two kinds of thinking: **divergent thinking** and **convergent thinking.** These are separate processes. During divergent thinking, there is an active search for ideas. Ideas are generated, explored, expanded, and recombined. During convergent thinking, on the other hand, ideas are evaluated and compared. Whereas divergent thinking enlarges and elaborates the range of ideas, convergent thinking winnows ideas by evaluating, synthesizing, and selecting. Research on group problem solving shows that groups often **plunge in** to make a decision before they have adequately probed their problem or elaborated a sufficient array of alternatives (Scheidel and Crowell, 1979). In other words, groups too often begin convergent thinking without first having engaged in enough divergent thinking.

CONCEPT CHECK

Common pitfalls in group decision making include social loafing, status influence, limited creative flexibility, and plunging in. Creativity can be enhanced by first using divergent thinking to generate and expand ideas, and then using convergent thinking to synthesize ideas and select among alternatives.

An entire consulting industry has grown to "facilitate" group decisions using techniques originally designed to circumvent one or more of the pitfalls discussed so far. The consulting organization's preferred technique is typically marketed as a magic bullet, capable of enhancing any group process. It is usually offered as a fixed formula whose efficacy depends on precise adherence to sequential steps and specific rules (with which the consulting organization is fully familiar). Alas, no single technique or process is appropriate to all groups or decision situations. However, specialized techniques can prove useful if the manager applies each to circumvent the pitfall it is designed to circumvent. In fact, the methods can often be tailored to specific situations through combination or modification. This point is illustrated in the following description of five techniques for group decision making and problem solving: brainstorming, the nominal group technique, ideawriting, dialectical decision making, and the Delphi technique.

Brainstorming

The technique of **brainstorming** was originally developed by the advertising executive Alex Osborn (1948) as a means to elevate the flow of ideas during meetings. It has since enjoyed substantial popularity as a method for assembling a volume of ideas about management problems that can be readily expressed as simple, discussable questions. For example, during the planning phases of Playmakers, brainstorming was used to develop ideas in response to the question, "What activities could a sports camp offer as selling features to parents?" Brainstorming has also been used to collect ideas for questions like, "How can we promote more attendance for this event?" and "How can we reduce our dropout rate?"

The key principle of brainstorming is to separate the phase of divergent thinking from the phase of convergent thinking. The process begins with *idea generation* (i.e., divergent thinking), during which all judgment and criticism (i.e., convergent thinking) are disallowed. There are four rules during the idea generation phase:

1. Every idea is welcomed, no matter how wild or silly.
2. No criticism or judgment of any kind is permitted.
3. Produce as many ideas as possible; the goal is quantity, not quality.
4. Combine ideas or piggyback onto an idea wherever possible.

During a brainstorming session, bursts of ideas are often followed by quiet periods. When everyone becomes quiet, it is sometimes assumed that the group has listed its full complement of possibilities, and the idea generation phase is called to an end. However, quiet periods can precede a new flurry of ideas. For this reason, it is usually better to set time boundaries in advance, rather than simply to stop when there seems to be a lull.

The idea generation phase requires a leader who will enforce the rules and encourage participation. It also requires a recorder to keep track of the ideas. Neither the leader nor the recorder should participate in idea generation. However, the leader should be prepared to offer an idea to prompt further thinking if there is a substantial lull during the meeting. For the group to combine ideas, it is preferable to have the recorder write each idea where it can be seen, such as on a blackboard or flip chart.

Once the idea generation phase is completed, the group begins *idea evaluation.* Now judgment and critical appraisal are permitted. Ideas can be eliminated, modified, or further combined.

Group members sometimes become impatient with the rigid separation of divergent thinking from convergent thinking. However, research shows that the technique is effective. In particular, groups using brainstorming produce more ideas and more high-quality ideas than do individuals or groups that generate and evaluate ideas simultaneously (Nijstad et al., 1999; Stein, 1975).

Nominal group technique

The **nominal group technique** (Delbecq et al., 1975) provides a useful variation on brainstorming. It is particularly useful if the time available to meet is too short for a full brainstorming session. Since it begins the group's activities with a period of individual work, it can also reduce the impact of social loafing, status influence, and group polarization. For these reasons, the technique is often used as a lead-in to other decision methods, such as brainstorming (cf. Madsen and Finger, 1978).

As with brainstorming, the nominal group technique begins with a *stimulus question.* Like brainstorming, it also requires a leader and a recorder. There are typically four steps for generating a group decision:

1. Each group member silently writes as many responses to the stimulus question as possible. This period of written response could be at the beginning of the meeting, or group members could be required to come to the meeting with written responses already prepared. It is expected that group members will not have discussed their individual ideas in advance.
2. Each member contributes one idea. The idea is recorded onto a blackboard or flip chart. There is no discussion of ideas. Rather, the leader calls on each member in turn until all ideas are recorded or until the group determines that a sufficient number of ideas have been collected.
3. The group discusses each idea on the list. Each idea is discussed separately. Discussion of each idea continues until members are clear about its meaning.
4. The group ranks the ideas and discusses its rankings. A final choice may be made by majority vote.

Research confirms that in most circumstances the nominal group technique is superior to informal methods of group problem solving (Fox, 1987; Hornsby et al., 1994). It generates a larger number of high-quality ideas and a more even distribution of contributions from members. It is also rated favorably by most participants.

Ideawriting

Ideawriting (Thissen et al., 1980) reduces social loafing, status influence, and group polarization by extending independent work into the phase of idea analysis and evaluation. The procedures for ideawriting are relatively simple. Each participant responds to the stimulus question by writing his or her ideas on a pad. The pad is then placed in the middle of the group. Each person takes each other person's pad and writes a response, analysis, evaluation, and/or extension. The original writer then reads the responses. Finally ideas and principles are discussed and summarized.

Although ideawriting does not promote the breadth of creativity fostered by brainstorming, it enjoys the unique advantage that it can be used with very large groups. Moore (1987) describes an application of ideawriting with 700 participants at an international conference. The participants were divided into small groups of between four and five persons each. Each group worked to identify community needs, such as the need for new sports facilities. Once a list of ideas had been generated, and everyone in the group responded, the ideas were discussed and the five most promising were selected. Each group then reported its conclusion to the full assembly.

When several small groups present their conclusions, it is common for their reports to be collated and assigned to appropriate committees for further work. Although anecdotal reports (Moore, 1987; Thissen et al., 1980) suggest this procedure to be useful during planning and policy making, it has not been subjected to empirical evaluation.

Dialectical decision making

Some decisions have major consequences for the organization. For example, the decision may result in substantial expense, or it may precipitate an irreversible choice among strategic alternatives. In such cases, the evaluation of ideas may be very important. In particular, it might be of interest to determine whether a decision is consistent. In other words, do different groups reach similar conclusions? If they do not, it can be helpful to probe the assumptions from which differences emerge. The best choice may be easier to identify after scrutinizing the assumptions on which different options are based (Byrnes, 1998).

Dialectical decision making (Mitroff and Emshoff, 1979) is a useful technique in such cases because it requires group members to engage in multiple phases of convergent thinking. This has the added advantage that it can foster the synthesis of several different options. Further, since the full group is divided into smaller subgroups, dialectical decision making can also reduce groupthink and group polarization (Macy and Neal, 1995; Schweiger et al., 1986).

The key to dialectical decision making is to develop two or more separate analyses of the decision problem. Each analysis is developed by a group working independently of other groups. At this phase, there are two possibilities: Each group can be instructed to develop its analysis in terms of what it deems the best possible alternatives. On the other hand, if it is important to examine fully a preexisting set of alternatives, each group could be assigned one alternative with the instruction to prepare an analysis that best supports it.

Once each group completes its analysis, group members are recombined to discuss the different analyses and to formulate a new analysis that builds on those of the small groups. At this phase, there are three possibilities: (1) The entire group can be convened to discuss the separate group analyses. (2) One new group can be constructed by assigning a member from each of the original groups. The new group consists of persons who did not work together during the preceding phase. (3) Several new groups can be constructed, each containing one member from each of the original groups.

If more than one new group is constructed, a further round of recombinations is possible. In this case, the process of analyzing, recombining, and reanalyzing can be continued for as many iterations as desired. Through successive recombinations and reanalyses, new insights may emerge, or an apparent consensus may develop.

One way this could be applied would be setting up a "Devil's Advocate" situation in which separately operating groups or individuals would articulate all of the opposing points of view that could be used against their desired outcome. This would accomplish several things: It would make group members more aware of the opposition's points of view and enable them to anticipate those arguments so that they could be addressed and overcome. Also out of such dialectical decision making would come a more informed decision, thus enabling group members to be more sensitive to others' points of view. When decisions address the concerns of those inclined to disagree, the resistance of the opposition is lowered and less enmity is generated.

For example, when it was decided that a new stadium would be built for the Philadelphia Phillies baseball team, several options for the location were considered. One was a location in the center of the city near Chinatown. Many contentious meetings with the business owners and residents of the area were held. The residents prevailed in their objections to this option because the decision, in part, took into consideration the wishes of the community. The final decision eliminating that site was likely made using the dialectical method of decision making.

Delphi

There are times when the persons required for a decision task cannot meet together. On other occasions, status differences among participating experts threaten the group's impartiality. In such instances, the **Delphi technique** (Delbecq et al., 1975) can be useful. It is an excellent tool for pooling expert judgment.

The first step of a Delphi process is to establish the **Delphi panel** of experts. Delphi panelists will work anonymously; they are not told who the other panel members are. All correspondence from them goes to a **facilitator** who is not a member of the panel. Panelists remain at their home sites and communicate by mail or electronic mail. Although any number of panelists can be included, execution becomes increasingly labor intensive as panel size grows.

Once the panel is selected, each panelist is sent the Delphi question. Relevant data may also be included. Imagine, for example, that we want to determine experts' best judgment about new directions for sport policy. We might send our panel data on recent trends in sport participation, attendance at sports events, and audience ratings for sports on television. The accompanying Delphi question might ask, "What are the keys to enhancing public interest in sport over the next decade?"

Each panelist prepares a written response. The responses are collated and sent to panelists along with any supporting material (articles, statistics, etc.) that one or more individuals want to share. (When necessary, the Delphi facilitator will remove names from material being shared to maintain panelist anonymity.) Each panelist then responds to the new material. The panelist can agree, rebut, clarify, expand, or synthesize. The process of responding, collating, and responding again continues through successive rounds (usually around five) until a group consensus or a clear majority and minority viewpoint have emerged.

Unlike the other methods discussed here, Delphi can take several weeks or months to complete. Even the process of obtaining a panel can prove time-consuming. Nevertheless, the technique continues to be widely used for planning and policy making (Linstone and Turoff, 1975; Tourism Forecasting Council, 1998).

CONCEPT CHECK

Group decision techniques can be divided into those useful in the divergent thinking stage and those useful in the convergent thinking stage. Brainstorming and the nominal group technique are used to avoid pitfalls during the divergent thinking phase of a group's work. On the other hand, dialectical decision making focuses primarily on the convergence of ideas. Ideawriting and the Delphi technique bring their methods to bear during divergent and convergent thinking phases. Components of several techniques can be combined as necessary to circumvent decision pitfalls.

FACILITATING GROUP DECISION MAKING AND PROBLEM SOLVING

Formal techniques for decision making do not relieve the manager from the task of facilitating the group's efforts. The adequacy of any decision depends, in part, on the adequacy of the processes by which the group reached its decision (Kleindorfer et al., 1993). Managing a group during decision making and problem solving is a key leadership skill. The requisite components are well studied and readily learned (Maier, 1963; Schwarz, 1994). Three pivotal skills are sequencing the process, assuring balanced participation, and maintaining a task-oriented climate.

Sequencing the process

Inadequate attention to the sequential elements of team building and problem deliberation is one of the most common causes of poor group performance. Although the necessary procedures and outcomes may seem self-evident to the manager, group members may not share the manager's expectations.

At the outset, the group's goals, purposes, and timetable must be clarified. Group members may arrive at a meeting with varied or fuzzy understandings of what it is the group is going to do. Communication is enhanced and misunderstandings are reduced if fundamental elements of the group's work have been agreed upon. For example, what is the problem to be solved? What choices are to be made? How much time is available for the group's efforts? How will the group's analyses and decisions be reported? To whom? Will implementation of the group's decision be delegated, or will it be the group's responsibility?

Once the group has agreed on its goals, purposes, and timetables, it must establish its methods for operation. The rules for group interaction must be specified, and a basic agenda outlined. Decision rules (e.g., voting, consensus) should be agreed on. If it is likely that the group will need to gather information during its deliberations, an appropriate procedure should be developed. If a formal decision technique (brainstorming, synectics, idea writing, etc.) is to be used, its methods and procedures should be described.

The group is now ready to begin its deliberations. Each of the decision techniques reviewed in this chapter is designed to prevent the group from plunging into choosing an option. When no formal technique is applied, the manager must make certain that the group spends sufficient time exploring members' thoughts about the problem. The group should first be directed to collect requisite information and to share ideas and opinions. Since it is useful to have a variety of proposals and viewpoints on the table, the group should be discouraged from evaluating each alternative as it is presented. Rather, the manager should encourage the group to elaborate and clarify each idea, and to find potential syntheses.

Figure 16-2 illustrates an ideal sequence of tasks when making a group decision. As the discussion

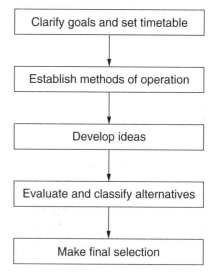

FIGURE 16-2   An ideal task sequence for group decision making.

progresses, more attention can be paid to evaluating and classifying the various proposals that have been formulated. At this stage, it may be useful to summarize the suggestions and concerns that have been forthcoming and to ask whether any additional matters require discussion. As the evaluation of ideas progresses, the manager can test group consensus by summarizing key points and asking whether these adequately reflect members' appraisal. The process is concluded when a consensus or a clear majority or minority viewpoint emerges.

Assuring balanced participation

The group's work can be compromised by social loafing or status influence. The group leader's task is to encourage the contribution and analysis of each member's best thinking. It is the leader's job to make certain that each member remains engaged and that each member's contribution receives adequate attention. To achieve those ends, it is useful to monitor who participates, how often, and with what impact. In this way, the leader seeks to identify persons whose ideas need to be queried or whose contributions require further examination. Four techniques are particularly useful for fostering balanced participation: *reinforcing, soliciting, prompting,* and *probing*.

The way in which points are received can affect members' subsequent willingness to contribute. Members are more willing to contribute when initial contributions have been welcomed. Body language (e.g., nodding, smiling) and verbal acknowledgment (e.g., "interesting point" or "that's something we should explore") encourage further participation. Writing the point on a blackboard or flip chart can also be reinforcing.

When members have not contributed for some time, the leader can reinvolve them by soliciting a contribution. The solicitations might be as simple as, "Fred, what do you think?" Or it might be useful to solicit a member's contribution in terms of the role he or she plays in the group. For example, the leader might ask, "Sally, how would that idea affect facility operations?"

If one or two members are dominating the discussion, the leader can prompt other views by saying something like, "So far we've spent a lot of time on Chris and Jim's suggestion, let's hear some other possibilities." If a member is preempting other discussion, the leader can point that fact out: "Bill,

you've made your point, now we'd like to hear some other views."

Probing can be useful when the group has ignored an idea or has neglected to explore one. If the group seems to be ignoring a contribution, the leader can say something like, "Joe's suggestion seems useful; let's explore it a bit more." If the group has failed to explore a previous idea, the leader can ask, "Jane, can you say a little more about that point you made a few minutes ago?" Sometimes a contribution is ignored because members failed to fully understand it. If that seems to be the case, the leader can ask, "Lee, could you elaborate more on that point?"

Maintaining a task-oriented climate

If group members have a stake in the outcome of the group's deliberations, the discussion can become emotional. High emotions can distract the group from a focus on its task. In other instances, the group may fail to address relevant hot topics to avoid conflict. In so doing, crucial components of the decision may be neglected. Sometimes a lack of conflict is more detrimental to the group's function than the conflict would be (Tjosvold, 1993; Dooley and Fryxell, 1999). The confrontation of divergent views can clarify requisite needs for information and foster an appreciation of alternative viewpoints.

It is useful for the group leader to state at the outset that diverse views will be important for the group's work. Later, if emotions begin to run high, tension can sometimes be diffused by orienting group members to their common goal. The leader can reaffirm the value of fully exploring diverse views. It may even be appropriate to compliment the group on its frank and open discussions and to restate the group's common goal. If the emotional tone is still high, it may be useful to put the controversial issue aside temporarily and to refocus the group's attention on other aspects of the problem until emotions have cooled.

On some occasions, it may be important to face emotions directly. If a dispute between members is taken personally, the residual resentment can interfere with subsequent deliberations. In such instances, it may be necessary to put the decision task aside, openly discuss the hurt feelings, and reestablish consensus on group goals and processes.

Social norms in most management contexts disallow expressions of anger. This in turn can cause the group to avoid potentially controversial elements of a decision. When group deliberations seem to be skirting a delicate issue, an effective instruction might be, "It would seem useful to expand our discussion to include [the delicate issue]." By using leadership authority to steer the group onto a touchy subject, the leader reduces group members' sense of risk. For one thing, members need not fear recrimination for having raised the matter (since they did not). For another, controversial discussion was mandated by the group leader, who thus bears primary responsibility. Peer relations seem less threatened than if the issue had been forced by a group member.

Concept Check

Managing group decision making and problem solving is a key leadership skill. A common source of poor group performance is inadequate sequencing of the decision process. Before beginning deliberations, the group should agree on its goals, purposes, timetables, and methods of operation. As the group works, the manager should ensure balanced participation by using such techniques as reinforcing, soliciting, prompting, and probing. Maintaining a task-oriented climate is vital, especially if the discussion has become emotional. The leader is responsible for seeing that controversial discussion and even conflict, when necessary, are not avoided.

SUMMARY

- In sport management, groups are involved in planning, generating ideas, problem solving, decision making, agenda setting, policy making, and governance.
- When compared with individual problem solvers, groups can generate more ideas, locate more information, identify more perspectives, and formulate a decision that seems fairer.
- When deciding whether to use a group for decision making, the manager should consider requisite decision quality, the amount of time available to make the decision, and

whether implementation of the decision will require subordinates to have helped formulate the decision.
- Persons who have requisite information or who must cooperate in decision implementation should be included on the decision team.
- Groupthink can be minimized by including outside experts, incorporating critical evaluators, or assigning someone the role of devil's advocate.
- The group's efforts can be compromised by social loafing, status influence, limited creative flexibility, and plunging in.
- Brainstorming is a useful technique for collecting a wide array of ideas. Brainstorming separates the phase of divergent thinking from the phase of convergent thinking. During the divergent thinking phase, members are encouraged to contribute as many ideas as they can.
- The nominal group technique also collects a wide array of ideas by separating the phase of divergent thinking from the phase of convergent thinking. Group members are required to begin by silently writing their ideas. The ideas are then discussed and evaluated.
- Ideawriting requires group members to write their idea, to read each other's ideas, and to respond in writing. It can be used with small or large groups.
- Dialectical decision making breaks the group into two or more smaller groups. The analysis and decision of each smaller group is then used as input to formulate a final decision.
- The Delphi technique obtains an estimate of expert consensus. Members of the Delphi panel work anonymously through several iterations of inquiry.
- The various decision techniques can be modified or combined as the situation warrants.
- The three pivotal skills for facilitating the group's work are sequencing the process, ensuring balanced participation, and maintaining a task-oriented climate.
- Appropriate decision sequencing consists of the following: (a) establishing goals,

purposes, and timetables; (b) presenting, elaborating, and clarifying ideas; and (c) classifying, summarizing, and evaluating.

- Methods for ensuring balanced participation include reinforcing, soliciting, prompting, and probing.
- To maintain a task-oriented climate, the group leader must see to it that the group does not skirt around important yet sensitive issues. When emotions run high, the leader must help the group to refocus on its common objectives.

 CRITICAL THINKING EXERCISE

1. You are the marketing manager of a professional baseball team that has moved to a new city. In order to develop the marketing plan to promote your team, you have brought your staff together for a planning session. What decision technique or sequence of techniques would you use?

 CASE STUDY

You have probably heard the old saying, "Two heads are better than one." This is particularly true in decisions made by groups. Group processes involving decision making often follow a pattern stemming from assumptions that may or may not be true. This is why the more input from the group members, the more likely it is that all perspectives on the issue have been considered before the decision is made.

In sports, decisions are often made by groups of varying sizes and functions. In professional sports, for example, decisions by management groups can determine the very existence of a team or the continuation or not of an athlete's or coach's career. Therefore, the choices must employ sound decision making and problem solving techniques.

Let's take the example of decision making in the battlefield conditions of a football game. Every play is strategized and considered from multiple perspectives, and most decisions are made not only by the head coach but also by the coordinating staff and key players. From moment to moment the situation changes; input must be processed and applied quickly.

Andy Reid, head coach of the Philadelphia Eagles, is the commander-in-chief, but he dare not ignore the advice of his valued quarterback and other members of the coaching staff and team. Their decisions use many of the critical-thinking and decision-making methods discussed in this chapter. When Andy Reid is talking behind his play card, he is not talking to himself; he is engaged in a group decision-making process. In sports, how decisions are made and by what methods has much to do with the success of the enterprise.

Watch a team sport on television or in person, and discuss the decision making you observed and any particular decision making or problem solving techniques that you think might have been employed.

 REVIEW QUESTIONS AND ISSUES

1. What are the relative pros and cons of group versus individual decision making and problem solving?
2. What criteria should be used to evaluate who should be included in the group?
3. List and describe six pitfalls to be wary of during group decision making and problem solving.
4. Explain the difference between divergent thinking and convergent thinking. Why is it useful for the former to precede the latter?
5. Briefly describe an appropriate task sequence for group decision making and problem solving.
6. Define the four techniques for ensuring balanced participation.
7. How should conflict be managed during group decision making and problem solving?
8. Give an example of a decision problem faced by sport managers that would benefit from technical decision support. What kinds of support would be most useful?
9. Write a stimulus question about a sport management problem. What kind of organization might seek to obtain an answer to such a question? If you were putting a group together to answer the question for such an organization, whom would you include? Why? What decision techniques would you apply? How? Why?

SOLUTION TO CRITICAL THINKING EXERCISE

1. The key techniques in this instance are those that foster divergent thinking. Therefore, brainstorming will probably be the key technique. It might be useful to use the nominal group technique as a means to minimize social loafing. If that were done, staff members would be asked to arrive at the meeting having done some initial work, or time would be allotted before the brainstorming begins for individuals to work independently. If the two techniques were combined, the sequence would be: nominal group technique followed by brainstorming. If the manager was concerned about the possible limitations that could be imposed by groupthink, then dialectical decision making might be a reasonable alternative to nominal group technique and brainstorming.

FOSTERING YOUR WORKPLACE SKILLS

1. You are an assistant athletic director who is traveling with the Collegiate Women's Basketball Team. One of the athletes discovers jewelry missing from her locker. What would be your role regarding the group decision-making process to resolve this situation?

WEBSITES

www.Olympic.org/IOC/e/facts/cities/candidate_city_intro_e .html—This site provides information about future host cities of the Olympic Games. It also provides detailed information about the processes and information required to bid to host an Olympic Games. It may be useful to consider the decisions that must be made in order to complete a bid. It may then be of interest to identify the stakeholders that would be implicated in each decision, and consider the decision techniques that might be applied to formulate each decision.

www.usbr.gov/Decision-Process/toolbox/pareitdo.htm— This site describes how to apply a decision process that uses polling and Pareto charts to reach a decision. It may be of some interest to consider the kinds of sport management problems to which this technique might be applied. It may also be useful to consider the pros and cons of this technique versus those discussed in this chapter.

REFERENCES

Cannon-Bowers, J. A., Salas, E., and Converse, S. (1993). Shared mental models in expert team decision making. In N. J. Castellan, Jr. (ed.), *Individual and group decision making: Current issues* (pp. 221–46). Hillsdale, NJ: Lawrence Erlbaum Associates.

Carroll, J. S., Sterman, J., and Marcus, A. A. (1998). Playing the maintenance game: How mental models drive organizational decisions. In J. J. Halpern and R. N. Stern (eds.), *Debating rationality: Nonrational aspects of organizational decision making* (pp. 99–121). Ithaca, NY: Cornell University Press.

Chalip, L. (1995). Policy analysis in sport management. *Journal of Sport Management*, 9, 1–13.

Chalip, L. (1996). Critical policy analysis: The illustrative case of New Zealand sport policy development. *Journal of Sport Management*, 10, 310–24.

Choi, J. N., and Kim, M. U. (1999). The organizational application of groupthink and its limitations in organizations. *Journal of Applied Psychology*, 84, 297–306.

Collins, A., and Gentner, D. (1987). How people construct mental models. In D. Holland and B. N. Quinn (eds.), *Cultural models in language and thought* (pp. 243–65). New York: Cambridge University Press.

Crawford, C. C. (1983). How you can gather and organise ideas quickly. *Chemical Engineering*, July 15, 87–90.

Davis, J. H. (1992). Some compelling intuitions about group consensus decisions, theoretical and empirical research, and interpersonal aggregation phenomena: Selected examples, 1950–1990. *Organizational Behavior and Human Decision Processes*, 52, 3–38.

Dawes, R. M. (1979). The robust beauty of improper linear models in decision making. *American Psychologist*, 34, 571–82.

Delbecq, A. L., Van de Ven, A. H., and Gustafson, D. H. (1975). *Group techniques for program planning: A guide to nominal group and Delphi processes*. Glenview, IL: Scott-Foresman.

Fox, W. M. (1987). *Effective group problem solving*. San Francisco: Jossey-Bass.

Gick, M. L., and Holyoak, K. J. (1980). Analogical problem solving. *Cognitive Psychology*, 12, 306–55.

Gick, M. L., and Holyoak, K. J. (1983). Schema induction and analogical transfer. *Cognitive Psychology*, 15, 1–38.

Hardin, R. (1982). *Collective action*. Baltimore: Johns Hopkins University Press.

Hollander, E. P. (1964). *Leaders, groups and influence*. New York: Oxford University Press.

Hornsby, J. S., Smith, B. N., and Gupta, J. N. D. (1994). The impact of decision-making methodology on job evaluation outcomes: A look at three consensus approaches. *Group & Organization Management*, 19, 112–28.

Janis, I. L. (1982). *Groupthink*. 2d ed. Boston: Houghton Mifflin.

Janis, I. L., and Mann, L. (1977). *Decision making: A psychological analysis of conflict, choice, and commitment*. New York: Free Press.

Johnson-Laird, P. (1983). *Mental models.* Cambridge, MA: Harvard University Press.

Kerr, N. L., MacCoun, R. J., and Kramer, G. P. (1996). Bias in judgment: Comparing individuals and groups. *Psychological Review, 103,* 687–719.

Koopman, P., and Pool, J. (1991). Organizational decision making: Models, contingencies, and strategies. In J. Rasmussen, B. Brehmner, and J. Leplat (eds.), *Distributed decision making: Cognitive models for cooperative work* (pp. 19–46). New York: Wiley.

Linstone, H. A., and Turoff, M. (eds.) (1975). *The Delphi method: Techniques and applications.* Reading, MA: Addison-Wesley.

Macy, G., and Neal, J. C. (1995). The impact of conflict-generating techniques on student reactions and decision quality. *Business Communication Quarterly, 58,* 39–45.

Madsen, D. B., and Finger, J. R. (1978). Comparison of written feedback procedure, group brainstorming, and individual brainstorming. *Journal of Applied Psychology, 63,* 120–23.

Maier, N. R. F. (1963). *Problem solving discussions and conferences: Leadership methods and skills.* New York: McGraw-Hill.

Mitroff, I. L., and Emshoff, J. R. (1979). On strategic assumption making: A dialectical approach to policy and planning. *Academy of Management Review, 4,* 1–12.

Moore, C. M. (1987). *Group techniques for idea building.* Newbury Park, CA: Sage.

Mulcahy, K. V. (1995). Rethinking groupthink: Walt Rostow and the national security advisory process in the Johnson administration. *Presidential Studies Quarterly, 25,* 237–50.

Nijstad, B. A., Stroebe, W., and Lodewijkz, H. F. M. (1999). Persistence of brainstorming groups: How do people know when to stop? *Journal of Experimental Social Psychology, 35,* 165–66.

Osborn, A. (1948). *Your creative power.* New York: Charles Scribner's Sons.

Putnam, L. L. (1986). Conflict in group decision-making. In R. Y. Hirokawa and M. S. Poole (eds.), *Communication and group decision-making* (pp. 175–96). Newbury Park, CA: Sage.

Schafer, M., and Crichlow, S. (1996). Antecedents of groupthink: A quantitative study. *Journal of Conflict Resolution, 40,* 415–34.

Scheidel, T. M., and Crowell, L. (1979). *Discussing and deciding.* New York: Macmillan.

Schwarz, R. M. (1994). *The skilled facilitator: Practical wisdom for developing effective groups.* San Francisco: Jossey-Bass.

Thissen, W. A. H., Sage, A. P., and Warfield, J. N. (1980). *A user's guide to public systems methodology.* Charlottesville, VA: School of Engineering and Applied Science.

Tjosvold, D. (1993). *Learning to manage conflict.* New York: Lexington Books.

Tourism Forecasting Council. (1998). *The Olympic effect: A report on the potential tourism impacts of the Sydney 2000 Games.* Canberra, Australia: Tourism Forecasting Council.

Vroom, V., and Yetton, P. (1973). *Leadership and decision making.* Pittsburgh: University of Pittsburgh Press.

CHAPTER 17

Human Resource Management in Sport

Frank Linnehan

In this chapter, you will become familiar with the following terms:

Affirmative action
Broadbanding
Compensation
Core competencies
Development
Downsizing
External competitiveness

Human resource development
Human resource planning
Internal consistency
Job posting system
Recruitment
Reliability
Selection

Strategic human resource
  management
Succession planning
Training
Validity

Learning Goals
By the end of this chapter, students should be able to:

• Identify the strategic role human resources plays in organizations today.

• Understand the importance of a firm's staffing (recruiting and selection) practices.

• Describe the difference between equal employment opportunity and affirmative action.

• Define two essential components of effective compensation strategies.

• Understand the importance of human resource development to the overall goals of an organization.

• Identify the relations between staffing, compensation, and human resource development strategy for today's professional sport teams.

Although what has been written about human resources' application to sport management is limited, the two disciplines have much in common. Human resource management (HRM) is the study of systems and activities in organizations that influence employee behavior. The human resources function in organizations can be thought of as a strategic, integrated collection of employee-centered activities and processes whose objective is to help the organization meet its short- and long-term goals. Typically, the human resource function includes such activities as staffing (recruiting and selecting personnel), rewards (i.e., compensation), and human resource development (HRD) (e.g., training and development, career development).

These activities are particularly relevant to sport and sport management. Administratively, coaches and their staffs are recruited and selected at every level, from high schools to the professional ranks. Not only must sport organizations be able to attract quality candidates and select the right person for the job, but the owners of the teams must know how to adequately reward their staff as well. From a team perspective, recruiting, selection, and personnel development are critical to the success of amateur and professional franchises, as well as the athletic departments at colleges and universities. These activities are also essential to the performance of companies in the health and recreational industries who must staff and manage their facilities.

This chapter will first present a strategic view of human resources. It will then discuss recent developments and the applicability of HR activities to sport management in three areas: staffing, compensation, and human resource development.

STRATEGIC HUMAN RESOURCES

In the past, human resources was considered to be a loose collection of employee-related activities whose purpose was to maintain or enhance the satisfaction of the company's employees. Often, personnel departments were the repositories of soon-to-be retired managers who had lost their value to the organization. Fortunately, this perspective of HR is no longer relevant today and has been replaced with the concept of **strategic human resources management.** Strategic human resources management takes a long-term view of the organization and its HR practices, recognizes that external conditions, such as competition and the labor market, will affect the firm, and tries to integrate HR activities with the firm's overall business strategy (Anthony et al., 1998).

HR professionals and researchers have advanced the notion that human resources can and must add value to an organization by becoming a strategic partner to management (Barney and Wright, 1998). As strategic partners, HR managers are not only involved in the development and execution of a firm's strategic plan, but also create an HR strategy that will help the organization meet its goals. This strategy is often developed through the process of **human resource planning,** which is a formal or informal process that forecasts the human resource needs of an organization and develops strategies to meet these needs. One objective of the planning process is to identify gaps between the current capabilities of the company and those needed to achieve the firm's objectives (Lam and Schaubroeck, 1998). These gaps are then used in the planning process to develop action plans to meet the firm's goals. This process helps a firm to build a competitive advantage in the marketplace through its human resources.

Why has the perspective of HR changed? To a great degree, it has been in response to increased competition in the marketplace. Much like an owner of a local sporting-goods store who now must compete against a national chain, all organizations are being challenged to find ways to distinguish themselves from their competitors. In order to do this, firms rely on the use of their distinctive resources, which are called **core competencies.** These distinctive resources or core competencies can be thought of as what organizations learn over time (Prahalad and Hamel, 1998). Increasingly, progressive human resource practices are being viewed as a way to either create or sustain a firm's core competencies, and they may even be considered a core competency of the firm itself (Cappelli and Crocker-Hefter, 1996).

In professional sports, for example, team performance is often crucial to the financial success of a franchise. Even the most loyal fans may lose interest in a team if it continues to post losing seasons. A subsequent decline in fan attendance will adversely impact the team's profitability. It could be argued that the truly successful franchises over the long term are those with the best front office or administrative staffs. These staffs are able to build unique, competitive advantages for the franchise through such HR-related practices as recruiting coaches and players, developing personnel, and structuring financial rewards that are competitive in the market, fiscally sound, and within league guidelines. These are the types of front office, human resource practices that can create a competitive advantage for successful sports franchises.

Focus on Research: Human Resource Strategy

Aligning human resources and strategy among NCAA basketball teams

Using team records and surveys from 143 Division I men's basketball team coaches, Wright et al. (1995) explored the effects on team performance of aligning human resource practices with the preferred strategy of the coach. They identified the coaches' preferred and actual strategies and classified them as strategies built on (1) speed, (2) power, or (3) finesse.

The researchers found that coaches who preferred a strategy based on speed rated the importance of a recruit's athletic ability and speed-quickness higher than the coaches who preferred the power or finesse strategies. Thus, the coaches' preferred strategy influenced the type of player that was recruited. Second, teams actually using the coaches' preferred strategy had better performance (as measured by a higher power rating) than teams that used a strategy inconsistent with the preferred strategy of the coach.

While recruiting and developing better players may improve a team's performance, can these and other HR practices actually help the performance of a business? In a study of over eight hundred firms, it was found that companies adopting high-performance HR practices had lower employee turnover, higher productivity, and higher profitability than companies that had not adopted these practices (Huselid, 1995). These HR practices included extensive employee training, the use of employee incentive plans, linking performance to future compensation, and the use of preemployment tests in making hiring decisions. What this study did not show is which of these practices were most effective or if certain practices were more effective for some companies than others. In addition, trying to replicate these findings has not been easy, and there is now some disagreement over the conclusion that implementing high-performance HR practices will lead to an improvement in organizational performance (Becker and Gerhart, 1996; Cappelli and Neumark, 1999; Way, 2002).

The idea that HR should be a strategic partner with business leads to the conclusion that the type of HR practices that will be most effective are those that are aligned with an organization's strategic plan. Conceptually, then, a close fit between a company's HR and business strategies should enhance a firm's overall performance. Evidence of this has been found and is the topic of the Focus on Research: Human Resource Strategy box.

From this strategic perspective of HR, we now turn our attention to a discussion of specific HR activities. We begin with the staffing process.

STAFFING

Perhaps the most common activities associated with human resources are those that pertain to the recruitment and selection of employees. Very simply, **recruitment** is the process firms use to attract a sufficient number of qualified candidates to fill their job openings, and **selection** is the process used to decide which candidates to hire. Similar to business and educational organizations, assessing the talents and skills of prospective players is often the most critical component of a team's success. Unlike in many business organizations, however, the team's ability to make these judgments is subject to immediate scrutiny by the public. The media coverage now given to the draft of college athletes, coupled with the subsequent performance of the players, make this a highly conspicuous activity in most sport organizations.

Recruitment strategies are developed through a continuous assessment of a firm's strategic goals and the human resource needs to meet these goals. Both internal and external factors will influence a company's recruitment strategy. Externally, one such factor is the supply and demand for labor. For example, when the demand for people with information technology skills far exceeded the supply, it led to a number of innovative recruitment strategies in the information technology industry. These included the use of smart agent software to actively search the World Wide Web for resumes of potential applicants (Greengard, 1998). These dynamics of the labor market, along with an increasingly competitive marketplace, have also caused many companies to look to nontraditional sources to fill their job openings. Today, more companies are making the decision not to recruit full-time workers and are using temporary employees to fill their needs. In fact, it is estimated that 20 percent of the new jobs that were created in the United States from 1991 to 1993 were filled by temporary workers (von Hippel et al., 1997).

When a company's recruitment strategy calls for hiring full-time workers, one of the first choices it must make is whether to look for applicants outside the firm or try to recruit from inside the company. This decision often depends on such factors as a company's level of commitment to the development of its employees, its business objectives, and the current capabilities of its workforce. If an organization is committed to developing its employees, it will first look internally for job candidates before searching outside the firm. One way to do this is through a formal **job posting system** that communicates present job opportunities to employees. These openings are posted, often using a company's intranet, and employees who are interested may then apply and compete for the positions.

While job posting systems may be used to fill lower-level positions, internal candidates for senior-level positions are often identified through **succession planning.** Succession planning is the process of identifying and developing employees for senior and executive-level positions. Colgate-Palmolive, for example, has created an extensive executive development program for employees with high potential (Conner and Smith, 1998). The program identifies employees early in their careers who Colgate-Palmolive believes have the ability to manage at an executive level. For development purposes, these employees are given assignments that have significant levels of managerial responsibility early in their careers. Colgate-Palmolive believes these experiences will prepare them for their future roles as executive leaders.

While employees are often used to fill job openings, not all positions can be filled from a company's current workforce. Accordingly, recruiting strategies will also identify external sources of job applicants as well. Traditionally, these sources have included advertisements in newspapers, on the radio, and in trade and professional publications; other external sources include employment agencies, executive search firms, colleges and universities, and, for many entry-level positions,

school-to-work programs at the high school or junior college level.

The Internet is now an established external recruitment source and promises to continue to grow in size and influence. The availability and accessibility of personal and job information online has helped to make the recruitment process of matching available candidates with job openings operate as a true, open marketplace (Cappelli, 2001; Greengard, 1998). Mega-Websites that post personal resumes and job openings, such as Monster.com (www.monster.com) and Career Builder (www.careerbuilder.com), are partly responsible for this phenomenon. It is estimated that Monster.com's 18,000 resumes and postings are equal to 13 percent of the entire U.S. labor force and, on a busy day, 4 million people access Monster's job board (Cappelli, 2001). In addition, there are now more than 5,000 smaller job boards that are used by both job seekers and employers. Of particular interest is Monster.com's subsidiary, MonsterTRAK.com (www.jobtrack.com), which is the largest online job-listing site for college students. In addition to these sources, many companies advertise openings on their own Website. Companies are now using their online resources to link their recruiting efforts to their product image and marketing campaigns (Cappelli, 2001).

The effectiveness of a recruitment strategy in attracting qualified applicants depends not only upon applicant sources, but also on other factors such as the organization's reputation, jobs, and the recruiters themselves (Turban et al., 1998). Recruiters will often influence the applicants' perceptions of the job and the company. In turn, these perceptions will influence the attractiveness of the company to the applicant (Turban et al., 1998).

Thus, a company must look at its recruitment process as a marketing effort, paying particular attention to the quality of the messages it sends applicants, as well as how, and by whom, its messages are sent. These messages act as signals to prospective employees that either attract applicants to the firm or motivate them to search for other opportunities (Rynes et al., 1991). When applicants are attracted to the company, the firm is then faced with the challenge of selecting the right candidates for their jobs.

Employee selection is one of the most challenging tasks faced by any organization. Selection is a complex process of assessing fit between the applicant and the organization. At the most fundamental level, companies must assess how well the applicants' skills, knowledge, and ability fit the requirements of the position. Professional teams, for example, will rely on scouting reports of college players to assess a player's skills and ability. However, selection is also based on an assessment of person-organization fit on levels other than skills and ability (Kristof, 1996). In choosing employees, companies will try to assess the fit between organizational values and culture and the applicant's personal values and work attitudes. Thus, scouting reports of a player's ability are not the only information used in making selection decisions. Prior to drafting a college player or signing a free agent, coaches and team officials will often meet with the athlete to assess such personal characteristics as character and work ethic. In addition to assessing the fit based on these personal characteristics, fit is also evaluated on more tangible issues such as the financial incentives the organization can offer, compared with the applicant's requirements.

A wide variety of selection techniques can be used to determine this fit between the organization's needs and the applicant. Interviews, background and reference checks, ability tests, and personality assessments are among the most common. In choosing which techniques to use, organizations must insure that these techniques are both valid and reliable. The concepts of *validity* and *reliability* of selection techniques are critical in the hiring process.

The **validity** of a selection technique is concerned with two issues, (1) what the test or procedure (such as an employment interview) is measuring and (2) how well it measures it (Cascio, 1998). For these reasons, validity can be thought of as a measure of the accuracy of the assessment tool.

While it is important that all selection tools have evidence of validity, it is equally important that there is evidence they are reliable as well. *Reliability* is concerned with the consistency of what is being measured. Formally, **reliability** is the absence of unsystematic errors of measurement (Cascio, 1998). If certain skills are measured at different times or by different people, there generally will be some differences between them. In order for an assessment to be reliable, however, any differences in measurement should be due to chance and not to an error in the measurement technique.

If a selection test is reliable, it means that test scores should be consistent between evaluators and consistent over time. If they are not, a pre-employment test or selection tool is unreliable and should not be used by a company to make its employment decisions.

CONCEPT CHECK

Selection techniques must show evidence of validity and reliability. Validity is concerned with the accuracy of a pre-employment selection tool, while reliability is concerned with the consistency of the technique.

Valid and reliable selection techniques not only help hiring managers identify the most qualified candidates for job openings, but they also help organizations minimize the legal risks associated with employee selection, specifically the risk of violating employment antidiscrimination law. To minimize these risks, an employer must demonstrate that its selection process is related to job performance, that is, the selection techniques it uses are both valid (accurate) and reliable (consistent) predictors of the candidate's future job performance.

U.S. public policy toward employment discrimination has been influenced by each branch of the federal government (executive, legislative, and judicial) (Konrad and Linnehan, 1999). All employers are required to comply with federal legislation, such as Title VII of the Civil Rights Act of 1964, which prohibits discrimination on the basis of race, color, or national origin. Although not the first or most recent antidiscrimination law, this act has had a far-reaching impact on U.S. employers, as it made employment discrimination against a member of a protected class of people illegal.

Antidiscrimination policy in the United States has not only been shaped by federal legislation, however. It has also been influenced to a great extent by the executive branch of government as well. A significant component of U.S. public policy toward employment discrimination is **affirmative action,** which was established through the issuance of a series of executive orders. Affirmative action has created a great degree of controversy and debate, and has also been the subject of a considerable amount of research (see for example,

Harrison, Kravitz, and Lev-Arev, 2001). Unfortunately, there is a great deal of misinformation and misconceptions about affirmative action plans and programs (Kravitz and Plantania, 1993).

Affirmative action (AA) is a program that is required of all federal contractors with 50 or more employees who have nonconstruction contracts of $50,000 or more with the U.S. government. Companies not conducting business with the federal government are not *required* to have affirmative action plans, but many do so on a voluntary basis. The program requires that an employer take a proactive approach to ensure that the demographic composition of its workforce is similar to the demographic composition of its local labor market or recruiting area. This necessitates collecting demographic data of the labor market and comparing it to the demographics of the organization's workforce. Affirmative action does not force employers to hire underqualified women or members of racial minority groups to fill employment quotas. If there are positions in which members of protected classes are underrepresented (when compared to their representation in the labor market), AA does require employers to take and document steps to find qualified members of the underrepresented group to be considered and hired for these positions.

Here is an example of how an affirmative action plan might influence a recruitment process. There is an opening for a defensive coordinator job on a Division I college football team. There are currently 10 assistant coaches on the team, one of whom is African American. According to NCAA statistics, 22.1 percent of all assistant football coaches at the Division I level in 2002 were African American (NCAA News release, 2003). Accordingly, African Americans are underrepresented (10 percent vs. 22.1 percent) on this team's coaching staff. As such, the university's affirmative action plan would have to show that the university took appropriate steps to find qualified African American candidates to fill this defensive coordinator opening.

While intended to redress past discrimination, affirmative action is not without its detractors. There is evidence that it may have unintended, negative consequences on those whom it intends to help, adversely impacting their self-esteem, self-confidence, and the perception of others about their qualifications (e.g., Heilman, Battle, Keller,

Implications of Recent Staffing Trends for Sport Management Students

Like most organizations today, sport-related industries are under significant financial pressure to reduce costs, which often translates into reduced employment opportunities. Athletic department budgets are under scrutiny by administrators who are sensitive to the public's concerns about tuition increases. Mega sporting-good outlets are squeezing many of the smaller retailers out of business. Actively recruiting through internal job posting systems, while providing promotional opportunities to current employees, severely limits the opportunities for students trying to enter the field. Given these trends, what can you do to find a career in sport management?

Perhaps the most important step is to obtain experience in the field while you are still a student. Internships (either paid or unpaid), co-op positions, and even work-study programs in athletic departments are excellent ways for you to obtain this experience, find out what these jobs and careers are really like, and make important contacts in the industry.

After graduation, the time it takes to find a job is often dependent upon the thoroughness of your job search. Begin your search early; don't wait until after graduation. Your search should tap into all recruitment sources used by organizations, such as advertisements in newspapers and professional journals, the Internet, corporate Websites, and search firms. One of the most important resources for you is a personal contact or personal networking list. Even today, with the Internet being such a large part of the recruitment and search process, many jobs are still found through word of mouth. Finding a job often depends on taking the initiative to make personal contacts. Your networking list can include professors at school who have contacts within the industry, colleagues with whom you worked, friends, relatives and even people who may have helped you in a project for one of your classes. Contact these individuals in your job search and use their knowledge to better understand the industry and their contacts to lead you to job opportunities that have yet to be advertised.

Focus on Research: Staffing

Manager/coach mid-season replacement and team performance

One of the most difficult decisions for the owner of a team is to replace a manager or coach. McTeer et al. (1995) studied the immediate and longer-term effects of a midseason manager/head coach change in four professional sports leagues: the NHL, the NBA, Major League Baseball, and the NFL. Across all four leagues, team performance improved for the remainder of the season. However, this improvement didn't last into the next season. In only one of the leagues (ice hockey) did team performance improve in the year following the change, compared to performance in the year prior to the change being made.

---

and Lee, 1998; Heilman, Block, and Lucas, 1992; Heilman, Block, and Stathatos, 1997). However, there is also evidence that firms using AA in recruitment attract a more diverse pool of applicants (Holzer and Newmark, 1999), and those that use AA in hiring select more women and minorities (Holzer and Newmark, 2000). Given its contradictory findings, research has not helped to ease the public controversy surrounding affirmative action, and AA's future in the United States as well as in other countries is still very much in doubt.

As we've seen, staffing strategies in organizations include decisions about employee selection and recruitment. However, staffing strategies also include a firm's decisions on the appropriate number of employees needed at any time. This assessment is done within the context of an organization's strategy, its competition and, perhaps most often, its profitability. Unfortunately, this assessment often leads firms to downsize their operations. **Downsizing** is a planned, systematic reduction in staff. Although earlier efforts at downsizing were simply intended to reduce the number of employees in an organization (and, along with that, its compensation and benefits expenses), many organizations now look to downsizing from a strategic perspective, to enable them to refocus on the areas of their competitive advantage (Bruton et al., 1996).

While these broad-based cuts in staff are endemic to many organizations today, other difficult staffing decisions must sometimes be made at the executive level. In professional sports, team owners and general managers are often faced with making the decision to change managers. The Focus on Research: Staffing box discusses the effects on a team's performance of managerial changes when they are made in the middle of a season.

Staffing processes, then, are one of the sets of HR activities that help a firm meet its strategic objectives. Another important set of these processes is related to the financial reward systems a firm develops. We now turn our attention to these reward systems.

COMPENSATION

In 1975 Steven Kerr, a professor of management and a consultant with General Electric Company, criticized the compensation schemes of many organizations for rewarding the wrong types of behavior. One of the examples he used to illustrate this was the sports contract that includes incentives that are based exclusively on individual accomplishments for players who participate in team sports. Unfortunately, many of Kerr's criticisms about company compensation systems are as relevant today as they were in 1975.

The heart of most companies' reward systems is **compensation,** which is any type of financial or tangible return given to an employee as a result of employment (Milkovich and Newman, 1996). In addition to base salary, compensation also includes rewards that vary with performance, such as commissions, incentives, or bonuses, as well as the cost of company benefits offered to employees. The allocation of these rewards and the productivity of the employees in exchange for them is of critical importance to a firm's profitability.

Among other factors, compensation strategies usually take both the external competitiveness and the internal consistency or equity of pay into consideration (Milkovich and Newman, 1996). **External competitiveness** is determined by comparing a firm's compensation with that paid by other companies. To make this evaluation, a firm will review compensation data from companies across many different markets. This means obtaining salary information not only from organizations that are in direct competition with the firm, but from other sources as well. For example, it may also be important to review salary data from a broad occupational area, or from companies who are in different industries but who recruit applicants from the same geographical area. Today, the dramatic increase in international sources for recruitment has significantly expanded the geographical recruiting areas of most companies (Laabs, 1998).

After competitive data are gathered, a firm must decide its strategy, that is, if it wants to lead, lag, or match the current market rates. This decision will have an impact on other HR outcomes such as employee turnover, applicant pool size and characteristics, acceptance rates, selection costs, and the attitudes of its current employees (Klaas and McClendon, 1996). Similar to other business organizations, a professional sports team's compensation strategy will be at least partially dependent upon its revenues. Revenues for professional teams are generated from attendance, broadcast rights, and licensing fees. Thus, the size of a team's market can be a strong determinant of its compensation strategy. Teams in smaller markets are often unable to compete for talent in the free agent market. It is clear that teams in major markets, such as the New York Yankees in professional baseball, have chosen a compensation strategy that leads the market. Putting aside the owner's personal financial status, this strategy can be sustained over the long term only if the market continues to support it.

Besides external competitiveness, another area compensation strategies must address is the **internal consistency** of salaries. Internal consistency is measured by the equity of salaries paid across similarly valued jobs within a firm. To achieve internal consistency, a firm will first assess the value or worth of all its positions and create a pay structure that insures that salaries are similar for jobs with equal value to the company. Determining the relative worth or value of a position is often done through a formal job evaluation system. While there are a number of ways to do this, jobs are most commonly evaluated by systems that assign points to indicate the value of each position to a company.

Salary structures are created using the results of the company's job evaluation system. Job levels are determined by placing similarly valued jobs (i.e., jobs whose points fall within a specific range) into salary grades. The midpoint of the salary range for each grade is set to the market rate and a minimum and maximum is established for each range. Typically, the difference between the minimum and maximum for a range may be 10 to 25 percent for lower-level jobs, but as high as 120 percent for upper-level jobs (Milkovich and Newman, 1996). This range spread for each salary grade allows the firm some flexibility in its individual pay decisions.

By using competitive market data (to set the midpoints of each range) and assessing the value of jobs with a point system, salary structures based on these systems try to develop compensation structures that are both externally competitive and internally consistent. Although still very widely used, these types of pay structures with their narrowly defined, multiple pay grades are rapidly losing favor (Risher, 1997). Intense competitive pressures, along with the constant change required to meet these pressures, have created a need for greater flexibility to be competitive in the market. Today, there is less emphasis on the goal of internal consistency and much greater use of group and individual incentive plans to more closely tie pay to individual performance (Risher, 1997).

One way firms have tried to be competitive is to allow managers more discretion in rewarding high performers. To do this, many organizations are implementing a salary structure that is based on **broadbanding.** Broadbanding is the consolidation of hierarchical, narrow pay grades into a very limited number of bands with much broader pay ranges. Pay surveys in both the United States and Great Britain have found that 19 to 20 percent of firms are using broadbanding now, and 27 to 30 percent are considering its implementation (Wagner and Jones, 1994).

The wide range spreads characteristic of broadbanding allow companies to be more competitive in the market, as managers are no longer constrained by narrow salary ranges. Placing jobs in only a few salary bands also allows managers greater flexibility to differentiate pay between employees in the same job, based on their performance and individual contributions. Additionally, broadbanding can also encourage lateral, developmental transfers across jobs that were previously in different salary grades (Brown, 1996). With the elimination of many management levels through downsizing and reengineering, the opportunity to move laterally within a company is particularly important.

CONCEPT ✓HECK

Broadbanding creates a salary structure that replaces multiple salary grades with a limited number of pay grades. The use of broader salary ranges gives managers more discretion in salary decisions and allows salaries to be more competitive with the market.

This emphasis on the external market and individual performance has also led to incentive pay becoming a larger component of an employee's total compensation. Although there are other factors that contribute to performance (Kohn, 1998), it has been argued that financial incentives are the single most influential factor (Jenkins et al., 1998). Typically, short-term financial incentive plans are based on goals established at the beginning of a plan year and tie the employee's pay to the achievement of these goals. Goals may be set at an individual, group, or team level, and even at the organizational level.

This emphasis on incentive-based pay, however, has contributed to considerable pay disparity between executive management levels and other employees. Despite the fact that the average executive pay of publicly held companies in the United States has decreased recently, this wide disparity still exists. According to the most recent data from *Business Week,* the highest paid executive in 2002 was Alfred Lerner. Lerner's total compensation was estimated to be $194.9 million; $9.0 million of this amount was paid in salary and bonuses, while the remaining consisted of earnings from incentives, such as exercising stock options, cashing in stock, and payments from long-term incentive plans (Lavelle, Jespersen, Ante, and Kerstetter, 2003).

Pay disparity exists in many of today's sports teams as well. Free agents are given enormous salaries, often creating significant disparity between the lowest- and highest-paid players on a team. Although the effects of pay disparity have not been studied extensively in business, they have been explored in professional baseball and are presented in the Focus on Research: Compensation box.

Compensation strategy, however, is not limited to organizational decisions regarding salary and bonuses; total compensation also includes the cost to the firm of employee benefits as well. Thus, the

---

Focus on Research: Compensation

Performance effects of pay dispersion on individuals and teams

Using data collected from professional baseball, Bloom (1999) looked at the effects on individual and team performance of wide variations in pay across team members. The difference between the lowest-paid person and the highest is a measure of pay dispersion in an organization. For organizations with hierarchical or high pay dispersion, there is a concentration of pay at the top levels. Compressed or low dispersion occurs when pay is more equally distributed and there isn't a large disparity between the highest and lowest pay levels.

Bloom examined the effects of pay dispersion on the performance of 1,644 professional baseball players and 29 teams during the years 1985 through 1993. He explored the effects of hierarchical pay dispersion on a player's offensive output and defensive performance, as well as on a team's winning percentage, fan attendance, and standing. He found that the greater the hierarchical pay dispersion, the lower the individual and team performance in every category except defensive performance. In explaining these results, he speculated that teams who actively participated in the free agent market and pay high salaries will increase pay dispersion, which may lower the performance of other players because of the feelings of inequity these high salaries create.

---

type and amount of benefits offered to employees are key components of a firm's overall compensation strategy. In the United States, federal law requires employers to offer such benefits as Social Security (the FICA deduction on a paycheck), Medicare, unemployment insurance, and workers' compensation to all employees. The cost of these legally required benefits is approximately 8 percent of total compensation (Bureau of Labor Statistics, 2003). To be competitive in the labor market, most employers also provide other benefits such as health, dental, and life insurance, retirement and savings plans, as well as short- and long-term disability insurance to their employees. The cost of these plans, however, continues to increase (health insurance alone now accounts for 7 percent of total compensation), and many employers today often share the expense of these plans with their employees.

Compensation systems, then, are important elements of a firm's human resource strategies. Ideally, these systems should promote and reinforce behavior that will lead to the accomplishment of an organization's objectives. Providing rewards for certain behavior on the job, however, will not be effective if employees don't possess the basic skills, knowledge, or ability to do their jobs. The third, and final, set of HR activities that will be discussed focuses on the development of a company's human resources.

HUMAN RESOURCE DEVELOPMENT

As organizations have been forced to change due to new technology, greater availability and access to information, and competitive global markets, scholars and organizational consultants are beginning to formulate different theories of the firm. One of these more recent theories views firms as learning organizations (Starkey, 1998) in which knowledge and the organization's ability to learn are seen as the firm's competitive advantages. While pure forms of learning organizations may not exist, these types of organizations share common characteristics, such as the belief that organizations and groups have the ability to learn, a commitment to continuous learning at every level, and the leadership and culture that support learning activities throughout the organization (Redding, 1997).

This view of the importance of knowledge and learning to a firm's success underscores the value of human resource development activities today. **Human resource development (HRD)** is the set of activities that promote learning and the acquisition of skills necessary to meet current and future job demands (Harris and DeSimone, 1994). HRD focuses on learning outcomes, specifically on the acquisition of knowledge, skills, and abilities (KSAs). It includes activities such as training and development as well as career development. While the definitions are often blurred, HRD professionals draw a distinction between training and development activities. **Training** is the process of trying to acquire KSAs for current or future jobs (i.e., the opportunity to learn), while **development** is the actual learning of KSAs (i.e., the results of learning) (Blanchard and Thacker, 1999).

Professional basketball offers a unique example of how decisions about an organization's HRD activities often need to be made in conjunction with recruitment and compensation strategies. In the NBA, first-round draft picks are given three-year contracts. When these contracts expire, the players become unrestricted free agents. This, along with the league's salary cap and the influx of players who enter the draft right out of high school, creates very challenging selection, compensation, and HRD decisions for NBA teams. Since most high school players (with the notable exception of LeBron James) need time to develop their skills before making substantial contributions to a team, drafting these younger players incurs investment costs associated with developing the team's human resources. Rather than incurring these costs, an alternative HR strategy is to choose not to draft high school players who will take time to develop, allowing other teams to incur the initial HRD investment costs and then attempting to sign these younger players after they become free agents and have developed their skills. As such, a team's selection and compensation decisions under the salary cap will heavily influence its HRD activities and costs.

Recognizing the importance of continuous learning, many companies have made substantial financial commitments to training and developing their employees. In its 2003 state of the industry report, the American Society for Training and Development reported that training expenditures and total hours of training in its benchmarking service organizations continue to grow. Expenses have now reached 2.2 percent of total payroll, and training hours per employee are now 28 per year (ASTD, 2003). Consistent with the growth in technology, the method by which firms deliver training is changing, as the total number of classroom hours have decreased, but the amount of training delivered via e-learning channels has significantly increased over the past few years.

How can e-training be used to better understand and perhaps improve performance in sports activities? The following Focus on Research: Hitting a Baseball describes a research project that explored the mechanics of hitting by using virtual simulation.

As knowledge is becoming obsolete faster today than ever before, many companies have established corporate universities to ensure that their employees have learning opportunities throughout

Focus on Research: Hitting a Baseball

Have you ever tried hitting a baseball or softball in a virtual batting cage at a video game arcade? Or perhaps you play video baseball games at home. Even for skilled baseball players, virtual hitting can be as frustrating as hitting a real baseball or softball. A recent study by Rob Gray (2002) of six college baseball players' experiences in a virtual batting task may shed some light on the reason why the virtual or real act of hitting a baseball is so difficult. Dr. Gray's experiments offers evidence that hitting success often depends as much, and sometimes more, on the batter's expectation of what the pitch will be (fastball, curve, etc.) based on the prior sequence of pitches, than the batter's visual perception of the pitch itself. However, his experiment also showed evidence that the prior sequence of pitches influence batting success in less experienced players more than experienced players who combine this knowledge with perceptual information (speed and location). So, as good hitting instructors know and teach, research has now shown evidence that success in hitting depends on both the cognitive functions of the batter (knowledge of the pitcher, expectations of the next pitch) and the split-second adjustments that a batter makes in timing and location of the swing based on the visual cues picked up after a pitch is released.

their careers. There are now more than 1,600 of these universities in operation (Meister, 1998) which provide not only specific job skill training but also training in such areas as leadership, communication, and problem-solving skills.

Training departments are increasingly being held accountable to measure their results. Kirkpatrick (1994) has identified four levels on which training evaluations can be conducted: (1) the immediate reactions of the participants, (2) an assessment of the learning that occurs, (3) measuring changes in behavior on the job, and (4) determining the results of the training. At the most basic level, participants' reactions are typically assessed by a questionnaire given at the end of the training. To assess whether any learning has taken place, tests may be adminis-

tered at the conclusion of the training, but these tests are not proof that the learning has been transferred to the job. The failure to transfer learning from the training environment to the job is a common problem of many corporate training programs (Rossett, 1997). The ultimate test of the training is not only its transfer to the work environment, but its result, that is, its impact on organizational performance. Unfortunately, despite the very limited correlation between trainees' reactions and the measurements on any of the other three levels (Alliger et al., 1997), many organizations continue to base their evaluation of training exclusively on the reactions of the participants alone.

Regardless of the extent to which they're used, formal training programs are not the only important HRD activities in organizations. HRD also includes activities focusing on career development. The traditional definition of a career was based on the premise of a long-term, relational contract between an employer and employee (Callanan and Greenhaus, 1999). This relationship was based on stability and mutual commitment, and career progress was defined as advancement through an organization's hierarchy. However, this type of psychological contract is no longer applicable, as such factors as shifts in employment opportunities, changing organizational structures and workforce characteristics have contributed to a dramatic shift in what is considered a career today (Greenhaus, Callanan, and Godshalk, 2000).

A career may be seen as a continual series of learning experiences over the course of one's life (Hall, 1996). Since these learning experiences will most likely not take place in a single organization, the responsibility for one's career has shifted away from the organization to the individual. Today, careers may more accurately be defined not by the progress one makes in a single organization, but by a feeling of psychological success, or the sense of accomplishment derived from achieving one's personal goals, whether these goals include professional achievement and/or personal happiness (Hall, 1996).

This need to achieve psychological success through one's career has a profound impact on the human resource practices of organizations that wish to motivate and retain their employees (Callanan and Greenhaus, 1999). Companies must strive to create environments in which continuous learning is encouraged and that offer the opportunity for self-assessment and evaluation. HR practices must help employees balance their work and family responsibilities and must be used to support the careers of their employees.

CONCEPT ✓ CHECK

The changing nature of the relationship between an employer and employee has had a significant impact on how careers are perceived. Although this new, shorter-term relationship has shifted the responsibility for career management to the individual, HRD activities in organizations are still used to facilitate personal growth, employee development, and career success.

While most HRD activities focus on the enhancement of individual knowledge and skills, there is also a need, at times, for entire organizations to change. These broader, organizational change efforts are often the result of an Organizational Development (OD) effort. OD specialists use an action research model to determine the need for and to implement organizationwide changes. This model includes diagnosing organizational issues, analyzing data to clearly identify organizational issues and problems, providing feedback of the data to help management understand the need for change, implementing the change, and reinforcing and evaluating its effects (Robbins, 2004). OD specialist often use training activities such as management development programs as part of their change efforts.

SUMMARY

- The human resource function is a collection of integrated, employee-centered activities whose objective is to help the organization meet its short- and long-term goals. Strategic human resource management takes a long-term, externally focused view of these HR activities.
- Employee recruitment strategies are influenced by factors external and internal to the company. Firms often recruit from their own employee base. A job posting system is used to fill lower-level jobs, while succession planning is used for upper-level positions.

- All employee selection techniques must show evidence of both reliability and validity.
- A compensation strategy is driven by the firm's desire for the external competitiveness of its salaries and the achievement of internal consistency between jobs within the company.
- To compete in the marketplace, many firms have switched from a narrowly defined salary grade system to broadbanding, which restricts the number of salary grades but uses wide salary ranges for each band. This structure offers greater discretionary judgment for managers.
- Incentive plans are becoming more prevalent in compensation, but they may contribute to pay disparity in many organizations.
- HRD activities promote learning and the acquisition of new skills. Training is the process of acquiring new KSAs, while development is the actual learning of these KSAs.
- A career is no longer based on a long-term, relational contract between an employee and employer.
- The new career concept of psychological success means that organizations must offer opportunities for continuous learning, self-assessment, and a balance between work and family.

 CRITICAL THINKING EXERCISES

1. As the owner and general manager of a new professional sports franchise, one of your most important decisions is the selection and hiring of the team's first coach. What issues should you consider before beginning the recruitment and selection processes?
2. You are the store manager of a family-owned retail sporting goods outlet. Last year, your store had very high turnover of its sales staff. You believe the main reason for this is that the national sporting goods chain that opened a store near you can pay higher salaries to their employees. What actions could you take to reduce this turnover?

CASE STUDY

Dr. Bill Watt was recently hired as the athletic director of a private university with a total student enrollment of 15,000. The athletic program has grown over the last five years and fields teams in men's and women's basketball and lacrosse, men's football and baseball, and women's softball and field hockey. The department currently employs thirty-six people, including administrative staff, faculty, coaches, and athletic trainers.

While he was being interviewed for the position, Dr. Watt learned that the men's and women's basketball teams are moving down from Division II to Division III next season. He also discovered that few of the employees in the department have been employed by the university for more than two years and that there are currently seven job openings that must be filled, one of which is the budget and finance manager of the department. The previous budget and finance manager was in the position only four months before leaving for another job.

The president of the university was very blunt with Bill during his job interview. She told him that morale in the athletic department was extremely low, and the previous AD was unsuccessful in his attempts to turn things around during his three-year tenure. She recommended that one of the first things Bill should do is to meet with the university's human resources director to discuss ways to address these issues. On this, his second day on the job, Dr. Watt is now preparing for this meeting.

REVIEW QUESTIONS AND ISSUES

1. List three external and three internal factors that influence employee recruitment strategies.
2. Define the term *psychological success* and explain how this can be achieved in today's corporate-driven society.
3. Identify the strategic role that human resources plays in organizations today.
4. Describe two essential components of effective compensation strategies.
5. What is the difference between *equal employment opportunity* and *affirmative action*?
6. How can an organization minimize the legal risks associated with employee selection?
7. Describe three benefits of using a broadband salary structure.

SOLUTIONS TO CRITICAL THINKING EXERCISES

1. Before choosing any HR activity, it is important to have a clear understanding of the business strategy of the organization. Is your plan for the team to be competitive right away? Or are you more interested in developing younger players, which will take the team more time to be competitive in the league? You must also consider your financial resources. Finally, you must consider the responsibilities of the job itself. Will the head coach have control over all player decisions or will someone else in the franchise have this responsibility? The answers to these questions will help decide the type of coach you want (someone who has been successful in developing young players, for example), the recruitment sources you choose (for example, coaches with or without professional experience), and the personal characteristics of the candidate.

2. First, you must find out why your employees are leaving. People leave jobs for many reasons, not just for higher salaries. One of the best ways to find this out is to conduct exit interviews with the employees who are leaving and ask why they have decided to leave. It may also be a good idea to find out the salaries being offered by the national chain. Think about the information you collect, why people work, and what they want from work. As a small store, what are your competitive advantages? Can you structure your jobs in such a way as to provide opportunities for your employees that the national chain is unable to do (flexible work hours, more responsibility in the store, or a chance to share in its profits)? Is it possible to create incentive plans for your employees that are based on individual or store performance?

FOSTERING YOUR WORKPLACE SKILLS

1. Gain relevant sports experience to enhance your resume. Check with your school's career center about internship or co-op opportunities with local sport teams or organizations.

Other employment opportunities you may look for include: working part-time in your school's athletic department, or in the sports department of a local newspaper, radio, or TV station. Other activities offer excellent relevant experience as well. For example, you could become the manager of the sports department at your school's radio station or newspaper. Write a regular sports column for the newspaper. Volunteer to participate in local youth sports associations as a coach, manager, referee, or umpire. Help start an intramural sport at your school.

2. Attend training to be certified in CPR. This is good to have on your resume and could become a lifesaving skill while participating in any athletic activity.

3. Begin developing your personal network list to use in your job search. In addition to your friends and relatives, stay in touch with colleagues from prior jobs and past coaches or gym teachers who may have contacts in the sports world.

 WEBSITES

www.shrm.org—This is the site for the Society of Human Resource Management. It is an excellent site for those interested in learning more about current trends in human resources.

www.astd.org—This is the site of the American Society for Training and Development. ASTD is the leading professional association and center of resources for workplace learning. ASTD currently has over 70,000 members.

www.monster.com—This is the largest job search site on the Internet. You can search for jobs and post your resume on the job board.

www.jobtrack.com—The largest job search site specifically designed for recent college grads.

www.salary.com—You may use this site to find competitive salary data, which is helpful information when negotiating starting salaries.

REFERENCES

Alliger, G. W., Tannenbaum, S. I., Bennett, W., Traver, H., and Shotland, A. (1997). A meta-analysis of the relations among training criteria. *Personnel Psychology*, 50, 341–358.

Anthony, W. P., Perrewe, P. L., and Kacmar, K. M. (1998). *Human resource management: A strategic approach.* 3d ed. Orlando, FL: Harcourt Brace & Company.

ASTD (2003). ASTD releases its 2003 state of the industry report. http://www1.astd.org/pressRoom/pdf/2003_SOIR %20press_rel.pdf.

Barney, J. B., and Wright, P. M. (1998). On becoming a strategic partner: The role of human resources in gaining competitive advantage. *Human Resource Management,* 37(1), 31–46.

Bassi, L. J., and Van Buren, M. E. (1999). The 1999 ASTD state of the industry report. *Training and Development,* 53(1), S3–S4.

Becker, B., and Gerhart, B. (1996). The impact of human resource management on organizational performance: Progress and prospects. *Academy of Management Journal,* 39: 779–801.

Blanchard, P. N., and Thacker, J. W. (1999). *Effective training systems, strategies and practices.* Englewood Cliffs, NJ: Prentice Hall.

Bloom, M. (1999). The performance effects of pay dispersion on individuals and organizations. *Academy of Management Journal,* 42(1), 25–40.

Brown, D. (1996). Broadbanding: A study of company practices in the United Kingdom. *Compensation and Benefits Review,* 28(6), 41–49.

Bruton, G. D., Keels, J. K., and Shook, C. L. (1996). Downsizing the firm: Answering strategic questions. *Academy of Management Executive,* 10(2), 38–45.

Bureau of Labor Statistics (2003). Employer cost for employee compensation—June 2003. Washington, DC: United States Department of Labor.

Callanan, G. A., and Greenhaus, J. H. (1999). Personal and career development. In A. I. Kraut and A. K. Korman (eds.), *Evolving practices in human resource management: Response to a changing world.* San Francisco: Jossey-Bass.

Cappelli, P. (2001). Making the most of on-line recruiting. *Harvard Business Review,* March, 139–146.

Cappelli, P., and Crocker-Hefter, A. (1996). Distinctive human resources are firms' core competencies. *Organizational Dynamics,* 24, 7–22.

Cappelli, P., and Neumark, D. (1999). Do "high performance" work practices improve establishment-level outcomes? Cambridge, MA: National Bureau of Economic Research (Working Paper No. 7374).

Cascio, W. (1998). *Applied psychology in human resource management.* 5th ed. Upper Saddle River, NJ: Simon & Schuster.

Conner, J., and Smith, C. A. (1998). Developing the next generation of leaders: A new strategy for leadership development at Colgate-Palmolive. In Edward M. Mone and Manuel London (eds.), *HR to the rescue: Case studies of HR solutions to business challenges.* Houston, TX: Gulf Publishing.

Frisby, W., and Kikulis, L. M. (1996). Human resource management in sport. In B. L. Parkhouse (ed.), *The management of sport: Its foundation and application.* 2d ed. New York: McGraw-Hill.

Gray, R. (2002). Behavior of college baseball players in a virtual batting task. *Journal of Experimental Psychology: Human Perception and Performance*, 28(5), 1131–1148.

Greengard, S. (1998). Putting online recruiting to work. *Workforce*, 77, 73–77.

Greenhaus, J. H., Callanan, G. A., and Godshalk, V. M. (2000). *Career management*. Fort Worth, TX: Dryden Press.

Hall, D. (1996). Proteam careers of the 21st Century. *Academy of Management Executive*, 10(4), 8–16.

Harris, D. M., and DeSimone, R. L. (1994). *Human resource development*. Orlando, FL: Dryden Press.

Harrison, D. A., Kravitz, D. A., and Lev-Arev, D. (2001, August). Attitudes toward affirmative action programs: A meta-analysis of 25 years of research on government-mandated approaches to reducing employment discrimination. Paper presented at the meeting of the Academy of Management, Washington, DC.

Heilman, M. E., Battle, W. S., Keller, C. E., and Lee, R. A. (1998). Type of AA policy: A determinant of reactions to sex-based preferential selection? *Journal of Applied Psychology*, 83, 190–205.

Heilman, M. E., Block, C. J., and Stathatos, P. (1997). The AA stigma of incompetence: Effects of performance information ambiguity. *Academy of Management Journal*, 40, 603–625.

Holzer, H., and Neumark, D. (1999). Are affirmative action hires less qualified? Evidence from employer-employee data on new hires. *Journal of Labor Economics*, 17, 534–569.

Holzer, H., and Neumark, D. (2000). What does affirmative action do? *Industrial and Labor Relations Review*, 53, 240–271.

Huselid, M. A. (1995). The impact of human resource management practices on turnover, productivity and corporate financial performance. *Academy of Management Journal*, 38(3), 635–672.

Jenkins, G. D., Gupta, N., Mitra, A., and Shaw, J. D. (1998). Are financial incentives related to performance? A meta-analytic review of empirical research. *Journal of Applied Psychology*, 83, 777–787.

Kerr, S. (1975). On the folly of rewarding A, while hoping for B. *Academy of Management Journal*, 18, 769–783.

Kirkpatrick, D. L. (1994). *Evaluating training programs*. San Francisco: Berrett-Koehler.

Klaas, B. S., and McClendon, J. A. (1996). To lead, lag, or match: Estimating the financial impact of pay level policies. *Personnel Psychology*, 49, 121–141.

Kohn, A. (1998). Challenging behaviorist dogma: Myths about money and motivation. *Compensation and Benefits Review*, March/April, 27, 33–37.

Konrad, A., and Linnehan, F. (1999). Affirmative Action: History, effects and attitudes. In G. Powell (ed.), *Handbook of Gender and Work* (pp. 429–453). Thousand Oaks, CA: Sage.

Kristof, A. (1996). Person-organization fit: An integrative review of its conceptualizations, measurement and implications. *Personnel Psychology*, 49(1), 1–48.

Laabs, J. (1998). Recruiting in the global village. *Workforce*, 77, 30–33.

Lam, S. S. K., and Schaubroeck, J. (1998). Integrating HR planning and organisational strategy. *Human Resource Management Journal*, 8(3), 5–19.

Lavelle, L., Jespersen, F. F., Ante, S., and Kerstetter, J. (2003, April 21). Executive pay: The days of fantasyland CEO pay package appear to be in the past. *Business Week*, 86.

McTeer, W., White, P. G., and Persad, S. (1995). Manager/coach mid-season replacement and team performance in professional team sport. *Journal of Sports Behavior*, 18(1), 58–68.

Meister, J. (1998). Ten steps to creating a corporate university. *Training and Development*, 52, 38–43.

Milkovich, G. T., and Newman, J. M. (1996). *Compensation*. New York: McGraw-Hill.

NCAA News Release (2003). http://www.ncaa.org/releases/divi/2002080201d1.htm.

Prahalad, C. K., and Hamel, G. (1998). The core competence of the corporation. In D. Ulrich (ed.), *Delivering results*. Boston: Harvard Business School.

Redding, J. (1997). Hardwiring the learning organization. *Training and Development*, 51(8), 61–66.

Risher, H. (1997). Emerging model for salary management. *Public Management*, 79, 10–14.

Robbins, S. (2004). *Organizational behavior*, 10th ed. Upper Saddle River, NJ: Prentice Hall.

Rossett, A. (1997). That was a great class, but. . . . *Training and Development*, 51, 18–24.

Rynes, S. L., Bretz, R. D., and Gerhart, B. (1991). The importance of recruitment in job choice: A different way of looking. *Personnel Psychology*, 44, 487–520.

Starkey, K. (1998). What can we learn from the learning organization? *Human Relations*, 51(4), 531–546.

Turban, D. B., Forret, M. L., and Hendrickson, C. L. (1998). Applicant attraction to firms: Influences of organization reputation, job and organizational attributes, and recruiter behaviors. *Journal of Vocational Behavior*, 52, 24–44.

von Hippel, C., Mangum, S. L., Greenberger, D. B., Heneman, R. L., and Skoglind, J. D. (1997). Temporary employment: Can organizations and employees both win? *Academy of Management Executive*, 11(1), 93–104.

Wagner, F. H., and Jones, M. B. (1994). Broadbanding in practice: Hard facts and real data. *Journal of Compensation and Benefits*, 10, 27–34.

Way, S. A. (2002). High performance work systems and intermediate indicators of firm performance within the U.S. small business sector. *Journal of Management*, 28(6): 765–785.

Who made the biggest bucks. *Wall Street Journal*, April 6, 2000.

Wright, P. M., Smart, D. L., and McMahan, G. C. (1995). Matches between human resources and strategy among NCAA basketball teams. *Academy of Management Journal*, 38(4), 1052–1074.

CHAPTER 18

Labor Relations in Professional Sports

Harmon Gallant
Revised by Lloyd Zane Remick, Esq.
and Bernard M. Resnick, Esq.

In this chapter, you will become familiar with the following terms:

Agency shop	Free agency	Players' associations
Cartel	Good faith collective bargaining	Reserve system
Collective bargaining	Grievance procedures	Revenue sharing
agreements	Lockout	Right of first refusal
Collusion	Merchandising	Salary cap
Commissioner	National Labor Relations Board	Scope of collective bargaining
Competitive balance	Negotiation impasse	Sports agents
Cross Promotions	Player strike	Standard player contract
Final offer salary arbitration		

Learning Goals
By the end of this chapter, students should be able to:

- Understand the economic structure of the major sports leagues and other sanctioning bodies.

- Comprehend the varying states of labor relations between management (owners, leagues, and coaches) and labor (athletes, referees, umpires, and judges).

- Identify the role of sports agents.

- Detail the overall relationship between management and labor by understanding the function of players' associations and sports agents within the collective bargaining system.

Despite a small controversy over accepting some free clothes while still in high school, teenage basketball phenom LeBron James was a millionaire before he ever tossed a ball toward the net in an official NBA game. James, like his NBA predecessors Kobe Bryant and Kevin Garnett, Olympic boxing gold medallists Oscar De La Hoya and Meldrick Taylor, and Olympic figure skating gold medallist Tara Lipinski, had the skills to compete at the highest level. The combination of early athletic development with these stars' corresponding mega salaries and endorsement contracts shows us the huge market value of professional athletes. The pressures of adult responsibilities and the temptations of the "fast life," however, often become too great for the young athlete whose physical maturity has outpaced his or her emotional maturity.

Each of the four major professional sports (football, ice hockey, baseball, and basketball) have well-organized **players' associations.** In ice hockey, for example, the NHLPA (National Hockey League Players' Association) represents the players as a labor union and also regulates the agents who represent the players. The origins of the Toronto, Canada–based NHLPA date back to 1967.

Similarly, basketball players are represented by the NBPA (National Basketball Players' Association), which is similarly situated to represent the players and to negotiate collective bargaining agreements on their behalf. These negotiations are complex procedures and require many individuals such as players, attorneys, financial experts, and elected negotiating leaders. After a new **collective bargaining agreement** is negotiated, it is the players who ultimately vote to accept or reject its terms. The NBPA also accredits player agents and monitors their activities as well as setting guidelines for their professional demeanor.

Collective bargaining

The law that governs workers involved in interstate commerce (which includes athletes in professional team sports) is the National Labor Relations Act of 1935, as amended. Section 7 of the NLRA provides for: (1) the right to self-organization, to form, join, or assist labor organizations; (2) the right to bargain collectively through representatives of their own choosing; and (3) the right to engage in "concerted activities" for employees' mutual aid or protection. This last element includes the right to strike and picket for legitimate ends. The law's provisions are administered by the National Labor Relations Board (NLRB) and enforced by the federal courts.

Unfair labor practices, by either management or labor, are prohibited by the NLRB. The Board also determines which issues are properly within the **scope of collective bargaining.** In professional sports, there are two areas that have been of special concern. One is the allegation that a team or employer has disciplined or discharged a player for participation in union activity. Another involves the allegation that an employer has refused to bargain in "good faith." In this context, the parties to negotiations are required to communicate through a series of back-and-forth proposals, while reasonably attempting to reach an agreement.

Individual teams negotiate collectively as a league for the purpose of reaching a contract with that sport's players' union. All active league players are bound by the actions of the bargaining unit, and nearly all players are union members. Since the clubs join together to bargain with the union, the negotiated agreement applies uniformly to each team. It is important to remember that, although certain issues are deemed *mandatory subjects* of collective bargaining by the NLRB in the four major sports leagues, the critical issue of individual player salaries has remained the province of individual club management. Salary caps have now been implemented pursuant to the collective agreements for basketball and football; as a result, individual salaries have come under the increasing scrutiny and intervention of league management. Other sports vary in their compensation schemes. Although prize money is very important, many professional golfers, track stars, tennis pros, "extreme" athletes, and race car drivers earn far more from product endorsement and appearance fees than what they receive in prize money. Athletes in sports such as volleyball are paid a uniform sum. Boxers are left to their own devices in their purse negotiations with the promoter to whom they are under contract. Many Olympic athletes are not paid at all.

Recently, the NBA has elected to extend the present collective bargaining agreement (CBA) through its 2004–2005 season. During the course of this time, representatives of the bargaining parties meet regularly to "iron out" a new long-term agreement. One of many issues that will be discussed is the minimum age for future NBA players. Many favor a minimum age of 20. Another stickier issue will be the length of "guaranteed" contracts (contracts where a sum of money is guaranteed to be paid regardless of whether or not the player continues to perform well, or at all), which are currently a maximum of seven years. The NBA wishes to shorten the time, which the NBPA will probably resist.

The third major players association is the MLBPA (Major League Baseball Players Association), which dates back to 1885. What remarkable changes since

Babe Ruth and Ty Cobb earned $8,000 per season to the players of today, who can earn the same amount per inning! Many players earn in excess of $10 million per season, and long-term guaranteed contracts have turned the tables to the players' advantage. In 2000, shortstop Alex Rodriguez stunned the baseball world when he signed with the Texas Rangers for an unprecedented 10-year, $252 million contract.

Today's highly compensated players owe a great debt to past heroes such as Curt Flood (who fought hard and gave much toward free agency, allowing a player to offer his or her services to more than one club) and Marvin Miller (who helped the players negotiate the first baseball CBA in 1968).

Fourth, the NFLPA (National Football League Players Association) is the officially recognized union for NFL players. The NFLPA, first established in 1956, represents players and negotiates on their behalf for the CBA. NFLBA negotiates issues such as insurance benefits and retirement and disability pay. Much thought and time goes into the regulation and monitoring of the players' contract advisors (agents). The NFLPA requires that new agents take a written examination, and all agents are required to attend annual seminars to keep current on the latest data and developments. The current fee for an agent, as set by the NFLPA, is a maximum of 3 percent of the value of the athlete's contract.

There are also other unions that represent other team sports, such as soccer, lacrosse, and others too numerous to mention. The overriding thought is that athletes are being protected more than ever. As of the time of this writing, the National Lacrosse League and players association have just agreed to extend their current collective bargaining agreement, averting a work stoppage until 2004.

College-level student-athletes also have very strict rules of adherence, as set forth under National Collegiate Athletics Association (NCAA) guidelines and policies.

Those wishing to enter the world of sports representation should be aware that in addition to the various unions representing player associations as a whole, players engage the services of personal contract negotiation representatives, called **sports agents.** To curb abuses and monitor agents, many states have enacted regulations and laws to govern the actions of sports agents. It is often necessary to register, post bond, and take exams in order to be licensed as an agent within multiple jurisdictions in order to open a sports agency. Many colleges also provide individualized rules and regulations issued to agents who wish to represent players as they turn professional.

ECONOMIC BACKGROUND

To understand labor relations in professional team sports, it is necessary to examine the economic structure of major sports leagues and the legal framework in which they operate.

Participation in and viewing sports as a spectator compete with film, theatre, music and other forms of entertainment for consumers' time and money. There are also the following elements to consider for each sport: the injury toll exacted on the players, how well the game is adapted to broadcasting (especially television), whether or not the sport is able to attract national interest, and whether merchandising and other "**cross promotions**" can add to profitability. As a result, the number of viable teams, and their total revenues, varies from one sport to another.

Considered as an industry, the sports industry in the past three decades has grown exponentially from small clusters of "cottage industries" to a multibillion-dollar, international business juggernaut. The teams have grown from small businesses with entrepreneurial ownerships (individual or partnerships) into corporate undertakings.

WHERE PROBLEMS OCCUR IN SPORTS LABOR RELATIONS

In the United States and Canada, there are four major sports leagues: the National Football League (NFL), the National Basketball Association (NBA), the National Hockey League (NHL), and Major League Baseball (MLB). There are also a myriad of other sports leagues and organizations, including but not limited to professional soccer (indoor and outdoor), so-called "extreme sports" such as street luge and snowboarding, various motor sports, such as NASCAR, and the WNBA (Women's National Basketball Association), minor league baseball and ice hockey, the arena league football, the Continental Basketball Association, women's beach volleyball, men's, women's and senior golf, tennis, and the "alphabet soup" of professional boxing and wrestling sanctioning bodies.

The basic working agreement between players and owners includes the collective bargaining agreement, the **standard player contract,** and league bylaws and rules. Team owners, general managers, and players, however, are not always familiar with their contents, and operating procedures often suffer as a result. Modern sports history contains many examples of owner-player conflicts resulting in litigation, when a careful consideration of the business relationship between owner and player might have avoided the need for court intervention. When agents and aggressive player unions are added to the equation, susceptibility to misunderstanding or simple miscalculation of interests during labor negotiations is greatly expanded. Some labor problems may be inherent in the basic structure of professional sports and prove less tractable. Within each sport, however, improvements in team and league administration should ameliorate many of the labor relations problems common in the professional sports environment (Staudohar, 1996). On the other hand, one can never underestimate the combination of risk of injury and greed, which continues to be the most divisive element in the labor relations equation.

CONCEPT CHECK

Because professional sports is a maturing industry, its principles of administration are still taking shape. Established industrial models are often inapplicable or improperly adapted to the operations of professional sports leagues.

COMPONENTS OF THE LABOR-MANAGEMENT RELATIONSHIP
Structure

Government. The principal issues in sports center on the distribution of money and power between players and owners. The government, through statutory enactments and court decisions, regulates the primary relationship, which is between management and labor. This relationship has been formalized under the NLRA-mandated system of union representation and collective bargaining and has in this way established the basic legal framework through which the sports industry is governed. The **National Labor Relations Board** and the federal courts have interpreted and applied laws pertaining

to collective bargaining, the right to strike and antitrust policy in a variety of industries.

Management. The league itself, and its individual clubs, including all nonplayer employees, make up the management component of the labor-management relationship. Players, their agents, and the players' association represent labor's side.

This alignment of interests remains relatively constant, although conflicts often arise within the ranks on each side.

Management operates through league offices, in conjunction with individual team ownerships. Questions of corporate planning and supervision are decided at this level. Leagues, operating through ownership committees, are responsible for the negotiation of collective bargaining agreements, national television contracts, setting procedures for player drafts, and rule-making to enforce various management prerogatives. Individual team owners have found it necessary to grant this authority to the league of which they are a part, but they retain power in several key areas. Team managements, we have seen, negotiate individual player contracts, but also establish rules for player movement between teams (subject to the collective bargaining agreement with the players' union), as well as hire their own front-office employees and coaches.

For example, occasionally individual club owners consider an action by the league contrary to their own interests. In the 1970s and early 1980s, Oakland Raiders owner Al Davis fought National Football League Commissioner Pete Rozelle and the other team owners over the right to relocate the franchise to Los Angeles. The right of an individual team owner to relocate a franchise over the objections of the league was an issue that affected the operation of the NFL far beyond this particular case. Since it affected the league's ability to govern its member clubs, the entire framework of labor relations within the league structure was also indirectly involved.

A similar case of conflict within management ranks occurred in baseball in 1992, when team owners decided to terminate the employment of Commissioner Fay Vincent and install Milwaukee Brewers owner Alan ("Bud") Selig as "acting Commissioner." Vincent was instrumental in ending the owners' 1990 **lockout** in spring training, and he was consequently perceived by the majority of owners as "pro labor" on the difficult labor relations issues then plaguing major league baseball. Public criticism of the Vincent firing extended to Congressional threats to repeal baseball's antitrust exemption unless a strong, independent commissioner was quickly appointed. The owners remained united in their determination to keep the commissioner's office out of their labor struggles. Their action, however, created a significant degree of player mistrust regarding their intentions in subsequent collective bargaining negotiations.

Labor. The labor component includes players, their agents, and the certified labor unions that represent the players in collective bargaining negotiations with management. Elements on the labor side of the equation sometimes come into conflict with each other, just as they do on the management side. The unions engage in five principal functions to further this objective: (1) organizing the membership to support union goals; (2) negotiating contract terms applicable to all players; (3) using pressure tactics, including strikes; (4) enforcing the terms of the collective bargaining agreement through grievance procedures under the NLRA; and (5) conducting meetings, voting on collective agreements and communicating with members, all of which provide internal union organization.

Labor has been subject to internal conflict. The dispute of the NFL players association over the national football league's collective bargaining agreement of 1993 is an example. Many players voiced resentment over the union's ratification process, complaining that they had inadequate time to consider all aspects of the complicated agreement, resulting in an uninformed and ill-advised player vote ratifying the agreement. Veterans and rookies within the NBA have faced off in acrimonious negotiations over the "rookie salary cap."

It is most common, however, for disputes to occur between elements on opposite sides of the labor-management equation. One source of conflict arises over the process by which sports agents negotiate contracts on behalf of individual players. Currently, league offices in football and basketball closely monitor individual player contracts, and nullify those deemed to violate the restrictions of current **salary cap** provisions.

A final concern involves the impact of external sources on the league's administration of operations, especially in labor relations. *Umpires* and *referees* are neither labor nor management elements according to our model, but they have become more active in union organization in recent years and they have a growing influence in their industries. *Television* and *radio broadcasts* have become absolutely vital to the revenue streams accruing to every professional sports team, and they have had a corresponding rise in influence over many administrative issues, including the time, locations, and even the way games are played and teams are operated. *Stadium* and *arena ownership* often involve municipalities, either in financing or operations or both, so that government becomes a crucial factor in a franchise's economic viability. Each of these external elements bears directly or indirectly on the relationship of labor and management in the classic model of the professional sports industries. One ignores a particular element at his peril (Berry, Gould, and Staudohar, 1986).

Commissioner. The **commissioner's** role, at least in theory, serves both management and labor. The league commissioner is held forth as a spokesperson on league matters and a guardian of the public interest on questions of the "integrity of the game." In reality, league commissioners are selected and paid by, and serve at the discretion of, management. In 1992 the owners of major league baseball dismissed Commissioner Fay Vincent and installed one of their members (Milwaukee Brewers owner Bud Selig) as "acting Commissioner." It was not until 1998, however, that Selig was given permanent status. Selig is part of the owners' Executive Council, and collective bargaining on behalf of management is handled through the council's Player Relations Committee. Critics have suggested that Vincent's intercession to end the 1990 lockout during spring training was responsible for his ouster as commissioner, illustrating the tenuous nature of the commissioner's role once labor disputes in a particular sport become heated or reach a **negotiation impasse.** Current threats from Congress to repeal baseball's antitrust exemption often emphasize the absence of an impartial commissioner, and this again points to the interconnected elements of the industrial model. The ultimate resolution of these issues is, at present, completely unsettled.

THE BASIC ELEMENTS OF MANAGEMENT AND LABOR

Leagues

Organized professional sports leagues in the United States began in 1876, when baseball's National League was formed. Friction between labor and management began soon thereafter. Individual clubs began by cooperating with each other regarding the market supply of producers and consumers. The producers were the players, who made the product by playing the games on the field, and the consumers were the fans, whose ticket purchases provided operating expenses and profits.

Each league allocates a territorial market to an individual member team, eliminating intraleague competition for the sports consumer within the territory. At the same time, the league expands to cover the major population centers throughout the country. In this way, a sports league becomes something of a *monopoly* and discourages the formation of rival leagues. The establishment of a viable team in a desirable market greatly decreases the chance a new league can be formed and succeed in that market. Nevertheless, the great expansion and shifts in American population centers in this century have given rise to a number of attempts to establish rival leagues. In basketball, football, and hockey, recent league mergers and expansions resulted from these attempts. In baseball, the American League in 1901 was the last successful attempt to challenge the monopoly enjoyed by an existing league.

To guarantee the league's overall health as an economic entity, each sport has a method of **revenue sharing.** Contracts with major commercial television networks are divided equally among the member teams in each league. With the great revenue increases in the past decade, the national television contracts have been the primary basis of team financial parity. Hockey has lagged behind the other three major team sports in the acquisition of network television contracts. It's quite difficult to follow the speedy movement of a small piece of vulcanized rubber, known as a "puck," across a television screen. Clubs contract individually for local broadcast revenue, and great discrepancies in these amounts (between so-called "big-market" and "small-market" teams) has been a divisive issue among team owners. Additionally, some leagues split gate receipts. The National Football League provides that 40 percent of regular-season and 50 percent of preseason gate revenues go to the visiting team. In baseball, the visiting team is given 20 percent, but in basketball and hockey there is no division of gate receipts between the home and visiting team, especially during playoffs.

A final allocation of league resources involves those necessary to make the product, which is the pool of player talent. A roughly equal division of these resources is necessary to ensure a competitive product from each team. It has been long established that a lack of **competitive balance** among the league's member teams will drive down fan interest and, ultimately, each team's revenues. Despite much ink being spilled over whether champion teams can "repeat" their glory so many times as to be considered a "dynasty," it's no fun being a fan of a team that has no realistic chance of ever winning a title. For this reason, a number of devices have been created, over time, to control the distribution of player talent to each team. Not every device is used simultaneously by each league, but they have included initial player allocations to new teams, drafts of available professional and amateur players, restrictions on player movement to new clubs, and compensation to old clubs for lost players.

Any restriction on player movement to new clubs has had the perhaps unintended effect of suppressing player salaries within a given league. Before the advent of the free-agency era in 1976, only the existence of rival leagues, aggressively competing for player services, effectively raised the level of player salaries within any professional sports league. Restrictions on mobility have been the primary concern of the players in modern labor negotiations. Players' unions consistently maintain that such restrictions illegally suppress player salaries by eliminating the market for their services (Staudohar, 1996).

CONCEPT CHECK

Sports leagues have the appearance of joint ventures between club owners, but they have in fact operated as **cartels.** *They have as a primary purpose to allocate and control the markets for production and distribution, and have therefore sought to eliminate, within the league, competition over producers (players) and consumers (fans). Imagine how you would feel if, after graduation, you only had one choice of where to reside and work in your chosen field.*

Member clubs

Individual clubs within a professional sports league are nominally independent legal entities, free to make or lose money depending upon how they operate their businesses. Each team, however, is signatory to a league agreement, which governs the team's actions as a member of the cartel. In this regard, each team is an equal partner with every other team in the league, subject to league rules and severe disciplinary action for any breach. Therefore each member club must be considered as *both* a private business entity and a franchise, operated in accordance with league-wide concerns.

In other industries, it is possible for one firm to withdraw to another market. A sports team, however, must have an opposing team to play against to create the game, which is its final product. A professional sports team must stay within its league to stay in business, unless a rival league exists or can be formed. Each league has rules providing for disciplinary action, including expulsion, against members.

Sanctions have been imposed against league clubs or their owners in a number of situations. For example, league rules were violated by owners trying to improperly lure a player away from another club, so that "tampering" penalties were invoked, on separate occasions, against Atlanta Braves owner Ted Turner, and Oakland A's owner Charles Finley. In 1994, NFL Commissioner Paul Tagliabue threatened to impose a $10,000 fine on any team owner who made public statements deemed unduly critical of the league's new collective bargaining agreement.

Traditionally, each club within a league endeavors to field the best team possible and thereby improve its economic performance. Some teams have sought to become more successful on the field through the acquisition of players in the free-agent player market, and this approach has driven up salaries in each sport. Clubs unable or unwilling to compete for these players will, in theory, direct their resources to develop players from their farm systems and future player rosters.

As the player's right to declare himself or herself a free agent has expanded, the pressures on each club to maintain performance levels by acquiring new players (usually other free-agent players) have also grown. But these pressures are balanced by certain economic realities. As a club approaches peak earnings, as determined by attendance, television revenues in its home market and merchandise revenues, there is a diminished incentive to spend money and improve the product. Spending more on player salaries would result in a reduction in short-term club profits, with no guarantee of improved on-field performance. Each league has a different proportion of owners who believe increased free-agent spending will translate into greater on-field success and consequently greater profitability. Each league has a different free-agent market as a result. Historically, owners have always claimed that an unrestrained free-agent market will destroy their league's viability in the long run (Berry and Wong, 1986).

Players

In each professional team sport, the players are the direct producers of the industry's product, the game; players *are* the product in the estimation of the public (the consumers). It is accurate to say the players are only a part of the game, but in many important respects, they are the most critical part.

With the advent of television, and the commercialization of the sports industries in the last quarter of the twentieth century, professional athletes have attained a cultural status at odds with their legal and economic status as mere employees. **Free agency** has given rise to a class of athletes properly considered independent contractors from a fan's viewpoint, and possibly in a strict legal sense as well.

From the players' perspective, since fans pay to see them perform, their compensation should be based on the revenues they generate. A player's career is also very short because of injury or the diminished performance of age, and this is another factor, in the players' view, entitling them to high salaries. Most players, therefore, are unified in their opposition to any club or league rules that suppress their salary levels. This is irrespective of any argument offered for their necessity, either the economic viability of certain teams or certain markets, fan loyalty, or competitive balance among clubs. As this chapter will explore more fully in considering the development of players' associations, these forces have had a powerful impact on the course of labor relations in modern professional sports (Berry, Gould, and Staudohar, 1986).

Agents and attorneys

With the advent of a free agency system in each of the major professional team sports, beginning with baseball in the mid-1970s, the marketing of players has been almost completely taken over by sports agents. A background in law or accounting is not required to become a sports agent. However, with the growing complexity and compensation of contracts, the players' need for the professional services of both attorneys and accountants has increased.

There are more sports agents than there are professional athletes. The frenzy over representation has caused a small but powerful breed of agents to surface, who will use whatever means necessary to obtain a percentage of their clients' earnings. Some agents have gone beyond their authority, defrauding professional athletes of portions of their hard-earned income, robbing collegiate student-athletes of their eligibility, and subjecting educational institutions to severe sanctions. This has caused an increase in the regulations governing agents. The NFLPA and the NCAA are leading the way in these regulations.

Under the NFLPA collective bargaining agreement, agents are regulated in numerous ways. The agent registration process requires that all agents must pass an entrance exam, disclose their professional and criminal histories, pay an annual registration fee of $1,200, and are limited to a 3 percent commission on their clients' contracts.

The NCAA has encouraged similar regulations. Under NCAA bylaws, a student-athlete or potential student-athlete becomes ineligible for intercollegiate competition when he or she accepts transportation, benefits, or anything of value from an agent, or

agrees to an agency contract. When these bylaws are violated, athletes lose their eligibility. Universities are sanctioned if they allow ineligible athletes to participate in intercollegiate competition. Such sanctions include a liability to return revenues for participation in postseason events, the loss of scholarships, and in the extreme, the "death sentence" (termination of the particular sport from the institution's athletic program).

Previously enacted state legislation over sports agents has proven to be less than effective. State laws varied tremendously, and some states did not even require registration. Thus, dubious agents often went unidentified, which in turn inhibited the states' ability to penalize such agents. This lack of effective legislation led the NCAA to ask the National Conference of Commissioners on Uniform State Laws (NCCUSL) to draft a uniform act for states to adopt. In the fall of 2000, the Conference introduced the Uniform Athlete Agents Act (UAAA). As of October 16, 2003, twenty-six states and territories have adopted the UAAA.

Under UAAA guidelines, agents must be registered with the state prior to contacting a student-athlete. However, if the student-athlete initiates the contact, the agent may negotiate with the athlete, providing he or she registers with the state within seven days. Furthermore, agents are required to disclose information regarding their professional and criminal history, and the secretary of state has the authority to issue subpoenas to obtain relevant information for compliance. Additionally, the UAAA prohibits agents from funneling benefits to student-athletes, all agency contracts must include a specific ineligibility warning to the student-athlete, and the student-athlete has the right to cancel the contract within fourteen days. Finally, the UAAA enforces its requirements through criminal and administrative penalties at the state level and gives institutions the right to seek civil remedies against agents or former student-athletes. The UAAA does not have uniform registration fees. Among the twenty-six states that have adopted UAAA legislation, the annual fees range between $100 and $500.

The influence of competent, ethical sports agents has been a positive one, resulting in higher salaries for their clients and the protection of the players' considerable financial resources. Problems and abuses in the player-agent relationship often result from a lack of professional requirements to enter the field. There currently exists a patchwork of individual state licensing provisions regulating sports agents.

If an agent acts in an unethical manner, the result may be any of the following: misappropriation of client funds, recommendation of investments that violate federal securities laws, overcharging of fees for contract negotiation (usually by charging an up-front percentage of an amount the player may never realize), renegotiation of a player's contract without prior authority, or negotiations contrary to a verbal agreement with the client. Agent abuses can be as varied as the imagination of the agent. College athletics, especially football, have had numerous problems in recent years as a result of the involvement of agents. Funds have often been furnished by agents to college athletes during their eligibility to play, in contravention of NCAA rules. Agents have been known to sign college athletes to contracts of representation before the end of their senior-year playing season, also a violation of NCAA rules. Another common prohibited practice is for an agent to loan money to a promising, but still eligible, college player in order to later represent him in professional contract negotiations. This is an incomplete list of the many devices sports agents have used to circumvent established rules and ethical practice. The player-agent relationship is an area where regulation by government licensing procedures, or self-governance by agents themselves, seems desirable. The role of the sports agent is substantial and can no longer be ignored by management. It affects the entire structure of professional team sports, and especially the structure of labor relations.

Players' associations

The historical development of the major professional sports leagues has resulted in a two-tier system. Through the collective bargaining process, the players' associations have each established a minimum player salary in their respective leagues. Players have also collectively negotiated several other financial considerations, notably pension payments and rookie salary structures. Individual players, on their own behalf or through agents, negotiate their own contracts. Salary, contract length, guaranteed payments, and bonuses are currently the province of individual negotiations between player and club (Staudohar, 1996).

To fully understand the development of players' associations, and the collective agreements they

have negotiated with ownership, we need to examine the reasons why professional athletes have considered it necessary to organize.

By 1966 it was evident that major league baseball's plan for player representation (in its decision-making executive council) did not adequately protect player interests. It was also clear that union membership had provided significant benefits for workers in diverse segments of American industry. Since player concerns over the **reserve system,** pensions, **grievance procedures,** and minimum salaries had gone unresolved for many years, the benefits of unionization became obvious. The prevailing attitude of players in all major sports was that ownership might not engage in **good faith collective bargaining** unless required to by law; it was, in fact, the establishment of player unions that created the mandate for collective bargaining. This process then transformed the employment relationship in professional team sports.

For many years, there was an active debate over whether player groups were really unions, capable of recognition under the NLRA. Even with official recognition, player unions have had a contentious relationship with management in the collective bargaining process. As a result, the recent history of each major professional sport has seen the players resort to three basic strategies to strengthen their position in the collective bargaining process: (1) antitrust litigation, (2) player strikes, and (3) arbitration of grievances. Antitrust litigation, which forms an essential part of the fabric of labor relations in sports, is considered elsewhere in the text (Jennings, 1990).

CONCEPT CHECK

In each of the four major professional sports, players' associations are now fully recognized as labor unions. As such, they are protected under the provisions of the National Labor Relations Act of 1935. Umpires and referees in these sports have, for the most part, organized in a similar manner. Players have gained greater economic power and freedom with respect to owners, largely through the efforts of player unions and sports agents. Management, labor, the commissioner, and agents all interact to create a model of labor relations built on collective bargaining procedures. Government regulations oversee the entire process, which is quite contentious.

CONTENTS OF THE COLLECTIVE BARGAINING AGREEMENT

Typical, but not exclusive, matters contained in collective agreements between the players' union and the league include:

1. *Contract length*, which, in general, has decreased over the past two decades.
2. *Compensation*, including wages, pensions, and fringe benefits. Unions in sports normally negotiate only minimum wage standards.
3. *Utilization of labor*, such as work practices, overtime and health and safety concerns. It is here that rules on player *free agency* are made part of the collective agreement.
4. *Individual job rights*, including seniority and discipline. Violence, gambling, and drug abuse by players are regulated in these provisions.
5. *Rights of the parties in the bargaining process*. The players' union is usually accorded status as an **agency shop,** so that players electing not to join can be assessed a "service fee" by the union (usually the equivalent of dues).

CONCEPT CHECK

The NLRA defines the scope of bargaining to include questions of wages (pay, benefits, and bonuses), hours, and working conditions. These areas are deemed "mandatory" subjects of collective bargaining, requiring good faith negotiating between employers and workers. The collective agreements in professional sports vary for each league.

BASEBALL AS A MODEL OF SPORTS LABOR RELATIONS

As America's oldest professional sport, baseball has provided a model of labor relations upon which the other major sports have been patterned. The modern players' union in baseball is the Major League Baseball Players Association (MLBPA). Formed in 1954, the union's early activities were primarily concerned with player pension and insurance issues. In 1966 Marvin Miller was hired as executive director of the MLBPA. Reflecting his background as a labor negotiator in the steel industry, Miller quickly transformed the MLBPA into an effective trade union. In 1968 he negotiated the first collective

bargaining agreement between players and owners, resulting in higher minimum salaries, pension increases, and disability and health insurance benefits. To secure a good faith collective bargaining relationship between the parties, the agreement provided for a grievance procedure for the resolution of disputes.

Before 1968, players were permitted to file grievances, but their final disposition was reserved to the commissioner of baseball. The new agreement instituted a system of impartial grievance arbitration, with participants chosen by both sides. In this manner, baseball became the first professional team sport with genuine collective bargaining procedures (Staudohar, 1996).

BASEBALL'S LABOR RELATIONS IN THE COLLECTIVE BARGAINING ERA

The MLBPA's apparent goal during Miller's stewardship was the modification or outright elimination of baseball's *reserve system*. The reserve system was named after the provision in baseball's standard player contract known as the *reserve clause*. The reserve clause stated that if a player failed to sign a contract for the following season, his club could unilaterally renew the contract for one additional season under the identical salary and conditions. During the history of the sport of baseball, the reserve system has proven to be the crux of over a century of near continued labor unrest. Together with the color barrier first broken by the heroic Jackie Robinson in 1947, the reserve system provided a consistent product year after year while denying players many of the basic labor rights that were taken for granted by their fans. A second collective bargaining agreement was ratified in May 1970 for a period of three years. The players, however, went on strike for thirteen days at the start of the 1972 season. The issue was the amount owners would contribute toward player pensions. Since the strike forced the cancellation of eighty-six league games, payment for games missed as a result of the strike was another point of contention. A compromise was reached in the February 1973 collective bargaining agreement, with the owners giving in on pension demands and the players agreeing to forfeit salaries for games not played during the strike. The new agreement broke important new ground, since it provided for **final offer salary arbitration** in cases where negotiations between owners and qualified individual players had reached an impasse. Under this new system, the club submitted the highest figure it was willing to pay, and the player submitted the lowest figure he was willing to accept, with an arbitrator choosing one figure or the other as a binding determination of the player's salary for the following season. The long-established practice of players negotiating salaries individually, with only minimum salary levels collectively bargained by the union, did not change.

Arbitration: The end of the reserve clause in baseball

Unilateral decisions by management on baseball's fundamental labor questions often result in harmful work stoppages. It was through the collective bargaining process that baseball's reservation system was finally toppled. In the 1973 agreement, the individual clubs and the players' union agreed to the use of a grievance-arbitration procedure, with a neutral third-party arbitrator presiding.

Jim "Catfish" Hunter brought a grievance against his Oakland A's club in 1974. Hunter claimed that the team's failure to purchase an annuity under the terms of his player contract was a breach allowing him to become a free agent, eligible to negotiate with any other club. The case went to arbitrator Peter Seitz, who ruled the A's owed Hunter the amount of the annuity plus interest and that Hunter was a free agent. The courts upheld the arbitration ruling, and Hunter signed a five-year, $3.75 million contract with the New York Yankees. This was the highest salary in baseball history at the time, and it emboldened players to test the reserve clause under the grievance-arbitration procedure.

In 1975 Andy Messersmith of the Los Angeles Dodgers and Dave McNally of the Montreal Expos played without renewing the signed contracts under which they had played the previous season. At the end of the season, each declared himself a free agent eligible to negotiate and sign with any other team in baseball. The players argued, in effect, that the reserve clause in their 1974 contracts only bound them for one additional year, while the owners maintained the reserve clause was perpetual.

In October 1975 the MLBPA filed a grievance on behalf of Messersmith and McNally, asking an arbitrator to declare both players free agents. The arbitrator, again Peter Seitz, sided with the players.

Seitz's final ruling declared that in the absence of an existing contractual relationship between team and player, the reserve clause had no effect. A signed contract allowed the team to exercise one option of the reserve clause per player for a period of one year. McNally and Messersmith were declared free agents who now could negotiate with any team in either league without restriction. The arbitration ruling was upheld on appeal in federal court, and the modern era of free agency in professional sports (and corresponding increases in player salaries) was born.

Baseball: Two decades of unrest

Once the existing reserve system had fallen, players and owners still had to negotiate a new reserve system that would fairly balance the needs of both parties. Nearly 30 years later, the issues remain.

In 1972 the players had struck briefly at the start of the season over a pension dispute, and eighty-six games were lost. In 1976, spring training was shut down for seventeen days because of a collective bargaining dispute over the free agency question. A similar lockout occurred during 1990 spring training. Before 1994, however, the only major disruption to a championship baseball season was the 1981 players' strike.

Baseball's owners and players reached an impasse on the free agency compensation question in 1981. When the owners announced they would unilaterally impose a compensation plan in the absence of an agreement with the players, the union set a strike date of May 29. The union then filed an unfair labor practice charge with the NLRB, claiming the owners had refused to bargain in good faith when they denied the union's request for financial data. The union delayed the strike for two weeks while the NLRB sought an injunction in federal court. An injunction would have prevented the owners from implementing the compensation plan and would have delayed the strike for another year. The court refused to intervene, and the players went on strike on June 12, 1981.

Once collective bargaining negotiations reach an impasse and breakdown, the ultimate weapon of the union is the **player strike.** Each of the major sports has a multiple-employer bargaining structure, so when the players strike, every team is shut down. Corollary businesses, such as network and local television companies and stadium concession stands, are adversely affected. Hotels, restaurants, bars, and airlines also lose revenue when games are cancelled due to a work stoppage. Baseball has endured five such stoppages since 1972, but none as catastrophic as the 1994 strike, described below.

Collusion

In 1985 the free-agent market collapsed when no contract offers for new free agents were forthcoming. The owners were eventually found by the courts to have engaged in **collusion,** agreeing among themselves not to bid for free agents and guaranteeing that no offers were made. The courts found that since an existing market had already been established, the owners had acted wrongfully. A $280 million damage award ($10 million per team assessed against all twenty-eight teams in Major League Baseball at the time) was split up among those players who had found no market for their services as free agents in the years 1985 to 1987. In essence, the court found that the owners had conspired to sacrifice winning for money in a secret, illegal attempt to artificially limit player salaries.

The 1994 impasse

By 1993, with the expiration of the current collective bargaining agreement, player salaries under free agency had increased to the point where the average player's salary was $1.2 million per season. Owners claimed that the continuation of several franchises in the game's current economic condition required revenue sharing between so-called "large-market" and "small-market" teams. The owners tied the plan to the acceptance of a salary cap by the players' union in a new collective agreement. The owners maintained they had to control player salaries to ensure the survival of the game. The players refused to accept a cap system, and when the owners threatened to unilaterally impose a salary cap at the end of the 1994 season, negotiations for a new agreement reached another impasse. On August 12, 1994, the players went on strike rather than complete the season and allow the owners to impose the new system. On September 14, 1994, the owners canceled the remainder of the season. Despite the owners' resolve to "explore all avenues to achieve a meaningful, structural reform of baseball's player compensation system," the collective bargaining mechanism had broken down, and the sport and business of major league baseball ground to a halt. For the first time in ninety years,

American baseball fans went from summer to fall without the World Series.

Months of unproductive negotiations ensued, and in late February 1995 labor negotiations between major league baseball's players and owners broke down.

On December 22, 1994, the owners announced they would unilaterally implement a salary cap provision after declaring an impasse in collective bargaining negotiations. The players had long maintained such an action was in violation of federal labor law, and in late January the general counsel of the National Labor Relations Board advised club owners he was about to file a complaint with the NLRB.

The owners took several contradictory steps in early February 1995. As matters deteriorated in early February, the two sides seemed more intransigent and irreconcilable than ever. The owners maintained that without a salary cap the economics of baseball were not viable, and the players' union steadfastly held that if a player and his club could not agree on what the player should be paid, the player should be free to seek employment with a new team.

On March 31, 1995, U.S. District Court Judge Sonia Sotomayor in New York granted the injunction sought by the NLRB, preventing the owners from implementing the salary cap system and its attendant provisions. The following week the Second Circuit Court of Appeals, acting through a three-judge panel, denied the owners' request for a stay of the injunction, and ultimately upheld the District Court's ruling. In response to this judicial action, the players' union announced it would voluntarily end its strike and return to the field to play the 1995 championship season.

After an abbreviated spring training, and the abrupt dismissal of replacement players prepared to proceed with a regular season schedule of games, major league players returned to begin a shortened 144-game schedule. Fans showed their displeasure with both sides by curtailing game attendance by about 20 percent. Other sports took advantage of baseball's missteps, effectively challenging baseball's position as the "national pastime."

With renewed popularity in 1998, baseball attendance drew closer to its average before the 1994–95 strike. By mid-1999, game crowds averaged 27,919, just under the 27,967 average a year earlier; attendance was up 10.5 percent from 1995 (25,260), but was off 11.7 percent from the pre-strike average (31,612).

Between 1972 and 1999, baseball had nine work stoppages, and the salary cap issue was the most divisive. The 1995 collective bargaining agreement avoided a salary cap by implementing a "luxury tax" on teams with the highest salaries. Some owners still feel a salary cap and revenue sharing system are necessary for the league's economic survival, but the players' union is still strongly opposed to the plan.

The umpires' lockout

As if the simmering dispute between baseball players and owners wasn't bad enough, problems arose with the umpires' union. The union had a four-year collective bargaining agreement which expired on December 31, 1994, and in the absence of a new agreement with the owners they were locked out of spring training camps as of January 1, 1995. Replacement umpires were then hired in contemplation of a 1995 major league season to be played by replacement baseball players.

At issue in the negotiations between the owners and the umpires was the existing salary structure for major league umpires, as well as corollary issues of severance and bonus pay. The union took the familiar tack of filing an unfair labor practices charge with the NLRB, alleging that American and National League owners had failed to bargain in good faith after the expiration of the old agreement.

The end of the players' strike, occasioned by an injunction prohibiting the owners' unilaterally imposed salary cap, led to a hastily restructured regular season. As regular-season games commenced they were staffed by replacement umpires. After several days, in which players expressed growing displeasure with the level of umpiring, the owners unceremoniously dismissed the replacements and reached an accord permitting the regular union umpires to return to work.

The owners faced a labor confrontation with umpires after the 1999 season. Selig wanted to shift control of umpires from the leagues to the commissioner's office, and the three-way relationship between owners, players, and umpires had deteriorated significantly since MLB acted indecisively in the 1996 Roberto Alomar spitting incident.

> ## CONCEPT CHECK
>
> *The concept of a standardized pay schedule, determined by age, position, and seniority, is common in many industrial settings, but has been consistently excluded from labor relations in professional sports. Sports has a two-tier system, and individual player salaries are not subject to collective bargaining. Note, however, that team challenges to salary cap strictures are blurring the traditional division of areas affected by collective bargaining.*

RECENT HISTORY: THE FREE-AGENT ERA IN THE OTHER PROFESSIONAL SPORTS
Football

Historically, each of the major professional sports has devised some form of reservation system to hinder a player's freedom to move from one team to another. Compensation systems and other league actions effectively destroyed the player's right to free agency, even with the one-year reservation system.

Beginning in 1947, football players had to sign a standard player contract, which bound them to their teams for an additional season at not less than 90 percent of their previous season's salary. In the National Football League, the compensation system was known as the *Rozelle Rule* because Commissioner Pete Rozelle was charged with the task of awarding compensation to those clubs that had lost players to free agency. The practice did have the owners' desired effect of discouraging free agent signings and holding down player salaries. Player dissatisfaction with the NFL's system led to strikes and antitrust litigation, which in turn led to a liberalized free agency system in the 1993 collective bargaining agreement.

The NFL players went on strike during the summer of 1974 to break the deadlock, but after six weeks the strike failed, and the players returned. Scabs and rookies had crossed the picket lines to enter training camp, and the 1987 player strike was broken in similar fashion. Nevertheless, the union in each instance had one weapon left in its arsenal—antitrust litigation. This is the one avenue unavailable to baseball players. From 1976 until 1993, NFL players won a series of court victories against the owners, and accomplished what the player strikes never could. The court decisions set the stage for the current free agency system in football.

Professional football survived its free agency crisis largely because of the John Mackey case, filed in a Minnesota federal court in 1975. The trial judge held that the Rozelle Rule was an illegal conspiracy in restraint of trade. As such, it violated antitrust law and denied the players the right to contract freely for their services.

It took another generation of court action to get rid of the successor to the Rozelle Rule, "Plan B" free agency. Plan B also undermined the free-agent market and unfairly held down player salaries, but it was successfully challenged by a 1993 antitrust suit (*McNeil v NFL*). This forced the owners back into collective bargaining negotiations with the players' union.

Of all the major sports leagues we have examined, the National Football League appears to have the most stable labor-management relationship. Considering the league's bitter legal battles and work stoppages of the past, this is surprising. But it is a testament to the determination of NFLPA executive director Gene Upshaw and NFL Commissioner Paul Tagliabue. Both men recognized the necessity of improving their relationship, and so were able to forge a sense of cooperation and mutual interest rarely present in the collective bargaining taking place in the other professional sports. In February 1998 the league owners and players' union agreed to extend the current collective bargaining agreement through the end of the 2003 season. This guarantees football's place as the only major sport that did not cancel games during the 1990s due to labor discord.

From 1989 to 1999, total league revenues increased from $970 million to $3.5 billion. The valuation of franchises also escalated throughout the decade. Between 1960 and 1988, Jack Kent Cooke paid $15 million to acquire sole ownership of the Washington Redskins. In 1999, the team was sold by his estate for $800 million. The expansion Cleveland Browns franchise was purchased from the league in the summer of 1998 for $530 million. The Dallas Cowboys, to take another example, were purchased by Jerry Jones for $95 million in 1988; ten years later, *Forbes* magazine (December 14, 1998) estimated the team's value at $413 million.

The average NFL team's player payroll is about $47 million per year. Players have shared in the league's sustained prosperity during the past decade; salaries have continued to rise despite restraints on free agency such as a hard salary cap. The huge television contracts of 1994 and 1998, spurred by network rivalries and a determination first by Fox then by CBS to participate in the league's broadcast packages, have been fundamental to the league's success. The inclination of cities and states to fund new stadium construction has also played a part. The other key element has been the lack of turmoil in the league's labor relations.

The working relationship of Upshaw and Tagliabue contrasts with the adversarial relationship between NBA commissioner David Stern and NBPA executive director Billy Hunter. The NFL principals meet regularly to discuss a wide range of issues, including all aspects of the governance of the game. By contrast, during the 1998 NBA lockout, Stern accused prominent player agents of sabotaging the negotiations, while Hunter accused Stern of trying to divide the union.

The National Football League is the new paradigm of positive labor relations in sport. (M. Freeman, "NFL Labor Peace Through 2003," *New York Times,* Nov. 8, 1998). Franchise values steadily appreciate, fan interest is high, and perhaps most essential, there is a working partnership between the league's commissioner and the head of the players' union. Accordingly, for sports leagues to ensure satisfactory collective bargaining it may be necessary for the principal negotiators to develop respect, trust, and the conviction that each side's interests are inextricably connected to their counterpart's.

It has been estimated that over 470 million people in the year 2002–2003 attended sporting events, and the prior ten years have shown an increase each year. It appears that baseball still accounts for the largest attendance at professional sports games; one should take into consideration, however, the number of games played in a baseball season. The highest percentage of growth of the major sports was 6.6 percent for football taking all factors into consideration.

It is a good idea to keep in mind that it was approximately ten years ago that Fox Network surprised and then outbid CBS for the rights to televise the NFL with their offer of 1.58 billion over four years.

The advent of high salaries has brought much attention to players, their agents and their lifestyles. It appears that each year the salaries increase; and professional football is illustrative of how payrolls have increased.

At the date of this writing, January of 2004, the NFL told its football clubs that the salary cap for 2004 should fall in the range of $78.7 million and $79.2 million per club. What this means, in effect, is that approximately 64.75 percent of the league's designated gross revenue will be allocated to players' salaries.

In 2003, according to the NFLPA (National Football League Players' Association), the league average was about $71.8 million, and eighteen teams paid out higher than that figure. The teams are listed in Table 18-1 with their payrolls for 2003.

Basketball

In the National Basketball Association, players signing the uniform player contract were originally bound to one team throughout their careers. If the player refused to sign a tendered contract, the team could unilaterally renew his contract for the following season at the same salary rate he was then earning.

Beginning in 1980, NBA players were allowed to become free agents, subject only to the **right of first refusal** by the team that the player sought to leave. This mechanism allowed the player's old team to resign him by matching any offer tendered to the player by a prospective new team.

In April 1983 the NBA brought professional sports into the salary-cap era.

The NBA lockout of 1998–99. Prior to the 1998–99 season, the National Basketball Association took great pride in the fact that no regular-season or play-off games had ever been lost to a work stoppage. The other major professional team sports, by contrast, suffered from serious labor discord throughout the 1980s and 1990s; often seasons were curtailed due to lockouts and strikes. In the case of Major League Baseball, the cancellation of the 1994 playoffs and World Series seriously undermined fan interest in the sport, creating a 20 percent decrease in attendance for the following two seasons.

In 1994, when the NBA began negotiations for a new collective bargaining agreement, the union leadership's primary goal was the elimination of

TABLE 18-1 *2003 NFL Team Payrolls*

Rank Team	Payroll
1. Saints	$85,886,810
2. Redskins	83,567,407
3. Bucs	81,196,551
4. Vikings	81,007,555
5. Cardinals	81,007,555
6. Seahawks	80,160,409
7. Rams	78,567,704
8. Cowboys	78,203,177
9. Bears	75,543,964
10. Patriots	74,778,384
11. Bengals	74,614,399
12. Titans	74,253,152
13. Chiefs	74,082,153
14. Giants	73,564,273
15. Texans	73,332,953
16. Eagles	71,951,211
17. Ravens	71,912,893
18. Colts	71,820,183
19. Bills	70,971,477
20. Packers	70,353,994
21. Lions	70,029,492
22. Jaguars	69,186,498
23. Raiders	68,322,739
24. Panthers	67,716,343
25. Broncos	65,885,132
26. Chargers	65,860,525
27. Falcons	64,184,794
28. Dolphins	63,844,606
29. Steelers	61,736,908
30. Jets	60,438,153
31. 49ers	56,526,337
32. Browns	56,016,540
'03 NFL AVERAGE:	**$71,772,275**

three provisions from the expiring contract: the salary cap, the college draft, and the "right of first refusal," which allowed a team to retain a free agent player by matching an opposing club's salary offer. The owners refused to reach a new agreement without these elements, and the 1994–95 season was played pursuant to a no-strike, no-lockout moratorium. The union then filed an antitrust lawsuit, alleging that the three provisions created an unlawful restraint of competition, and constituted an unlawful price-fixing agreement among horizontal competitors, in violation of the Sherman Antitrust Act. The players also argued that by collectively imposing terms of employment after the prior agreement had expired, the owners were acting as an illegal cartel.

The players' claims were rejected in court. This set the stage for some unusual developments at the bargaining table. A tentative agreement was reached between owners and the union. Several influential player agents objected to the proposed agreement because it greatly restricted the growth of the top player salaries.

On June 30, 1995, the owners declared a lockout, the first in league history, and froze all dealings with players. They also moved to restructure the proposed collective bargaining agreement to make it more acceptable to the dissident players and their agents. At the urging of several powerful agents, a number of players (including superstars Michael Jordan and Patrick Ewing) tried to have the union decertified; the goal was to nullify the proposed collective bargaining agreement. This strategy was also designed to destroy the owners' antitrust immunity under the "nonstatutory labor exemption." In early September, the players voted emphatically (63 percent) not to decertify, the lockout was lifted, and the 1995–96 season proceeded on schedule without the cancellation of any games.

One result of the 1995 negotiation was that top player agents and the union's legal counsel became part of the collective bargaining process. The union was still in turmoil; the owners saw that a lockout could be an effective technique in conducting negotiations, and they would soon use it again as a preferred tactic in dealing with an uncooperative union.

In 1998 the owners voted to reopen negotiations at the conclusion of the season, claiming that nearly half of its twenty-nine franchises were losing money.

Over the next three months, the owners' and players' negotiating committees met a total of nine times. The final meeting between the sides ended after only thirty minutes, and a few days later the league announced a lockout beginning on July 1.

The NBA enjoyed tremendous popular growth throughout the 1980s and 1990s; though overall attendance was stable during 1997–98, some teams experienced 15 to 20 percent attendance declines and decreased sales of licensed apparel. Much of the league's success was due to the extraordinary popularity of Michael Jordan and the Chicago Bulls, who became a worldwide marketing phenomenon. But steadily increasing aberrant behavior by NBA players, including domestic violence, on-court violence, and weapons, traffic, drug, and alcohol charges, reflected negatively on the sport and disaffected many fans.

Still, the single most polarizing issue in the labor negotiations of 1998 was the explosive rise in player salaries. We have traced the growth of player salaries in professional team sports during the collective bargaining era, but basketball posed an especially dramatic case. In 1977, for example, Kareem Abdul-Jabbar's $625,000 annual salary with the Los Angeles Lakers was the league's highest. In 1987, Patrick Ewing of the Knicks topped the list with an annual salary of $2.75 million, and in 1997, Chicago's Jordan was the highest paid at $30 million per year.

Long-term contracts were part of the problem. In 1996, Shaquille O'Neal signed with the Los Angeles Lakers for seven years at $123 million. The following year the Minnesota Timberwolves signed 21-year-old Kevin Garnett for $126 million over seven years. Garnett had entered the NBA directly from high school and was still establishing himself as a player; his salary represented potential value rather than compensation for proven performance. By 1997, 15 percent of total salaries were going to the nine highest-paid players, while about 20 percent of the players made the league's minimum salary. As always, the issue boiled down to how to divide the revenues between the players and owners.

The five principal issues in the 1998 negotiations were: the salary cap, free agency, minimum salaries, the rookie pay scale, and discipline of "aberrant" player behavior.

Most negotiating was done through the media. Face-to-face bargaining was rare, and usually hostile. The league's strategy was to secure itself economically and wait the players out. The league's television contracts were guaranteed in the event of a lockout, with repayment for lost games interest-free and not due for three years. The issue of whether players with guaranteed contracts would be paid during the lockout was referred to an arbitrator. In this case, the arbitrator ruled that the owners were not responsible for paying the "guaranteed" contracts. (*In the Matter of National*

Basketball Players Association and National Basketball Association, arbitration decision issued October 19, 1998.) The media consensus was that this decision gave the owners significant leverage in the dispute.

On November 1, 1998, the regular season was scheduled to begin, but on that date the NBA lost its unblemished record regarding games lost to work stoppages. The two sides were close on a number of issues as the year ended, but the league announced that if no agreement was reached by January 7, 1999, the entire season would be cancelled. Stern directly mailed to each player a nine-page letter outlining the owners' most recent proposal; Hunter then sent each player a nineteen-page union response. Stern declared that his letter included the owners' final offer, and he asked that the rank-and-file union members be allowed to vote on it. The union leaders agreed, seeking to prevent the players' growing unhappiness over negotiating tactics. A vote was scheduled for January 5, 1999.

A media poll of player attitudes towards the owners' proposal indicated a probable 2–1 vote against ratification. With the season, and perhaps the viability of the league, depending upon the vote's outcome, Hunter and Stern met for a marathon bargaining session. They reached a compromise agreement, and within hours the union ratified 179–5, and the owners approved 29–0. The season, comprised of fifty regular-season games per team rather than the regular 82-game schedule, began on February 5, 1999.

After the NBA's shortened 1999 season was completed (fifty regular-season games per team and a normal playoff schedule), the union announced that the average NBA salary increased to $2.64 million from $2.37 million, and the median salary increased from $1.4 million to $1.68 million. The number of players earning $1 million or more increased; players earning between $1 million and $4 million annually rose from 44 percent to 50 percent. Young star players who signed six-year extensions, such as Allen Iverson and Ray Allen, can earn upwards of $200 million over their careers if they maintain their level of excellence.

Another result of the lockout was that NBA owners acquired more control over player salaries than any other sport's owners. During the lockout, NBA teams lost about $1 billion in revenues and players about $500 million in salaries, but because

the season and playoffs were salvaged, further losses were avoided. Paul Staudohar, a leading observer of labor relations in professional sports, believes the new collective bargaining agreement could reduce the influence of agents. The fixed salaries for long-term contract extensions eliminated agents from that aspect of negotiations. Since the objective of collective bargaining is to represent all players, it is desirable that the process restores this function to the union instead of individual player agents.

Salaries, though moderated, are likely to continue to rise. Staudohar suggests the following to improve the league's labor prognosis: avoid union decertification and antitrust litigation, maintain a stable union leadership, keep agents on the collective bargaining sideline, encourage players to improve on- and off-court behavior, and restore the lost notion of a cooperative partnership between owners and players (Staudohar, 1999).

Effect of the new collective bargaining agreement.

The WNBA collective bargaining agreement of 1999. In 1997, two new professional basketball leagues were created: the American Basketball League (ABL) and the Women's National Basketball Association (WNBA). Both were women's leagues seeking to capitalize on the growing interest in women's college basketball and the success of the U.S. women's basketball team at the 1996 Olympics in Atlanta. The WNBA was set up as a summer league, while the ABL played a fall/winter schedule in direct competition with men's college and professional basketball. From their inception, the two women's leagues competed for the best players, and for supremacy in an untested sports market.

Originally there were eight teams in the WNBA. Instead of individually owned franchises, each team was owned by the league itself. The WNBA was organized as a joint venture of the NBA team owners. An operating agreement was granted by the WNBA to local management groups designated to run the teams, in exchange for a share of the profits. This allowed the new league to benefit from the NBA's marketing capital and know-how, and proved decisive in the competition with the American Basketball League. In December 1998, after its second season, the ABL declared bankruptcy and ceased operating. About 90 ABL players were left to seek employment in the WNBA, the sole remaining American professional women's basketball league, or in the professional women's leagues in Europe.

The WNBA was created and operates on the "single entity" ownership model, that is, individual franchises are owned by the league. Players are not employees of the team they play for; rather, they are employed by the WNBA itself. This marks a critical difference from the men's professional leagues in the four major sports. The U.S. Supreme Court has ruled that a company and its subsidiaries are not treated as separate entities regarding antitrust law, and so can't violate the statute's prohibition of "conspiracy, contract or combination" in restraint of trade; see *Copperweld Corp. v Independent Tube Corp.,* 467 U.S. 752 (1984). This allows the WNBA to conduct its operations without fear of antitrust scrutiny.

After its second year, the players of the WNBA voted to affiliate with a certified players' union. The new union then designated the NBPA, and executive director Billy Hunter, as its authorized representative in collective bargaining negotiations with the league. The WNBA was represented in collective bargaining negotiations by President Val Ackerman. The key issue involved salaries: the league minimum was $15,000, with incremental raises dependent upon draft position and seniority, up to a maximum salary of $50,000. Bonuses could be earned for most valuable player awards and other incentives. The overall pay structure was much less than the standard of the defunct ABL, whose league average was about $80,000 for forty-four regular-season games. With a thirty-two-game schedule and twelve teams set to play in 1999, the WNBA was unwilling to significantly increase salaries, and WNBA players were still marginally "professional" (i.e., able to earn a living solely from their sport). Many WNBA players continued to play overseas to supplement their earnings.

The minimum pay scale remains as originally agreed. Each player will each get a 401(k) retirement plan with mandatory team contributions, graduate school tuition, a $100,000 life insurance plan, plus year-round health and dental benefits (including maternity leave). Salaries are guaranteed for players who appear in sixteen games. Finally, the union will receive $100,000 annually from WNBA licensing royalties.

The WNBA's first experience in collective bargaining succeeded because the NBA's nearly disastrous 1998–99 labor negotiation was still fresh in the minds of the parties. The principal actors were essentially the same, and the issues involved were very similar, albeit on a much smaller scale. If the WNBA continues to survive and prosper, the players' union will aggressively seek a bigger share of the economic benefits. As in each of the other major sports leagues, the central issues will be what is a fair division of revenue and power, and whether league management and the union can foster the idea of a cooperative enterprise between players and owners. These questions will require further consideration as the league matures.

Hockey

The National Hockey League also had a standard player contract that granted the team a right to own a player's services in perpetuity. In every sport the standard player contract is incorporated into the collective bargaining agreement. Hockey players relied on the collective bargaining process to eliminate the "perpetual" player reservation system. In 1975 the *Philadelphia World Hockey Club* case (351 F. Supp. 462) struck down the NHL's reserve system, and the owners subsequently recognized the players' right to become free agents after playing out an option season. Hockey retained the compensation award for teams losing free agents, a system referred to as equalization. An arbitrator awarded the compensation if the two clubs could not agree, although after 1982 no compensation was required for free agents aged 33 and over.

The National Hockey League's collective bargaining agreement expired in 1994. The owners declared a lockout on October 1. Two months earlier, Commissioner Gary Bettman had announced major cutbacks in the package offered to the players by the owners. These included pension and medical benefit reductions, as well as reduced arbitration rights and roster sizes. The commissioner and owners were responding to what they perceived as a refusal to bargain by the players' association. The players, however, claimed that the owners' proposed wage structure was merely a disguised salary cap system, and they did not intend to proceed with negotiations until it was withdrawn.

One week before the lockout, Bettman announced that the 1994–1995 regular season would not begin without a new labor agreement, in order to protect the sport from a mid-season strike similar to the one which had recently damaged baseball. The players responded by promising not to strike during the season and playoffs if the owners would promise in return not to lock them out. The union's counterproposal to the owners featured a complex payroll tax, whereby club salaries beyond a determined amount would be taxed at a specified rate and the revenues derived from the tax would then be transferred to small-market, low-payroll clubs. The payroll tax was rejected by the owners on October 11, and the NHL season was formally postponed.

In mid-November 1994, as games were cancelled and lost revenues were mounting, a group of player agents entered the negotiations by advising league executives the payroll tax was unworkable. In its place, the owners substituted a revised free-agent provision that would allow less player movement between clubs. The owners also empowered the commissioner to cancel the remainder of the season if no agreement was reached by January 16, 1995; the theory was that a minimum fifty-game regular season was needed, and that playoffs had to be completed prior to July 1.

As the January 16 deadline approached, the owners resubmitted the payroll tax plan, and the union solidified in its opposition. On January 4, the union submitted its "final offer," with the payroll tax eliminated, and three days later the NHL Board of Governors responded with its own "final offer," dropping the payroll tax but raising to 32 the age for unrestricted free agency in the first half of the six-year agreement. The owners approved the amended proposal by a 19–7 vote, and on January 11, 1995, the players' union leadership, led by Robert Goodenow, accepted it pending ratification by the union membership. After a short training period, the league proceeded to play out a forty-eight-game regular season (pared down from its standard eighty-four-game length), and began the Stanley Cup playoffs just in time to conclude the season by the end of June.

The NHL has a hard salary cap which places an absolute ceiling on each team's payroll and puts downward pressure on player salaries. The salary tax concept imposes a tax on each team whose payroll exceeds a specified amount. The revenues generated by the tax are then apportioned to the smaller-market teams, who by necessity have lower payrolls. In baseball and hockey labor negotiations, both sides agree that revenue sharing in some form is needed to ensure the economic survival of the small-market franchises; the issue is whether the salary cap accomplishes the desired result in the most efficient way.

The NHL also has a system of salary arbitration wherein the owners and the union jointly appoint eight arbitrators from a national academy. Unlike baseball's system, in which the arbitrator must choose from one or the other salary proposals submitted by each side, the NHL's panel can set a fair salary regardless of the proposals submitted to them. Only restricted free agents are eligible for salary arbitration, and while the arbitrator sets the amount, the owner selects the contract's duration (one or two years). Salary arbitration is binding, *except* the owner can refuse to enter into any three contracts in a two-year period if the arbitration salary exceeds $550,000 (Staudohar, 1996).

The full intricacies of the NHL's collective bargaining agreement are beyond the scope of this chapter. When the current agreement expires, the issues of salary cap/salary tax, revenue sharing, and free agency restrictions will return to the negotiating table. The NHL's prolonged work stoppage of 1994–95 destroyed a golden opportunity for hockey to fully capitalize on the labor woes of baseball and basketball, but it did impress both sides with the need to conclude negotiations before a season is completely lost by strike or lockout. If the owners and the players' union successfully navigate the next bargaining round, hockey will continue to grow.

League salaries

Tables 18-2a, b, and c chart the highest individual salaries, median salaries, and total payrolls in the professional baseball league in 2003.

Salary changes

Tables 18-3a, b, and c chart the median salaries, highest individual salaries, and total payrolls in the professional basketball leagues in 2003–2004. Tables 18-4a and b chart top salaries and team payrolls in professional hockey in 2003–2004.

TABLE 18-2a   *MLB Salary Data, 2003*

Rank	Player	Salary	Team
1	Rodriguez, Alex	$22,000,000	Texas Rangers
2	Ramirez, Manny	20,000,000	Boston Red Sox
3	Delgado, Carlos	18,700,000	Toronto Blue Jays
4	Vaughn, Mo	17,166,667	New York Mets
5	Sosa, Sammy	16,000,000	Chicago Cubs
6	Brown, Kevin J	15,714,286	Los Angeles Dodgers
7	Green, Shawn	15,666,667	Los Angeles Dodgers
8	Jeter, Derek	15,600,000	New York Yankees
9	Piazza, Mike	15,571,429	New York Mets
10	Bonds, Barry	15,500,000	San Francisco Giants
11	Martinez, Pedro	15,500,000	Boston Red Sox
12	Johnson, Randy	15,000,000	Arizona Diamondbacks
13	Maddux, Greg	14,750,000	Atlanta Braves
14	Hampton, Mike	13,625,000	Atlanta Braves
15	Jones, Chipper	13,333,333	Atlanta Braves
16	Bagwell, Jeff	13,000,000	Houston Astros
17	Belle, Albert	13,000,000	Baltimore Orioles
18	Gonzalez, Juan	13,000,000	Texas Rangers
19	Mondesi, Raul	13,000,000	New York Yankees
20	Park, Chan Ho	13,000,000	Texas Rangers
21	Walker, Larry	12,666,667	Colorado Rockies
22	Griffey Jr. Ken	12,500,000	Cincinnati Reds
23	Dreifort, Darren	12,400,000	Los Angeles Dodgers
24	Williams, Bernie	12,357,143	New York Yankees
25	Burnitz, Jeromy	12,166,667	New York Mets

http://asp.usatoday.com/sports/baseball/salaries/top25.aspx?year=2003.

ANTITRUST CONSIDERATIONS

Before the 1970s, players remained subject to the reservation systems imposed by each sport. This was not changed by early unionization attempts or the periodic appearance of rival leagues, which introduced competition for player services. As a result, players sought relief from the reserve clause through antitrust law prosecutions; their argument was that reservation was anticompetitive and a violation of the Sherman Act.

Baseball players were completely unsuccessful in this strategy. A 1922 U.S. Supreme Court decision by Justice Holmes held that baseball was a sport rather than a business, and as such was not covered by the antitrust laws. Subsequent legal challenges to the reserve clause by baseball players were denied, as the Supreme Court continued to uphold the earlier exemption and suggested Congress should be the one to abolish it.

The other major sports have been more successful in this tactic because the Supreme Court has refused to extend baseball's antitrust exemption to cover any other professional sport. The lack of an antitrust exemption has been the primary cause of eliminating player reservation systems in professional football, basketball, and hockey. The courts have taken the position that jointly bargained agreements, as contemplated by the National

TABLE 18-2b *Major League Baseball Median Salaries, 2003*

Team	Median salary
New York Yankees	$4,575,000
Seattle Mariners	3,150,000
Los Angeles Dodgers	2,605,834
Boston Red Sox	2,000,000
San Francisco Giants	1,937,500
Arizona Diamondbacks	1,750,000
New York Mets	1,300,000
Florida Marlins	1,225,000
Baltimore Orioles	1,200,000
Houston Astros	1,200,000
Texas Rangers	1,150,000
Chicago Cubs	1,125,000
Oakland Athletics	1,032,500
Anaheim Angels	1,000,000
St. Louis Cardinals	900,000
Philadelphia Phillies	850,000
Pittsburgh Pirates	825,000
Atlanta Braves	800,000
Minnesota Twins	750,000
Cincinnati Reds	694,000
Toronto Blue Jays	600,000
San Diego Padres	592,500
Colorado Rockies	550,000
Chicago White Sox	475,000
Milwaukee Brewers	428,000
Montreal Expos	333,500
Cleveland Indians	330,000
Detroit Tigers	320,000
Kansas City Royals	313,500
Tampa Bay Devil Rays	300,000

http://asp.usatoday.com/sports/baseball/salaries/
mediansalaries.aspx?year=2003.

TABLE 18-2c *Major League Baseball Payrolls, 2003*

Team	Total payroll
New York Yankees	$152,749,814
New York Mets	117,176,429
Atlanta Braves	106,243,667
Los Angeles Dodgers	105,872,620
Texas Rangers	103,491,667
Boston Red Sox	99,946,500
Seattle Mariners	86,959,167
St. Louis Cardinals	83,486,666
San Francisco Giants	82,852,167
Arizona Diamondbacks	80,640,333
Chicago Cubs	79,868,333
Anaheim Angels	79,031,667
Baltimore Orioles	73,877,500
Houston Astros	71,040,000
Philadelphia Phillies	70,780,000
Colorado Rockies	67,179,667
Cincinnati Reds	59,355,667
Minnesota Twins	55,505,000
Pittsburgh Pirates	54,812,429
Montreal Expos	51,948,500
Toronto Blue Jays	51,269,000
Chicago White Sox	51,010,000
Oakland Athletics	50,260,834
Detroit Tigers	49,168,000
Florida Marlins	49,050,000
Cleveland Indians	48,584,834
San Diego Padres	47,928,000
Milwaukee Brewers	40,627,000
Kansas City Royals	40,518,000
Tampa Bay Devil Rays	19,630,000

Labor Relations Act, are the proper method of resolving labor questions in professional sports. How well the collective bargaining method actually works to resolve sports labor conflicts is still an issue, but the public policy of encouraging arm's length bargaining between the parties remains.

COLLECTIVE BARGAINING AND ANTITRUST

The Sherman Act, an 1890 federal law prohibiting agreements that unfairly restrain trade, was clearly instrumental in helping players radically alter existing player reservation systems in football, basketball and hockey. The 1976 *Mackey* case in professional

TABLE 18-3a   *National Basketball Association Median Salaries, 2003–04*

Team	Median salary
New York Knicks	$5,394,000
Dallas Mavericks	4,464,286
Detroit Pistons	3,950,000
Philadelphia 76ers	3,900,000
Indiana Pacers	3,800,000
Memphis Grizzlies	3,380,000
Portland Trail Blazers	3,300,000
Sacramento Kings	3,287,500
Chicago Bulls	3,080,000
Golden State Warriors	2,800,000
Toronto Raptors	2,800,000
Houston Rockets	2,460,000
Cleveland Cavaliers	2,458,500
Denver Nuggets	2,256,000
New Orleans Hornets	2,179,000
Minnesota Timberwolves	1,987,500
Washington Wizards	1,980,242
Seattle SuperSonics	1,935,000
Los Angeles Clippers	1,900,000
Milwaukee Bucks	1,898,000
Phoenix Suns	1,725,000
New Jersey Nets	1,586,000
San Antonio Spurs	1,543,500
Boston Celtics	1,500,000
Los Angeles Lakers	1,500,000
Orlando Magic	1,500,000
Utah Jazz	1,053,980
Atlanta Hawks	1,000,000
Miami Heat	813,679

http://asp.usatoday.com/sports/baseball/salaries/totalpayroll.aspx?year=2003.

football is the leading precedent. The federal court (Eighth Circuit) ruled that a reservation system was not a per se violation of the Sherman Act, but the NFL's system was deemed improper because it was not a product of bona fide arm's-length bargaining between owners and players.

As stated, the National Labor Relations Act of 1935 granted workers the right to form and join unions, and to engage in collective bargaining with employers. As player associations became certified unions under the provisions of the statute, they acquired the power to use the collective bargaining process in order to negotiate conditions of employment. Through this mechanism, and bolstered by the court's willingness to apply antitrust law to the league's operation, football, basketball, and hockey players achieved a more equal position with the owners. A new era of collective bargaining began in this way.

Baseball owners continue to have the benefit of an antitrust law exemption. There have been periodic Congressional hearings into the matter, and revocation has been often threatened, but as of 2003 no action had been taken.

COLLEGE ATHLETICS

Should college athletes be considered employees of the universities they attend? If so, a model of labor relations will need to be applied to college, as well as to professional sports. Currently they are treated as "student-athletes" with amateur status, and there are strict rules promulgated and enforced by the National Collegiate Athletic Association (NCAA) governing the source and amount of permissible income.

Since major college sports have become significant revenue producers in football and basketball, a question of fairness is raised if the players are prohibited from sharing in the profits they generate for their schools. Additionally, if a scholarship athlete is injured while performing, his or her right to worker's compensation benefits will hinge on whether he or she is considered an employee in the estimation of the courts.

Proposals to make student-athletes employees of their academic institutions have met varied responses from both the NCAA and legislative bodies. The current system is under intensive NCAA review, in an attempt to correct the most serious flaws, but a constant stream of violations and sanctions continue to result. For the foreseeable future, however, no fundamental change in the system should be expected.

In theory, the employment rights of college athletes could be created by a university initiative, but this has never been attempted. Similarly, college athletes could organize into a union and undertake

TABLE 18-3b   *The NBA's Highest Paid Players*

Rank	Player	Salary	Team
1	Garnett, Kevin	$28,000,000	Minnesota Timberwolves
2	O'Neal, Shaquille	26,517,858	Los Angeles Lakers
3	Wallace, Rasheed	16,990,000	Portland Trail Blazers
4	Houston, Allan	15,937,500	New York Knicks
5	Webber, Chris	15,937,500	Sacramento Kings
6	Stoudamire, Damon	14,375,000	Portland Trail Blazers
7	Abdur-Rahim, Shareef	13,500,000	Atlanta Hawks
8	Allen, Ray	13,500,000	Seattle SuperSonics
9	Baker, Vin	13,500,000	Boston Celtics
10	Hardaway, Anfernee	13,500,000	Phoenix Suns
11	Ilgauskas, Zydrunas	13,500,000	Cleveland Cavaliers
12	Iverson, Allen	13,500,000	Philadelphia 76ers
13	Marbury, Stephon	13,500,000	Phoenix Suns
14	McDyess, Antonio	13,500,000	New York Knicks
15	Sprewell, Latrell	13,500,000	Minnesota Timberwolves
16	Walker, Antoine	13,500,000	Dallas Mavericks
17	Bryant, Kobe	13,498,000	Los Angeles Lakers
18	Finley, Michael	13,281,250	Dallas Mavericks
19	McGrady, Tracy	13,279,500	Orlando Magic
20	Rose, Jalen	13,279,500	Chicago Bulls
21	Hill, Grant	13,279,250	Orlando Magic
22	Van Horn, Keith	13,279,000	New York Knicks
23	Kidd, Jason	13,152,000	New Jersey Nets
24	O'Neal, Jermaine	13,140,000	Indiana Pacers
25	Duncan, Tim	12,676,125	San Antonio Spurs

http://www.usatoday.com/sports/basketball/nba/salaries/mediansalaries.aspx?year=2003–04.

collective bargaining but have not yet done so. For the present, court decisions considering these matters on a case-by-case basis are the only avenues open to college athletes. Legislation and NCAA regulations have been spotlighted by the media, but have offered no tangible results in this area.

OTHER PROFESSIONAL SPORTS

Playing for a team in a league whose labor relations are negotiated through the collective bargaining process can be a blessing or a curse, depending on the individual athlete's status, accomplishment and fame, and the corresponding negotiating leverage that may or may not result.

Motor sports, including the most popular spectator sport in America, NASCAR (National Association of Stock Car Auto Racing), provide an excellent example. The NASCAR governing body sets specifications and standards for its competitors in such areas as engine size, fuel economy, and event sanctioning. Prize money for top finishes in each race is set by the individual race promoter. Drivers, however, assemble their own pit crews, and must solicit corporate sponsors in order to maintain the enormous cost of maintenance and transportation of sophisticated machinery and personnel. This is coupled with the sheer danger of high-speed auto racing, which makes life and disability insurance virtually unobtainable. In this sport, the ability of a

TABLE 18-3c *NBA Salary Data, 2003–04*

Team	Total payroll
New York Knicks	84,523,891
Portland Trail Blazers	84,304,778
Dallas Mavericks	79,099,293
Minnesota Timberwolves	72,385,947
Sacramento Kings	69,567,889
Los Angeles Lakers	65,510,147
Phoenix Suns	65,176,684
Atlanta Hawks	63,536,207
Toronto Raptors	60,307,176
Boston Celtics	59,112,919
Memphis Grizzlies	58,233,851
Philadelphia 76ers	57,763,301
Indiana Pacers	57,548,489
Detroit Pistons	52,942,639
Houston Rockets	52,354,437
Chicago Bulls	52,150,699
Golden State Warriors	51,804,638
Seattle SuperSonics	50,624,368
New Jersey Nets	48,579,883
New Orleans Hornets	48,125,452
Orlando Magic	47,696,731
San Antonio Spurs	46,879,322
Cleveland Cavaliers	46,513,187
Washington Wizards	45,681,942
Miami Heat	45,529,862
Milwaukee Bucks	42,452,361
Los Angeles Clippers	37,547,054
Denver Nuggets	36,004,731
Utah Jazz	28,320,329

http://www.usatoday.com/sports/basketball/nba/salaries/totalpayroll.aspx?year=2003–04.

driver to engage in competition may have little connection with that driver's actual performance on the racetrack.

Tennis and golf have until recently been sports dominated by the elite and wealthy. Long considered to be the sports of "ladies" and "gentlemen," many tournaments offer scant economic reward for success. One cannot survive on a silver plate or gilded trophy. Like motor sports, athletes in professional tennis and golf do not enjoy the type of collective bargaining representation seen in the major sports leagues. Consequently they depend on corporate sponsors to supplement their incomes.

The myriad of events in these sports, in combination with a complicated rating system and the necessity of good weather conditions for top competition, ensure that there is no "season" in the sense of a typical team sports league. Individual event promoters, often unable to advertise that the event has anything to do with an overall championship, frequently resort to negotiation and payment of "appearance fees" to the sport's current stars. Therefore, golfers like Tiger Woods and tennis players like Venus and Serena Williams frequently do not have to win an event in order to realize a handsome profit. Their mere appearance at the event allows the promoter to charge fans a hefty admission fee, and to justify significant corporate sponsorship packages which make such events financially profitable.

Boxing is an insular world completely unto itself. Similar to motor sports, golf, and tennis, boxing events do not have a traditional championship season. Boxers, like gold pros and tennis players, can command substantial appearance fees to ply their trade. There is often a huge disparity between the purse paid to the champion versus that offered to the challenger in the same match.

Individual boxing promoters often contract with certain boxers for multibout or even multiyear terms. Boxers then share their purses with their staff, which may include employees as varied as managers, trainers, assistant trainers, a "cut man," agents, attorneys, masseuses, barbers, tailors, sports psychologists, publicists, bodyguards, and even cheerleaders.

"Club fighters" at the beginning of an obscure boxing career earn as little as $100 per round for their professional matches, while their champion counterparts command multimillion-dollar purses for the same number of rounds. The difference in pay is directly linked to the value each participant brings to the promoter, sponsor, and broadcast network involved in staging the match.

Over the past century, boxing has thrived and grown despite countless attempts to "clean up" the sport. At the time of this writing, no less than four major sanctioning bodies (IBF, WBA, WBC, WBO) and literally dozens of minor sanctioning bodies (for example, IBC, IBO, NABF, USBA, etc.) all exist. These bodies govern events, rank competitors, set variable rules, and recognize "champions" and

TABLE 18-4a   *2003–04 Top Salaries in the NHL*

	Player name	Team	Position	Compensation
1	Forsberg, Peter	Colorado Avalanche	C	$11,000,000.00
2	Jagr, Jaromir	Washington Capitals	R	11,000,000.00
3	Fedorov, Sergei	Mighty Ducks of Anaheim	C	10,000,000.00
4	Bure, Pavel	New York Rangers	R	10,000,000.00
5	Lidstrom, Nicklas	Detroit Red Wings	D	10,000,000.00
6	Tkachuk, Keith	St. Louis Blues	L	10,000,000.00
7	Sakic, Joe	Colorado Avalanche	C	9,880,939.00
8	Pronger, Chris	St. Louis Blues	D	9,500,000.00
9	Blake, Robert	Colorado Avalanche	D	9,326,519.00
10	LeClair, John	Philadelphia Flyers	L	9,000,000.00
11	Modano, Michael	Dallas Stars	C	9,000,000.00
12	Sundin, Mats	Toronto Maple Leafs	C	9,000,000.00
13	Guerin, Bill	Dallas Stars	R	8,866,445.31
14	Holik, Robert	New York Rangers	C	8,850,000.00
15	Weight, Doug	St. Louis Blues	C	8,500,000.00
16	Yashin, Alexei	New York Islanders	C	8,400,000.00
17	Joseph, Curtis	Detroit Red Wings	G	8,000,000.00
18	Allison, Jason	Los Angeles Kings	C	8,000,000.00
19	Turgeon, Pierre	Dallas Stars	C	7,500,000.00
20	Iginla, Jarome	Calgary Flames	R	7,500,000.00
21	Roenick, Jeremy	Philadelphia Flyers	C	7,500,000.00
22	Palffy, Zigmund	Los Angeles Kings	R	7,000,000.00
23	Belfour, Ed	Toronto Maple Leafs	G	7,000,000.00
24	Stevens, Scott	New Jersey Devils	D	6,916,747.25
25	Brodeur, Martin	New Jersey Devils	G	6,891,103.13
26	Bertuzzi, Todd	Vancouver Canucks	R	6,800,000.00
27	Kovalev, Alex	New York Rangers	R	6,600,000.00
28	Leetch, Brian	New York Rangers	D	6,600,000.00
29	Demitra, Pavol	St. Louis Blues	L	6,500,000.00
30	Prospal, Vaclav	Mighty Ducks of Anaheim	C	6,500,000.00

http://www.hockeynut.com/0304/salaries0304.html.

"worthy contenders." It is fair to say that none of these "alphabet soup" sanctioning bodies truly represents or recognizes "undisputed" champions in each weight class. In reality, other acronyms such as HBO, ESPN, TVKO, and SHO rule the roost in boxing, because payments by television networks to promoters for broadcast rights eventually provide the purse for which the boxers compete.

Consequently, it is unfortunate that competitors in a sport so dangerous to human health have virtually no collective voice in labor negotiations. Not only is a boxer alone in the ring, there is no labor union to provide a voice for the boxer on issues such as health care, retirement benefits, disability insurance, job security, or occupational safety. Without such a voice, and without the financial means to employ the entourage to accomplish these tasks, club fighters often spend their middle-aged years crippled and destitute.

There are numerous state athletic commissions that attempt to provide additional safeguards for

TABLE 18-4b   *NHL Team Payrolls, 2002–03 Season*

Rank	Team	Payroll (in millions)
1	N.Y. Rangers	$69.2
2	Detroit	68.0
3	St. Louis	61.8
4	Dallas	61.8
5	Colorado	60.8
6	Philadelphia	55.7
7	Toronto	54.9
8	New Jersey	51.2
9	Washington	50.4
10	Monteal	48.6
11	San Jose	45.1
12	Chicago	44.4
13	Phoenix	43.9
14	Los Angeles	41.8
15	N.Y. Islanders	41.5
16	Anaheim	38.8
17	Carolina	38.4
18	Boston	36.9
19	Vancouver	35.3
20	Calgary	33.6
21	Buffalo	31.5
22	Edmonton	31.5
23	Florida	31.2
24	Pittsburgh	31.2
25	Ottawa	28.5
26	Tampa Bay	28.9
27	Columbus	27.4
28	Atlanta	27.0
29	Nashville	23.3
30	Minnesota	21.1

Source: National Hockey League, www.twincities.com/mld/twincities/sports/507:546.htm.

boxers. From time to time, federal legislation has been proposed to further protect the health and livelihood of professional boxers.

SUMMARY

- Because players were historically denied the right to choose which team to play for, and to switch teams to raise their salary level, the owners were in a much more powerful position. They benefitted from the new revenues radio and television brought into the game, while players' salaries were suppressed far below the level a competitive labor market would have brought them.
- In response to the reservation system, players in each sport formed players' associations, which evolved into labor unions. This in turn led to the system of collective bargaining between players and owners, which is where labor relations in most sports stand today.
- The main focus of this chapter has been how employer-employee relationships have developed in America's four major professional team sports—baseball, football, basketball, and hockey.
- The employer in each situation is the club, or team, and in each sport individual clubs have been organized into professional sports leagues. The employee is the professional athlete who performs on the playing field.
- Occasionally, competing leagues have come into existence to challenge established operations, and they always have a significant impact on the employment relationships of their rivals.
- At present, there is only one major league operating in each of the four major sports. While there is competition among the teams in a particular sport for free-agent players, championships and revenues, it is more accurate to view individual teams within a sport as joint venturers with a common interest in the competitive balance and financial soundness of the league as a whole.
- Players have gained more power in recent years through the organization of player associations into effective labor unions. They have also realized substantial income escalation through the establishment of various free agency mechanisms in each sport, allowing them to change teams under certain conditions and thereby require employers to bid among themselves for player talent.
- Free agency for players and the existence of rival leagues have been the two driving

forces behind rising player salaries in the modern era of professional sports.

- The labor crisis that each sport faces revolves around the question of the proper balance between the rights of team owners and professional athletes.

- The current situation raises these key questions: What role, if any, should government play in regulating the employment relationship, particularly when labor negotiations between the parties reach an impasse? What rights should players and owners each have in the equation, and what is the public's interest (especially the fans') in the employment relationship?

- These issues have moved to center stage in the last several years, as players and owners have become more adversarial and less trusting of each other's motives during collective bargaining negotiations.

- The case of baseball illustrates how destructive the breakdown of labor relations can be. Each sport must answer the critical questions of the employment relationship for itself, but neglecting them jeopardizes their ability to put on the games, which constitute the economic product of professional sports.

- College athletes have not been recognized as employees by their universities, nor have they organized into unions. Courts consider their status on a case-by-case basis.

- Athletes in other sports, such as auto racing, extreme sports, golf, tennis, and boxing do not enjoy the benefits of the collective bargaining system. On the other hand, this class of athlete has much more latitude to negotiate his/her individual compensation package with event promoters and corporate sponsors.

 CRITICAL THINKING EXERCISES

1. From the perspective of the commissioner of baseball, how crucial is the decision to take control over MLB umpires away from the American and National League presidents? Does your answer change if the transfer of authority causes the National League president to tender his resignation?

2. As head of an agency representing pro athletes, how much regulatory authority do you feel should be vested in the respective professional leagues' player associations? Should union employees participate in external investigations of sports agents, that is, by the government, the NCAA, or college athletic departments?

 CASE STUDIES

Player-Agent-Union Relations: A Case Study

We have examined how the creation and growth of viable players' unions led to free agency and, in turn, higher player salaries. Now we will look at union attempts to regulate the agents who represent player interests. Our case study involves a player agent and the NFL Players' Association.

Regulatory Background. *After the* Powell *case, the NFLPA was recertified as the authorized union for collective bargaining. The union also restored a regulatory program for player agents, requiring them to be union-certified. This created a dual role for the union. In late 1996, the union sent all registered player agents a voluntary test on the terms of the new collective bargaining agreement; only one-third of the agents reportedly took the test, but most who did scored poorly.*

Another concern is that agents are violating SEC rules by acting as financial advisors and giving their clients investment advice. The SEC has also investigated agent referrals; the NCAA restricts agent activities on college campuses, and some agents use financial planners to recruit new clients. An agent who signs a player referred by a planner gives them a "finder's fee" and also exclusive management of the player's finances. Failure to disclose the agent–financial planner relationship to the player in advance constitutes fraud.

The NFLPA has instituted safeguards for its players in the past few years. In 1996 it reduced the maximum allowable percentage charged by agents for contract negotiation from 4 to 3 percent, the lowest in the major professional sports. In early 1997, the union instituted a stricter application process and mandatory testing of agents. But not all problems are caused by the agent's misbehavior. Some players have failed to pay earned commissions to their agents, and this results in arbitration. Players also have been known to quickly drop an agent when a lower fee is offered by a competing agent.

By 1998, 800 different agents represented the NFL's 1,200 active players. This is nearly twice the number of player agents in 1990. During this period, player salaries have nearly tripled, but the number of arbitration complaints between NFL players and their agents also rose significantly, a total of 88 cases between 1996 and 1998. This number far exceeds player vs. agent disputes in the other major sports leagues. Since 1996, according to the union's disciplinary summary statement, seven agents were found guilty of violating union rules, and two were suspended for a year and fined $5,000 for improperly providing money to college players. In conjunction with stricter union rules, several states have enacted laws making it illegal for agents to improperly contact college players. One of those states is Florida.

The "Tank" Black Case. William "Tank" Black is head of Professional Management, Inc. (PMI), one of the leading sports agencies representing professional football players. He offers players the following services: contract negotiations with team management, personal management services, marketing and public relations services, and post-career planning. PMI currently has forty players under contract and earns between $10 million and $15 million annually. In mid-April 1999, five of Black's clients were selected in the first round of the NFL draft.

In early May, the NFLPA announced that Black was under investigation since late January for possible violations of their sports agent regulations, though neither Black nor any of his clients were questioned until the week of the draft. The union announced Black was accused of having an employee try to bribe a Louisiana State University assistant football coach in order to sign tackle Anthony McFarland as a client. The University of Florida and Florida attorney general also announced investigations into Black's activities regarding four players at that school. NFLPA representative Trace Armstrong was reportedly present during the university police's questioning of the players. Black faces up to five years in prison and a $5,000 fine if he is found guilty of violating the state's agent law.

On May 19, 1999, the NFLPA issued a five-page complaint against Black detailing eight different types of alleged violations. Possible penalties extend from the agent's suspension and fine, to a lifetime ban on representing NFL players in contract negotiations. The NFLPA complaint alleged Black told an LSU assistant coach he had purchased a car for a University of Florida athlete still playing collegiate football, using the money of one of Black's professional clients. A Black employee allegedly offered the LSU coach $30,000 to persuade McFarland to sign with Black. McFarland subsequently signed with another agent.

The complaint further charged Black with selling his clients shares in BAOA, Inc., a publicly traded company, for $1 per share. The stock price was 5 cents per share when the complaint was issued. Another allegation was that Black provided cash to football players at Florida, LSU, and the University of South Carolina, through an employee, Alfred "Tweet" Twitty. Black was accused of arranging the purchase of a Mercedes-Benz automobile for Florida's Jevon Kearse on December 31, 1998 (two days before Kearse played his final college game in the Orange Bowl), as well as acquiring cars for three other Florida players who still had college eligibility. One player, Johnny Rutledge, said under oath that he accepted $500 payments from Black while still enrolled at Florida. Rutledge and former Florida players Kearse and Reggie McGrew made sworn statements admitting to receiving payments from Black. All four Florida players named in the complaint fired Black as their agent prior to the draft.

On June 22, 1999, Black filed a federal lawsuit in Washington, D.C., claiming the NFLPA's disciplinary proceedings violated his civil rights. The suit claimed that Black lost $10 million due to the termination of his representation of the four players, and that other potential clients were scared away. The suit asked that the court issue an injunction to suspend the NFLPA investigation and take over complete jurisdiction in the matter.

In early July 1999, Black's attorney filed a reply with the NFLPA, which included statements from the four former Florida players and affidavits from three other Black clients, all denying that payments had been made to entice them to sign with Black. A sworn affidavit from Twitty was also submitted, denying that he worked for Black or in any way induced players to sign with Black's agency. In addition to denying each of the eight allegations of wrongdoing in the NFLPA complaint, Black's response included bank records and sworn statements from car dealers that the car purchases in question were made on January 4 and 6, 1999, after the eligibility of the players involved had expired.

Black again claimed that the union and other agents had conspired to force him out of business. He stated that the sworn statements by players claiming he had provided them with cash were the result of undue pressure applied by the police during the Florida criminal investigations.

When Black's lawsuit against the union was filed, NFLPA general counsel Richard Berthelsen stated Black was being treated no differently than the fifteen other agents investigated by the union in the past two years. "We don't have time for witch hunts. They've apparently chosen to make the media the forum for the issue instead of our internal arbitration procedures."

1. Should the union's investigation procedures for alleged agent misconduct also include due process guarantees for the accused? If so, how should they be worded?
2. How should the courts rule on sports agent Black's request for injunctive relief? Are the state and federal courts a better forum for the resolution of agent misconduct allegations and counter-claims, or should the matter remain within the union's internal arbitration procedures?
3. What is the proper role of the union concerning investigations conducted by state police agencies under a state sports agent law? Did the NFLPA overstep its bounds by being present during state police questioning of players?
4. Given the pressures put on top college players by sports agents, what is the proper regulatory function of the union regarding the player-agent relationship? What should be the NCAA's role in this process?

The Labor Dispute between the Umpires and MLB

One of the most unusual labor-management disputes in the history of professional team sports occurred during the summer of 1999. In mid-July the Major League Umpires Association, a certified labor union, voted to tender the resignations of fifty-seven of the union's sixty-eight members (eleven did not participate), effective September 2, 1999.

Recall that the MLBPA players' union struck on August 12, 1994, and forced the cancellation of the playoffs and World Series at the end of that season.

The umpires found themselves in a similar negotiating position with owners regarding their collective bargaining agreement, about to expire at the end of the 1999 calendar year. Instead of striking, however, the umpires adopted a mass-resignation strategy to force the owners to begin early negotiations on a new labor agreement. But the umpires were not unified behind their executive director, Richie Phillips, nor did they accurately gauge the response of their negotiating counterparts. It is customary for unions to begin collective bargaining a month or two prior to the expiration of an existing agreement. An added consideration for the umpires was the no-strike clause in the agreement then in effect.

At the time of the "resignation vote," Phillips announced the umpires' intention of forming a new corporation as soon as the resignations took effect, requiring the two major leagues to contract for umpiring services with the new entity. The union's goal was to win for the umpires the right to supervise themselves and make their own work schedules, including postseason assignments.

The union made an apparent miscalculation as to what response MLB would have to the resignation vote. Earlier in 1999, Commissioner Selig announced his office would assume responsibility for umpire supervision, a power previously residing in the two league presidents. (In September, National League president Leonard Coleman would resign in protest over this transfer of power over umpires.) But even in mid-July, Selig's newly appointed "executive vice president of baseball operations," Sandy Alderson, was acting on behalf of baseball's owners in the umpires dispute. Alderson announced the leagues would accept twenty-two of the resignations that had been submitted to his office, nine in the American League and thirteen in the National, and would hire twenty-five replacement umpires from the minor leagues to begin work in early September.

In March 1999, Phillips had been granted a new five-year contract by the umpires' union; after the events in July, it was clear that a faction of umpires, mostly in the American League, were opposed to his continued presence. Once management made clear its intention to accept resignations and hire replacements, twenty-seven umpires withdrew previously tendered resignations, or refused to submit letters in support of the union's plan. By early August, Alderson accepted the resignations of twenty-two union umpires and announced twenty-five new umpires would be hired from the minor leagues.

With the situation rapidly deteriorating and pro-Phillips umpires publicly exchanging recriminations with the dissident umpires, the union filed an unfair labor practice charge with the National Labor Relations Board. A complaint was also filed on July 26 in the federal court in Philadelphia, challenging MLB's attempt to replace the twenty-two umpires and seeking an injunction to prevent it. Phillips argued the resignation strategy was merely an attempt to circumvent the current labor agreement's prohibition against umpire strikes.

The 1995 agreement had been reached after a lockout that had caused the umpires to miss eighty-six games at the start of the season. Tensions between labor and management were heightened by a September 1996 incident in which Baltimore's Roberto Alomar spat on umpire John Hirschbeck, and received a penalty regarded as unduly lenient by the umpires. (Hirschbeck, ironically, later emerged as one of the leaders of the anti-Phillips faction.) Then on July 2, 1999, tension escalated when umpire Tom Hallion was suspended for three days by NL president Coleman as punishment for bumping a player during an on-field argument. The umpires were prepared to strike then, according to Phillips, but he was able to substitute the resignation tactic in order to comply with the no-strike provision.

The umpires' union voluntarily withdrew its federal lawsuit on August 10th, pursuing instead the NLRB complaint and submitting the matter to binding arbitration pursuant to the terms of the current bargaining agreement. The union's argument was that of the twenty-two resignations that MLB had accepted, the determining factor was apparently union support rather than seniority or performance rating. This, if proven, would support the union's contention that the action constituted an unfair labor practice, and should be enjoined.

By late August, the union discussed whether to call a strike before the resignations were to take effect in early September. Instead they chose to seek an injunction in federal court, to keep MLB from accepting their resignations and fielding the replacements who had been hired. The federal judge in Philadelphia, J. Curtis Joyner, declined to intervene on the umpire's behalf. On September 2, the twenty-two umpires were relieved of their positions, and the replacement umpires began working major league games without incident. The displaced umpires accepted a settlement by which they would be paid the remaining portion of their 1999 salaries, along with health benefits and termination pay, in exchange for their voluntary waiver of any rights to continue working as umpires in 1999, including pursuit of the unfair labor charge with the NLRB. The terminated umpires are to share in a post-season bonus pool, but may not engage in any strike or work stoppage as per the collective bargaining agreement.

MLB terminated the twenty-two umpires, by which their careers as umpires ended. The remaining umpires fired Phillips as union counsel.

1. What tactics, if any, should the umpires' union have adopted to force management to the bargaining table in July? Why didn't the union wait for the customary bargaining phase to begin one month prior to expiration?

2. What impact did the apparent lack of union solidarity have on the effectiveness of the "resignation strategy"?

3. If you were the commissioner, would you have taken the same action regarding the transfer of authority over umpires? What effect did the National League president's resignation have, if any?

4. What do you think MLB's negotiating posture will be when the collective bargaining agreement expires? What will the umpires' union do in the wake of the failed resignation strategy, and their acceptance of the "settlement agreement" in September?

5. How will the arbitrator rule on the union's claim that the resignations should be rescinded and the twenty-two terminated umpires be restored to their jobs?

6. "Good faith bargaining" does not require either side to make concessions or agree to proposals against their will, only that each side communicate to the other through proposals and counterproposals. The extreme tactics of strike and lockout are justified only after an impasse is reached, and an impasse can occur only when one side insists on the acceptance or removal of a provision and refuses to modify its position. Do you think there is sound logic behind the NLRA's scheme for (1) good faith bargaining and (2) reaching impasse before invoking certain tactics?

REVIEW QUESTIONS AND ISSUES

1. What devices can be invoked by each side when an impasse is reached during the collective bargaining process?
2. Is it desirable that players continue to perform when negotiations break down, or is their strike weapon the ultimate guarantee that a collective bargaining agreement will be reached?
3. Should government agencies intervene when collective bargaining negotiations reach an impasse? If so, at what level?
4. What is the proper role, if any, of a league commissioner in labor negotiations between players and owners?
5. Are player salaries too high or too low? What standard of comparison is appropriate?
6. Is a salary cap a viable method of controlling operating costs of professional sports teams? Is it the best method? Should teams be required to reveal their financial information, especially their profitability, to the players' union when a cap on salaries is sought? To the public?
7. If a percentage of ownership revenues is designated for player salaries under a cap system, which revenues should be included? What is a fair percentage?
8. Should the free market alone determine player salaries in professional sports? What about the fans' need to have players stay with one team for a certain period to encourage team loyalties and rooting interest?
9. Has the development of players' unions been a positive influence in the history of professional team sports? Can you think of a better system to protect the interests of the major factions, specifically the players, owners, and fans?
10. Is the two-tier system of contract negotiations desirable?
11. What labor issues do you think should be resolved through the collective bargaining process?
12. How can collective bargaining negotiations be encouraged when an impasse occurs between management and players?
13. Assume collective bargaining negotiations reach an impasse. When, if ever, should players call a strike? When, if ever, should owners field replacement players?
14. In the event of a players strike, is a player-owned league a rational economic decision? How would fans respond?
15. In the 1994 baseball strike, were the owners' actions designed to undermine, or "break," the players' union? How can this analysis be made?

SOLUTIONS TO CRITICAL THINKING EXERCISES

1. MLB Commissioner Selig felt the transfer of control over umpires to his office from the respective leagues was a necessary element in consolidating management control over the game into a central office. His action led directly to the resignation of National League president Leonard Coleman, the highest-ranking black official in an American professional sports league; a variety of management issues were thereby raised.
2. The players' associations in each of the professional sports leagues have asserted their right to regulate agents who represent active league players. Requirements vary from league to league, and include devices such as posting bonds and passing written tests to substantiate a knowledge of the league's collective bargaining agreement. In the "Tank" Black case, it was argued that it was improper for the NFLPA to assist state authorities in an investigation, or even to be present during interrogations.

FOSTERING YOUR WORKPLACE SKILLS

You are a senior in college living in a dormitory. Your on-campus job is to assist the media relations office in your school's athletic department. The star of the football team, senior Charles "Crusher" Matwell, lives in the room next door to you. While at your job in the athletic department, a sports agent's associate, "Sleezy Dave" Simpson, offers you $100 and a pair of tickets to a rock concert if you can "hook him up" with

Crusher for a meeting in your dorm room. Sleezy Dave makes it clear that there is "more to come" if you can persuade Crusher to sign with Dave's boss's agency before the NFL draft. Crusher, meanwhile, is focused on the team's final home game of the season; if the team wins, there will be a good chance the team will be invited to a post-season bowl game.

What should you do?

A. Help Dave set up the meeting with Crusher in your room and share the $100 and tickets with Crusher?
B. Decline Dave's offer?
C. Tell the coach?
D. Tell the athletic director?
E. Call the NCAA for advice?
F. Call Dave's boss?
G. Ask for more money and tickets?
H. Other?

If both of you meet with Dave and keep the money and tickets, are you in any trouble? Is Crusher in trouble? Is your school in trouble? Is Dave in trouble? Is Dave's boss in trouble? What possible difficulties or penalties does each person or the institution face?

 WEBSITES

www.nytimes.com—The *New York Times*. The sports section of this Website provides an excellent source of news reporting on labor relations developments in each of the four major professional sports leagues. It also will provide links to timely Associated Press wire stories by Ronald Blum, the sports labor relations reporter.

www.sportserver.com—The Sports Server. This site is a service of the *Charlotte News & Observer* ("Nando"), and it allows the student to select each major sport. After choosing a sport, go to the desired sports league, or the link to NCAA college football or basketball. Once chosen, the link to "News and Features" will provide a daily list of wire service stories, archived for two weeks. Labor relations developments can be tracked this way, and the student can be sure to stay current.

REFERENCES

Berry, R., and Wong, G. (1986). *Law and business of the sports industries.* Vol. I: Professional Sports Leagues. Dover, MA: Auburn House.

Berry, R., Gould, W., and Staudohar, P. (1986). *Labor relations in professional sports.* Dover, MA: Auburn House.

Burk, R. (1994). *Never just a game: players, owners, and American baseball to 1920.* Chapel Hill, NC: The University of North Carolina Press.

Cosell, H., and Whitfield, S. (1991). *What's wrong with sports?* New York: Pocket Books.

Dworkin, J. (1981). *Owners versus players: Baseball and collective bargaining.* Dover, MA: Auburn House.

Jennings, K. (1990). *Balls and strikes: The money game in professional baseball.* New York: Praeger.

Johnson, A., and Frey, J. (eds.) (1985). *Government and sport: the public policy issues.* Totowa, NJ: Rowman and Allanheld.

Kochan, T., and Katz, H. (1988). *Collective bargaining and industrial relations.* 2nd ed. Homewood, IL: Irwin.

Lowenfish, L. (1990). *The imperfect diamond: A history of baseball's labor wars.* New York: Da Capo Press.

Miller, M. (1991). *A whole different ball game: The sport and business of baseball.* New York: Birch Lane Press.

Noll, R. (ed.) (1974). *Government and the sports business.* Washington, D.C.: The Brookings Institution.

Quirk, J., and Fort, R. (1992). *Pay dirt: the business of professional team sports.* Princeton, NJ: Princeton University Press.

Sands, J., and Gammons, P. (1993). *Coming apart at the seams.* New York: Macmillan.

Scully, G. (1989). *The business of major league baseball.* Chicago: The University of Chicago Press.

Shropshire, K. (1995). *Agents of opportunity: sports agents and corruption in collegiate sports.* Philadelphia: University of Pennsylvania Press.

Sommers, P. (ed.) (1992). *Diamonds are forever: The business of baseball.* Washington, D.C.: The Brookings Institution.

Staudohar, P. (1996). *Playing for dollars: Labor relations and the sports business.* Ithaca, NY: ILR Press.

Staudohar, P. (1999, April). Labor relations in basketball: The lockout of 1998–99. *Monthly Labor Review,* 3–9.

Staudohar, P. (1998, Spring). Salary caps in professional team sports. *Compensation and Working Conditions,* 3–11.

Staudohar, P. (1997, Fall). Baseball's changing salary structure. *Compensation and Working Conditions,* 2–9.

Wolff, A., and Keteyian, A. (1990). *Raw recruits,* New York: Pocket Books.

Zimbalist, A. (1998, July 5). Perspective: Team profits and labor peace. *The New York Times,* A13.

PART VI

Field Experiences and Careers in Sport Management

Discussion Topic One

As the new Community Relations Director for the Chicago Cubs, you are considering reinstating an internship program for sport management students. The previous director discontinued the program because of "incompatibilities between college/university and franchise calendars." These incompatibilities included: (1) interns wanted grades at the end of an academic term; (2) many students were not interested in continuing their internship at the conclusion of the academic term and either expected their pay or left the organization; (3) having an intern for only part of the season did not allow the Cubs organization to reap the benefits of the program.

Group Discussion Question: Suggest solutions to the problems the former director faced. Consider the interests of all primary stakeholders in an internship situation: the student, the internship agency, and the college/university.

Discussion Topic Two

When you begin considering options for a senior internship, you may find that several agencies hosting interns do not operate on a semester or quarter basis. For example, interns with many professional sport teams must remain with the franchise throughout the entire season. Site supervisors may not be comfortable with assigning a grade or evaluating performance until the internship is completed.

Group Discussion Questions: What will you do if the internship that you desire follows this format? Are you prepared to delay graduation in order to complete this type of internship? What factors will you consider when making this decision?

CHAPTER 19

Experiential Learning Through Field Experiences

M. Elizabeth Verner, Bette B. Keyser, and Marilyn J. Morrow

In this chapter, you will become familiar with the following terms:

Academic service-learning
Alternating cooperative
  education
Chronological résumé
Cooperative education
Discrete experiential
  education
Experiential education
Experiential learning

Field experience
Formal sources
Informal sources
Internship
Nondiscrete experiential
  education
Parallel/extended day
  cooperative education
Pedagogical approach

Practicum/Practica
Reflective statement
Service-learning
Showcase portfolio
Sport Management Program
  Standards and Review
  Protocol
Vocational self-concept
Working portfolio

Learning Goals
By the end of this chapter, students should be able to:

- Become acquainted with experiential learning and the role experiential learning plays in the professional preparation of sport managers.

- Realize the benefits field experiences can offer to students, the university, and the sponsoring organization.

- Identify potential field experience opportunities in sport management.

- Learn the intern competencies desired by agency supervisors.

- Utilize career advancement materials to market oneself.

- Develop strategies to search for, secure, and solidify the field experience.

- Understand the stages of an internship.

CONCEPTUAL BACKGROUND
Learning theory

In a very fundamental way, learning theory literature acknowledges that people learn in at least two ways, through academic learning and experiential learning. For the purpose of this discussion, academic learning refers to learning from activities such as listening to lectures, reading materials, and watching films. These types of learning activities are obviously more physically passive than those associated with experiential learning. Experiential learning refers to learning by doing, and is almost always associated with active engagement. Examples of experiential learning include role-playing, field experience, and volunteerism. "In general terms, the distinguishing features of experiential learning are that it refers to the organizing and construction of learning from observations that have been made in some practical situation, with the implication that the learning can then lead to action (or improved action)" (Moon, 1999, p. 20).

Even though activity, or actually doing, is a central tenant for experiential learning, the theory suggests that cognition or mental structures are a byproduct of experiential learning and participants learn by mentally connecting what is learned through experience with what was previously known to the learner, including convictions or beliefs acquired through either academic or experiential means. In this way, experiential and academic approaches to learning become natural allies in the process of constantly changing and reformatting thought structures. For example, enlightenment occurs when something read in a textbook comes to life as the learner makes the connection between the idea and its execution. Likewise, revelation is apparent when the learner comprehends the textbook explanation for phenomena previously observed but never understood (Cross, 1994).

Dr. David Kolb is one of the most well-known authors whose work supports the use of experiential learning. He maintains that experience plays a central role in learning and that learning is "the process whereby knowledge is created through transformation of experience" (Kolb, 1984, p. 38). Kolb's learning theory synthesizes the work of Dewey, Lewin, and Piaget; it emphasizes adapting, creating, and re-creating, as well as insight and application (Hesser, 1990).

Experiential learning is frequently explained by reference to Kolb's Experiential Learning Cycle of Development (see Figure 19-1 for a graphic representation), which progresses the learner (1) from an actual experience, (2) through reflection about the experience, (3) to conceptualization or generalization that relates the experience to theories and to

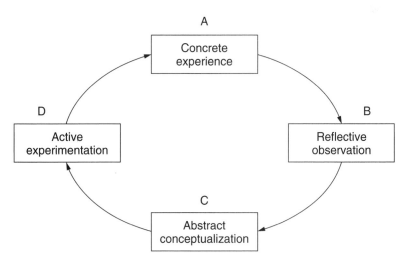

FIGURE 19-1 Kolb's experiential learning cycle.
From Kolb, D. A. (1976). *Learning style inventory technical manual.*

other experiences, and finally (4) on to active experimentation with changed practice based on these considerations.

To enhance this process of *learning by doing*, theorists and experiential learning advocates emphasize the important role played by reflection (Boud, 1995; Eraut, 1994; Jacoby, 1996; Kolb, 1984; Moon, 1999). Examples of reflective activities include student-generated logs, weekly reports, or other types of periodic updates that encourage learners to mentally process what's going on around them. Baker, Jensen, Kolb (2002) stress the importance of conversation as a meaningful reflective tool. In addition to conversing with the university supervisor and professionals in the workplace, attending seminars that bring interns together to discuss their experiences can stimulate reflection. When face-to-face conversation is not possible, technology provides reflective opportunities through the use of electronic blackboards and chat rooms. Regardless which reflective mode is utilized, self-assessment and critical thinking are key elements to achieving maximum benefit from experiential learning.

Experiential learning and experiential education

Thus far we have established that **experiential learning** refers to learning in which the learner is directly in touch with the realities being studied. It is contrasted with learning in which the learner only reads about, hears about, talks about, or writes about these realities, but never comes into contact with them as part of the learning process (Keeton & Tate, 1978).

Now let's apply the concept of experiential learning to the process of education. **Experiential education** is a form of pedagogy, or teaching methodology, employed to facilitate experiential learning. Therefore "'Experiential education' refers to learning activities that engage the learner directly in the phenomena being studied. This learning can be in all types of work or service settings by undergraduate and graduate students of all ages . . . [Experiential education is] carefully monitored, experience-based learning" (Kendall et al., 1986).

There are two basic categories of **experiential education activities: discrete and nondiscrete.** Discrete activities are those that are self-contained and constitute a separate entity. Examples of discrete experiential education activities include field study, internships, practica, student teaching, clinical experiences, cooperative education, and service-learning.

Nondiscrete experiential education activities are more often than not extensions or components of a course or program. As such they are not self-contained, separate entities. Many of the nondiscrete experiential education activities are considered to be innovative classroom instruction techniques. Examples of nondiscrete experiential education activities include: field trips, simulation/games, group process, role play, laboratory work, oral interviews, and participatory observations. Table 19-1 provides a more complete list of the most common types of experiential education activities.

No matter which activity becomes the vehicle, experiential learning is that transformation which "occurs when changes in judgments, feelings, knowledge, or skills result for a particular person from living through an event or events" (Chickering, 1976). The value inherent in learning through experience is amply expressed in the adage, "No man's knowledge here can go beyond his experience" (John Locke, 1690, *Essay Concerning Human Understanding*).

Field experiences, internships, practica, cooperative education, service-learning, and academic service-learning

Experiential learning in the form of field experiences, defined more specifically as practica and internships, are the types of experiential education activities that will be discussed in this chapter. **Field experience** is "an off campus learning activity, generally for credit, in which a student accepts a large share of the responsibility for his/her own learning" (Davis et al., 1978).

Internships are a type of field experience. They are "structured and career-relevant work experiences obtained by students prior to graduation from an academic program" (Taylor, 1988). Because they are most often pursued during the later stages of an academic degree program, internships are frequently the culminating experience for the plan of study. As such, they provide the student with an opportunity to experience the fusion of principles and theories with the solution of practical problems (Hoekstra, 1975; Rex, 1961). Because each should inform the other, the relationship between theory and practice

TABLE 19-1 *Types and Forms of Experiential Education*

1. Discrete experiential education courses or programs	2. Experiential education as one or more components of a course or program	3. Other experiential techniques incorporated into a course or program
Cooperative education	Field projects	Role playing
Field study, fieldwork, field research	Field trips	Laboratory work
	Participatory observations	Simulation games and exercises
Independent study	Oral interviews	Student-led class sessions
Internships	Site visits/field observations	(presentations or discussions)
Practica	Use of primary source or raw	Group learning activities
Service-learning	data	Other active forms of learning
Work-learn	Others	
Others		

From *Strengthening Experiential Education Within Your Institution* by Kendall, J. C., Duley, J. S., Little, T. C., Permal, J. S., Rubin, S. National Society for Experiential Education, 3509 Haworth Drive, Suite 207, Raleigh, North Carolina 27609, 1986, page 31.

can be realized as a result of participating in an internship (Sweitzer and King, 1999).

Similar to internships, **practica** are "academically credited field experiences designed to meet specific academic objectives. They may be general and interdisciplinary in nature or oriented toward specific preprofessional training. These experiences are often degree requirements" (Stanton and Ali, 1987). Practica, however, are typically shorter than internships and frequently occur earlier in the academic degree plan of study.

On occasion, internships, and to an even lesser degree practica, are classified as **cooperative education** (co-op) experiences. To qualify as cooperative education, the field experiences must be "paid work experiences closely related to [the student's] academic and career pursuits" (U.S. Department of Education, 1991).

Cooperative education typically subscribes to one of two basic formats. The first is **alternating cooperative education,** which is a "plan of providing full-time, paid periods of work, balanced with full-time periods of study in institutions of higher education" (Gould, 1987). The second is **parallel or extended-day cooperative education,** which is a pattern allowing "attendance in classes, day or night, concurrent to a co-op placement" (Sheppard, 1987). Whether or not the experience is alternating or parallel/extended-day, receipt of payment in

some form is usually necessary for the endeavor to be considered a cooperative education experience.

A concept that has evolved since the late 1960s, **service-learning** as defined by Jacoby (1996, p. 5), "is a form of experiential education in which students engage in activities that address human and community needs together with structured opportunities intentionally designed to promote student learning and development. Reflection and reciprocity are key . . . to service-learning." Due to its "commitment to social justice" (p. 10), service-learning could be confused with volunteer or community service programs. A striking difference is that service-learning includes intentional goals for student learning and development. Volunteer or community service programs, on the other hand, may lack the reflective component and intentional learning goals inherent in service-learning. (Jacoby, 1996).

The collaboration that results from entering into a bona fide partnership is critical to creating high-quality service-learning opportunities (Jacoby, 2003). True partnership exists only when representatives from academic institutions, including students engaging in service-learning activities, realize they are entering a *partnership with* the community to meet collective needs, rather than providing services to the community as an *outreach on behalf* of the community. To be effective, service-learning "must be reciprocal: it must serve the community while establishing learning opportunities" (London, 2001, p. 13).

"**Academic service-learning** is a pedagogical model that intentionally integrates academic learning and relevant community service" (Howard, 1998, p. 22). Within this context, service-learning is a teaching methodology where there is an *intentional* effort made to utilize community-based learning to enhance academic learning, and to utilize academic learning to inform community service. There is an *integration* of the two kinds of learning, experiential and academic; each works to strengthen the other. Additionally, the community service experiences must be *relevant* to the academic course of study (Howard, 1998). In short, academic service-learning is a teaching methodology whereby service is integrated into the course by means of an assignment (or assignments) that requires reflection in light of course objectives (Weigert, 1998, p. 7).

CONCEPT CHECK

*Both contexts, experiential and academic, are important as allies in the cyclic process whereby knowledge is created through the transformation of experience. Experiential education as a **pedagogical approach** refers to learning activities that engage the learner directly in the phenomena being studied. Field experiences are a type of experiential education and are often defined in terms of internships and practica. For a field experience to qualify as a co-op experience, the intern is typically paid. In an effort to link service-learning and academic study, academic service-learning is a field experience that provides community service through the achievement of course/curriculum objectives.*

Application to sport management curriculum

In the professional preparation of sport managers, experiential learning most commonly exists as field experience in the form of internships and practica. National curriculum standards require and describe each:

Practica are part-time work experiences in the sport industry, which may or may not be offered for credit. Practica are

often performed in proximity to the campus and usually involve observing and providing assistance to another professional. They must be directed and evaluated by a qualified faculty member with appropriate supervision by an on-site professional. (NASPE–NASSM, 2000, p. 9)

Internships are a full-time work experience in the sport industry (40 hours/week) that are offered for academic credit. This experience is actual work in a sport management setting in which management practices are applied. Final agreements and arrangements are completed by a member of the faculty. They must also be directed and evaluated by a faculty member with appropriate supervision by an on-site professional. (NASPE–NASSM, 2000, p. 10).

Field experience plays an essential role and is highly valued in the preparation of both undergraduate and graduate sport management students (Brassie, 1989; Chouinard, 1993; Cuneen, 1992; Cuneen and Sidwell, 1993; DeSensi et al., 1990; Li et al., 1994; Parks and Quain, 1986; Sutton, 1989; Parkhouse, 1987). In fact, the internship has historically been a core curricular component and is one of the most commonly found elements among undergraduate sport management programs in the United States (Cuneen, 2004; Stier 2002).

As cornerstones of the curriculum, practica and internships take students beyond the classroom by placing them in a real work environment, thus providing the opportunity to bridge theory and practice. Participation in these activities helps students develop professional attitudes, behaviors, and values while providing the opportunity to problem solve and link theory to real world occurrences. At the heart of these activities is *learning by doing*. Because they take place in the "real" workplace, practica and internships ensure opportunities to "practice the profession" while being immersed in the work behaviors and social culture of the host organization (Verner, 1993).

BENEFITS OF THE INTERNSHIP EXPERIENCE

The internship is a triangular relationship entered into by three principal parties. These include the student, university, and sponsoring organization. Each one of the three helps to define the internship expectations. As a result, each has the potential to benefit from the unique educational opportunity that can develop. Students most notably desire to accomplish academic, personal, and career-related goals. The university and sponsoring organization theory and practice. Further, the sponsoring organization can help to strengthen the profession by enhancing the workforce through the development of more capable entry-level employees. Following are benefits of specific value to the student, university, and sponsoring organization that can evolve from the internship relationship.

Value for students

Inherent in an internship experience for students is the opportunity to function as a professional and to become a part of the organization's culture through experiential awareness not only of its structure, resources, and purpose, but also the other internal and external factors that shape the organization. This includes becoming immersed in the behaviors, attitudes, beliefs, and values of the organization, an occurrence that can happen only when the internship experience duplicates or closely approximates that which is experienced by a full-time employee. Therefore, outside commitments such as coursework or other employment should not be pursued during the internship (Sutton, 1989). Interns should expect to follow all rules, regulations, and policies of the sponsoring organization to acquire the values, behaviors, and attitudes that constitute the culture of a professional in the organization. Granted, students pursuing full-time internships who are totally involved with the host organization may be making a considerable sacrifice. However, tremendous benefits can be realized by those who accept the challenge (Verner, 1993). Following are some of the benefits that may be realized by students.

A new learning environment. Knowledge and skills are acquired in different ways by different people. The practical settings that internships offer may be more effective learning environments for some students than the traditional classroom. Problem solving associated with an internship occurs in the "real world." The circumstances are not fictitious or contrived. Therefore lessons learned from the decision process can have a greater impact when experienced during an internship. For many students, the implications of problem solving and decision making have greater meaning and are longer lasting when associated with an internship rather than a simulated situation within the classroom.

desire to provide practical, on-the-job experience for students to help them meet their goals (Lanese and Fitch, 1983). Additionally, the university can help students reinforce the connection between

Realization of the meaning of professional commitment. Misconceptions often exist related to the totality of a career. It is not uncommon for the enjoyable and interesting parts of the job to be amplified at the expense of diminishing the less desirable tasks. A full-time internship places students in organizations where they are confronted daily with both the positive and negative sides of their career choice.

Assessment of skills and abilities by practitioners. Because of the environment in which they function, practicing professionals often view things from a more pragmatic and realistic perspective than college professors do. As a result, practitioners' assessment of interns' strengths and weaknesses can provide additional insight into the interns' potential for that particular career. This may help students progress toward greater crystallization of **vocational self-concept** and work values by facilitating the identification of vocationally relevant abilities, interests, and values (Taylor, 1988).

"Experience" as a category on the résumé. One of the most frustrating obstacles for neophyte professionals to overcome is lack of experience. Internships provide the opportunity to gain invaluable work experience and as a result create another entry on the résumé. Researchers have documented the value of work experience and internships in securing a job. Evaluation of résumés, including background as well as presence or absence of an internship for six college women graduates, indicated that the most common reasons for success in being selected for a job was relevant work experience and completion of an internship related to the job (Avis and Trice, 1991).

Two-way screening process. Students can determine whether they feel suited for the career choice during the internship, and those with whom they work can evaluate the performance of interns within the context of the real work environment. This is not to say that interns should expect to be hired by the host organization, although this does happen on occasion. Evaluation of an intern's potential is more valuable when based on how the student performed on the job rather than on the

evaluator's perceptions of how the student *may* function on the job.

New mentor/mentee relationships. New relationships develop as a result of contact with people encountered during the internship. These new relationships can help interns learn more about themselves, both professionally and personally. Through guidance, direction, and suggestion, mentors can help interns develop attitudes and behaviors necessary for success in their career. Many insights can be gained when interns learn from the mistakes and successes of those who have preceded them. Administrators advocate that all young professionals seek to establish mentor/mentee relationships (Young, 1990). Quality internships in sport management provide a forum for the development of strong mentor/mentee relationships (Brassie, 1989; Parks and Quain, 1986).

Networking. Being on the inside of the organization allows interns to be a part of the informal employee network. Students can learn of potential job openings before they are advertised, and they can develop important contacts as well as possible references for future career opportunities. Young (1990) found "administrators agreed that recommendations by network contacts often take precedence over a candidate's experience in a job search [which] reinforces the adage 'it's *who* you know that counts.' "

Information regarding vacancies or job availability can be from formal or informal sources. **Formal sources** are the traditional mechanisms for attaining job information, such as placement office bulletins and employment ads. **Informal sources** include friends and professional contacts. Greater access to informal sources of information regarding the job search is available to students who complete an internship (Parks, 1991; Taylor, 1988). According to Taylor (1984), the use of informal, as opposed to formal, sources of job information produces more satisfying job opportunities. Parks (1991) found the job placement strategy most frequently used by sport management majors was personal contact.

Mirror feedback and evaluation. Internships offer students the chance to discover whether theoretical ideas and textbook principles work in actual situations. The resulting successes and failures help establish a personal, critical assessment of how effective different strategies may be in a realistic environment.

Dealing with crises and critical decisions. In the real work world, daily incidents are not always predictable, and some situations may occur in which interns have had no experience. The conditions of the moment may not allow for consultation with mentors, the university supervisor, or textbooks. Action and decision making in such realistic dilemmas can accelerate the maturation process. Professional growth and development become evident as interns move away from reacting as students and assume the posture of young professionals.

Springboard for a career. An internship is the intermediate step between being a student and being a full-time professional. Depending on what the intern makes of the opportunity, it can be either a springboard or a barrier to a valued career position. A successful internship experience provides the basis for an excellent reference for future employment.

Value to university
Keeping in touch with the "real world." As new techniques and technology are developed and incorporated into the profession, it is helpful for university faculty to have exposure to what is and is not working in real-life situations. As visits and contacts are made with professionals who supervise student interns, faculty have the opportunity to discuss and witness both the effective and the ineffective procedures, equipment, and methodologies. This allows faculty to remain closer to the cutting edge of the profession (Verner, 1990).

Updating curriculum. Sport management educators believe one of the most valued characteristics of an effective graduate program is that the program is "updated to include current areas of subject matter in sport management" (Li et al., 1994). The university may improve its educational programs

and test "its curricula through feedback" associated with the internship (McCaffrey, 1979).

Faculty who supervise interns have tremendous opportunity to remain abreast of current developments in the profession. Additionally, feedback can be gained not only from student interns but also from sponsoring organization supervisors. Based on their exposure during the field experience, interns can inform faculty of the strengths and weaknesses of the curriculum. Likewise, feedback can be provided by supervisors in sponsoring organizations regarding how well prepared the intern was to accept responsibility and function in the organization (Konsky, 1976). Information from all of these sources can be useful to faculty as they update their lectures and revise the curriculum. Enriched by feedback from the field and subsequent reformulation of the curriculum, professional preparation programs will remain in step with the industry, and better prepared students will emerge to join the workforce.

Exposing students to new equipment. Even though it is relatively inexpensive to update the curriculum based on various forms of feedback, at a time when technology is changing so rapidly, it is quite expensive to keep college/university teaching laboratories up to date. Higher education institutions often experience financial limitations, prohibiting replacement or addition of new equipment so that students can be exposed to the latest available. It is particularly difficult to remain current with the most advanced equipment in the fitness industry because manufacturers are constantly designing and producing updated cardiovascular and resistive weight training apparatus. Internship experiences can provide students with the opportunity to work with equipment that may not be available on the campus.

Enriching classroom instruction. Classroom instruction can be enriched through the process of students relating their field experiences to the content being discussed (Gryski et al., 1992). Because they have been a part of the organization and have experienced what happens there on a day-to-day basis, the relationship between theory and practice may be more apparent for a student who has completed or is enrolled in a practicum or internship. Students who have not yet completed a field experience can become enlightened when fellow students who have completed an internship share their experiences and relate them to topics of instruction.

Developing research contacts. Faculty who supervise interns network with professionals in the field. Extensions of these relationships may lead to developing new ideas or strategies for research, as well as solidifying contacts that may be valuable in other endeavors (Cottrell and Wagner, 1990). Particularly enhanced through these faculty/practitioner relationships are opportunities related to applied research. Interaction with practicing professionals can provide faculty the opportunity to engage in research, possibly using the organization, its clients, or employees as the population to be studied. A few examples of applied research opportunities that may promote collaboration among the intern, faculty advisor, and sponsoring organization supervisor include study related to the following: (1) fan recognition of identified advertising displays in a sports venue, which may influence an advertiser's marketing approach; (2) client preference for cardiovascular equipment in a fitness environment, which may influence management's purchasing pattern; (3) donor motivation characteristics of those who, through gift-giving, financially support the organization, which may help the fundraiser better relate to current donors as well as know how to approach new donors.

Enhancing public relations. Through interaction with sponsoring organizations, universities can disseminate information about the strength of their programs and the capabilities of their graduates (Gryski et al., 1992). This interaction provides a valuable basis upon which to build relationships between the university and potential employers for graduates. It may also increase the likelihood that future interns may be placed with the sponsoring organization (Sink and Sari, 1984).

Value to sponsoring organization

Expanding the available workforce. It should not be expected that motivation on the part of an organization for hosting an intern is completely altruistic. In return for the time and energy invested in

helping students advance their knowledge, skill, and ability, sponsoring organizations with an effective intern will gain an additional staff member. This aspect can be particularly appealing when budget constraints have inhibited hiring practices (Bjorklund, 1974; Conklin-Fread, 1990).

Even in the beginning of the experience, when interns would not be expected to be full contributors, simple tasks and responsibilities can be assigned, thus allowing regular employees to direct their attention to higher-order tasks. As the interns become acclimated to the agency, greater responsibility can be assumed (Verner, 1990).

Bringing new ideas into the organization. Periodically introducing new ideas into the organization promotes variety and vitality. With each change in staff, new ideas are introduced to the agency. Such is also the case when hosting interns. "Students may sometimes serve as agents of change as they bring some of the latest information and innovation from the academic world into the field" (Gryski et al., 1992). Though they often have not had the opportunity to try many of their ideas, interns can offer a new perspective and a fresh outlook on tradition-laden policies and procedures. Because of their recent classroom exposure to literature and theories, interns are an excellent source of creative ideas (Verner, 1990).

Evaluating potential employees. Throughout the internship experience, personnel within the agency have the opportunity to evaluate the intern's capability to become a regular employee. Agency personnel can preview, with "no strings attached," preprofessionals who may be candidates for future job vacancies. Thus the internship can provide assistance in identifying talent among potential employees.

Assisting higher education to develop more-qualified employees. Through the sponsorship of internship opportunities, organizations blend their efforts with those of academic institutions to develop a more qualified workforce. The value of field experiences in accomplishing this goal was substantiated by DeSensi et al. (1990) when business or agency personnel in sport management organizations "indicated that both practica and internship experiences were very important" (p. 49). No doubt sport management curricular improvements since the late 1970s have narrowed the gap between employer expectations and entry-level employee abilities, but at that time Parkhouse and Ulrich (1979) found employers believed that "on-the-job training rather than formal preparation, better serves the organization's needs."

CONCEPT CHECK

Internships and practica can benefit everyone involved in the triangular relationship—the student, university, and sponsoring organization. However, the student probably gains the most.

POTENTIAL INTERNSHIP OPPORTUNITIES FOR SPORT MANAGEMENT STUDENTS

Before evaluating and selecting an internship site, students can narrow the search by creating a list of objectives they hope to accomplish during the internship experience. This process will enhance self-direction, which, according to Shipton and Steltenpohl (1980), promotes higher quality in experiential learning endeavors. By clarifying goals and planning a program to attain those goals, essential skills in self-direction are developed. Becoming self-directed related to one's education requires the following: (1) "learning how to plan"; (2) "learning how to assess personal values, interests, skills, aptitudes, and developmental needs [that contribute] to goal setting"; and (3) "knowing how to identify alternative learning activities and resources in relation to purposes." Having an environment in which to practice what is expected to be learned is requisite to developing ability in self-direction. Determining the most appropriate environment can be accomplished, in part, by subscribing to sound evaluation and selection criteria.

When considering potential organizations, it is helpful to be both creative and futuristic. Rather than being restrained by considering only typical placement sites, students should also look for organizations that could benefit from the knowledge, skill, and experience the intern could provide. Conversely, interns should evaluate whether potential sites offer appropriate opportunities to fulfill their internship objectives. The following types of organizations may meet the objectives of interns in fitness, leisure, and sport management. This partial list is offered to stimulate ideas. It is not intended to be comprehensive.

1. Fitness/Wellness
   a. Clinic/hospital programs for apparently healthy or diseased populations
   b. Commercial programs, franchises or independently owned establishments
   c. Community programs, e.g., YM/WCA, park districts, community centers
   d. Corporate/worksite programs for employees
   e. Cruise ships, large hotels, and resorts
2. Recreational Sport and other Leisure Endeavors
   a. Commercial programs, franchises or independently owned establishments
   b. Community programs, e.g., YM/WCA, park districts, community centers
   c. Corporate/worksite programs for employees
   d. Cruise ships, large hotels, and resorts
   e. Parks, including state and national, amusement and theme
3. Sport Management (either within sport organizations themselves or governing organizations that span the levels of sport below, or within organizations that facilitate sport delivery, e.g., broadcasting and journalism, career advancement and management, facility and professional management, marketing and public relations, sporting goods and equipment).
   a. Collegiate
   b. Extreme
   c. Olympic, including able-bodied, Para and Special Olympics
   d. Professional
   e. Youth

CONCEPT CHECK

Prospective interns should create a list of objectives to help define what they hope to accomplish during the internship. The process of developing objectives will assist in self-direction by clarifying goals and assist in planning to accomplish those goals. As a result, prospective interns should not be hesitant to make known their desires related to the type of internship placement.

COMPETENCIES DESIRED OF INTERNS

Two research studies documented potential employers' perceptions of desired competencies for sport management interns. Cuneen and Sidwell (1993) surveyed personnel who interview and select interns in major and minor league professional sports, college and university athletics, associations and conferences, resorts and clubs, event management, and the media. The respondents ($N = 215$) reacted to six fictitious potential intern résumés providing a rank order and identifying the one they would select for placement in their organization. From this assessment, nine intern qualifications emerged as the most desirable. In order of preference, the desired competencies were "(1) marketing/promotion experience, (2) evidence of computer skills, (3) evidence of writing skills, (4) sales experience, (5) internship goal, (6) practical/work experience, (7) athletic/sport background, (8) well-rounded, and (9) sports reporting experience."

Klein (1994) completed doctoral dissertation research, which led to the development of a "top ten" list of criteria for sport management interns as perceived by college athletic internship supervisors, nonprofit organization internship site supervisors, and sport management faculty advisors ($N = 143$). From an initial group of twenty knowledge competencies, eight technical skills, seventeen personal qualities, and seven selection criteria (fifty-two possible qualifications), the "top ten" list evolved and included seven personal qualities, two knowledge competencies, and one technical skill. The "top ten" criteria (actually there were eleven because of a tie for tenth place) for sport management interns emerging from this study in rank order were (1) reliable, (2) responsible, (3) willing to learn, (4) positive attitude, (5) verbal skills, (6) ethics, (7) communications, (8) cooperative, (9) adaptable to situations, (10) attention to detail, and (11) demonstrates initiative.

The two lists of competencies differ considerably in the items identified, most likely because of the differences in populations surveyed and the methodologies employed for the studies. Nonetheless, the results provide a point of departure for determining desirable intern characteristics.

As the internship coordinator for an agency that ran numerous large-scale sporting events, Williams (2004) emphasized quality student preparation as one of the most highly desired intern characteristics. While screening résumés and interviewing candidates, Williams looked for students who understood the business, industry, and particular organization. She stressed, "no fans please," meaning the interns' attraction to the agency had to be more than an infatuation. They had to be willing to roll up their sleeves, dig in, and work long hard hours for the duration of the internship. To be selected as the successful candidate from the interview process, interns had to demonstrate to Williams that they were committed and had direction. The latter is believed by some to be missing among many of today's graduating seniors. Lack of focus and absence of a clear career objective is quite common among students seeking internships or entry-level positions (Palomares, 2000). Some of the skills most highly valued among prospective interns include: interest, enthusiasm, strong communication skills, maturity, team, skills, independence, initiative, and a positive work ethic (Cuneen & Sidwell, 1993).

CONCEPT CHECK ✓

Sport management intern competencies have been identified in recent research and include as the top three work-related skills: marketing/promotion experience, computer skills, and writing skills. The top three personal qualities include reliability, responsibility, and willingness to learn.

UTILIZING CAREER ADVANCEMENT MATERIALS TO MARKET ONESELF

With consideration given to desirable intern characteristics and after spending introspective time to assess personal and professional strengths and weaknesses, students should develop materials to market themselves. Three pieces of marketing material are often used to kick off this million-dollar marketing campaign: cover letter, résumé, and student portfolio. (Consider this a million-dollar marketing campaign because today's graduates may expect to make a million dollars or more in a lifetime of work.)

Cover letter and résumé preparation is briefly discussed in the following section, while considerably more space is dedicated to the development and use of a student portfolio. Excellent resources on career advancement are noted at the end of this chapter.

Cover letter, résumé, and thank-you letter

Prospective interns should design a **chronological résumé** and prepare a cover letter that connects their professional skills and personal abilities with the tasks believed to be important to successful completion of the internship in question. When applying for an internship listed on the Web, follow the individual agency's formatting requirements for receiving applicant's e-mail cover letter and résumé (Smith, 1999). The cover letter and résumé should look professional because they are the first impression given by the potential intern. Make the cover letter specific, concise and well constructed with correct grammar, punctuation, spelling, and appropriate word choice. The résumé should provide all information that will help the agency staff become familiar with the candidate, including contact information, educational background, experiences related to the internship, and previous employment and volunteer experiences. According to Cuneen and Sidwell (1993), specificity regarding work-related skills is of tremendous value. For example, it is preferable for the résumé to identify the type of computer hardware and software used rather than simply indicating that the candidate is computer literate. Professional organization memberships, as well as school affiliations, should be listed. Leadership positions held in professional organizations and school affiliations should be highlighted. A handwritten thank-you letter sent to an agency interviewer immediately following a telephone or personal interview is common courtesy. A follow-up letter expresses appreciation for the interviewer's time, and also offers the potential intern an opportunity to add any information not shared during the interview (Garber, 2000). Refer to Websites describing career advancement materials at the end of the chapter for examples of résumés and cover letters.

Student portfolio

Recently, faculty from several fields of study have suggested that student portfolios are beneficial in assisting students in their preparation for internships and job interviews, as well as their entry into chosen careers. Professions where student portfolio development have been recommended include business, teacher education, health education, and applied health professions. Faculty from several fields of study have stated that student portfolio development contributes in a positive manner to success in undergraduate coursework as well.

Portfolio definitions and purposes. Although the definition and purpose of the student portfolio are often described differently by those representing various fields of study, it is agreed by most writers that a portfolio is a collection of student work gathered over time. In the early 1990s, researchers at the Northwest Regional Educational Laboratory in Oregon defined the student portfolio as "a purposeful collection of student work that tells a story of the student's efforts, progress, or achievement in a given area (Arter & Spandel, 1992, p. 36). The student portfolio has been described as having many purposes. "Why develop a student portfolio?" is a fair question to ask. One purpose is to document one's learning and growth during the undergraduate professional preparation program (Stone, 1998). Stone describes such a portfolio as the best work that a student can show others to demonstrate accomplishments over time and across a variety of contexts. Second, a portfolio may be a means for a student to reflect upon the successes and failures during experiences of applying knowledge and skills in classroom simulations or practica. For example, Stone suggests that logs, journals, self-evaluations, and reflective captions on items selected for portfolio inclusion can provide a student an opportunity for introspection and reflection. A third purpose of a portfolio is for showcasing to prospective internship supervisors and employers what a student knows and can do. Prospective employers find that this collection of work provides much more information than is given on a résumé, and thus it is seen as an important marketing tool that accompanies the résumé (Ellery & Rauschenbach, 1997).

Typically, interest by faculty has been increasing to use the student portfolio in yet another manner. It is seen as a tool for assessing and evaluating what a student knows and can do, and how well a student is progressing. Because this latter purpose involves controversy, especially within the field of education, research and development projects have been ongoing to determine the reliability and validity of the portfolio in assessing student achievement (Storms, Nunez, and Thomas, 1996).

Student portfolio types. The type of portfolio to be developed is determined by the audience for which it is intended. One type of portfolio is the **working portfolio** that contains cumulative work collected by the student in a purposeful manner according to stated guidelines or criteria. Selected work accumulated during enrollment in a single course and from many courses over a period of time shows one's efforts and progress toward the achievement of specific goals or standards. For example, the NASPE-NASSM Sport Management Program Standards provide specific areas of knowledge requisite for a student to enter into a career in sport management. The sport management working portfolio would contain samples of work selected by the student from undergraduate courses with the inclusion of the following areas: behavioral dimensions of sport; management and organizational skills in sport; ethics in sport management; marketing in sport; communication in sport; finance in sport; economics in sport; legal aspects of sport; governance in sport; and field experiences in sport management (NASPE-NASSM Joint Task Force on Sport Management Curriculum and Accreditation, 1993). This type of portfolio often includes student reflections and is most likely intended for the student, classmates, and course instructors.

A second type of student portfolio is the **showcase portfolio,** a purposeful collection of the student's best works as documentation of mastery of content and skills standards. A portfolio of this type provides evidence that links coursework to skills directly related to core competencies defined by a discipline (Waishwell et al., 1996). Such a portfolio can be presented to prospective practicum or internship supervisors and employers as evidence clearly documenting a student's readiness to enter the profession.

Selecting items for the portfolio. A wide variety of materials should be gathered for a portfolio (Hansen, 1992; Cleary, 1993). Suggested items include videotapes, writing samples, presentations and performances, individual and group projects, and career goal statements. Specific examples

from the field of sport management might include marketing plans, budgets, and evidence of Website development. The student may wish to include a **reflective statement,** which is an introspective process of describing one's philosophy, values, or beliefs to others. For example, the sport management student might develop a reflective statement describing his or her personal leadership style.

In developing a showcase portfolio for either an internship or the employment interview, the student should select documents that demonstrate the link between classroom experiences and the knowledge and skills required for an internship or professional position. Products should be selected that demonstrate the ability to apply the theory and content of academic coursework to the "real life" skills needed by a sport management professional. Throughout the process of developing the showcase portfolio, it is important to remember that each portfolio is a unique effort, a tool designed to help students to market themselves. Although guidelines for portfolio development are often suggested, each student, with guidance from faculty members, should carefully select the documents to be included.

Items that demonstrate the student's acquisition of sport management content and skills should also be incorporated. Although any item can be included, a student might utilize the NASPE-NASSM Sport Management Program Standards during the selection process. Class projects and assignments that document the acquisition of knowledge and skills in one or more core content areas of the Program Standards would be especially relevant and appropriate. For example, a student might select an item that demonstrates competence in finance in sport or legal aspects of sport.

A recent survey of sport management professionals provides additional direction for the selection of portfolio items. In a study by Kadlecek and Thoma (1999), 186 sport management professionals were asked to identify the essential components of a portfolio. The five items that were identified as being most important for a portfolio included a marketing plan, a budget project, a sponsorship proposal, an ad media campaign, and a ticket sales campaign. Other items identified as important included evidence of Web page development, an

I. One-Page Résumé
II. Table of Contents (listing page numbers)
III. One- to Two-Page Reflective Statement
IV. Documentation of Content and Skills
    Acquisition
    a. Budget Project
    b. Marketing Plan
    c. Sponsorship Proposal
    d. Ad and Media Campaign
    e. Ticket Sales Campaign
    f. Press Release
    g. Legal Aspects of Sport Management
       Issue Presentation

FIGURE 19-2 Sport management student portfolio.

event bid, a risk management assessment, and a press release.

Organizing the showcase portfolio. The keys to a successful showcase portfolio are the types of documents included and the way in which they are presented, not the amount of material accumulated (Ellery & Rauschenbach, 1997). In fact, a portfolio that is too bulky or not carefully organized may be counterproductive. It is important to remember that a person who is conducting interviews to choose the best candidate for an internship or employment may be pressed for time. Few will have the time to review a lengthy portfolio, especially if there are a number of applicants.

Figure 19-2 provides an example of how a student portfolio for sport management might be organized and the types of documents that could be included. One technique to begin the portfolio is to start with a current one-page résumé. This reminds the interviewer of important information about the candidate, including academic preparation, relevant work experiences, and appropriate certifications and volunteer experiences. A table of contents is often then presented. Listing all portfolio items with page numbers can serve as an important organizational tool. This organization will help someone to easily locate a relevant document as opposed to searching needlessly through all documents. Several portfolio experts suggest that a brief reflective statement be included next (Montgomery, 1997; Ellery & Rauschenbach, 1997). This statement should be

limited to one or two pages and should describe one's strengths as a sport management professional and one's leadership/management style.

Incorporating the portfolio during an interview. Following the development of an organized, quality portfolio documenting that one has the skills and knowledge essential for entry into sport management, the student faces yet another challenge. This challenge is to successfully integrate the portfolio into the interview process. In addition to getting the portfolio into the interviewer's hands, the student must also draw the attention of the interviewer to those items that best market the interviewee as the best candidate. During the interview, the student should listen very carefully to identify an early question that provides the opportune moment to hand the portfolio to the interviewer. Before offering the portfolio, the student needs to open it without difficulty to the specific section or item that contains evidence of the professional quality or skill, knowledge, or experience the interviewer asked about. Throughout the rest of the interview, the interviewee should continue to make references to documented work in the portfolio while encouraging the reader to take time to view it. It takes forethought and planning to be prepared to then elaborate on how and why the piece of work being viewed is important to one's future performance in sport management. Helping the interviewer see the value and worth of one's portfolio can enhance the overall interview experience and the impending outcome.

Electronic portfolios

A new trend in portfolio development is the electronic portfolio. Although specialized software is available, a student can place the reflective statement, résumé, and various artifacts demonstrating professional skills on a personal Web page. The potential internship coordinator can review the Web pages in preparation for the interview. The advantage of an electronic portfolio is a sports management student can present information about relevant skills and experiences without overwhelming the internship coordinator with a large, heavy binder at the time of the interview (Kimeldort, 1997). As with electronic cover letters and résumés, internships sites may vary as to their preference for portfolio format. A student should inquire as to the preferred method of submission, either paper or electronic or a combination of both.

CONCEPT CHECK

In the past ten years, the student portfolio has emerged as a method to document the acquisition of specific skills that are essential to entering the profession. The working portfolio combines many examples of student work that are completed during the undergraduate or graduate experience. As the student prepares for the internship or practicum, he or she will develop a showcase portfolio that contains the best work and documents essential skills needed in sport management. The portfolio can be continued throughout the internship/practicum, adding new work from that experience. More and more employers regard the portfolio as a useful supplement to the interviewing and hiring of a sport management professional.

SECURING AN INTERNSHIP

In their book, *Sport Management Field Experiences*, Cuneen and Sidwell (1994) answer questions often asked by sport management students, their families, friends, and support groups. Intended to be an introduction to the purposes of field experiences, site search methods, credentials preparation, interview processes, conduct of field experiences and appropriate academic exercises, Cuneen and Sidwell's work is a key resource that should be consulted by sport management students before they seek practica and internships.

There are four basic steps to securing an internship: (1) identifying potential internship organizations; (2) contacting those of greatest interest; (3) interviewing with several organizations to find out more about their offerings; and (4) selecting the organization best suited for personal objectives. Before embarking on the process of securing an internship, students should become familiar with the expectations, resources, and requirements at their universities. By working closely with a university adviser or internship coordinator, the student will benefit by suggestions and become aware of approved university procedures.

Awareness of potential sites

Internship opportunities can be discovered by reviewing professional literature and web sites (several appear at the end of this chapter), listening to speakers who share their professional experiences, participating in class or club activities designed to introduce new career opportunities, or attending professional conferences. Students can do more in-depth exploration by interviewing, observing, or shadowing a professional in the field. Finally, students can experience various career options by volunteering or completing practica in work-related environments (Verner, 2004). In exchange for providing person power, practicum students or volunteers get the opportunity to assess their fit with various segments of the sport industry while functioning as a part of a sport organization. This *inside perspective* helps students make better-informed decisions when choosing an internship.

In some segments of the sport industry, such as minor league baseball, job fairs are held annually to connect employers and job/internship seekers. During the 2003 Baseball Winter Meetings in New Orleans, the Professional Baseball Employment Opportunities Fair listed approximately 300 jobs, including internships, and hosted approximately 500 job/internship seekers (J. A. Bell, personal communication, December 30, 2003).

Initial contact

Initial contact should be made by sending the cover letter and résumé to preferred organizations. Allow approximately ten working days to receive a response. If no response is received, follow up the initial contact with a phone call. During this conversation, students can provide additional information or arrange to meet with someone from the agency to discuss the possibility of an internship.

Interview

The purpose of the initial contact is to arrange for an interview or to discuss the possibility for an internship. Try to obtain interviews with different agencies to compare the various opportunities. When visiting these organizations, tour the facilities and meet as many staff members as possible to evaluate the organizational culture and climate. Questions should be asked by both the interviewer and the interviewee to provide the information needed to help each make the appropriate choice to facilitate a good fit between the intern and the agency. Expectations held by the student, the agency, and the university should be discussed.

After the interview, it is wise for the interviewee to follow up with a thank-you letter to the interviewer. Consistent with the preparation of all application materials, this communication should be professional in appearance and message. The thank-you letter allows the interviewee to: (1) show appreciation for the time taken by the interviewer to review materials and conduct the interview, (2) keep his/her name in the interviewer's thoughts, (3) make a point that was forgotten/overlooked during the interview, or (4) reiterate an item of importance.

Selection

Internship site selection should occur only after the student has given considerable thought to the information collected during the interview, as well as from conversations with previous interns and the university internship supervisor. Information from these sources should be balanced against the student's objectives for the internship experience. Factors to consider when making the selection should include the following:

Position identity. The agency selected for the internship should be similar to that desired for an entry-level position. If that is not possible, the agency should be one that will provide the experience needed to be competitive for the desired entry-level position. The anticipated tasks and responsibilities should be transferable. At a minimum, the skills used in the internship should be similar to those required by the desired entry-level position (Sutton, 1989).

Compensation. Remuneration, or the lack thereof, should be the pivotal point for site selection only if financial compensation is absolutely required to be able to pursue the internship. However, significant financial compensation is not typical; in most internship situations, there is no remuneration.

Time span. The length of the internship will be determined in part by university and organizational requirements. Typically, internships occur within the semester; however, some are six months to one year in duration. The time of year should be considered, since organizations may be involved in cyclic work patterns and may only accept interns during specific times of the year.

Location. Students seeking permanent residence in particular parts of the country may want to consider obtaining internships in the desired regions. This not only provides the opportunity to learn more about a selected area but also can help students make professional contacts with knowledge of future job opportunities.

New experience. Internships are perfect times to try something unfamiliar and challenging. During this period, experiment and explore new aspects of the profession. There is little risk on the part of either the intern or the host organization in terms of an extended commitment or obligation.

Compatibility. Cuneen (2002) described five cohort groups that have a vested interest in the internship: the student; host site; and the academic institution, which she subdivided into academic faculty and administrators. Our discussion addresses the *major* stakeholders who enter into the three-way internship agreement: the student, host site, and university supervisor as a representative of the academic institution. The majority of our attention is directed toward student concerns.

While all parties have deeply vested interests, most agree that the student is the primary stakeholder. Even so, students must realize the constraints imposed by a host site's bottom-line necessity to serve its clientele. Within those constraints, prospective interns should be forthcoming about what they hope to accomplish during the internship (Verner, 1993).

Prospective interns should identify their needs, interests, and desires, and define the parameters they feel are necessary for a successful internship. This is the first step in taking an active role to shape the experience by determining compatibility between their professional/personal goals and opportunities available at various internship sites. By taking initiative and being proactive in this way, students approach the internship from the confident perspective of "I'm going to make this experience happen FOR me, rather than letting it happen TO me" (Verner, 2004, p. 25).

Stier (2002) poses a list of questions that soon-to-be interns can answer to help determine compatibility between their goals and a potential internship site. It should be remembered, however, that these questions should be considered only after students give tremendous thought to their interests, needs, and desires for the internship and develop objectives to guide the search process.

1. Is there a good match between the intern and the host site in terms of interests, job assignments, and general responsibilities?
2. Are the proposed duties and responsibilities of the intern meaningful and appropriate?
3. Is the length of the internship appropriate for the student in light of the proposed assignments and responsibilities?
4. Has the organization (and the host site supervisor) successfully utilized interns in the past?
5. Does the host site view interns as candidates for future employment or merely as free labor?
6. Does the host site have a history of hiring past interns as regular employees following the internship?
7. Has the host site actually helped former interns secure meaningful employment with other appropriate organizations following the internship?
8. Will the intern be working with skilled and experienced professionals within the host site?
9. Will the host site assist in making living arrangements (if required) for the intern?
10. Will the overall internship experience facilitate the student's career goals? (Stier, 2002, p. 8)

Providing students a voice through interviews and qualitative research techniques to determine their criteria for accessing the compatibility of potential internship sites, Stratta (2004) offers a model depicting the aspects students deem significant. Developed entirely from the feedback from undergraduate and graduate sport management students currently enrolled in or who had recently completed an internship, this model clarifies students' needs and concerns associated with each internship stakeholder, that is, students themselves, academic institutions, and host sites. Figure 19-3 depicts the working model that evolved from Stratta's four-year study. It offers additional focus for prospective interns' consideration when determining compatibility along with answering the questions posed by Stier (2002).

CONCEPT CHECK

There are recommended steps to be followed in seeking an internship placement. However, before embarking on the search process, potential interns should contact the university internship coordinator or academic adviser who coordinates the internship program to become familiar with university policies, procedures, expectations, and resources.

SOLIDIFYING INTERNSHIP EXPECTATIONS

After the intern, university representative, and supervisor from the sponsoring organization have concurred that the internship can take place, an agreement should be developed to solidify the parameters and expectations of the internship experience. A document signed by the three parties is often used for this purpose. Although many universities and sponsoring organizations have used the term *learning contract* to refer to this document, there is reason to believe that *learning agreement* or other terminology that excludes the term *contract* might be a better choice. The preference for refraining from using *contract* is to avoid any legal implications that may be inherent in the term. The intent to identify expectations related to the internship can be accomplished without using the term *contract*; so as a measure of caution, the document specifying these conditions should not include this term.

Items covered by the learning agreement include anything that aids in clarifying the intentions and expectations of the student, university, and sponsoring organization supervisor. These include, but are not limited to, criteria related to educational goals, work-related objectives, learning activities, evaluation and grading techniques, academic credit, supervision support, and insurance coverage. Often, organizations that sponsor internship programs require some type of learning agreement

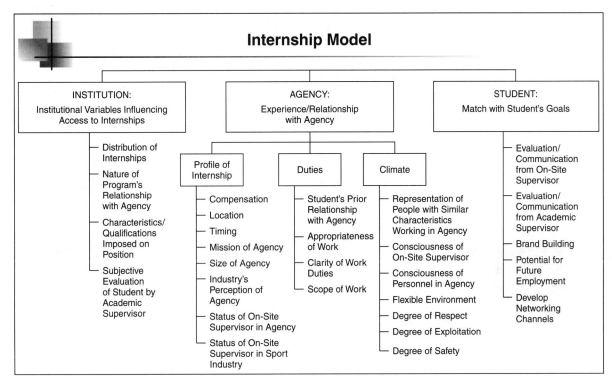

FIGURE 19-3   The internship model.

before the experience can begin. This ensures that all parties clearly understand and agree to the role each will play in the internship relationship (Stanton and Ali, 1987). (Figure 19-4 provides an example learning agreement.)

STAGES OF AN INTERNSHIP

While each intern's experience subscribes to a certain element of uniqueness, some faculty who have supervised internships over a period of many years believe threads of similarity exist among most internship experiences. Some of the concerns and challenges that confront interns seem to occur in a predictable order. One of the similarities that cuts across various internship experiences is the phases students progress through as the internship unfolds. Sweitzer and King (1999) typify the five stages of an internship and call the stages anticipation, disillusionment, confrontation, competence, and culmination. While the order in which interns

migrate through these stages is fairly predictable, the length of time spent in each stage differs considerably from intern to intern. Additionally, the end of one stage and the beginning of the next are not completely separate. Overlap often exists from one stage to the other. Sweitzer and King's explanation of what to expect during the course of an internship may be helpful as the interns prepare for and progress through the internship experience: (1) *anticipation:* looking forward to the internship and dealing with the accompanying anxiety; (2) *disillusionment:* a sense of despair when reality falls short of desire, a lack of certainty or affirmation about the experience; (3) *confrontation:* dealing with issues that are causing disillusionment, working through the difficulties; (4) *competence:* increased confidence resulting from successfully confronting and dealing with issues; (5) *culmination:* a sense of uneasiness that surfaces near the end of the experience as reflection clarifies what has transpired and anticipation seeks what the future may hold.

Illinois State University Department of Health, Physical Education, and Recreation Professional Practice – Cooperative Education & Internship **LEARNING AGREEMENT**	

PART I

A. NAME	SOCIAL SECURITY NO.

CAMPUS ADDRESS *Street*	HOME ADDRESS *Street*

City	*State*	*Zip*	*City*	*State*	*Zip*

PHONE	EMAIL	PHONE	EMAIL

ADDRESS WHILE DOING CO-OP/INTERNSHIP   *Street*

City	*State*	*Zip*	PHONE *(include area code)*

DATE CO-OP/INTERNSHIP COMMENCES	*DATE CO-OP/INTERNSHIP TERMINATES*

B. CO-OP/INTERNSHIP ORGANIZATION

ADDRESS   *Street*

City	*State*	*Zip*	PHONE *(include area code)*

NAME OF AGENCY SUPERVISOR	EMAIL

STUDENT POSITION

STUDENT POSITION IS –
☐ Paid *or* ☐ Unpaid

C. FACULTY SPONSOR/ADVISER

PROGRAM

ADDRESS   *Street*

City	*State*	*Zip*	PHONE *(include area code)*

CREDITS TO BE AWARDED

PROGRAM	COURSE NO.	NO. OF CREDITS

Copies:	White - *Faculty Adviser*	Pink - *Dept. P.P. Coordinator*
	Canary - *Agency Supervisor*	Gold - *Student*

FIGURE 19-4   Sample learning agreement.

Adapted by Illinois State University from Stanton, T., and Ali, K.: *The experienced hand: A student manual for making the most of an internship*. National Society for Experiential Education, 3509 Haworth Drive, Suite 207, Raleigh, North Carolina 27609, 1987, pp. 63–65. Reprinted with permission.

Professional Practice Learning Agreement

PART II. The Professional Practice Co-op/ Internship Experience

A. Job Description: Describe in as much detail as possible your role and responsibilities while on your internship or co-op. List duties, projects to be completed, deadlines, etc., if relevant.

B. Supervision: Describe in as much detail as possible the supervision to be provided. What kind of instruction, assistance, consultation, etc., you will receive from whom, etc.

C. Evaluation: How will your work performance be evaluated? By whom? When?

PART III. Learning Objectives/ Learning Activities/ Evaluation

A. Learning Objectives: What do you intend to learn through this experience? Be specific. Try to use concrete, measurable terms.

FIGURE 19-4   (cont.) Sample learning agreement.

B. Learning Activities

(1) On-the-Job: Describe how your internship/co-op activities will enable you to meet your learning objectives. Include projects, research, report writing, conversation, etc., which you will do while working, relating them to what you intend to learn.

(2) Off-the-Job: List reading, writing, contact with faculty sponsor, peer group, discussion, field trips, observations, etc., you will make and carry out that will help you meet your learning objectives.

C. Evaluation: How will you know what you have learned, or that you have achieved your learning objectives? How do you wish to evaluate your progress toward meeting these objectives? Who will evaluate? When? How will a grade be determined? By whom? When?

PART IV. Agreement

This agreement may be terminated or amended by student, faculty supervisor, or worksite supervisor at any time upon written notice which is received and agreed to by the other two parties.

STUDENT SIGNATURE		DATE
FACULTY ADVISER		DATE
AGENCY SUPERVISOR		DATE

FIGURE 19-4   (cont.) Sample learning agreement.

SUMMARY

- Over the last few decades, there has been considerable growth in the endorsement of field experiences as valuable components in the academic degree preparation for a number of professions. Curricular standards developed by the NASPE-NASSM Task Force require both a practicum and an internship experience in the preparation of sport managers.

- The internship represents a three-way agreement. Tremendous benefits can be gained by each of the three principal parties involved in the internship experience—the intern, university, and sponsoring organization.

- Desirable competencies of sport management interns have been identified in recent research. After considering these competencies, prospective interns should consult with their university internship program coordinator, and begin the process of preparing career advancement materials and selecting an internship site. There are recommended ways to market oneself as well as search for, select, and solidify an internship placement.

- When an organization decides to offer an internship, it should specify in writing the expectations and intent for the internship. It is advisable that this document not be called a "learning contract"; a better title may be "learning agreement."

 CRITICAL THINKING EXERCISES

1. On your résumé you indicate the availability of both references and a portfolio. An employer calls you to set up an interview, and during the conversation asks you to explain the portfolio and its purpose. In a paragraph, provide your response to the prospective employer.

2. During the new millennium, many undergraduate and graduate sport management programs will begin to require student portfolios. What might be the impact of this practice from the perspective of the student? internship supervisor? prospective employer? the sport management profession?

 CASE STUDY

The following case study was written by a student during the final few weeks of his internship experience. It is offered as a testimonial to the value of developing and using a student portfolio. As you become aware of this student's perspective, consider the suggestions he offers as a seasoned intern:

Each year, thousands of graduates enter the job market to compete for employment. These students have completed their degrees in hopes of attaining a job related to their field of expertise. Unfortunately for these students, there are fewer jobs than there are students. Students must find ways to present themselves to the employers using as many techniques as possible. One such approach that is currently being used on college campuses is student portfolios.

As a college freshman, I spent most of my time taking courses to satisfy university requirements and practicing poor study habits. I had no real idea what I wanted to do after graduation, and after all, it seemed so far away. I remember thinking to myself; "I will have no problem getting a job because I will have a college degree." To say I was a bit naive would be completely accurate. However, time passed and before I knew it, I was a sophomore.

As a sophomore, I chose the sport management major, as it seemed the right fit for my interests. So I began taking sport management courses, not knowing what to expect or even what was ahead for me. I remember being in my major class thinking, "is this the area I really want to be involved with for the rest of my life?" At the completion of the class, my instructor advised us to update four specific items for our "portfolios." I, like many others, thought the idea was just another assignment and nothing to be too concerned about. The portfolio I developed lacked effort and importance. My classmates and I felt if we "just got it done," it would not be an issue anymore and we could move on.

My junior year rolled around and I continued taking the sequences of courses, studying and learning more about the field of sport management. I completed projects and kept them filed away for some reason. Like the previous semesters, there was some importance placed on the portfolio, but nothing to prepare us for the future.

My senior year came and with it a new outlook on school and life. I was finally realizing it was about time to step out into the real world. I thought continuously about being out there and not being prepared or not having the knowledge necessary for employment, so I can honestly say that I applied myself 100 percent. As part of this experience of being a senior who would be graduating in just two short semesters, I took great pride in doing everything that I could do to prepare for the future. One such preparation was the development of my personal portfolio. I am not speaking of the portfolio required by the professors early on in the program, but a product of my work and success as a college student.

I was introduced to the concept of portfolios by one of my instructors, who provided suggestions on developing a showcase portfolio. She provided the class with a handout to help us to structure and organize our portfolios. As students we were responsible for meeting certain criteria for the portfolio, but at the same time we had great liberty to use creativity to tailor our portfolios to our personalities.

As I began to develop my portfolio, I reevaluated all of my projects, papers, and assignments from courses throughout the program. As I looked through these items, I took time to correct and modify them for accuracy, currency, and thoroughness. Next, I decided to organize the portfolio based on the NASPE-NASSM Sport Management Program Standards. I felt this was the best way for the items to be organized for both me and for employers. A key to successful portfolio design is ease of reading. You want to catch the viewer's attention by selecting content that is meaningful and providing relevant evidence of your acquired knowledge, skills, and experiences. I also wanted the portfolio to be professional, yet exciting. I completed this task by placing a fair amount of color in the portfolio, using protector sheets, and organizing it with divider sheets and tabs in a leather binder. The items I included were as follows: projects, assignments, papers, certifications, reflective statement, volunteer work résumé, table of contents, and presentations. Throughout the process I kept in mind my own personality and my intended viewer/reader.

When it came time to use my portfolio, I was thankful for all the time and effort I put into developing the total package. It definitely has proven to be an asset to my career opportunities thus far. For example, as part of the final requirement for my undergraduate degree, I was to complete a sport management internship. The process required me to schedule and complete an interview with my site supervisor. At this time we discussed one another's expectations during my internship, my strengths and weaknesses, and specifics about the site. For the interview, I brought my portfolio that I had developed throughout my college career. As we talked and time went on, I realized that I had to incorporate my portfolio into the interview. The most difficult task is not developing the portfolio but finding a smooth transition to using it in an interview. The answer to this problem is, "there is no perfect time!" You must just have a feel for the interview and the conversation to determine when to share your portfolio with the interviewer.

Currently, I use my portfolio to support my work in my internship. It is nice to have a handy reference on my desk to help me navigate my way through problems. Also, I have used my portfolio to help me generate ideas for new projects.

As I move on in my professional career, I plan to continue adding to and replacing materials in my portfolio. By this I mean I will add new project materials that I am especially proud of and feel would be beneficial to a future employer as well as me. Second, I will replace dated work with current work that could aid me in future projects. Finally, I would like to keep my portfolio updated as evidence of personal achievement.

For those of you contemplating a portfolio, I would without a doubt recommend developing one. I have gained much from developing my portfolio, and I offer you the following suggestions when beginning your own professional portfolio:

- *Seek the assistance of a professor for support.*
- *Organize your portfolio so it is easy for the viewer to read.*
- *Develop your portfolio to represent you and your personality.*
- *Use your creativity to gain interest and maintain the viewer's attention.*
- *Use materials that will be beneficial for an employer to see.*
- *Start development of the portfolio EARLY in your program.*

- *Keep all materials from each class in your program and any other course material you feel would be appropriate.*
- *Update your materials as you go through the program; DO NOT wait until you begin to use your portfolio.*
- *Seek ideas by browsing through former students' portfolios.*
- *Do your very best to make it what you want it to be.*
- *And . . . good luck!*

Your future is not going to rest on your decision to not develop a portfolio. However, the job market continues to be saturated with college graduates. As this happens, employers can continue to be more selective in whom they choose to hire. A portfolio is an excellent way to market yourself and place yourself a step higher on the employer's candidate list. As a college student, you have all that is needed to develop a quality portfolio, but you must provide the effort and determination to make it useful and complete. The portfolio is an excellent tool for graduates entering the job market to showcase their abilities and to seek promotion or career advancements.

 REVIEW QUESTIONS AND ISSUES

1. What role do experiential and academic learning play in the process of creating knowledge through transformation?
2. Describe Kolb's experiential learning theory in terms of its structure and relate the four components to one another.
3. What are the two field experience components required by the NASPE-NASSM curriculum standards? How do they differ and how are they similar?
4. Identify and describe three possible benefits for the intern that can result from an internship experience.
5. What are three university/faculty benefits that can be realized from an internship experience? Name and describe them.
6. An organization that sponsors internship opportunities can benefit in numerous ways. List and describe three possible benefits that can result from hosting an intern.

7. Competencies desired by sport management interns have been documented in two research studies (Cuneen and Sidwell, 1993; Klein, 1994). Name any six of the desired competencies identified among the top five on either of the two lists generated by these two studies.
8. Describe the major differences between a working and a showcase portfolio. What are the benefits of each type?
9. Identify the three purposes of a student portfolio. Which of the three is the most important to you as a student? Explain why.
10. What term is *not* recommended for use in the document that specifies arrangements and expectations for the internship? Why should this term not be associated with the document that solidifies the internship relationship?

 SOLUTIONS TO CRITICAL THINKING EXERCISES

1. Sample answer: The portfolio is a representative collection of my best work from all sport management classes. It provides evidence of my sport management skills, writing style and problem-solving abilities. The reason why I would like you to review it is that it demonstrates my professional skills as well as my commitment to high-quality work.
2. Sample answer: The student feels prepared for the entry-level job, the internship supervisor confirms the skills of the new intern, the prospective employer can better compare two job applicants, and the sport management profession supports common entry-level skills through student documentation.

FOSTERING YOUR WORKPLACE SKILLS

1. Develop a résumé "master" that could be customized for an e-mail résumé.
2. Write a cover letter highlighting information from your résumé that you want the internship contact person to pay special attention to.
3. In preparation for an interview:
   a. Identify your strengths and weaknesses.
   b. Name two activities to date that helped you develop skills desired by agency supervisors. Elaborate on the skills you developed

in each situation. Remember to consider your practicum and volunteer experiences.

c. List adjectives you believe former employers/supervisors would use to describe you.

d. Create a list of 10 verbs to use during an interview that describe your accomplishments in the field of sport management, e.g., evaluated, supervised, etc.

 WEBSITES

Sport Management Internship and Career Resources

www.canadiansport.com/jobs—Canadian Sport Canadian sport-related job opportunities from around the country.

http://personal.bgsu.edu/~jparks/ExSport/—ExSport II: An interactive sport management career interest system made available through Bowling Green State University to help students learn more about sport management careers.

www.hpcareernet.com—HPCAREER.NET: Career resources in health promotion, providing *real-time* advertising services to employers seeking candidates and support to professionals seeking career advancement.

www.iaam.org—International Association of Assembly Managers: Resources, including job and internship listings for professionals in the entertainment, sports, trade, hospitality, and tourism industries.

www.internsearch.com—Internsearch.com: Match qualified students with quality internship positions (and vice versa) by publishing a National Internship Directory which includes detailed descriptions of available internships, including sport management. Students and university access is free of charge.

www.jobsinsports.com—Jobs in Sports: Membership fee required to search a job, internship, and contact data bases, and post a résumé. Some sample openings are visible without membership.

www.MonsterTRAK.com—Monster Track: Internship opportunities listed locally or nationally. State and university affiliation and job descriptors required to access the database.

www.ncaa.org—National Collegiate Athletic Association: The *NCAA News* offers both online and hard copy job opportunities in intercollegiate athletics called The Market. Registry for receiving e-mail updates is available.

www.BlueFishJobs.com—National Intramural-Recreational Sports Association: Lists jobs, graduate assistantships, and internships in recreational sport.

www.sportsemploymentnews.com—National Sports Employment News: Membership required for a twice-monthly publication (weekly via e-mail) of sports industry positions including internships, entry-level, management, and executive-level positions.

www.nassm.com/resume—North American Society for Sport Management: NASSM Service Center Career offers a free résumé bank, membership posting, professional village, and a bulletin board for internship, graduate assistantship, and job opportunities.

www.onlinesports.com—Online Sports: Online directory of sport products and services, including job and internship postings.

www.pbeo.com—Professional Baseball Employment Opportunities: A career network for job seekers looking to gain employment in professional baseball by providing continuous access to minor league baseball and Major League Baseball clubs.

www.rsinternships.com—Rising Star Internships: Employers and internship seekers alike can post under an array of categories, including sport management.

www.sportscareers.com—Sports Careers: Describes career opportunities within the sports industry and profiles jobs in various sectors, including qualifications, education, responsibilities, and a general salary range.

www.sportsbusinessdaily.com—Sports Business Daily: SBD's Sports Business Resources provides Web links to the home pages of international sports teams, leagues, and governing bodies grouped by sport. Internship or job opportunities may be posted on the various home pages.

www.sportsemployment.com—Sports Employment: Membership fee required to access results of a Web crawler that searches over 25,000 sports, recreation, and health- and fitness-related company Websites searching for recently posted sports jobs. These jobs are filtered and merged into the SportsEmployment.com sports job bank.

www.sportmanagementclub.com—Sport Management Club: Membership fee required for access to an internship database, career tips, interviews with executives, network opportunities, contact information for industry leaders, and e-mails containing business news and industry trends.

www.sportsweb.com—Sports Web: Recruitment service for the health, fitness, and leisure industries in the United Kingdom.

www.teamworkonline.com—TeamWork Online: Powers job boards of teams in the NBA, NHL, National Football League, Major League Soccer, Arena Football League, as well as sports conglomerates such as AEG, Palace Sports and Entertainment, Comcast-Spectacor Pro Rodeo Cowboys Association, SMG's Louisiana Superdome & New Orleans Arena, and World Wrestling Entertainment.

www.toxiclemon.co.uk/d/management-jobs/sports-management-jobs.htm—Toxic Lemon UK: Toxic Lemon UK search engine searchs ten different search engines at once with a UK web portal.

www.athleticlink.com—Women's Sports Foundation: WSF career and resources site.

www.womensportsjobs.com—Women Sports Jobs Powered by Women's Sports Services: Jobs and internships in sales, marketing, broadcasting, public relations, coaching, officiating, health and fitness, athletic administration, event management, journalism, and sporting goods; provides assistance with writing and submitting résumés, career counseling and events; offers testimonials and answers to FAQs.

www.workinsports.com—Work In Sports: Requires a weekly, monthly, or three-month membership fee to access sports industry jobs and internships.

Career Advancement Materials

http://staff.wm.edu/career/02/Student/Resume/ResumeIndex.cfm—College of William and Mary: Students are provided a detailed description of each section of an effective résumé as well as several examples of good résumés. Information on professional portfolios is also included.

www.jobhuntersbible.com—Job Hunter's Bible: Supplement to *What Color Is Your Parachute? A Practical Manual for Job-Hunters and Career-Changers.*

www.jobweb.com—JobWeb: Career development and job-search information for college students and new college graduates sponsored by the National Association of Colleges and Employers.

www.jobweb.com—National Association of Colleges and Employers: Combining the interest of college graduates and business, this site provides students with résumé development information. Valuable information about developing a reference list and interviewing skills are also available.

http://owl.english.purdue.edu—Purdue University Online Writing Lab (OWL): Résumé development and cover letters are addressed. In addition, this site provides information concerning professional writing skills.

www.wpi.edu/Admin/CDC/Students/Marketing Yourself—Worchester Polytechnic Institute: Students can find useful tips on marketing themselves throughout the entire internship process including the résumé, interviewing, and phone calling.

REFERENCES

Arter, J. A., and Spandel, V. (1992). Using portfolios of student work in instruction and assessment. *Educational Measurement: Issues and Practice,* 11(1), 36–44.

Avis, R. K., and Trice, A. D. (1991). The influence of major and internship on the evaluation of undergraduate women's résumés. *College Student Journal,* 25, 536–38.

Baker, A. C., Jensen, P. A., Kolb, D. A. (2002). *Conversational learning: An experiential approach to knowledge creation.* Westport, CT: Quorum Books.

Bjorklund, C. (1974). *A feasibility study of internships in educational management and innovation.* Boulder, CO: Western Interstate Commission for Higher Education.

Boud, D. (1995). *Enhancing learning through self-assessment.* London: Kogan Page.

Brassie, P. S. (1989). Guidelines for programs preparing undergraduate and graduate students for careers in sport management. *Journal of Sport Management,* 3(2), 158–64.

Chickering, A. W. (1976). Developmental change as a major outcome. In M. T. Keeton (ed.), *Experiential learning: Rationale, characteristics, and assessment* (pp. 62–109). San Francisco: Jossey-Bass.

Chouinard, N. (1993). Some insights on meaningful internships in sport management: A cooperative education approach. *Journal of Sport Management,* 7(2), 95–100.

Cleary, M. J. (1993). Portfolio development for health education students. Paper presented at annual convention of American Alliance for Health, Physical Education, Recreation, and Dance, Washington, D.C.

Conklin-Fread, M. T. (1990). An investigation of the direct, indirect, and intangible benefits which accrued to hospital dietetic departments sponsoring an internship for student dietitians (Doctoral dissertation, New York University, 1990). *Dissertation Abstracts International,* 51/08B, 3785.

Cottrell, R. R., and Wagner, D. I. (1990). Internships in community health education/promotion professional preparation programs. *Health Education,* 21(1), 30–33.

Cross, K. P. (1994). The coming of age of experiential education. *NSEE Quarterly,* 19(3), 1, 22–24.

Cuneen, J. (1992). Graduate level professional preparation for athletic directors. *Journal of Sport Management,* 6(1), 15–26.

Cuneen, J. (2004). Adding vigor to the sport management internship. *Journal of Physical Education, Recreation, and Dance,* 75(1), 20–21, 27.

Cuneen, J., and Sidwell, M. J. (1993). Sport management interns: Selection qualifications. *Journal of Physical Education, Recreation and Dance,* 64(1), 91–95.

Cuneen, J., and Sidwell, M. J. (1994). *Sport management field experiences.* Morgantown, WV: Fitness Information Technology.

Davis, R. H., Duley, J. S., and Alexander, L. T. (1978). *Field experience.* East Lansing, MI: Instructional Media Center.

DeSensi, J. T., Kelley, D. R., Blanton, M. D., and Beitel, P. A. (1990). Sport management curricular evaluation and needs assessment: A multifaceted approach. *Journal of Sport Management,* 5, 31–58.

Ellery, P. J., and Rauschenbach, J. (1997). Developing a professional portfolio. *Strategies,* 11(2), 10–12.

Eraut. M. (1994). *Developing professional knowledge and competence.* London: Falmer Press.

Gould, P. (1987). Alternating cooperative education programs. In D. C. Hunt (ed.), *Fifty views of cooperative education* 5th ed. Detroit: University of Detroit.

Graber, S. (2000). *The everything online job search book.* Atolbrook, MA: Adams Media.

Gryski, G. S., Johnson, G. W., and O'Toole, L. J. (1992). Undergraduate internships: An empirical review. In A. Ciofalo (ed.), *Internships: Perspectives in experiential learning* (pp. 195–210). Malabar, FL: Krieger.

Hansen, J. (1992). Literacy portfolios: Helping students know themselves. *Educational Leadership,* 49(8), 66–68.

Hesser, G. (1990). *Experiential education as a liberating art.* Raleigh, NC: National Society for Experiential Education.

Hoekstra, R. B. (1975). *Internships as a means of training educational leaders: An historical and contextural perspective.* ERIC Document Reproduction Service No. ED 103 999.

Houle, C. O. (1976). Deep traditions of experiential learning. In M. T. Keeton (ed.), *Experiential learning: Rationale, characteristics, and assessment* (pp. 19–33). San Francisco: Jossey-Bass.

Howard, J. P. F. (1998), Academic service learning: A counternormative pedagogy. In R. A. Rhoads and J. P. F. Howard (eds.), *Academic service learning: A pedagogy of action and reflection* (pp. 21–29). San Francisco: Jossey-Bass.

Jackowski, M., and Gullion, L. (1998). Teaching sport management through service-learning: An undergraduate case study. *QUEST, 50,* 251–65.

Jacoby, B. (1996). Service-learning in today's higher education. In B. Jacoby and associates (eds.), *Service-learning in higher education: Concepts and practices* (pp. 5–25). San Francisco: Jossey-Bass.

Jacoby, B. (2003). Fundamentals of service-learning partnerships. In B. Jacoby and associates (eds.), *Building partnerships for service-learning* (pp. 1–19). San Francisco: Jossey-Bass.

Kadlecek, J., and Thoma, J. E. (1999). Sport management student portfolios: What practitioners want included. Paper presented at the annual conference of the National American Society for Sport Management, Vancouver, Canada.

Keeton, M. T., and Tate, P. J. (1978). *Editor's notes:* The bloom in experiential learning. In M. T. Keeton and P. J. Tate (eds.), *New directions for experiential learning: Learning by experience—what, why, how* (pp. 1–8). San Francisco: Jossey-Bass.

Kendall, J. C., Duley, J. S., Little, T. C., Permaul, J. S., and Rubin, S. (1986). *Strengthening experiential education within your institution.* Raleigh, NC: National Society for Experiential Education.

Kimeldorf, M. (1997). *Portfolio power: The new way to showcase all your job skills and experiences.* Princeton, NJ: Peterson's.

Klein, D. C. (1994). *Knowledge, technical skills, personal qualities, and related selection criteria for sport management internships.* (Doctoral dissertation, University of New Mexico.)

Kolb, D. A. (1984). *Experiential education: Experience as the source of learning and development.* Englewood Cliffs, NJ: Prentice Hall.

Konsky, C. (1976). Practical guide to development and administration of an internship program: Issues, procedures, and forms. Normal, IL: Illinois State University. ERIC Document Reproduction Service No. ED 249–539.

Lanese, L. D., and Fitch, W. C. (1983). How to get an intern off and running: A model. *Performance and Instruction Journal,* 22(1), 30–32.

Li, M., Cobb, P., and Sawyer, L. (1994). Sport management graduate programs: Characteristics of effectiveness. *Journal of Physical Education, Recreation and Dance,* 65(5), 57–61.

London, S. (2001). *Higher education and public life: Restoring the bond.* Dayton, OH: Kettering Foundation.

McCaffrey, J. T. (1979). Perceptions of satisfaction and dissatisfaction in the internship experience. *Public Administration Review,* 39, 241–44.

Montgomery, K. K. (1997). Student teacher portfolios: A portrait of the beginning teacher. *The Teacher Educator,* 32, 216–25.

Moon, J. (1999). *Reflection in learning and professional development: Theory and practice.* London: Kogan Page.

National Association for Sport and Physical Education–North American Society for Sport Management (2000). *Sport management program standards and review protocol.* Reston, VA: Author.

Palomares, A. (2000). Employer expectations of students attending job fairs. *Journal of Career Planning and Employment,* 60(2), 20–23.

Parks, J. B. (1991). Employment status of alumni of an undergraduate sport management program. *Journal of Sport Management,* 5(2), 100–110.

Parks, J. B., and Quain, R. J. (1986). Sport management survey: Employment perspectives. *Journal of Physical Education, Recreation and Dance,* 57(4), 22–26.

Parkhouse, B. L. (1987). Sport management curricula: Current status and design implications for future development. *Journal of Sport Management,* 1(2), 93–115.

Parkhouse, B. L., and Ulrich, D. O. (1979). Sport management as a potential cross-discipline: A paradigm for theoretical development, scientific inquiry, and professional application. *Quest,* 31(2), 264–76.

Peterson's (2002). *Internships, 2003.* Princeton, NJ: Peterson's.

Rex, R. G. (1961). A theory of the internship in professional training. (Doctoral dissertation, Michigan State University, 1961.) *Dissertation Abstracts International,* 23/02.

Sheppard, J. (1987). Parallel and extended-day cooperative education programs. In D. C. Hunt (ed.), *Fifty views of cooperative education,* 5th ed. Detroit: University of Detroit.

Shipton, J., and Steltenpohl, E. (1980). Self-directedness of the learner as a key to quality assurance. In M. T. Keeton (ed.), *New directions for experiential learning: Defining and assuring quality in experiential learning* (pp. 11–27). San Francisco: Jossey-Bass.

Sink, K. E., and Sari, I. F. (1984). Internships: A mutually beneficial relationship. *Performance and Instruction Journal,* 23(10), 23–25.

Smith, R. (1999). *Electronic resumes and online networking,* Franklin Lakes, NJ: The Career Press.

Stanton, T., and Ali, K. (1987). *The experienced hand: A student manual for making the most of an internship,* 2d ed. Cranston, RI: Carroll Press.

Stier, W. F. (2002). Sport management internships: From theory to practice. *Strategies,* 15(4), 7–9.

Stone, B. (1998). Problems, pitfalls, and benefits of portfolios. *Teacher Education Quarterly,* 25, 105–14.

Storms, B. A., Nunez, A. M., and Thomas, W. H. (1996). Using portfolios to demonstrate student skills. *Thrust for Educational Leadership,* 25, 6–9.

Stratta, T. M. P. (2004). The needs and concerns of students during the sport management internship. *Journal of Physical Education, Recreation, and Dance,* 75(2), 25–29, 33–34.

Sutton, W. A. (1989). The role of internships in sport management curricula: A model for development. *Journal of Physical Education, Recreation and Dance,* 60(7), 20–24.

Sweitzer, H. F., and King, M. A. (1999). *The successful internship: Transformation and empowerment.* Pacific Grove, CA: Brooks/Cole.

Taylor, M. S. (1984). Strategies and sources in the student job search. *Journal of College Placement,* 45(1), 40–45.

Taylor, M. S. (1988). Effects of college internships on individual participants. *Journal of Applied Psychology,* 73(3), 393–401.

Ulrich, D., and Parkhouse, B. L. (1982). An alumni-oriented approach to sport management curriculum design using performance ratings and a regression model. *Research Quarterly,* 53(1), 64–72.

U.S. Department of Education. (1991). *Cooperative education program: Guide for the preparation of applications fiscal year 1992.* Washington, DC: U.S. Department of Education.

Verner, M. E. (1990, September). The internship advantage. *Fitness Management,* pp. 34–35.

Verner, M. E. (1993). Developing professionalism through experiential learning. *Journal of Physical Education, Recreation and Dance,* 64(7), 45–52.

Verner, M. E. (2004). Internship search, selection, and solidification strategies. *Journal of Physical Education, Recreation, and Dance,* 75(1), 25–27.

Waishwell, L., Morrow, M., Micke, M., and Keyser, B. (1996). Utilization of the student portfolio to link professional preparation to the responsibilities and competencies of the entry level health educator. *Journal of Health Education,* 27(1), 4–9.

Weigert, K. M. (1998). Academic service learning: Its meaning and relevance. In R. A. Rhoads and J. P. F. Howard (eds.), *Academic service learning: A pedagogy of action and reflection* (pp. 3–10). San Francisco: Jossey-Bass.

Williams, J. (2004). Sport management internships: Agency perspectives, expectations, and concerns. *Journal of Physical Education, Recreation, and Dance,* 75(2), 30–33.

Young, D. (1990). Mentoring and networking: Perceptions by athletic administrators. *Journal of Sport Management,* 4, 71–79.

CHAPTER 20

Sport Management: Scope and Career Opportunities

Packianathan Chelladurai

In this chapter, you will become familiar with the following terms:

Association with excellence
Consumer, professional, and
  human services
Contest
Context, or situational
  contingencies
Human resources

Job dimensions
Market access
Participant services
Spectacle
Spectator services and
  sponsorship services

Sport industry
Sport products and services
Support units
Technologies
Third place

Learning Goals
By the end of this chapter, students should be able to:

- Describe the broad field of sport management.

- Categorize the sport-related services and their production and marketing.

- Outline the factors that need to be coordinated in the production and marketing of those services.

- Describe the various forms of organizations in which sport services are produced and marketed, and where sport management students can find employment.

- Outline both the external focus of career (i.e., job description, organizational type, and geographic location) and internal focus of career (i.e., the fit between the job and organizational factors and the individual's personal skills, needs, and values).

SCOPE OF SPORT MANAGEMENT
Many students are likely to be bewildered by the various terms used to describe the field of sport management. First, the use of the term *sport* engenders some confusion. The term has been used in a generic sense to denote those kinds of physical activities that concern those of us in the field, including competitive sports, recreational sports, exercise, and dance. For instance, the constitution of the North American Society for Sport Management

(NASSM) defines the field as "the theoretical and applied aspects of management theory and practice specifically related to sport, exercise, dance, and play as these enterprises are pursued by all sectors of the population." Others use the term to refer to a specific form of physical activity. For instance, Snyder and Spreitzer (1989) implicitly distinguish between sport and other forms of physical activity when they state:

We define sport as (1) a competitive, (2) human physical activity that requires skill and exertion, (3) governed by institutionalized rules. With this definition in mind, it is clear that some activities can be classified as sport under some conditions but not under others.

In our own field, Mullin's (1980) view of sport management is confined to an activity that "is play-like in nature, is based on physical prowess, involves physical skill, strategy or chance, is uncertain of outcome, is governed by rules and has specialized equipment and facilities." From this perspective, although sport is a form of physical activity, not all physical activities are sport. For the purpose of this text, I will follow the lead of NASSM and use the term *sport* in a global sense covering various forms of physical activities.

Yet another term that might confuse the reader is **sport industry.** Many scholars and practitioners tend to use the term in its singular form. Considering that an industry is a group of organizations that produce the same or similar products that are substitutable for each other, the question arises whether we are indeed a single industry. From this perspective, Mullin (1980) noted that "we have a collection of sport management occupations. The sports industry is fragmented. It is in fact a number of sports industries."

CONCEPT CHECK

The term sport *is used to refer to all recreational and competitive sports, exercise and fitness activities, and dance. Management encompasses the activities associated with administration, supervision, and leadership.*

The view of sport management as dealing with different products and different industries suggests that the best way to define the field is to catalogue and describe its various products. This approach is consistent with the modern view that (1) all organizations are mechanisms that have evolved to facilitate the process of exchange of products, and (2) the types of organizational arrangements needed to support any particular exchange will depend on the inherent characteristics of the exchange (Hesterly et al., 1990). As noted elsewhere, "if we can define, describe, and classify the products of exchange within the context of sport, then we should be able to capture the essential nature of the field and its boundaries" (Chelladurai, 1994). Based on this view, Chelladurai (1994) defined sport management as "a field concerned with the coordination of limited human and material resources, relevant technologies, and situational contingencies for the efficient production and exchange of sport services." This definition incorporates the notions of (1) **sport products (services),** (2) the production and exchange of those products, and (3) the coordination of the processes of such production and exchange. (Also refer to the definition of sport in Chapter 1.)

SPORT PRODUCTS AND SERVICES

Products can be either goods or services. Goods within the context of sport are tangible things such as golf clubs, tennis balls, soccer shoes, weight training sets, basketball boards, and volleyball uprights. In many instances, sports equipment is needed to engage in sporting activities. Typically, however, sport management has not been concerned with goods per se except in their purchase, care, and maintenance. The production of these goods has been left to conventional manufacturing industries. On the other hand, most products are services, which are intangible, perishable, heterogeneous, and simultaneous (see Table 20-1 for a description of these characteristics).

An earlier elaborate classification of sport products (Chelladurai, 1992, 1994) can be meaningfully collapsed into fewer classes as shown in Figure 20-1. The major classes of sport products and services are **participant services, spectator services,** and **sponsorship services.** These services can be broken down into smaller categories as follows.

Participant services

Participant services are broken down on the basis of two criteria: (1) the distinctions among **consumer,**

TABLE 20-1   *Characteristics of a Service*

Characteristic	Service
Intangibility	A service is intangible because the client or customer cannot judge its quality before experiencing it. Also, because the sensual and psychological benefits (feelings such as comfort, status, and a sense of well-being) are individualistic, the services offered will remain intangible.
Perishability	A fitness consultant cannot produce service without customers, nor can services be stored for future use. In contrast, a manufacturer can continue to produce fitness equipment and inventory it for future sales.
Heterogeneity	Services are likely to be heterogeneous because (1) two clients with different psyches may perceive the quality of the service and the same fitness instructor differently, (2) one client may perceive the service differently at different times because of changes in frame of mind or mood, (3) two fitness instructors with different education, experience, expertise, and leadership style may not provide the same quality of service, and (4) the same instructor may not provide the same quality services at different times. Students should be familiar with variations of the quality of lectures by different professors or by the same professor at different times.
Simultaneity	Because a service is perishable, it has to be used as it is produced, and because of this simultaneity of production and usage, the interface between the employee (the producer) and the client (the consumer) becomes critical. In contrast, a tennis racket is produced at one point and sold to a customer at another.

From Chelladurai, P. (1992). A classification of sport and physical activity services: Implications for sport management. *Journal of Sport Management, 6,* 38–51.

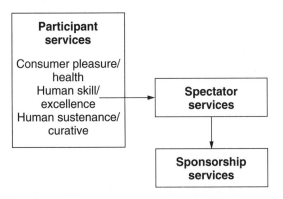

FIGURE 20-1   A classification of sport products.

professional, and **human services** (Table 20-2), and (2) the client motives for participation in sport and physical activity (Table 20-3).

Consumer-pleasure and health services. Consumer-pleasure and health services involve scheduling or reserving facilities and/or equipment as requested by clients who seek pleasure in physical activity. This class of service includes organizing and conducting different kinds of competitions for clients. Bowling alleys are prime examples of this service. The same type of service also can be provided to those who engage in physical activity for fitness and health reasons. For example, an enterprise may allow clients to use its fitness equipment and facilities for a membership or user fee.

Human skills and excellence. This class of service requires the expert application of teaching technology and leadership in developing the skills (including techniques and strategies) of clients in various forms of sport and physical activity. Clients may be satisfied with developing their skills to a level where they enjoy the activity. When clients want to excel in an activity, expert guidance and coaching need to be provided. In our culture, the pursuit of excellence in sports is highly valued and practiced, thus the importance attached to coaching various age groups at various educational and professional levels.

TABLE 20-2   *Description of Consumer, Professional, and Human Services*

Service	Description
Consumer	Consumer services are largely based on renting facilities or retailing goods. For example, when a university permits its students to use its gymnasia and playing fields on a drop-in basis, it is offering a consumer service. A racquetball club may restrict its operations to renting its courts and selling sporting goods. Such services require very little expertise on the part of the first-line operators. For instance, the clerk in the front office need only know the appropriate reservation procedures for the facilities or equipment and guidelines for their use.
Professional	Professional services are largely based on knowledge, expertise, and special competencies of the employee, the service provider (e.g., lawyer, accountant, architect). Direct and active leadership is provided by the service worker in assessing clients' needs and making appropriate decisions.
Human	Application of knowledge can transform *people's* view to enhance personal well-being (e.g., educating the child, coaching the athletes, and enhancing the spiritual life). The input in these services are people; the output are people whose attributes have been changed in a predetermined manner.

From Chelladurai, P. (1992). A classification of sport and physical activity services: Implications for sport management. *Journal of Sport Management, 6,* 38–51.

TABLE 20-3   *Client Motives for Participation in Physical Activity*

Motive	Description
Pursuit of pleasure	People may participate to enjoy the kinesthetic sensations experienced in a physical activity or the competition posed by certain activities (e.g., a game of squash). The pleasures they seek can be enjoyed only during participation.
Pursuit of skill	The desire to acquire physical skills may compel people to participate in physical activity. That is, individuals may focus on perfecting their skills through continued vigorous physical activity.
Pursuit of excellence	People may participate in a form of physical activity with a desire to excel in that or another activity. A basketball player and a discus thrower may train with weights to enhance performance capability in their sports.
Pursuit of health and fitness	People may participate in vigorous physical activity mainly for health-related benefits (e.g., fitness, stress reduction, longevity) that accrue as a consequence of such participation.

From Chelladurai, P. (1992). A classification of sport and physical activity services: Implications for sport management. *Journal of Sport Management, 6,* 38–51.

Human sustenance and curative. Human sustenance and curative services require organizing and conducting exercise and fitness programs on a regular basis under the guidance and supervision of experts. When healthy individuals want to participate in this class of service, their intention is to maintain and sustain present levels of fitness and health. This form of service also can be extended to rehabilitate those deficient in fitness, health, and/or physical appearance (e.g., cardiac rehabilitation, relaxation and stress reduction, and weight loss programs). This latter form of service is more curative and requires careful attention to scientific knowledge relevant to these clients.

This classification covers only those services in which clients actively participate in an activity. Sport management is concerned with much more than these participant services. We need to consider spectator services, sponsorship services, donor services, and social ideas to more clearly delineate the boundaries of sport management (Chelladurai, 1994).

Spectator services

First note that spectator services are fundamentally an offshoot of the pursuit of excellence, a participant service as described earlier. The second caveat is that spectator services also entail entertainment. These spectator/entertainment services are based on (1) the contest, (2) the spectacle, and (3) the notion of third place.

A **contest** exists when two opponents (individuals or teams) strive to demonstrate excellence by winning an event. The excitement and entertainment generated by a contest are derived from the excellence of the contestants; the unpredictability of the outcome; and fans' loyalty to the sport, team, and/or athlete.

Spectacle refers to the sight and splendor of opening parades, halftime shows, and closing ceremonies provided by the organization presenting the contest. These may be considered product extensions of the contest itself. Spectacle also includes the grandeur and vastness of the stadium, gymnasium, or playing surface; the ambience of the total setting—the large number of spectators, their colorful outfits, and their antics.

The concept of **third place** in the context of a sport contest was highlighted by Melnick (1993), who argued that modern life, both at home and at work, is characterized by reduced and tenuous primary social ties with family and friends. Therefore individuals seek the satisfaction of their social needs in less personal ways in "casual encounters with strangers of a quasi-primary kind" (Melnick, 1993). And the places where such casual encounters can take place are called *third places* (in contrast to the home and workplace).

Although there are several examples of third places (e.g., bars), "sports spectating has emerged as a major urban structure where spectators come together not only to be entertained [by the contest] but to enrich their social psychological lives through the sociable, quasi-intimate relationships available" (Melnick, 1993). In essence, spectator services include the excitement of a contest and the offering of the stadium or gymnasium as third place for the spectator.

The third place as just defined also serves as a forum for BIRGing—*basking in reflected glory* (Cialdini et al., 1976; Wann and Branscombe, 1990)—and CORFing—*cutting off reflected failure* (Snyder et al., 1986; Wann and Branscombe, 1990). It is argued here that the presence of quasi-intimate relationships in a third place permits unmitigated expression of reflected glory and distancing from reflected failure.

Sponsorship services

There are two elements in the sponsorship services. First is the **market access.** The organization that seeks sponsorship offers the sponsor, in return, access to a market of its own; that is, the access to communication with the direct and indirect consumers of a sport. For example, for those who sponsor the Olympic Games, the payoff is access to the billions of people who watch the event. In some cases the sponsor seeks **association with excellence** related to an athlete, team, or event. Sponsors of the Olympic Games emphasize their association with the best and biggest sporting event in the world. Similarly, for those who sponsor Michael Jordan or seek his endorsements, the return is association with perhaps the most talented and accomplished basketball player of all time. In these cases, such association projects the sponsoring organization as excellent in its own right.

From a different perspective, some sponsors may wish to be associated with a worthy cause such as special sports events organized by community and charitable organizations. In this case, the sponsor is projected as a socially responsible enterprise.

The emphasis on the services produced is just one way to describe the sport management field. As the definitions by different authors suggest, there are other ways of describing the field. For instance, Parks and Zanger (1990) and Parks, Zanger, and Quarterman (1998) have listed as segments of the sport industry the following areas: intercollegiate athletics, professional sports, international sport, campus recreation, community-based sport, physical fitness industry, facility management, event management, sport marketing, sports information, sports communication, sports journalism, athletic training, sports medicine, health promotion, sport tourism, health promotion, sports club management, aquatic management, sport tourism, sport management and marketing agencies, and consulting and entrepreneurship. Similarly, Masteralexis, Barr, and Hums (1998) divide the sport industry into (a) amateur sport industry, including high school and youth sports, collegiate sport, the European sport club system, and international sport; (b) professional sport industry, including sport agency and professional sport; (c) sport industry support segments, including facility management, event management, media relations, sport broadcasting, sporting goods industry, and sale of licensed products; and (d) lifestyle sports, including health and fitness industry and recreational sport.

CONCEPT CHECK

The services in sport management include participant services (consumer-pleasure and health, human skill and excellence, and human-sustenance and curative services), spectator and entertainment services, and sponsorship services.

PRODUCTION AND MARKETING

The next essential thrust in the definition of sport management is the inclusion of both the production and marketing of services. That is, management is seen as the coordination of the factors and processes of both production and exchange—that is, marketing is seen as one, albeit a major, function of management.

The distinction between the production of a service and the marketing of that service is clearly evidenced in the case of certain services. Take, for example, the spectator services where the production of entertainment largely rests with the players and the coaches of both contesting teams. The marketing of the players, the teams, and the contests can be carried out by others independent of the production of that entertainment. Similarly, sponsorship services can be independent of a team cultivating its fans and its own market. Along the same vein, it can be argued that the consumer-pleasure and health services, which involve only the renting of facilities and/or equipment, can be marketed independently of the production of these services. In this case, the producers of the service are separated from the consumers of the service.

On the other hand, the distinction between production and marketing is not so clear in the case of human services. This is because the production of human services requires the simultaneous involvement of the client and the service provider. Moreover, client involvement in the production of human services is physical and at times agonistic, as in the case of human-excellence services. In other words, the client is at least partially responsible for the production of that service. The interface between the employee and the client in a human service is the forum for both the production and the exchange of a service—that is, the service provider is simultaneously the producer and marketer of that service. Even in these cases, it is useful to keep the distinction between production and marketing in mind for analytical purposes.

CONCEPT CHECK

Although most services are produced and consumed simultaneously, the marketing of some services can be separated from the production of them, as in the case of spectator services.

MANAGEMENT AS COORDINATION

The third significant element in the definition is coordination of those factors associated with the production and marketing of products. Management has been described from various perspectives, e.g., the functions a manager has to carry out (Fayol, 1949), the skills a manager has to have (Katz, 1974), and/or the roles one has to play as a manager (Mintzberg, 1975). When these descriptions are analyzed, we notice that the central thrust of each of them is the idea of coordinating the activities of individuals and groups toward the attainment of organizational goals with limited resources. For example, the managerial functions of planning, organizing, leading, and evaluating are all focused on the coordination of human and material resources. In summary, coordination is the name of the game managers play.

The significant factors that need coordination for the production of sport services can be grouped into (1) **human resources** (e.g., paid employees, volunteer workers, and the clients themselves), (2) **technologies** (e.g., exercise physiology, sport

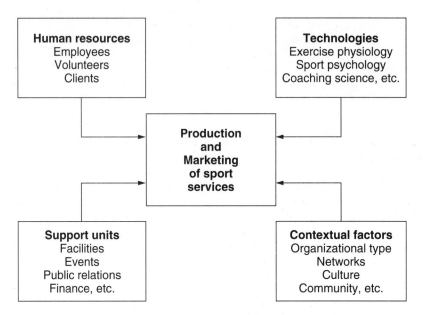

FIGURE 20-2 Factors of coordination in sport management.

psychology, pedagogy, coach education, and sport nutrition), (3) **support units** (e.g., the units dealing with facilities, events, ticket sales, legal affairs, finance, public relations), and (4) **context** or **situational contingencies** (e.g., organizational types, interorganizational networks, government regulations, cultural norms, and community expectations). The various factors that need to be coordinated in sport management are illustrated in Figure 20-2.

HUMAN RESOURCES

Although human resources management is a fundamental task in every organization producing any form of product, the task is made onerous in the case of human services, where clients also must be managed. The human resources of any venture offering sport and physical activity service should involve the clients of that service, since service cannot be produced without active client participation (Chelladurai, 1992). Clients may vary in their orientation toward sport and physical activity (pursuit of pleasure, health, and/or excellence) and in the degree of commitment to such programs. Motivating clients and gaining their compliance is a challenge to service providers.

Paid employees may be further classified into consumer service or professional service employees.

Consumer service employees engage in simple, routine activities requiring little training, whereas professional service employees provide complex, knowledge-based, and individualized service to clients.

Sport organizations also are characterized by heavy involvement of volunteers. These volunteers are the mainstay of projects such as the Special Olympics and youth sport organized by city recreation departments. The conventional approaches to managing paid workers have to be considerably modified in the case of volunteers. The coordination of volunteer contributions with those of paid employees is a critical area of sport management. In summary, motivating these different types of employees and coordinating their activities is a highly significant component of sport management, which offers both challenge and opportunity for sport managers.

TECHNOLOGIES

Technology refers to *the processes that transform organizational inputs into desired outputs* (Pierce and Dunham, 1990). Technology includes all equipment used, techniques employed, and knowledge units derived from different subject areas. For example, fitness assessment and exercise prescription involve sophisticated equipment, specific organizational arrangements for the production of this service, and the knowledge derived from physiology, nutrition, and psychology. Coaching a high school pole vaulter would entail the modern fiberglass poles, and the knowledge units derived from biomechanics, sports medicine, and coaching science, for example. The more critical component of technology as defined here is the knowledge units that are generated in other allied fields. Those who use these knowledge units are professional people. Coordinating their activities with those of other organizational activities is the essence of sport management.

The relative significance of these technologies obviously varies from service to service (and with quality levels expected of a service). For example, human services aimed at enhancing excellence and/or health entails greater application of relevant knowledge as compared with consumer services. Following this argument, we can expect a high school coach to be more highly trained in the application of knowledge than a volunteer youth coach.

SUPPORT UNITS

In a small enterprise, all of the necessary activities can be carried out by a few individuals. For example, there may be only one physical educator or coach in a small rural school. That person, apart from coaching the school team, may also carry out all arrangements for a game to be played on Saturday afternoon. Of course, a coach may recruit some students to assist in the process. However, as the organization grows in size and scope, several subunits may have to be created. Take the case of a Division I university athletic department. In this case, the coaches are assigned only coaching duties. All other necessary activities are assigned to specialized units. Thus we are likely to find separate units for facility management, event management, ticket sales, media relations, legal affairs, compliance to rules, etc. Coordinating the activities of these units is the responsibility of the top manager, the athletic director.

The term *support units* may be misleading. It is used here to emphasize that these units do support the fundamental purpose and activities of the department, that is, to provide student athletes the opportunity to pursue excellence. However, the term does not minimize their importance. That is why nearly every sport management degree program includes specialized courses in these areas.

CONTEXT

No organization operates in a vacuum. A host of environmental factors have an impact on the organization and its activities. These external forces may facilitate or constrain the organization in the production and marketing of its services. A successful sport manager would effectively coordinate the activities of the organization with the demands and constraints of these external factors. These factors may be classified as organizational types, interorganizational networks, market conditions, government, culture, and community.

Sport organizations differ in their profit orientation (e.g., a high school athletic department vs. a professional sport franchise). The emphasis on profit orientation imposes a different set of demands and constraints on managers of professional sports than it does on a high school athletic director.

A funding source is another factor that may affect the coordination process. In private organizations, which are sustained by membership fees, donations, and/or shares, the manager will be more influenced by the needs and desires of the members, clients, and donors. In contrast, the manager in a public organization such as the city recreation department will have to coordinate the department's activities with not only the preferences of taxpayers but also the pressures exerted by city politicians.

Interorganizational networks such as the National Collegiate Athletic Association (NCAA) and the U.S. Olympic Committee link those organizations producing the same services. Other examples are the professional leagues, such as the National Football League (NFL) and the National Hockey League, national and international sports federations such as the U.S. Tennis Association (USTA) and the International Federation of Basketball Associations (FIBA), and industry associations such as the Aerobic and Fitness Association of America (AFAA) and Club Managers Association of America (CMAA). These networks, or governing bodies, control member organizations and their operations to varying degrees.

The context would also include market conditions such as the rise and decline in the demand for services, and the organizations competing for clients and customers and resources. Thus a professional sport franchise has to coordinate its own activities, tactics, and strategies to counteract those of the competitors, which provide the same or similar services.

By the same token, operations should be consistent with government regulations, cultural norms, and societal expectations. For instance, the recent societal thrusts in favor of diversity and gender equity have affected the practice of management in general, and sport management in particular. The growing sport management literature on considerations of gender equity is a case in point, emphasizing the need for sport managers to alter their employment practices.

The need to coordinate the operations of a sport organization with a local community's interests and desires is best illustrated by the influence exerted by alumni associations in intercollegiate athletics. Similarly, professional sport franchises depend on local governments for building and/or renting stadiums and arenas (Johnson, 1993). Even smaller sport organizations look up to local communities for concessions and tax exemptions.

CONCEPT CHECK

Sport management is concerned with the coordination of material and human resources (clients, paid and volunteer workers); technologies (facilities, equipment, process, and knowledge units underlying the production process); support units dealing with facilities, events, legal affairs, etc.; and contextual factors such as organizational type, interorganizational networks, government regulations and community expectations.

CAREER PLANNING

Many who read this text will step into the world of organizations and work related to sport and physical activity. Career opportunities in this field are well described in Parks and Zanger's (1990) *Sport and Fitness Management: Career Strategies and Professional Content.* Several authors contributing to this text have discussed careers in intercollegiate athletics and professional sport, facility management, campus recreation programs, community-based sport, sports information, sport marketing, sports journalism, sports club management, the physical fitness industry, athletic training and sports medicine, and consulting and entrepreneurship. Kelley

et al. (1991) have elaborated on sport and fitness management careers clustered according to similarity of objectives and profit orientation. In addition, other authors have discussed issues of career patterns in sport management (Fitzgerald et al., 1994); gender and careers in sport management (Cuneen and Sidwell, 1993; Inglis, 1988; Lovett and Lowry, 1988, 1994; Pastore, 1991, 1992; Pastore and Meacci, 1994); roles, responsibilities, and stress associated with jobs in sport and recreation (Cuskelly and Auld, 1991; Danylchuk, 1993; Hatfield et al., 1987; Quarterman, 1994); and the employment status of sport management graduates (Kjeldsen, 1990; Parks, 1991; Parks and Parra, 1994). This list does not exhaust all relevant information about careers in sport management. Students should consult other sources including trade journals. The following sections outline some general concerns in selecting a job or career.

Once students enter the work world, they are likely to move from one job to another. This movement may be vertical in the sense that they get promoted to higher level jobs in the same line of work. Consider the careers of May and June reported in the case study at the end of this chapter. Both women joined an intercollegiate athletic program as clerks. In time, May was promoted to the position of assistant director of the ticket office. In contrast, June left that athletic department to become a coach in a smaller four-year college. This progression through various jobs in one or several organizations is known as *one's career*. But every career begins with a first job, which is where our interests lie at the moment.

The descriptions of the jobs in these two organizational contexts contain information available to everyone. Also, the progression through various jobs to higher positions in each organization is known to everybody (or can be gleaned from the records). This aspect of one's career is rightfully known as the *objective* or *external career* (Johns, 1988).

What is not evident to observers is the personal experiences and reactions felt by two individuals in their career tracks. It is not clear to others why Person Y chose to leave athletics altogether and enter the field of parks and recreation. It may be presumed that Person Y did not like the experiences with the athletic program, and therefore preferred to move to another field where the experiences were more acceptable. However, the meanings Person Y had attached to the experiences in the two fields, and the reactions to those experiences were personal, and imperceptible or misunderstood by others. This aspect is called *subjective* or *internal career.*

Focus on external career

In making decisions about a job in sport management, the graduate has to consider several factors. Some of them, as noted earlier, would be objective factors such as job description, organizational type, and geographical location. Many questions related to these factors can be verified through objective analysis.

Job descriptions should contain information on organizational philosophy and policies; organizational type and size; tasks and activities associated with the job, working conditions, including supervision, salary, and fringe benefits; and promotional opportunities. The prospective applicant should carefully peruse all of this information. If necessary, the student may write or call the prospective employer for more information.

Although written job descriptions are useful, a one- or two-day visit to the organization may provide additional information. It may also be useful to interview one or more employees of the organization to get their personal feelings about the organization and their jobs. Such visits and interviews will help the applicant to verify the job description and assess the mood and spirit of the organization. An institution may advertise its employment practices as equal opportunity, but the student may find that all employees of the organization are of one race or gender. Again, the working conditions such as room size, lighting, ventilation, seating arrangements, and parking facilities may not be as good as advertised. In summary, a thorough analysis of the job description and the organization would be worthwhile.

Organizational type. Consider that you are contemplating a job as manager of a racquetball club. Such a club may be operated by a branch of the YMCA; a city recreation department; a university intramural department; a private, exclusive nonprofit organization; or a private profit-oriented commercial firm. Although the same tasks need to be carried out in all of these settings, there are other factors that affect the employees.

Some differences among organizations were discussed earlier. To extend that discussion, city recreation department personnel are likely to enjoy relatively greater job security and higher salaries than those in a private, profit-oriented commercial club. On the other hand, there are probably many levels of hierarchy through which a proposal has to be processed, which may impede the decision-making process. This is known as *red tape* in governments.

As another example, personnel working in a university intramural department may have higher social status than those carrying out the same activities in a commercial club. After all, the university is the ivory tower! Also, the university department personnel are exposed to students' youthful, energetic, and carefree lifestyles. Some may feel that is a reward in itself. Similarly, those who work in a Division I university athletic department or a professional club may gain satisfaction from the association with excellence in sport irrespective of the nature of their jobs or their remunerations.

Geographical location. People have preferences for particular geographic locations. Preferences may be based on the proximity of family and friends, or even health. Some may prefer an urban center, whereas others may enjoy life in a less thickly populated locale. These are important considerations inasmuch as they will enhance one's quality of life. After all, a job is only a tool to enjoy one's life.

Focus on internal career

The internal career simply implies a fit between the job and its context, and the personal characteristics of the individual. The job and the context refer to what the individual is required to do in a job and the parameters of a particular organization, including its policies, procedures, working conditions, supervision, and work group. The personal characteristics include the person's personality, needs, values, beliefs, and preferences, along with abilities, skills, and talents. Abilities, skills, and specialized knowledge required for a successful job performance can be increased through general education and specialized professional preparation programs. Personality, needs, values, and preferences are relatively more stable.

The central issue for people who desire a job in sport management is to assess the fit between their personal characteristics and the characteristics of the job as well as those of the organization offering the job. Let us consider job characteristics. Obviously, salary, fringe benefits, the chance for advancement, and the location are important considerations. Salary may be the primary consideration for a student who has incurred enormous debt while in college. If only one job were available, such a student might be forced to take it without any consideration of the other job characteristics. On the other hand, if more than one job were available, the applicant should evaluate the jobs in terms of their characteristics and choose the one that offered the best fit.

It is not our intent to discuss the ways in which people differ. It will be useful, however, to point out some ways in which jobs differ. Consider the differences and decide whether those **job dimensions** are consistent with personal needs, values, and preferences.

Job dimensions. There are several schemes to define and describe the attributes of job dimensions (Campion and Thayer, 1985; Hackman and Oldham, 1980; Stone and Gueutal, 1985). This section outlines some of the more significant dimensions of a job.

In discussing the differences between consumer services and the professional and human services (see Table 20-2), I alluded to the differences in the degree to which jobs may be simple or complex. The complexity of a job increases as the variety of activities increases. For example, a secretary in an athletic department may be assigned only the task of typing, whereas another secretary may be involved in typing, answering telephones, and taking notes in departmental meetings. The latter person enjoys a variety of tasks, and, therefore, a relatively more complex job. The more important element in complexity is the variability of the tasks, that is, an employee is required to make different decisions based on different pieces of information. A coach may use different techniques to motivate athletes based on individual differences among those athletes. Similarly, the director of a city recreation department may use varying approaches when dealing with politicians, taxpayers, or participants. In contrast, the job of locker room attendant is not as complex as that of a coach. Consider a racquetball club that simply rents its premises and equipment to its clients. The necessary tasks in such a club may relate to keeping the courts and equipment in good repair, reserving the courts according to some specified criteria, budgeting and accounting, legal affairs, and marketing the club and its activities. As you can see, the activities in the first two tasks can be clearly specified and made routine.

From a different perspective, simpler jobs can be made routine and standardized. Everything required of the job may be specified by rules and regulations. What is to be done, when it is to be done, how should it be done, and who should do it can be stated in advance in the first two tasks. Also, monitoring and controlling these activities are easily carried out. On the other hand, the activities in the next three tasks are more complex in that every situation may entail different information, and therefore different decisions.

It must be noted that a job may contain some tasks that are routine and others that are more complex. Therefore the prospective applicant would do well to verify if the degree of simplicity or complexity in the job is consistent with personal preferences. There are those who prefer a structured and orderly setting. Others may feel restricted in such jobs, and prefer more flexibility, autonomy, and challenge of deciding how the job should be carried out.

The degree of interaction with other people required may vary from job to job. Take two individuals in the athletic department's public relations office. One may be involved in collating all the department's media coverage. The same person may also engage in preparing advance material for the media. In all these activities, he or she may not be required to interact with the media people or other clients to any great extent. On the other hand, the second person's job may require both contact with the media and response to queries on a regular basis. Some people would like a job that requires interaction with people, whereas others may be uncomfortable in that position.

There is also the question of feedback. Some jobs provide clear and immediate feedback, and others delayed feedback. For example, when a fitness club employee sets out to recruit more members, feedback is likely on a daily, weekly, or monthly basis relative to the success rate. It is immediate and clear in terms of the exact number of new members recruited. Consider the same individual who is also in charge of a program of weight loss through physical activity. Feedback is going to be delayed because weight loss takes time. Also, feedback may not be clear-cut in the sense that some of the clients may lose weight, others may not. In addition, the weight one loses or gains is a function of many other factors such as diet and activity patterns away from the club.

In some jobs, one can identify the outcome of his or her efforts. If a marketing specialist in a university athletic department garners a few rich sponsorships, that particular outcome is attributable to that individual's efforts. On the other hand, if a person is one of several employees in charge of crowd control in a game, personal contribution to the total effort cannot be identified easily.

In the previous example, those in charge of crowd control realize and enjoy the significance of their jobs. Can you imagine what would happen if their collective responsibility falters in a game with 80,000 or so spectators? Some of you might have heard some of the gruesome tales of tragedies during sporting events in other parts of the world. Their job is so significant because people's welfare and lives are at stake. From this perspective, other jobs may not be so significant.

CONCEPT CHECK

A job can be evaluated on its relative complexity, requirement of interaction with other people, feedback available from the job itself, the possibility of identifying one's own contribution, and its significance.

After careful analysis of the job and the organization that offers the job, the student has to evaluate the extent to which the characteristics of the job and the organization match his or her personal skills and abilities, needs, and values. In this assessment the student should consider the various higher level jobs one may move through in one's career. It is conceivable that the first job may be quite routine and devoid of any autonomy. Although this situation may not be acceptable immediately, subsequent promotions may land that person in a more complex and autonomous job. For example, the first job in a professional sport club may involve simply selling tickets at the counter. Although this may not be very appealing, the opportunity exists for that person to move up in the hierarchy to a job such as the marketing director. That position may offer considerable flexibility and freedom of operation for the incumbent. Therefore students are well advised to consider not only the immediate job that is offered but also the other jobs that the present one may lead to.

Students should also note what Hums and Goldsbury (1998) identify as myths surrounding careers in sport management. Three of them serve as reality checks for those aspiring to enter sport management. In dispelling the myth that "most employment opportunities are in professional or college sport," these authors note that the job opportunities in professional or collegiate sport are limited because only a few organizations deal with this segment of sport. Another myth is that "sport management jobs are glamorous and exciting." Hums and Goldsbury (1998) note that "sport managers labor in the background so others can enjoy the spotlight. A typical work week for that event coordinator is fifty to sixty hours per week, including lots of late nights and long weekends" (pp. 479–80). Yet another myth is that "sport management jobs pay well." As Hums and Goldsbury note, because of the high number of applicants for jobs in sport management, the salaries tend to be low for most jobs in sport management. It must also be noted that with necessary ability and perseverance, some people rise to the top positions that pay high salaries.

Sample of organizational types with sport management jobs

Jobs in the sport industry can be found in such organizations as:

1. The professional sports, such as the National Football League (NFL), National Basketball Association (NBA), Major League Baseball

(MLB), National Hockey League (NHL), and Major League Soccer (MLS).

2. Intercollegiate athletics (e.g., NCAA, Division I, II, III universities, two- and four-year colleges, including subareas such as administration, academic counseling, compliance, etc.).

3. High school sports (e.g., state and regional high school athletic associations; athletic departments in high schools).

4. Recreational sports in universities and colleges.

5. City and community recreation departments.

6. National and state sport governing bodies (e.g., Amateur Athletic Union—AAU; USA Judo; United States Field Hockey Association; U.S. Figure Skating Association).

7. International sports federations (e.g., the International Swimming Federation—FINA; International Association of Athletics Federation—IAAF; International Basketball Federation—FIBA; International University Sports Federation—FISU).

SUMMARY

- The products (i.e., the services) with which sport management is concerned are varied. Some of them are *participant services* wherein clients participate vigorously in some form of sport and physical activity. The other services labeled *spectator* and *sponsorship services* are nonparticipant services.

- Sport management was defined as "a field concerned with the coordination of limited human and material resources, relevant technologies, and situational contingencies for the efficient production and exchange of sport services" (Chelladurai, 1994).

- The coordination was said to involve human resources (clients, paid employees, and volunteer workers), technologies (the processes and knowledge units employed in the production of a service), support units (dealing with facility management, event management, legal affairs, public relations), and contextual factors (organizational type, interorganizational networks, government rules and regulations, community expectations, and social norms).

- The objective and subjective aspects of a career were described. It was emphasized that a match between one's personal characteristics and the characteristics of the job and the organization is the critical factor that a student should consider before accepting a job. In this regard some of the job and organizational characteristics were outlined.

 CRITICAL THINKING EXERCISES

1. You have the good fortune to get two job offers. The first job is that of a supervisor of ticketing operations in an athletic department of a Division I institution. The second job is that of a coordinator of youth sport programs in the recreation department of a mid-sized city. Which one would you take? And why?

2. Imagine that you are the assistant to the event manager of a large athletic department. What kinds of tasks would you be involved in? Who are the people you are most likely to interact with in performing your duties?

 CASE STUDY

May Baxter and June Armstrong were good friends. They both went to the same school in a rural setting and graduated with good standing. Both played on the high school basketball team and were members of the school track team. They went to the same university and graduated with degrees in sport management. They were lucky to get jobs in the athletic department of a neighboring university.

May's first job was as a ticket office clerk. Her superiors, noting her diligent work and her interpersonal skills, promoted her to the position of supervisor of clerks. The same hard work and positive attitude in successive jobs facilitated her promotion to the position of assistant director of the ticket office within six years. She enjoyed her work very much and took great pride in being associated with an organization that had a high profile within the university and the community. She looked forward to possible promotions such as the assistant or associate athletic director either in the same university or in another. To equip herself better for the future, she enrolled part time in an MBA program.

June's first job was as a clerk in the media relations office. Like May, June impressed her bosses with her work effectiveness and pleasant manner. She was promoted to a supervisory position within her department. Everybody assumed she was happy in her job and had expectations that she would quickly move up in her career. However, June was becoming restless with her current job and future prospects. She felt that she was removed from where the action was, that is, she realized that she was not directly involved in the production of the fundamental service of the department—the production of excellence in sports. She perceived her own job and those in her department as only supplementary to that fundamental task. In short, she felt that her own abilities, interests, needs, and values would be best served if she were to become a coach. With this in mind, she volunteered to assist the coach of the women's basketball team. In that role, she assiduously learned everything she could from the coach. In addition, she began taking courses such as sport psychology and coaching science. Subsequently, she applied for and got a job coaching the women's basketball team at a four-year college. She soon proved to be an effective coach with a winning tradition. She enjoyed her present status and was looking forward to being a coach at a big university. The media and the community began noticing her achievements and winning ways.

1. *Compare and contrast the careers of May Baxter and June Armstrong.*
2. *What are the differences between the first jobs of May (ticket office clerk) and June (media relations clerk)?*
3. *How would you distinguish between May's present job (assistant director of the ticket office) and June's present job (coach in a four-year college)?*
4. *In this chapter, sport management was defined in terms of various services. Discuss the services in which May and June are currently engaged.*

 REVIEW QUESTIONS AND ISSUES

1. Define the field of sport management. Describe the various categories of services produced and marketed in the field. Explain the significance of defining the field from the perspective of its products.

2. Select a service (e.g., fitness service, youth soccer) offered by an organization (e.g., commercial fitness club, local YMCA, city recreation department). Describe the human resources, technologies, support units, and contextual factors associated with the production and marketing of the chosen service.
3. Distinguish between objective and subjective careers.
4. Consider any sport-related job. Describe it in terms of the job dimensions referred to in the chapter.
5. Evaluate the job in terms of how it matches your abilities, education, needs, and values.

 SOLUTIONS TO CRITICAL THINKING EXERCISES

1. The choice of one of those jobs will be based on your personal orientation and your assessment of the job. The factors that could influence your choice would include the geographical location (e.g., large and crowded city), the reputation of the organization (e.g., treatment of employees), opportunities for advancement to higher-level positions, and similar considerations. One other difference between the two jobs is that the ticketing operations may be limited to supervising the employees of the unit who are involved with routine tasks. On the other hand, the coordinator of youth programs is likely to be more involved with participants, coaches, parents, and volunteer workers. This aspect of the job may be more appealing to some.
2. Obviously, as an assistant to the event manager, you will do everything the manager assigns or delegates to you. Some of those tasks may be routine, such as checking the media booths and/or concessions for cleanliness and necessary supplies, assigning paid and volunteer workers to different gates of entry, and verifying the arrangements for the arrival of dignitaries. While these tasks are routine, your interactions with other workers (e.g., volunteers), other units (e.g., facility management or security), and the patrons themselves could be exciting. As noted in the chapter, event managers and their assistants

are responsible for the safety of the spectators and their enjoyment of the event.

FOSTERING YOUR WORKPLACE SKILLS

1. How would you describe your current career orientation? Are you focusing on a career in a particular organizational context such as professional sports, intercollegiate sports, or commercial golf clubs? Explain your preferences and the reasons for them.
2. As you are thinking about a career in sport management, you may choose to enter a specific line of specialization such as event management, facility management, ticketing operations, public relations, communications, marketing, and so on. Which line of work do you prefer and why?
3. Explain your own personal skills and discuss how they match the requirements of different jobs in sport management.

 **WEBSITES**

www.ncaa.org/market/ads/
www.ncaa.org/human-resources/—These two sites contain information on jobs within the NCAA and links to jobs in the field at their member institutions. Organized by category, such as coaching, administration, marketing, etc.
www.coolworks.com/showme/—coolworks has a site featuring seasonal jobs at ski areas, resorts, national parks, cruises, and camps.
www.sponsorship.com/jobBank/jobBank.html—IEG jobBank has a place for résumés. It also lists executive-level jobs available in event and sports marketing.
www.onlinesports.com/pages/Resumes.html—Online Sports Career Center has a place to post brief résumés.
www.sportlink.com/employment/jobs/index.html—This is the Website of the Sporting Goods Manufacturers Association Career Center, which provides a list of jobs available in the sporting goods industry.
http://www.SportManagementClub.com—This site serves its members by providing access to an internship database, career tips, and interviews with executives. It also provides news and current trends in the industry.
http://www.womensportsjobs.com—This site is a platform that connects sports enterprises and career-minded individuals. Members can get detailed job descriptions and contact information for jobs in enterprises such as the LPGA, WNBA, NIKE, NCAA, U.S. Olympic Committee, ESPN, Vans, Sports Illustrated, Sportsline, etc. The enterprise also

helps a member prepare his or her résumé, and post the résumé in its Web page for employers to see.
www.teamworkonline.com—TeamWork Online lists several sport management jobs available with major league sports teams in the NFL, NBA, NHL, Arena Football, MLS, and other sport organizations.

Students may also check out the following sites:

www.bluefishjobs.org—for jobs in recreational sports
www.chronicle.com—for jobs in higher education
www.higheredjobs.com—for jobs in higher education
www.ymca.net—for jobs in community recreation

REFERENCES

Campion, M. A., and Thayer, P. W. (1985). Development and field evaluation of an interdisciplinary measure of job design. *Journal of Applied Psychology, 70,* 29–43.

Chelladurai, P. (1992). A classification of sport and physical activity services: Implications for sport management. *Journal of Sport Management, 6,* 38–51.

Chelladurai, P. (1994). Sport management: Defining the field. *European Journal for Sport Management, 1,* 7–21.

Cialdini, R. B., Borden, R. J., Thorne, A., Walker, M. R., Freeman, S., and Sloan, L. R. (1976). Basking in reflected glory: Three (football) field studies. *Journal of Personality and Social Psychology, 34,* 366–75.

Cuneen, J., and Sidwell, M. J. (1993). Effect of applicant gender on rating and selection of undergraduate sport management interns. *Journal of Sport Management, 7,* 216–27.

Cuskelly, G., and Auld, C. J. (1991). Perceived importance of selected job responsibilities of sport and recreation managers: An Australian perspective. *Journal of Sport Management, 5,* 34–46.

Danylchuk, K. E. (1993). Occupational stressors in physical education faculties. *Journal of Sport Management, 7,* 7–24.

Fayol, H. (1949). *General and industrial management.* London: Pitman. First published in French in 1916.

Fitzgerald, M. P., Sagaria, M. A. D., and Nelson, B. (1994). Career patterns of athletic directors: Challenging the conventional wisdom. *Journal of Sport Management, 8,* 14–26.

Hackman, J. R., and Oldham, G. R. (1980). *Work designed.* Reading, MA: Addison-Wesley.

Hatfield, B. D., Wrenn, J. P., and Bretting, M. M. (1987). Comparison of job responsibilities of intercollegiate athletic directors and professional sport general managers. *Journal of Sport Management, 1,* 129–45.

Hesterly, W. S., Liebeskind, J., and Zenger T. R. (1990). Organizational economics: An impending revolution in organization theory? *Academy of Management Review, 15*(3), 402–20.

Hums, M. A. Q., and Goldsbury, V. R. (1998). Strategies for career success. In L. P. Masteralexis, C. A. Barr, and M. A. Hums (eds.), *Principles and practice of sport management* (pp. 476–96). Gaithersburg, MD: Aspen.

Inglis, S. E. (1988). The representation of women in university athletic programs. *Journal of Sport Management, 2,* 14–25.

Johns, G. (1988). *Organizational behavior: Understanding life at work.* 2d ed. Glenview, IL: Scott, Foresman.

Johnson, A. T. (1993). Rethinking the sport-city relationship: In search of partnership. *Journal of Sport Management, 7,* 61–70.

Katz, R. L. (1974). Skills of an effective administrator. *Harvard Business Review, 52,* 90–102.

Kelley, D. R., Beitel, P. A., DeSensi, J. T., and Blanton, M. D. (1991). In B. L. Parkhouse (ed.), *The management of sport* (pp. 12–26). St. Louis: Mosby.

Kjeldsen, E. K. M. (1990). Sport management careers: A descriptive analysis. *Journal of Sport Management, 4,* 121–32.

Lovett, D. J., and Lowry, C. D. (1988). The role of gender in leadership positions in female sport programs in Texas college. *Journal of Sport Management, 2,* 106–17.

Lovett, D. J., and Lowry, C. D. (1994). "Good old boys" and "good old girls" clubs: Myth or reality. *Journal of Sport Management, 8,* 27–35.

Masteralexis, L. P., Barr, C. A., and Hums, M. A. (1998). *Principles and practice of sport management.* Gaithersburg, MD: Aspen.

Melnick, M. J. (1993). Searching for sociability in the stands: A theory of sport spectating. *Journal of Sport Management, 7*(1), 44–60.

Mintzberg, H. (1975). The manager's job: Folklore and fact. *Harvard Business Review, 53,* 49–61.

Mullin, B. J. (1980). Sport management: The nature and utility of the concept. *Arena Review, 4*(3), 1–11.

Parks, J. B. (1991). Employment status of alumni of an undergraduate sport management program. *Journal of Sport Management, 5,* 100–110.

Parks, J. B., and Parra, L. F. (1994). Job satisfaction of sport management alumni. *Journal of Sport Management, 8,* 49–56.

Parks, J. B., and Zanger, B. R. K. (1990). Definition and direction. In J. B. Parks and B. R. K. Zanger (eds.), *Sport and fitness management: Career strategies and professional content* (pp. 1–4). Champaign, IL: Human Kinetics.

Parks, J. B., Zanger, B. R. K., and Quarterman, J. (1998). *Contemporary sport management.* Champaign, IL: Human Kinetics.

Pastore, D. L. (1991). Male and female coaches of women's athletic teams: Reasons for entering and leaving the profession. *Journal of Sport Management, 5,* 128–43.

Pastore, D. L. (1992). Two-year college coaches of women's teams: Gender differences in coaching career selections. *Journal of Sport Management, 6,* 179–90.

Pastore, D. L., and Meacci, W. G. (1994). Employment process for NCAA female coaches. *Journal of Sport Management, 8,* 115–28.

Pierce, J. L., and Dunham, R. B. (1990). *Managing.* Glenview, IL: Scott, Foresman/Little, Brown Higher Education.

Quarterman, J. (1994). Managerial role profiles of intercollegiate athletic conference commissioners. *Journal of Sport Management, 8,* 129–39.

Snyder, C. R., Lassegard, M. A., and Ford, C. E. (1986). Distancing after group success and failure: Basking in reflected glory and cutting off reflected failure. *Journal of Personality and Social Psychology, 51,* 382–88.

Snyder, E. E., and Spreitzer, E. A. (1989). *Sociological aspects of sport.* 3d ed. Englewood Cliffs, NJ: Prentice Hall.

Stone, E. E., and Gueutal, H. G. (1985). An empirical derivation of the dimensions along which characteristics of jobs are perceived. *Academy of Management Journal, 28,* 376–96.

Wann, D. L., and Branscombe, N. R. (1990). Die-hard and fair weather fans: Effects of identification on BIRGing and CORFing tendencies. *Journal of Sport and Social Issues, 14*(2), 103–17.

Index

Page numbers in italic type refer to figures. Tables are indicated by "t" following the page number.

Date Due